THE WELLNESS ENCYCLOPEDIA OF FOOD AND NUTRITION

by Sheldon Margen, M.D.,
and the Editors of the University
of California at Berkeley
WELLNESS LETTER

REBUS
NEW YORK

DISTRIBUTED BY RANDOM HOUSE

University of California at Berkeley

The Wellness Encyclopedia of Food and Nutrition

How to Buy, Store, and Prepare Every Variety of Fresh Food

THE UNIVERSITY OF CALIFORNIA AT BERKELEY WELLNESS LETTER

The Wellness Encyclopedia of Food and Nutrition, the single most authoritative guide to shopping and eating for better health and a longer life, comes from the editors of America's top-rated health newsletter, the *University of California at Berkeley Wellness Letter.*

The *Wellness Letter* is a monthly eight-page newsletter that delivers brisk, useful coverage on health, nutrition, and exercise topics—in language that is clear, engaging, and nontechnical. It's a unique resource that covers fundamental ways to prevent illness. For information on how to order this award-winning newsletter from the world-famous School of Public Health at the University of California at Berkeley, write to Health Letter Associates, Department 1103, 632 Broadway, New York, New York 10012.

Library of Congress Cataloging-in-Publication Data

Margen, Sheldon
The wellness encyclopedia of food and nutrition : how to buy, store, and prepare every fresh food / by Sheldon Margen and the editors of the University of California at Berkeley wellness letter.
p. cm.
Includes index.
ISBN 0-929661-03-6
1. Food. 2. Nutrition. I. University of California, Berkeley, wellness letter. II. Title.
TX353. M344 1992 92-13017
613.2—dc20 CIP

Printed in the United States of America
10 9 8 7 6 5 4 3 2
Distributed by Random House, Inc.

This book is not intended as a substitute for medical advice. Readers who suspect they may have specific medical problems should consult a physician about any suggestions made in this book.

The publisher would like to thank Frieda's, Inc. in Los Angeles, California for supplying some of the fruits and vegetables pictured in this book.

THE WELLNESS ENCYCLOPEDIA OF FOOD AND NUTRITION

Thomas Dickey
Editorial Director

Patricia A. Calvo
Executive Editor

Bonnie J. Slotnick
Writer

Judith Henry
Art Director

Dean Bornstein
Leah Lococo
Design Associates

Dale A. Ogar
Managing Editor

Grace Young
Contributing Editor/Food

Josh Waldman
Editorial Assistant

Marie Baker-Lee
Kitchen Coordinator

All photographs by
Steven Mays

Rodney M. Friedman
Editor and Publisher

Barbara Maxwell O'Neill
Associate Publisher

THE UNIVERSITY OF CALIFORNIA AT BERKELEY
WELLNESS LETTER

Rodney M. Friedman
Editor and Publisher

Shirley Tomkievicz and Michael Goldman
Medical Writers

Dale A. Ogar
Managing Editor

Bette Ponack Albert, M.D.
Medical Editor

Jeanine Barone, M.S.
Sports Medicine and Nutrition Editor

Jane Margaretten-Ohring, R.N.
Associate Medical Editor

Barbara Maxwell O'Neill
Associate Publisher

Tom R. Damrauer
Librarian/Researcher

Contents

4
EXOTIC FRUITS AND VEGETABLES

5
GRAINS AND GRAIN PRODUCTS

6
LEGUMES, NUTS, AND SEEDS

7
MEATS AND POULTRY

8
FISH AND SHELLFISH

9
DAIRY AND EGGS

Appendixes

Introduction

AMERICANS TODAY HAVE a greater variety of foods to choose from than ever before. Yet many people are confused and anxious about the impact of their eating habits on their health; they are also concerned about the quality and safety of foods. One of the ironies of modern life is that as the technology of food production has advanced, Americans have come to rely increasingly on processed convenience foods that are often stripped of nutrients and fiber. In the belief that there are shortcuts to good nutrition, many people also take vitamin pills and other nutritional supplements that contain "pure" nutrients. Some of these products may provide health benefits, but in terms of a healthful daily diet, they aren't adequate substitutes for whole, fresh foods. The substances in foods exist in an astonishingly complex balance that can't be reproduced in a pill or a heavily processed food product; therefore, eating fresh or minimally processed foods is the best way to be sure of obtaining all of the nutritional benefits that food offers. The information on the following pages emphasizes the richness and variety of fresh foods, including the culinary rewards and satisfactions they provide.

A unique aspect of this book is that it deals not only with the nutrients in food, but with many non-nutrient substances that scientists are discovering can have a profound impact on health. Consumers tend to hear about additives used to make foods more palatable or attractive—for example, the sodium added to many canned foods or the wax sometimes used on fruits and vegetables. But numerous other substances, many of which occur naturally, are at work in various ways. Some appear to be highly beneficial. For example, dietary fiber, though it is not absorbed by the body, performs a number of valuable functions and may help prevent such chronic health problems as heart disease and certain types of cancer. Similarly, chemical substances known as indoles, which occur in cruciferous vegetables such as broccoli and cauliflower, have been linked to cancer prevention, as has ellagic acid, which is found in certain types of berries.

On the other hand, solanine, a substance in sprouting potatoes, is toxic; hydrazines (which occur in raw mushrooms) and aflatoxin (found in a mold that grows on peanuts) are both known carcinogens. Foods are also subject to contamination from bacteria (for example, salmonella) as well as man-made chemical agents (such as the residues from pesticides) that can have adverse effects on health. One purpose of this book is to put these substances into perspective. There is more to be learned, of course, but enough research has been done to provide safety guidelines where appropriate.

Given our present knowledge, the most important step you can take to maintain a healthy diet is to eat a wide variety of foods. This not only helps ensure that you get a proper balance of nutrients, but also minimizes your exposure to any substances in food that may be hazardous. Vegetables, fruits, grains, and legumes are preferred foods, since they are typically low in fat and rich in complex carbohydrates, dietary fiber, vitamins, and minerals. But meats, poultry, fish, and dairy products also contain a wealth of nutrients. Some of these foods are high in fat, and so should be consumed in moderation. But there is no reason to give them up entirely.

A varied diet also increases the pleasure you take in food. In the serving suggestions provided, you'll find that it's possible to eat delicious foods and not abandon good nutrition; you will also have a reason to try unfamiliar foods as well as new ways of preparing foods you eat every day.

HOW TO USE THIS BOOK

Along with helping you plan your shopping and your daily menus, the information herein will give you expertise in healthy methods for preparing food. You will see that many foods need little enhancement: The simplest cooking techniques (explained in the Cooking Glossary on page 490) can bring out a food's natural goodness while minimizing any loss of nutrients. The book will also answer any questions you have about the nutritional makeup of the foods you eat and the healthiest, most appetizing ways to incorporate them into your diet. You can either look up a subject in alphabetical order in the appropriate chapter, or turn to the index, which will also guide you to any related topics.

Each entry is accompanied by one or more nutritional profiles (highlighted in green and red boxes). Their purpose isn't to prod you to add up calories or monitor cholesterol content, but to allow you to determine and compare the nutritional value of foods with ease. The profiles will also help you evaluate foods that don't carry nutrition labeling. The values given are based on the United States Department of Agriculture (USDA) Handbook 8, which uses 3½ ounces (100 grams) of food as the standard portion size.

Standardizing the portion sizes by weight makes it possible to compare the nutritional content of foods fairly. Three and a half ounces turns out to be a reasonable serving size for many foods, and in any case the equivalent volume or quantity is usually indicated.

Because cooking vegetables and fruits changes their nutritional content, the values given are for raw foods. Grains, legumes, meats, poultry, and seafood are less affected by cooking, so the cooked values are shown. Values for dairy products and nuts are for the products as they are sold. (Bear in mind that these values are averages: The nutritional content of any particular food depends on where and when it was grown, and how it was shipped, stored, and displayed, as well as how it has been prepared.)

The top part of the profile box always shows values for the same categories: calories, protein, carbohydrates, dietary fiber, fat, saturated fat, cholesterol, and sodium. Since methods for measuring dietary fiber vary widely, the values for fiber are presented as High (over 5 grams), Medium (3 to 5 grams), and Low (2 grams or less). If 40 percent or more of the fiber is soluble—the kind that helps lower blood cholesterol levels—an "S" appears. A lack of fiber is indicated by "None."

The lower section of the box, called Key Nutrients, highlights the vitamins and minerals supplied by 3½ ounces of the food in amounts equal to or greater than 10 percent of the Recommended Dietary Allowances (RDAs) for adults. The box shows the amount of each nutrient, as well as the percent of the RDA it represents.

There is no RDA for beta carotene, copper, manganese, or potassium. The recommendations for these nutrients, developed from a variety of health associations, are presented on pages 16-17. They are included under Key Nutrients if a food provides 10 percent of the smallest amount recommended.

Most of the nutritional values in these profiles are rounded to the nearest whole number. However, certain vitamins and minerals are needed in such minute amounts that rounding to the nearest whole number would grossly misrepresent the amounts supplied by the food. These nutrients—thiamin, riboflavin, vitamin B_{12}, vitamin B_6, copper, and manganese—are rounded to the nearest tenth decimal place.

Chapter 1

A NUTRITION DIRECTORY

Many Americans are aware that making some changes in their diet would benefit their health, particularly with regard to lowering their risk of chronic disease. Scientists now estimate that that 40 percent of all cancer incidence in men, and 60 percent in women, is related to diet. Diet has also been implicated in two of the three major risk factors linked to the development of heart disease—high blood cholesterol levels and hypertension (smoking is the third)—and it is often a crucial aspect of being seriously overweight (which increases a person's risk of heart disease and certain cancers) and can aggravate the development of type II (adult-onset) diabetes. Fortunately, there is now a consensus among experts as to which dietary elements play a role in promoting or preventing disease. Yet it isn't always clear to the public which dietary guidelines are important or how to apply them on a day-to-day basis.

Which foods have been implicated in the prevention or promotion of disease? Actually, it isn't foods *per se* that contribute, but substances contained in foods. These range from fats—which in excessive amounts can contribute to heart disease and certain cancers—to antioxidant compounds that can protect against cancer and other diseases and may enhance immune system functioning. At the same time, these substances interact and carry out their functions best not as individual nutrients, but as part and parcel of a nutritional package—that is, when they are present in food. This chapter identifies these various substances, the roles they play in our bodies, and the foods where they are found. It will also sort out some of the more common misconceptions about nutrients that Americans have been bombarded with over the past decade or so.

FOOD AND ENERGY

The nutrients in food are broken down into three types. *Macronutrients*—which include carbohydrates, protein, and fats—are those which are present, and needed, in large amounts. *Micronutrients*—the vitamins and minerals—are present in much smaller amounts. *Water,* though normally not thought of as a nutrient, is a basic component of all foods, and is essential to life.

Each type of nutrient has specific functions, though every nutrient interacts with others to carry out those functions. The macronutrients provide energy and help maintain and repair the body. Vitamins regulate the chemical processes that take place in the body. Minerals assist with this, and play a role in body maintenance as well, notably in the formation of new tissue, including bones, teeth, and blood. Water provides a fluid medium for all chemical reactions in the body, and for the circulation of blood and removal of waste. It is a lubricant, and plays a critical role in regulating body temperature.

Your body is always burning a mixture of macronutrients for energy. The production of energy—and the potential for a food to supply energy—is measured in calories. (The caloric content of a food is determined by measuring the amount of heat produced when the food is burned in a laboratory device called a calorimeter. The heat that is generated is analogous to the energy produced in the human body.) At rest and at low levels of activity, carbohydrates provide 40 to 50 percent of the body's energy needs. Carbohydrates are the most efficient fuel for the body because they can be broken down to produce energy almost instantly. Fat—either from food or from body fat stores—also provides energy, but not as readily as carbohydrates. Only after 20 to 30 minutes of continuous activity does your body begin to rely more on fat than on carbohydrates. The longer the activity and/or the longer you go without food, the more your body uses fat for fuel. And any dietary fat that is not burned is converted to body fat (as are any unused carbohydrates or proteins).

THE BASICS OF A HEALTHY DIET

Developing healthy eating habits isn't difficult: It merely requires choosing foods that offer the best balance of nutrients for your body's needs. Based on guidelines established by the National Academy of Sciences, the National Institutes of Health, and the American Heart Association, here are basic rules you should try to stick to in planning your daily diet. (Each of the dietary elements mentioned here is covered in greater detail in the following pages.)

- Keep your total fat intake at or below 30 percent of your total calories, and limit your intake of saturated fats—which contribute to high blood cholesterol levels—to no more than 10 percent of your total calories.
- Limit your intake of dietary cholesterol to no more than 300 milligrams per day.
- Get at least 55 percent of your total daily calories from carbohydrates, preferably complex carbohydrates—the starches in grains, legumes, vegetables, and some fruits. These foods can also provide you with the 20 to 30 grams of dietary fiber that experts recommend you consume each day, as well as vitamins and minerals.
- Protein should make up only about 12 to 15 percent of your daily calories—and the protein should come from low-fat sources.
- Balance the calories you consume with the calories you expend in physical activity, to maintain a desirable body weight. The more active you are, the more you can eat to maintain this balance.
- Avoid too much sugar; it contributes to tooth decay, and many foods high in sugar are also high in fat.
- Limit your intake of sodium to no more than 2,400 milligrams per day, the equivalent of a little more than a teaspoon of salt.
- Maintain an adequate intake of vitamins and minerals—particularly of iron and calcium. And obtain your vitamins and minerals from food, not from supplements.
- If you drink alcohol, do so in moderation—no more than 1 ounce of pure alcohol a day. While some studies have linked moderate alcohol consumption with a lowered risk of heart disease, drinking alcohol beyond these limits can lead to health problems.

Given this prescribed balance of nutrients, what's the best way to achieve it in your daily diet? As a fundamental ground rule, your diet will likely be very healthy if you avoid foods that are high in fat, refined sugar, and sodium, and eat mostly those that are high in complex carbohydrates. Obviously, it is helpful to be aware of the nutritional make-up of the foods you are eating, and such information is included in most of the food entries in this book. The chart on page 14, which is based on recommendations established by the United States Department of Agriculture (USDA), presents a more detailed picture of a healthy diet, which will be useful in planning daily menus.

DAILY FOOD GUIDE

Nutrient and calorie needs vary from person to person, depending on age, sex, body size, and level of physical actvity. The chart here presents recommendations from the USDA for planning daily menus. Adults of all ages should consume at least the lower number of servings from each food group. However, most adults will need more calories than this, depending on body size and degree of physical activity. Most men, for example, can have the middle to upper number of servings that are shown.

The needs of children vary widely, but they, too, should eat at least the lower number of servings from each group. Teenagers need at least three servings of milk, cheese, or yogurt each day to meet their calcium needs. Adolescent boys can eat the higher number of servings from each food group, while girls usually can eat a middle range of servings, and more if they are quite active. Very young children, pregnant or lactating women, and other people with special needs may have higher nutritional requirements.

Food Group	**Suggested Daily Servings**	**What Counts as a Serving?**
Breads, Cereals, and Other Grain Products *(whole grain; enriched)*	6 to 11 servings Include several servings of whole-grain products daily.	1 slice of bread; ½ hamburger bun or English muffin; a small roll, biscuit, or muffin; 3 to 4 small, or 2 large crackers; ½ cup cooked cereal, rice, or pasta; 1 ounce of ready-to-eat breakfast cereal
Fruits *(citrus; melons; berries; other fruits)*	2 to 4 servings	A whole fruit such as a medium apple, banana, or orange; a grapefruit half; a melon wedge; ¾ cup of juice; ½ cup of berries; ½ cup of cooked or canned fruit; ¼ cup of dried fruit
Vegetables *(dark green leafy; deep yellow; dry beans and peas; starchy vegetables; other vegetables)*	3 to 5 servings Include all types regularly; use dark green leafy vegetables and dry beans and peas several times a week.	½ cup of cooked vegetables; ½ cup of chopped raw vegetables; 1 cup of leafy raw vegetables, such as lettuce or spinach
Meat, Poultry, Fish and Alternates *(eggs; dry beans and peas; nuts; seeds)*	2 to 3 servings	Amounts should total 5 to 7 ounces of cooked lean meat, poultry, or fish a day. Count 1 egg, ½ cup cooked beans, or 2 tablespoons of peanut butter as 1 ounce of meat.
Milk, Cheese, and Yogurt *(low- or nonfat types)*	2 servings 3 servings for women who are pregnant or breastfeeding, and for teens; 4 servings for teens who are pregnant or breastfeeding	1 cup of milk; 8 ounces of yogurt; 1½ ounces of natural cheese; 2 ounces of process cheese
Fats, Sweets, and Alcoholic Beverages	Avoid too many fats and sweets. If you drink alcoholic beverages, do so in moderation.	One ounce of pure alcohol equals: two 12-ounce beers, two small glasses of wine, or 1½ fluid ounces of spirits.

THE RDAs

How much of a particular vitamin or mineral do you need to consume to maintain good health? In the United States, the Recommended Dietary Allowances, or RDAs, for most nutrients have been developed by the Food and Nutrition Board of the National Research Council, a committee funded in part by the federal government. This group, made up of scientists from many specialties, evaluates the current research on nutrition to establish estimates of nutrient recommendations for protein, carbohydrates, fats, energy, eleven vitamins, and seven minerals.

In addition, the committee has established a range of safe and adequate intakes for two more vitamins and five more minerals for which insufficient scientific evidence exists to establish an RDA, but which are known to be toxic at levels only several times the upper limit of the committee's recommended range. The RDAs are designed to apply to healthy individuals and are adjusted for men, women, and children, and for different age groups, as well as for pregnant women. They are revised about every five years to include any new information about human nutrient needs. The RDAs were developed for health professionals; consumers may benefit more from following dietary guidelines, like the ones on pages 12-14, rather than trying to build a diet around the RDAs.

On food labels you will find an older and simplified version called the U.S. Recommended Daily Allowance, or U.S. RDA. Whereas the RDA gives specific guidelines based on age and sex, the U.S. RDA is the highest RDA value given for a nutrient (except for children age four or younger and pregnant or lactating women).

It is important to note that the RDAs are recommendations, not requirements. Individual dietary needs vary greatly, and the RDAs are set at a level that is assumed to cover the nutrient needs of most people, plus a generous margin of safety. Over a period of time, an intake well below the RDA may leave some people deficient in a particular nutrient, and in some cases, and for some nutrients, a regular intake far in excess of the RDA may have unpleasant side effects, or even be toxic. But if you eat a low-fat diet that includes plenty of vegetables, grains, legumes, and fruits, you should have no trouble meeting the RDAs, and it is almost impossible to get toxic amounts of vitamins and minerals from foods.

RECOMMENDED DIETARY ALLOWANCES[a]

Category	Age	Weight[b] (lb)	Height[b] (in)	Protein (g)	Vitamin A (mcg RE)[c]	Vitamin D (mcg)[d]	Vitamin E (mg α-TE)[e]	Vitamin K (mcg)	Vitamin C (mg)	Thiamine (mg)
Infants	0-6 months	13	24	13	375	7.5	3	5	30	0.3
	6-12 months	20	28	14	375	10	4	10	35	0.4
Children	1-3	29	35	16	400	10	6	15	40	0.7
	4-6	44	44	24	500	10	7	20	45	0.9
	7-10	62	52	28	700	10	7	30	45	1.0
Males	11-14	99	62	45	1000	10	10	45	50	1.3
	15-18	145	69	59	1000	10	10	65	60	1.5
	19-24	160	70	58	1000	10	10	70	60	1.5
	25-50	174	70	63	1000	5	10	80	60	1.5
	51 plus	170	68	63	1000	5	10	80	60	1.2
Females	11-14	101	62	46	800	10	8	45	50	1.1
	15-18	120	64	44	800	10	8	55	60	1.1
	19-24	128	65	46	800	10	8	60	60	1.1
	25-50	138	64	50	800	5	8	65	60	1.1
	51 plus	143	63	50	800	5	8	65	60	1.0
Pregnant women				60	800	10	10	65	70	1.5
Lactating women	1st 6 months			65	1,300	10	12	65	95	1.6
	2nd 6 months			62	1,200	10	11	65	90	1.6

[a] *The allowances, expressed as average daily intakes over time, are intended to provide for individual variations among most normal persons as they live in the United States under usual enviromental stresses. Diets should be based on a variety of common foods in order to provide other nutrients for which human requirements have been less well defined.*

[b] *Weights and heights of Reference Adults are actual medians for the U.S. population of the designated age. The use of these figures does not imply that the height-to-weight ratios are ideal.*

[c] *Retinol equivalents. 1 retinol equivalent= 1 mcg retinol or 6 mcg beta carotene. To calculate IU value: for fruits and vegetables, multiply the RE value by ten; for animal-source foods, multiply the RE value by 3.3.*

OTHER RECOMMENDED INTAKES

The following nutrients have no RDA or Estimated Safe and Adequate Daily Dietary Intake. Instead the daily recommendations listed below are based on guidelines established by various health organizations and experts.

Beta Carotene	5 to 6 milligrams
Cholesterol	no more than 300 milligrams
Dietary Fiber	20 to 30 grams
Potassium	3000 milligrams
Sodium	no more than 2400 milligrams

Riboflavin (mg)	Niacin (mg NE)[f]	Vitamin B_6 (mg)	Folate[g] (mcg)	Vitamin B_{12} (mcg)	Calcium (mg)	Phosphorus (mg)	Magnesium (mg)	Iron (mg)	Zinc (mg)	Iodine (mcg)	Selenium (mcg)
0.4	5	0.3	25	0.3	400	300	40	6	5	40	10
0.5	6	0.6	35	0.5	600	500	60	10	5	50	15
0.8	9	1.0	50	0.7	800	800	80	10	10	70	20
1.1	12	1.1	75	1.0	800	800	120	10	10	90	20
1.2	13	1.4	100	1.4	800	800	170	10	10	120	30
1.5	17	1.7	150	2.0	1200	1200	270	12	15	150	40
1.8	20	2.0	200	2.0	1200	1200	400	12	15	150	50
1.7	19	2.0	200	2.0	1200	1200	350	10	15	150	70
1.7	19	2.0	200	2.0	800	800	350	10	15	150	70
1.4	15	2.0	200	2.0	800	800	350	10	15	150	70
1.3	15	1.4	150	2.0	1200	1200	280	15	12	150	45
1.3	15	1.5	180	2.0	1200	1200	300	15	12	150	50
1.3	15	1.6	180	2.0	1200	1200	280	15	12	150	55
1.3	15	1.6	180	2.0	800	800	280	15	12	150	55
1.2	13	1.6	180	2.0	800	800	280	10	12	150	55
1.6	17	2.2	400	2.2	1200	1200	320	30	15	175	65
1.8	20	2.1	280	2.6	1200	1200	355	15	19	200	75
1.7	20	2.1	260	2.6	1200	1200	340	15	16	200	75

[d] *As cholecalciferol. 10 mcg cholecalciferol=400 IU of vitamin D.*

[e] *α-tocopherol equivalents. 1 mg d-α tocopherol=1 α-TE.*

[f] *1 NE (niacin equivalent) is equal to 1 mg of niacin or 60 mg of dietary tryptophan.*

[g] *Folacin*

ESTIMATED SAFE AND ADEQUATE DAILY DIETARY INTAKES OF SELECTED VITAMINS AND MINERALS[a]

		Vitamins		Trace Minerals[b]				
Category	**Age**	**Biotin** (mcg)	**Panthothenic acid** (mg)	**Copper** (mg)	**Manganese** (mg)	**Fluoride** (mg)	**Chromium** (mcg)	**Molybdenum** (mcg)
Infants	0-6 months	10	2	0.4-0.6	0.3-0.6	0.1-0.5	10-40	15-30
	6-12 months	15	3	0.6-0.7	0.6-1.0	0.2-1.0	20-60	20-40
Children and adolescents	1-3	20	3	0.7-1.0	1.0-1.5	0.5-1.5	20-80	25-50
	4-6	25	3-4	1.0-1.5	1.5-2.0	1.0-2.5	30-120	30-75
	7-10	30	4-5	1.0-2.0	2.0-3.0	1.5-2.5	50-200	50-150
	11 plus	30-100	4-7	1.5-2.5	2.0-5.0	1.5-2.5	50-200	75-250
Adults		30-100	4-7	1.5-3.0	2.0-5.0	1.5-4.0	50-200	75-250

[a] *Because there is less information on which to base allowances, these figures are not given in the main table of RDAs and are provided here in the form of ranges of recommended intakes.*

[b] *Since the toxic levels for many trace elements may be only several times usual intakes, the upper levels for the trace elements given in this table should not be habitually exceeded.*

Carbohydrates

An immense variety of foods, nearly all of them derived from plants, supply us with carbohydrates—the body's principal source of energy. Table sugar, whole grains, pears and strawberries, pasta, popcorn, green peas, kidney beans, dates and figs, and apple pie are all sources of carbohydrates. In fact, all sugars and starches that we consume are carbohydrates, as are most types of dietary fiber. The fiber is not strictly a nutrient, since it is not essential for the body's metabolic functioning. It is, nevertheless, a crucial item in the carbohydrate package, as explained on page 19. Most starches and sugars, however, are transformed by the body into one substance, glucose—a form of sugar that is carried in the blood and transported to the cells for energy. Any glucose not used by the cells is converted into glycogen, another form of carbohydrate that is stored in the muscles and liver, or converted to body fat. The body's glycogen storage capacity is limited to about 3/4 of a pound, so most unused glucose is converted to fat.

In the chronicle of American dietary fads, carbohydrates have had their ups and downs. Today, however, carbohydrates, especially "complex" carbohydrates, are back in favor—a reflection of a better understanding of what's good for us. Moreover, carbohydrates are in bountiful supply on the American table, as in most parts of the world, and—unless purchased in highly processed forms—are the most economical of foods.

Nutritionists distinguish between two types of carbohydrates:

Simple carbohydrates are the sugars. To most people sugar means refined, white table sugar (sucrose), made from cane or beets. However, there are actually dozens of sugars: In their pure form they have such names as fructose, glucose (also called dextrose), maltose, lactose, and sugar alcohols like sorbitol and xylitol. Sugars are often identified by their sources, such as maple syrup, honey, corn syrup, and molasses. Simple carbohydrates turn up in some unlikely places—processed foods such as soups, spaghetti sauces, fruit drinks, frozen dinners, cereals, and yogurts—as well as in breads, condiments, canned goods, and, of course, soft drinks and what we call "sweets." Sugar also occurs naturally in fruits, vegetables, and dairy products.

Complex carbohydrates, which are primarily starches, are large chains of glucose molecules. Starch is the storage form of carbohydrates in plants, comparable to the glycogen in humans and animals. The major sources of complex carbohydrates are grains such as bread, rice, and pasta, and vegetables such as potatoes and beans.

CARBO-LOADING AND EXERCISE

Since carbohydrates in the form of glycogen are stored in the liver and muscles and provide energy for muscle contraction, some athletes believe they can enhance their performance by manipulating the body's carbohydrate stores before a competition. The classic "carbo-loading" regimen called for depleting the body's glycogen through exercise and diet, and then eating very high levels of complex carbohydrates. Most sports nutritionists now advise against this extreme diet. Instead they recommend simply increasing your complex carbohydrate intake during the two or three days before *long-duration* events such as marathons. However, for most types of exercise, the balanced, high-complex-carbohydrate diet that is recommended on a daily basis will supply adequate energy.

If both forms of carbohydrate end up as glucose or glycogen, why does it matter which one you eat? For one thing, they come in different nutritional packages. Many sugary "sweets" are high in calories and relatively low in other nutrients (with the possible exception of fat, which is all too plentiful in many cookies and candies). By contrast, foods high in complex carbohydrates usually contain a lot of nutritional extras—vitamins and minerals, and in many cases appreciable amounts of water and dietary fiber. Some, like legumes, contain protein as well. Ounce for ounce, foods high in complex carbohydrates supply a far better balance of nutrients than sugar-laden foods, and are usually less fattening. It's true that many fruits contain the simple sugars fructose and sucrose, but they also contain vitamins, minerals, and fiber that processed or refined sweets lack.

If you are trying to control your weight or lose several pounds, you have probably heard contradictory things about carbohydrates. Some dieters avoid starchy foods (such as beans, bread, potatoes, and pasta), as well as sugary foods, believing they are highly "fattening." It may come as a surprise that—gram for gram—both simple and complex carbohydrates contain exactly the same number of calories as protein, 4 calories per gram, compared to 9 calories per gram of fat. Rich desserts are not fattening because of the sugar and starches they contain, but because they are loaded with fat. Foods high in complex carbohydrates tend to be low in fat and are thus not particularly fattening. In fact, because fruits and vegetables, which are rich in complex carbohydrates, have a high water content and relatively few calories, they can be useful in any weight-control program. They also help satisfy your appetite.

Fiber

A healthy diet is usually described negatively—consume less fat, cholesterol, and salt, for instance, or less red meat, eggs, and chips. Yet the same diet can be given a positive slant: eat more fiber in the form of whole grains, fruits, and vegetables. Though interest in high-fiber foods goes back to Hippocrates' day, our understanding of fiber's health benefits has been greatly enhanced by research done during the last twenty-five years. Formerly called roughage or bulk, fiber was once thought of primarily as filler—in other words, if you eat high-fiber foods, you'll have less room for high-fat, high-calorie items. That is still seen as one of fiber's potential benefits, as is the fact that it is generally found in foods rich in vitamins and minerals. But scientists now recognize that fiber itself may play a role in reducing the risk of the leading chronic diseases—heart disease, cancer, and diabetes.

Fiber is hard to peg down because it isn't a single substance, but rather a large group of widely different compounds with varied effects in the body. What all types of fiber have in common is that they are the parts of plants that can't be digested by enzymes in the human intestinal tract. For simplicity, fiber can be divided into two broad categories: those that are insoluble in water and those that are soluble. Most plant foods contain both types in varying amounts, but certain foods are particularly rich in one or the other.

Until a few years ago, food chemists would measure only insoluble fiber, and the result was called "crude fiber." Today, better laboratory techniques now provide a more complete measurement of fiber, called "dietary fiber," which includes the soluble as well as insoluble kind. Still, there is as yet no single "correct" way to measure dietary fiber, so results from different labs can vary substantially, although methods are becoming more standardized. Currently, manufacturers are not required to list fiber on nutrition labels unless they make a claim concerning it.

New labeling regulations proposed by the FDA would require dietary fiber content to be listed on food labels.

Fiber's benefits

In the late 1960s studies began to link a high-fiber intake among rural peoples in non-industrial countries with a low incidence of diseases all too common in industrialized Western countries, where people tend to eat more meats and fats. It has been difficult, however, to prove the protective effects of fiber because fiber isn't consumed in isolation. High-fiber foods may be beneficial because they tend to be low in fat and calories and usually replace meats and other fatty foods that may increase the risk, for instance, of colon cancer or coronary artery disease. Foods rich in fiber also tend to be high in antioxidants (such as beta carotene and vitamin C) and other substances that may protect against a variety of cancers, and it is hard to separate the effects of fiber from those of these other components. People who eat a high-fiber diet may also make other healthy choices in their lives, such as exercising regularly and not smoking, that may lower their risk for some chronic diseases. In many studies, scientists use statistical techniques to adjust their data for some or most of these complicating factors, but even the best studies can't control for all known variables. Though extremely promising, the evidence concerning fiber's protective effects remains inconclusive, and research is continuing.

Consuming a healthy amount of dietary fiber may lessen the risk of developing the following diseases and conditions:

Constipation Insoluble fiber, consumed with adequate fluids, is the safest, most effective way to prevent or treat constipation—by increasing the frequency, bulk, and ease of bowel movements. This fiber is like a sponge: It absorbs many times its weight in water, swelling within the intestines and producing a larger, softer stool that the digestive system can pass quickly and easily. Also, when fiber enters the large intestine, some of it is broken down by bacteria, yielding compounds that in turn produce intestinal gas and initiate bowel movements.

Diverticulosis About one American in ten over age forty and at least one in three over age fifty suffers from diverticulosis, a condition in which tiny asymptomatic pouches, called diverticula, form within the wall of the colon. When the pouches trap food, they may become painfully inflamed (diverticulitis). Insoluble fiber may help prevent the formation of diverticula by reducing constipation and strained bowel movements, thus alleviating pressure in the colon, or relieving the inflammation once it occurs.

Colon and rectal cancer This is the second leading cause of cancer deaths in the U.S., but is rarer in countries with a diet low in meat and rich in high-fiber foods. Dozens of studies have supported the hypothesis that a fiber-rich diet protects against colon cancer (a few studies have not). One of the strongest pieces of evidence came from New York Hospital in 1989 in a four-year study that found that a diet high in insoluble fiber significantly inhibited the development of precancerous colon and rectal polyps (which tend to gradually enlarge and become malignant) in subjects with an inherited predisposition to them. In 1992 the *Journal of the National Cancer Institute* published a large study also showing that a high-fiber, low-fat diet helps prevent the growth of precancerous polyps.

No one knows exactly how insoluble fiber may protect against colon cancer, but several theories have been proposed. By moving foods faster through the system, fiber may lessen the exposure of colon walls to potential carcinogens. Or fiber may dilute the carcinogens or inactivate them in some way. Studies have also confirmed that insoluble fiber reduces bile acids in the intestines as well as bacterial enzymes, both of which are possible cancer promoters.

Heart disease Numerous studies have indicated that soluble fiber (as in oat bran, barley, and fruit pectin) helps reduce total blood cholesterol, primarily by lowering LDL ("bad") cholesterol. The debate continues, however, about how much soluble fiber you have to consume to get a significant reduction—and, again, the typical high-fiber diet is low in fat and that alone may reduce blood cholesterol. Most attention has focused on oatmeal or oat bran, thanks to research funding (and ad campaigns) from cereal companies, but there have also been studies about other sources of soluble fiber, such as grapefruit and apples. Most have shown modest positive effects. But rather than looking at any single food as a magic bullet against cholesterol, you should get your fiber from a variety of sources. Reducing your intake of saturated fat (from fatty meats, whole milk, cheese) and maintaining a healthy weight are even better ways to control blood cholesterol.

Diabetes Some studies have suggested that soluble fiber improves control of blood sugar and can thus reduce the need for insulin or medication in people with diabetes. Exactly why isn't clear, but soluble fiber (specifically gums and pectin) seems to delay the emptying of the stomach and slow the absorption of glucose in the intestine.

Obesity Most high-fiber foods are also high in complex carbohydrates (starch) and low in fat—a good combination for weight control. Many take longer to chew, which slows you down at the table. Fiber also fills you up temporarily without adding calories.

Breast cancer Research into the effects of fiber on the risk of breast cancer is still in its early stages. A recent study at the American Health Foundation in New York City found that wheat bran (rich in insoluble fiber) reduces blood estrogen levels, which, the researchers theorize, may affect the risk of breast cancer. However, there has been no conclusive epidemiological evidence to support this. When people eat more fiber they tend to eat less fat, and it has often been proposed (though never proven) that a high-fat diet increases the risk of breast cancer.

Even though it's too early to say for sure whether fiber can cure or even prevent disease, it's clear that a high-fiber, low-fat diet is healthful. Most authorities agree that, on average, Americans should at least double their consumption of dietary fiber—to 20 to 30 grams a day. Some even recommend 40 to 50 grams a day, an amount many vegetarians safely consume.

IS FIBER SAFE?

Yes, although eating enormous amounts of fiber in a short time can result in intestinal gas, bloating, and cramps caused by fermentation of fiber and indigestible sugars in the colon. Usually this isn't serious and subsides once the bacteria in your system adjust to the fiber increase. You can reduce the chances of gas or diarrhea by adding fiber-rich foods gradually to your diet. One potential problem of an extremely high-fiber diet is fiber's ability to bind some trace minerals, such as zinc, iron, magnesium, and even calcium, thus lessening their absorption by the body. This effect is minimal, however, and high-fiber foods tend to be rich enough in minerals to more than compensate for any losses. In contrast, fiber pills, which contain no nutrients, are more likely to create mineral deficiencies in people whose diet is nutritionally poor.

To ensure an adequate fiber intake, eat a variety of foods—the less processed, the better. Don't rely on fiber supplements, which may be unbalanced or incomplete and have no other nutrients in them. Instead, eat more fruits, vegetables, whole grains, cereals, and legumes—these are all excellent low-calorie sources of fiber and provide essential vitamins, minerals, and other nutrients as well.

Be sure to drink plenty of liquids; otherwise, fiber can slow down or even block proper bowel function. And don't try to get all of your fiber at one sitting, which can cut the benefits and increase the chances of unpleasant side effects. As a rule of thumb, try to eat foods high in both insoluble and soluble fiber at every meal.

Protein

Aptly enough, the word "protein" is derived from a Greek root meaning "of first importance," and protein is the basic material of life. Protein constitutes three-fourths of our body tissue (if you don't count the water in the tissue). Muscles, organs, antibodies, some hormones, and all enzymes (the compounds that direct cell chemical reactions) are largely composed of protein.

Yet protein is not a single, simple substance, but a multitude of chemical combinations. The basic structure of protein is actually a chain of amino acids that can form many different configurations and can combine with other substances. There have been twenty-two amino acids identified in the proteins of the human body. The possible arrangements are almost infinite, and thousands of different proteins have been identified.

Proteins are constantly being broken down in our bodies. Most of the amino acids are reused, but we must constantly replace some of those that are lost. This process is known as protein turnover. Our need to keep this process going begins at conception and lasts through life. Without dietary protein, growth and all bodily functions would not take place.

Government surveys show that the typical American consumes about 100 grams of protein a day—nearly twice as much as the Recommended Dietary Allowance. In general, the RDA is easily met when 12 to 15 percent of your total caloric intake comes from protein.

While plants and some bacteria can manufacture all the amino acids they need, the human body can manufacture only thirteen. The amino acids we can make are known, somewhat confusingly, as the "nonessential" amino acids. They are in fact essential, but not as part of our diet. The nine "essential" amino acids are those we have to eat. They are histidine, isoleucine, leucine, lysine, methionine, phenylalanine, threonine, tryptophan, and valine. We can either get them from plant protein directly or by eating animals that consume plants.

When we eat foods containing protein, the digestive system breaks it down to the constituent amino acids, which enter the body "pool" of amino acids. Each cell then assembles the proteins it needs using the building blocks available. If, however, one or more of the amino acids is in short supply, others that may be on hand cannot be utilized. This is why it is important to eat a diet that contains all of the essential amino acids, plus enough additional amino acids to allow for synthesis of the "nonessential" amino acids.

Complete and incomplete

Nutritionists use the phrases "complete protein" and "incomplete protein" to describe the proteins provided by various foods. If the protein of a food supplies a sufficient amount of the nine essential amino acids it is called a complete protein. Virtually all proteins from animal foods are complete. Proteins in foods—such as fruits, grains, and vegetables—that are low in one or more of the essential amino acids are called incomplete proteins. Such plant-derived foods can still be excellent sources of protein if eaten in combinations that supply all of the essential amino acids. For example, the amino acids missing in a vegetable can be provided by eating a grain product, another vegetable, or an animal-derived protein, at the same meal or later that day.

Bread, a staple of the human diet for thousands of years, is rich in the amino acid methionine, but low in lysine. Legumes are rich in lysine, but poor in methionine; when legumes and bread are eaten together, however, you get a complete protein. That lunchbox favorite the peanut butter sandwich is an example of this complementarity. The peanuts provide the amino acids that the grain lacks, and vice versa. Without understanding the chemical reasons for what they were doing, cooks the world over have come up with complementary combinations of proteins: beans or peas or lentils and rice, beans and brown bread or cornbread, corn and lima beans. Most of the diets in the world contribute adequate amino acids and protein.

Protein sources

That meat and other animal products are the most readily available sources of complete protein is perhaps the reason why humans have been such ardent hunters and fishers, as well as domesticators of animals. The protein content, by weight, of cooked meat, fish, poultry, and milk solids is between 15 and 40 percent. The protein content of cooked cereals, beans, lentils, and peas ranges from 3 to 10 percent. Potatoes, fruits, and leafy green vegetables come in at 3 percent or lower. Soybeans and nuts have a protein content comparable to meat, but in the past the protein was considered less digestible. However, recent research suggests that in a mixed or even totally vegetarian diet, the issue of digestibility is not too important. For someone eating a whole-grain and vegetable diet, the decrease of availability due to nondigestibility would be no more than 5 to 15 percent.

Luckily for the ability of the human species to survive, we are omnivorous, that is, we can eat both meats and plants. But many authorities regard meat eating in America as excessive, since it is a primary source of saturated fats, which may contribute to coronary heart disease, cancer, and stroke. Moreover, a diet high in meat but not dairy products—the typical diet for adult Americans—increases the loss of calcium in the body. Another potential problem with such a high-protein diet may be the strain it puts on the kidneys in having to excrete extra waste products from the protein, since the end product of protein metabolism has to be excreted in the urine.

Yet given that the cells of muscles, tendons, and ligaments have to be maintained with protein, many people try to eat more protein in their quest for a stronger body or to improve athletic performance. Up until ten or fifteen years ago, athletes at many training tables would typically wolf down steaks or raw eggs to achieve this. Today, they're more likely to take protein supplements in powder form, or amino acid tablets, in the belief that these can increase their muscle mass. However, regardless of the degree of exercise, even professional athletes do not require additional protein if their caloric intake is adequate.

"MIRACLE" AMINO ACIDS

Numerous claims have been made for the curative powers of various amino acids, some of which are sold over-the-counter in drugstores and health-food stores. For example, lysine was once thought to be useful in treating herpes, but since the positive results of early tests could not be duplicated, lysine is no longer recommended.

As a general rule, taking amino acid supplements is unnecessary, unless there is a deficiency in the digestive system. Studies with animals have shown that abnormally large intakes of amino acids can create imbalances of those substances in the body. For that reason the Food and Drug Administration in 1974 took them off the list of substances generally recognized as safe (GRAS).

The body does not make more protein than usual just because you increase your consumption of amino acids or protein-rich foods. Studies of athletes have not found that protein supplements improve strength, power, or endurance. Excess protein simply breaks down in the body and the amino acids are mostly burned for energy or turned into fat—the protein doesn't build additional muscle. (Strength-building exercise is the only way to accomplish that.) Moreover, taking protein supplements can cause diarrhea and can worsen dehydration. Like almost all nutrients, excessive amounts of protein can do more harm than good.

You need adequate protein intake to build muscles, but if you eat a normal, balanced diet, it is hard not to get enough protein. Even strict vegetarians get enough if they eat grains and vegetables in the proper quantities and combinations to insure that their protein is complete.

Fats

By now, the health effects of too much fat in the diet have been fairly well established. A high-fat diet has been linked in study after study with heart disease, cancer, and other ills. Since fat contains about twice as many calories by weight as carbohydrates and protein, high-fat foods can also contribute to obesity.

As a result, fat, in most people's minds, is a nutritional villain to be shunned at all costs. What people generally forget, however, is that fat is essential to the proper functioning of the body, and humans need to consume some fat to remain healthy. Fats supply "essential" fatty acids, so named because the body can't make them and must get them from foods. Linoleic acid is the most important of these, especially for the proper growth and development of infants. Essential fatty acids are the raw materials for several hormonelike compounds, including prostaglandins, that help control blood pressure, blood clotting, inflammation, and other bodily functions.

Fats perform many other important functions. They serve as the storage substance for the body's excess calories, filling the balloonlike adipose cells that insulate the body. Extra calories from carbohydrates and proteins as well as from fats are stored as body fat. Carbohydrates are considered to be the body's primary source of energy, but when the body has depleted its carbohydrate stores—which can happen after the first 20 minutes of aerobic exercise—it draws on fat. Thus, fat is as important as carbohydrates for energy.

In addition, fats help maintain healthy skin and hair, transport the fat-soluble vitamins (A, D, E, and K) through the bloodstream, regulate blood cholesterol levels, and promote a sensation of feeling full when eaten, probably because they slow the emptying of food from the stomach.

From granola cereals to packaged rice and potato mixes, processed foods containing vegetables and grains are often high-fat rather than low-fat foods. In fact, the bulk of fat in the American diet—about 44 percent—comes from vegetable oils, shortenings, butter, and margarine, as compared to 34 percent from meat, poultry, and fish, and 15 percent from dairy products. Many of the "hidden" fats that lurk in processed foods are in the form of tropical oils or hydrogenated vegetable oils that are highly saturated.

Yet, Americans consume more fat than is necessary to remain healthy. Our fat intake has increased dramatically: About 41 percent of all calories consumed today come from fats, up from 32 percent at the start of the century. Most of this rise has occurred at the expense of carbohydrates. Nutritionists recommend that no more than 30 percent of our total daily calories come from fat, and we should pay special attention to the types of fat we eat, too.

Types of fat

Technically called lipids, fats come in solid or liquid (oil) form. All are insoluble in water, unlike carbohydrates. Most fats in foods are triglycerides, which consist of three fatty acids attached to a glycerol molecule. These fatty acids vary in length and in degree of saturation by hydrogen atoms—and it is these variations that determine the properties of different fats. All fats are combinations of saturated and unsaturated fatty acids, and depending on their proportions, may be called "highly saturated" or "highly unsaturated."

A manufacturing process called *hydrogenation* adds hydrogen atoms to unsaturated fats, thus making them more saturated. It can also change the form of unsaturated fats to different configurations, so even if the fat remains unsaturated, it can still act as a saturated fat in the body. The fats in margarines and shortenings are often hydrogenated because this makes them harder and more stable. Depending on the degree of hydrogenation, these artificially saturated vegetable fats are no better for you than comparably saturated animal fats.

Saturated fatty acids are loaded with all the hydrogen atoms they can carry. Fats that are largely saturated are usually solid at room temperature and keep well. Such fats come chiefly from animal sources—butter, dairy products, and meats. Two vegetable oils—coconut and palm oils—are also highly saturated. A diet high in saturated fat can result in high blood cholesterol levels, which in turn can lead to heart disease.

Unsaturated fatty acids do not have all the hydrogen atoms they can carry. Depending on the number of missing hydrogen atoms, these fatty acids are called either *monounsaturated* (olive, canola, peanut, and avocado oils are largely monounsaturated) or *polyunsaturated* (corn, safflower, and sesame oils are primarily polyunsaturated). The important dietary unsaturated fats come from plants and fish. They generally are liquid at room temperature and may become rancid quickly. The majority of our fat intake should come from these unsaturated fats.

Fats and blood cholesterol

All of our tissues contain some cholesterol, but it is the cholesterol that circulates in the blood—sometimes referred to as "serum cholesterol"—that is so often discussed and measured. And it is this cholesterol that can accumulate in the walls of blood vessels, leading to atherosclerosis and possibly heart attack or stroke. A high blood cholesterol level is especially dangerous when combined with other risk factors, such as smoking, hypertension, diabetes, obesity, and a family history of heart disease.

CALCULATING FAT CALORIES

To determine the percentage of calories from fat in a food, follow these steps:

Example: 250 calories, 9 grams of fat

1. **Multiply the number of grams of fat in a serving by 9 (the number of calories in a gram of fat).**
   9 x 9 = 81
2. **Divide the result by the number of calories in a serving**
   81 ÷ 250 = 0.324
3. **Multiply your answer by 100, then round to the nearest whole number**
   0.324 x 100 = 32.4 or 32

This food would get 32 percent of its calories from fat.

Some cholesterol, though, is necessary; it is a vital constituent of cell membranes and nerves, and is also a building block for certain hormones. Though cholesterol is found in some of the foods we eat, it isn't an essential nutrient for humans—our bodies manufacture most of the cholesterol that we need. However, the average American consumes about 400 to 500 milligrams of cholesterol in food every day. This dietary cholesterol, as it is called, comes only from animal sources—such as eggs, meat, and dairy products—which tend to be also rich in saturated fats. If it were only a matter of the cholesterol from food going directly into our bloodstream, all we would have to worry about is how much cholesterol we eat. But the liver usually synthesizes most of the

HOW MUCH FAT SHOULD YOU EAT?

Though knowing the percentage of calories from fat in a food can be helpful in identifying foods high in fat, what really matters is the percentage of your *total daily caloric intake* that comes from fat. This means, then, that you can include some higher fat foods in your daily diet as long as you compensate for them the rest of the day and do not exceed 30 percent of your daily calories from fat. (About one third of your calories should come from polyunsaturated fat, one third from monounsaturated fat, and no more than one third from saturated fat.) To figure out the maximum amount of fat you should be eating, estimate how many calories you consume each day. Then use the guide below to see how many grams of fat you can eat without exceeding 30 percent calories from fat.

Caloric intake	Grams of fat
1200	40
1500	50
1800	60
2000	66
2500	83

cholesterol in the body—a process only partly regulated by the amount of cholesterol eaten.

Surprisingly, there does not appear to be a simple direct relationship between *dietary* intake of cholesterol and *blood* cholesterol levels. Researchers theorize that only about 20 to 30 percent of the population is genetically hypersensitive to dietary cholesterol—that is, their blood cholesterol levels increase when they eat high-cholesterol foods. There's no simple test for cholesterol hypersensitivity, but experts still recommend that healthy people consume no more than 300 milligrams of cholesterol a day.

Dietary changes, especially regarding fats, *can* have a significant effect on blood cholesterol levels. Saturated fats usually stimulate the production of low-density lipoproteins (LDL), or "bad" cholesterol, and raise overall cholesterol levels. That's why limiting your cholesterol intake but not your consumption of saturated fats can still result in high blood cholesterol levels.

For example, the citizens of Finland, who have the highest levels of saturated fat in their diets of any national group, have the highest cholesterol levels as well as the highest rate of heart disease. Americans, with a slightly less rich diet, have the second highest level of heart disease. The Japanese have the lowest levels of blood cholesterol and of heart disease of any developed nation—and their diet, at least in the past, has been very low in saturated fat.

In contrast, polyunsaturated fats tend to lower the amount of LDL cholesterol, thus reducing the amount of artery-clogging cholesterol in the bloodstream. Moreover, the unique polyunsaturated fats in fish oil offer an additional benefit: They make the blood's platelets less likely to clot, thus reducing the chances of an artery blockage and heart attack.

Monounsaturated fats, such as olive oil, may also be able to reduce the amount of damaging LDL cholesterol in the blood, according to some recent studies.

High-density liproproteins (HDL) are often known as "good" cholesterol because, as they circulate in the bloodstream, they seem to have the beneficial capacity to pick up cholesterol and bring it back to the liver for reprocessing or excretion. However, reducing the saturated fat in your diet does not seem to have an effect on HDL cholesterol in your bloodstream (though some other factors, such as exercise, seem to help boost it). Nor can you eat "good" cholesterol; no type of cholesterol you eat is good for you.

Fats and health risk

While saturated fat has the greatest impact on heart disease risk, any kind of fat increases your chance of becoming overweight or obese, which is another risk factor in cardiovascular disease. In addition, some animal studies have indicated that a *large* intake of polyunsaturated fats is implicated in the development of certain types of cancer. The relationship between fat intake and cancer is more controversial than the link to heart disease. Many scientists have noted that, with a few exceptions, countries with a high national fat intake also have the highest cancer rates. And some studies have suggested that a diet high in fat—whether saturated or unsaturated—increases the risk of cancer of the colon and breast, and possibly of the ovary, uterus, and prostate.

The mechanism for the link between a high-fat diet and cancer has not been determined, but there are theories. A diet high in fat affects the secretion of some sex hormones, which might cause cancer in the reproductive organs. Moreover, high-fat diets increase the amount of cholesterol and bile acids in the colon, which may be converted there by bacteria into carcinogenic by-products.

Reducing overall fat intake is no guarantee of protection against heart disease or cancer, but it does significantly increase the odds in your favor (especially for heart disease). Such a diet is especially recommended if you have high blood pressure or are in another high-risk group for heart disease, or if you smoke, which is a risk factor for both heart disease and certain types of cancer.

Vitamins

A vitamin is an organic substance (meaning it contains carbon) that your body requires to help regulate functions within cells. For the most part, vitamins must be obtained from food; except for vitamins D and K, which the body can't synthesize. Only very small amounts of vitamins are needed to carry out their functions, but these small amounts are absolutely essential. Without vitamins, higher animal organisms—like humans—could not exist. Vitamins affect all functions in the body. Among the myriad tasks vitamins perform are promoting good vision, forming normal blood cells, creating strong bones and teeth, and ensuring the proper functioning of the heart and nervous system. While vitamins themselves do not supply energy, some of them do aid in the efficient conversion of foods to energy.

Thirteen vitamins are needed by humans: A, C, D, E, K, and eight B vitamins—thiamin, riboflavin, niacin, pantothenic acid, B_6, B_{12}, folacin, and biotin. In addition, vitamin A, which comes from animal sources such as meat and eggs, is present in the form of a precursor, beta carotene, when manufactured by plants. Carrots, for example, are rich in beta carotene, and the body converts this nutrient to vitamin A. It appears that beta carotene may also have its own effects as an antioxidant apart from this vitamin A conversion.

Fat- and water-soluble

Vitamins can all be categorized as either fat-soluble (A, D, E, and K) or water-soluble (the B vitamins and vitamin C). The distinction is important because the body stores fat-soluble vitamins for relatively long periods (usually in the liver and in fat tissue), whereas water-soluble vitamins, which are stored in various tissues, remain in the body for only a short time and so need to be replenished frequently. Otherwise, symptoms associated with a deficiency of water-soluble vitamins can occur within weeks to several months.

Most vitamins are sensitive in varying degrees

ANTIOXIDANT VITAMINS

Recent research has suggested that besides their other contributions to health, two vitamins, C and E, along with beta carotene, may play important roles in averting or delaying coronary artery disease, cancer, cataracts, and other ills, and may even delay the effects of aging. These vitamins are now often referred to as "antioxidants" because they seem to neutralize a class of atomic particles known as "free radicals." All cells require oxygen to generate energy, and in the process they create certain unstable oxygen molecules—free radicals—that seek to combine with other compounds, creating a chain reaction and, over the course of time, cracking or damaging cell walls and structures within the cells. The process never stops and is in-fluenced from inside and outside the cells. Just as normal chemical processes in the cells create free radicals, so can heat, radiation, cigarette smoke, alcohol, and certain pollutants.

However, cells have orderly systems for battling free radicals and repairing molecular damage—systems that subdue or inactivate dangerous molecular by-products and stitch up the molecular "holes." Vitamins C and E and beta carotene are part of this process for fighting free radicals, along with enzymes and certain other compounds manufactured by the cells themselves. Since all these processes take place at the sub-atomic level, they cannot be observed by even the strongest microscope—and thus no one is sure exactly how free radicals may cause chronic disease and aging, or how antioxidant vitamins delay the process.

to heat and light, and there is always some loss of vitamins when food is being stored, handled, and cooked. These losses can be accelerated when food isn't stored away from light or properly refrigerated. Fat-soluble vitamins are more stable during cooking than water-soluble ones, which can easily be leached from foods that are cooked in boiling water. Short cooking times, and the practice of cooking foods in minimal amounts of water (as explained in the Cooking Glossary that starts on page 490), can help conserve nutrients.

Supplements and megadoses

Between 35 and 40 percent of American adults take vitamin supplements. But current scientific evidence suggests that a healthy person who eats a well-balanced diet, like the one described on page 14, has no need for vitamin supplements. Extra vitamins won't make you live longer, give you a better sex life, or make you a better athlete, despite all the claims. Researchers have investigated the functions of vitamins in thousands of carefully controlled studies, and in almost every case they have found that vitamins simply cannot perform the miracles that some people say they will. Nor are supplements a lazy person's path to good nutrition. Vitamins work with other nutrients in food; they cannot replace food or necessarily turn a junk-food diet into a healthy one.

As for megadoses of vitamins, these are not only wasteful, but also potentially dangerous. For every popular report on the benefits of megadoses, the medical literature can respond with documented cases of harm from large doses. Recent studies have shown that most vitamins are toxic when taken in large doses, although the differences between the RDAs and toxic levels may vary greatly. The fat-soluble vitamins, especially vitamins A and D, are toxic in doses close to the RDAs, but most water-soluble vitamins can be taken in very large doses without apparent harm. Unless you know about relative toxicities and dosages of vitamins, taking high-level supplements may be dangerous. In contrast, it is almost impossible to reach megadose levels if you get your vitamins through the foods you eat.

There are certain groups of people who may be prone to vitamin deficiencies. In many cases, these needs can be met through a normal diet, but you should seek nutritional advice if you fall within one of the groups listed below.

Pregnant women need more vitamins than other adults, but not megadoses. Some physicians recommend supplements during pregnancy, though a woman can generally meet her increased vitamin needs through a good diet. According to the RDAs pregnant women should get 15 to 50 percent more vitamins each day (but 100 percent more vitamin D and folacin). Recent research indicates that vitamin supplements containing folic acid can decrease the incidence of neurological tube defects (for example spina bifida) in the fetus. This is probably due to a low intake of folic acid in the American diet.

Elderly people may need supplements because they reduce their consumption of foods that are good sources of vitamins.

Frequent aspirin takers, such as people with arthritis, should ask their physicians about supplements since aspirin interferes with the metabolism of vitamin C and folacin.

Heavy drinkers may need extra B vitamins and vitamin C since heavy alcohol consumption often depletes these vitamins in the body.

Smokers use up vitamin C at a faster rate than nonsmokers. A committee of the National Academy of Sciences recommends that the RDA for vitamin C for smokers be 100 milligrams (as compared to 60 milligrams for nonsmoking adults). A balanced diet—indeed, even an 8-ounce glass of orange juice—will easily satisfy this RDA.

Functions and sources

Each vitamin carries out specific functions, and if a certain vitamin is lacking or is improperly used by the body, a particular deficiency disease usually results. In such cases vitamins have worked miracles. Vitamin C has cured scurvy; vitamin A has cured night blindness; B vitamins have restored stamina and alleviated mental disturbances—but only when the lack of these vitamins in the diet, or in rare cases a metabolic inability to utilize them, was the cause in the first place.

Vitamin A Vitamin A promotes good vision, particularly vision in dim light, by generating pigments necessary for the proper workings of the retina (it is also known as retinol). This fat-soluble vitamin helps form and maintain healthy skin, teeth, mucous membranes, and skeletal and soft tissue. In addition, it may be essential for reproduction and lactation, and may inhibit the development of tumors as well. Another possible function, suggested by preliminary research, is to increase resistance to infection in children.

Vitamin A deficiency can increase susceptibility to infectious diseases, as well as causing vision problems. Potent forms of vitamin A have recently been used as a treatment for acne. Large doses, however, can be toxic and quite dangerous; for example, they can cause abnormal development of the fetus in pregnant women.

A number of animal foods contain vitamin A. But most of our vitamin A comes from plant sources, namely dark green and yellow vegetables and fruits that contain beta carotene, a vitamin A precursor that is converted into the vitamin in the body's intestinal wall.

Sources: Cod and halibut fish oil, liver, kidney, and other organ meats, milk, cream, and cheese. All these sources except skim milk (which is fortified with vitamin A) have the disadvantage of being high in fat or cholesterol or both. Vegetable sources (see *beta carotene*) are fat and cholesterol free.

Beta carotene One of a larger group of substances known as carotenoids, beta carotene has been overshadowed by vitamin A. Scientists once thought that the benefits of beta carotene were due to its conversion into vitamin A, but research suggests that it actually is a potent substance on its own, with antioxidant properties that may protect against cancer. Unlike vitamin A, beta carotene is nontoxic even in large amounts. The body regulates the conversion of beta carotene to vitamin A at the rate the body requires. The worst a large amount of beta carotene could do is turn your skin yellow or orange, even if you were to eat enormous quantities of it (for example, a pound or two of carrots a day).

Sources: Carrots, sweet potatoes, pumpkin and other orange winter squashes, canteloupe, pink grapefruit, spinach, apricots, broccoli, and most dark green leafy vegetables. The more intense the green or yellow-orange color, the more beta carotene the fruit or vegetable contains.

Vitamin D The "sunshine vitamin"—so-called because deficiencies are rare in sunny climates—promotes the absorption of calcium, which is necessary for the normal development of bones and teeth. (Vitamin D is also known as "calciferol.") It also helps maintain proper blood levels of calcium and phosphorus. A deficiency leads to soft bones, or rickets. Although vitamin D is classified as a nutrient—that is, it comes from foods—it is also manufactured by the body after exposure to daylight or sunshine. (Ten or fifteen minutes of sunshine three times weekly is sufficient to produce the body's requirement for vitamin D.)

Megadoses can be toxic and dangerous, since too much vitamin D can result in calcium reabsorption from bone and subsequent deposition in soft tissues, such as the heart or lungs.

Sources: Fortified milk (all milk is fortified with vitamin D in the United States), butter, margarine, cheese, cream, fish, oysters, and fortified cereals.

Vitamin E Also called tocopherol, this vitamin is an antioxidant that protects tissue against the damage of oxidation, as well as helping in the formation of red blood cells and in the utilization of vitamin K. As an antioxidant, it helps destroy or neutralize free radicals (unstable oxygen molecules), and thus may play some role in preventing cancer or slowing the aging process, though much remains to be learned about its functions. Preliminary research suggests it may help prevent cardiovascular disease, including heart attack and stroke, by reducing the harmful effects of LDL cholesterol and by preventing blood clots. But no clinical studies have ever shown that it can prevent or cure any disease in humans (though vitamin E supplements have been heavily promoted by manufacturers in recent years, along with vitamin C). Nor can supplements counteract the effects of smoking.

Topical vitamin E (applied to the skin) has no unique properties. Because it's an oil, it coats the skin and keeps natural moisture from evaporating. But it's no more effective than mineral oil or other moisturizing ingredients. There's no evidence that applying it to wounds promotes healing or prevents the formation of scar tissue (contrary to the claims made by some cosmetics manufacturers) or that it counteracts the damaging effects of sunburn or ultraviolet rays.

Researchers have not discovered any toxic effects of megadoses (ten times the RDA), though side effects such as headaches have occasionally been reported. Since longterm effects, as well as any potential benefits, of megadoses are unknown, they are not recommended.

Sources: Vegetable oils (soybean, cottonseed, sunflower, corn) and products made from them such as margarine; also wheat germ, corn, nuts, seeds, olives, asparagus, spinach and other green leafy vegetables.

Vitamin K Without this vitamin, blood would fail to clot. Preliminary studies suggest it also plays a role in maintaining strong bones in the elderly. Bacteria in the body's intestines manufacture about 80 percent of the vitamin K we need, and the rest comes from the diet. Deficiencies are almost unknown, and are usually caused by an inability to absorb the vitamin, rather than an inadequate intake. Infants, for example, may not have the bacteria that produces the vitamin, and patients taking antibiotics may become deficient because the drugs can destroy the bacteria.

Sources: Cabbage, cauliflower, spinach and other leafy vegetables, cereals, soybean and other vegetable oils.

Thiamin (vitamin B_1) Thiamin plays an essential role in metabolism, helping cells convert carbohydrates into energy. It is also necessary for healthy brain and nerve cells as well as heart function. Deficiencies can cause fatigue, weakness, nerve damage, even heart failure, and, at its most extreme, the disease beriberi. However, thiamin deficiency is rare in the United States.

Thiamin is especially sensitive to heat, and, like some other water-soluble vitamins, quickly leaches into cooking water.

Sources: Whole grains (especially wheat germ), lean meats (especially pork), fish, peas, dried beans and soybeans, peanuts, fortified breads, pasta, and cereals. Milk and other dairy products, fruits, and vegetables are not high in thiamin, but when consumed in quantity they become a significant source.

Riboflavin (vitamin B_2) Like thiamin, riboflavin helps release energy from carbohydrates. It interacts with other B vitamins and is essential for growth and for the production of red blood cells. A deficiency can cause skin to become dry and cracked and the eyes to be sensitive to bright light, but riboflavin is abundant in foods, and so deficiencies are rare in the United States.

Sources: Milk and other dairy products, lean meats, eggs, nuts, green leafy vegetables, and legumes. Bread and cereal are often fortified with riboflavin, as well.

Niacin (vitamin B_3) Niacin is shorthand for nicotinic acid, a vitamin that is crucial for the conversion of food into energy. It also helps maintain normal functioning of the skin, nerves, and digestive system. The body can manufacture niacin from tryptophan (a component of protein) or can get it preformed in foods. Deficiency of niacin causes pellagra, a disease characterized by inflammation of the skin, digestive problems, and mental impairment.

Megadoses can be dangerous, causing rashes, liver damage, ulcers, and other side effects. There's no truth to the contention that niacin boosts energy and strength. However, niacin is sometimes prescribed to lower blood cholesterol, in which case it should be used only under medical supervision; in large doses, the vitamin acts as a drug, not simply a supplement.

Sources: Nuts, dairy products, lean meats, poultry, fish, and eggs. Legumes and enriched breads and cereals also supply some niacin.

Vitamin B_6 Vitamin B_6, also called pyroxidine, is important in many chemical reactions of proteins and protein components. The more protein a person eats, the more B_6 is required to utilize it. B_6 helps maintain normal brain function and aids in the formation of red blood cells. It also plays a role in synthesizing antibodies in the immune system. Deficiency of B_6 is rare in this country. Long thought to be harmless at any level, B_6 taken in megadoses can cause numbness and other neurological disorders.

Sources: Meats, fish, nuts, beans and other legumes, bananas and some other fruits, eggs, whole grains, and fortified cereals and breads.

Vitamin B_{12} Like all B vitamins, B_{12} is important for metabolism. It aids in red blood cell formation and helps maintain the central nervous system. Vitamin B_{12} is made from bacteria and is only present in foods that contain the bacteria or foods from animals that have ingested the bacteria. Thus, almost all the vitamin B_{12} in the diet comes from animal products; strict vegetarians who consume no dairy products or eggs may need a B_{12} supplement. Soy sauce and other fermented products may contain some of the vitamin. A deficiency of vitamin B_{12} causes a disease called pernicious anemia, but usually this results from an inability to absorb the vitamin rather than from a nutritional deficiency. It can be treated with injections of B_{12}. There is no evidence, however, that B_{12} injections boost energy or well-being, and no evidence that large doses of B_{12} can confer any health benefits.

Sources: Milk and milk products, eggs, meat, poultry, and shellfish.

Pantothenic acid and biotin No deficiencies of either of these B vitamins have been observed outside of experimental settings, so requirements for them have never been established. Pantothenic acid, or vitamin B_5, is found in all living tissue (its name means "widespread"); it is essential for metabolizing food and in synthesizing various body chemicals, such as hormones and cholesterol. Megadoses produce no toxic effects, other than possible diarrhea.

Like the other B vitamins, biotin is essential for metabolism of proteins and carbohydrates. It also helps build and oxidize fatty acids and has other chemical functions similar to those of pantothenic acid and vitamin B_{12}. Found in many foods, biotin is also manufactured in the human intestine.

Sources: Eggs, milk and milk products, fish, whole-grain cereals, legumes, yeast, lean beef, broccoli and other vegetables in the cabbage family, white and sweet potatoes, and most other foods that supply B vitamins.

Folacin Important in the synthesis of DNA, which controls cell function and heredity as well as tissue growth, folacin (or folic acid) also acts with B_{12} to produce red blood cells. Because folacin is plentiful in foods, most people get an adequate intake, but pregnant women should be extra careful to consume enough of this vitamin since it is so important to the growth and function of new cells. Preliminary studies suggest folacin may play some role in lowering the risk of such birth defects as spina bifida and may possibly be helpful in preventing cancer of the cervix.

Sources: Dark green leafy vegetables, citrus fruits and juices, beans and other legumes, wheat bran and other whole grains, pork, poultry, shellfish.

Vitamin C (ascorbic acid) Vitamin C plays many roles in the body, including helping to promote healthy gums and teeth, aiding in iron absorption, maintaining normal connective tissue (collagen), and healing wounds. Recent research suggests that an intake of vitamin C three to five times the RDA (easily obtained from foods) may be helpful to health. An adequate intake may help protect against cataracts. A chronic low intake is associated with cancers of the stomach and esophagus. However, it's not true that huge doses of vitamin C cure any of these conditions, nor will vitamin C supplements help ward them off. And any excess amounts are simply excreted.

Contrary to myth, no well-controlled studies have consistently shown that megadoses of vitamin C can significantly prevent, cure, or shorten the duration of a cold. Megadoses from supplements can cause diarrhea and distort the results of some medical tests.

Sources: Citrus fruits, strawberries, tomatoes, broccoli, turnip greens and other greens, sweet potatoes, white potatoes, and cantaloupe. Most other fruits and vegetables contain some vitamin C; meats, fish, and milk have small amounts.

Minerals

The minerals that act as nutrients are absolutely essential to a host of vital processes in the body, from bone formation to the functioning of the heart and digestive system. Many are necessary for the activity of enzymes (proteins that serve as catalysts in the body's chemical reactions). In recent years, scientists have been paying great attention to minerals, looking for links between them and the major chronic diseases—high blood pressure, osteoporosis, cardiovascular disease, and even cancer. This research has been very promising. Encouraged by this research, as well as ads by manufacturers of supplements, millions of Americans now take a variety of mineral pills, sometimes in large doses, in the the belief that "if a little is good, a lot is better." Does anyone need these supplements?

Most people don't need supplements, and no one needs megadoses. The interactions among minerals, vitamins, other nutrients, and various substances in the body are so complex that taking too much of any mineral (or other supplement) can interfere with the body's use of other nutrients. The key to good health lies in maintaining the proper percentages—not too little, not too much. The National Academy of Sciences has issued Recommended Dietary Allowances (RDAs) for just seven minerals; for five others it has offered what it more cautiously terms "estimated safe and adequate dietary intakes." Since there is a danger of overdosing (some minerals, taken in large amounts, can be fatal), no one should self-prescribe mineral supplements in amounts greater than these recommended intakes. The best way to ensure an adequate supply of minerals—with the few possible exceptions discussed below—is to eat a varied and balanced diet. That way you'll also get a supply of vitamins and fiber, along with any nutrients that haven't been identified yet.

Minerals are basic elements of the earth's crust (in contrast to vitamins, they are inorganic matter—they contain no carbon). Carried into the soil, groundwater, and sea by erosion, they are taken up by plants and consumed by animals and humans. The minerals in foods are indestructible—even if you burn your food to a cinder, it will retain all its original minerals. However, when food is boiled, some of its minerals may dissolve into the water and be discarded. Minerals can also be processed out of foods, as when grains are refined to make flour.

There are more than sixty minerals in the body (making up about 4 percent of its weight), but only about twenty-two are considered essential. Of these, seven—calcium, chlorine, magnesium, phosphorus, potassium, sodium, and sulfur—are called macro-minerals because they are present in the body in relatively large quantities. The other essential minerals are termed trace or even ultratrace nutrients because they are present in such minute quantities.

Three key minerals

Sodium, calcium, and iron are of particular concern in the American diet. On average, we consume too much of one (sodium), and too little of the others.

FINDING THE SODIUM

For most people, cutting back on sodium means reducing their salt (sodium chloride) intake. Salt is the main form of sodium added to foods and is probably the worst sodium offender. In general, however, anything with sodium in its name is a source. A few of the sources of sodium commonly added to packaged foods include: baking powder, baking soda, brine, garlic salt, kelp, monosodium glutamate (MSG), onion salt, sea salt, sodium chloride, sodium citrate, sodium nitrate, sodium phosphate, sodium saccharin, and soy sauce.

Some minerals, such as phosphorus, are so plentiful in the American diet that deficiencies are virtually unknown. In the case of sodium, the average American consumes two to three times as much as health officials generally recommend (mostly in the form of salt, or sodium chloride). An estimated 5 to 10 percent of all people (and about half of all hypertensives) are sensitive to sodium: their blood pressure rises when they consume more sodium, increasing the risk of stroke, kidney disease, and heart disease. And sensitivity to sodium increases with age. But sodium isn't the only mineral that affects blood pressure. Many studies have found that potassium, calcium, and magnesium may actually help prevent or control elevated blood pressure.

On the other hand, most Americans don't consume enough calcium. The typical American woman, in particular, consumes only about half as much calcium as is recommended. The body builds bone mass during childhood and young adulthood. It appears that peak bone mass is not reached until age twenty-five or later. Though it is most crucial to consume adequate calcium in these formative years, you still need substantial amounts as an adult, since bones constantly take up and release calcium throughout life. Yet many adults drink little or no milk and shortchange themselves on other sources of calcium, too.

Beginning about the age of thirty-five to forty, bone mass usually begins to decline—this is not debilitating if you have built adequate amounts of bone during your first three decades. But for many older people, especially women, a shortfall in calcium, combined with the body's reduced ability to absorb the calcium efficiently, contributes to the development of osteoporosis, a more drastic loss of bone mass and density that increasingly makes bones fragile. The decline in a woman's estrogen production during and after menopause may impair the bones' ability to retain calcium or actually lead to its significant loss. It's true that other hormones, as well as heredity, drugs, exercise, and other life-style factors also affect the health of a woman's bones. Still, one recent study found that adequate calcium intake may reduce the risk of hip fractures by 50 to 60 percent.

In recent years some studies have also suggested that a low calcium intake (especially less than 600 milligrams a day) increases the risk of high blood pressure. The mineral may help control blood pressure by decreasing contraction of muscles in the walls of blood vessels or by affecting certain hormones.

Like a lack of calcium, a deficit of iron is also one of the most common nutritional shortfalls: Up to 15 percent of American women of childbearing age have some degree of iron deficiency. The deficiency is most common in women because of the physiological demands of menstruation and childbearing. Initially there are no symptoms when the body's iron stores are depleted. But as the iron supply to the bone marrow dwindles, so does the marrow's ability to produce healthy red blood cells. Eventually this can result in iron-deficiency anemia, characterized by weakness, paleness, shortness of breath, and an increased susceptibility to infection.

Cooking in cast-iron pots is one way to increase the iron content of food. The more acidic the food (such as spaghetti sauce) and the longer it cooks, the higher the increase in iron content.

An iron deficit isn't necessarily due to poor eating habits. An otherwise balanced diet *may not* supply adequate iron, particularly if you are in one of these groups:

Menstruating women, especially those who bleed heavily, since blood losses increase the need for iron.

Pregnant women, whose iron needs increase because of the demands of the fetus and placenta.

Dieters, especially women, since the less they eat, the more likely it is that they will not get enough iron.

Endurance athletes, such as marathoners, who tend to have a higher incidence of iron depletion, which may impair top performance. This iron shortfall has been attributed to a variety of reasons, including the increased elimination of iron during prolonged exercise.

Strict vegetarians, since the animal products they don't eat are the best sources of iron. These vegetarians have to make a special effort to eat other foods that contain fair amounts of iron, such as legumes, dried fruits, leafy greens, and enriched cereals and grains.

Infants and children, because of their rapid growth; deficiencies may adversely affect their learning capacity.

Even if you fall into one of these groups, consult your doctor before taking iron supplements, since you may not be lacking in iron. Large doses of iron supplements can damage the liver, pancreas, and heart. Prolonged use of iron pills can even be fatal for about one million Americans who have the genetic disorder known as hemochromatosis, in which the body overabsorbs the mineral.

Functions and sources

The list below highlights what the important macro- and trace minerals do in the body and which foods are the best sources. Remember, if you *do* take supplements, do not exceed the RDA or "estimated safe and adequate intake" given on pages 16-17. Pregnant and lactating women have special nutritional needs and should get professional dietary advice.

Boron Several studies have suggested that boron may help regulate the body's use of calcium, phosphorus, and magnesium.

Sources: Fruits and vegetables, especially apples, pears, broccoli, and carrots.

Calcium In addition to building and maintaining strong bones and teeth, calcium also helps regulate heartbeat and other muscle contractions and is necessary for proper blood clotting. Adequate calcium intake (preferably from foods) can help prevent or minimize osteoporosis—and may also help prevent hypertension. Vitamin D and lactose (milk sugar) help improve calcium absorption by the body. Oxalic acid, found in some leafy green vegetables (notably spinach), reduces the absorption of calcium somewhat from that particular food.

Sources: Milk and milk products, dark green leafy vegetables, broccoli, some tofu, canned sardines and salmon (eaten with their bones), and some fortified cereals. Grain products also supply a small amount of calcium.

Chlorine (chloride) Essential in maintaining the body's fluid and acid-base balance, chloride is also a necessary component of gastric juices.

Sources: Primarily table salt (sodium chloride); also fish.

Chromium This mineral is important in the metabolism of carbohydrates and fats. A deficiency in chromium may impair the action of insulin and the regulation of glucose in the blood.

Sources: Meat, whole grains, brewer's yeast, and fortified cereals.

Copper Along with iron, copper helps in the formation of red blood cells. It also helps keep bones, blood vessels, nerves, and the immune system healthy.

Sources: Shellfish (especially oysters), beans, nuts, organ meats, whole grains, and potatoes.

Fluorine (fluoride) Fluoride helps form bone and teeth. Some studies suggest it may help prevent osteoporosis.

Sources: Fluoridated water and foods grown or cooked in it, canned fish (eaten with their bones), and tea.

The daily intake of minerals is minuscule, and some are measured in micrograms, which is one-thousandth of a milligram (or one-millionth of a gram, which is about 1/28 of an ounce). However, the tiny amounts are in no way indicative of the relative importance of minerals to your health. For instance, the .00004 percent of your body that is iodine is no less critical to survival than the 1.5 to 2 percent that is calcium.

Iodine Iodine is necessary for normal cell metabolism. It is necessary for the thyroid gland to synthesize and secrete the thyroid hormones thyroxine and levothyroxine. A sufficient intake of iodine helps prevent goiter (enlargement of the thyroid), which is now rare in developed countries primarily due to the use of iodized salt.

Sources: Primarily iodized salt, but widely dispersed in the food supply—notably in seafood, seaweed, dairy products, and crops from iodine-rich areas. So even if you eat little iodized salt, you probably get enough iodine.

Iron Iron is essential to the formation of hemoglobin (which carries oxygen in the blood) and myoglobin (which carries oxygen in muscle). It is also part of several enzymes and proteins in the body. Heme iron, the type found in meat and other animal products, is better absorbed by the body than nonheme iron, the type found in foods derived from plants. To enhance the absorption of nonheme iron from grains and vegetables, consume a food high in vitamin C at that meal, or else eat even a small amount of meat or other source of heme iron with it.

Sources: Liver, kidneys, red meat, poultry, fish, eggs, peas, beans, nuts, dried fruits, leafy green vegetables, enriched pasta and bread, and fortified cereals.

Magnesium Vital to many basic metabolic functions, magnesium also aids in bone growth and the function of nerves, bones, and muscles, including the regulation of normal heart rhythm. A low intake has been linked to high blood pressure, heart-rhythm abnormalities, and, consequently, heart attack.

Sources: Wheat bran, whole grains, leafy green vegetables, meat, milk, nuts, beans, bananas, and apricots.

Manganese Reproduction and energy production are among the roles played by this trace mineral, which also may be as essential as calcium for building bones. Excess manganese may interfere with iron absorption.

Sources: Whole grains, nuts, beans, vegetables, fruit, instant coffee, tea, and cocoa powder.

Molybdenum Molybdenum is needed to activate certain enzymes in the body. No deficiency in humans has ever been documented.

Sources: Whole grains, liver, beans, and leafy vegetables.

Phosphorus Vital for energy production, phosphorus also helps build bone and teeth as well as forming cell membranes and genetic material. Excess phosphorus, which may impair the body's use of iron and calcium, may be a problem for people who habitually consume soft drinks.

Sources: Almost all foods: especially plentiful in fish, meat, poultry, dairy products, eggs, peas, beans, and nuts.

Potassium Potassium is vital for muscle contraction, nerve impulses, and the proper functioning of the heart and kidneys. Together with sodium, calcium, and magnesium, it helps regulate blood pressure and water balance in cells. There is some evidence that a high-potassium diet may reduce the risk of hypertension and stroke.

Sources: Most foods, especially oranges and orange juice, bananas, potatoes (with skin), dried fruits, yogurt, meat, poultry, and milk.

Selenium Selenium is part of certain enzymes that act as antioxidants—that is, they help fight cell damage caused by oxygen-derived compounds and thus may protect against certain cancers. The mineral is also needed for proper immune response and the proper functioning of the heart muscle. Large doses, as supplied by some supplements, can be extremely toxic.

Sources: Fish, shellfish, red meat, grains, eggs, chicken, garlic, and liver. The amount in vegetables depends on the soil they are grown in.

Sodium Sodium helps regulate blood pressure and water balance in the body. In people who are sensitive to it, sodium can elevate blood pressure.

Sources: Table salt and salt added to prepared foods, especially cheese, smoked meats, soups, salty snacks, and "fast food."

Zinc Next to iron, zinc is the second most abundant trace mineral in the body. It is important in the activity of enzymes needed for cell division, growth, and repair (wound healing), as well as proper functioning of the immune system. Zinc also plays a role in acuity of taste and smell, the metabolism of carbohydrates, and the replication of DNA. Zinc deficiency is rare, but several groups are at risk—heavy drinkers (alcohol speeds zinc excretion), endurance athletes (sweating causes significant zinc depletion), and strict vegetarians (fruits and vegetables contain little zinc). Zinc is relatively nontoxic except in extremely high doses, which can cause nausea, impaired immunity, and increased LDL ("bad") cholesterol.

Sources: Seafood (especially oysters), meat, liver, eggs, milk, brewer's yeast, whole wheat bread, wheat germ.

Water

Without the nutrients in food, we can live for several weeks; without water we would die in a few days. More than half the weight of the human body is water, which is the basis of all body fluids, including digestive juices, blood, urine, lymph, and perspiration. All cell processes and all organ functions depend on it. It's essential as a lubricant, and it's the basis of saliva, mucous secretions throughout the body, and the fluids that bathe the joints. Water is needed to keep food moving through the intestinal tract and to eliminate wastes; it helps prevent constipation, which may occur if you're eating high-fiber foods. Water also helps regulate body temperature by distributing heat and cooling the body via perspiration.

The body loses and needs to replace, under average circumstances, two to three quarts of water every day. If you're exercising or doing physical work in the heat, the loss can be much more. We get some water from the foods we eat, most of which are 85 percent to 96 percent water. Some water is produced as a by-product of metabolism. But six to eight glasses of liquid—which can include juice, milk, and soup—are usually needed to make up the balance. Alcoholic and caffeinated beverages (coffee, tea, and cola) are not ideal for this purpose because they have a diuretic effect—that is, they increase urine production. The best source is generally plain old drinking water.

Fluoridation

Fluoride in the water sometimes occurs naturally, as in Colorado Springs and other communities. And sometimes local governments, usually cities, add it to the water supply in controlled quantities. As medical science has known for decades, fluoride interacts with tooth enamel and hardens it, making it less susceptible to decay—50 to 70 percent less susceptible. In the generations born since the 1950s, when fluoridation came into wide use, toothaches and tooth extractions are almost an oddity.

Fluoridated water may also play a role in building strong bones and warding off osteoporosis. Studies have shown that women who live in areas with naturally fluoridated water suffer fewer osteoporotic fractures and have generally greater bone strength than those who drink nonfluoridated water.

Research shows that cool drinks—40° to 50°—are absorbed more quickly than lukewarm ones.

As early as 1908, fluoride's properties as a tooth-decay preventive were deduced from observing dental health patterns in communities where the water supply was naturally fluroidated. According to a number of long-term studies, such communities have no greater incidence of cancer, heart disease, liver disease, or other ills than other places. One well-known side effect of fluoride, however, is dental fluorosis, a light mottling of the tooth enamel that may be cosmetically unappealing. This occurs in some people in areas where the natural fluoride content of the water is very high.

Bottled water

Sales of bottled water have quadrupled during the past decade. There may be a good reason to drink this product—perhaps your tap supply is temporarily shut off or is contaminated. Or your tap water may simply have an "off" taste, and you prefer the taste of bottled water. But many people think bottled water is "healthier" and "purer," which in most cases is nonsense. In fact, about 25 percent of bottled water in the United States is just processed tap water from municipal systems. Some bottled waters are high in sodium, and may lack fluoride. Some may also contain contaminants that aren't allowed in public drinking water. If your tap water comes from a municipal system, there is no reason to forsake it for the bottled variety.

When you exercise

Even if you don't feel thirsty when exercising, it's important to replace the water you lose through sweating. (Thirst is satisfied long before you have replenished lost fluids.) In hot weather, you should drink at least 16 to 20 ounces of fluid—three glasses or so—2 hours before exercising and another 8 ounces 15 to 20 minutes before. While you exercise, drink 4 to 8 ounces every 10 to 20 minutes. And after exercise, you should, of course, be sure you have drunk enough to replace the fluid you've sweated out.

Chapter 2

VEGETABLES

If the key to good nutrition is consuming a variety of foods, then vegetables can truly stand as the cornerstone of a healthy diet. Of all foods, they offer the most diversity: There are literally hundreds of varieties available to us, and because of careful plant breeding, today's vegetable harvest is continually being expanded and improved. In addition, vegetables are replete with nutrients. They supply nearly all of the vitamins and minerals required for good health, and many of them—especially starchy vegetables like potatoes and winter squash—contain complex carbohydrates, which furnish us with energy. Most also provide dietary fiber, and a few, such as lima beans and potatoes, can contribute significantly to your protein intake. At the same time, vegetables contain no cholesterol, have little or no fat, and are low in calories. (Even half a cup of boiled potatoes or squash contains fewer calories than a tablespoon of butter.) In nutritional parlance, vegetables are "nutrient dense"—that is, their store of nutrients is relatively high for the number of calories they supply. When you consider how inexpensive most vegetables are compared to meats and other animal foods, you really are getting the most out of the calories you consume when you emphasize vegetables in your diet.

OUT OF FAVOR, IN FAVOR

With such diversity of choice, it's nearly impossible for anyone to say categorically, "I don't like vegetables." Along with an impressive range of sizes and shapes, vegetables offer a rich mix of colors—among them green, yellow, orange, red, white, and purple in dozens of shades—and a correspondingly wide array of flavors and textures. Moreover, most vegetables are easy to prepare, and can be eaten raw or cooked. Yet in the United States, vegetables have typically been served as accompaniments to meat or fish, rather than as equal partners or as the main course (as they are in Asian and Middle Eastern cuisine, for example). According to a 1990 survey by the National Cancer Institute, the average American eats less than two servings of vegetables a day (including salad) rather than the recom-

mended three to five servings. Furthermore, the vegetables that Americans favor are, as often as not, among the lowest in vitamins and minerals. Together with potatoes, carrots, and broccoli, which are packed with nutrients, the most popular vegetables include iceberg lettuce, cucumbers, and celery, which are far less nutrient-dense.

Still, the demand for vegetables has been rising. Following several decades during which per-capita consumption of vegetables declined, Americans have been steadily eating more fresh vegetables during the past twenty years. Excluding potatoes, which are in significantly greater demand than any other vegetable, consumption of a dozen fresh vegetables increased from 65 pounds per person annually in 1970 to about 92 pounds in 1989. The biggest gains were for lettuce, onions, tomatoes, and broccoli.

There has also been increased interest in new or unusual vegetables. Some are familiar foods in different guises—white eggplants or baby squashes, for example. Other "new" vegetables have been around for some time and are simply being rediscovered by imaginative cooks—beet greens and kale, to mention two traditional American favorites, or bok choy and daikon radish, which were once found only in Asian markets and are now available at corner greengrocers and in many supermarkets. (The production of Asian vegetables in California increased by 41 percent between 1988 and 1989.) You will find these less-familiar foods covered in this chapter as well as in Chapter 4, which treats even more exotic varieties of vegetables and fruits.

TYPES OF VEGETABLES AND THEIR NUTRIENTS

Most of the vegetables that we eat today are descended from ancient wild plants that were domesticated centuries ago and have been widely cultivated over the last few hundred years. There are several ways to classify vegetables, but two of the most basic are by their botanical families, or by which part of the plant is eaten—the root, stalk, or leaves, for example. Although the botanical designation of a vegetable is sometimes useful, it doesn't

determine the vegetable's nutrient content. That depends largely on what part of the plant it comes from.

Leafy vegetables—including spinach, salad greens, collards, kale, radicchio, and watercress—may grow in tight or loose heads or individually on stems; a few leafy greens are actually the tops of root vegetables, like turnips and beets. Lettuces and other salad greens are nearly always served raw, while sturdier, more flavorful greens, like kale, are generally cooked. Some greens can be eaten either way. All leaves contain lots of water and few carbohydrates (or calories). Most green leaves are excellent sources of beta carotene and vitamin C, and good sources of fiber and folacin (a B vitamin). They also supply varying quantities of iron and calcium.

Flowers, buds, and stalks range from the ordinary, such as celery, broccoli and cauliflower, to some of the aristocrats of the vegetable kingdom—asparagus and artichokes, for example. These plants tend to be rich in vitamin C, calcium, and potassium, as well as dietary fiber. Cauliflower and broccoli also offer cancer-fighting compounds. Their mild to slightly sweet flavors are appealing alone, or with a range of sauces or accompaniments.

Seeds and pods are the parts of plants that store energy. Snap beans, lima beans, peas, and sweet corn have more protein than other vegetables, and also contain more carbohydrates than do leafy, stalk or flower vegetables. When the vegetables are immature (and freshly picked), the carbohydrates are in the form of sugars; with time—on the plant or after harvesting—these sugars turn to starch. The B vitamins, zinc, potassium, magnesium, calcium, and iron are also nutritional strong points of these foods.

Roots, bulbs, and tubers grow underground and act as nutrient storehouses. Onions, turnips, potatoes, beets, carrots, radishes, and parsnips are sturdy and dense, making them satisfying foods. Interestingly, however, in some cases—such as beets and onions—the tops of the plant (beet greens and scallions) are richer in vitamins and min-

erals than the roots or bulbs. Because of their high starch content, some of these vegetables are higher in calories than most of their aboveground counterparts. The foods in this group make various other nutritional contributions: Potatoes are good sources of vitamin C and potassium; both sweet potatoes and carrots contain abundant amounts of beta carotene; radishes and turnips are good sources of fiber and vitamin C; and a number of studies suggest that onions and garlic may lower blood pressure and cholesterol levels.

Fruit vegetables, which include eggplants, squashes, peppers, and tomatoes, are the pulpy, seed-bearing bodies of the plants on which they grow. Technically speaking, these are fruits rather than vegetables (because the fleshy part of the plant contains seeds), but we use them like vegetables and refer to them as such. Generally higher in calories than leafy vegetables, stalks, or flowers, they also tend to be good sources of vitamin C. These vegetables offer a myriad of flavors and textures, which makes them useful as seasonings and accents (think of tomato paste or chili sauce), as well as staple foods.

Color is a good clue to nutrient content. Most yellow and orange vegetables, such as carrots, winter squashes, or sweet potatoes, get their color from beta carotene and other carotenoids, which are precursors to vitamin A. Dark green leafy vegetables also contain carotenoids (as well as the pigment chlorophyll, which gives them their green color). The more intense a vegetable's green or yellow color, the more beta carotene it contains.

CRUCIFERAE—THE DISEASE FIGHTERS

One group of vegetables has received a great deal of attention from researchers for its role in disease prevention. Named after the Latin word for "cross" because they bear cross-shaped flowers, cruciferous vegetables include cabbage and close relatives such as broccoli, Brussels sprouts, cauliflower, kale, and collards as well as mustard greens, rutabagas, and turnips. All are part of a botanical genus known as *Brassica.* Studies of cruciferous vegetables have shown that they contain nitrogen compounds called indoles, which appear to

be effective in protecting against certain forms of cancer, particularly cancers of the stomach and large intestine. More recent recent research has revealed other promising anticancer compounds in these vegetables: Some of them seem to stimulate the release of anticancer enzymes, while antioxidant nutrients—such as carotenoids and vitamin C—help to sweep up cancer-promoting unstable oxygen molecules known as free radicals. In addition, most cruciferous vegetables are good sources of dietary fiber. A few—chiefly kale, collard greens, and turnip greens—also supply calcium, while others such as Brussels sprouts provide iron.

AVAILABLE YEAR ROUND

At one time the vegetables consumers bought were grown on local farms (or came from the family garden), but today the major vegetable crops are part of the vast American industry called "agribusiness," which began developing after World War II. Advances in agricultural and food-handling technology created a movement toward large-volume production. Small farmers expanded their land holdings if they could, or entered into cooperative marketing ventures with other farms. As a result, farm acreage increased tremendously in warm-weather states, such as California, New Mexico, Arizona, Texas, and Florida, which now produce the bulk of the domestic vegetable crop. (California alone supplies more than 50 percent.) Growers in these states, aided by machinery at nearly every stage of cultivation, can harvest a steady, year-round stream of vegetables, which are then dispatched in refrigerated train cars and trucks to food brokers and wholesalers nationwide. Consequently, consumers are never limited to seasonal foods from their own locality.

This development doesn't mean that all vegetables are readily available throughout the year. Asparagus and artichokes, for example, are more difficult to cultivate than broccoli or cabbage, and so are raised in smaller quantities in more limited seasons.

Increasingly, though, less-abundant vegetables are supplemented by imports—asparagus and eggplant from South American countries, for example—during off-seasons in the United States.

Greater availability, however, has come at a price. Mechanized growing and handling methods, combined with the rigors of long-distance shipping, have prompted large-scale commercial growers to emphasize hardiness over flavor and texture in developing many vegetable varieties. Vegetables displayed in supermarkets often appear fresh and sturdy, and are of a uniform size, but they probably don't equal the taste of produce grown locally. An appreciation for flavor and freshness on the part of consumers has prompted a resurgence of small farms that send their harvests to greenmarkets in nearby cities, allowing urbanites to take advantage of local crops. Residents of suburbs and small towns can often buy local vegetables at roadside farmstands or directly at the farms. And, more and more, Americans are growing their own vegetables, allowing them to cultivate flavorful varieties, pick them as soon as they're ripe, and cook them almost immediately.

If you have access to local sources of produce, by all means take advantage of them. But remember that most vegetables sold in supermarkets have perfectly adequate flavor and nutritional quality, and will probably be very good if they have been properly shipped and handled. Even vegetables transported a thousand miles and left in bins for a day or two are full of nutrients. It's important, however, to be able to distinguish between such vegetables and those that may have lost half of their vitamins because of careless storage and display. The shopping and storage guidelines in the entries that follow should help you in your selection.

FRESH, FROZEN, OR CANNED

If vegetables are truly farm fresh—harvested the same day you serve them—they will offer maximum nutritional value. To get the most from fresh vegetables, shop frequently and

use them as soon as possible. Some types of vegetables, however, if stored incorrectly (or for too long) before use, will lose a significant amount of their nutrients. If produce looks or feels wilted and pallid, or if you have inadvertently allowed the green beans to sit in the refrigerator for a week, you'll be better off with the frozen or even the canned version.

In general, frozen vegetables are preferable to canned. Once vegetables are harvested, a loss of nutrients starts to occur. But if the vegetables are flash-frozen soon after picking, they retain most of their nutrients, except for small amounts of vitamin C and other water-soluble vitamins. However, their texture probably won't be equal to that of well-prepared fresh vegetables, and they may suffer further nutrient loss if improperly stored or overcooked.

Canned vegetables, on the other hand, undergo a heating process that can destroy some of the vitamin C and B vitamins. Minerals aren't destroyed, but they may be lost if the canning liquid is not saved and used. In addition, large amounts of sodium are often added during processing. Though they have enough nutrients to be worth eating if nothing else is available, most canned vegetables lack the flavor and texture of produce that is fresh or frozen.

PESTICIDES AND WAXES

Pesticides and other "agrichemicals" kill insects that can damage crops, thus helping to ensure the huge volume and variety of vegetables on the market today. These chemicals have been accepted for years as a necessity of modern farming, but now they are being perceived as, perhaps, an unnecessary evil—a health risk that might not outweigh the advantages gained from eating fresh vegetables. The residues of scores of these compounds remain on the food we eat, while their toxic effects remain in question.

The Food and Drug Administration (FDA) monitors samples of domestic and imported foods for pesticide residues. In 1989 they found residues in 31 percent of the

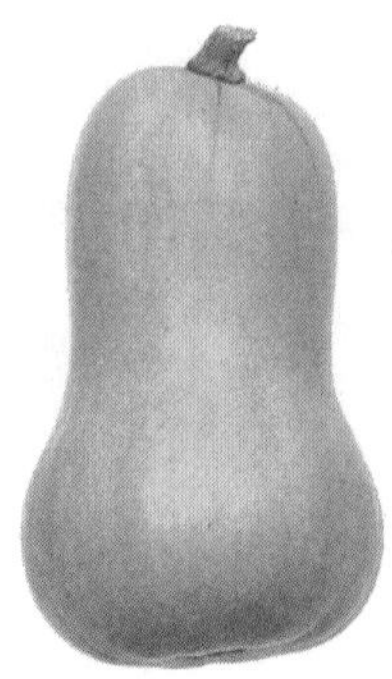

3,699 domestic vegetable samples tested. Less than 2 percent of the samples, however, contained levels of residues that exceeded tolerances set by the FDA. (About 5 percent of imported samples were found to contain excessive levels.) Yet the FDA tests only 1 percent of vegetables marketed in the United States. Even if a greater proportion were examined, some scientists believe that the FDA's acceptable levels are, in fact, too high.

Associated with the use of pesticides is the practice of waxing vegetables before sending them to market. Wax coatings keep food fresh and bright looking; they also slow moisture loss and thus extend shelf life. But waxes also seal in pesticide and fungicide residues (sometimes the chemicals are combined with the wax). Washing or scrubbing removes some, but not all, of these surface chemicals; the only way to completely remove them is by peeling the skin, which means discarding the portion richest in fiber and some nutrients. Vegetables that are commonly waxed include cucumbers, squashes, sweet and white potatoes, tomatoes, peppers, beets, and rutabagas. Sometimes, as with rutabagas and cucumbers, the layer of wax is visible on the surface—you can scrape some off with your thumbnail. But it isn't so obvious on potatoes or tomatoes. The FDA requires retailers to post signs identifying waxed produce (and the type of wax used), but few comply with the regulation.

PROTECTIVE STEPS

Despite the gaps in current research, enough evidence of toxicity in these residues has been gathered to justify concern. Fortunately, there are a number of sensible measures you can adopt.

- Try to buy fresh vegetables in season. When prolonged storage and long-distance shipping are not required, there's less need for antispoilage chemicals.
- Wash vegetables carefully. Many water-soluble residues rinse away with thorough washing. Peel vegetables with wax coatings, which washing does not remove. If you're not

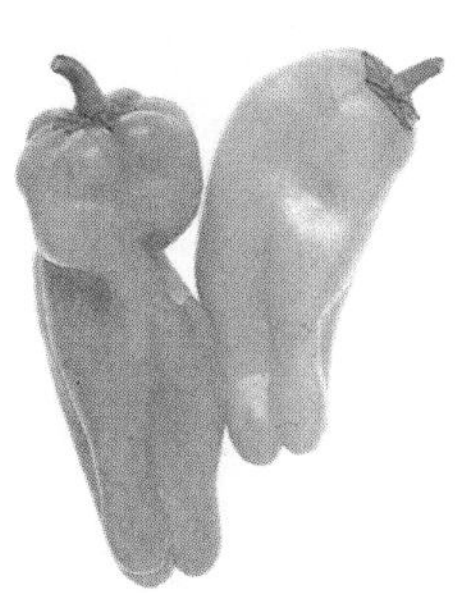

sure whether a vegetable has been waxed or not, check with the produce manager.

- Trim away tops and the very outer leaves from celery, lettuces, cabbages, and other leafy vegetables, which may contain the bulk of a vegetable's toxic residues. Be sure to wash the inner leaves.
- To avoid chemical residues in vegetables as much as possible, you can buy organic produce, which is available not only in health-food stores, but also in some farmers' markets and big-city supermarkets. "Organic" usually means that the food has been grown without chemical fertilizers or pesticides. However, not every state regulates that foods labeled "organic" must actually be raised without pesticides. Check with produce sellers to ascertain that you are actually getting organically grown vegetables; be aware, though, that they may not really know for certain.

PREPARATION AND COOKING

The nutritional content of vegetables, as well as their taste and texture, is affected by how you store and handle them, and especially by how you cook them. Specific guidelines are given in the individual entries that follow, but here are some general rules to keep in mind.

Nutrient loss occurs when vegetables are exposed to light and air; therefore, don't wash, chop, or slice vegetables until you are ready to use them. While vegetables should always be washed before you cook or serve them raw, long soaking is not recommended, as it can leach out water-soluble vitamins. You can quickly but thoroughly rinse vegetables under cold running water, or dunk them in several changes of water in a basin. Use a soft brush to remove dirt that clings; lukewarm water also helps to release sand and grit from leafy vegetables.

When peeling and chopping vegetables, remember that many nutrients are concentrated just beneath the skin. If possible, do not peel vegetables such as potatoes and beets; or, cook them in their skins and peel them after cooking, when their thin skins will

slip off. (Even if you don't eat the skin, leaving it intact during cooking helps preserve nutrients.)

In general, most vegetables should be cooked until they are barely tender or crisp-tender. Only then will they retain most of their nutrients, bright colors, and fresh flavors. Of course, this rule does not apply to every vegetable: Potatoes, for instance, need to be cooked until tender, or they will be unpalatable. But they can be baked, or boiled, unpeeled, thereby conserving nutrients that might otherwise be lost.

Among the various cooking methods, long boiling takes the severest toll on vegetable nutrients, causing most of the vitamin C and other water-soluble vitamins to leach into the cooking liquid. The heat can also destroy vitamin C, and if thiamin is present, it converts this B vitamin into a form that the body cannot utilize. If you still prefer to boil vegetables, do so as quickly as possible, using a small amount of water in a covered pan. To further minimize nutrient loss, cook vegetables whole, or in large pieces, rather than diced or finely sliced or chopped. Snap beans cut into 1-inch pieces retain almost twice as much vitamin C as French-cut (slivered) beans.

Better yet, employ methods that use minimal liquid (or none at all), or in which the liquid does not touch the vegetables. Steaming, microwaving, pressure cooking, and boiling in a covered pot in a small amount of water have all been shown to conserve nutrients about equally. Boiling vegetables in enough water to cover them, however, causes a loss of more nutrients than these other methods, sometimes by as much as 100 percent in the case of vitamin C.

Naturally, techniques that require little or no fat are preferable to any kind of frying, although a version of sautéing or stir-frying can be done with very little fat, or with broth substituted for oil. Since heat destroys nutrients, the less time the vegetables stay in the pan, the better.

The rules for minimal water, a covered pot, and short cooking time also apply

to frozen and canned vegetables. Package directions usually suggest that frozen vegetables be heated in 1/4 cup of water or less. Canned vegetables should be reheated in their packing liquid to avoid nutrient loss, but if you wish to avoid excess sodium, it may be wiser to pour off the liquid and reheat the vegetables with a little fresh water, if necessary, or to buy low-salt canned vegetables.

Finally, serve cooked vegetables promptly: The longer they stand, whether at room temperature or in the refrigerator, the higher their nutrient losses.

Artichokes

In certain respects, the artichoke might be regarded as the vegetable equivalent of lobster. A culinary delicacy, it requires using your hands to get at the delicious parts, which must be eaten bit by bit. It can be boiled, baked, or steamed, and eaten hot or cold. In addition, the artichoke can be served whole or trimmed down to the heart, which, like the lobster's tail, is often considered the tastiest morsel. Moreover, both foods are traditionally eaten with liberal amounts of melted butter—though there are certainly healthier ways to enjoy an artichoke, as explained below.

Globe artichokes

Baby artichokes

Because of its seemingly intricate structure, many people have never tried this vegetable—an unfortunate omission, since the artichoke is not only delectable, but is also a rich source of vitamin C and dietary fiber. And while eating it demands attention, the effort is rewarding. The artichoke has a noble history. Pliny, the early Roman scholar and writer, noted that it garnered more esteem—and fetched a higher price—than any other garden vegetable. It was avidly cultivated in fifteenth-century Florence and was reputedly taken to France by Catherine de Médicis, wife of Henry II. The French and Italians, along with the Spanish, continue to be the leading growers—and consumers—of artichokes. European immigrants brought artichokes to the United States in the nineteenth century, first to Louisiana and later to the midcoastal regions of California, where the cool, foggy climate has proven ideal for its cultivation—fully 99 percent of the commercial crop is grown in this area. More than two-thirds of the domestic artichoke crop is sold fresh; much of the rest is canned or frozen, usually in the form of artichoke hearts or bottoms.

A single artichoke is actually an unopened flower bud from a thistlelike plant with the Latin name of *Cynara scolymus.* Each green cone-shaped bud consists of several parts: overlapping outer leaves that are tough and inedible at the tip, but fleshy and tender at the base; an inedible choke, or thistle, which is enclosed within a light-colored cone of immature leaves; and a round, firm-fleshed base. Although this latter part is often referred to as the "heart" of an artichoke, it is more accurately called the bottom. This meaty base, minus the leaves and choke, is the part that you work your way toward when eating a large artichoke. An artichoke heart is actually the tender central portion of a small artichoke (which has no choke)—the bottom with some of the innermost leaves attached. Commercially packaged artichoke hearts come from tiny whole artichokes that have almost no choke.

Artichokes vary greatly in size. Differences are not related to quality or maturity, but are determined by the part of the stalk the buds grow on—large ones on the center stalk, smaller ones on side branches, and "baby" artichokes (weighing about 2 ounces) at the base. The largest artichokes—entrée-sized specimens weighing a pound or more—are best when stuffed with a savory filling and served hot or cold; the medium-sized ones are recommended for eating with sauces as an appetizer; and the babies—which are completely edible when properly trimmed—are often marinated and served in salads and in hot or cold antipastos.

The shape of this vegetable also varies. While spherical and oval-shaped artichokes are preferred for market, a more cylindrical shape is quite common. Even conical-shaped artichokes have been produced.

When you eat an artichoke, it makes the food you have immediately afterward taste sweet. Cynarin, a substance present in artichokes, stimulates the taste buds responsible for detecting sweet flavors.

VARIETIES There are probably as many as fifty different artichoke varieties grown in warm climates around the world, but only the Green Globe, an Italian type, is cultivated commercially in the United States. Ideally, it has a spherical or slightly elongated bud that is solidly green (many European artichoke varieties have purplish or reddish leaves) and grows to about 4 inches in diameter. (Jerusalem artichokes, by the way, are not from Jerusalem, nor are they really artichokes—see page 171.)

AVAILABILITY Artichokes are harvested year round. The crop peaks in the spring—March through May—and again, to a lesser extent, in October.

SHOPPING TIPS Whatever its size or shape, an artichoke should be compact and heavy for its size, with leaves, or scales, that are fleshy, thick, firm, and tightly closed; if they look dry and woody, or have begun to spread apart, the artichoke is past its prime. Check the stem end for tiny holes—these are signs of worm damage, which will probably be even more extensive inside the artichoke.

Spring artichokes should be a soft green; those picked in the fall and winter tend to be olive green, and may have bronze-tipped leaves or a slightly blistered, whitish outer surface. This "winter-kissed" effect, as it is called by the growers, is the result of exposure to a light frost in the fields; it does not affect the taste or tenderness of the artichoke. Don't, however, confuse blackened or wilted leaves, or dark bruised spots, with the normal bronzing of frost-touched artichokes.

If you're not sure about the freshness of an artichoke, squeeze it: You'll hear a squeaky sound if the leaves are still plump and crisp.

Many supermarkets sell artichokes either packaged in cans and jars or frozen. These have the advantage of being ready to eat, as all the inedible parts have already been removed. Canned artichoke hearts usually come packed in brine; rinse and drain them before serving to reduce their high sodium content. Marinated artichoke hearts, sold in jars, are preserved in a seasoned oil or oil-and-vinegar mixture, which will add to their calorie count. However, you can remove some of the fat by pouring off the oil and letting the artichokes drain in a colander; much of the sodium can then be reduced by rinsing them with cold water.

Frozen artichoke hearts have no added ingredients and need only brief cooking to heat them through.

STORAGE Although artichokes appear hardy, they are quite perishable; store them in the refrigerator, in a plastic bag, for no more than four or five days. To keep them moist, sprinkle a few drops of water into the bag and then close the top, but do not rinse or wash the vegetables (or cut or trim them) before storing.

Whole cooked artichokes should be wrapped in plastic wrap or placed in plastic bags; they will keep in the refrigerator for four to five days.

PREPARATION If artichokes are to be served whole with a dipping sauce, they need little preparation—it's the eating itself, of course, that is labor intensive.

Wash each artichoke under cold running water or hold it by the stem and swish it vigorously in a basin of water. Cut off the top inch of the bud, which consists of inedible leaf tips, with a large, sharp knife. If you prefer, clip the sharp tips off the remaining outer leaves, using kitchen shears. Don't cut an artichoke with a carbon-steel knife; it will turn the cut parts black. Rub the cut parts with lemon juice to keep them from darkening or drop the prepared artichoke into a bowl of cold water to which a tablespoon of lemon juice or vinegar has been added.

Pull off any short, coarse leaves from the bottom and cut off the stem flush with the base so the artichoke can stand upright in a pot while it cooks. After cooking, serve the artichokes either hot, at room temperature, or cold, with a dipping sauce; be sure to supply plates for the discarded leaves. For easier eating, whole cooked artichokes may be halved lengthwise and the chokes removed.

Some recipes call for the choke to be removed to form an artichoke "cup" for stuffing; others require only the artichoke bottoms. Preparing these are easiest after cooking whole artichokes.

With small or baby artichokes, cut off the stems and the top parts of the leaves before sautéing or stir-frying. Remove the outer leaves by bending them back until they snap (the meaty portion will remain attached); stop when you reach the inner, pale green leaves. Pare the outer layers from the artichoke bottoms. Halve each vegetable lengthwise, scoop out the thin center petals, then slice the artichoke halves lengthwise.

To make artichoke cups, prepare the vegetable as for serving whole. Boil, steam, or microwave, then let stand until cool enough to handle. Spread the outer leaves apart with your fingers, pull out the petals covering the choke, and then use a teaspoon to scrape out the choke. The artichoke can then be stuffed and served as is, or baked.

To prepare artichoke bottoms, remove all the leaves from the cooked artichoke; you can eat them separately or scrape off the flesh from the base of each leaf to incorporate in the dish. Discard the thin petals covering the choke, then you can just scrape off the choke with a paring knife. Trim around the bottom with a knife to neaten it.

HOW TO EAT AN ARTICHOKE

Eating your first artichoke can be daunting: What do you do with all those leaves? Once you know how to tackle it, though, you'll find the experience greatly rewarding. Here is a food, however, that can't be eaten quickly: You simply have to relax and savor it one leaf at a time. An artichoke is an excellent choice when you're trying to cut down on rich foods, yet want to treat yourself to something special. Just be sure the dipping sauce you use is a low-fat one.

When you are served a whole artichoke, remove the outer leaves, one at a time, beginning at the bottom. Pull off a leaf and dip its fleshy base into the sauce. Place the bottom half of the leaf, curved-side down, in your mouth and draw it between your teeth so that you scrape off the tender flesh and pull out the fibrous portion of the leaf.

Continue eating the fleshy leaves until you encounter the inner petals, which are thin (like flower petals), rose colored, and bunched to a point at the top. The bases of these can be bitten off rather than scraped through your teeth. Underneath the petals you'll find the choke, a tuft of slender hay-colored fibers resembling cornsilk. Pull or scrape off the choke to expose the artichoke bottom, which resembles the center of a daisy (the artichoke is a member of the daisy family). That is your reward—dense and velvety, the entire bottom can be cut into quarters, dipped and eaten.

Baking Make "cups" from cooked artichokes as described above, then fill the cavity and the spaces between the leaves with stuffing. Stand the filled artichokes in a baking dish; add some chicken stock, white wine, or tomato sauce to the dish to keep the vegetables from drying out, cover with foil, and bake until the filling is heated through and the artichokes are tender throughout. *Cooking time:* 20 to 30 minutes.

Boiling Place trimmed artichokes, stem end down, in a nonreactive pot of boiling water; the addition of 2 tablespoons of lemon juice or vinegar will help keep the artichokes from darkening and also add flavor. Cover the pan and return the water to a boil; when done, an inner leaf can be pulled out easily. Lifting the lid a few times during cooking will help the vegetables retain their color. Invert the artichokes in a colander so that they drain thoroughly before serving. *Cooking time:* 20 to 40 minutes.

Microwaving Trim the artichokes; rinse but do not dry, then wrap each in plastic wrap. Place each wrapped artichoke, upside down, in a microwavable cup and cook on high power, rotating halfway through the cooking time. Remove them from the microwave and let stand, wrapped, for 5 minutes. *Cooking time:* for one artichoke, 4 to 7 minutes; add 3 minutes for each additional artichoke.

Sautéing and stir-frying Sliced artichoke bottoms or hearts can be sautéed or stir-fried in a small amount of oil or stock, alone or with vegetables such as mushrooms or summer squash. *Cooking time:* 5 minutes.

Steaming Stand trimmed artichokes in a vegetable steamer and cook over boiling water. Or, stand several artichokes in a nonreactive pan just large enough to hold them upright. Add an inch of boiling water and 2 tablespoons of lemon juice (or a lemon wedge). Cover and simmer until the bases of the artichokes can be easily pierced with a sharp knife, and you can readily pull out one of the inner leaves. If the vegetables are not done when first tested, cook them for 5 minutes longer and test again. Invert and drain the artichokes for a few moments before serving. *Cooking time:* 25 to 40 minutes.

ARTICHOKE 3½ oz raw (⅔ large artichoke)

Calories	47	Fat	<1 g
Protein	3 g	Saturated Fat	<1 g
Carbohydrate	11 g	Cholesterol	0 mg
Dietary Fiber	High	Sodium	94 mg

KEY NUTRIENTS		% RDA Men	% RDA Women
Vitamin C	12 mg	20%	20%
Copper	0.2 mg	N/A	N/A
Folacin	68 mcg	34%	38%
Iron	1 mg	10%	7%
Magnesium	60 mg	17%	21%
Manganese	0.3 mg	N/A	N/A
Phosphorus	90 mg	11%	11%
Potassium	370 mg	N/A	N/A

S=40% or more soluble N/A=Not Applicable N=Not Available

SERVING SUGGESTIONS When eating whole artichokes, avoid dipping the leaves and bottoms in melted butter or Hollandaise sauce. Instead, try one of these appetizing but healthy choices: a plain oil-and-vinegar dressing; a Japanese-style dip made by combining soy sauce, lemon juice, minced garlic, grated fresh ginger, and a dash of dark sesame oil; or a low-fat garlic dip made by cooking several unpeeled garlic cloves along with the artichokes, then mashing them to a paste before adding a little vegetable oil and lemon juice.

Artichoke leaves and quartered bottoms or hearts make good dippers on an appetizer tray. Some tasty dips: plain yogurt flavored with garlic, lemon juice, and mustard; puréed roasted red peppers; tomato sauce (fresh or cooked); buttermilk-based salad dressing. Quartered artichoke hearts—fresh, frozen, or canned—are also a delicious addition to baked pastas, chicken or tuna casseroles, warm potato salad, or rice pilaf. Serve them in a green salad or toss them with pasta and tomato sauce, or use them as an omelet filling.

Stuff steamed artichokes with a well-seasoned breadcrumb or mushroom stuffing, or a mixture of cooked rice (or other grains) and chopped vegetables, or a spinach or broccoli purée, and bake as directed above. Or, fill cooked, cooled artichokes with a cold salmon, tuna, shrimp, or chicken salad.

A purée of canned or frozen artichoke bottoms or hearts, flavored with garlic and lemon juice, makes an excellent spread for whole-wheat bread or crackers. If this seems too Spartan, the purée can be blended with "lite" cream cheese for a richer hors d'oeuvre.

When preparing whole artichokes, cook some extras and keep them in the refrigerator for a quick, tempting meal or snack.

Asparagus

Sometimes referred to as the aristocrat of vegetables, asparagus has been prized since the days of the ancient Greeks and Romans, who not only appreciated its taste but also believed it possessed medicinal properties—from alleviating toothaches to preventing beestings. Such attributes are mythical, but asparagus—a member of the lily family, and thus related to onions, leeks, and garlic—does contain a good supply of vitamins and minerals. Two basic types of asparagus, white and green, are cultivated, though only the green variety is grown on a commercial scale in the United States (Martha Washington and Mary Washington are the principal varieties).

Many consider asparagus a delicacy, at least in its fresh state: Its season is short and its price is relatively high, primarily because it must be harvested by hand. However, frozen spears approach fresh in flavor and in nutritiousness. Although canned asparagus is less expensive than fresh or frozen, a significant amount of its vitamin content, particularly vitamin C, leaches out into the canning water. (You can conserve the nutrients by using the water in soups or stocks.) A 10-ounce can may also contain up to 350 milligrams of sodium (although low-sodium versions are available).

AVAILABILITY Asparagus appears in markets as early as February, when the first crops are picked in California (the largest asparagus-producing state). There and in other western states, the peak months are April and May; in the Midwest and East, the growing season extends from May through July. In fall and winter, some stores carry asparagus from South America. While its taste is acceptable, its price is generally high.

SHOPPING TIPS After harvesting, asparagus deteriorates rapidly unless it is kept cold. In stores, therefore, asparagus should either be refrigerated or displayed on trays with the stalks standing in several inches of cold water. In outdoor markets, the trays should be shaded from the sun.

The best-quality spears are firm yet tender, with deep green or purplish tips that are closed and compact; partially open or wilted tips are the most obvious signs of aging. Avoid excessively sandy spears (sand grains can lodge within the tips and be difficult to wash out). Stalks should stand straight, be green for most of their length, and have a nicely rounded shape; flat or twisted stalks are often tough and stringy.

THE WHITE VARIETY

White asparagus (actually cream- or ivory-colored) is planted under heaps of soil, which is piled on the plants as they grow, thereby blocking the sunlight necessary for them to produce chlorophyll. The process yields spears that are more fibrous than the green ones and have a stronger, slightly bitter flavor. While you can find fresh white asparagus in the United States at gourmet food shops and local markets, it remains more popular in Europe. Some domestic asparagus growers, however, cultivate white asparagus specifically for canning.

Size is not directly related to quality, but stalks that measure at least ½ inch in diameter at the base are usually preferable. Asparagus is usually sold in bundles, but if you can buy it loose, select spears of uniform size, which will cook evenly.

When deciding on quantity, remember that asparagus loses about half of its total weight once it's been trimmed and cooked. For a main dish, buy at least a pound of asparagus for two people; as a side dish, a pound serves three to four.

STORAGE Keep fresh asparagus cold to preserve its tenderness and as much of its natural sweetness and vitamin C content as possible. Wrap the stalk bottoms in a damp paper towel and store in the refrigerator crisper; if you don't have a crisper, put the spears in a plastic bag and store in the coldest part of the refrigerator. It's best to eat asparagus the day you buy it—the flavor can diminish noticeably with each passing day—but it will keep for four to five days if refrigerated.

When kept at room temperature rather than refrigerated, asparagus loses roughly half of its vitamin C content within two days. It also loses some of its residual sugars (which impart flavor), and the stalks become tougher and stringier.

PREPARATION Wash asparagus in cool running water. If the tips have any sand on them, dunk them in and out of water, then rinse thoroughly. Cut or break off the tough white ends.

Whatever cooking method you choose, cook asparagus quickly; overdone asparagus will be unappetizingly limp and discolored and have a bitter taste. The spears should be firm-tender, so that you can pierce the butt end with the point of a paring knife. Another test of doneness is to pick up a spear with kitchen tongs: If it bends over slightly, it's done. After cooking, lift out the spears with tongs or two spatulas and let them drain for a minute on a paper towel. If you plan to serve the asparagus cold, plunge it immediately into cold water to stop it from cooking further and then refrigerate.

Boiling This method can be more convenient than steaming for cooking whole spears. Because the cooking time is brief and only a small amount of water is needed, flavor and texture as well as nutritional content are virtually the same as with steaming. Use a pan in which you can lay the asparagus flat; try a large skillet. Add about an inch of water and bring to a rapid boil. Drop in the asparagus, adding the thickest stalks first and letting them cook for a minute before adding the rest. Quickly bring to a second boil and cook, uncovered. *Cooking time:* 3 to 5 minutes, depending on thickness.

Microwaving Arrange a pound of spears in an oblong microwavable dish, with the tips pointing toward the center. Add 1/4 cup of water and cover with microwave plastic food wrap. Halfway through the cooking time, rotate the dish. *Cooking time:* 5 to 7 minutes.

Roasting For a simple but more unusual approach, trim the stalks, then place them in a baking dish and lightly drizzle with a small amount of olive oil. Roast them uncovered. *Cooking time:* 3 to 5 minutes in a 500° oven.

THAT TELLTALE ODOR

Eating asparagus can cause some people temporarily to excrete urine with an odd smell. This happens because a sulfur compound contained in the vegetable is converted during digestion in their bodies into a closely related compound that has the same distinctive sulfurous odor. For years it was assumed this happened to anyone who ate asparagus, but a study conducted with asparagus eaters indicated that of 800, only 344 produced the odorous substance. The researchers thus concluded that only about 40 percent of people have a gene that somehow causes this apparently harmless reaction.

Steaming One of the best ways to cook asparagus is to steam it upright in shallow water. Then the stalks will be heated more intensely than the delicate tips, thus insuring evenly cooked spears as well as minimizing nutrient loss. You can use a tall, lidded pot in which the stalks will stand upright or a double boiler with the upper portion inverted over the lower. There are also special asparagus cookers designed for this purpose. (A conventional basket-shaped steamer is perfectly adequate, too, but if it isn't a large model, you will have to cut the spears into 3- to 4-inch lengths.)

To handle the asparagus easily, tie the spears into bundles of ten with kitchen string and place upright in the cooking vessel. Add 2 inches of water, bring to a rapid boil, then cover. For a delicate seasoning, place a clove of garlic, a slice of onion, or a lemon wedge in the water before steaming. *Cooking time:* 5 to 8 minutes, depending on the thickness of the spears. Very thick spears may require more time.

Stir-frying Cut the spears into 1- to 2-inch pieces and cook in vegetable oil; add in a drop or two of sesame oil to complement the flavor of the asparagus. (For every dozen spears, use 2 teaspoons of oil, to keep calories and fat per serving low.) *Cooking time:* 3 to 5 minutes.

SERVING SUGGESTIONS Avoid a heavy cream or butter sauce; instead, serve the spears with a simple light seasoning such as lemon juice, mustard sauce, herbs such as dill or savory, a topping of crumbled hard-cooked egg whites, or a sprinkling of toasted breadcrumbs or Parmesan cheese. Another appetizing variation is to cut the spears into shorter lengths and, after cooking, combine them with pasta or with vegetables such as cauliflower, mushrooms, or peas.

You can serve cold asparagus as a first course dressed with a light vinaigrette, or add it—chopped or sliced—to a tossed green salad. Many people also enjoy eating raw asparagus tips (but the asparagus must be quite fresh).

Use any leftover asparagus as the basis for a low-fat cream of asparagus soup.

ASPARAGUS 3½ oz raw (8 spears)

Calories	22	Fat	<1 g
Protein	3 g	Saturated Fat	<1 g
Carbohydrate	4 g	Cholesterol	0 mg
Dietary Fiber	Low	Sodium	2 mg

KEY NUTRIENTS		%RDA Men	%RDA Women
Vitamin A	897 IU	18%	22%
Vitamin B_6	0.2 mg	10%	13%
Beta Carotene	0.5 mg	N/A	N/A
Vitamin C	33 mg	55%	55%
Copper	0.2 mg	N/A	N/A
Vitamin E	2 mg	20%	25%
Folacin	119 mcg	60%	66%
Manganese	0.2 mg	N/A	N/A
Potassium	302 mg	N/A	N/A

S=40% or more soluble N/A=Not Applicable N=Not Available

Beans (Edible Pods)

Of the many types of beans that we consume, only a few varieties are eaten fresh. These beans aren't a distinct species, but are simply picked at an immature stage, when the inner seed (also referred to as the bean) has just started to form; left on the plant, the seeds eventually grow to full size and dry in the pod. Nutritionally, one major difference between the two stages is that immature pods contain good amounts of beta carotene and vitamin C, whereas the dried seeds are high in protein and carbohydrate in the form of starch.

Though they belong to a number of plant species, fresh beans can be classified into two broad categories: those with edible pods and those that are shelled. Green and other snap beans belong to the first category, while lima beans and other so-called shell beans belong to the second. The fact that we call these beans "fresh," by the way, doesn't mean they are always marketed fresh—actually, we eat the bulk of fresh beans in canned or frozen form.

VARIETIES Snap beans are the most popular beans with edible pods. There are, however, many other delicious varieties of edible-pod beans on the market. (For edible-pod peas, see page 132.)

Chinese long beans Originally from the Orient, these mild-tasting, thin green beans—also called "yard-long" or "asparagus" beans—can measure up to 18 inches long. When young and tender, long beans are good for stir-frying.

Haricots verts For many years, the French cultivated snap beans more enthusiastically than Americans—snap beans are also referred to as French beans—and, as a result, developed this slender variety of green bean. It is increasingly available in American specialty markets.

Italian green beans Also called Romano beans, these are distinguished by broad, flat, bright green pods. They are often available only in frozen form.

Purple wax beans Similar to small yellow wax beans, these have a dark purple pod that turns green when cooked.

Scarlet runner beans The pods are broad, flat, and green; the seeds are scarlet. These beans also have an edible blossom that may be red or white.

Snap beans A great favorite of cooks as well as home gardeners, snap beans are so called because

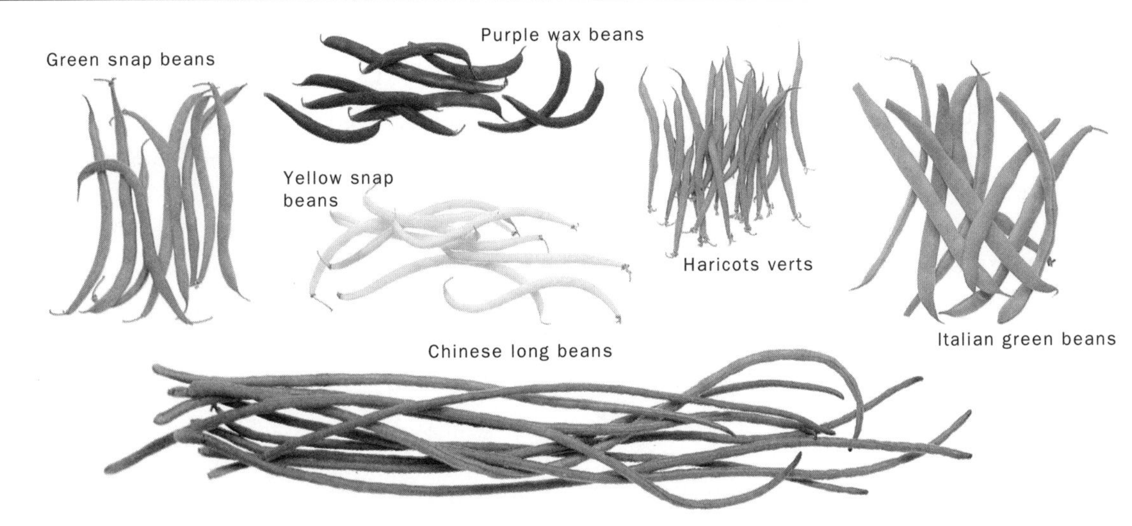

of their tender, crisp pods that snap when bent (the ends are snapped off before cooking). The most familiar types are green beans and yellow wax beans, which are identical in taste and texture, though yellow wax beans are lower in beta carotene. Both are actually immature kidney beans, and their pods can be flat, oval, or rounded, depending on the variety. These beans were formerly known as string beans because the varieties developed in the nineteenth century had a long, tough string down the seam of the pod that had to be stripped off. However, the string has been bred out of most snap bean varieties; occasionally, though, a bean does need stringing.

BY THE BUSH OR THE POLE

One way of classifying snap beans is by how they grow. There are two main varieties: bush beans and pole beans. Bush beans are short plants—about a foot and a half high—that develop many flowers on each stem. This growth pattern is called branching and results in a plant with a bushlike appearance. The pods of the bush bean plant all reach maturity at the same time. As a consequence, this variety is preferred by commercial growers since it is easier to harvest.

Pole beans, on the other hand, grow like vines and can reach heights of eight feet or more. Each stem develops only a single flower. Pods of pole bean plants reach maturity at different times, so you can have flowers and pods on the same plant simultaneously.

AVAILABILITY Snap beans are available year round in good volume, but the supply—and the quality—of most varieties tends to be best in summer and early fall.

SHOPPING TIPS The best way to choose beans is at a market that sells them loose so that you can pick out pods of equal size (for uniform cooking), free of rusty spots or scars. The beans should have a fresh, vivid color and a velvety feel, and they should be straight and slender (no thicker than a pencil), with a firm texture. When broken, they should snap crisply (although the very thin haricots verts are not as crisp). If snap bean pods are very stiff, or the seeds are visible through the pod, the beans are overly mature and will be tough and leathery.

STORAGE Keep beans in plastic bags in the refrigerator crisper; they'll stay fresh for three to five days.

PREPARATION Wash the beans, then snap or trim both ends of each bean. Leave the beans whole for cooking or cut them crosswise or diagonally into 1- to 2-inch lengths. Slicing them lengthwise, "French style," should be necessary only with beans that are old and tough; it robs young beans of their crisp texture and allows their sweet flavor to cook out.

There are many ways to cook snap beans; whatever method you use, be sure not to overcook them. Otherwise, they will lose their brilliant color and crisp-tender bite, and you'll end up with limp, gray beans depleted of much of their vitamin content.

Blanching A relatively brief immersion in lots of rapidly boiling water will insure that snap beans retain their bright color while also tenderizing them. Snap beans can be precooked by blanching, then quickly reheated in a little stock at mealtime. Drop a few beans at a time (whole or cut-up) into a large pot of boiling water so that the water continues to boil; cook to the desired doneness. Drain and serve them while they are still al dente, or cook them until they are more tender, as you prefer. Drain the beans (cool them under cold water if you are going to serve them cold). *Cooking time:* 5 to 8 minutes.

Microwaving Place a pound of cut-up snap beans in a microwavable dish with 1/4 cup of water or broth; cover and cook until tender. *Cooking time:* 5 to 10 minutes.

Steaming Use a steamer basket over boiling water or cook the beans in a small amount of boiling water in a tightly covered pot. *Cooking time:* about 3 to 5 minutes.

Stir-frying Cut beans into 1-inch lengths and stir-fry with thin strips of beef or poultry, or in combination with vegetables such as broccoli, mushrooms, or water chestnuts. *Cooking time:* 2 to 5 minutes.

SERVING SUGGESTIONS For a side dish, simmer beans with chopped onion or garlic and chopped tomatoes. Blanched beans will be more flavorful if reheated in a combination of stock and lemon juice, or served with a sprinkling of lemon juice; omit butter, and season with herbs such as fresh parsley or dill, or dried thyme or basil. Consider tossing them with mild vinegar and prepared mustard. Try topping cooked beans with a tablespoon of chopped or slivered almonds, peanuts, pecans, or cashews. You can also serve snap beans with tomato sauce (or add them to fettuccine or other pasta and top with sauce); you may, if you like, add a sprinkling of Parmesan or another sharp grating cheese.

For an interesting cold salad, cook the beans until crisp-tender, then chill and mix them with tossed greens. Or, combine the beans with diced tomatoes, fresh herbs, and an oil-and-vinegar dressing. If you prefer a hearty main-dish salad, toss cooked beans with a vinaigrette and thinly sliced red onions. Then add warm potato slices and/or tuna or turkey.

To make a tasty casserole, layer snap beans with chopped onion, diced tomatoes, bell peppers, or other vegetables. Season to taste, add some stock, cover tightly, and bake in a 350° oven for about an hour, or until the beans are very tender.

SNAP BEANS 3½ oz raw (1 cup)			
Calories	31	Fat	<1 g
Protein	2 g	Saturated Fat	<1 g
Carbohydrate	7 g	Cholesterol	0 mg
Dietary Fiber	Low	Sodium	6 mg

KEY NUTRIENTS		% RDA Men	% RDA Women
Vitamin A	668 IU	13%	17%
Vitamin C	16 mg	27%	27%
Folacin	37 mcg	19%	21%
Iron	1 mg	10%	7%
Manganese	0.2 mg	N/A	N/A

S=40% or more soluble N/A=Not Applicable N=Not Available

Beans (Shell)

In addition to snap beans, there is another broad category of beans that are sold fresh or frozen. Often called shell beans, these are mature fresh seeds that are midway in development between snap and dried. Many of the varieties listed below are also available dried, but their nutritional content differs. Both shell and dried beans are good sources of protein, potassium, and iron. Dried beans, however, contain more of these nutrients, while shell beans are higher in vitamin C (though not as high as beans with edible pods).

Shell beans can be used interchangeably with dried beans in many recipes. Just remember that shell beans keep the same bulk whether they're raw or cooked, whereas dried beans—which usually require soaking—swell up, so you'll need to adjust recipes accordingly.

VARIETIES There are four popular types of shell beans:

Cranberry beans These beans—so named because of the red markings on both the white pods

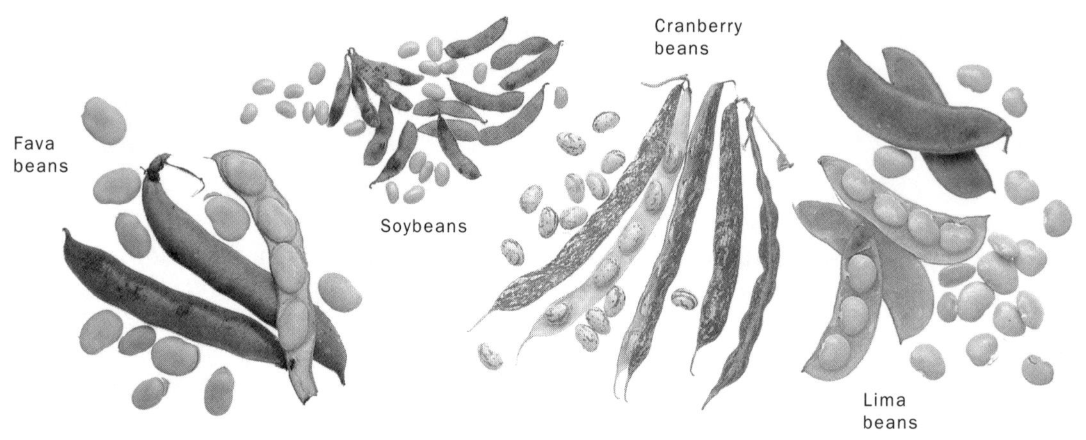

and the beans themselves—are occasionally available fresh. They are usually served as a side dish or added to soups and stews.

Fava beans Some people prefer the taste and texture of these beans to lima beans, which favas closely resemble. Also called broad beans, their pods are longer than those of limas—up to 18 inches—with larger beans. Young favas can be cooked and eaten in their pods, but more mature favas must be shelled. Favas can be enjoyed cold in salads or hot as a side dish.

Lima beans The most common shell bean in the United States, limas are named after the capital of Peru, where they have been cultivated since about 5000 B.C. Nearly all of the domestic crop is marketed frozen or canned, but you can sometimes find fresh limas sold in their pods. As do their dried counterparts, limas come in two varieties: Fordhooks (also called butter beans) and baby limas, which are not really young lima beans but are a smaller, milder-tasting variety.

Soybeans In the United States, soybeans are more commonly available dried. Since they are widely consumed fresh in Asian countries, they can often be found fresh in local Asian markets. Distinguished by their small, fuzzy dark green pods, fresh soybeans have a mild flavor, along with a higher protein and fat content than other beans (but the fat is unsaturated). Moreover, the protein is complete—meaning that it provides enough of the essential amino acids needed in one's diet—so soybeans are equivalent to animal products in terms of protein quality.

Lima beans supply 65 percent more iron than fava beans, and almost twice the potassium, but fava beans supply 182 percent more folacin and 43 percent more vitamin C.

AVAILABILITY Fresh shell beans are generally available for only a few months of the year—lima beans and cranberry beans from mid-summer through early fall; fava beans from late spring though early summer; and soybeans in summer and fall.

SHOPPING TIPS Shell beans should bulge through a tightly closed pod; feel the pods to be sure the beans inside are firm. If they're sold shelled, the beans should be plump and tight-skinned. Shelled limas should be grass green (chalky white limas will be starchy), favas should be a lighter gray green, and cranberry beans should be splashed with bright color. Soybean pods contain two to four beans per pod and should be plump and well filled, with no signs of browning.

STORAGE Keep shell beans in plastic bags in the refrigerator crisper. Those in their pods will keep for two or three days; if they are already shelled, refrigerate them in a plastic bag and use them within a day or two.

PREPARATION To remove shell beans from the pod, split the pod open and push out the beans with your thumb; rinse the shelled beans before cooking. It may be easier to open the pod if you shave the seam of the curved side with a paring knife or vegetable peeler. Large fava beans not only need to be shelled, but their tough skins must be peeled either before or after cooking; small, young favas need not be skinned. To peel the raw beans, split the skin with your thumbnail or a sharp paring knife. The skins of cooked favas will slip off easily.

Boiling Shell beans can be simmered in water or stock. Place the beans in a pot with boiling liquid to cover. Cover the pot, reduce the heat, and simmer the beans until tender. *Cooking time:* 5 to 20 minutes (the shortest time is for baby limas; the longest is for large fava beans).

Microwaving Place 2 cups of shell beans in a dish with 1 tablespoon of water, cover, and cook until tender. *Cooking time:* 4 to 8 minutes.

Steaming Steam shell beans over boiling water. *Cooking time:* 5 to 20 minutes.

SERVING SUGGESTIONS When boiling shell beans to serve as a side dish, add a sprinkling of fresh herbs, or a few cloves of garlic, or a whole small onion to the cooking liquid for extra flavor.

LIMA BEANS 3½ oz raw (¾ cup)

Calories	113	Fat	1 g
Protein	7 g	Saturated Fat	<1 g
Carbohydrate	20 g	Cholesterol	0 mg
Dietary Fiber	Medium	Sodium	8 mg

KEY NUTRIENTS		% RDA Men	% RDA Women
Vitamin B_6	0.2 mg	10%	13%
Vitamin C	23 mg	38%	38%
Copper	0.3 mg	N/A	N/A
Folacin	34 mcg	17%	19%
Iron	3 mg	30%	20%
Magnesium	58 mg	17%	21%
Manganese	1.2 mg	N/A	N/A
Phosphorus	136 mg	17%	17%
Potassium	467 mg	N/A	N/A
Thiamin	0.2 mg	13%	18%

S=40% or more soluble N/A=Not Applicable N=Not Available

Serve the beans whole or purée them. Add shell beans to minestrone or other vegetable soups, then mash some of the beans against the soup pot to thicken the cooking liquid. Substitute fresh shell beans for kidney, pinto, or other dried beans in recipes for chilies, stews, soups, and baked beans. Lima beans are one of the basic components of succotash and its many variations (see Corn, page 87). Warm cooked shell beans, tossed with a well-seasoned vinaigrette, will add interest to a spinach salad. Or, you can combine different kinds of snap and shell beans in a marinated mixed bean salad.

Beets

Beets are notable for their sweetness—they have the highest sugar content of any vegetable, but are, nevertheless, very low in calories. Their sweet flavor comes through whether the beets are fresh or canned (which is the way most beets are packaged in the United States). Unlike many other processed vegetables, canned beets are perfectly acceptable in both taste and texture; if not pickled, their sweet flavor is largely unaffected by the canning process. Fresh beets, however, are higher in vitamin C and folacin, and have a distinctive flavor and a crisp texture that you don't find in canned versions. Fresh beets also supply a nutritional bonus—their green tops are an excellent source of beta carotene, calcium, and iron.

.Like turnips, beets (also called red beets, root beets, and table beets) are a root vegetable with two parts, the root and the edible green leaves. They belong to the botanical species *Beta vulgaris,* which also includes sugar beets (which are processed for sugar, and thus not eaten), mangelwurzels (very large bulbs that are used as animal fodder), foliage beets, and Swiss chard (the latter two are grown for their greens, not their roots). All five vegetables are descended from a wild slender-rooted plant that grew abundantly in southern Europe, especially in sandy soil near seacoasts. In ancient civilizations, only the green part of the beet plant was eaten; the roots—which did not look like modern beets—were used medicinally to treat headaches and toothaches. Beets with rounded roots, like those we eat today, were probably developed in the sixteenth century, though it took another two hundred years before they gained any popularity as a food.

Beets

BEET RED

Many people cannot metabolize betacyanin, a group of pigments that is responsible for the purplish-red color of beets. After eating beets, these nonmetabolizers pass the bright red pigments through their urine and feces, turning these waste products pink or red for a couple of days. When this occurs, it may seem alarming if you aren't aware of the cause (the trait is genetically determined), but it's perfectly harmless.

Beets can be prepared as a hot side dish, used as an ingredient in soups (including *borscht,* the classic Russian peasant soup) and salads, or pickled or made into a relish. About 95 percent of the domestic beet crop is processed for canning and sold plain, pickled, spiced, and cut into various sizes. Beet greens, which are akin to spinach, can be prepared in the same way as other greens.

The beets you are likely to see in the market are globe-shaped roots, with deep red flesh and green leaves that have either green or red veins. Other less common varieties have golden or white flesh, but these are mainly raised by local growers and home gardeners.

AVAILABILITY Fresh beets are always in good supply. They are grown in more than thirty states, and crops are harvested and shipped year round. June through October, however, are peak months, and at the start of the season you can find young beets with small, tender roots, which are suitable for cooking whole. The roots get larger—and tougher—as the season goes on. In the off-peak months, you may also find clip-topped beets that have been in storage, but these are less tender than freshly harvested beets.

SHOPPING TIPS Beets are marketed in a range of sizes. Early crop beets are usually sold in bunches with the tops attached, or as clip-topped beets in perforated plastic bags. If those you buy are bunched, choose equal-sized ones so that they will cook evenly. Very small "baby" beets—radish-sized immature roots that have been pulled to thin the farmer's rows—are a delicacy. Sold (and cooked) with the tender leaves attached, they may be found in early summer at farmers' markets, roadside stands, and specialty greengrocers. Small, young beets (about 1½ inches in diameter) are pleasingly tender and cook in less time than larger ones; their fine texture is also an asset if you intend to use them raw in a salad. Medium-sized beets are fine for most cooking purposes, but very large specimens (over 2½ inches in diameter) may be tough, with unpalatable woody cores.

Look for smooth, hard, round beets; a healthy deep red color is an indicator of quality. The surface should be unbruised and free of cuts; avoid beets with soft, moist spots or shriveled, flabby skin. The taproot, which extends from the bulbous part of the beet, should be slender.

If the leaves are attached—and especially if you're planning to eat them—it's preferable that they be small, crisp, and dark green. Leaves that are larger than about 8 inches are probably too mature to be palatable; limp, yellowed leaves have lost their nutritive value. However, beets with wilted greens may still be acceptable, because the leaves deteriorate much more quickly than the roots. If the leaves on the beets offered at your market look less than fresh, just be sure to check the roots extra carefully for soundness. If the beets are clip-topped, at least ½ inch of the stems (and 2 inches of the taproot) should remain, or the color will bleed from the beets as they cook.

STORAGE To reduce moisture loss from the roots, cut off beet greens before storing, but leave at least an inch of the stem attached (tiny leaf-topped baby beets can be stored for a day or two with their tops intact). Place the unwashed roots in a plastic bag and store in the refrigerator crisper for up to three weeks. Store the greens separately in the same fashion and use them as soon as possible; they are perishable and will keep for only a few days.

PREPARATION In England, greengrocers sell cooked beets—a convenience, to be sure, but beets are not difficult to cook. Generally speaking, to preserve their color and nutrients, beets should never be cut or peeled before cooking them in liquid; otherwise, the beets will "bleed" their rich red juices while cooking and turn an unappetizing dull brown. Scrub the beets very gently and rinse well, but be careful not to break the skin, which is quite thin. Leave at least an inch of stem and don't trim the root.

Beets are done when you can easily pierce them with the tip of a sharp knife. Once cooked, drain the beets, cool them briefly under cold running water, and peel them. Then cut in quarters, slices, cubes, or in long, thin strips—or, if they're small, serve whole.

SUGAR BEETS

By weight, sugar beets are about 20 percent sucrose—twice the sugar content of table beets. Still, about 100 pounds of sugar beets are needed to produce 5 pounds of sugar. But advances in harvesting techniques have reduced the cost of producing beet sugar so that it is competitive with cane sugar, and today the sugar beet (which is grown in mild climates) provides about a third of the world's sugar.

Cooked beets are at their most colorful if some acid ingredient has been added; vinegar or lemon juice, used in many beet recipes, will keep them a beautiful crimson.

Baking Dry-heat cooking locks in nutrients and intensifies the natural sweetness of beets. It's not a quick method, though: To save time, cook a large quantity of beets at once, then chill some for later use in salads. Or bake beets when you're baking or roasting something else. Wrap beets in foil, place them in a baking pan, and bake in a 350° to 400° oven until tender. Unwrap and let stand until they're just cool enough to handle, then peel them while still warm. *Cooking time:* 1½ to 2 hours, depending on size.

You can also slice peeled beets, then layer them with thinly sliced onions or apples in a casserole. Add a little stock to keep them moist and cover tightly, then bake/braise. *Cooking time:* 30 to 60 minutes.

Boiling This is the most common way of cooking beets, but some of the color (and nutrients) will be lost in the cooking water. Place beets in a pot of boiling water, cover, and simmer until the beets are just tender. *Cooking time:* 40 minutes to 2 hours, depending on the size and the age of the beets.

Microwaving Place 1 pound of whole beets in a microwavable dish with ¼ cup of liquid. Cover and cook until tender. *Cooking time:* 10 minutes.

Steaming Beets can be cooked in a vegetable steamer over boiling water. Tiny beets can be steamed with their leaves attached in a little water with lemon juice and herbs added. *Cooking time:* 40 minutes.

SERVING SUGGESTIONS In most dishes calling for cooked beets, you can substitute canned beets. Sliced cooked beets are good simply sprinkled with lemon or orange juice, ground pepper, and herbs; a touch of butter enhances their flavor. Or, toss warm cooked beets with a vinaigrette or a sweet-and-sour dressing (based on cider vinegar and sugar in a 4-to-1 ratio). Warm or chilled cooked beets are even tastier when coated with a creamy yogurt sauce flavored with horseradish or dill. Other seasonings that work well include fresh or ground ginger, orange or lemon zest, caraway seeds, cloves, nutmeg, and cinnamon.

A handsome multicolored composed salad can be easily made by arranging separate mounds of cooked, cubed, or grated beets, potatoes, and carrots on a platter. The vegetables can be served warm, at room temperature, or chilled, with a lemon vinaigrette on the side. A diced onion or apple or cooked vegetables such as sweet potatoes, green beans, or yellow wax beans can also be substituted or added.

Sliced chilled beets, oranges, and onions make a refreshing summer salad. Beets complement tart or bitter greens very well; try them with watercress, endive, or chicory. (When adding beets to a *tossed* salad, wait until the last minute to mix them in, so that the beet juice won't color the rest of the salad.)

For a cool summer version of the Eastern European beet soup called *borscht* (in Russian) or *barscz* (in Polish), purée cooked beets, chunks of peeled cucumber, and chicken stock in a food processor or blender. Season to taste with lemon juice or cider vinegar, horseradish, and/or dill. Refrigerate until ice cold and stir in yogurt just before serving.

BEETS 3½ oz raw (¾ cup sliced)

Calories	44	Fat	<1 g
Protein	1 g	Saturated Fat	<1 g
Carbohydrate	10 g	Cholesterol	0 mg
Dietary Fiber	Medium	Sodium	72 mg

KEY NUTRIENTS		%RDA Men	%RDA Women
Vitamin C	11 mg	18%	18%
Folacin	93 mcg	47%	52%
Manganese	0.4 mg	N/A	N/A

S=40% or more soluble N/A=Not Applicable N=Not Available

Broccoli

The name "broccoli" comes from the Latin word *brachium,* which means "branch," or "arm"—an apt description for a vegetable with numerous thick, fleshy stalks supporting a head of compact florets. A close relative of cauliflower, broccoli has grown wild in Mediterranean areas for hundreds of years, but domestic broccoli probably dates from the seventeenth or eighteenth century and was first cultivated in the United States in the 1920s. Since then, it has become one of the best-selling members of the *Brassica* genus (which also includes cabbage, Brussels sprouts, and other so-called cruciferous vegetables). Fortunately, broccoli is one of the healthiest foods you can eat. Along with a rich supply of vitamins and minerals, it contains nitrogen compounds called indoles, which various studies seem to indicate are effective in protecting against certain forms of cancer. In addition, broccoli contains special enzymes and good amounts of beta carotene and vitamin C—all of which help fight cancer.

The most common type in the United States is called sprouting, or Italian green, broccoli; its light green stalks are topped by umbrella-shaped clusters of purplish green florets. It is also known as Calabrese, after the Italian province of Calabria, where it was first grown. (The other type is heading, or cauliflower, broccoli, which has dense white buds.)

Packaged frozen broccoli differs slightly from fresh in nutritional makeup. While still a low-sodium food, frozen broccoli has twice as much sodium as fresh—up to 68 milligrams per 10-ounce package.

AVAILABILITY Most broccoli is grown in California, and it has become one of the few vegetables available fresh year round, though it is most abundant (and least expensive) from October through May.

SHOPPING TIPS For fresh broccoli to taste its best, it must be picked young. Left growing too long, the plant begins converting its sugar to lignin, a type of fiber that cannot be softened by cooking. (Broccoli that has been stored too long after harvesting also develops lignin.) Overly mature broccoli, no matter how it's prepared, will be tough and woody, and have an unpleasantly strong cabbagy odor.

FROZEN BROCCOLI AND BETA CAROTENE

Before packaging frozen broccoli, manufacturers typically cut off most or all of the plant's thick stalks in favor of the tender flower buds, or florets. These are richer in beta carotene than the stalks, and so frozen broccoli may contain about 35 percent more beta carotene by weight than fresh specimens with their stalks intact. However, frozen versions have about half the calcium of fresh and moderately smaller amounts of iron, thiamin, riboflavin, niacin, and vitamin C.

Examine the stalks attached to the florets; they should be on the slender side and be so crisp that if you broke one, it would snap clean. The florets should be tightly closed and uniformly green; yellowing florets are a sign that the broccoli is past its prime. Good color also indicates nutritional quality. Florets that are dark green or purplish or bluish green have more beta carotene and vitamin C than paler florets. The leaves, if any, should have good color and not appear wilted. Avoid broccoli with soft slippery spots on the florets or with stalk bottoms that are brown or slimy. Fresh broccoli has a clean smell.

Broccoli is usually sold in bunches that weigh 1½ to 2 pounds, which will yield about a pound when trimmed—enough to serve two if used as a main dish, or, as a side dish, three to four.

STORAGE Refrigeration slows the conversion of sugar to lignin, thereby preserving texture and

flavor, and also protects vitamin C content. Store broccoli in an open plastic bag in the refrigerator crisper, which will provide the right balance of humidity and oxygen. Do not wash broccoli before storing; although it needs moisture to remain fresh, any water on its surface will encourage the growth of mold.

Fresh broccoli is at its best if used within a day or two of purchase, but it will keep for up to four days in a crisper. Once cooked, any leftovers may be refrigerated for two to three days in a tightly covered container.

PREPARATION Very fresh young broccoli can be served raw as an hors d'oeuvre or in salads. Its taste and texture, however, don't agree with all palates; in general, most people prefer broccoli cooked. Whichever way you serve the vegetable, first rinse it thoroughly under cold running water to remove surface dirt and debris. If you see dirt embedded in the florets, soak the broccoli in cold water for several minutes to flush it out.

Most people cut off and discard the leaves; however, they are eminently edible and contain even more beta carotene than the florets. (If you decide to remove them, consider using them in soups, purées, or stir-fries.) If you wish, peel the stalks—which get tougher the longer you keep the broccoli—but remove only a thin layer to preserve the nutrients.

Cooked broccoli should be tender enough so that you can pierce it with a sharp knife, but still remain crisp and bright. You can achieve this level of doneness with any of the methods covered below; however, steaming and microwaving preserve more of the nutrients. Because the broccoli florets tend to cook much faster than the stalks, either split the stalks about halfway up or cut an "x" in the bottom of each stalk. Another option is to cut off the florets and add them to the pot after the stalks have cooked for 2 to 3 minutes. You can also cut both the florets and stalks into smaller pieces for fast, even cooking.

For boiling or steaming, use a non-aluminum pot or pan, since aluminum appears to heighten broccoli's cooking odors.

Boiling Boiling broccoli, uncovered, in a large pot with plenty of water has the greatest dispersing effect on the chemical compounds released by cooking, and can thereby yield a milder taste. But boiling in a large amount of water results in a loss of vitamin C and allows about half of the indole content to escape. If you choose this method, however, bring the water to a rapid boil before adding the broccoli. *Cooking time:* 5 to 8 minutes.

By weight, fresh broccoli that has been boiled and drained has 16 percent more vitamin C than an orange, and roughly as much calcium as milk.

Microwaving Arrange one pound of broccoli, in wheel-spoke fashion, on a microwavable plate or platter, with the florets pointing toward the center. Add 1/4 cup water and cover with microwave plastic food wrap. Halfway through the cooking time, rotate the container. *Cooking time:* 6 to 10 minutes.

Steaming Not only does steaming preserve the most nutrients, but it also keeps the florets from breaking apart. After steaming for 1 to 2 minutes, uncover the pot for 10 to 15 seconds, to disperse the strong-tasting sulfurous compounds that form in cooking. *Cooking time:* 5 to 7 minutes.

WHAT HAPPENS WHEN YOU OVERCOOK
Heating broccoli (or any cruciferous vegetable) causes chemicals in the vegetable to break down and release various strong-smelling sulfur compounds, including ammonia and hydrogen sulfide (the culprit behind the smell of rotten eggs). As broccoli cooks, more of these compounds are released, intensifying (rather than weakening) the odors. Some of the compounds also interact with chlorophyll (which makes broccoli and other vegetables green), gradually turning the broccoli brownish the longer it cooks. As a result, it is best to cook broccoli rapidly in a small amount of water to minimize these chemical interactions (and also to maximize the retention of nutrients).

Stir-frying Stir-fry for 2 minutes, then add a little broth or water, cover the pan and let steam until crisp-tender. *Cooking time:* 4 to 5 minutes.

SERVING SUGGESTIONS All too often, broccoli is presented in a cheese or cream sauce that is high in fat, calories, and cholesterol. Served with 1/4 cup of shredded Cheddar cheese, for example, a cup of cooked broccoli contains 158 calories, 57 percent of them derived from fat, much of it saturated. For a satisfying yet simple topping, just squeeze some lemon juice over the vegetable, or add a sprinkling of slivered almonds, sesame seeds, chopped hard-boiled egg whites, toasted breadcrumbs, or Parmesan cheese. Cut-up broccoli spears will enhance any pasta dish, while leftover broccoli stalks, florets, and leaves—puréed or chopped—are wonderful additions to soups. Or, consider using a pound of broccoli as the main ingredient in a hot soup.

BROCCOLI 3½ oz raw (1 cup chopped)

Calories	28	Fat	<1 g
Protein	3 g	Saturated Fat	<1 g
Carbohydrate	5 g	Cholesterol	0 mg
Dietary Fiber	Medium (S)	Sodium	27 mg

KEY NUTRIENTS		% RDA Men	% RDA Women
Vitamin A	1542 IU	31%	39%
Vitamin B_6	0.2 mg	10%	13%
Beta Carotene	1 mg	N/A	N/A
Vitamin C	93 mg	155%	155%
Folacin	71 mcg	36%	39%
Manganese	0.2 mg	N/A	N/A
Potassium	325 mg	N/A	N/A

S=40% or more soluble N/A=Not Applicable N=Not Available

Brussels Sprouts

Named after the capital of Belgium, where they may have first been cultivated, Brussels sprouts look like diminutive heads of cabbage. The resemblance is not surprising, since both belong to the same botanical family. A relative newcomer to the cabbage family (standard cabbage has been around for some three thousand years, Brussels sprouts for about five hundred), sprouts are one of the few vegetables to have originated in northern Europe. In the nineteenth century, Brussels sprouts were introduced to France, then to England—where they are still highly popular—and later to America, where French settlers grew them in Louisiana. They are similar to cabbage in taste, but are slightly milder in flavor and denser in texture; nutritionally, they

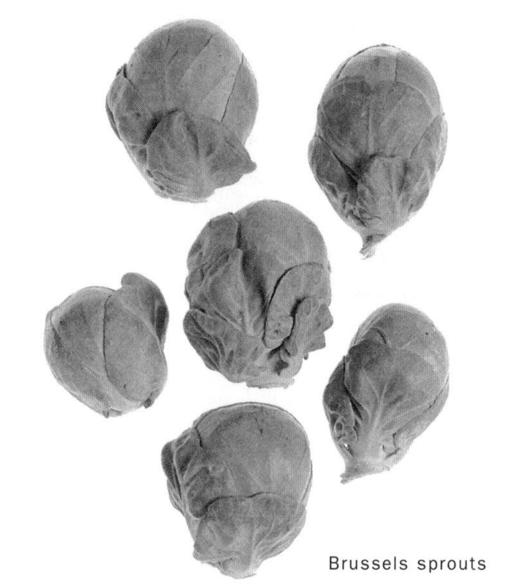
Brussels sprouts

have the same cancer-inhibiting potential as cabbage and other cruciferous vegetables (such as broccoli and cauliflower) by virtue of containing the nitrogen compounds called indoles and a significant amount of vitamin C and beta carotene (which the body converts to vitamin A). These and other nutrients are available, with only a minimal loss, in frozen Brussels sprouts.

Like other members of the cabbage family, Brussels sprouts have a reputation for tasting bitter or turning mushy when they are cooked. You can avoid either outcome as long as you use fresh sprouts and cook them just until tender. Then, their flavor will be fresh and their texture pleasingly crisp.

Brussels sprouts are a good vegetable source of protein, with 31 percent of their calories coming from protein. Although the protein in Brussels sprouts is incomplete—that is, it's low in some essential amino acids—you can complement it by eating animal products or whole grains during the course of the day.

AVAILABILITY You can find fresh Brussels sprouts year round, but their peak growing season is autumn through early spring; most are cultivated in California. There are several varieties, but the differences among them are minor.

SHOPPING TIPS Fresh Brussels sprouts should be displayed under refrigeration; if kept at room temperature, their leaves will turn yellow quickly. Although sprouts are commonly sold in pint or quart tubs, it's easier to choose sound sprouts if you can select them individually from a bulk display. Choose sprouts of comparable size so that they will cook evenly.

Bright green color is the best guide to freshness and good condition; yellowed or wilted leaves are a sure sign of age or mishandling. Old sprouts also have a strong, cabbagy odor. Avoid puffy or soft sprouts; choose small, firm, compact ones with unblemished leaves. Tiny holes or sootlike smudges on the leaves may indicate the presence of worms or plant lice. The stem ends should be clean and white.

STORAGE Don't wash or trim sprouts before storing them, except for removing any yellow or wilted outer leaves. Don't remove fresh outer leaves, since these contain the most nutrients. If you've purchased sprouts in a cellophane-covered container, take off the wrapping and examine the sprouts, then return them to the container, re-cover with the cellophane, and refrigerate. (If the sprouts aren't fresh, return them to the store.) Place loose sprouts in a perforated plastic bag. Fresh Brussels sprouts will keep for three to five days.

PREPARATION Drop the sprouts into a basin of lukewarm water and leave them there for 10 minutes; this easy step will eliminate any insects hidden in the leaves. Then rinse the sprouts in fresh water. Trim the stem ends, but not quite flush with the bottoms of the sprouts, or the outer leaves will fall off during cooking.

Many cooks cut an "x" in the base of each sprout; this nick helps the heat penetrate the solid core so that it cooks as quickly as the leaves.

Whichever cooking method you choose, test for doneness by inserting a knife tip into the stem end, which should be barely tender.

HOW BRUSSELS SPROUTS GROW

If you have only seen sprouts in a store, you probably don't know how unusual they look growing in the garden. Whereas other members of the cabbage family form a single large head on a short stem, a Brussels sprout plant consists of a tall, thick stem from which many tiny "cabbage" heads sprout. The heads grow closely together on the stalk from the bottom up in a circular fashion, so that on any given plant the bottom sprouts are the most mature. Between the sprouts (and at the top of the plant), large palmlike leaves grow sporadically to shelter the sprouts from excessive sun or heavy rains. The plants grow to a height of 2 to 3 feet, depending on the variety. Most Brussels sprouts are clipped off their stalks and packaged in containers for sale. But you can sometimes find sprouts attached to their stems at farmers' markets and roadside stands.

Boiling Use a cup of water for every cup of Brussels sprouts. Bring the water to a rapid boil in a large pot, add the sprouts, and quickly return the water to a boil. Cook the sprouts just until tender. Drain them, return them to the warm pot, and shake for a few seconds until dry. A little parsley added to the cooking water can subdue the taste of the strongly flavored Brussels sprouts. *Cooking time:* 7 to 10 minutes.

Braising If you cook sprouts slowly in stock, you can reduce the liquid after the vegetable is done and use it as a sauce, thereby conserving nutrients. Place the sprouts in a casserole or baking dish and pour in enough stock to cover them. Cover and bake in a 350° oven. Or, braise the sprouts in a heavy skillet on the stovetop. *Cooking time:* 25 to 35 minutes.

Microwaving Place ½ pound of Brussels sprouts in a microwavable dish; add ¼ cup of liquid, cover, and cook. *Cooking times:* for medium sprouts, 4 minutes; for large ones, 8 minutes.

Steaming Sprouts should be steamed rapidly in a small amount of water to minimize the chemical interactions that cause them to develop a strong flavor (and also to maximize the retention of nutrients). This cooking method also keeps the sprouts intact. Just add the sprouts to an inch of already-boiling water and cover, or place them in a vegetable steamer. After steaming for 1 to 2 minutes, uncover the pot for 10 to 15 seconds to disperse the strong-tasting sulfurous compounds that form when sprouts (and other members of the cabbage family) are cooking. Cover and finish steaming. *Cooking times:* in boiling water, 5 to 10 minutes; in a steamer, 6 to 12 minutes, depending on size.

SERVING SUGGESTIONS The hearty flavor of Brussels sprouts can overshadow very mild or delicate foods such as poached fish or chicken; sprouts tend to go better with flavorful foods such as beef and sharp cheeses or with assertive seasonings. Mustard, caraway, poppy or dill seeds are popular choices, as are dillweed, sage, and garlic. Any of these can be added to an accompanying yogurt-lemon sauce. Or, consider just sprinkling the sprouts with lemon juice and nutmeg. Toasted sesame seeds provide yet another top-

BRUSSELS SPROUTS 3½ oz raw (1 cup)

Calories	43	Fat	<1 g
Protein	3 g	Saturated Fat	<1 g
Carbohydrate	9 g	Cholesterol	0 g
Dietary Fiber	Medium	Sodium	25 mg

KEY NUTRIENTS		% RDA Men	% RDA Women
Vitamin A	883 IU	18%	22%
Vitamin B_6	0.2 mg	10%	13%
Beta Carotene	1 mg	N/A	N/A
Vitamin C	85 mg	142%	142%
Vitamin E	1 mg	10%	13%
Folacin	61 mcg	31%	34%
Iron	1 mg	10%	7%
Manganese	0.3 mg	N/A	N/A
Potassium	389 mg	N/A	N/A

S=40% or more soluble N/A=Not Applicable N=Not Available

ping. Sauté steamed sprouts briefly in a small amount of olive oil in which a few cloves of garlic have been sautéed, then add a squeeze of lemon. For an attractive contrast, toss cooked sprouts with grated Parmesan or Cheddar cheese before adding strips or squares of sautéed or roasted red bell pepper or canned pimiento.

Nuts work well with sprouts, too. Either sliced almonds or chopped pecans will make a crunchy topping for the cooked sprouts. A traditional English recipe combines Brussels sprouts with chestnuts (which, unlike other nuts, are low in fat); cook the two separately, then toss them together, season as desired, and serve at once.

Blanched whole sprouts are perfect for shish kebab: Thread them on a skewer with meat or chicken cubes and other vegetables, then grill. Or, halve or slice sprouts, toss them with a vinaigrette or other salad dressing, and serve warm or at room temperature as a side dish or salad. In winter, quartered sprouts will make a tasty addition to a hearty vegetable soup or stew.

Remember that young, tender Brussels sprouts can be eaten raw; lengthwise slices, which reveal an attractive cross section, are suitable for salads or for dipping.

Cabbage

A sturdy, abundant vegetable that is rich in vitamin C, cabbage is almost on a par with potatoes or corn as a long-standing dietary staple. It has been domesticated for at least twenty-five hundred years, probably first in the eastern Mediterranean, where it was immensely popular among the ancient Greeks and Romans—though the cabbage eaten then seems to have been a non-heading variety with loose leaves. During the Middle Ages, farmers in northern Europe developed compact-headed varieties with overlapping leaves—the cabbages familiar to us today. These heading cabbages were capable of thriving in cold climates, and people who had little else to eat came to rely primarily on them to survive the winter. Cabbage continues to be an inexpensive food that is easy to grow, is tolerant of cold, keeps well, and—as a member of the large family of cruciferous vegetables—is rich in nutrients. Like Brussels sprouts, cauliflower, broccoli, and other cruciferous vegetables, which are characterized by thick, water-storing stalks and leaves, cabbage is high on the list of anti-cancer foods. Along with vitamin C, it contains significant amounts of nitrogen compounds known as indoles, as well as fiber—both of which appear to lower the risk of various forms of cancer. And despite a reputation for tasting strong or turning mushy when cooked, cabbage can be prepared so that it is well flavored and crisp.

VARIETIES Hundreds of varieties of cabbage are grown throughout the world, but in American markets you will find three basic types: green, red,

CABBAGE 3½ oz raw (1½ cups shredded)			
Calories	24	Fat	<1 g
Protein	1 g	Saturated Fat	<1 g
Carbohydrate	5 g	Cholesterol	0 mg
Dietary Fiber	Medium (S)	Sodium	18 mg

KEY NUTRIENTS		% RDA Men	% RDA Women
Vitamin C	47 mg	78%	78%
Folacin	57 mcg	29%	32%

S=40% or more soluble N/A=Not Applicable N=Not Available

and Savoy. (For information on the various types of Chinese cabbage, see the box on page 72.)

Green This cabbage has smooth, dark to pale green outer leaves; the inner leaves are pale green or white. (Sometimes the outer leaves are tied around the head as the cabbage grows to keep the interior white; cabbage also turns white if it is kept in cold storage.) Three types of green cabbage—Danish, domestic, and pointed—account for most commercially marketed cabbage. Danish types—which are grown for late fall sale, and for storage over the winter—are very compact and solid, with round or oval heads. Domestic types form slightly looser, round or flattened heads, with curled leaves that are more brittle than any of the Danish types. Pointed varieties, which are grown mainly in the Southwest for spring marketing, have small, rather conical heads and smooth leaves.

Red Similar in flavor to green cabbage, red cabbage has solid deep ruby red to purple outer leaves, with white veins or streaks on the inside. Its texture may be somewhat tougher than green, but red cabbage has more vitamin C, providing nearly 100 percent of the RDA in a 3½ ounce serving.

Savoy This cabbage has crinkled, ruffly yellow-green leaves that form a less compact head than other types; it is about as hard as iceberg lettuce. Savoy cabbage contains a significant amount of beta carotene—enough to supply 20 percent of the RDA for vitamin A; green and red cabbage have very little. It also has a more delicate texture and milder flavor than other varieties, making it a good choice for salads and coleslaw.

A HALF A HEAD A DAY

A half a head of cabbage a day may be enough to help prevent certain forms of cancer. Researchers believe that indoles—nitrogen compounds in cabbage and other cruciferous vegetables—play an important protective role. Studies of animals fed a daily dose of indole compounds equal in amount to that found in half a head of cabbage show that there was a significant increase in the rate at which the active form of estrogen—which may trigger the growth of breast tumors—was converted to a safer, inactive form of the hormone. Hopefully, scientists will be able to prove that indoles actually prevent breast cancer in humans (though this next step may take years).

Other studies have found a lower incidence of colon and rectal cancer in people who frequently eat cabbage. Research has also demonstrated that animals fed a diet rich in cabbage and collard greens (a member of the cabbage family) had less growth of cancer when injected intravenously with tumor cells, compared to animals not fed these vegetables.

CHINESE CABBAGE

Chinese cabbage is a name used interchangeably for two very different types of cabbage: napa and bok choy. Napa cabbage (or nappa, also called pe-tsai) looks like a paler version of a tightly closed head of romaine lettuce. The bottoms of the leaves are white; at the top of the head, the leaves are pale green and somewhat crinkly. Napa cabbage has a more delicate taste than standard cabbage varieties and is crispy and juicy. Bok choy (also called Chinese mustard cabbage) resembles a cross between celery and green Swiss chard. The head consists of white celery-like stalks that are topped with deep green, veined leaves. Raw leaves have a slightly sharp tang while the stalks are not as bitter; cooking turns the leaves milder and the stalks sweeter.

Bok choy and napa have some nutritional advantages over other types of cabbage. They are higher in calcium, for example, with 3½ ounces (about 1½ cups shredded) of bok choy supplying 13 percent of the RDA; the same amount of napa cabbage provides 10 percent. In addition, bok choy furnishes 60 percent of the RDA for vitamin A in the form of beta carotene, while napa is on a par with Savoy cabbage in vitamin A value (about 20 percent of the RDA). Both types of Chinese cabbage are similar to green cabbage in vitamin C, folacin, potassium, and fiber content.

Both raw napa and bok choy taste delicious in salads and slaws. Chinese cabbage cooks in less time than standard cabbage varieties but can be prepared in the same ways—steamed, boiled, braised, microwaved, stuffed, or stir-fried. The last of these methods is the one most generally used in preparing these vegetables. When stir-frying either bok choy or napa (or cooking them by any other method), cook the stems for a few minutes before adding the thinner, more tender leaves.

To prepare bok choy, you must cut off the leafy top from the celery-like stalk; for napa, you will have to separate the thick central part of the leaf from the frilly, delicate leaf that surrounds it. To stir-fry, slice the stalks crosswise or on the diagonal, then cut the leaves into thick shreds. Cook the Chinese cabbage in a little oil (or a blend of oil and broth) with meat or poultry, or with other vegetables—red bell peppers, onions, bean sprouts, mushrooms, or tomatoes. You can season it with either soy sauce, rice vinegar, ginger, hot peppers, or toasted sesame seeds.

The sturdy white stems of bok choy can also be treated like celery, and the leaves cooked like greens. Bok choy leaves are tasty in broth—chicken or miso—with scallions and cubes of chicken or tofu. Both the leaves and stalks of any variety of Chinese cabbage are also marvelous in thick soups or stews; add the shredded leaves at the very last minute for a colorful, crisp contrast.

AVAILABILITY Cabbage grows in a variety of climates and conditions; in fact, it is cultivated commercially in almost every state for local markets, and since it also stores well, there is always a good supply. During the winter, most cabbage comes from California, Florida, and Texas. Savoy, less common than other cabbages, is most widely available from September through March.

SHOPPING TIPS Look for solid, heavy heads of cabbage, with no more than three or four loose "wrapper" (outer) leaves. These wrapper leaves should be clean and flexible but not limp, and free of discolored veins or worm damage, which may penetrate the interior of the head. The stem should be closely trimmed and healthy looking, not dry or split. The inner and outer leaves should be tightly attached to the stem.

A head of cabbage should not look puffy, although Savoy types are normally looser and lighter than smooth-leaved types. Fall and winter cabbage from storage is usually firmer than the fresh picked types sold in spring and summer. Don't buy halved or quartered heads of cabbage, even if well wrapped: As soon as the leaves are cut or torn, the vegetable begins to lose vitamin C.

Two pounds of cabbage will serve four to six as a side dish. A 2-pound head of cabbage yields about 10 cups of shredded raw cabbage.

STORAGE Cabbage keeps well—and retains its vitamin C—if kept cold. Place the whole head of cabbage in a perforated plastic bag and store it in the refrigerator crisper. An uncut head of green or red cabbage will keep for at least two weeks; the more delicate Savoy will keep for about one week.

Once a head of cabbage is cut, cover the cut surface tightly with plastic wrap and use the remainder within a day or two. Rubbing the cut surface with lemon juice will prevent it from discoloring.

PREPARATION Don't wash cabbage until you are ready to use it. The interior of a tight head of cabbage is nearly always clean, but if you want to rinse it, do so after cutting or chopping the vegetable. Avoid slicing or shredding cabbage in advance, which causes a loss of vitamin C. If you must prepare the vegetable an hour or so before cooking or serving it, seal it tightly in a plastic bag and refrigerate.

When cutting cabbage into wedges, trim the stem but leave part of the core intact, as it will help hold the leaves together. However, when cabbage is to be cut up into smaller pieces, the first step is to quarter and core it. Using a large, heavy knife, cut the cabbage in quarters through the stem. Then cut out a wedge-shaped section from each quarter to remove the stem and core. If the core is tender, it can be cut up and cooked. Or, you can nibble on it raw while you're cooking.

To slice or shred cabbage, place a quarter wedge on the cutting board so that it's resting on its side. Slice the wedge vertically, gauging your cuts to produce wide ribbons or fine shreds, as desired. Or, grate cabbage by hand on the coarse side of a grater, or shred it in the food processor, using the grating disk.

Use a stainless steel (not carbon steel) knife when cutting cabbage; the vegetable's juices react with carbon steel and will turn the cut edges of green cabbage black, and red cabbage blue. To further preserve its bright color, red cabbage should also be cooked in a nonreactive vessel—not an aluminum or cast-iron pot.

COLESLAW: VEGETABLE OR FAT?

Coleslaw (from the Dutch *kool sla,* or cabbage salad) is a deli favorite that often shows up on salad plates in restaurants, and it may be the only vegetable—besides french fries—served in some fast-food outlets.

Unfortunately, it can be a nutritional disaster—a cup may contain up to 200 calories and 16 grams of fat, usually because it has been dressed with prodigious amounts of mayonnaise.

But when you prepare coleslaw at home, you can ensure that it is tasty and nutritious, without a high fat content. Use both red and green cabbage for a colorful salad, and enliven it with ingredients such as crushed pineapple, raisins, shredded apple or pear, grated raw carrots, sliced radishes, bell peppers, chopped scallions, cooked kidney beans, grapes, slivered almonds, or chopped walnuts. For an interesting variation, toss in very thinly sliced sweet onions and a handful of chopped fresh parsley. If you like a mayonnaise dressing, try mixing a little "light" mayonnaise with an equal amount of nonfat plain yogurt. And if you prefer an oil-and-vinegar dressing, just mix olive oil with apple cider or herbed vinegars. Then, garnish the slaw with a squeeze of lemon and a sprinkling of any of the following herbs or spices: caraway, celery seed, dillweed or seed, ginger, mint, thyme, parsley, or coriander.

For a cooked "coleslaw," marinate steamed shredded cabbage and other vegetables in a vinaigrette for a few hours, then drain the vinaigrette and cook it down to form a thicker sauce. Stir the sauce back into the slaw.

For salads, Savoy cabbage can be torn like lettuce rather than cut with a knife.

To remove single leaves for stuffing, cut the base of each leaf with a sharp knife, then carefully peel the leaf from the head to avoid tearing it.

Although many old-fashioned cabbage recipes require long cooking, cabbage should be cooked quickly, then served as soon as possible. Allow slightly longer cooking times for red cabbage, the leaves of which are somewhat thicker than green cabbage, and slightly shorter times for Savoy cabbage, which is more delicate.

Boiling The pungent smell for which cabbage is notorious is caused by sulfur compounds released when the vegetable is heated. Cooking cabbage quickly, in a large quantity of water, in an uncovered pot, will minimize this problem; just don't use an aluminum pot, which promotes the chemical reaction. Dropping a whole, unshelled walnut or a slice of bread into the water may also reduce the odor.

Another advantage to cooking cabbage as briefly as possible in an uncovered pot is that it will prevent the leaves from turning a drab grayish green. To conserve its high vitamin C content, add the cabbage to water that's already boiling. Once it's cooked, save the water to use in stock or soup. *Cooking times:* for quarters or large wedges, 10 to 15 minutes; for shredded cabbage, 3 to 5 minutes.

Braising Any type of cabbage can be braised in stock, apple juice, cider, or wine. Thinly sliced onions will enhance the flavor. Place the shredded cabbage and just enough liquid to cover it in the pan, bring to a boil, cover, and simmer until tender. You can also braise the vegetable in a casserole in the oven. If you like, after cooking the cabbage, reduce the cooking liquid and stir in lowfat plain yogurt to make a sauce.

Braising red cabbage with acid ingredients helps to preserve its color; a classic dish cooked this way is sweet-and-sour red cabbage. Use lemon juice or wine vinegar (about 1 tablespoon per cup of cooking liquid), or braise the cabbage in red wine or cider. Cook sliced apples and onions with the cabbage, and balance the sourness with brown sugar or honey and nutmeg. *Cooking times:* 30 to 60 minutes.

Microwaving Cut a head of cabbage into wedges and place them in a microwavable baking dish with 2 tablespoons of water or chicken stock. For shredded cabbage, add ¼ cup liquid to 2 cups of the vegetable. *Cooking time:* for wedges, 5 to 7 minutes; for shredded, 8 minutes, stirring halfway through.

Steaming This method is the best way to conserve the nutrients, color, and crisp-tender texture of cabbage. If cabbage is steamed with no added water—that is, cooked in the vegetable's own moisture—it will retain 68 percent of its vitamin C content, compared to 44 percent when it is cooked in water to cover. Place quartered, sliced, or shredded cabbage in a vegetable steamer over boiling water, or in a pan with ½ inch of boiling water. To help hold in the steam, place one of the "wrapper" leaves on top of the cabbage while it cooks. If this leaf is tender enough, shred or chop it and add it to the rest of the steamed cabbage after cooking; the dark green outer leaves are rich in nutrients. *Cooking times:* for quarters or large wedges, 10 to 15 minutes; for shredded cabbage, 5 to 10 minutes.

SAUERKRAUT

The most famous way of preserving cabbage is by pickling it. Pickled cabbage, known as sauerkraut, is likely to be found bottled on your grocer's shelf, refrigerated in jars and plastic bags, or sold loose in the deli case. Shredded cabbage that has been salted and aged produces lactic acid, which gives sauerkraut its distinctive sour taste.

To reduce some of its very high sodium content (780 milligrams per ½ cup of canned sauerkraut), you should rinse and drain the sauerkraut before serving. Heating sauerkraut enhances its taste, and it can be further flavored with caraway or dill seeds, chopped onions, or a pinch of brown sugar. Cooked sauerkraut, like cooked cabbage, can be combined with other vegetables, meat, or poultry to make a substantial main dish.

Stir-frying Sliced or shredded cabbage can be stir-fried on its own, combined with vegetables such as red bell peppers, or added to a number of Chinese dishes. *Cooking time:* 1 to 2 minutes.

Stuffed cabbage Cabbage leaves make appealing wrappers for a filling of rice or other grains, such as barley or kasha, mixed with chopped vegetables or small amounts of meat. It's easiest to use a precooked filling, although some recipes call for raw beef or uncooked rice.

To prepare leaves for stuffing, remove them from the head and blanch them until they are limp (3 to 5 minutes). Allow to cook and then shave off the thick part of the central rib from the back of each leaf, or it may cause the leaf to break when you roll it. Place the filling at the bottom of the leaf's cuplike hollow, then fold the bottom and the two sides of the leaf over the filling and roll the leaf up firmly. Secure the rolls with toothpicks (or tie them with scallion greens) and arrange them snugly in a baking dish just large enough to hold them. Add stock, tomato sauce, or other liquid and bake until the leaves are tender and the filling is heated through.

SERVING SUGGESTIONS You can season raw cabbage salads or cooked green cabbage with dillweed or dill seed, caraway seeds, curry powder, or mustard.

Shredded cabbage adds satisfying texture to any homemade vegetable soup; it cooks quickly, but should not be added until the last 5 to 10 minutes of cooking. It imparts a fresh flavor to canned vegetable or tomato soup.

Cabbage and pasta make good partners. Cut a cabbage into strips the same width as wide noodles or fettucine, and cook them with the pasta. Then toss the cabbage and pasta with cottage cheese and poppy seeds, or with grated sharp cheese, or top with your favorite sauce.

Carrots

Vitamin A is derived from beta carotene—and carrots are the leading source of this substance in the American diet. In fact, carotenoids, the group of plant pigments of which beta carotene is a member, are so named because they were first identified in carrots. With the exception of beets, carrots contain more sugar than any other vegetable, which makes them a satisfying snack eaten raw and a tasty addition to a variety of cooked dishes.

The carrot belongs to the *Umbelliferae* family, and is recognizable by its feathery leaves as a relative of parsley, dill, fennel, celery—and the wildflower Queen Anne's Lace, from which it first may have been domesticated. In earlier times, carrots were small red, yellow, or purple roots; the elongated orange carrot, forerunner of today's familiar vegetable, was probably developed in the seventeenth century.

Eating carrots may lower blood cholesterol levels, according to a study by researchers at the USDA. Study participants who ate 7 ounces of carrots a day for three weeks had, on average, an 11 percent reduction in cholesterol levels. This effect was probably due to calcium pectate, a type of soluble fiber present in carrots.

There are many varieties of carrots, but most of them are 7 to 9 inches long and 3/4 to 1 1/2 inches in diameter; carrots in this range are commonly sold in plastic bags at the supermarket. Larger ones are sometimes peeled and trimmed to 1 1/2- to 2-inch

lengths and packaged as baby carrots. But true baby carrots are pulled from the ground early, and actually look like miniature carrots. They are sold in specialty shops or local markets, usually with their green tops attached.

AVAILABILITY The majority of carrots are grown in California and Michigan. The vegetable is shipped nationwide all year round, and in the summer and fall, you may find locally grown fresh carrots at farmers' markets or produce stands.

Carrots are also available canned and frozen. The nutritional differences between frozen and fresh are generally minor, except that fresh carrots have almost twice as much vitamin C and potassium as frozen. Canned carrots contain even less vitamin C and about half the beta carotene of fresh or frozen; in addition, they are much higher in sodium than fresh unless they are labeled "no salt added."

SHOPPING TIPS Since the 1950s, almost all carrots in the United States have been sold in plastic bags. "Topped" or "cliptop" carrots—with their leafy greens cut off—are usually packaged in 1- or 2-pound bags that often have thin orange lines printed on them. This decoration gives the illusion of brighter, fresher-looking carrots. Other bags have a dark band at their bottoms, thus obscuring the stem ends of the carrots, which provide an important visual clue to freshness. In certain states, however, carrots bags are required to have a "window" that affords the consumer a clear view of the contents.

Many markets sell carrots in bunches with their tops still on, but usually at a higher price than bagged carrots. Some consumers see the tops as an indication of freshness, which indeed they are—if crisp and bright green. However, refrigeration and moisture-retaining packaging are the best preservers of freshness: If carrots are displayed unwrapped at room temperature, they will lose sweetness and crispness, with or without their leafy crown.

CARROTS AND VISION

As children, most of us were told that eating carrots is good for our eyes—a health claim that is only partially true. The beta carotene in carrots is converted by the body to vitamin A, a nutrient essential for the functioning of the retina of your eye. And some studies suggest that carotenoids, such as beta carotene, can help prevent or delay the development of cataracts because of their antioxidant properties (though this evidence is far from conclusive). But vitamin A or beta carotene won't preclude or improve any other vision problems (including nearsightedness or farsightedness), unless they result from a vitamin A deficiency, a rare condition in this country.

Look for well-shaped carrots; they should not be gnarled or covered with rootlets. Their color should be a healthy reddish orange, not pale or yellow, from top to bottom (the darker the orange color, the more beta carotene is present). The top, or "shoulder," may be tinged with green, but should not be dark or black, both indications of age. However, the green part is likely to be bitter (it should be trimmed before eating); if carrots are very green on top, they should not be purchased. Also, avoid carrots that are cracked, shriveled, soft, or wilted.

Fairly young carrots are likely to be mild flavored and tender, but, surprisingly, mature carrots are often sweeter, with a dense, close-grained texture. Regardless of its age, the smaller a carrot's core—the fibrous channel that runs the length of the vegetable—the sweeter the carrot, as the vegetable's natural sugars lie in the outer layers. Usually, you can't see the core until you cut the carrot, but any carrots that have large, thick shoulders are likely to have large cores, too.

STORAGE To preserve their flavor, texture, and beta carotene content, carrots should be refrigerated. Keep them in the refrigerator crisper, in their original plastic bag. If they were purchased loose, place them in a perforated or loosely closed plastic bag. You should not store carrots together with apples, pears, or other fruits that produce ethylene gas as they ripen (even in the refrigerator, ripening of such fruits slows, but does not cease).

If you buy carrots with "tops," twist or cut off the leaves before storing. Otherwise, the greens will wilt and decay quickly; furthermore, moisture will be drawn from the roots, turning them limp and rubbery.

PREPARATION Although carrots may look clean, bacteria from the soil may be present on the surface. So whether eating the carrots raw or cooked, be sure to scrub them with a vegetable brush under running water, or peel them with a swivel-bladed vegetable peeler or paring knife, then rinse thoroughly.

If you enjoy crunching on raw carrots, then do so. However, since carrots have tough cellular walls that the body cannot easily break down, cooking them just until crisp-tender actually makes their nutrients (including beta carotene) more accessible—although *overcooking* them can significantly decrease the carotene level.

Proper cooking brings out the sweetness in carrots. They can be left whole or cut into short lengths; halving them lengthwise will reduce cooking time. If you prefer, cut them straight or diagonally crosswise into "coins," or slice them into julienne (matchstick-sized) strips. Grated or shredded carrots also cook very quickly. A food processor is handy for slicing or shredding.

Baking When you are baking or roasting other foods, place whole carrots in a shallow baking dish, cover, and bake them at the same time. *Cooking time:* 40 to 45 minutes in a 350° oven.

TOO MANY CARROTS?

Eating excessive quantities of carrots can cause the skin to turn yellow because of the high intake of carotenoid pigments. This condition—called carotenemia—is perfectly harmless, and affected skin will return to normal within a few weeks if carrot consumption is reduced. Carotenemia affects only the skin; if the whites of the eyes turn yellow or if urine is discolored, it may be a sign of a more serious condition, such as jaundice.

Blanching There is no reason to boil carrots until tender; for fully cooked carrots, steaming or microwaving are better alternatives. But blanching helps to preserve color and nutrients, yet makes carrots a bit less crunchy and easier to eat when they are being served raw. Bring a large pot of water to a boil and drop in the carrots. When the water returns to a boil, cook the carrots briefly. Drain, then cool them under cold running water. *Cooking time:* 3 to 4 minutes.

Microwaving Fruit juice or broth, rather than water, can be used as the cooking liquid in this method. Place a pound of carrots, cut into 1-inch pieces, in a covered microwavable dish with 2 tablespoons of either liquid. *Cooking time:* 4 to 6 minutes.

Steaming Place the carrots in an inch or less of water or other liquid (orange juice or chicken broth, for instance) in a heavy pan with a tight-fitting lid. The liquid should be completely absorbed by the end of cooking time. Or, you can use a conventional vegetable steamer. Cook until just tender for serving as is; or until fully tender if you wish to mash or purée the carrots. *Cooking times:* for whole carrots, 5 to 8 minutes; for slices, 3 to 4 minutes.

CARROTS 3½ oz raw (1⅓ carrots)			
Calories	43	Fat	<1 g
Protein	1 g	Saturated Fat	<1 g
Carbohydrate	10 g	Cholesterol	0 mg
Dietary Fiber	Medium (S)	Sodium	35 mg

KEY NUTRIENTS		% RDA Men	% RDA Women
Vitamin A	28,129 IU	563%	703%
Beta Carotene	17 mg	N/A	N/A
Vitamin C	9 mg	15%	15%
Potassium	323 mg	N/A	N/A

S=40% or more soluble N/A=Not Applicable N=Not Available

Eat carrots with tomatoes. Lycopene, the red coloring of tomatoes, enhances the body's absorption and utilization of beta carotene. Add sliced or grated carrots to a lettuce and tomato salad or combine carrot sticks with wedges of tomato as part of a vegetable platter.

SERVING SUGGESTIONS Toss cooked carrots with a squeeze of lemon juice, or add a little honey and orange juice and continue to cook, stirring frequently, until the carrots are coated with a light glaze. Try sautéing cooked carrots with curry powder or its component spices, such as cumin, dried coriander, and mustard seed; then stir in some golden raisins or chopped dried fruits. You can also purée cooked carrots and season them with sweet or savory spices. Serve with other purées such as turnip, potato, squash, or beet. Julienned carrots can be steamed with green beans; sliced carrots with cauliflower florets.

Add chopped or grated carrots to soups and tomato sauces for sweetness, and to meatloaf to "stretch" the meat and make it juicier. Grated carrots are frequently included in potato pancake, quick bread, and muffin recipes to increase moistness and sweetness without increasing their fat, sugar, or calorie content. Grated carrots are also a good source of extra fiber; ½ cup of grated carrots will add approximately 2 grams of fiber to any recipe.

Carrots may be a healthful food, but carrot cake is not. A typical recipe may contain up to a cup of oil. A 3½-ounce slice of carrot cake with cream cheese frosting has 385 calories, with 49 percent of them from fat.

Vary carrot salad recipes and coleslaw by mixing in some dried fruits—golden or dark raisins, chopped dried apricots, or pears. Top the slaw with a sprinkling of poppy seeds or chopped walnuts; perk up carrot salad with coconut, grated apple, or grated fresh ginger. Some grated carrot mixed in with peanut butter or cream cheese makes a nutritious sandwich filling and helps to reduce its fat content.

Cauliflower

Cauliflower is, indeed, a flower, one growing from a plant that in its early stages resembles broccoli, its closest relative. Like broccoli, cauliflower is a cruciferous vegetable; members of this family have been associated with reducing the risk of cancer. However, while broccoli opens outward to sprout bunches of green florets, cauliflower forms a compact head of undeveloped white flower buds. As it grows on a single stalk, the head (known as the "curd") is surrounded by heavily ribbed green leaves that protect it from sunlight, so that the flower buds don't develop chlorophyll. With some types of cauliflower, however, the head pokes through the leaves and the grower periodically will tie the leaves over the head to shield it from the sun. Otherwise, exposure to sunlight would discolor the florets and also cause them to develop an undesirable flavor.

Some markets sell a cauliflower-broccoli hybrid that looks like cauliflower but has a green curd. Less dense than white, this recently developed variety cooks more quickly and has a milder taste. Still, white cauliflower remains more plentiful in the United States.

Fresh and frozen cauliflower are virtually equivalent nutritionally except that frozen versions have a third less vitamin C and about half the potassium. Frozen cauliflower can also look and taste watery, no matter how it's cooked.

AVAILABILITY You can usually obtain cauliflower year round, though it is typically more abundant in autumn. (California and New York are the major producers.) Before they are shipped, the heads are trimmed of their outer leaves and packed in protective plastic wrap that has been perforated to allow carbon dioxide to escape. (If the gas builds up, the cauliflower will discolor and taste unpleasant when cooked.)

SHOPPING TIPS Select clean, firm, compact heads that are white or creamy white. (The size of the head doesn't affect its quality.) Any leaves that remain should be green and crisp. Avoid heads with major spots, speckles, bruises, or loose, open floret clusters. Some stores also sell packaged florets that have been trimmed off the head, and these, too, should be free of bruises or spots. Small leaves growing between the florets are not a sign of poor quality; just pull them out before you cook the cauliflower.

A medium-sized head is 6 inches in diameter and weighs about 2 pounds—enough to serve 4 to 6 people after trimming off the leaves and stem.

STORAGE Refrigerate cauliflower in the crisper, where it will keep for up to five days (though you should eat it as soon as possible for the best flavor). If the head is unwrapped, store it in an open or perforated plastic bag. Keep the head stem-side up to prevent moisture from collecting

on top. Precut florets don't keep well, so use them within a day of purchase.

PREPARATION The head can be easily separated into florets for serving raw or cooked. (Raw cauliflower is milder tasting than raw broccoli.) For cooking, you can also leave the head whole, which some people prefer because of its appearance; however, it takes longer to cook than the florets and so more nutrients may be lost.

First, trim the cauliflower: Pull off any outer leaves and cut off the protruding stem end close to the head. If you find that the florets have started to turn brown at the edges, trim off these areas. To cook the head whole, remove the base of the core by cutting around the stem with a small knife; this step allows for faster, more even cooking. To prepare florets, hollow out the inner core. Then you will be able to separate the head into florets, or slice off the florets around the inner core. Split any larger florets in two and slice up the inner core pieces. Rinse the cauliflower thoroughly before cooking.

Like broccoli, cauliflower contains plant acids that form odorous sulfur compounds as the vegetable is heated; these odors become more intense the longer the cauliflower cooks. Rapid cooking not only reduces the odors, but keeps the texture crisp, preserves the vegetable's color, and reduces the loss of nutrients. Cook until crisp-tender, but be aware that cooking times vary considerably, depending upon the size of the head or florets.

Don't cook cauliflower in an aluminum or iron pot. Because of the chemical compounds in cauliflower, contact with aluminum turns the vegetable yellow, while an iron pot turns it brown or blue-green.

Boiling Using a large open pot filled with water to cover disperses the odorous compounds and produces a mild flavor, but this method destroys about half the vitamin C content. If you do boil the vegetable, keep the cooking time short. For a whole cauliflower, submerge the entire head by lowering it into the water with the stem side up, so that the florets don't bob above the surface. Add lemon juice or vinegar to retain whiteness. *Cooking times:* for florets, 3 to 6 minutes; for whole cauliflower, 10 to 15 minutes.

SAVING THE FOLACIN

Like broccoli, cauliflower is a good source of folacin—but it loses nearly all of its B vitamin content if cooked too long. In a study testing the effect of cooking on vegetables considered good sources of folacin, cauliflower that was boiled vigorously for 10 minutes lost 84 percent of its folacin content—more than any other vegetable. (Asparagus, by comparison, lost only 22 percent.) All the folacin is not destroyed, but most leaches into the cooking water. By using this water in a sauce or soup, you would conserve a significant amount of the vitamin.

Microwaving Put 2 cups of florets in a 9-inch microwavable dish, add 1/4 cup of water, and cover. For a whole 1½-pound cauliflower, cover it in plastic wrap. *Cooking times:* for florets, 3 minutes on high, then let stand 2 more minutes, covered, to complete cooking; for whole cauliflower, 3 minutes on high, then turn it over and cook for 2 to 4 minutes, then test underside for doneness with a fork. Let stand for 3 more minutes to complete cooking.

Sautéing Cauliflower needs no precooking if the florets are thinly sliced. Use a small amount of oil in a skillet or wok, or lightly coat the pan with a vegetable oil spray. If you need to add more liquid to prevent sticking, you can use 1 or 2 tablespoons of water, broth, or vinegar. *Cooking time:* 3 to 4 minutes.

Steaming Use a conventional steamer basket for florets. For steaming cauliflower whole, place the vegetable, stem-side down, in a steamer basket or simply lower it into a pot containing 2 inches of boiling water. Cauliflower may turn yellow in alkaline water; to keep it uniformly white, add the juice of half a lemon or a teaspoon of vinegar to the cooking water. After the first few

CAULIFLOWER 3½ oz raw (1 cup florets)			
Calories	24	Fat	<1 g
Protein	2 g	Saturated Fat	<1 g
Carbohydrate	5 g	Cholesterol	0 mg
Dietary Fiber	Medium	Sodium	15 mg

KEY NUTRIENTS		% RDA Men	Women
Vitamin B_6	0.2 mg	10%	13%
Vitamin C	72 mg	120%	120%
Folacin	66 mcg	33%	37%
Manganese	0.2 mg	N/A	N/A
Potassium	355 mg	N/A	N/A

S=40% or more soluble N/A=Not Applicable N=Not Available

minutes of steaming, remove the cover for 10 to 15 seconds to allow the odorous compounds to escape. *Cooking times:* for florets, 3 to 5 minutes; for a whole trimmed cauliflower weighing 1½ pounds, 15 to 20 minutes, but begin checking for tenderness after 12 minutes.

SERVING SUGGESTIONS Raw florets make a crunchy, nutritious appetizer—they are especially good served with a low-fat dip—and are an excellent addition to salads. Season cooked cauliflower with dillweed or nutmeg, or toss with parsley, chopped chives, or almonds. Mix cooked florets with such vegetables as carrots, peas, tomatoes, Brussels sprouts, bell peppers, or broccoli florets. (Cauliflower can be substituted for broccoli in many dishes.) Add chopped florets to pasta sauce instead of meatballs or stir them into mashed potatoes to enhance their texture. Use any leftovers in soups and stews.

Celery

As much a household staple as onions or potatoes, celery is valued for its crisp texture and distinctive flavor. It is widely used as an appetizer, a salad ingredient, and a flavorful addition to many cooked dishes. A bunch of celery is more accurately called a stalk, which is made up of individual ribs. These ribs are naturally crisp due to the rigidity of the plant's cell walls and the high water content within the cells. In fact, celery is mostly water and therefore exceptionally low in calories, making it a first-rate snack food for people trying to control their weight.

Celery was first cultivated in the sixteenth century in northern Europe, though another two hundred years passed before modern-looking varieties with large, fleshy ribs appeared. Most celery grown commercially in the United States belongs to several green varieties that range in color from light to dark green; all are referred to as Pascal.

DOES CELERY HAVE "NEGATIVE CALORIES"?

Celery is very low in calories, but not so low that chewing it burns more calories than the vegetable contains. An 8-inch rib has only 6 calories, but chewing celery burns about the same number of calories per minute as just sitting. Basically celery, like iceberg lettuce and cucumbers, is nearly calorie free—not because of the energy required to chew the vegetable, but because of its high water content. If you're on a diet, munching celery is better for you than eating a candy bar. But no food has negative calories.

In addition to loose stalks of celery, you'll often find grocery stores selling prepackaged celery

Celery

hearts. This term refers to the tender, innermost ribs of the celery, but many of the packaged ones are actually just small stalks of celery that have been washed and trimmed. (You can also make your own celery hearts; see instructions under braising, below.)

AVAILABILITY Celery is available year round. California and Florida produce about 90 percent of the domestic crop, with California supplying the majority. Some celery is grown in Michigan, Texas, and New York; a small amount of celery is imported, primarily from Canada.

SHOPPING TIPS Light green celery ribs with a glossy surface tend to taste best. (Dark green ribs have slightly more nutrients, but are apt to be stringy.) If not wrapped, celery should be sprinkled with water to prevent wilting. Look first at the bunch—it should be compact and well shaped—and then examine the leaves, which should be green and fresh-looking. The leaves are a good guide to the celery's overall condition. The ribs and leaf stems should feel firm and crisp, as if they would snap when broken in half, and should be free of cracks or bruises.

Inspect both the outer and inner surfaces of ribs for discolored spots or bruises, or for patches that appear to be trimmed off—grocers sometimes slice off bruised or rotting areas, and such stalks won't keep as long as undamaged celery.

STORAGE Refrigerate celery in a plastic bag in the crisper, where it can keep for up to two weeks. Keep the vegetable away from the coldest areas of the refrigerator—the back and the side walls—since celery freezes easily, thus damaging the cell walls. Once thawed, the celery will be limp and watery. Sprinkle the ribs occasionally with water to maintain freshness, since celery dehydrates easily. If the ribs have begun to wilt by the time you want to use them, refresh them by separating the ribs and submerging them in ice water for several minutes.

PREPARATION Rinse celery thoroughly to remove sand and dirt. To serve it raw, cut the ribs to the desired length just before serving them. (If you want to cut the celery in advance, let the pieces stand in ice water for an hour before serving—this immersion, however, will cause some loss of vitamin C content.) Should the outer ribs in a bunch be coarse and stringy, just peel them away with a vegetable peeler. Trim off the leaves and knobby tops—and if you wish, save them to add flavor and texture to salads, broths, soups, and stews.

When added to other dishes, raw or cooked celery is generally cut into smaller pieces—you can slice the ribs diagonally, chop or dice them, or slice them lengthwise into ¼-inch-wide julienne strips.

Boiling This method, if done with a small amount of water, keeps nutrient loss to a minimum; however, it can dilute texture and flavor. For best results, cut the celery into ½- to 1-inch pieces. Place them in ½ to 1 inch of boiling water or broth. Reduce heat and simmer, covered, until

CELERY 3½ oz raw (2½ stalks)			
Calories	16	Fat	<1 g
Protein	1 g	Saturated Fat	<1 g
Carbohydrate	4 g	Cholesterol	0 mg
Dietary Fiber	Low (S)	Sodium	87 mg

KEY NUTRIENTS		% RDA Men	% RDA Women
Vitamin C	7 mg	12%	12%
Folacin	28 mcg	14%	16%

S=40% or more soluble N/A=Not Applicable N=Not Available

crisp-tender. *Cooking time:* 3 to 6 minutes, depending on the amount of celery.

Braising Although braising takes longer than other methods, it can yield a more tender, flavorful result. If you braise celery by the bunch, separate the ribs and cut them into uniform lengths 6 to 8 inches long. Many cooks prefer to braise celery hearts. To make the hearts, trim the ribs to a length of about 5 inches and remove the outer ribs to reveal the tender innermost ribs, or hearts; then cut each heart in half lengthwise.

CELERY TRANSPLANTS

Celery sprouts from the tiniest of seeds—a pound numbers more than a million. To take root and grow, the seeds must be planted in soil that is kept constantly moist. Most commercially grown celery is first planted in greenhouses or outdoor seedbeds so that watering can be controlled. After about two months of early growth, when the young plants are 4 to 6 inches high, they are transplanted to fields, where they mature in three to four months.

Lay the celery in a heavy pan. (To enhance the flavor, peel and chop several onions and carrots, spread them over the bottom of the pan first, and place the celery on top.) Add enough water, or defatted beef or chicken broth, to just cover the vegetables, bring to a boil, and simmer, covered, until tender. Cut celery pieces can also be braised in this way and will take less time. *Cooking time:* for whole stalks or hearts, 20 to 30 minutes; for pieces, 10 to 12 minutes.

Microwaving Trim a pound of celery and cut the ribs into 2- to 3-inch pieces. Place in a microwavable baking dish, add 2 tablespoons of water, and cover with a lid or vented plastic wrap. Stir pieces halfway through cooking time. *Cooking time:* 9 to 10 minutes.

Stir-frying Celery is a favorite ingredient in Chinese cooking; it can be sautéed or stir-fried, alone or with other vegetables, in a small amount of oil. In a skillet or wok, heat a small amount of oil until hot. Add 2 cups of thinly sliced celery. Cook and stir over medium-high heat until crisp-tender. *Cooking time:* 2 to 3 minutes.

SERVING SUGGESTIONS As a snack or appetizer, sticks of raw celery are refreshing whether served alone with lemon juice or a vinaigrette dressing, or filled with chopped tomatoes and parsley. Even better, arrange them on a platter with carrots, cucumbers, cauliflower, mushrooms, and other raw vegetables, with a healthy dip made from a low-fat cottage cheese flavored with horseradish, chopped scallions, and herbs. (Good seasonings to use include basil, thyme, rosemary, and dill.)

Raw celery, chopped or sliced, adds crispness to virtually any green salad as well as to egg, potato, tuna, or chicken salad. Cooked celery can be served as a main vegetable, though more often it is used as part of a vegetable dish and in stuffings for poultry and fish dishes. When offering celery on its own, try seasoning it with either ginger, garlic, nutmeg, paprika, dill, tarragon, dry mustard, curry powder, or cilantro. The leaves and tops, as well as the ribs, can be be added to stews and soups, or puréed and made into a sauce for vegetable or fish dishes. For a creamy low-fat soup, cook celery and potatoes in defatted chicken broth and pureé in a blender or food processor until smooth.

Corn (Sweet)

A high-carbohydrate food, corn has been an important nutritional resource for thousands of years. It was probably first cultivated in areas of southern Mexico or Central America, perhaps as early as 3400 B.C., and became a staple among Native American civilizations throughout the Western Hemisphere. When European colonists arrived in the New World in the seventeenth century, the grains they brought with them didn't grow well, and initially they depended upon corn for their survival. The Native Americans taught them not only how to cultivate corn, but how to cook the kernels for succotash and corn chowder, and how to grind them into cornmeal for bread and puddings.

BOOSTING CORN'S NUTRIENTS

Although corn is high in protein, it is deficient in the essential amino acids lysine and tryptophan. However, you can compensate for the low levels by combining corn with plant foods high in these amino acids—such as legumes—or with animal products.

Corn is similarly "deficient" in niacin: Although it contains a reasonable amount of this B vitamin, most of it is in a form that is unavailable to the body. However, when corn is mixed with an alkaline substance—for example, when it is ground with lime to make corn tortillas—much of the niacin seems to be released.

The corn of that day was a starchier, less tender version of the sweet corn that ranks as one of America's favorite fresh vegetables. Corn, of course, is a grain—actually, the corn plant is a grass, and the kernels themselves grains, like wheat or oats—and most of today's crop isn't intended to be served as a vegetable. *Field corn,* as nonsweet varieties are generally referred to, is picked at a mature, predominantly starchy stage, dried to a more hardened state, and used in a multitude of ways—as livestock feed and, after refining, in a wide array of processed foods and drinks, from cornstarch to whiskey, as well as in many nonfood products, such as fuel, paper, and plastics. *Popcorn* is a field-type corn with thick-walled kernels; when heated, steam is trapped inside the dried kernels, causing them to "explode." Sweet corn—which was not widely cultivated until the mid-1800s—is harvested at an immature stage, so that its kernels are tender and juicy; at their peak of flavor, they contain 5 to 6 percent sugar by weight.

Presumably, it is the sugar in sweet corn that accounts for its popularity among Americans. They eat about 25 pounds of it per person annually, most of it frozen or canned. Except for being lower in vitamin C, canned and frozen corn are about equal in nutritional value to fresh corn. However, frozen corn—which includes corn on the cob (whole ears or sections) and cut corn kernels—sometimes is packaged in a butter sauce or in other rich ingredients that increase its fat and sodium content. Canned corn usually has both salt and sugar added, making it marginally high-

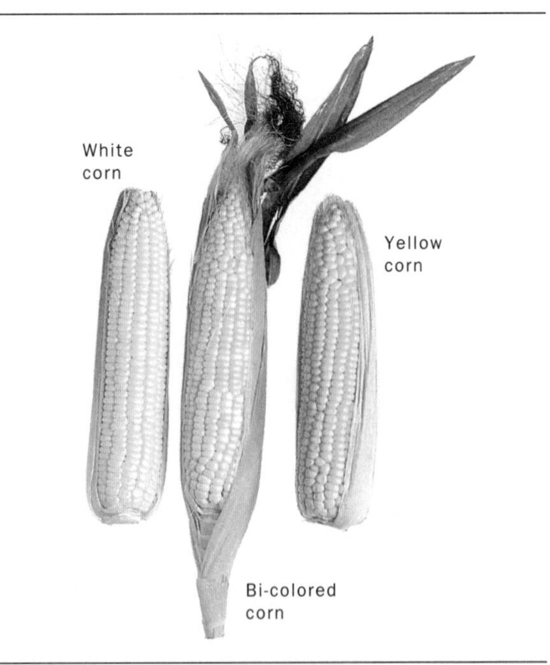

Baby corn

er in calories and sometimes substantially higher in sodium than fresh cooked kernels. Vacuum-packed canned corn is somewhat crisper and more like fresh corn than other canned types. Despite its name, canned "cream-style" corn has no milk or cream added; it is prepared with sugar and cornstarch, which further raise its calorie (but not its fat) content.

VARIETIES Most varieties of sweet corn—there are more than two hundred—have yellow kernels; smaller local crops often include white or bicolor corn (which has a mixture of white and yellow kernels). All varieties are good sources of vitamin C, but only yellow kernels contain small amounts of vitamin A in the form of beta carotene.

Recent work in corn genetics has produced varieties called "supersweet," bred to have more than twice the sugar content of regular corn. Much of the corn now grown in Florida—the leading producer of fresh market sweet corn—is a supersweet variety known as "Florida Sweet." Some supersweet varieties also convert their sugar into starch more slowly after the corn is picked—a highly desirable trait in corn that must be shipped to distant markets. Supersweets, like standard sweet corn, may be yellow, white, or bicolor.

AVAILABILITY Although it is traditionally a summer vegetable, you'll find fresh sweet corn in many supermarkets all year round. Most of the corn sold from December through May comes from Florida, where the harvest season runs from fall through spring. Corn is harvested in much of the rest of the country in the late summer and early fall, and at these times you will probably find locally grown corn in your market. New York and Ohio are among the largest producers of summer sweet corn.

***Maize,* which Americans often think of as the Native American word for corn, is the term used for corn in countries other than the United States. *Corn,* in turn, denotes whatever happens to be the most popular cereal grain. In England, for example, corn refers to wheat, and in Scotland and Ireland it refers to oats.**

SHOPPING TIPS For corn, freshness means staying cool, since warmth converts the sugar in the kernels into starch. In the supermarket, therefore, corn should be displayed in a refrigerated bin; at a farmstand or a farmer's market, it should be kept in the shade or on ice. Shop early in the day for the best selection of locally grown corn; ideally, it should have been picked the morning you buy it. The corn should not be piled high in the bin, or it will generate its own heat, hastening the conversion of sugar to starch. If you're making a trip to the country to get fresh-picked corn, take along an ice chest or cooler in which to pack it.

Check that the husks are fresh-looking, tight, and green (not yellowed or dry); strip back part of the husk to see whether tightly packed rows of plump kernels fill the ear. The kernels at the tip should be smaller (large kernels at the tip are a sign of overmaturity), but still plump rather than shrunken. Pop a kernel with your fingernail: Milky juice should spurt out. If the liquid is watery, the corn is immature; if the skin of the kernel is tough and its contents doughy, the corn is overripe. The stalk of a freshly picked ear of corn will be green and moist; if it is opaque and white, or dry and brown, the corn is several days old and will not be very sweet. The silk should be moist, soft, and light golden, not brown and brittle.

SWEETENING WITH CORN

Aside from feeding animals, the single largest industrial use of American corn is the production of corn sweeteners for beverages—carbonated drinks, fruit juices and fruit drinks, beers and ales, and even wines. A bushel of corn, which weighs about 56 pounds, can be processed to produce 33 pounds of sweeteners, enough to sweeten 324 cans of cola. Corn sweeteners have surpassed other types of sugar in the nondiet sweetener market.

STORAGE To best enjoy fresh corn's flavor, "the sooner the better" is a rule of thumb. Try not to store corn for more than a few hours; cook it as soon as possible after it is picked, and be sure to refrigerate it the moment you get home if you are not cooking it immediately. (At room temperature, sweet corn loses its sugar six times faster than at 32°—up to half its total sugar in one day.) Refrigeration also helps the corn retain its vitamin C content.

If the corn is unhusked, leave it that way to keep it moist until you are ready to cook it. If the ears are already fully or partially husked, place them in a perforated plastic bag. If you have more corn on hand than you can use within a day or two, parboil it for just a minute or two (this step stops the conversion of sugar to starch); then you then can refrigerate it for up to three days. Finish the cooking process by dropping the corn into a pot of boiling water and boiling it for a minute. Or, cut the kernels from the cob (see below) and reheat them in a small saucepan.

PREPARATION Unless you are grilling or roasting corn in its husk, strip off the husk and snap off the ends (or leave them on to use it as "handles," if you like). Pull off the silk, using a dry vegetable brush to remove strands of silk caught between the kernels.

If you prefer to eat the kernels *off* the cob, there are two basic ways to remove them:

To cut whole kernels from the cob, hold an ear of corn vertically, resting the tip on the work surface. Slide a sharp knife down the length of the cob to slice off the kernels. Don't press hard, or you will also cut off part of the cob.

For cream-style corn, slit each row of kernels with a sharp knife, then run the back of the knife down the length of the cob, to squeeze out the pulp and juice, leaving the skins of the kernels on the cob.

Alternatively, drop the corn into a pot of boiling water, cover, and boil until tender. *Cooking time:* 4 to 7 minutes, depending on the maturity and freshness of the corn.

Boiling There are many schools of thought as to the best way to cook corn on the cob, but two basic rules apply: Do not add salt, as it will toughen the corn (although a little sugar will enhance the corn's sweetness); and cook the corn only long enough to tenderize it—a matter of minutes.

One method is to add husked ears of corn to a pot of boiling water, cover it, and let the water return to a boil. Turn off the heat and let stand for 5 minutes. (You can leave it in the hot water for up to 10 minutes.)

Microwaving Individually wrap one or two ears of husked corn in waxed paper or place several ears in a covered microwavable dish with 2 to 3 tablespoons of water. *Cooking times:* for wrapped, 3 to 6 minutes; in a dish, 5 to 7 minutes.

Roasting If the corn is unhusked, first pull back the husks so that you can remove the silk, then replace the husks and tie them with kitchen string. Soak the corn in cold water for 5 minutes. (If the corn is already husked, you can wrap each one in foil.) Bury the ears of corn in the hot coals of a barbecue fire, or place them on the grill and cook, turning occasionally. To oven-roast corn, place the ears in a 375° oven. *Cooking times:* in the coals, 10 to 15 minutes; on the grill, 15 to 20 minutes; in the oven, 20 to 30 minutes.

POPCORN: THE BEST SNACK

In terms of snack food, popcorn is the nutritional winner. It's high in both complex carbohydrates and fiber: Ounce for ounce, popcorn has about three times as much fiber as chickpeas, and about six times the fiber found in cooked broccoli. One cup of popped corn, prepared in an air popper, contains just 30 calories and virtually no fat.

Popcorn ceases to be a healthful choice, however, when it is popped in oil and doused with butter and salt. A cup of oil-popped popcorn, tossed with a tablespoon of butter and sprinkled with a small pinch of salt, contains 155 calories, 14 grams of fat (over 80 percent of the calories come from fat), and 200 milligrams of sodium. Microwave popcorns are usually no healthier; many are packed in highly saturated coconut or palm kernel oil; some also come with additional butter. There are even "light" microwave versions that derive 45 percent of their calories from fat. In general, it's better to airpop your own popcorn and season it to taste with garlic or onion powder, a small amount of grated cheese, or cinnamon-sugar instead of butter and salt.

Steaming Place whole or cut-up ears of corn in a vegetable steamer and cook, covered, over boiling water. Or, place them in a heavy pot with an inch of cold water, cover tightly, and simmer. *Cooking time:* 6 to 10 minutes.

SERVING SUGGESTIONS The traditional way of eating corn is with plenty of butter; yet each teaspoon of butter (or margarine) adds about 34 calories of almost pure fat, and a tablespoon would more than double the modest calorie count of an average ear of corn. Many people also salt corn liberally. Instead, try seasonings such as lemon or lime juice, pepper, fresh herbs, or a light dressing of vinegar and oil.

Corn kernels combine nicely with other cooked or raw vegetables. The time-honored mixture of corn and lima beans, known as succotash, makes a nutritious vegetable side dish; it can also serve as a good starting point for variations. Prepare the basic succotash with fresh, frozen, or canned corn and lima beans, or use cooked dried beans (such as kidney or pinto beans); for a more colorful, crunchy version, add green beans, chopped red bell peppers, milder varieties of hot peppers, tomatoes, scallions, or chopped onions. And rather than using cream as a thickener, substitute a little evaporated skim milk or stir in some plain yogurt after removing the pan from the heat. Season the mixture with herbs (experiment with dill, basil, or coriander leaf) or with the more pungent flavors of chili powder or hot pepper sauce. Serve hot, warm, or cold as a side dish or salad.

Uncooked or frozen corn kernels are always welcome additions to stir-fries, baked beans, bean salads, and chicken or tuna salad. Fresh, frozen, or canned corn kernels also lend an interesting texture and flavor to cornbreads, muffins, and cornmeal pancakes.

When grilling or roasting corn, place sprigs of fresh herbs on the kernels before rewrapping the corn in its husk (or in foil). One-inch sections of corn on the cob (fresh or frozen) will sweeten any chowder, stew, or vegetable soup (they are typically used this way in Portuguese dishes). Dried sweet corn, which is cooked in liquid to reconstitute it, is an old-fashioned dish still enjoyed by the Pennsylvania Germans.

CORN, yellow 3½ oz raw (⅔ cup kernels)

Calories	86	Fat	1 g
Protein	3 g	Saturated Fat	<1 g
Carbohydrate	19 g	Cholesterol	0 mg
Dietary Fiber	Medium	Sodium	15 mg

KEY NUTRIENTS		%RDA Men	%RDA Women
Vitamin C	7 mg	12%	12%
Folacin	46 mcg	23%	26%
Magnesium	37 mg	11%	13%
Phosphorus	89 mg	11%	11%
Thiamin	0.2 mg	13%	18%

S=40% or more soluble N/A=Not Applicable N=Not Available

Cucumbers

As you will quickly recognize when you bite into one, cucumbers are not only crisp, but also cool and moist—attributes due to their exceptionally high water content. Cut up into slices, they are well suited for summer salads and refreshing low-calorie sandwiches and snacks (though they can also be cooked and eaten as a vegetable on their own). The cucumber belongs to the same vegetable family as pumpkin, zucchini (a close look-alike), watermelon, and other squashes. First cultivated in Asia in ancient times, it was brought to America by Columbus, and was eventually grown by both Native Americans and colonists from Florida to Canada. Today, "cukes," as they are popularly called, grow in a wide variety of shapes and sizes, from the inch-long ones sold as gherkins to mammoth greenhouse varieties that reach 20 inches or longer.

THE QUEST FOR STRAIGHT CUCUMBERS
Unlike the long cylindrical cucumbers of today, cucumbers of the eighteenth and early nineteenth centuries grew bent and twisted. Unhappy with crooked cucumbers, George Stephenson—the inventor of the locomotive and an avid cucumber gardener—developed a device to force them to grow straight. He placed young cucumbers inside a hollow, long glass cylinder—which he called a cucumber glass—and as they grew, the cucumbers took on the shape of the tube. Fortunately for modern gardeners, today's varieties grow practically straight on their own.

VARIETIES There are two basic types of cucumbers, those eaten fresh (called slicing varieties) and those cultivated for pickling. The slicing cucumbers most commonly seen in supermarkets are field-grown varieties that are usually 6 to 9 inches long and have glossy, dark green skin and tapering ends. After harvesting, the skin is often waxed for longer shelf life.

In recent years, slicing cucumbers grown in greenhouses have become widely available. Most of these varieties originated in Europe (they are sometimes called European or English cucumbers), and they tend to be thin, smooth skinned, and 1 to 2 feet in length. The majority are also seedless, or nearly so. For that reason, many people find greenhouse cucumbers easier to digest and milder (or blander, depending on your taste buds) in flavor than field-grown varieties. Greenhouse cukes are usually more expensive.

A single 8-inch cucumber (weighing 10½ ounces) provides 12 percent of the minimum amount of fiber experts recommend for daily consumption.

Other less common slicing varieties include Armenian (pale green skin, curled end, soft seeds); Sfran (compact cukes from the Persian Gulf); and Japanese (long and slender with warty bumps). Most distinctive is the lemon cucumber, which looks like a large lemon with pale greenish yellow skin.

Pickling varieties are smaller and squatter, and have bumpy, light green skins. Most are processed into pickles, but one type—the kirby, which is used to make commercial dill pickles—is also sold fresh (and usually unwaxed). Cucumber-lovers appreciate fresh kirbies for their thin skin, crisp flesh, and tiny seeds.

AVAILABILITY The familiar dark green slicing varieties are produced in all states (the majority of the crop comes from Florida) and are available throughout the year. However, they are at their best (and least expensive) from May through July. In fall and winter months, the domestic harvest is supplemented by imports from Mexico. Greenhouse cucumbers are also available year round, as are Armenian and Japanese cucumbers. Other specialty cucumbers tend to be more seasonal.

SHOPPING TIPS Cucumbers and coolness are natural partners—at least in the sense that the vegetable must be kept cool, or it will quickly wilt to soggy limpness. (Overchilling or freezing, however, will reduce the inside of a cucumber to slush). At the supermarket, cucumbers should be kept under refrigeration; at a farmer's market or roadside stand, they should always be displayed in the shade.

No matter what kind you buy, look for cucumbers that are very firm and rounded right to the ends; avoid any with withered, shriveled tips. Although the overall size varies with the type, slender cukes typically have fewer seeds than thick or puffy ones. Beware of cucumbers that bulge in the middle, since they are likely to be filled with large seeds and have watery, tasteless flesh. Waxed or not, their skin should be a rich green—not extremely pale and definitely not yellow. Watch out for bruises or dark spots.

Greenhouse cucumbers are usually sealed in a tight plastic wrapping.

STORAGE Store cucumbers in the refrigerator crisper. Uncut, waxed cucumbers will keep for about one week. Check unwaxed cukes every day or so and discard any that show signs of decay. Wrap cut cucumbers tightly in plastic wrap and use within a day or two of purchase.

PREPARATION If a cucumber is unwaxed, you can leave the skin on; it's best to wash the cucumber before eating it, though. All waxed cukes should be peeled; slice off the ends first, to make the job easier.

Even if the seeds are small, some people prefer to remove them before serving cucumbers. Simply halve the cucumbers lengthwise and scoop out the seeds with the tip of a teaspoon. Then slice, dice, julienne, or grate the flesh.

There are several ways to remove the bitterness cucumbers sometimes have. Try cutting off the ends and peeling the skin. If that does not work, sprinkle the peeled cucumbers with a pinch of salt, a pinch of sugar, and a few drops of vinegar, and let stand for 20 to 30 minutes. (Avoid this method if you are on a low-sodium diet.)

The delicate flavor of cooked cucumbers nicely complements fish and poultry. Season the cukes after cooking with herbs—dill, mint, tarragon or basil, for instance—lemon juice, or a favorite dressing or sauce.

Baking Halve cucumbers lengthwise or cut whole cucumbers into 2-inch sections; remove the seeds. Stuff the cucumber "boats" or sections with a cooked meat, vegetable, or breadcrumb stuffing. Place them in a baking dish, add broth to a depth of about ½ inch and cover. *Cooking time:* 35 to 45 minutes in a 350° oven.

Boiling Cook thick cucumber slices in an inch of boiling water or broth; drain well. *Cooking time:* 3 to 5 minutes.

Braising Peel the cucumbers and halve them lengthwise; scoop out the seeds. Cut into thick crosswise slices. Bring about ½ inch of broth to a boil in a skillet, add the cucumbers, cover and cook over low heat. *Cooking time:* 5 minutes.

Sautéing Peel, halve, and seed cucumbers, then slice them about 1/4 inch thick. Sauté over medium-high heat in a few tablespoons of broth, stirring constantly; cook just until crisp-tender. *Cooking time:* 3 to 4 minutes.

Steaming Here is an excellent way to precook cucumber halves or sections before you stuff and bake them. Place the cucumbers in a vegetable steamer and heat over boiling water. *Cooking time:* 5 to 8 minutes.

CUCUMBERS 3½ oz raw (1 cup sliced)			
Calories	13	Fat	<1 g
Protein	1 g	Saturated Fat	<1 g
Carbohydrate	3 g	Cholesterol	0 mg
Dietary Fiber	Low	Sodium	2 mg

S=40% or more soluble N/A=Not Applicable N=Not Available

SERVING SUGGESTIONS Cucumber salad recipes are legion. To prepare an Indian salad, just mix chopped cucumbers, tomatoes, and onions, then spice it with cumin, cayenne pepper, and lemon juice; a popular Japanese version uses julienned cucumbers sprinkled with soy sauce, rice vinegar, and sesame seeds. To assemble a sweet-and-sour cucumber salad, marinate very thinly sliced cucumbers and onions in a dressing of vinegar, sugar, salt and pepper; chill for at least 2 hours and drain before serving. Distilled, wine, cider, or herbed vinegar will each produce a slightly different flavor. If you like, stir some low-fat or nonfat yogurt into the drained salad.

There are many refreshing variations on the pairing of cucumbers and yogurt. The Indian condiment called *raita*—which frequently accompanies a hot curry—is a blend of yogurt and grated cucumbers, seasoned with fresh coriander or mint, ground cumin, and pepper. Near Eastern versions of this dish include golden raisins, almonds, or walnuts. You could further enliven it with some minced garlic or hot pepper sauce. Thinly sliced cucumber and chopped dill in yogurt also makes a delicious sauce for hot or cold fish, especially salmon.

COOL AS A CUCUMBER

Cucumbers are refreshing because they are mostly water and are often served ice cold, not because—as some sources claim—their internal temperature is cooler than the outside air. The myth probably arose when someone measured the temperature of cucumbers in the early morning, and did not allow time for the effect of the cooler nighttime temperatures to wear off.

For an icy summer soup, purée peeled cucumber chunks with yogurt or buttermilk, garlic, and fresh mint or dill. Season with vinegar or lemon juice, salt and pepper. Or, prepare a quick gazpacho by stirring together tomato juice, chopped cucumbers, bell peppers, scallions, and garlic. Refrigerate until very well chilled.

For a light, hot soup, add julienned cucumbers to a boiling, well-seasoned broth and cook for just 45 seconds; remove from the heat and serve while the cucumbers are still crisp.

Eggplants

Many people would agree that eggplant, with its elegant pear shape and glossy purple skin, is one of the most attractive vegetables. In fact, until this century, Americans valued it more as an ornament or table decoration than as a flavorful, versatile food. Eggplant is not high in any single vitamin or mineral. However, it is very filling, while supplying few calories and virtually no fat, and its "meaty" texture makes eggplant a perfect vegetarian main-dish choice.

A member of the nightshade family, and therefore related to potatoes, tomatoes, and peppers, eggplant is a native of India. It was apparently little known in Europe until the twelfth century, when Arab traders introduced it into Spain. The first plants that English-speaking people came into contact with bore egg-shaped fruits, probably white ones, hence the vegetable's name. In various parts of Europe, eating eggplant was suspected of causing madness, not to mention leprosy, cancer and bad breath, which prompted its use as a decorative plant. But by the eighteenth century it was established as a food in Italy and France (where it is known as aubergine). Today, it is grown in most warm regions of the world, and is widely used in Asian and Middle Eastern cookery, as well as in many Mediterranean cuisines.

Eggplant is astonishingly adaptable, as Americans have discovered. It can be served individually as a main dish, an appetizer, a side dish, or mingled with other ingredients. Many traditional recipes, however, call for cooking eggplant in fat; certainly there are healthier alternatives, as shown below.

VARIETIES In the United States, the familiar dark purple eggplants, weighing 1 to 5 pounds, are the most common types sold commercially. They come in two basic shapes, oval and elongated; the latter is sometimes referred to as Japanese or oriental eggplant. Increasingly, you will find white eggplant sold at greengrocers and specialty markets; these are usually 6 to 8 inches long and tend to have firmer, moister flesh than purple varieties.

Other specialty varieties include miniature eggplants that come in a range of shapes and colors: deep purple ones that are either round or oval (sometimes called Italian or baby eggplants); pale violet ones, usually slim and light (known as Chinese eggplants); and violet-white Italian Rosa Biancos; and Japanese eggplants, which are

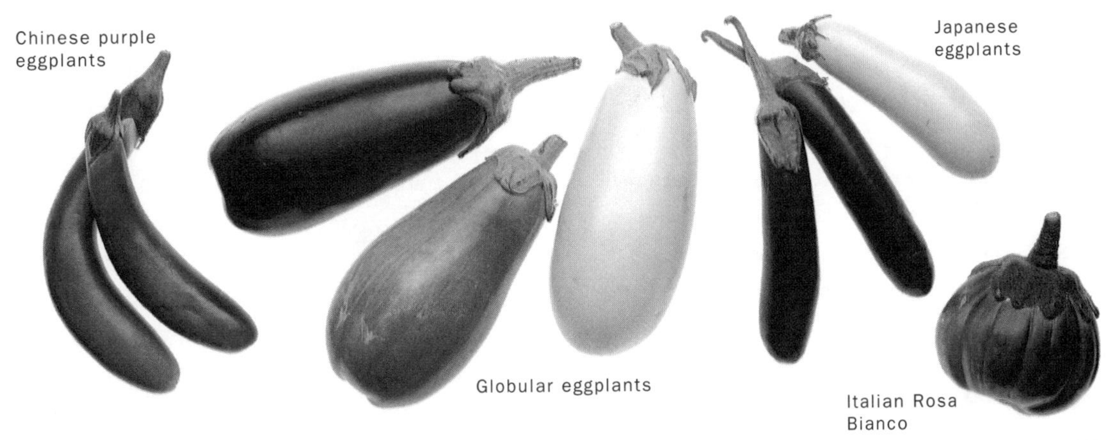

younger versions of the larger commercial types. These small eggplants are generally sweeter and more tender than the larger varieties; they also have thinner skins and contain fewer seeds.

AVAILABILITY Eggplants are available all year, with their peak growing season extending from July to October. Florida provides the bulk of the domestic harvest; New Jersey is a major supplier during the summer months; California and Mexico are relied on to supplement the winter's supply.

SHOPPING TIPS Look for a well-rounded, symmetrical eggplant with a satin-smooth, uniformly colored skin; tan patches, scars, or bruises on the skin indicate decay, which will appear as discolorations in the flesh beneath. An eggplant with wrinkled or flabby-looking skin will probably be bitter. If you press the vegetable gently with your thumb, the indentation should refill rapidly if the eggplant is fresh. A good eggplant will feel fairly heavy; a light one may be woody. The stem and calyx (cap) should be bright green. A medium-sized eggplant, 3 to 6 inches in diameter, is likely to be young, sweet, and tender; oversized specimens may be tough, seedy, and bitter.

SEXING AN EGGPLANT

A good eggplant should not be seedy. Some people believe that they can tell the seed content, as well as the sex, of an eggplant by checking the size and shape of the scar at the blossom end. According to the theory, male eggplants have fewer seeds than female ones. But this method is a myth. An eggplant is self-pollinating; that is, it has both male and female characteristics and can reproduce on its own. A better way to judge seediness is by size. Small- and medium-sized eggplants have fewer seeds than large, overmature ones, which are practically guaranteed to be seedy.

STORAGE Ideally, eggplant should be stored at about 50°. Cold temperatures will eventually damage it, as will warm conditions. You can store an uncut, unwashed eggplant in a plastic bag in the refrigerator crisper for three to four days. If the eggplant won't fit easily in the crisper, don't try to squeeze it in; the vegetable is so delicate that any undue pressure will bruise it. The skin is also easily punctured, leading to decay.

PREPARATION Wash the eggplant just before using, and cut off the cap and stem. (Use a stainless steel knife for cutting eggplant; a carbon steel blade will blacken it.)

Eggplant may be cooked with or without its skin. If the eggplant is large, the skin may be tough, so you may want to peel it with a vegetable peeler. White varieties tend to have thick, tough skins, and should always be peeled. (If you're baking the eggplant, the flesh can be scooped from the skin after cooking.)

Many recipes call for salting eggplant before cooking it. This step draws out some of the moisture and produces a denser-textured flesh, which means the eggplant will exude less water and absorb less fat in cooking. Salting also seems to eliminate the vegetable's natural bitter taste. Rinsing the eggplant thoroughly after salting will remove most of the salt; however, if you are following a sodium-restricted diet you should not use this method.

To salt eggplant, cut it in half lengthwise (or slice or dice it, depending on the recipe) and sprinkle the cut surfaces with salt; ½ teaspoon is sufficient for a pound of eggplant. Place the salted eggplant in a colander and let stand for about half an hour. You can then rinse the eggplant, squeeze out the excess moisture, and pat dry with paper towels.

Unlike many vegetables, eggplant is not really harmed by long cooking. Its nutrient content is minimal, so you don't have to worry about destroying vitamins. And undercooked eggplant has a chewy texture that can be quite unpleasant, whereas overcooked eggplant simply becomes softer. Just don't cook eggplant in an aluminum pot; otherwise, the vegetable will discolor.

Baking A whole eggplant that is baked yields soft flesh that's easy to mash or purée, and it requires no attention while cooking. Pierce the eggplant with a fork several times (otherwise it may explode as the interior heats up). *Cooking time:* 30 to 40 minutes in a 400° oven.

For baked eggplant halves, cut off the stem, then halve the eggplant lengthwise. Score the surface of the cut sides. Place the eggplant halves, cut-side up, on a baking sheet and brush the cut sides lightly with oil. The halves can be filled with a meat or vegetable stuffing; after baking, scoop out some of the flesh and use it in the stuffing. *Cooking time:* 20 to 30 minutes in a 425° oven.

Sliced eggplant can also be layered and baked with other vegetables, such as onions and tomatoes, or with tomato sauce.

Like nearly all vegetables, eggplant contains virtually no fat. But according to an Australian study, it absorbs more fat than any other vegetable. When researchers deep-fried a serving of eggplant, they found that it absorbed 83 grams of fat in just 70 seconds—four times as much as an equal portion of potatoes—adding more than 700 calories.

Broiling or grilling Either of these methods can be used whenever the recipe calls for frying, as both tenderize the vegetable without using lots of fat. Prepare eggplant slices this way when serving it on its own, or before using it in casseroles, such as eggplant Parmesan or moussaka. Charcoal grilled eggplant is a delicious accompaniment to a barbecue meal.

Cut the eggplant into thick lengthwise slices and score them lightly with a sharp knife. Place the slices on a broiler pan or barbecue grill and brush them lightly with oil; sprinkle with chopped garlic and herbs. Broil about 5 inches from the heat; turn the slices when they begin to brown. Cubes of eggplant can also be broiled in the oven. *Cooking time:* about 5 minutes per side.

Microwaving Pierce a whole eggplant with a fork and cook, rotating every 2 minutes. Or, place a pound of cubed eggplant in a microwavable dish, cover, and cook. *Cooking times:* for whole, 6 to 8 minutes; for cubed, 3 to 4 minutes.

Roasting Eggplant that is roasted has a rich, meaty flavor, which is especially recommended for dips and spreads. The vegetable can be roasted under the broiler or over a barbecue fire. Prick the skin with a fork, then halve the unpeeled eggplant lengthwise. Place the halves, cut-side down, on a broiler pan (or, skin-side down, on a barbecue grill). Broil or grill until the skin is blistered and blackened, then enclose the halves in a paper bag for a few minutes; the steam will loosen the charred skin, making it easy to peel and scrape off with a knife. The flesh is then ready to be chopped and combined with other ingredients. (Whole small eggplants can be grilled until charred, then eaten from their skins like baked potatoes.)

Sautéing Eggplant cooked this way acts as a veritable sponge for the fat, so sautéing (or any other form of frying) is not recommended. If you do sauté, use olive oil or another highly unsaturated vegetable oil; 2 tablespoons should be enough for about 2 cups of salted eggplant (see page 92).

Dip eggplant slices into flour or breadcrumbs, if desired, then sauté until lightly browned. Drain the cooked eggplant on paper towels. Or, sauté well-blotted cubes of eggplant until tender; cook in batches, if necessary, to avoid crowding the pan. Otherwise, the vegetable will be steamed rather than sautéed. Drain the sautéed eggplant in a colander. *Cooking times:* for slices, 3 to 4 minutes per side; for cubes, 6 to 8 minutes.

Stewing Eggplant can be stewed alone, or with other vegetables, to form the colorful Provençal stew called ratatouille. Sauté eggplant chunks in a little oil, then add stock, tomato juice, or other liquid. Simmer, covered, until the eggplant is tender. *Cooking time:* 20 to 25 minutes.

SERVING SUGGESTIONS For an appetizer spread of Mediterranean and Balkan origins, coarsely chop roasted or broiled eggplant and combine it with chopped roasted bell peppers, onion, garlic, chopped black olives, and a little oil and vinegar (or lemon juice). For the Middle Eastern version of this dish, *baba ghanoush,* mash or purée the eggplant until smooth and mix it with tahini (sesame butter), lemon juice, parsley, and garlic. Serve either mixture with crackers or crudités, or use it to fill pita pockets. Mashed, baked eggplant, seasoned with Indian spices such as cumin and coriander seed, goes well with plain low-fat yogurt, either stirred in or served as an accompaniment.

Ratatouille is a colorful Provençal blend of unpeeled eggplant, bell peppers, tomatoes (fresh or canned), summer squash, onions, and garlic. Cut the vegetables into large cubes or chunks, sauté them in a little olive oil until they begin to express their juices, then cover the pan and simmer until tender. Season with Provençal herbs, such as oregano, basil, and thyme. Serve ratatouille warm, at room temperature, or cold. It can be used as a side dish, entrée, appetizer, or as a delicious omelet filling or satisfying pasta sauce; leftovers can be puréed to make a soup.

EGGPLANT 3½ ounces raw (1¼ cup sliced)			
Calories	26	Fat	<1 g
Protein	1 g	Saturated Fat	<1 g
Carbohydrate	6 g	Cholesterol	0 mg
Dietary Fiber	Low	Sodium	4 mg

KEY NUTRIENTS		%RDA Men	%RDA Women
Folacin	18 mcg	9%	10%

S=40% or more soluble N/A=Not Applicable N=Not Available

Cover broiled or sautéed eggplant slices with chopped tomatoes, fresh herbs, and a sprinkling of cheese, then place under the broiler until the cheese melts. Or, fill baked eggplant halves with a mixture of their diced flesh (scooped out after baking to leave a thick shell), onions, garlic, ricotta cheese, herbs, and a sprinkling of mozzarella, Parmesan, or Romano cheese. If you prefer, add other vegetables, such as mushrooms, tomatoes, summer or winter squash. Ratatouille makes a perfect eggplant filling. For a heartier meal, make a spicy cooked ground turkey or rice stuffing. Fill the prebaked eggplant halves with the stuffing and return to the oven until heated through.

Fennel

With its rounded pale green bulb, short stems, and feathery green leaves, fennel could be mistaken for a plump bunch of celery. The texture, too, is similar, but fennel's flavor emphatically sets it apart from celery and other stalk vegetables. The overlapping layers of bulb, the stems, and the leaves all impart a mild sweet flavor akin to licorice or anise. Because of its taste, fennel is called "anise" in many markets; however, the vegetable is an entirely different plant from the herb anise, which is grown for its seeds and the oil secreted by its leaves (both of which are used as flavorings.) A member of the parsley family, fennel is also known as sweet fennel, Florence fennel, and, in Italian neighborhoods, *finocchio.* Europeans, particularly the Italians and the French, have been enthusiastic about fennel for many years—they cultivate more of it than anyone else—but the vegetable is becoming more widely appreciated in the United States. Like celery, it is filling and yet very low in calories, so that it provides an excellent snack food for weight watchers. It is also well suited to cooking.

AVAILABILITY Fennel is available through the fall and winter at many supermarkets and greengrocers.

SHOPPING TIPS The fennel bulbs should be firm and clean, the stalks straight, and the leaves fresh and green; if flowers are present on the stalks, the bulb is overmature. The top of the bulb should be compact, with the stalks closely spaced rather than spread out. If the stalks are cut off (which may indicate that the fennel is not perfectly fresh), the cut ends should be fresh looking, not dry and white. Avoid bulbs that show any brown spots or signs of splitting.

STORAGE Fennel dries out more quickly than celery. Cut off the stalks and wrap the stalks and bulb separately in plastic bags. Store in the refrigerator crisper, where the vegetable should keep for three to four days; the stalks may not keep quite as well as the bulb, though, so use them first, if possible.

Fennel

PREPARATION If you've bought a fennel bulb with the stalks attached, trim them off at the point where they meet the bulb. Set aside the stalks to use in soups and stews, and save the frondlike leaves to use as an herb (as you would use dillweed). Wash the fennel bulb and halve it. Trim the base (but not too closely, or the layers will fall apart), then cut the bulb as needed: into slices (vertically), dice, or chunks for braising or use in soups, or into slivers or sticks for stir-frying, sautéing, or eating raw. You can also carefully remove individual layers of the fennel bulb and cut each into strips or squares. If slicing the bulb vertically, leave the central core intact so that it holds the layers together; if halving, quartering, or slivering the bulb, cut out the dense core, or cut around it and discard.

Fennel adapts well to several cooking methods, all of which soften its crispness and mellow its rather striking flavor.

Baking First, braise the fennel for about 5 minutes. Transfer the vegetable to a baking dish and add just ½ cup of the cooking liquid. Cover tightly and bake in a 350° oven until just tender and beginning to brown. If desired, uncover the baking dish toward the end of the cooking time, to allow any excess liquid to evaporate, then sprinkle the fennel with breadcrumbs and grated Parmesan, and brown under the broiler before serving. *Cooking time:* about 1 hour.

Braising For a variety of flavors, braise fennel in broth, tomato sauce, or in vermouth or sherry (diluted in a one-to-one ratio with water); add lemon zest, garlic, or onion for extra flavor. Braised fennel is delicious hot, warm, or chilled. Place fennel slices, or halved or quartered small fennel bulbs, in a saucepan and add just enough boiling liquid to barely cover the vegetable. Simmer uncovered, turning occasionally, until the fennel is tender, adding more liquid if necessary. *Cooking time:* 25 to 40 minutes.

Sautéing Cut fennel into slivers and heat in a small amount of stock, tossing and stirring it frequently. For extra flavor, cook chopped onion and garlic along with fennel. A sprinkling of lemon juice and zest makes a nice finishing touch. *Cooking time:* 10 to 15 minutes.

Steaming Fennel steamed until crisp-tender can be covered with your favorite sauce or marinated in a vinaigrette, chilled, and served as a salad. To steam it, place whole or halved fennel bulbs in a vegetable steamer and cook over boiling water until just tender. *Cooking time:* 20 to 30 minutes.

SERVING SUGGESTIONS Cut fennel stalks into sticks and serve as you would celery stalks, with a dressing or dip. In general, fennel can be substituted for celery: Try it in poultry stuffing, tuna or chicken salad, or any green salad. When using fennel in a mixed salad, dress the ingredients with a mustard vinaigrette flavored with the chopped fennel leaves.

For a vegetable dish, sauté fennel with thinly sliced red bell peppers, zucchini, or mushrooms; serve the mixture as a side dish, or toss with pasta and your favorite sauce.

Fennel marries well with fish. In France, whole fish are grilled over fennel stalks. For a similar flavor, you can oven-bake fish on a bed of blanched whole or chopped fennel stalks or on a sliced fennel bulb. When poaching fish, flavor the cooking liquid with slices of fennel; add chunks of fennel to any fish or seafood chowder.

Chop leftover fennel and add it to ground-meat dishes, such as meatloaf or hamburger, or to soups. Its anise flavor particularly enhances tomato soup, homemade or canned.

The delicate sweetness of fennel also lends itself to last-course dessert salads—for example, serve crisp, chilled slices of fennel with figs, apple slices, or juicy oranges.

FENNEL 3½ oz raw (1 cup chopped)			
Calories	23	Fat	<1 g
Protein	2 g	Saturated Fat	<1 g
Carbohydrate	3 g	Cholesterol	0 mg
Dietary Fiber	Medium	Sodium	86 mg

KEY NUTRIENTS		%RDA Men	%RDA Women
Vitamin A	1411 IU	28%	35%
Beta Carotene	0.8 mg	N/A	N/A
Vitamin C	93 mg	155%	155%
Calcium	109 mg	14%	14%
Iron	3 mg	30%	20%
Magnesium	49 mg	14%	18%
Potassium	494 mg	N/A	N/A

S=40% or more soluble N/A=Not Applicable N=Not Available

Garlic

There is probably more folklore associated with garlic than any other food. By virtue of its pungent odor—similar to that of the onion, its close relative, but stronger and more distinctive—garlic was reputed in ancient times to supply strength and courage to those who ate it. The Egyptians fed it to the slaves who labored on the pyramids, while the Roman nobility—who disdained garlic themselves—gave it to their soldiers and workers. The Egyptians also used it for embalming, and in many parts of the world where garlic was cultivated—particularly India and China—the vegetable was credited with warding off evil spirits and curing all sorts of ills, including broken bones, tuberculosis, bronchitis, and the common cold. (The Roman writer Pliny touted garlic as a remedy for no less than sixty-one ailments.) In contemporary societies, claims are still being made for garlic's medicinal powers, and even in the United States certain garlic products are sold as health foods.

Research into whether garlic (or the oil derived from it) has any actual health benefits is still inconclusive (see page 99). But the daily amount of garlic needed to produce any benefits appears to be much greater than the quantities most people can comfortably consume.

By weight, garlic is slightly more nutritious than onions. Since we use it primarily to season dishes, and therefore consume it in small amounts, it doesn't contribute significantly to our nutritional requirements.

Like the onion, garlic is a member of the *Allium* genus—it is classified as *Allium sativa*—and it consists of a bulb wrapped in a loose, crackly outer skin. However, the garlic bulb has several small sections called cloves, or buttons, that are individually enclosed by tight-fitting papery sheaths. Garlic's characteristic odor and flavor, which stem from sulfur compounds, are used to enhance many different dishes. Its popularity, though, is not as universal as the onion's. In Middle Eastern and Mediterranean countries, and in India and China, it is a practically indispensable cooking ingredient, whereas in Scandinavia and Britain, it is largely or completely ignored. In the United States, its use has increased rapidly in recent years; Americans consume 250 million pounds of garlic a year.

About two-thirds of the domestic crop is dehydrated to produce garlic-based flavorings. Garlic in the form of salt or powder is at best a poor substitute for fresh garlic, as the processing destroys much of the flavor. And garlic salt may contain over 900 milligrams of sodium per teaspoon. Garlic chips and instant minced garlic are dried or freeze-dried versions and somewhat closer to fresh garlic.

Jars of chopped or crushed garlic preserved in oil and tubes of oil-based garlic paste are other convenient stand-ins for fresh; however, they add unnecessary fat calories to recipes.

VARIETIES Some three hundred varieties of garlic are grown around the world, but most garlic grown in the United States—about 90 percent of it in California—is of two types, "early" and "late." The early variety, harvested in mid-summer, is white or off-white in color; the late variety, harvested a few weeks later, has a similarly colored outer skin, but the sheaths covering the individual cloves are pinkish. This variety is slightly denser than the early one and also has a longer storage life. A third harder-to-find type, Chileno, is a reddish, sharp-tasting garlic imported from Mexico. Elephant garlic, an allium with large cloves, resembles garlic, but is actually a form of leek and has a milder flavor than regular garlic.

AVAILABILITY Thanks to staggered harvests and its good keeping qualities (dry-curing after harvest prolongs its shelf life), garlic is available all year round. The California harvest begins in June, and that state sends garlic to market from July through December. Garlic imported from

Mexico and South America takes up the slack when the California supply wanes.

SHOPPING TIPS It might seem odd that garlic—a vegetable with a natural double "coat"—would be packaged for sale in a cardboard box with a cellophane wrapper. But you'll find it sold this way in many supermarkets. The packaging is a more eye-catching feature than a loose display, but the box makes it difficult for the consumer to judge the quality of the garlic. Look for garlic sold loose, so you can choose a healthy, solid bulb.

Garlic bulbs should be plump and compact, free of damp or soft spots; the outer skin should be taut and unbroken. The garlic should feel heavy and firm in your hand; if it is light, or gives under your fingers, the contents may have dried to dust. The cloves should appear well formed. A bulb of garlic may contain a "standard" eight cloves, or as many as forty: Choose a bulb with large cloves if you're a garlic lover—peeling a large number of small ones to flavor your favorite dishes can be tedious.

STORAGE Garlic will keep from a few weeks to a few months, depending on its variety, its age when purchased, and storage conditions. Garlic has the potential to sprout. If it does, the compounds responsible for its pungency will partly seep into the new sprouts, leaving the bulb itself diminished in flavor. Cloves that have sprouted can still be used, although you may need to include more of them in your recipe to compensate for the milder taste. (The sprouts can be cut up like scallions or chives, as they sometimes are in Chinese dishes.) To prevent sprouting, garlic should be kept in a cool, dark spot. A loosely covered container, out of the sun and away from the stove or any other heat source, will make a good storage place.

Special garlic "cellars"—small unglazed ceramic vessels with vent holes and covers—can be found at gourmet cookware shops, but you can devise your own garlic keeper, using a ceramic dish or even a small terra-cotta flowerpot. Cover with a saucer, and leave the container slightly ajar to admit air. A small wooden box, a basket, or a loosely lidded glass jar or similar vessel will serve the same purpose.

As you remove cloves for use, be careful not to pierce the skin on those remaining; even a slight nick will speed decay. Check your stored garlic from time to time and remove any cloves that have become shriveled, dried, or moldy.

Some experts advise against storing garlic in the refrigerator, but it should keep perfectly well there for at least a week or two. (To guard against its aroma seeping into other foods, store it in a separate compartment.) Don't put uncooked garlic in the freezer, which will destroy its texture and give it an acrid flavor.

GARLIC AND OIL: A WARNING

If not handled properly, garlic-in-oil preparations carry the risk of botulism. Garlic can pick up the bacterium that causes botulism from the soil in which it grows; then once the garlic in oil is covered, spores will have an ideal oxygen-free environment in which to germinate. The resulting toxin cannot be detected by taste or smell.

Commercial garlic-in-oil products are safe when they contain an antibacterial or acidifying agent, such as phosphoric or citric acid. Those that do not contain such ingredients, and thus require refrigeration, have been banned by the FDA. Although they should no longer be available, if you do find one that says "keep refrigerated," or doesn't list a bacterial inhibitor on the label, don't buy it. Discard similar preparations you may have at home.

There is still a risk from homemade preparations. If you're making a garlic-in-oil or garlic-in-butter blend or a salad dressing or marinade that contains garlic, be sure to keep it refrigerated and do not store it longer than 10 to 14 days. Or, prepare a fresh batch each time you need it.

Although braided strands of garlic look attractive hanging in the kitchen, they are probably not worth buying unless you use a lot of garlic. The

THE POWER OF GARLIC

What are garlic's health benefits? No one really knows, but some research findings are interesting. Garlic does contain a substance (also found in onions) that interferes with the formation of blood clots and in addition may help reduce blood cholesterol. This might support its age-old reputation as a weapon against heart disease. Some studies also suggest that garlic has anti-cancer properties. For example, as reported in the *Journal of the National Cancer Institute,* about sixteen hundred people in China, a third of whom had stomach cancer, were interviewed about their consumption of garlic and onions (including chives and scallions). Those who had eaten the most garlic and onions (53 pounds a year) were 60 percent less likely to have stomach cancer than those who had consumed these foods rarely. Laboratory studies have also indicated that some substance in garlic can reduce the incidence of some tumors and inactivate some cancer-causing chemicals.

But so far most studies have been too small or flawed in some other way, or have involved animals instead of people. Nobody seems to know whether cooking destroys or reduces any medicinal properties garlic may have. Most people could not manage to consume the 53 pounds of garlic and onions a year (about a pound a week) that the Chinese study suggests may protect against cancer—particularly if it all must be eaten raw. It would be a special challenge for anyone living and working among people who don't eat raw garlic and onions regularly. There is another problem, too; large quantities of raw garlic may make the mouth burn or cause stomach distress.

Nevertheless, the National Cancer Institute, among other institutions, is currently studying the anticancer effects of garlic and many other foods. In a "designer foods" project, NCI will try to find out what elements in foods actually protect against cancer and perhaps formulate special anticancer foods. Promoters of garlic often point to studies showing that men in Greece, Italy, and other Mediterranean countries eat large amounts of garlic and have a lower heart-attack rate than in northern European countries. However, other dietary, life-style, and genetic factors could be at work here besides the comsumption of garlic. The bottom line: Eat as much garlic and onions (raw or cooked) as you find palatable. And remember that regular exercise and a diet low in fat and high in fruits, grains, and vegetables are already known to help prevent heart disease and cancer.

majority of the bulbs are apt to go bad before you get around to cooking with them.

PREPARATION To remove individual cloves, peel off the outer layers of skin from the bulb, then pull back on the top of a clove and snap it off at the base.

To peel garlic cloves, place them on a cutting board and lay the flat side of a broad knife on top. Tap the knife with your closed fist: A fairly gentle impact is all that's required to split the peels without smashing the cloves.

If you need to peel several cloves at once, either blanch them in boiling water or put them in the microwave for 5 seconds and then the skins will come off easily. Cut off the root end after blanching, then slip off the skin. (Incidentally, longer blanching—a few minutes' worth—will also subdue garlic's potency.)

Many people assume that garlic's flavor is too intense, but you can temper its pungency in a number of ways. For a light garlic flavor, add whole cloves (impaled on toothpicks for easy retrieval) to food while it cooks or marinates, then discard them before serving the meal; unpeeled cloves will yield the subtlest possible taste. Placing a garlic clove on the tines of a fork and then stirring food with it (beating eggs for an omelet, for example), is another way to impart a gentle garlic flavor. For a more assertive bite, chop garlic by hand to release its aromatic oils. The more finely it is chopped, the more flavorful it will be.

To chop garlic, cut the cloves in half lengthwise (if there is a green core—a sign of incipient sprouting—remove and discard it, as it may be bitter). Make several cuts the length of the clove with the tip of the knife, then cut crosswise.

A garlic press is quick and easy to use, but many cooks feel that squeezing garlic through a press gives it a strong (and unpalatable) taste; others don't seem to notice any difference in flavor. One clear drawback to a press is that the gadget often takes much more time to clean than it does to use. A self-cleaning press, however, may make that chore easier.

Cooking—or not cooking—garlic affects its pungency because heat destroys some of the flavor- and odor-producing compounds. Garlic is most robust when raw, milder when quickly sautéed, and sweetly delicate when boiled or baked. Cooking with garlic "indirectly" also tames its strength: Sauté whole cloves in oil, then discard them; the garlic-scented oil will make a flavorful addition to many recipes. Or, toss an unpeeled garlic clove into the water used for cooking vegetables; just remember to discard the clove before serving the vegetables.

Garlic's strength also varies with the season and variety, so you may have to accommodate these differences in your cooking. And, of course, you always have the option of altering the amount of garlic called for in a recipe: Choose a larger or smaller clove, or double or halve the amount, depending on your personal preference.

Baking Slow baking produces a sweet, nutty flavor and a buttery consistency. Baked garlic can be used as a low-fat spread on bread or as part of a sauce. To bake, place whole, unpeeled bulbs, rounded-side down, in a shallow baking dish. Drizzle with a little oil, cover with foil, and bake in a 325° oven. *Cooking time:* 1½ hours.

Sautéing Be careful not to burn garlic when sautéing, as it will turn bitter. If the recipe calls for onions and garlic to be cooked together, add the garlic after the onions have been sautéed for a few minutes. Garlic takes less time to cook and the juices exuded from the onions will help to protect the garlic from scorching.

SERVING SUGGESTIONS To give salad a mild, fresh garlic flavor, rub the serving bowl with a cut clove before adding the ingredients. Salad can also be seasoned with what the French call a *chapon:* Rub a sizable chunk of stale bread (a firm type such as French or Italian) with garlic and toss it with the salad; remove the *chapon* just before serving the salad.

When making salad dressing that will be kept for longer than 24 hours, use whole cloves and remove them before storing the dressing (keep it refrigerated); otherwise, the garlic will turn strong and unpleasant. You can also flavor dressings with garlic vinegar. Place several peeled cloves in a bottle of wine vinegar. Cover and let stand for three days, then remove the garlic.

One way to enjoy garlic is in garlic bread. Try preparing it with oil, rather than butter, to cut down on cholesterol and saturated fat. Or, for a

GARLIC 3½ oz raw (33 cloves)

Calories	149	Fat	<1 g
Protein	6 g	Saturated Fat	<1 g
Carbohydrate	33 g	Cholesterol	0 mg
Dietary Fiber	N	Sodium	17 mg

KEY NUTRIENTS		%RDA Men	%RDA Women
Vitamin B_6	1.2 mg	60%	75%
Vitamin C	31 mg	52%	52%
Calcium	181 mg	23%	23%
Copper	0.3 mg	N/A	N/A
Iron	2 mg	20%	13%
Manganese	1.7 mg	N/A	N/A
Phosphorus	153 mg	19%	19%
Potassium	401 mg	N/A	N/A
Thiamin	0.2 mg	13%	18%

S=40% or more soluble N/A=Not Applicable N=Not Available

completely fat-free version, heat the bread in the oven, then slice the loaf open, rub the inside with a halved garlic clove or spread with baked garlic and crisp the loaf under the broiler.

Meat and poultry take on a delicious flavor when cooked with garlic. For roast beef, veal, or lamb, cut slits in the meat and insert slivers of garlic into each gash. The garlic will "melt" into the meat as it cooks. You can also roast whole garlic cloves along with meat or poultry; the most famous such dish is chicken cooked with forty cloves of garlic. For this recipe, unpeeled cloves of garlic (about forty, or to taste) are roasted in a pan with a chicken. The garlic bakes to a buttery mildness, and after roasting, the cloves are squeezed from their skins and puréed to make a sauce. (If you pass them through a food mill instead, the skins will be removed by the mill.)

For garlic soup, a delicious twist on onion soup, simmer a bulb's worth of peeled cloves with some onions and herbs in a few cups of stock for 20 minutes. Purée the solids in a blender or food processor and return the purée to the pan. Add low-fat milk and heat through.

Greens (Cooking)

Plant leaves and stems are the basic makers of nutrients. Many types of leafy plants—especially kale, collards, and others in the cabbage family—are rich in beta carotene, vitamin C, and other substances that may protect against cancer. They are also good sources of fiber and of various minerals, particularly iron and calcium; ounce for ounce, fresh collard greens, kale, and mustard greens have about as much calcium as whole milk, and dandelion and turnip greens have more. (In some countries whose populations eat primarily vegetarian diets, such as China, greens can supply their total calcium needs.)

The level of beta carotene and other nutrients in leafy green vegetables appears to be linked to the presence of chlorophyll, the green pigment produced by photosynthesis. Hence, the dark outer leaves of greens—which are the richest in chlorophyll—may contain as much as 50 percent more beta carotene than the inner leaves, and several times as much vitamin C and calcium.

For years, "cooking greens"—a term referring to a group of leafy green vegetables from several different plant families that are distinguished by their pungent bite and abundant nutrients—have been appreciated mainly in southern-style cuisine. It's odd that until recently they have not had more widespread appeal. Perhaps they seem difficult to cook, but they aren't. Some varieties can be eaten raw; others are easy to prepare.

VARIETIES Now that greens are gaining greater recognition for their nutritional benefits, they are no longer considered a regional item, and have become available throughout the country. Those listed below come from several different plant families, chief among them the the cabbage family. Most of these greens can be eaten raw when young and tender, but as they mature, their strong flavors benefit from a brief cooking.

Beet greens These are the green tops of a root vegetable, and they may be sold attached to full-sized or baby beets, or in bunches by themselves. The long-stemmed large green or greenish red leaves are significantly more nutritious than the roots. Beet greens are at their best when young and tend to become tougher as they mature.

Collards
Red Swiss chard
Turnip greens
Green Swiss chard
Dandelion greens
Beet greens
Kale
Purple kale
Sorrel
Mustard greens
Broccoli raab

THE GREENS VERSUS THE ROOTS

While turnips and beets are nutritious vegetables, their green tops are even better sources of vitamins and minerals, as the chart below shows.

VEGETABLE (3½ oz raw)	PERCENT OF RDA FOR Vitamin A Men	Vitamin A Women	Vitamin C	Calcium	Iron Men	Iron Women	Folacin Men	Folacin Women
Beet greens	122%	152%	50%	15%	33%	22%	8%	9%
Beets	<1%	<1%	18%	2%	9%	6%	51%	46%
Turnip greens	152%	190%	100%	24%	10%	7%	97%	108%
Turnips	0%	0%	35%	4%	3%	2%	7%	8%

Broccoli raab Also called broccoli rape or rabe, rapini, and Chinese flowering cabbage, this green resembles thin broccoli stalks with small clusters of buds. Broccoli raab has a strong, somewhat bitter taste, however, and it is usually cooked to mellow the flavor.

Collards A cruciferous vegetable with anticancer potential, collards, along with kale, are among the oldest members of the cabbage family to be cultivated. Their large, smooth leaves, deep green in color, don't form a head, but grow outward from a central axis. Each leaf is attached to a long, heavy stalk (which is inedible). Collards are one of the milder greens; its flavor is somewhere between cabbage and kale.

Dandelion greens Whether wild or cultivated, these greens come from the common lawn weed, which is a member of the sunflower family. The leaves—pale green with saw-toothed edges—are picked before the yellow flower develops, and they have a faintly bitter taste, similar to chicory. The dandelion greens sold in markets have been cultivated for eating and are longer and more tender than wild greens; before picking wild dandelion leaves from lawns or meadows, be sure that the area has not been treated with weed killer or fungicides, and that it is not close to a heavily traveled road, where exhaust pollutants are likely to have tainted it.

Kale Kale resembles collards, except that its leaves are curly at the edges. In addition, it has a stronger flavor and a coarser texture. When cooked, it doesn't shrink as much as other greens. The most common variety is deep green, but other kales are yellow-green, red, or purple, with either plain flat or ruffled leaves. The colored varieties—sometimes called salad savoy—are most often grown for ornamental purposes, but they are edible. Kale is a hearty plant; it can be left in the ground over the winter, and the flavor actually improves after a frost.

Mustard greens Yet another cabbage-family member, mustard greens resemble a more delicate version of kale, but they have a stronger bite. They are the leafy part of the plant from which we get mustard seed. The leaves, which are light green (sometimes with a bronze tinge) and slightly ruffled, taste best when they are 6 to 12 inches long and have no seeds attached: Seeds are a sign of overmaturity. In some markets, you may also find "oriental" mustard greens, which are a milder variety.

A cup of cooked beet greens has 340 milligrams of sodium; a cup of cooked Swiss chard has 313 milligrams. The amount of sodium is not great when compared to some processed foods and snacks. But if you're on a low-sodium diet, you should be aware of the sodium content of these vegetables when planning your meals.

Sorrel This relative of rhubarb has small, smooth, arrow-shaped leaves and a lemony (some would say sour) taste that provides a good accent to salads. Most often, sorrel is puréed and used to

COMPARING GREENS **3½ ounces raw (2 to 3 cups)**

TYPE	Calories	Beta Carotene (mg)	Vitamin C (mg)	Calcium (mg)	Iron (mg)
Beet Greens	19	4	30	119	3
Collards	19	2	23	117	0.6
Dandelion greens	45	8	35	187	3
Kale	50	5	120	135	2
Mustard greens	26	3	70	103	1
Swiss chard	19	2	30	51	2
Turnip greens	27	5	60	190	1

flavor cooked vegetable dishes. The paler the leaves are, the gentler the flavor. The stems are tough and should be removed.

Swiss chard Also known as chard, these greens come from a variety of beet grown for its tops, not its root. The dark green leaves are wider and flatter than beet greens, and they have a distinctive but not sharp flavor and a full-bodied texture similar to spinach (for which chard is a good substitute). The fleshy stalks and ribs are either white or, less commonly, a rhubarblike red. Unlike many greens, the stalks of Swiss chard don't have to be discarded; in fact, in European countries, they are considered the best part of the plant. Unless the chard is young, though, the stalks are often separated from the leaves and cooked as you would celery or asparagus.

Turnip greens The leafy tops from turnips are one of the sharpest-tasting greens, and like mustard greens, they are generally too assertive (and tough) for eating raw. Don't expect to find them with turnip roots attached: Most varieties grown for their tops don't develop full-grown roots. If you find roots with their tops attached, the greens are perfectly edible, but they may be too bitter and tough to eat unless they are quite young.

AVAILABILITY All of the greens discussed here are available year round, except Swiss chard, which is available from April through November. Most greens have seasonal peaks: Collard, dandelions, kale, and mustard greens are at their best from approximately January through April; beet greens from June through October; and turnip greens from October through March.

SHOPPING TIPS Greens should be kept in a chilled display case or on ice in the market, as they will wilt and become bitter if left in a warm environment. Whatever the type of green, it is best to choose smaller-leaved plants for tenderness and mild flavor, especially if the greens are to be eaten raw; coarse, oversized leaves are likely to be tough. Look for a fresh green color—leaves should not be yellowed or browned—and purchase only moist, crisp, unwilted greens, unblemished by tiny holes, which indicate insect damage.

When buying greens with edible stems, select those with fine stems. Make sure that dandelion greens have their roots attached, and that broccoli raab has small buds and no open flowers. Check that mustard greens are free of seed stems.

STORAGE Wrap unwashed greens in damp paper towels, then place them in a plastic bag; store them in the refrigerator crisper for three to five days. Sturdy greens, such as collards, are better keepers than delicate ones like sorrel. Some greens, such as kale, develop a stronger flavor the longer they are stored; use them within a day or two of purchase.

PREPARATION Whether serving them raw or cooked, wash greens before using, as they are likely to have sand or dirt clinging to them. Trim off any roots, separate the leaves, and swish them around in a large bowl of cool water; do not soak. Lift out the leaves, letting the sand and grit settle; repeat if necessary.

Pinch off tough or inedible stems, and also the midribs (the part of the stem that extends into the leaf) if they are thick and tough. You can easily stem tender greens by folding each leaf in half, vein-side out, and pulling up on the stem as you hold the folded leaf closed. Tougher stems, such as those on kale leaves, may need to be trimmed off with a paring knife. The thick, edible stems of Swiss chard and broccoli raab should be cut off and saved for cooking. (The stems of broccoli raab may need to be pared with a vegetable peeler if the skin seems tough.)

Dry greens well in paper towels or a salad spinner if serving them in salads; for cooking, leave them damp.

Whenever possible, use the cooking liquid from greens in a sauce or add it to a soup; a significant percentage of the nutrient content of greens is released into the liquid as they cook. Don't heat oxalate-containing greens, such as sorrel and Swiss chard, in aluminum pots; otherwise, the pot will discolor. When cooking the stems and leaves of Swiss chard, heat the stems for a few minutes before adding the leaves.

Cooking greens quickly will help to preserve their color as well as their nutrients, and for members of the cabbage family, such as kale and collards, it will prevent them from releasing odorous compounds.

Greens cook down considerably from their raw volume: One pound of raw greens will yield about ½ cup cooked.

The relatively wide range of cooking times given below reflects the variety of greens covered here: Small, young, tender greens, such as sorrel, require minimal cooking time, while large collard leaves or mustard greens need considerably longer to become tender.

Blanching To soften greens and mellow their flavor, or to prepare them for sautéing or braising, drop them into a large pot of boiling water and cook just until wilted. Drain and cool before squeezing out excess moisture (cool under cold water if not serving immediately or continuing with another cooking process). *Cooking time:* 5 to 15 minutes.

Braising To make greens more tender, after sautéing, add a little broth, cover the pan, and continue cooking the greens, then uncover the pan and cook, stirring, until the liquid evaporates. *Cooking time:* 10 to 30 minutes.

Microwaving This method is a good substitute for blanching, as a preliminary step before sautéing or braising greens. Place ½ pound of greens (washed but not dried) in a microwavable dish; cover loosely and cook until tender. *Cooking time:* 4 to 7 minutes.

Sautéing If greens are blanched first, they can be sautéed quickly in a small amount of oil. Whenever you use a nonstick pan, 2 teaspoons of oil should be sufficient for 3 cups of chopped greens. In addition, greens can be sautéed in stock, if you are careful to stir and toss them constantly; be prepared to add more stock to the pan as it evaporates. A generous quantity of finely chopped garlic is the traditional seasoning for sautéed greens; chopped onions or leeks are tasty alternatives. *Cooking time:* 3 to 15 minutes.

Simmering This method works well with such fairly sturdy greens as collards or kale. Simmer the greens, covered, in seasoned broth until tender; to preserve nutrients, after the greens are cooked, set them aside and reduce the cooking liquid to use in a sauce. *Cooking time:* 10 to 30 minutes.

Steaming Tender greens cook quickly enough to be steamed in just the water that clings to the leaves after washing. Steam greens whole or coarsely chopped. Place the washed greens in a heavy skillet (for sturdier greens, add ½ inch of water or broth to the skillet); cover and cook, shaking the pan occasionally, until the greens are wilted. Sorrel heated in this way reduces almost instantly to a purée and is usable as is for a sauce. Greens can also be steamed in a vegetable steamer over boiling water. *Cooking time:* anywhere from 2 to 15 minutes.

KALE 3½ oz raw (1½ cups chopped)			
Calories	50	Fat	<1 g
Protein	3 g	Saturated Fat	<1 g
Carbohydrate	10 g	Cholesterol	0 mg
Dietary Fiber	Medium	Sodium	43 mg

KEY NUTRIENTS		% RDA Men	% RDA Women
Vitamin A	8900 IU	178%	222%
Vitamin B_6	0.3 mg	15%	19%
Beta Carotene	5 mg	N/A	N/A
Vitamin C	120 mg	200%	200%
Calcium	135 mg	17%	17%
Copper	0.3 mg	N/A	N/A
Vitamin E	5 mg	50%	63%
Folacin	29 mcg	15%	16%
Iron	2 mg	20%	13%
Magnesium	34 mg	10%	12%
Manganese	0.8 mg	N/A	N/A
Potassium	447 mg	N/A	N/A

S=40% or more soluble N/A=Not Applicable N=Not Available

SERVING SUGGESTIONS Tender greens, particularly dandelions, are traditionally served with a hot dressing to wilt them. In place of the classic French dressing made with warm bacon fat, heat some tart, garlic-laced vinaigrette, then pour it over the greens. Add recently cooked sliced red potatoes for a more substantial dish.

Use sorrel and other tart greens as you would herbs: Toss fine raw shreds over a mixed green salad. Or, substitute tender greens for lettuce in sandwiches. For a salad, blanch greens and serve them cold, with olive oil and lemon juice.

Cooked or wilted greens are delicious when topped by a crunchy garnish of toasted (rather than fried) croutons, toasted pine nuts, slivered almonds, or sesame seeds. Crisp-crusted cornbread is the traditional southern accompaniment for greens—an excellent choice even if you don't cook the greens with a ham hock, the old-fashioned way.

Many cabbage recipes can be prepared with cooking greens. Be adventurous and try one of the following suggestions: Use chopped greens in stuffings for other vegetables (summer or winter squash, bell peppers); add them to bread- or grain-based stuffings for poultry or fish; add torn greens to broth, or to hearty bean, lentil, or barley soups; blanch or steam whole large leaves and use them, like cabbage or grape leaves, to wrap fillings; layer greens into baked pasta casseroles such as lasagna; mix chopped greens with brown rice that has been cooked in stock, or with mashed potatoes; toss garlicky sautéed broccoli raab or other flavorful greens with pasta.

One of the best-known uses of sorrel is as the main ingredient of *shchav,* an Eastern European-Jewish soup made from sorrel purée and enriched with cream and beaten egg; served cold, its tart flavor is refreshing in summer. For a similar soup, minus the fat and cholesterol, blend sorrel purée, broth, and a little plain yogurt or buttermilk; serve well chilled. For a more full-bodied soup, purée some diced cooked potatoes along with the sorrel (a variety of greens could be substituted for the sorrel); serve hot or chilled. Sorrel purée blended with yogurt makes a tasty sauce for fish, chicken, or vegetables.

Kale, highlighted above, is one of the more nutritious cooking greens.

Greens (Salad)

As people have become more nutritionally conscious, salads have gained in favor as an essential part of a healthy meal—or even as the meal itself. Americans now consume about thirty pounds of lettuce a year—five times what they ate at the turn of the century. Undoubtedly, part of the reason for the popularity of salads is the freshness of the principal ingredients. Lettuce and other salad greens are seldom canned, frozen, or dehydrated; moreover, due to improved methods of shipping and storage, they are the most widely available of fresh vegetables. The other great appeal of salads is that they lend themselves to an almost endless combination of ingredients, from a simple mix of lettuce leaves to main-course salads that contain a selection of chicken, turkey, fish, grains, beans, and cheese as well as other vegetables.

For years, iceberg lettuce dominated the choice of salad greens, but today other lettuces are gaining favor; greens from other botanical families are becoming frequent additions to fresh salads, as well. If iceberg is the only type of lettuce you eat, you are choosing the least-nutritious member of a family of nutritional champions. Any other lettuce or leafy green vegetable would be a better choice. Most other greens are excellent sources of vitamin C and beta carotene—vitamin A's precursor—as well as iron, calcium, folacin, and dietary fiber.

As a general rule, the darker green the leaves, the more nutritious the salad green. Romaine and looseleaf lettuce, for example, have up to six times as much vitamin C and five to ten times as much beta carotene as iceberg lettuce. And arugula has about four times the vitamin C and three times the beta carotene of romaine. Indeed, most of the nonlettuce greens covered on pages 109-110 are higher in nutrients than the basic types of lettuce. By varying the greens in your salads, you can enhance the nutritional content as well as vary the taste and texture.

VARIETIES The greens listed here are primarily enjoyed in salads, but they can also be cooked to make delicately flavored hot vegetables.

Lettuces

Lettuce has been cultivated for more than twenty-five hundred years. The Romans—for whom romaine lettuce is named—grew many varieties, and the vegetable (which is a member of the sunflower family) came to be widely appreciated throughout Asia and Europe. In the United States, an 1885 agricultural report listed no less than eighty-seven varieties. Today, there are four basic types of lettuce you are likely to find in most produce sections of supermarkets or at greengrocers. A fifth type—stem lettuce—is a comparatively new vegetable and less commonly available. When making salads, use more than one type to create a medley of different textures and flavors—and to boost nutritional value.

Lettuces rank a close second to potatoes as the most popular fresh vegetable in the United States.

Butterhead This type includes Boston and Bibb lettuces, which are characterized by a loose head and grass green leaves; both have a soft "buttery" texture and a sweet, mild flavor. A head of Boston lettuce resembles a flowering rose; Bibb lettuce—also called limestone—forms a smaller, cup-shaped head.

Iceberg More accurately called crisphead, this familiar pale green lettuce forms a tight, cabbage-like head. Its texture is crisp and its flavor very mild.

Looseleaf This type of lettuce comprises a number of varieties that don't form heads, but consist of large, loosely packed leaves joined at a stem. The leaves are either green or shaded to deep red at the edges, and may be ruffled or smooth. Their degree of crispness is midway between romaine

Romaine
Green oak leaf
Red oak leaf
Iceberg
Boston
Bibb
Red leaf
Green leaf

and butterhead, their taste is mild and delicate. Oak leaf, red leaf, and green leaf are popular varieties. For home gardeners, looseleaf lettuce has an advantage over other types: If you pick leaves individually instead of pulling the whole head from the ground, the leaves will continue to replace themselves throughout the season.

Romaine Also called cos, this lettuce has long, deep green leaves that form a loaf-shaped head. Some varieties develop a closed head, others are more open. The main ingredient in Caesar salads, romaine has a crisp texture and a strong, but not bitter, taste. Romaine and iceberg lettuce have somewhat similar textures, but romaine is more nutritious.

Caesar salad is traditionally made with raw eggs, and thus can be a source of salmonella bacteria, which can cause food poisoning. (Bottled "Caesar" dressing does not contain raw eggs, but like most bottled dressings, it is very high in fat.)

Stem A thick edible stem, 6 to 8 inches long, is what distinguishes stem lettuce from other types. It is widely grown in China (it is also known as Chinese lettuce), but the only variety available in the United States is celtuce. Stem lettuce has a mild flavor that is sometimes described as "nutty cucumber." Good raw or cooked, celtuce is popular in Chinese cooking.

Other greens

The following greens, each of which has a distinct flavor, can be used alone or mixed with lettuce to heighten the flavor of a salad as well as increase its nutritional content: Some of them contain significantly more vitamins and minerals than lettuce. Two of these greens—chicory and escarole—are often confused with one another or are referred to by different names in different localities. The descriptions here should help you identify them.

Arugula Also called rocket or roquette, this green—rich in beta carotene and higher in Vitamin C than any of the greens listed here—used to be sold only in Italian markets, but is now widely available. Arugula consists of small, flat leaves on long stems—it resembles dandelion greens—and is often displayed with the roots attached. It has a distinct peppery taste and aroma; the more mature the green, the stronger and more mustardlike the taste. In fact, arugula grown during the summer can have a very sharp flavor, so taste it to determine how much you want to use. A cruciferous vegetable, arugula may help to protect against cancer.

HEALTHY SALAD BAR CHOICES

Greens are among the healthiest salad bar choices. But offered alongside these and other nutritious foods are many high-fat, high-calorie items, and choosing too many of these can give your salad the same fat and calorie count as a cheeseburger. In addition to greens, healthful choices include fresh vegetables, fruits, and legumes, such as kidney beans. Don't eat too many avocados, hard-boiled eggs, and meats, and use cheese in moderation. Avoid marinated vegetables, bacon bits, butter-fried croutons, and creamy salad dressings. Be advised that coleslaw and prepared salads made from pasta, potatoes, chicken, or tuna are likely to be loaded with oil or mayonnaise, and therefore be high in fat. Use dressing sparingly; two ladles-full of blue cheese dressing (about 4 tablespoons), for example, could add 300 calories and 32 grams of fat to your salad.

Belgian endive This smooth, pale, elongated vegetable is known in Europe by its botanic name, "witloof chicory." A relative of chicory and escarole, it is also sometimes called French endive (though most of it is imported from Belgium). Each plant is forced from roots that have had soil piled on them or else have been kept in darkness and warmth so that no chlorophyll develops. This time-consuming growing process yields bulletlike heads of tightly closed creamy yellow or white leaves. Belgian endive has fewer vitamins and minerals than iceberg lettuce, although it has much more flavor. The taste is slightly bitter,

COMPARING SALAD GREENS 3½ ounces raw (2 cups)

TYPE	Calories	Beta Carotene (mg)	Vitamin C (mg)	Calcium (mg)	Iron (mg)
Arugula	23	4	91	309	1
Belgian endive	15	trace	0	18	1
Bibb	13	0.6	8	35	2
Boston	13	0.6	8	35	2
Chicory (curly endive)	23	2	24	100	1
Escarole	17	1	7	52	1
Iceberg	13	0.2	4	19	1
Looseleaf	18	1	18	68	1
Mâche	21	4	38	38	2
Romaine	16	2	24	68	1
Watercress	11	3	43	120	<1

while the texture is both crisp and velvety.

Chicory Also called curly endive or simply endive, chicory forms a loose bunch of ragged-edged leaves on long stems. The outer leaves are deep green and have an assertive, slightly bitter taste; the leaves in the center are yellow and milder tasting.

Escarole This member of the chicory family is actually a variety of endive, with loose, elongated heads and broad wavy leaves with smooth edges. The flavor is slightly bitter, but milder than chicory—though the inner leaves, as with chicory, do not have as sharp a bite as the outer leaves.

Mâche This expensive and delicate green, which is extremely perishable and therefore not widely available, has several names: lamb's lettuce, field salad, and corn salad. The leaves are fingerlike and velvety, with a mild taste. Mâche is usually sold in small bunches with its roots attached. It is high in beta carotene.

Radicchio Another chicory-family member, radicchio resembles a small head of red cabbage. The leaves come in various shades of red, white, and green: In the United States, a variety of purplish red and white is most common. The flavor of radicchio—most of which is imported from Italy—is similar to Belgian endive, but the texture is not as crisp. Although domestic growers are beginning to cultivate radicchio, it is still much more expensive than other salad greens and so tends to be used as a color and flavor accent rather than as the basis for a salad.

Watercress A member of the family of cruciferous vegetables—and thus a potential protector against cancer—watercress grows in streambeds, forming masses of pungent dark green sprigs. Sold in bunches, it has a sharp mustardlike flavor that makes it popular as a garnish and sandwich or salad ingredient.

AVAILABILITY Lettuce and other greens are available in fairly constant supply all year. Much of the domestic harvest comes from California. Belgian endive is at its peak from September through May; at other times, it may be harder to find and more expensive. In season, local farmers' markets often sell "baby" greens, which are generally sweeter and more tender than their mature counterparts.

SHOPPING TIPS Above all, salad greens should be fresh and crisp. It is easy to spot wilted greens; watch out for limp, withered leaves that have brown or yellow edges, or dark or slimy spots. Once greens have passed their prime, there is no way to restore them to crisp freshness. Lettuce

Mâche
Watercress
Arugula
Radicchio
Belgian endive
Chicory
Escarole

and other greens should be displayed under refrigeration, or on ice; they are among the more perishable vegetables.

Try to choose lettuce with healthy outer leaves; these are likely to be the most nutritious part of the green, containing much more beta carotene and vitamin C than the pale inner leaves. Unfortunately, the outer leaves are usually the most damaged part of the head, but from a nutritional standpoint, it's best to salvage as many as you can.

Iceberg and other head lettuces should be symmetrically shaped. Choose a head with its dark green outer leaves intact and healthy looking. The stem end of a head of iceberg lettuce may look brown; this discoloration is the natural result of harvesting and does not indicate damage. If the head is not wrapped, sniff the stem end: It should smell slightly sweet, not bitter.

Iceberg lettuce should be compact and firm, yet springy: Very hard heads may be overmature and bitter. Avoid overly large heads of romaine, which may have tough, fibrous leaves.

Even delicate greens, such as watercress and arugula, should be crisp, especially the stems. The leaves should be dark green, never yellow. Select radicchio heads that are small and tight, with a firm, unblemished base.

Belgian endive, delicate and light-sensitive, is usually displayed in boxes, wrapped in dark-colored paper. If the heads at the top of the box have emerged from the wrappings, don't purchase them. Exposure to light causes the vegetable to discolor and turn bitter. Reach deep into the box and choose small, pale heads for the sweetest flavor. Check that the leaf tips are light yellow, not brown or green.

STORAGE Most lettuces and other greens keep best in a plastic bag in the refrigerator crisper. Soft-leaved lettuces do not keep as well as firm greens, such as romaine or iceberg lettuce: Iceberg should keep for up to two weeks, Romaine for about ten days, and butterhead and leaf lettuces for about four days. Store Belgian endive for no more than three to four days; radicchio will keep for up to a week. Delicate greens, such as arugula and mâche, are very perishable: Buy only enough for immediate use, or keep them for no more than a day or two.

Don't store greens near fruits, such as apples or bananas, which give off ethylene gas as they ripen. Otherwise, the greens will develop brown spots and decay rapidly. For appetizingly crisp greens—and to minimize last-minute preparation at mealtime—wash and dry them, then layer the leaves in clean paper towels and place in a plastic bag. Refrigerate in the crisper drawer until serving time, but not more than a few hours, for optimal nutrient retention.

If you purchase a cellophane-wrapped head of iceberg lettuce, leave it in the wrapper until you are ready to use it. Untie bunches of greens, such as watercress, and check them for insects. Arugula (and other greens sold with their roots intact) keeps best if you wrap the roots in damp paper towels, then place the whole bunch in a plastic bag. Greens with their roots attached can also be placed upright in a glass of water (like a bouquet of flowers), covered with a plastic bag, and refrigerated.

PREPARATION Even if greens look clean, they should be washed—and in some cases trimmed—before you put them in the salad bowl.

Although it often comes wrapped in protective cellophane, iceberg lettuce should be rinsed to remove any sand or grit that may have penetrated the leaves. It's best to core it first: Cut the head in half lengthwise and then remove the core with a stainless steel knife; or, rap the head, core-end down, on the counter, then twist and lift the core out. If you're using the whole head, rinse it by running cold water into the cored end, then invert the lettuce to drain it well.

Since grit tends to collect at the stem end of looser-headed greens, it's important to twist off the stem and separate the leaves before washing them. (If you're not using the entire lettuce at one

HOW TO DRESS A SALAD

The numerous nutritional advantages to eating a variety of salad greens will be negated if you drown them in a high-fat dressing. Mixing your own dressing allows you to control the fat content and, of course, the flavor.

Next to a simple sprinkling of oil and vinegar, a classic vinaigrette is the simplest of dressings. This blend of oil and vinegar can be seasoned with salt, pepper, garlic, herbs, spices, mustard, soy sauce, ginger, poppy seeds or whatever you like. Lemon, lime or orange juice can be substituted for the vinegar. The classic proportions are three to four parts oil to one part wine vinegar, but for a lower-fat version, try using a mild vinegar (such as Japanese rice vinegar or balsamic vinegar) and a strong-flavored oil, such as dark sesame oil or walnut oil and experiment until you find the proportions of oil and vinegar you like; two to one (or less) is a healthy compromise. If you like, add some chicken broth or wine to "stretch" a vinaigrette without increasing its fat content.

It's easiest to mix a vinaigrette in a small jar. Just pour in all the ingredients, cover the jar tightly, and shake until blended. To thicken a low-oil vinaigrette, place an ice cube in the jar once the dressing is blended, and shake again; serve immediately. The ice cools the oil and thickens the mixture. If you like garlic in your dressing, and are preparing more than you'll need at one meal, use a whole, lightly crushed clove instead of mincing the garlic. Then remove the clove from the jar before storing the dressing, as its flavor may become unpleasantly strong over time. (The dressing itself keeps well in the refrigerator.)

If you want a creamier dressing, substitute yogurt or buttermilk for mayonnaise. For instance, you can make a mock Thousand Island dressing that's low in fat by stirring a little ketchup or tomato paste and some chopped dill pickles (which will add some sodium) into plain yogurt. Mock Green Goddess can be prepared by combining yogurt with garlic, lots of chopped chives and parsley, lemon juice, and some minced anchovy. Tomato juice or chopped or puréed tomatoes (either fresh or canned) also provide good bases for flavorful dressings. (Whenever you use whole tomatoes, it's best to mix the dressing in a blender.) Experiment with some Mexican seasonings, such as ground cumin, coriander, lime juice, and hot pepper sauce; add a few chopped fresh coriander leaves.

Don't use too much dressing. Otherwise, you will weigh down the greens and destroy the lightness and freshness that are the most appealing features of a good salad. Three to four tablespoons of dressing should be sufficient for two quarts of greens. The more delicate the greens, the less dressing needed. For a well-balanced salad, coat the greens lightly with dressing; then dress heavier ingredients (such as artichoke hearts, tomato wedges, or radishes) separately before adding them to the salad. Toss at serving time.

meal, just tear as many leaves as you need from the stem.)

To wash small-leaved greens on stems, such as watercress and arugula, cut off the roots, hold the greens by the stems, and swish them around in a large bowl of cool water. Lift out the leaves, letting the sand and grit settle, then empty and refill the bowl and repeat the process. Belgian endive is usually very clean and requires only a quick rinse of the outer leaves.

A salad spinner greatly simplifies the preparation of greens by drying them quickly and thoroughly—and dry leaves are a must if the dressing is to adhere properly.

If the center ribs of the outer leaves of romaine are very thick, cut them away before using the leaves. (Save these portions to use in soup or stock.) To separate the leaves of Belgian endive, cut off the stem end and they will come apart easily. If cooking the heads of endive whole, trim a cone-shaped section from the stem end to remove the core, which may be slightly bitter. Radicchio should also be cored before use.

You can either tear greens into bite-sized pieces by hand or cut them with a knife; each method has its proponents. Kitchen shears are useful for snipping leaves, too. As long as you use a stainless steel blade (carbon steel can cause blackening and alter the flavor) and serve the salad soon after it's prepared, it's safe to cut most greens. However, delicate leaves, such as butterhead lettuce, mâche, and arugula, are more appealing when torn (or left whole). Iceberg lettuce can be cut into thick slices ("rafts"), wedges, chunks, or shreds, or simply torn.

In addition to their use in salad, many types of greens can be briefly cooked and served as main-dish or side-dish vegetables. The firmer and more strongly flavored greens, such as escarole, chicory, or radicchio, benefit the most from cooking, as it mellows their taste. But even butterhead lettuce can be braised.

Braising When braised in broth, Belgian endive, escarole, and radicchio—and even mild lettuces—make delicious and unusual hot side dishes that are low in fat. Blanch trimmed, washed heads of greens in boiling water for about 2 minutes, then cool under cold water. Halve the heads lengthwise. Place the greens in a heavy skillet and add enough broth (chicken, beef, or vegetable) to almost cover them. Add lemon juice, onion, garlic, or herbs for flavor, if you like. Cover the pan tightly and simmer until tender. When the greens are done, you may remove them and reduce the cooking liquid to a thick sauce. *Cooking time:* 10 to 15 minutes.

Grilling Brush heads of radicchio or Belgian endive, halved lengthwise, with a little oil and grill them until softened and beginning to brown. *Cooking time:* 6 to 10 minutes.

Sautéing Cut heads of sturdy lettuce or greens in half, or separate into leaves or small bunches, and sauté in broth (with some chopped garlic, if desired) until wilted. Belgian endive, escarole, chicory, and radicchio work well. Season with herbs or sprinkle with a little grated Parmesan. *Cooking time:* about 5 minutes.

Steaming The water that clings to individual leaves when they are washed but not dried should be sufficient to steam them. Place the wet leaves in a tightly covered skillet and cook over low heat, shaking the pan occasionally, until just tender. Or, place whole heads of lettuce or greens in a vegetable steamer and cook over boiling water. Season with lemon juice and herbs. *Cooking time:* about 8 to 15 minutes.

SERVING SUGGESTIONS If you usually serve salad as a first course, try it with or after the main course, for a change. And, of course, a substantial green salad that includes high-protein foods, such as poultry, fish, or legumes, makes a satisfying meal in itself, especially when accompanied with some crusty bread.

To prevent a salad from turning brown and limp, dress it at the last minute or serve the dressing separately.

The most interesting salads offer a judicious mixture of tastes and textures: Mix soft lettuces and crisp ones, mild greens and sharp or bitter ones, then garnish with sliced onions, croutons, or nuts. Chilled, cooked vegetables, such as asparagus, snow peas, or green beans, also make wonderful salad additions. And don't forget to use fresh herbs: Parsley, chives, basil, and dill are considered "greens," too.

Delicate, mild-flavored greens are usually best with a mild dressing, while more assertive greens can stand up to a more robust flavor. Butterhead lettuce and mâche, for example, need only a light coating of an herbal vinaigrette, while greens such as Romaine, escarole, and arugula benefit from a bolder, mustard- or garlic-based dressing. The sturdier greens also combine well with warm ingredients: Try topping greens with warm sautéed mushrooms, freshly blanched snow peas, or well-seasoned broiled chicken, fish, or seafood, such as shrimp or scallops. If you have any leftover chicken or turkey, sauté the sliced poultry quickly in some vinaigrette before arranging it on the greens. Pour the warm dressing over the salad and serve immediately.

Although iceberg lettuce has few nutrients, its texture is ideal for certain culinary purposes. Only iceberg shreds into the crisp strands favored for garnishing Mexican dishes, and no other lettuce can be cut crosswise into crunchy rafts to hold other foods, such as sliced chicken or tuna salad.

Parsley is most often used as a garnish or seasoning, but it can also serve as a flavorful and nutritious addition to salads. Just an ounce of parsley provides 43 percent of the RDA for vitamin C and 18 percent of the RDA for iron for men (12 percent for women) and a milligram of beta carotene.

Watercress and other small-leaved greens make appetizing garnishes as well as tangy salad ingredients. Citrus compliments pungent greens. Pair arugula, watercress, chicory, or escarole with grapefruit or orange slices or sections, or simply toss them with a dressing containing some citrus juice. These greens are good choices for wilted salads; toss with a hot dressing or quickly sauté the greens in vinaigrette. You can also enliven a bland potato salad with watercress and arugula leaves, or chop and blend them into low-fat cream cheese to make a delicious sandwich spread. Cook watercress briefly in chicken broth, then purée it and you'll have an appetizing soup. Or, mix this zesty ingredient with chicken or cheese to create a more interesting sandwich. For a light, fresh pasta dish, sauté some escarole or radicchio with garlic, then combine it with the hot fettuccine.

Belgian endive leaves make elegant scoops for dips. The rich flavor and texture of this green goes well with fruit (sliced apples or pears, or mashed avocado) and nuts (top an endive salad with chopped walnuts or pecans). Radicchio can be readily substituted for Belgian endive. Either of these greens, as well as arugula and and watercress, are delicious served with a little crumbled blue cheese or goat cheese.

Use the curving leaves of butterhead lettuce, Belgian endive and radicchio to hold salad ingredients, cooked vegetables, sandwich fillings, or condiments. Peas can be cooked in a lettuce cup, or with shredded lettuce (see page 135). Both vegetables can also be heated together in chicken broth and then puréed to make a delicate, spring-like soup. Add any leftover salad greens, once past their peak, to a vegetable soup or stockpot, or cook them along with other vegetables and purée for a side dish.

Steamed or blanched lettuce leaves can be used to encase a whole fish or fillet; these wrappers will keep it moist during baking. A chicken placed on a bed of lettuce leaves will also stay juicy while roasting.

Romaine lettuce, highlighted below, is a more nutritious substitute for iceberg.

ROMAINE LETTUCE 3½ oz raw (2 cups shredded)

Calories	16	Fat	<1 g
Protein	2 g	Saturated Fat	<1 g
Carbohydrate	2 g	Cholesterol	0 mg
Dietary Fiber	Low	Sodium	8 mg

KEY NUTRIENTS		% RDA Men	% RDA Women
Vitamin A	2600 IU	52%	65%
Beta Carotene	2 mg	N/A	N/A
Vitamin C	24 mg	40%	40%
Folacin	136 mcg	68%	76%
Iron	1 mg	10%	7%
Manganese	0.6 mg	N/A	N/A

S=40% or more soluble N/A=Not Applicable N=Not Available

Leeks

The leek is a versatile vegetable that has not received the same appreciation in the United States as it has in Europe, where it is a favorite (France, Belgium, and the Netherlands are the world's leading producers). Like onions, to which they are related, leeks are most commonly used to add flavor to various dishes, particularly stews and soups (the best known of which is vichyssoise, the classic cold potato and leek soup). But leeks have a milder, sweeter flavor than onions and a crunchy texture when cooked, which is why they are also delicious served on their own. As the chart on page 117 shows, leeks are surprisingly nutritious, supplying more vitamins and minerals than an equal-sized serving of onions or scallions.

AVAILABILITY Although leeks are most plentiful from fall to early spring, they can be found year round. (California, Florida, and New Jersey are major suppliers.) There are several commercially grown varieties available, all similar.

Leeks

SHOPPING TIPS Leeks resemble overgrown scallions, but are usually displayed in bunches of three or four; sometimes they are sold separately. While the white ends of scallions may be bulbous, those of leeks should be relatively straight and not exceed 1½ inches in diameter—larger leeks are often tough and woody. Check each leek at both ends: The leaf tops should be fresh and green, while the white root end should show a firmly attached fringe of rootlets and several inches of unblemished skin, which will give very slightly to pressure. Avoid leeks with obvious signs of age or mishandling, such as wilted or torn greens or split or oversized bulbs. Some markets also carry baby leeks, which can be pencil thin and are usually more tender than medium-sized leeks.

STORAGE In the refrigerator, leeks keep for up to a week. Store them loosely wrapped in plastic—this precaution not only helps them retain moisture, but also prevents their odor from spreading to other foods. Don't trim the leeks until you are ready to cook them.

PREPARATION Leeks often require careful cleaning, since soil and grit can collect in between the layers of the broad overlapping leaves. Remove any withered or toughened outer leaves, and trim off the green tops and the rootlets at the base. If cooking leeks whole, insert a knife about an inch from the base and slice lengthwise to the top end. Then roll the leek a quarter turn and make a second lengthwise slit perpendicular to the first. Fan the leaves apart and wash under cool running water. If any grit remains, swish the leeks in a bowl of water, changing the water until it stays clear.

(Chopping the leeks into 2- or 3-inch pieces can make them easier to rinse.)

Cooked and served whole, leeks make an excellent side dish or appetizer; they can also be chopped or sliced for use as an ingredient in other dishes. Leeks can quickly overcook, which turns them soft and slimy. Also, they continue to cook after they are removed from heat (unless you plunge them into cold water). If serving them hot, therefore, cook until barely tender—you should be able to just pierce the base with the point of a sharp knife. Since cooking times vary, depending upon the size and age of the leeks, you will need to keep testing for doneness.

Braising This is a popular method for cooking leeks, but typically the vegetable is simmered in a large amount of butter; one recipe calls for 6 tablespoons for twelve leeks, adding 66 grams of fat to an otherwise low-fat food. Instead, braise them in low-sodium chicken or veal stock to enhance the flavor. (For eight leeks, use 2 to 3 cups of stock.) Or, use water instead of stock and add ⅓ cup of white wine. Arrange leeks in a casserole dish or sauté pan, cover with liquid, bring to a boil, then partially cover and simmer until done. Reduce the liquid if necessary and pour over leeks. *Cooking times:* for whole, 10 to 30 minutes, depending on size; for chopped, about 10 minutes.

Microwaving Whole leeks do not cook evenly, so it's better to chop them. Add 2 tablespoons of water to the dish, and stir the pieces halfway through the cooking time. *Cooking time:* 5 to 8 minutes.

LEEKS 3½ oz raw (1 cup chopped)

Calories	61	Fat	<1 g
Protein	2 g	Saturated Fat	<1 g
Carbohydrate	14 g	Cholesterol	0 mg
Dietary Fiber	N	Sodium	20 mg

KEY NUTRIENTS		% RDA Men	Women
Vitamin B_6	0.2 mg	10%	13%
Vitamin C	12 mg	20%	20%
Folacin	64 mcg	32%	36%
Iron	2 mg	20%	13%
Magnesium	28 mg	8%	10%
Manganese	0.5 mg	N/A	N/A

S=40% or more soluble N/A=Not Applicable N=Not Available

Steaming and boiling Use a conventional steamer or submerge leeks in boiling water. Drain immediately after cooking (or the leeks will be watery). Baby leeks (½ inch or less in diameter) should be tied in bundles like asparagus. *Cooking times:* for whole, 10 to 15 minutes; for cut up, 5 minutes or less; for baby leeks, 3 to 5 minutes.

SERVING SUGGESTIONS You can serve leeks in ways similar to asparagus—with lemon juice, or a sprinkling of dill or savory, or combined with other vegetables, such as carrots, squashes, beets, Brussels sprouts, or mushrooms. Cover with a lightly braised topping of chopped tomatoes, onion, or black olives, and dress with a reduced-oil vinaigrette. Sliced or puréed leeks can be added to stews or soups, and be substituted in recipes that call for onions. Raw young leeks, thinly sliced, lend flavor and texture to salads.

Mushrooms

Mushrooms are not usually thought of as a particularly good source of nutrients, perhaps because they lack the brighter colors of so many other vegetables. But actually mushrooms rank rather high in nutritive value. They have a good deal of protein, and although lacking any beta carotene or vitamin C (because they have no chlorophyll), they contain a substantial amount of B vitamins, copper, and other minerals. Despite their somewhat meaty texture, mushrooms are low in calories (a cup of raw mushrooms has about 20 calories). Moreover, researchers have discovered that they contain antibacterial and other medicinal substances; the most commonly cultivated variety has been reported to contain an anti-tumor substance.

The mushroom's distinctiveness stems, in part, from the fact that it isn't truly a vegetable but a fungus—a plant that hasn't any roots or leaves, that doesn't flower or bear seeds, and that doesn't need light to grow (although some do need light to fruit). Instead, it proliferates in the dark and reproduces by releasing billions of spores. There are about 38,000 varieties of mushrooms, some of them edible, others highly toxic. Most varieties grow wild; in fact, their earthy flavor has been appreciated for thousands of years, dating back to the time of the Egyptian pharaohs, who decreed them a royal food. But perhaps no one has been as appreciative of mushrooms as the French, who were the first to cultivate them by growing them in caves, beginning in the seventeenth century. By the late 1800s, mushrooms were being grown on a commercial scale in other European countries as well as in the United States, where farmers in Pennsylvania eventually developed new methods for growing mushrooms indoors.

While some mushrooms are still cultivated in caves or cellars, most are grown year round in specially designed buildings in which all aspects of the environment—light, temperature, humidity, and ventilation—can be controlled. As a result, cultivated mushrooms—which were once considered an expensive delicacy—are affordable and widely available in fresh and canned form.

It may be tempting to gather wild mushrooms; however, a number of them are highly toxic, even deadly, and some of these are similar in appearance to edible mushrooms—to such an extent that even experienced mushroom foragers cannot always tell the difference. Therefore, leave wild mushrooms to the experts and gather your own mushrooms from the market.

Cooked fresh mushrooms are more nutritious than canned mushrooms: They have almost three times the niacin and potassium, twice the iron, and fifteen times the riboflavin of the same amount of canned. But if you use the canning liquid in your recipe, you will be able to conserve the niacin and riboflavin. Just be sure to check the label listing the other ingredients in the can. Sometimes canned mushrooms contain more than four times the sodium of fresh cooked mushrooms, and if packed in a butter sauce, the fat content will be significantly increased.

VARIETIES For many years, the only commercial mushrooms grown in the United States were the familiar smooth, round-capped button mushrooms. In fact, they still make up most of the domestically cultivated crop. Buttons can be found in several different colors—white, off-white, and brown (called Cremini)—but they all belong to a single species, *Agaricus bisporus*. These mildly flavored mushrooms are sold prepackaged in supermarkets or in bulk, and are also available canned and frozen.

Increasingly, though, other varieties of mushroom are becoming popular, and these offer a wider range of tastes and textures. Some are cultivated versions of wild mushrooms, now called

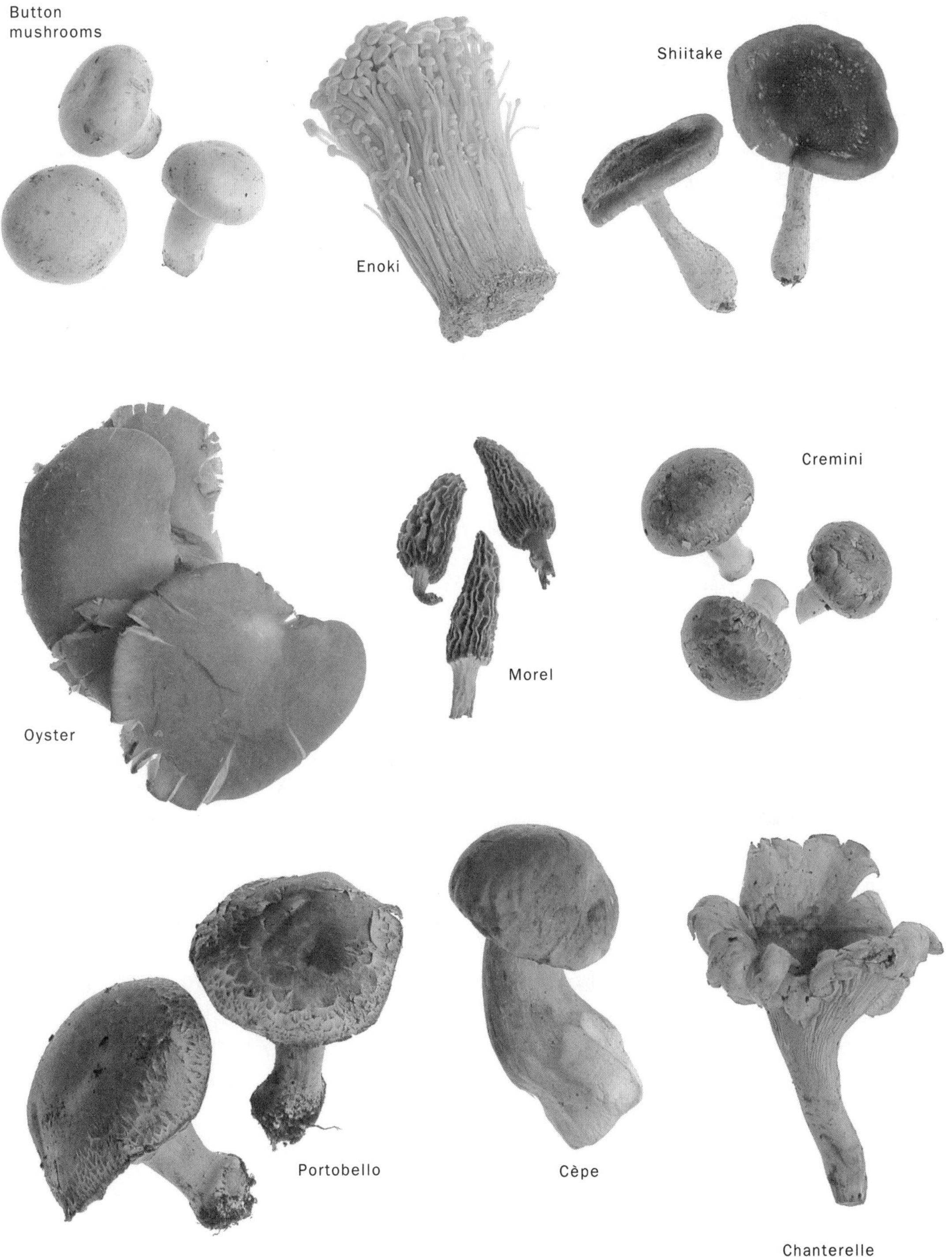
Button mushrooms
Enoki
Shiitake
Oyster
Morel
Cremini
Portobello
Cèpe
Chanterelle

TRUFFLES

Truffles are fungi, but they have taken on a value far beyond any type of mushroom. Prized for their flavor, truffles have proven nearly impossible to cultivate, and they are very difficult to harvest in the wild. The plants grow underground, attaching themselves to the roots of host trees (usually oaks or hazels), and they must be sniffed out by pigs or dogs trained specifically to detect their scent. Consequently, they have always been treated as an expensive delicacy.

Truffles have a textured surface and dense flesh; their earthy, sometimes garlicky flavor is imparted to any food with which they're stored, cooked, or served. Two types of truffles exist: black (from France and Italy) and white (from northern Italy). Fresh truffles are in season in the late fall and winter, and are imported into the United States. They are also available canned and, in paste form, in tubes; these versions are more widely available and less expensive.

Because of their intense flavor and high price, truffles are used sparingly, sliced or grated raw over hot foods. Black truffles are usually peeled before serving and the peelings are saved to flavor soups and stocks.

specialty mushrooms, while others are varieties that haven't yet been domesticated and so must be picked wild (and, therefore, tend to be relatively expensive). Like buttons, most of these are available in processed form as well as fresh. Indeed, because of new flash-freezing techniques, mushrooms can be preserved for up to a year with much of their flavor and texture intact.

DRIED MUSHROOMS

Dried mushrooms have an intensely concentrated flavor and therefore are considered more a seasoning than a vegetable. To reconstitute them and bring out their flavor (and to remove any grit), they should be soaked before use: Rinse the mushrooms, then place them in a bowl, pour hot water over them, and let stand for 30 minutes. Lift the mushrooms out, leaving the liquid in the bowl, then strain the flavorful soaking liquid through a cheesecloth-lined strainer. Rinse the mushrooms, chop them, and add both the mushrooms and soaking liquid to the dish you're cooking, if possible. If not, save the liquid for a soup or stew. To duplicate the taste and meatiness of fresh wild mushrooms in soups or dishes such as chicken cacciatore, use dried mushrooms for flavor and fresh button mushrooms for texture.

Fresh varieties that are not commercially cultivated have a short season; they are more costly than buttons, but each is distinctly flavorful on its own or added to other foods. The following types are the ones most likely to be sold in greengrocers or specialty stores:

***Cèpe* (*also known as bolete, cep, porcino*)** A stout stem and a spongy surface underneath the brown cap (rather than gills) are distinguishing features of cèpes, which range in size from 1 to 10 inches in diameter. Grown in Washington and Oregon, or imported from France or Italy during the summer and fall, they are expensive but are generally considered the finest-tasting wild mushrooms.

***Chanterelle* (*girolle, pfifferling*)** Shaped like trumpets, these large mushrooms with frilly caps range from gold to yellow-orange in color. They vary in flavor as well: Some are reminiscent of apricots, while others taste more earthy. Chanterelles are gathered wild in the Pacific Northwest; they are also cultivated domestically, and some are imported from Europe.

***Enoki* (*enokitake, enoki-daki*)** Sproutlike enoki have small caps on a long, thin trailing stem. They are creamy white and have a mild, almost sweet, taste that is best appreciated when enoki are served raw in salads or soups. Native to Japan (and commonly used in Asian dishes), they are now cultivated in California.

Italian brown A popular variety that was once

imported, but is now cultivated domestically, Italian browns are among the less-expensive specialty mushrooms. Not much larger than buttons, they have a rich flavor, yet are quite tender.

Morel Among the highest-priced varieties because they are usually picked in the wild (though they are grown commercially in Michigan), morels are small, dark brown mushrooms with conical, spongy caps. They have an especially intense, earthy flavor, and their honeycombed surface makes them ideal for sauces.

Oyster (pleurotus, tree oyster, phoenix, sovereign) These mushrooms are a wild variety that have become easy to cultivate and therefore are more widely available (and less expensive) than other specialty mushrooms. Ranging in color from off-white to gray brown, they grow in clusters and have a dense, chewy texture. Although you can eat them raw, they are more flavorful when cooked, and are often used in meat dishes.

Portobello (Roma) Produced domestically or imported from Italy, these hearty-flavored mushrooms have circular flat tops and long, thick stems that may retain some of the black soil in which they're grown.

Shiitake (golden oak mushroom, forest mushroom, black forest, oriental black, Chinese black) Once grown only in Japan, shiitake mushrooms are now available from a number of states, where they are cultivated on artificial logs. These large, umbrella-shaped mushrooms are brown-black in color and have a rich flavor that goes well with many types of dishes. They are especially satisfying in sauces. Several packaged commercial brands are now available in supermarkets.

Wood ear (tree ear, black tree fungus) Health claims have been made for this specialty mushroom. Although there is some evidence that wood ear acts as an anticoagulant to thin the blood, no studies have been conducted to show whether its consumption will help to prevent heart attacks. Sold mostly in dried form until recently, fresh wood ear is becoming easier to obtain. Fresh versions have flattened caps that vary greatly in size; the mushroom's almost crunchy texture provides an interesting contrast with other foods in stir-fries, casseroles, and stews.

AVAILABILITY Button, shiitake, oyster, and enoki mushrooms are available all year, while other specialty varieties are on the market more sporadically, with supplies best in summer and fall. (Some, like the wood ear, are mainly sold in Asian markets.) Pennsylvania grows about half of the domestic crop; California, Florida, and Michigan are also leading suppliers.

CAUTION ON RAW MUSHROOMS

Practically all food plants contain natural substances that protect them against predators. Some of these have been shown to have adverse effects on animals, and a few on humans. Among this group are hydrazines, which are contained in mushrooms. A study from the University of Nebraska Medical School found that mice allowed to eat unlimited amounts of common raw mushrooms (*Agaricus bisporus*) during the course of their lifetimes developed malignant tumors at a significantly higher rate than mice in a control group.

Many hydrazines are highly volatile, and, according to some studies, most of them (including the most harmful types) can be destroyed by cooking or drying. Moreover, the amount contained in a serving of raw mushrooms appears to be small (and most of the hydrazines are in the stems). However, if you eat mushrooms often, it is probably prudent to eat them cooked, not raw.

SHOPPING TIPS When buying fresh button mushrooms, choose plump, clean ones that are a fresh white, cream or tan, depending on the variety; mushrooms darken as they age. Reject those that appear slimy, bruised, or pitted. Look for mushrooms with closed "veils"—the area where the cap meets the stem: A wide-open veil indicates that the mushroom has aged and will have a shorter storage life. If the veils are slightly open, the gills—the spore-bearing chambers visible under the cap—should be pink or tan, not brown or black.

If you're not fussy about appearance, slightly older mushrooms—which actually have a richer flavor—may be bought for immediate use.

To minimize waste in recipes that call for caps only, choose mushrooms with short stems.

For garnishing, or for cooking whole in a stew or braise, choose small mushrooms; for general cooking purposes, select medium-sized ones; and for stuffing, look for those with caps large enough to hold a generous amount of filling.

Specialty mushrooms, such as oysters and cèpes, differ in shape from button mushrooms. They are sold with open caps (or do not have separate caps or gills), and particularly if gathered in the wild, will not have the clean, uniform appearance of cultivated button mushrooms. They should, however, be firm and meaty, as well as dry to the touch but not withered. Even uncooked, they should have a pleasantly earthy fragrance.

People who are sulfite sensitive needn't worry about eating mushrooms. Though packaged mushrooms used to be treated with sulfites to keep them white, these chemicals have been banned by the FDA and are no longer used.

STORAGE It is important to conserve just the right amount of moisture when storing mushrooms. If left completely uncovered, they will dry out; if enclosed in moisture-proof wrapping, they will become soggy and begin to decay. A good compromise is to place mushrooms purchased in bulk in a loosely closed paper bag or in a shallow glass dish covered with a kitchen towel or a lightly moistened paper towel. Leave prepackaged mushrooms in their unopened package. Don't wash or trim mushrooms before storing them.

Keep mushrooms on the refrigerator shelf—not in the refrigerator crisper, which tends to be humid—for no more than a few days. Unopened, prepackaged mushrooms will stay for up to a week. If mushrooms begin to darken (and their caps open) with age, they can still be used for cooking and flavoring foods.

Dried mushrooms will keep almost indefinitely if wrapped in plastic or placed in a tightly closed jar and stored in the refrigerator or freezer. They can also be stored in a cool, dark place for up to six months.

PREPARATION Since mushrooms are very absorbent, try to minimize their contact with water when cleaning them. You can simply wipe them with a dry paper towel or a damp sponge or cloth, or use a soft brush (you'll find special mushroom brushes at shops that sell kitchen gadgets, or you can use a new soft-bristled paintbrush). If the mushrooms have a lot of soil adhering to their stems, just trim off the stem bottoms. If absolutely necessary, place the mushrooms in a colander and rinse them quickly under cold running water; if soaked, they will absorb water, only to release it later during cooking, turning a sauté or stir-fry into a soup.

Do not peel button mushrooms, or you will rob them of much of their flavor. Trim the woody tip of the stems and break or cut off the stems if the recipe requires it. Do not discard the stems; if you cannot use them immediately, then chop, wrap, and freeze them for later use in a stock or soup. Shiitakes are an exception to this rule; their stems are often too tough and fibrous to eat. But if you want to use the stems, cut them lengthwise into thin slices and cook them longer than the caps. You can also use the stem to flavor stock. About ½ inch of stem should be cut from enoki mushrooms.

Generally, mushrooms need just a few minutes of cooking; overcooking toughens them. Use stainless steel, ceramic, or enamel pans; mushrooms will discolor aluminum cooking utensils.

Baking Arrange mushrooms in a single layer in a baking pan; brush with a little oil. *Cooking time:* 12 to 15 minutes in a 375° oven.

Broiling/grilling These methods bring out the meaty flavor of mushrooms. Thread whole mushrooms on skewers with vegetables—cherry tomatoes, bell peppers, and summer squash chunks, for instance—and grill. Or, place mushroom caps stem-side down, on a pan and broil, turning them halfway through the cooking time. Brush them lightly with oregano- or basil-flavored olive oil before broiling, and again when you turn the mushrooms. *Cooking times:* broiling, about 5 minutes; grilling, 10 minutes.

Sautéing Mushrooms will soak up whatever liquid they are cooked in. If possible, sauté them in broth or wine, or, initially, use a small amount of olive oil and then add more if the mushrooms begin to stick. Never cover the pan when sautéing, as the liquid the mushrooms exude should be allowed to evaporate. *Cooking time:* 3 to 5 minutes.

Steaming Place whole mushrooms in a vegetable steamer and cook over boiling water (the water should not touch the bottom of the top pan). Use this method to precook mushroom caps for stuffing. *Cooking times:* in a steamer, 3 to 8 minutes; in a double boiler, about 20 minutes.

Stir-frying Add sliced, halved, or whole mushrooms to stir-fries, but remember that they will release some water as they cook. *Cooking time:* 3 to 4 minutes.

SERVING SUGGESTIONS Sliced raw mushrooms add pleasing texture to mixed green salads, sandwiches, or appetizers. Substitute raw enoki mushrooms for sprouts in salads and sandwiches.

Mushrooms partially owe their flavor to glutamic acid, a natural version of the flavor enhancer monosodium glutamate (MSG). However, whereas monosodium glutamate contains sodium, fresh mushrooms are virtually sodium free.

Try seasoning cooked mushrooms with any of the following: fresh or dried tarragon, dillweed, thyme, oregano, basil, chopped fresh parsley, sherry, soy sauce, garlic, shallots, lemon juice, or pepper. Or, sauté mushrooms with chopped onions or garlic; add lemon juice, pepper, and dillweed, then remove from the heat and stir in plain yogurt. You can also make a tempting side dish by tossing sautéed mushrooms with a little goat cheese or low-fat cream cheese, then sprinkling them with chives or tarragon. Use "creamed" mushrooms as a topping for baked potatoes.

Stuffed mushroom caps make an appealing edible garnish, appetizer, or main dish. Stuff the caps with a mushroom filling containing the stems; with finely chopped or puréed vegetables (try peas or spinach); with tuna or crab meat; or with an herbed breadcrumb and Parmesan mixture. Serve broiled or grilled mushroom caps or sliced, sautéed mushrooms on toast for a light lunch.

Cut broiled mushrooms into strips and stir into cooked brown or wild rice, barley, or kasha. For a double-mushroom tomato sauce, add chopped mushrooms when you begin to make the marinara sauce, then toss in sliced mushrooms just before the sauce is done. Add whole or quartered mushrooms to stews 5 to 10 minutes before serving, so they do not overcook.

For an easy soup with a rich mushroom flavor, prepare dried mushrooms, then cook the mushrooms in beef broth, including the soaking liquid in the broth. A few minutes before serving, add thinly sliced fresh mushrooms. Finish the soup with some sherry and chopped herbs.

Button mushrooms, profiled below, are the most popular type of mushroom in the United States.

MUSHROOMS, button 3½ oz raw (5 mushrooms)

Calories	25	Fat	<1 g
Protein	2 g	Saturated Fat	<1 g
Carbohydrate	5 g	Cholesterol	0 mg
Dietary Fiber	Low	Sodium	4 mg

KEY NUTRIENTS		% RDA Men	% RDA Women
Copper	0.5 mg	N/A	N/A
Folacin	21 mcg	11%	12%
Iron	1 mg	10%	7%
Niacin	4 mg	21%	27%
Phosphorus	104 mg	13%	13%
Potassium	370 mg	N/A	N/A
Riboflavin	0.4 mg	24%	31%

S=40% or more soluble N/A=Not Applicable N=Not Available

Okra

Long popular in the South, where it is integral to many Creole dishes, okra is now becoming increasingly common in supermarkets and greengrocers in other parts of the country. This small green pod is best known as a key ingredient in the thick piquant soup called gumbo, a word derived from the African dialect names given okra when it was first brought to America in the early 1700s. There is some question as to who actually introduced the vegetable here—West African slaves or the French colonists of Louisiana—but the plant (which is related to cotton) probably originated in Ethiopia and spread to North Africa and the Middle East before reaching the American colonies. The name *okra* itself is of African origin, though in other parts of the world where the vegetable is popular—the Caribbean, South America, the Middle East, India, Africa—it is still referred to as gumbo, among other regional names.

Okra's flavor and texture are unique. Its taste falls somewhere between that of eggplant and asparagus, and, not surprisingly, it marries well with other vegetables, particularly tomatoes, peppers, and corn. Cooked sliced okra exudes a sticky juice that is a combination of complex-sounding chemical substances, such as acetylated acidic polysaccharide and galaturonic acid. This juice will thicken any liquid to which it is added, a characteristic that helps to explain okra's long-standing use in soups and stews. Not everyone finds this mucilaginous texture pleasing, but cooking the vegetable quickly will reduce the gumminess, allowing okra to be enjoyed on its own as an interesting and nutritious side dish.

This unusual vegetable has a lot to offer nutritionally. It's a good source of vitamin C, folacin and other B vitamins, magnesium, potassium, and calcium. Okra is high in dietary fiber, supplying over 5 grams per 3½ ounce serving.

Okra is marketed in processed form as well as fresh: About half of the domestic crop is frozen, and smaller amounts are canned or pickled. Frozen okra makes an acceptable substitute for fresh when used in soups and stews, but lacks the raw vegetable's crispness when served alone.

VARIETIES You can find okra in varying shades of green or white and in chunky or slender shapes, with either a ribbed or smooth surface. Varieties with green, ribbed pods are the most common.

AVAILABILITY Okra is grown in warm climates—Florida, Georgia, and Texas are leading producers—and is available all year, with supplies peaking in the summer months.

SHOPPING TIPS Small, young pods—no more than about 3 inches long—are the most tender; as the vegetable matures, it becomes fibrous and tough. Choose pods that are clean and fresh (overmature ones will look dull and dry), and that

Okra

snap crisply when broken in half; avoid okra pods that are hard, brownish, or blackened.

STORAGE Don't wash okra until just before you cook it; moisture will cause the pods to become slimy. Store untrimmed, uncut okra in a paper or plastic bag in the refrigerator crisper for no longer than three or four days.

PREPARATION Wash the okra; if the pods are very fuzzy, rub them in a kitchen towel or with a vegetable brush to remove some of the "fur."

If you are cooking whole okra pods, trim just the barest slice from the stem end and tip, without piercing the internal capsule; prepared this way, the juices won't be released and the okra won't become gummy. When you're cutting okra into slices, however, you can trim the stem end more deeply.

In general, when okra is to be served separately as a vegetable side dish, cook the whole pods rapidly—until crisp-tender or just tender—to minimize the thickening juices. The same principle applies when you're adding okra to any cooked dish in which you want to retain its crisp, fresh quality: Add the vegetable during the last 10 minutes of cooking time. On the other hand, when okra is to be used in a soup, stew, or casserole that requires long cooking, it should be cut up and allowed to exude its juices.

Don't cook okra in a cast iron or aluminum pot, or the vegetable will darken. The discoloration is harmless, but makes the okra rather unappetizing.

Blanching You can blanch okra you intend to serve cold in a salad, or before stir-frying. Drop whole okra pods in a large pot of boiling water. If serving okra cold, cool it in a bowl of ice water. *Cooking time:* 3 to 5 minutes.

Boiling Okra can be boiled when you want to serve it simply, with a seasoning or sauce. Cook whole okra pods in about an inch of boiling water; boil just until crisp-tender. *Cooking time:* 5 to 10 minutes.

Microwaving Place a pound of whole okra, rinsed but not dried, in a covered microwavable dish. *Cooking time:* 6 minutes.

Sautéing First, sauté some onions and garlic in a little vegetable oil, then add whole or sliced okra and sauté. *Cooking time:* 3 to 5 minutes.

Steaming Brief steaming keeps okra very crisp. Place whole pods in a vegetable steamer and cook over boiling water. *Cooking time:* 3 to 6 minutes.

SERVING SUGGESTIONS As a side dish, serve steamed or boiled okra with lemon juice and ground black pepper. Since okra's flavor has been likened to that of asparagus or eggplant, prepare it as you would those vegetables. (Adjust cooking times as necessary.)

Tomatoes, in particular, are an ideal partner for okra because their acidity seems to cut okra's gluey consistency. Okra stewed with tomatoes is a classic southern dish. To make a "pilau"—a southern-style pilaf—combine stewed okra and tomatoes with partially cooked rice, then continue cooking until the rice is done. Add shrimp or crab meat, if you like.

Okra is also popular in India; add it to curries, or sauté it with Indian spices, such as cumin, coriander, turmeric, or curry powder.

OKRA 3½ ounces raw (1 cup sliced)

Calories	38	Fat	<1 g
Protein	2 g	Saturated Fat	<1 g
Carbohydrate	8 g	Cholesterol	0 m
Dietary Fiber	High	Sodium	8 mg

KEY NUTRIENTS		% RDA Men	% RDA Women
Vitamin A	660 IU	13%	16%
Vitamin B_6	0.2 mg	10%	13%
Vitamin C	21 mg	35%	35%
Calcium	81 mg	10%	10%
Folacin	88 mcg	44%	49%
Magnesium	57 mg	16%	20%
Manganese	1 mg	N/A	N/A
Potassium	303 mg	N/A	N/A
Thiamin	0.2 mg	13%	18%

S=40% or more soluble N/A=Not Applicable N=Not Available

Use sliced okra in vegetable soups, chicken, beef or lamb stews, and fish or seafood chowders to thicken the broth. For a crisp counterpoint, save some of the okra and stir it in a few minutes before serving.

Blanched, chilled okra is delectably crunchy. For an appetizer, offer blanched okra pods with salsa or a spicy yogurt dip. For a salad, toss the okra and some tomato wedges with an herbed vinaigrette. Or, marinate blanched okra and some sliced onions for several hours in a vinaigrette, and serve well chilled.

Onions

Onions have always been popular. One of mankind's earliest foods, they originated in prehistoric times and were widely consumed in ancient Egypt, Greece, and Rome. By the seventeenth century, Europeans were enjoying them as a salad ingredient and a breakfast "health" food. Today, onions are used as seasonings in a tremendous range of dishes, and, cooked or raw, they are also appreciated as vegetables in their own right. In fact, they rank sixth among the world's leading vegetable crops.

Onions and their relatives—which include leeks, garlic, and shallots—are known botanically as alliums, a plant genus that has been classified at different times as belonging to the lily family, the amaryllis family, or to a family all their own called Alliaceae. There are more than five hundred alliums, and all of the edible species are bulbing plants that have a characteristic pungent smell or taste, which is produced once their layers of skin are cut. The act of chopping or slicing an allium brings its sulfur-containing amino acids into contact with enzymes to form volatile compounds, one of which strikes the tongue, while another irritates the eye, apparently by turning into sulfuric acid. The older an allium is, the stronger these compounds become. Fortunately for our taste buds, cooking produces further chemical changes that render them much milder. (Some of the odor compounds appear to be converted into a substance that is fifty to seventy times sweeter than table sugar.)

Onions are low in calories and in most nutrients (though green onions can be an excellent source of vitamin A). But a number of studies indicate that they may produce certain health benefits, including lowering blood pressure and cholesterol levels. Onions also contain a substance that interferes with the formation of blood clots.

Onions are a low-fat food, but the same can't be said for onion rings. Sixty percent of the 160 calories in four onion rings (about 1½ ounces) come from fat.

VARIETIES Onions (their botanical name is *Allium cepa*) come in an impressive array of sizes, colors, and shapes. Because onions are easily crossbred, growers are continually developing new varieties and hybrids. The ubiquitous medium-sized yellow globe onions, which are available year round, encompass many different varieties, with subtle differences in taste or texture. (The globe shape is popular with consumers, so growers have emphasized it.) Whatever names are bestowed upon onions, though, they fall into two general categories: spring/summer onions and storage onions.

Spring/summer onions Grown primarily from fall to spring in warm-weather states, such as Texas, Georgia, and Arizona, these onions have soft flesh and a mild or sweet taste. Some are des-

ignated by names referring to their growing areas, such as California Italian Red, Vidalia (from Georgia), or Maui Sweet (from Hawaii). Granex and Grano are other names denoting sweet onions with flattened or top-shaped bulbs. Unlike storage onions, the spring and summer varieties generally are not stored, but are shipped almost immediately after harvesting. Many of them are quite juicy and, because of their relatively high sugar content, mild enough to be eaten raw.

Storage onions These have firm flesh, dry, crackly outer skins, and pungent flavors. Grown in northern areas of the United States, such as Idaho, Colorado, and New York, they are harvested in late summer and early fall. After a brief period of drying out (a process known as "curing"), they are stored for several months; they are available at markets from late fall to early spring. In stores, these onions may simply be labeled by color—yellow, red, or white. "Spanish" onions are a variety of very large storage onion, distinguished by their mild flavor and skin color, which ranges from yellow to purple. There are no nutritional differences among these types.

Pearl onions Also called white onions, these are actually white pearl-shaped bulbs from different varieties. They are so densely planted that they attain a size of only an inch or less in diameter. "Boiling" onions are larger pearl-like onions that grow to 1 to 1½ inches in diameter.

SHALLOTS

A small, mild-tasting allium, the shallot resembles both the onion and garlic. Its bulb is wrapped in an onionlike yellowish or brownish skin but it is divided into small segmented cloves like garlic. However, unlike garlic, the cloves are not enclosed by a sheath and so are easier to separate. The guidelines for buying and storing garlic also apply to shallots—select those that are firm, dry, and free of sprouts; store them (for up to a month) in a cool, well-ventilated space. They will also keep in the refrigerator in a tightly closed jar. Shallots are available year round. Those produced domestically are grown chiefly in New Jersey and New York, but many of our shallots are imported from France. Use shallots with, or in place of, onions to impart a delicate savory flavor.

AVAILABILITY Onions can be found year round in ample quantities. The mild spring and summer onions are in greatest supply from March until September, at which time new crops of storage onions are shipped to markets. These are generally available until March or April, depending on your locality. Pearl and boiling onions are in good supply year round.

SHOPPING TIPS Consider how you plan to use the onions. As a rule, the large, mild spring and summer onions are good for eating raw or for cooked dishes in which you want a subtle flavor. The crisp, assertive character of storage onions makes them better-suited for dishes that require long cooking, since they can hold their flavor. An onion's flavor is not only determined by its variety, but also by the local soil and climatic conditions where it grew. Consequently, onions with the same appearance can taste considerably different, depending on where and when they were grown. If possible, ask the produce manager for assistance in gauging the flavor of the onions at your local market. But you may have to experiment, particularly when it comes to choosing the mildest onions.

Many shoppers prefer a particular color, though color is not a reliable guide to flavor or texture. (White onions tend to be more pungent than yellows or reds, but this rule of thumb may not be true in your area.) Size is another consideration: For raw onion slices in salads and sandwiches, select large onions. They are also a more efficient choice for peeling and chopping. For cooking whole or in wedges, choose small- to medium-sized onions.

Most onions are sold loose by the pound, though globe and pearl onions also come in mesh bags. (Pearls are frequently packaged in small boxes.) Whatever type you choose, look for ones that feel dry and solid all over, with no soft spots (a sign of rot) or sprouts. The neck should be tightly closed, and the outer skin should have a crackly feel and a shiny appearance. Onions should smell mild, even those that are pungent when you cut into them; a strong odor is a sign of decay. Also avoid onions with green areas, which can taste unpleasant, or with dark patches, which may indicate a mold.

STORAGE Whole onions should be kept in a cool, dry, open space, away from bright light (which can turn their flavor bitter.) They do best in an area that allows plenty of air to circulate around them; either spread them out in a single layer or hang them in a basket. Onions will absorb moisture, causing them to spoil more quickly, so don't store them under a sink (which can be damp) or place them near potatoes, which give off moisture and produce a gas that causes onions to spoil more quickly. Storage onions can last three to four weeks under these conditions, spring and summer onions about half as long. High humidity, though, will considerably reduce storage time. If an onion begins to sprout, use it quickly, since it's probably started to turn mushy. The sprout itself can be substituted for a scallion.

You can extend the life of onions, particularly spring and summer varieties, by storing them unwrapped in the refrigerator crisper. Leftover cut portions of fresh onion, wrapped tightly in plastic, will keep for two to three days if refrigerated. Cooked onions, tightly covered, can be kept for up to five days; store them in glass or plastic containers (metal can discolor the onions).

PREPARATION Onions can be sliced, chopped, diced, or grated, but first they must be peeled. To make this task easier, trim off the tops and bottoms and place the onions in boiling water for about a minute. Drain them and pull off the outer skin, which should be loose, then peel off the slippery membrane underneath. To lessen eye irritation, hold the onions under cold running water as you peel; this trick carries away the sulfur compounds before they can reach your eyes. Chilling the onions beforehand may also help. With small white boiling onions, cut a cross in the root end of each one, which keeps the onion intact once you slip off the skin.

Although some recipes call for raw onions to be cooked with other ingredients, others require them to be cooked beforehand. Virtually every cooking method has been used with onions; since they are low in nutrients, the length of cooking time is not a problem. But often, recipes call for too much fat to be added to them. The following methods avoid or minimize the use of fat.

Baking Use whole, unpeeled onions. Cut off the root ends, so the onions will stand upright in the baking pan, prick them with a fork, and place in a baking pan lightly coated with nonstick spray. Or, peel the onions, pierce them, and wrap in foil. Cook in a 350° to 375° oven; test for doneness by pressing the onions, which should give easily without feeling mushy. *Cooking times:* for medium-sized onions, 45 to 60 minutes. Storage onions generally take longer than the more loosely layered spring and summer onions.

Boiling This method is best for whole and half onions, but also works for sliced onions. *Cooking time:* 10 to 35 minutes, depending on size and density of the onions.

Braising This method works well for small white pearl or boiling onions. Place the onions in a pan and cover with ½ inch of water or broth. Simmer, covered, over low heat until the liquid is absorbed and the onions are tender. (Add more liquid if necessary.) *Cooking time:* 25 minutes.

Microwaving Peel and quarter a pound of small- to medium-sized onions. Arrange them in a microwavable casserole dish, adding 2 tablespoons of water or stock. Rotate once during cooking. *Cooking time:* 7 to 8 minutes.

Sautéing A popular method, sautéing can be done in only a little oil, or you can use stock or wine. The key is to keep the heat low and stir constantly. If the onions begin to brown too quickly, reduce the heat further and add 1 to 2 tablespoons of water. *Cooking time:* 5 to 10 minutes, depending on how finely chopped the onions are.

SERVING SUGGESTIONS You can use raw or cooked onions to season stews, soups, tomato sauces, cooked vegetables, meat and vegetable casseroles, and bean and grain recipes—there are innumerable dishes they can accompany. For stocks and stews, many cooks prefer yellow onions, peels and all, because of the lovely color they impart. Small boiling onions make a tasty, low-fat side dish when cooked by one of the above methods and then seasoned with thyme and fresh chopped parsley. Enjoy onions on their own, stuffed and baked. Use onions at least 3 inches in diameter and hollow out the tops with a knife or sharp-edged spoon. Then stuff with a mixture of chopped vegetables (and breadcrumbs or cooked rice, if you wish) and bake.

Creamed onions—traditionally made with whole milk, light cream, or both, as well as butter and flour—are too high in calories and fat to be a regular part of a healthy diet. Substituting skim milk for the whole milk, and reducing the amount of butter, can cut the calories nearly in half and the fat by two-thirds.

Raw onions, particularly the sweet-flavored variety, go well with raw vegetables in salads or on appetizer platters, and they can be relied on to add flavor and crunch to various dressings, relishes, and sauces. Slices of large sweet onion are marvelous with sliced tomatoes. (If only strongly flavored onions are available, you can lighten their pungency. Cut them into very thin slices, place them in a dish, and pour boiling water over them. Let them stand for a few minutes, then drain and refrigerate for several hours to restore crispness.)

ONIONS 3½ ounces raw (½ cup chopped)

Calories	38	Fat	<1 g
Protein	1 g	Saturated Fat	<1 g
Carbohydrate	9 g	Cholesterol	0 mg
Dietary Fiber	Low (S)	Sodium	3 mg

KEY NUTRIENTS		%RDA Men	%RDA Women
Vitamin C	6 mg	10%	10%
Folacin	19 mcg	10%	11%

S=40% or more soluble N/A=Not Applicable N=Not Available

Parsnips

Parsnips—cold-weather root vegetables that are relatives of carrots—served as a good source of starch for four thousand years. In Europe and colonial America, parsnips were a nutritious and ubiquitous staple until the nineteenth century, when potatoes replaced them. Unjustly neglected by many of us today, this hardy root vegetable is easy to prepare and offers a healthy stand-in for potatoes as a side dish. It also makes an excellent addition to soups and stews.

The vegetable resembles a top-heavy, ivory-colored carrot, but it has a mild celerylike fragrance and a sweet, nutty flavor. Unlike carrots, parsnips contain no beta carotene; instead they are a good source of vitamin C. Their flavor is best in winter, when they are most abundant. Planted in the spring, they take a full three to four months to mature. Then, they are left in the ground until a hard frost occurs in late fall, which initiates the conversion of the starches in the vegetable to sugars, giving parsnips their pleasantly sweet flavor. Some gardeners and farmers leave parsnips in the ground over the winter, rather than picking and storing them; they believe that parsnips dug up the following spring are the sweetest.

Parsnips

Commercial growers harvest parsnips in the late fall and place them in cold storage for at least two weeks to allow for the conversion of starch to sugar. (Parsnips properly stored at between 32° and 34° will be just as sweet as those left in the ground for two months of cold weather.)

There are several common varieties, among them All American, the most popular, which is distinguished by its broad shoulders, white flesh, and tender core.

AVAILABILITY Parsnips are not a major commercial crop, but they are available year round, although the supply is lowest during the summer months. Northern California is the major producer, Michigan the second largest. You can also find parsnips at local farmers' markets.

SHOPPING TIPS Parsnips range in color from pale yellow to off-white. Although they can grow up to 20 inches long, they are most tender when about 8 inches—roughly the size of a large carrot. Very large parsnips are likely to be overmature and have tough, woody cores. The characteristic "broad-shouldered" shape is not a sign of overmaturity, but the wide top should taper smoothly to a slender tip.

The roots should be firm and fairly smooth; an abundance of hairlike rootlets is undesirable. Soft, withered parsnips are likely to be fibrous. Irregularly shaped parsnips are acceptable, but wasteful, as you'll have to trim away a good deal while preparing the vegetables for cooking. Parsnips with moist spots should also be avoided.

Most parsnips are sold "clip-topped," but if the leafy tops are still attached, they should look fresh and green. When buying parsnips in a 1-pound plastic bag (most are sold this way), be sure to take a close look at the vegetables through the wrapping; the bag may have fine white lines printed on it in an effort to enhance the appearance of the parsnips.

Sometimes you'll find parsnips sold in a package of soup greens (a "soup bunch"), along with a carrot, turnip, some celery tops, or other greens. It's fine to buy a parsnip this way for flavoring stock, and it needn't be in prime condition.

STORAGE Like carrots, parsnips keep best in a perforated plastic bag in the refrigerator crisper. They can last for up to three to four weeks. If the green tops, or parts of them, are attached, remove them before storing, or they'll draw moisture from the roots.

POISONOUS PARSNIPS?

Folklore gives us two contradictory myths about parsnips. One notion is that parsnips left in the ground over the winter are poisonous; the other is that parsnips are poisonous until the first frost. Both are false. There have been reported cases of people being poisoned by what they thought were wild parsnips, but the plants turned out to be water hemlock, which resembles the parsnip (the two are in the same botanical family). It is true that parsnips left in the ground until the first frost will taste sweeter and have a better texture than those harvested before then. But the latter aren't poisonous, they just lack flavor.

PREPARATION Unlike carrots, parsnips are almost always eaten cooked, as they tend to be quite fibrous. Be careful not to overcook them, however; their flavor is sweetest when just tender. Brief cooking also helps to preserve nutrients. Just before cooking, cut off the root and leaf ends; trim any major rootlets or knobs. Either scrub or peel the parsnips, depending on how you plan to prepare them.

Parsnips can be peeled before or after cooking. Peel them *before* if you're going to cut them into chunks for a stew, or if you simply want to shorten the cooking time. Peel as thinly as possible with a paring knife or vegetable peeler. (If the skin is thin, it can be scraped like a carrot.) Then cut the parsnips as you wish: Halve them crosswise and then quarter each half lengthwise; dice them; or, cut them into "coins" or julienne strips.

Peel parsnips *after* cooking if you're going to purée them; this technique helps to preserve their color and flavor, and also saves nutrients since you'll be able to remove a thinner layer of peel. Make a lengthwise cut through the skin down one side, then pull the peel off with your fingers. Halve the cooked parsnips lengthwise; if you find a fibrous, woody core, pry it out with the tip of a sharp paring knife.

If the tops of the parsnips are much thicker than the bottoms, halve the vegetables crosswise and cook the top halves for a few minutes before adding the bottom halves. Then the slender tips will not cook through before the bulbous tops.

Whenever you cook parsnips in liquid, save the flavorful liquid for making a sauce or adding to a stock or soup; the liquid contains any nutrients that may have leached out in cooking.

Baking Place whole or cut-up parsnips in a baking dish with a cover. To serve as a savory dish, season with stock and herbs, or cook as you would sweet potatoes, with orange or apple juice, brown sugar, ginger, and nutmeg. The parsnips may be parboiled for 5 minutes first to make them cook more quickly. *Cooking time:* 20 to 30 minutes in a 350° oven.

Boiling Drop whole or cut-up parsnips into a pan of boiling water and simmer until tender. *Cooking time:* 5 to 15 minutes.

Microwaving Cut parsnips into large chunks and place them in a microwavable dish with 2 tablespoons of liquid. Cover with a lid or vented plastic wrap. *Cooking time:* 4 to 6 minutes.

Steaming This method is by far the best way to cook parsnips, as it brings out their sweetness without turning them mushy. Place trimmed, well-scrubbed parsnips—whole or cut up—in a steamer and cook over boiling water. Or, place them in a saucepan with ½ inch of boiling water, cover, and cook until tender. When done, let cool (or cool briefly in cold water) and peel. *Cooking times:* for whole parsnips, 20 to 40 minutes; for cut-up pieces, 5 to 15 minutes, depending on their size and age.

SERVING SUGGESTIONS Traditionally, parsnips tend to get buttered, fried, and frittered. But the gentle flavor of steamed parsnips takes well to a wide range of low-fat or nonfat seasonings. Sprinkle them with savory herbs such as tarragon, rosemary, thyme, parsley, or chives; try covering them with a sauce of yogurt and curry powder. To bring out their sweetness, accent parsnips with nutmeg, ginger, mace, or cinnamon and a little brown sugar. Garnish with orange zest, which will provide an excellent counterpart to these sweet spices.

You can purée cooked parsnips in a food processor or food mill and add seasonings of your choice. Or, combine the parsnip purée with other puréed vegetables, such as white or sweet potatoes, carrots, turnips, or winter squash. Scatter chopped nuts or fresh herbs over the purée to enliven the texture and color of the dish.

Add parsnip chunks to soups and stews, but remember that they don't need to cook for more than 15 to 20 minutes; mushy parsnips in stews can be quite off-putting. Thinly julienned parsnips will enrich a clear chicken soup, while parsnips and potatoes can be combined into a hearty chowder.

Cut parsnips and carrots into coins or logs and steam together. Season and serve as a hot vegetable side dish, or as a salad: Either use your favorite potato-salad recipe, substituting the parsnips and carrots for the potatoes, or simply toss the vegetables while warm with a lemon vinaigrette. Serve at room temperature or chilled. Parsnips nicely complement other cooked vegetables such as green beans or peas.

Fresh parsnips that are not too tough and fibrous can be thinly grated or shredded and dressed like coleslaw. And if you slice the roots thinly, you can serve them as crudités.

PARSNIPS 3½ ounces raw (¾ cup sliced)

Calories	75	Fat	<1 g
Protein	1 g	Saturated Fat	<1 g
Carbohydrate	18 g	Cholesterol	0 mg
Dietary Fiber	High	Sodium	10 mg

KEY NUTRIENTS		% RDA Men	% RDA Women
Vitamin C	17 mg	28%	28%
Vitamin E	1 mg	10%	13%
Folacin	67 mcg	34%	37%
Magnesium	29 mg	8%	10%
Manganese	0.6 mg	N/A	N/A
Potassium	375 mg	N/A	N/A

S=40% or more soluble N/A=Not Applicable N=Not Available

Peas

Technically, green garden peas are legumes—plants that bear pods enclosing fleshy seeds. But, unlike dried legumes such as chick-peas and split peas, which require long cooking times, green peas are packaged and prepared like other fresh vegetables. As is true of all seeds, though, they are storehouses of nourishment for potential new plants, and provide low-

fat, low-calorie protein for people, too: Green peas are second only to lima beans as a fresh vegetable source of protein. A 100-calorie serving of peas (about 3/4 cup) contains more protein than a whole egg or a tablespoonful of peanut butter—but less than half a gram of fat.

Peas in their dried form have been used as a food since ancient times—archaeologists found them in Egyptian tombs—but it was not until the sixteenth century that tender varieties were developed to be eaten fresh. In the seventeenth century, Louis XIV and his courtiers discovered the delights of eating young fresh peas. And Gregor Mendel, an Austrian monk, used peas as the basis for his famous plant breeding experiments in the latter half of the nineteenth century; his work with pea plants is considered the foundation of modern genetics.

Today, only about 5 percent of all green peas grown come to the market fresh; more than half the crop is canned, and most of the rest is frozen. Frozen green peas retain their color, flavor, and nutrients better than canned and are low in sodium. If just thawed and not cooked, frozen peas can be substituted for fresh peas in salads and other uncooked dishes. Canned peas lack the appetizing color and delicate texture of fresh or frozen, and their flavor is stronger. In addition, most canned peas have added salt and sugar.

VARIETIES Also known as English peas because of the many varieties developed in England, *green peas* possess a large, bulging, grass green pod enclosing peas that are typically round and sweet; some homegrown varieties are more strongly flavored. The pods are not palatable. Packaged green peas differ from fresh garden varieties in appearance, color, texture, and flavor. Moreover, different varieties are grown for freezing and canning. And there are even some variations among canned peas: Baby green peas, or *petits pois*—French for "little peas"—are tiny and sweet. "Early" or "June" peas are larger and starchier.

Snow peas and *sugar snap peas* are in greater supply than fresh green peas and are meant to be eaten—cooked or raw—with the pod intact. Snow peas (also called sugar peas and Chinese pea pods) have pale green flat pods with small, immature-looking peas (they are picked before the seeds have developed in the pod). Probably developed in Holland in the sixteenth century, snow peas are most familiar today as a component of Chinese stir-fries. Sugar snaps were created in the 1970s as a cross between the snow and green pea. They have plump pods filled with extremely sweet, tender peas.

Snow peas supply less protein than green shelled peas because they are eaten when their seeds are still immature. However, snow peas provide almost twice the calcium (though just 5 percent of the RDA) in 3½ ounces and slightly more iron (21 percent of the RDA for men, 14 percent for women) than green shelled peas. They are also higher in vitamin C, supplying 100 percent of the RDA in 3½ ounces, but lower in the B vitamins.

AVAILABILITY Fresh green peas have a very limited season: Their peak is April through July, and they are least plentiful from September through December (though California, Florida, and Mexico provide some peas for the market in winter). Snow peas are sold year round in Asian neighborhoods and markets; some supermarkets carry them during the period from May to December, when they are most abundant. Frozen snow peas (but not sugar snaps) are also more widely available these days. Sugar snaps are not yet commonly stocked in supermarkets, but you may be able to buy them at roadside farm stands and farmers' markets in late spring and early summer.

SHOPPING TIPS At the market, fresh peas should be refrigerated; if kept at room temperature, half their sugar content will turn to starch within six hours. Low temperatures also help to preserve their texture and nutrient content. Look for firm, glossy pods with a slightly velvety feel, filled almost to bursting; the peas should not rattle loosely in the pod. Choose medium-sized pods rather than overlarge ones. The stem, leaves, and tip should be soft and green. Toss back pods that are puffy, dull, yellowed, or heavily speckled. If possible, crack open a pod and taste a few peas for sweetness. You may find trays of preshelled peas in the market; though these will save you time and labor, such peas are likely to be mealy and not very sweet because of the rapid conversion of their sugar to starch.

Snow peas should be shiny and flat, with tiny peas barely visible through the pod; small ones will be the sweetest and most tender. Old snow peas often appear twisted. Sugar snaps should be bright green, plump, and firm; the pod should tightly encase small peas. Avoid limp or yellowed sugar snaps; break a pod in two if you can to see if it snaps crisply.

A pound of peas in the pod will yield about 1 cup of shelled peas; a quarter pound of snow peas or sugar snaps will usually be sufficient for one serving as a side dish.

STORAGE It's preferable to serve all types of fresh peas the day you buy them. If you must store them, place the pods in a perforated plastic bag and refrigerate them for no more than a day or two. Don't shell green peas until just before you plan to cook or eat them, and don't wash them before storing.

PREPARATION Rinse green peas before shelling them. To shell peas, pinch off the stem with your fingernails and pull the string down the length of the pod. Immediately, the pod will pop open, then you can push out the peas with your thumb. If the pods are clean on the outside, you need not wash the peas. (When cooking the peas, you can add three or four pods for extra flavor. Or, save the pods for flavoring chicken or vegetable stock; discard them with any other solids when the stock is strained.)

Snow peas and sugar snaps should also be rinsed before use. With snow peas, simply cut the tips from both ends of the pod; kitchen shears are perfect for this job. Sugar snaps should have the string removed whether they are to be eaten raw or cooked. Unlike green peas, the string on a sugar snap runs around both sides of the pod. It's easiest to start at the bottom tip and pull the

Green peas

string up the front, then snap off the stem and pull the string down the back. Snow peas and sugar snaps, as well as shelled green peas, can be eaten raw. But if you cook them, do so briefly so that they retain their flavor and texture.

The quickest way to thaw frozen peas (for use in salads or in dishes that require further cooking, such as casseroles) is to place them in a strainer or colander and pour boiling water over them. When you prepare frozen green peas or snow peas, according to package directions, on the stovetop or in the microwave, check them after just a minute or two; they are unlikely to require the full cooking time suggested on the package. If overcooked, they will turn mushy and gray, and look unappetizing—and lose much of their vitamin C content.

Blanching This method works especially well for sugar snaps and snow peas because they are boiled in a pot that is not covered, and so you can more easily check the vegetables to prevent them from being overcooked. Blanching both tenderizes them and brings out their brightest color. Bring a large pot of water to a boil over high heat and drop in the peas. From the time the water returns to a boil, it should be a matter of seconds until the pods begin to turn a vibrant green. Drain them and cool immediately in ice water to stop the cooking process. *Cooking time:* 30 seconds to 1 minute.

If peas are cooked too long or in too much water, they can lose one-third or more of their vitamin C content.

Braising in lettuce leaves This classic French cooking method, which keeps the peas moist in a nest of lettuce leaves, can be used for fresh or frozen peas; it will enhance the flavor and tenderness of fresh peas that are slightly past their prime.

Wash but do not dry leaves of a soft lettuce, such as Bibb or Boston. (If the leaves are large or coarse, shred them.) Line a saucepan with several layers of leaves and place the peas in this nest. Add seasonings (pepper, herbs, and a pinch of sugar if you like), layer the peas with more lettuce leaves, and cover the pan. The peas can steam-cook in the moisture clinging to the leaves, but you can also add a few tablespoonfuls of water or broth. Cook the peas over medium heat until they are tender. Discard the lettuce before serving, or chop it and serve it with the peas. *Cooking time:* 15 to 20 minutes.

Microwaving Place 1 cup of shelled peas or ½ pound of snow peas in a covered dish with 1 tablespoon of liquid. Stir the peas halfway through the cooking time. *Cooking times:* for green peas, 5 minutes; for snow peas, 8 to 10 minutes.

Steaming Fresh green peas, sugar snaps or snow peas can be "steam cooked" in a small amount of liquid: The less liquid you use, the more vitamin C the vegetables retain. Place ½ inch of water in a pan, cover tightly, and bring to a boil. Fresh or dried herbs can be added, but omit salt, as it toughens the peas. Add the peas, cover the pan, and simmer until the green peas are just tender; sugar snaps and snow peas should be a brilliant emerald green and barely crisp-tender. For extra flavor, use broth instead of water; add some chopped onion, celery, or scallions. *Cooking times:* for shelled peas, 5 to 10 minutes; for snow peas and sugar snaps, 1 to 2 minutes.

Snow peas and sugar snaps can also be cooked in a vegetable steamer placed over boiling water. *Cooking time:* 2 to 3 minutes.

Stir-frying Snow peas are frequently used in Chinese stir-fries. You can use either oil or broth in the skillet or wok. Slice each pod diagonally into two or three pieces, if you wish. Just be sure to cook both fresh and frozen snow peas only until the pods turn bright green, so that they stay crisp. Sugar snaps can also be quickly stir-fried. *Cooking time:* 1 to 2 minutes.

SERVING SUGGESTIONS Season cooked peas with fresh or dried mint, chopped fresh parsley, curry powder, or lemon zest. Peas nicely complement most other vegetables, particularly pearl onions or sautéed mushrooms.

With their bright color and sweet flavor, peas are a welcome addition to many other foods. Stir peas and a little grated Parmesan into cooked rice for an easy version of *risi e bisi,* a classic Italian dish. For a warm pea-and-potato salad, mix cooked (or thawed frozen) peas and sliced mushrooms with sliced boiled potatoes; dress with a light vinaigrette. At lunch, toss green peas with pasta and your favorite sauce, or add cooled, blanched snow peas or sugar snaps to cold pasta or vegetable salads. In addition, thawed frozen peas go well in tuna or chicken salad, while puréed cooked peas make a satisfying accompaniment to chicken breasts, fish fillets, or veal scallops. You can even thin the purée with chicken stock and a little skim milk for a quick but tasty pea soup.

For a colorful side dish, stir-fry snow peas or sugar snaps with water chestnuts, red bell pepper strips, julienne carrots, or sliced mushrooms. When entertaining, offer sugar snaps or snow peas alongside carrot sticks and an herbed yogurt or yogurt-cheese dip.

PEAS, green 3½ ounces raw (⅔ cup)

Calories	81	Fat	<1 g
Protein	5 g	Saturated Fat	<1 g
Carbohydrate	15 g	Cholesterol	0 mg
Dietary Fiber	Medium	Sodium	5 mg

KEY NUTRIENTS		% RDA Men	% RDA Women
Vitamin A	640 IU	13%	16%
Vitamin B_6	0.2 mg	10%	13%
Vitamin C	40 mg	67%	67%
Copper	0.2 mg	N/A	N/A
Folacin	65 mcg	32%	36%
Iron	2 mg	20%	13%
Magnesium	33 mg	9%	12%
Manganese	0.4 mg	N/A	N/A
Niacin	2 mg	11%	13%
Phosphorus	108 mg	14%	14%
Thiamin	0.3 mg	20%	27%

S=40% or more soluble N/A=Not Applicable N=Not Available

Peppers

Peppers are not pepper: The plant that produces dried peppercorns, the spice we grind and use as a seasoning, is native to Asia and is entirely unrelated to the shrubby plant that gives us the familiar green and red bell peppers and their many relatives, including hot chile peppers. Members of the genus *Capsicum,* peppers are native to the western hemisphere and have been domesticated in its tropical regions for several thousand years. They were given their name by Spanish explorers who had set out with Columbus on his second voyage in search of the peppercorns of India. When they landed in the New World and encountered these vegetables, perhaps they thought their flavor resembled that of peppercorns, and so misnamed them. They returned home with the capsicum peppers, which quickly became popular in Europe as a food, spice, and condiment. Over the next two hundred years, peppers were introduced to many other parts of the world, becoming one of the most widely appreciated of all vegetables.

Perhaps the most surprising feature of peppers is their nutritiousness: They are excellent sources of many essential nutrients, especially vitamin C—by weight, green bell peppers have twice as much as citrus fruit (red peppers have three times as much). Hot peppers contain even more vita-

Habanero
Poblano
Chile de árbol
Pimento
Anaheim
Banana
Hungarian wax
Cayenne
Serrano
Mexi-Bell
Jalapeño
Cubanelle
Cherry
Bell

min C, 357 percent more than an orange. Moreover, red peppers are quite a good source of beta carotene.

Red peppers are higher in beta carotene than green peppers: A sweet red pepper provides nearly 11 times as much beta carotene as a sweet green one; hot red peppers contain nearly 14 times as much as their green counterparts. Furthermore, sweet red peppers have one and a half times as much vitamin C as sweet green peppers; the vitamin C content of red and green hot peppers is the same.

Peppers also offer an exceptional range of flavors. Some are sweet, while others exhibit varying degrees of pungency—a distinctive burning sensation (caused by a chemical substance called capsaicin) that can range from mild to fiery. Found in a panorama of red, green, yellow, and purple hues, peppers are guaranteed to add visual zest to any dish. (In fact, very hot peppers have often served as ornaments as well as seasonings, and certain peppers are even used in food processing to color a variety of products, from salad dressings to meat products.)

VARIETIES Today, peppers are cultivated in a range of sizes, shapes, and shades. While almost all of them belong to one species, *Capsicum annuum,* the number of varieties is daunting, and the names are confusing, as they vary from region to region. The basic categories are simple: sweet and hot. (Hot peppers are also known as chile peppers, or chiles.) While the following listing can help you distinguish the most common pepper varieties, it can be tricky, if not impossible, to determine just how hot a pepper is. The amount of heat in a hot pepper depends on the variety; within an individual variety the more mature the pepper, the hotter it will be—for example, a red Anaheim will pack more punch than a green one. (Redness does not indicate heat in bell peppers, however, since they do not contain capsaicin. A red bell pepper is simply a mature pepper and will be sweeter than a green one.) Soil, climate, and other conditions also affect the amount of capsaicin in a pepper, so that peppers of the same variety—even those on the same plant—can differ in hotness.

Sweet peppers

The most popular pepper in the United States is the bell, which accounts for more than 60 percent of the domestic pepper crop. While hot peppers are primarily used to season foods, it's possible to consume sweet peppers in sufficient quantities so that they make a significant nutritional contribution to your diet.

Bell With three to four lobes, these sweet bell-shaped peppers can be green, red, yellow, orange, brown, or purple, depending on the variety and the stage of ripeness. Most are sold in the mature green stage—fully developed, but not ripe. As they ripen on the vine, most bell peppers turn red and become sweeter. Bell peppers have no "bite" at all, since they contain a recessive gene that eliminates capsaicin. Instead, they have a mild tang and a crunchy texture that makes them suitable for eating raw; their size, shape, and firmness allow them to be stuffed whole. (*Mexi-Bell,* a cross between bell peppers and hot peppers, look like small bell peppers, but have a hotter bite.)

Banana These mild yellow peppers, resembling bananas in shape and color, are available fresh or pickled in jars. It's important to taste one before using it in a recipe because of its resemblance to a moderately hot twin called Hungarian wax. Both banana and Hungarian wax peppers may be labeled "yellow wax" in stores, with no indication of their pungency.

Cubanelle These long, tapered peppers, about 4 inches in length, are either light green or yellow; occasionally, you will find red ones that have been fully matured. Cubanelles are more flavorful than bells and are perfect for sautéing.

Pimento Large and heart-shaped, pimentos (sometimes spelled "pimientos") are generally sold in jars, but every so often you can find them fresh—fully ripe and red—in specialty markets. These sweet peppers are mild yet flavorful; their thick, meaty flesh makes them good candidates for roasting; in fact, the pimentos sold in jars are usually roasted and peeled. Large red bell peppers are sometimes packaged as pimentos. You can tell the difference by the shade of red; true pimentos will have an orangy tomato cast, but bells are bright red.

The leading pepper producer is China, which harvests nearly six times the number of peppers as does the United States.

Hot peppers (chiles)

In many areas of the world, and particularly in tropical climates, hot peppers are liberally used to add spice to dishes. Though Americans still prefer sweet peppers, the hot varieties have become increasingly popular in ethnic cooking—Mexican, Indian, Thai, Vietnamese, Arab, and Spanish. While they can give food a pleasurable bite, the most pungent peppers are powerful, and need to be used with care and restraint. As indicated below, most of the leading varieties are marketed in dried or canned form as well as fresh.

Anaheim Among the most commonly used chiles in the United States, with a bite ranging from mild to moderately hot, these long, slender, lobed peppers come in varieties also known as New Mexican, long green, long red, or California. Anaheims are eaten in both the green and red stages of development; when mature and red, they are often made into a *ristra*—a strand of peppers that are strung together on a cord—and left to dry. Anaheims are the peppers of choice for the classic Mexican dish called *chiles rellenos,* or stuffed chiles.

Ancho Technically, ancho refers to a dried poblano pepper, but many distributors and markets also apply the term to the fresh version. Dried anchos are flat, wrinkled, and heart shaped, ranging in color from oxblood to almost black. Considered one of the mild to moderately hot peppers (like poblanos), anchos are often soaked and ground for use in cooked sauces.

Cascabel These moderately hot chiles are mostly available dried. In their fresh state, they are green or red and shaped like a small tomato. Dried, their skin turns a brownish red and becomes translucent, and their seeds rattle around inside. The name cascabel means "jingle bell" in Spanish.

Cayenne Among the hottest chiles, cayenne peppers are long, thin, sharply pointed red pods that are either straight or curled at the tip; they grow to a length of 6 to 10 inches. (The *chile de árbol* is closely related and similar in shape, but grows only 2 to 3 inches in length and usually does not have a curled tip; it is also slightly less pungent.) Ground, dried cayenne is a popular spice.

Cherry So named for their resemblance to the familiar fruit, cherry peppers are round and red. They range in pungency from mild to moderately hot. Cherry peppers are sold fresh, and also are commonly pickled and sold in jars.

In England, all peppers are known as chiles; hot ones are called hot chiles. In Latin America, hot peppers are also called chiles, while mild peppers are known as pimentos. And in the United States, pimentos are simply one variety of sweet red pepper.

Habanero These lantern-shaped peppers, measuring about 2 inches by 2 inches, are of a different species—*Capsicum chinense*—than the predominant *Capsicum annuum* peppers. Their color is most often yellow-orange, but can be yellow, orange, or red. Habaneros hold the distinction of being the most fiery of all domesticated peppers; however, their heat can sneak up on you, so beware of taking a second bite if you think the first one wasn't hot (which is unlikely). Furthermore, rather than dissipating quickly, the heat of habaneros persists. They are also called Scotch bonnets.

Hungarian wax These are the hot version of

WHY THE HEAT—AND WHY WE LIKE IT

All hot peppers contain capsaicinoids, natural substances that produce a burning sensation in the mouth, causing the eyes to water and the nose to run, and even induce perspiration. Capsaicinoids have no flavor or odor, but act directly on the pain receptors in the mouth and throat. The primary capsaicinoid, capsaicin, is so hot that a single drop diluted in 100,000 drops of water will produce a blistering of the tongue.

Capsaicinoids are found primarily in the pepper's placenta—the white "ribs" that run down the middle and along the sides of a pepper. Since the seeds are in such close contact with the ribs, they also are often hot. In the rest of the vegetable, capsaicinoids are unevenly distributed throughout the flesh, so it is likely that one part of the same pepper may be hotter or milder than another. You can reduce the amount of heat in a chile pepper by removing the ribs and seeds, but you must wear gloves while doing so.

Capsaicinoid content is measured in parts per million. These parts per million are converted into Scoville heat units, the industry standard for measuring a pepper's punch. One part per million is equivalent to 15 Scoville units. Bell peppers have a value of zero Scoville units, whereas Habaneros—the hottest peppers—register a blistering 200,000 to 300,000. (Pure capsaicin has a Scoville heat unit score of 16 million.)

Why do we enjoy the sensations all this heat produces? Psychologist Paul Rozin, a researcher at the University of Pennsylvania, has suggested that eating hot peppers is an example of "constrained risk." The reactions we experience are similar to the ones the body produces in times of fear or anxiety, but since there really is no danger, we can enjoy the experience for its own sake, much like riding a roller coaster or making a parachute jump. Rozin also hypothesizes that in response to the discomfort produced by the burning peppers, the brain releases endorphins—the same substances responsible for producing so-called "runner's high"—which at high levels can create a sensation of pleasure.

sweet banana peppers. They are never green—the peppers start out yellow and ripen to orange or red—and are mostly sold when yellow, either fresh or pickled in jars.

Jalapeño Probably the most familiar hot peppers—and almost as frequently used as the Anaheims—jalapeños are tapered, about 2 inches in length, and have slight cracks at their stem ends. They are very hot, with a bite that you notice immediately. Most often, these peppers are consumed at the mature green stage, but sometimes you will find fully ripe red jalapeños on the market. In addition, they are sold canned, sliced, and pickled, and are processed into a wide array of products, such as sausage, cheese, and jelly. Canned types may be milder than fresh because they are usually peeled, seeded, and packed in liquid—but they will still pack a punch.

Poblano These are ancho peppers in the green state; they look like small bell peppers at the stem end, tapering to a thin point at the blossom end. Ranging from mild to hot, poblanos are usually roasted and peeled before using, either in casseroles, soups, and sauces, or stuffed with meat or cheese for *chiles rellenos.*

Here is some indirect evidence that hot peppers and upset stomachs don't go hand in hand. El Paso, Texas, is a town whose inhabitants consume a great deal of spicy food that is seasoned with hot peppers. Yet, when researchers at Northeastern University, in Boston, Massachusetts, conducted a nationwide survey on people's use of antacids, El Paso had the lowest per-person consumption of the two hundred cities taking part.

Serrano Very popular in Mexico and the southwestern United States, these small (1 to 4 inches long) torpedo-shaped peppers are primarily consumed fresh, usually in salsas. Serranos are very hot and are typically sold in their mature green state, though they are also sometimes available when red.

AVAILABILITY Sweet bell peppers are on the market all year in good supply, but they are slightly more plentiful in the summer months. California and Florida produce most of the domestic crop; bells are also imported from Mexico, the Dominican Republic, Belgium, and the Netherlands (which exports some intensely colored greenhouse varieties). Hot peppers are also generally available year round. They are grown in California, New Mexico, and Texas; some are imported from Mexico.

SHOPPING TIPS Fresh peppers come in a wide variety of shapes, sizes, and colors, but the guidelines for choosing them are practically the same. Whether they are sweet or hot, peppers should be well shaped, firm, and glossy. Their skins should be taut and unwrinkled, and their stems fresh and green. Bell peppers are best when they are thick walled and juicy, so they should feel heavy for their size. Watch out for soft or sunken areas, slashes or black spots. Except for jalapeños, which often have shallow cracks at their stem ends, peppers should be free of cracks.

If a green bell pepper shows streaks of red, it will be slightly sweeter than a totally green one; however, once picked, it won't get any redder—or sweeter, either.

Dried hot peppers should be glossy and unbroken, not dusty or fragmented.

STORAGE Store unwashed sweet peppers in a plastic bag in the refrigerator for up to a week; green peppers will keep somewhat longer than red or other ripe peppers. Check them frequently; immediately use any peppers that have developed soft spots.

Fresh hot peppers should be wrapped in paper towels rather than plastic; moisture will cause them to decay. You can refrigerate them for up to three weeks.

Store dried hot peppers in an airtight container at room temperature for up to four months. If you are keeping them longer, place them in the refrigerator.

PEPPERS AND HEALTH

Are hot peppers bad for you? Probably not, according to recent studies. A common concern is that hot peppers or other spicy foods cause ulcers, but there's no evidence that they do. Studies of areas where hot peppers are used extensively in cooking, such as Brazil and Thailand, have found no higher incidence of stomach ulcers among their populations. And in a study conducted at a Veterans Administration hospital, researchers ground up about an ounce of jalapeño pepper and injected it directly into the stomachs of volunteers. Follow-up observation showed no damage to their stomach linings. Nor do hot peppers aggravate or cause hemorrhoids, as has often been claimed, since capsaicinoids (the chemicals responsible for a pepper's heat) are broken down before they reach the lower intestine.

Actually, evidence has shown that peppers may have some beneficial properties. Capsaicin—the predominate capsaicinoid—has been found to work as an anticoagulant, thus possibly helping to prevent heart attacks or strokes caused by a blood clot. Small amounts of capsaicin can produce numbing of the skin and have a slight anti-inflammatory effect. In some countries, peppers are used in salves. Moreover, peppers are high in vitamin C, which, in turn, may be effective in protecting against cancer. Vitamin C is an antioxidant, a chemical substance capable of removing the threat from free radicals, which can cause cells to mutate.

PREPARATION Wash sweet peppers just before you use them and before coring or cutting them. Some bell peppers are waxed, and these should be peeled before eating. Although not truly hot, the seeds of sweet peppers can be bitter and need to be removed. It's simple to stem, core, and seed sweet peppers all at once: Starting at one side of the stem, run a knife around the pepper to halve it. Separate the halves, then pull out the stem and core, which should come out as a unit. Tap or rinse the pepper halves to shake out any remaining seeds.

HANDLING HOT PEPPERS

Capsaicin, the substance that makes these peppers feel hot in your mouth, can cause extreme pain if it gets into your eyes. In fact, whenever you handle the seeds and membranes of hot peppers, you must take precautions, or the capsaicin will irritate and burn the skin on your hands.

When cutting hot peppers, it is best to wear thin rubber gloves. If gloves aren't available, be sure to wash your hands very thoroughly with soap and water (a mild bleach solution is even better) after working with the peppers. And never touch your hands to your face—especially to your eyes—when they have come into contact with capsaicin. Don't forget to wash the utensils and cutting board after use, or you may taint other foods with undesired pungency.

The same caveats apply for dried hot peppers, with one additional caution: When grinding them (by hand or in a food processor or blender), be careful not to inhale the fumes or let them waft into your eyes.

Pepper skin can be unpleasantly tough in cooked dishes; you can easily peel peppers by blanching or roasting them, as explained below. For most recipes, the various colors of bell peppers are interchangeable (keep in mind that reds and yellows are sweeter than green peppers). However, jewel-like purple bells turn a dull grayish green when heated, so reserve them for salads and other uncooked uses.

When using hot peppers, you will find that even those of the same type vary in hotness. Consequently, you may need to use a different amount each time you prepare a favorite recipe. Sample a bit of the hot pepper before deciding how much to use in a particular dish. It's best to add hot pepper a small amount at a time, until the food reaches the degree of hotness you desire.

Exercise caution when handling hot peppers. If the capsaicin contained in their inner flesh and seeds comes into contact with your skin or eyes, you will experience a painful burning sensation. Wash the hot peppers, cut them open, and remove the seeds and ribs, if desired (this procedure tempers their pungency; soaking hot peppers in cold salted water for an hour further diminishes their hotness). For a milder flavor, cut a few slits in a whole pepper, impale it on a toothpick, then add it to food that is already cooking. When the dish is done, remove and discard the hot pepper. If you prefer, roast the whole pepper first, then peel and seed it.

Baking Cut bell peppers into large chunks and place them in a baking dish (alone or with other vegetables). Bake in a 350° oven until tender. For baking with a stuffing, choose solid, thick-walled

SEASONINGS FROM PEPPERS

Whole peppers are not the only means of enlivening dishes. You can also substitute a wide variety of seasonings and condiments made from hot peppers:

Cayenne **This spice—very hot and orange red or deep red in color—is based on very pungent peppers grown in Louisiana, Africa, India, and Mexico. However, sauces marketed as cayenne may also contain other hot red peppers and spices.**

Chili powder **Dried ground Anaheim peppers are the basis for the typical seasoning used to flavor chili con carne. Usually the peppers are mixed with other spices, such as garlic, cumin, and cayenne.**

Curry powder **A number of variations of this Indian spice are available; all of them contain dried hot peppers as their base. The pungency varies, depending on how much hot pepper is used.**

Paprika **Originating in Hungary, this spice is made by grinding dried mild red peppers into a powder. Sweet paprika contains just the pods; a hotter version may also include the ground seeds and ribs.**

Red pepper **The spice labeled simply "red pepper" is generally made from the dried pods of mild to moderately hot red peppers, but the term can also refer to the more pungent cayenne pepper.**

Salsa **A spicy sauce with texture, salsa contains chopped tomatoes, hot peppers, onions, herbs and spices, such as garlic or cilantro (coriander). It is sold bottled in varying degrees of pungency.**

Tabasco sauce **Only one company, based on Avery Island in Louisiana, makes this hot spicy sauce (the name is a registered trademark). Tabasco peppers—so-called because of the region they originally came from in Mexico—are exceptionally hot red chiles in the shape of elongated Christmas tree lights. (They are also a different species—*Capsicum frutescens*—from other peppers.) The sauce is made by soaking the peppers with salt and letting the mixture age for at least three years. It is then mixed with vinegar and strained before bottling. (Similar hot sauces are made from other red chiles, such as cayenne.)**

peppers so that they will hold their shape. Cut off a ½-inch "lid" and a thin slice from the bottom of each pepper so that each one will stand without tipping; or, halve each pepper lengthwise to form two "cups." Stuff the peppers, replace their cups, and place them in a baking pan in which they will fit snugly upright. Bake in a 375° oven until the filling is heated through and the peppers tender. *Cooking time:* 20 to 25 minutes.

Blanching Blanched sweet peppers can be used without further cooking as cases for cold salads or cottage cheese mixtures. Cut off the caps and core the peppers, then blanch them in boiling water. Blanching also makes peppers easier to peel. *Cooking time:* 5 minutes.

Microwaving For stuffed peppers, first microwave the cored pepper shells for 2 minutes to soften them. The precooking ensures that the shells will be done at the same time as the filling. Then fill the peppers and cook until the filling is heated through. *Cooking time:* 7 to 8 minutes.

Roasting Both sweet peppers and fresh green hot peppers take on a wonderful smoky flavor when charred over a flame. You can fire-roast whole peppers over the flame of a gas stove, in a broiler, or on a barbecue grill; halved or sliced sweet peppers can be roasted under the broiler.

Cut a small slit near the stem of each pepper. One at a time, impale each pepper on a long-handled cooking fork and hold over the flame, or grill or broil 4 inches from the heating element or fire, turning frequently until the skin is blackened. Immediately place the charred peppers in a paper or plastic bag to steam for about 15 minutes, then remove them and scrape off the skin with a table knife. Cut around the stem, pull out the stem and core, and scrape out any remaining seeds. *Cooking time:* 6 to 10 minutes.

Sautéing Strips or squares of bell pepper can be sautéed in oil or stock. They are good alone or in combination with other vegetables. *Cooking time:* 10 to 15 minutes.

Stir-frying Add 1-inch squares or strips of bell pepper to Chinese meat or poultry stir-fries, or cook the peppers with broccoli, water chestnuts, green beans, or other vegetables. *Cooking time:* 4 to 6 minutes.

Preparing dried hot peppers Wipe the peppers with a damp cloth. They can be pulverized in a mortar and pestle or food processor, for use as chili powder. To soften their texture and flavor, heat whole dried hot peppers on an ungreased griddle, or tear them into pieces and soak them in hot water for half an hour. Purée the peppers (with the soaking liquid, if any) and use as directed with your recipe.

Preparing hot peppers for stuffing Fire-roast and peel Anaheims or other large, mild chiles as directed above. Cut a 2-inch slit near the stem. Holding onto the stem, reach into the chile and detach the core with the seeds attached. Scrape out any remaining seeds.

SERVING SUGGESTIONS Sweet peppers will enhance almost any kind of green salad; cut the peppers into strips, squares, or julienne strips to complement the other ingredients. They will also perk up cooked vegetables. Try them with zucchini, yellow squash, green beans, corn, or asparagus. Tomatoes, onions, and sweet peppers are another excellent combination: Either sauté the vegetables together, or roast the peppers first, cut them into strips or squares, and add to steamed vegetables.

It is easy to prepare a delicious relish or sandwich filling based on roasted sweet peppers. Just combine peeled, chopped peppers with chopped onion, black pepper, and a dash of oil and vinegar. Or, spread sliced roasted peppers on Italian bread and sprinkle on a little oil and vinegar.

For a delicious fat-free sauce to accompany poultry or pasta, purée roasted red bell peppers with garlic, onion and herbs; for a creamy version, add yogurt. Chopped red bell peppers will lend

PEPPERS, hot, red 3½ oz raw (2 peppers)

Calories	40	Fat	<1 g
Protein	2 g	Saturated Fat	<1 g
Carbohydrate	10 g	Cholesterol	0 mg
Dietary Fiber	Low	Sodium	7 mg

KEY NUTRIENTS		% RDA Men	Women
Vitamin A	10,750 IU	215%	269%
Vitamin B_6	0.3 mg	15%	19%
Beta Carotene	6 mg	N/A	N/A
Vitamin C	243 mg	405%	405%
Copper	0.2 mg	N/A	N/A
Folacin	23 mcg	12%	13%
Iron	1 mg	10%	8%
Manganese	0.2 mg	N/A	N/A
Potassium	340 mg	N/A	N/A

S=40% or more soluble N/A=Not Applicable N=Not Available

PEPPERS, sweet, red 3½ oz raw (1 cup chopped)

Calories	27	Fat	<1 g
Protein	1 g	Saturated Fat	<1 g
Carbohydrate	6 g	Cholesterol	0 mg
Dietary Fiber	Low	Sodium	2 mg

KEY NUTRIENTS		% RDA Men	Women
Vitamin A	5700 IU	114%	142%
Vitamin B_6	0.3 mg	15%	19%
Beta Carotene	3 mg	N/A	N/A
Vitamin C	190 mg	317%	317%
Folacin	22 mcg	11%	12%

S=40% or more soluble N/A=Not Applicable N=Not Available

crunchiness to a tomato-based pasta sauce, and a red-pepper purée can serve as the base for a flavorful soup.

Sweet peppers provide excellent cases for a variety of fillings: Stuff them with cooked ground meat, poultry, canned tuna, salmon, or leftover cooked fish; or, if you prefer, substitute cooked rice, pasta or grains, such as barley or kasha. Vegetarian chili or leftover cooked vegetables (whole or puréed) also make tasty stuffings.

Hot peppers can be used to make Mexican *chiles rellenos*. These are usually filled with cheese or ground meat, then deep fried; a Southeast Asian version of filled hot peppers calls for a mixture of rice and fish, seasoned with scallions, garlic, and ginger. Vegetables can be used in place of fish.

If you taste some food laced with hot peppers and find it intolerably hot, eat a bit of rice or bread, rather than have a drink of water. Water, or just about any other beverage, will only spread the fire. The one liquid that seems to work is milk. It contains a protein called casein, which literally wipes away capsaicin, the fiery compound in peppers.

Just a sprinkling of chopped hot peppers will add zest to such everyday favorites as macaroni and cheese, corn bread, meat loaf, or tomato sauce. To prepare *salsa* in its familiar Mexican form, mix chopped hot peppers, tomatoes, onions, garlic, cilantro, and lime juice or vinegar. It is delicious as an accompaniment to grilled fish or poultry, or as a dip or salad dressing. A similar Asian condiment, which is based on tropical fruits such as pineapple or mango, contains lime juice, onions, and hot peppers.

Nutritional profiles of the average sweet red pepper and the average hot red pepper are provided on page 144. Red peppers contain more nutrients than green ones.

Potatoes

Only a few other foods are as wholesome as a potato. Not only does it contain complex carbohydrates, but it also supplies protein and ample vitamins and minerals. In addition, this nourishing food may have changed the course of history. The potato was first brought to Europe from South America around 1570, where it contributed needed calories and nutrients to the diet of the poor, particularly in Ireland. Dependence on potatoes in that country became so great that when the crop failed in the 1840s, it led to widespread famine and massive emigration to the United States.

A half of a large baked potato with skin (about 3½ ounces) contains more potassium than a 6-ounce glass of orange juice.

A member of the nightshade family of plants, the potato is a tuber—a swollen underground stem (not a root) that stores surplus carbohydrates to feed the leafy green plant sprouting above the soil. Left undisturbed, the plant will bear fruit resembling small green tomatoes. But unlike its relatives—including bell peppers, tomatoes, and eggplants—the fruit isn't edible; the stem is.

Today the potato is the world's most widely consumed and economically important vegetable. It is grown in at least eighty countries, and the United States alone produces about 35 billion pounds of potatoes annually. Americans consume about 126 pounds per person per year, on average—far more than any other vegetable. In fact, simply by virtue of the quantities eaten, the potato is the leading source of vitamin C in the American diet. Unfortunately, about 65 percent of America's potatoes are not sold fresh, but in various "convenience" forms that increase their fat and sodium content. Although canned potatoes are nearly the nutritional equivalent of boiled,

peeled potatoes, they may contain more than 400 milligrams of sodium per cup, compared with about 6 milligrams of sodium per cup of freshly cooked potatoes.

Many people think of potatoes as a fattening food, but they are not. It is the fat added in processing and in toppings for potatoes—such as the butter, sour cream, mayonnaise, or gravy—that give them this bad reputation. You can prepare potatoes in a number of delicious ways without adding fat.

Three ounces of conventional French fries contain about 345 calories; the same amount of potatoes fried as hash browns has 240 calories; and the same amount served plain boiled has only 85 calories.

VARIETIES Potatoes are often differentiated according to age. They may be sold soon after they are dug, or kept in cold storage for up to a year before sale. But only potatoes that are freshly harvested may be called "new." Many consumers believe that "new" simply denotes a small, round red or white potato, but true new potatoes have thin "feathering" skins that can be brushed off with your fingers. Mature potatoes, by contrast, have thick skins, frequently with a meshlike netting on their surface. New potatoes may be as small as marbles or as large as full-sized mature potatoes. They have a high moisture and sugar content, so they cook quickly and have a delicately sweet flavor.

Moreover, potatoes can be found in dozens of shapes. Both the skin and flesh of potatoes come in a range of colors, from yellow and tan to blue and purple. In the United States, however, the most common varieties grown commercially fall into one of four categories:

Long russets Typified by the Russet Burbank, they are the favorites among baking potatoes and are the leading variety grown. (Most Idaho baking potatoes are Russet Burbanks.) These large, oval-shaped potatoes, which may often weigh up to 18 ounces each, have a hard brown skin and starchy flesh.

Long whites The White Rose is one of the better-known varieties of these all-purpose potatoes. When new, they are thin skinned and waxy; when mature, they are starchy and weigh an average of half a pound.

Round reds These red, smooth-skinned potatoes, notably the Red LaSoda and Red Pontiac, are most commonly sold "new"; when more mature, they are waxy and good for boiling.

Round whites The Katahdin (the predominant variety grown in Maine) is representative of these multipurpose potatoes. They have a light tan skin and are smaller than the long whites, averaging three per pound.

Special potato varieties are sold at some specialty greengrocers and farmers' markets. They include the Finnish Yellow Wax, which has deep yellow flesh; its rich taste and "buttery" appearance may convince you to forgo butter when you serve it. Both the Blue Carib and All Blue have grayish blue skin, dark blue flesh, and a delicate flavor. The Rose Fir is a small, waxy potato with a pink to red skin.

AVAILABILITY Potatoes are harvested somewhere in the United States in every month of the year—they are a commercial crop in forty-eight states—and they also keep well if stored under the proper conditions. As a result, there is an endless peak season, with no periods of short supply. The principal growing states with an autumn harvest include Idaho, Washington, Oregon, Maine, and New York; major winter and spring crops are harvested in the South and Southwest. New potatoes are not stored, but the overlapping growing seasons mean that they, too, may be found in stores throughout the year, though in limited quantities.

WHAT GETS ADDED TO POTATOES

Frozen french fries, hash browns, or potato puffs contain a lot of added fat and sodium; special microwavable versions are usually even higher in fat. Instant mashed potato flakes or granules have a moderately high sodium content and can also be high in fat, if prepared according to package directions. Other dried potato mixes—for scalloped, creamed, or au gratin potatoes—are high in both sodium and fat. Potato chips take unhealthy processing to the extreme—just 2 ounces of chips (about thirty chips) contain about 300 calories and 20 grams of fat, as compared to 220 calories and no fat in a 7-ounce fresh baked potato.

SHOPPING TIPS If possible, choose individual potatoes from a bulk display. Buy a large bag (5 or 10 pounds) only if you can check the condition of the potatoes through the packaging—and if you are sure of using all of them before they spoil. Look for clean, smooth, well-shaped potatoes, free from sprouts. (A sprouting potato, though edible, has started to age and may contain increased amounts of solanine, a naturally occurring toxin.) Potatoes should feel firm, the "eyes"—the buds from which sprouts can grow—should be few and shallow, and the skins should be free of cracks, wrinkles, or dampness. Reject any with green-tinged skins, indicating improper storage (and the presence of solanine), and those with black spots, bruises, or other discolorations.

The USDA has established grades for potatoes, according to appearance and size. "U.S. Extra No. 1" is a premium grade, followed by "U.S. No. 1," which is the most common grade and denotes potatoes that have few defects and must be at at least 1¾ inches in diameter. However, grade labeling is not required, and many potatoes are not marked.

STORAGE Few modern homes have root cellars, but a cool (45° to 50°), dark, dry place makes the best storage area, as light and warmth encourage sprouting. Don't put potatoes in the refrigerator, or anywhere below 45°. Their starch will turn to sugar, giving them an undesirable sweet taste (although leaving them at room temperature for a few days allows the sugar to reconvert to starch). Keep the potatoes in a burlap, brown paper, or perforated plastic bag. Check them occasionally and remove any that have sprouted, softened, or shriveled; a bad one can adversely affect the condition of the ones remaining.

Mature potatoes will keep for up to two

months under optimum conditions; new potatoes are more perishable and should be used within a week of purchase. Don't wash potatoes before storing, or they will spoil more quickly. And don't store onions together with potatoes: The gases given off by onions accelerate the decay of potatoes, and vice versa. Neither raw nor most cooked potatoes freeze well; however, mashed potatoes may be packed into containers and frozen.

PREPARATION Nutritionally speaking, the less you do to potatoes, the better. The skin is an excellent source of fiber, so try to leave it on. But if you decide to peel it because you don't like the taste of the skin, do so carefully. Use a swivel-bladed vegetable peeler to remove the thinnest possible layer, and thus preserve the nutrients just below the skin. Better yet, simply scrub unpeeled potatoes under cold water before cooking; remove any sprouts, green spots, or deep eyes with a sharp paring knife.

Generally speaking, low-starch, high-moisture "waxy" potatoes, such as round reds, are best for boiling or steaming. They remain firm-textured when sliced or diced (before or after cooking), and are therefore a good choice for stews, casseroles, or salads in which you want the potato pieces to hold their shape. Starchy potatoes, such as Russet Burbanks, have a drier flesh. They turn out fluffy when baked or mashed and may fall apart if cut into chunks or slices after cooking. They are best used in soups and stews in which the potatoes are meant to break up and thicken the cooking liquid.

Potatoes occasionally turn gray or dark after they are boiled; this color change may be caused by the conditions under which they were grown or stored. It's impossible to tell which potatoes will turn dark, but the discoloration does not affect flavor, texture, or nutritional value. Contact with aluminum or iron will also discolor potatoes, so cook them in stainless steel pots. For the same reason, raw potatoes should not be cut with a carbon steel (nonstainless) knife. If exposed to air, peeled raw potatoes will also discolor. Cook the potatoes immediately in a pot of water that has already been brought to a boil. And if you are interrupted while preparing them, place them in a bowl of cold water, then add a few drops of lemon juice or vinegar. This trick will help to keep the potatoes white.

WHAT TO DO ABOUT THE SKIN

Eat potatoes with their skins whenever possible—ounce for ounce, the skin is richer in fiber, iron, calcium, phosphorus, potassium, zinc, and B vitamins than the flesh. However, don't eat the skin if it has a greenish tinge. The green is chlorophyll, and although not harmful in itself, it may signal a high concentration of a toxic alkaloid called solanine. Potatoes normally contain harmless quantities of this bitter compound, small amounts of which contribute to the vegetable's characteristic flavor; it's only when exposed to light or extreme temperatures after harvesting that they develop larger amounts. Eating such damaged potatoes can cause cramps, diarrhea, and fatigue. Potato sprouts also contain lots of solanine; however, the concentration in undamaged potatoes is so low that you would have to eat about 12 pounds at one sitting to be adversely affected.

If you find that your potatoes have turned green or sprouted, peel away the sprouts and green areas of skin along with at least ⅛ inch of the flesh beneath. Potatoes that are excessively soft or sprouted should be discarded.

Baking Russets are truly the best for baking. Do not wrap them in foil, however, as the covering traps moisture, which will steam rather than bake the potatoes. Pierce their skin in a few places with a fork before baking; it will allow steam to escape, thus producing dry, fluffy potatoes. Thick-skinned potatoes may actually burst if baked without piercing.

A large baking nail inserted lengthwise into a potato will conduct heat to the interior of the vegetable and speed the baking process. If you do not have one of these nails available, use a metal skewer. Test for doneness by squeezing the potato: It should give slightly. *Cooking time:* 45 to 60 minutes in a 400° oven.

Boiling To reduce the loss of vitamin C, boil small to medium potatoes whole. Cut larger ones into halves or quarters and leave the skins on; if you want to remove the skins for eating, they will slip off easily while the potatoes are still warm. To keep unpeeled potatoes from bursting, pare a band of skin around the circumference with a paring knife or vegetable peeler. Drop the potatoes into a pot of boiling water; do not start them in cold water, or you'll destroy more of their vitamin C content. (Adding garlic, onion, or herbs to the water will give the boiled potatoes a subtle flavor.) Cover and cook until they can be easily pierced with the tip of a sharp knife. Drain the potatoes, return them to the pot, and toss gently over the still-warm burner to dry them. *Cooking times:* for small new potatoes, 10 to 15 minutes; for cut-up potatoes, 15 to 20 minutes; for medium to large whole potatoes, 20 to 40 minutes.

Microwaving Pierce the potatoes several times with a fork—they can explode if the skins are left intact. Set them on a double thickness of paper towels, placing a single potato in the center of the oven, and two or more in a circle or spoke pattern. Turn or rotate the potatoes halfway through cooking time; wrap or cover after removing them from the oven and let stand for 5 minutes. *Cooking times:* for one 8-ounce potato, 5 minutes; for two potatoes of that size, 7 minutes; for four potatoes, 13 minutes.

Steaming This method conserves more nutrients than boiling, since the potatoes are in minimal contact with water. Arrange a single layer of small, whole potatoes, thick slices, or chunks in a steamer basket and cook over boiling water. *Cooking times:* for cut-up potatoes, 15 to 20 minutes; for whole ones, 30 to 40 minutes.

Mashed potatoes For fluffy mashed potatoes, boil and dry the potatoes. Don't overheat the potatoes or mash them in a food processor, which may turn them gummy; it's best to use a potato masher or mill.

SERVING SUGGESTIONS As a topping for baked potatoes, try plain nonfat yogurt or low-fat cottage cheese blended with herbs, scallions, or chives; chopped broccoli or other cooked vegetables; or a spoonful or two of leftover soups or stews. Toss boiled potatoes with herbed stock or nonfat yogurt and then top with parsley. For added zest, mix in some salsa, or sprinkle with a small amount of grated Parmesan or Cheddar.

LOW-FAT CHIPS AND FRIES

Scrub and very thinly slice a baking potato (a vegetable peeler makes the thinnest slices). Lightly coat a baking sheet with nonstick cooking spray or cooking oil, place the slices in a single layer, spray or brush them lightly with oil, and sprinkle with paprika. Bake in a 400° oven for 30 minutes, turning the chips halfway through the cooking time. Reduce the oven temperature to 300° and bake for 15 to 20 minutes longer, or until the chips are crisp. For oven fries, cut the potatoes into ½-inch-thick sticks and proceed as above, but bake the potatoes in a 450° oven for 35 to 40 minutes, turning them over occasionally.

For flavorful but low-fat mashed potatoes, whisk in nonfat yogurt or buttermilk, then season with pepper, herbs, chopped chives, or scallions.

POTATO 3½ oz baked (½ potato)

Calories	109	Fat	<1 g
Protein	2 g	Saturated Fat	<1 g
Carbohydrate	25 g	Cholesterol	0 mg
Dietary Fiber	Medium	Sodium	8 mg

KEY NUTRIENTS		% RDA Men	% RDA Women
Vitamin B_6	0.3 mg	15%	19%
Vitamin C	13 mg	22%	22%
Copper	0.3 mg	N/A	N/A
Iron	1 mg	10%	7%
Magnesium	27 mg	8%	10%
Manganese	0.2 mg	N/A	N/A
Niacin	2 mg	11%	13%
Potassium	418 mg	N/A	N/A

S=40% or more soluble N/A=Not Applicable N=Not Available

If you yearn for the taste of butter, use a small amount or try a powdered butter substitute. Or, boil a couple of whole garlic cloves along with the potatoes. By the time the potatoes are done, the garlic will be soft and sweet tasting, and you can mash it in with the potatoes. A nutritious alternative is an Irish dish called colcannon: Combine hot mashed potatoes with shredded, steamed cabbage and chopped scallions. Leftover mashed potatoes can be used to thicken sauces or stews, or thinned with broth to make a soup.

Instead of serving a mayonnaise-laden potato salad, make a dressing with nonfat yogurt, vinegar, prepared mustard, and herbs. A variety of ingredients can be added to this basic recipe, such as chopped celery, diced green pepper, shredded carrot, diced apple, minced green onion, or ripe tomatoes, and then tossed in with the potatoes. A cup of this mixture has about one-third the calories of potato salad made with mayonnaise. Or drizzle a vinegar-and-oil dressing, flavored with mustard and herbs, over the potatoes while they are still hot; they will absorb the liquid more fully. For extra flavor, sprinkle the warm potatoes with white wine, broth, or vinegar before adding any dressing; you can also mix in other cooked vegetables, such as zucchini, asparagus, or green beans. If there are any leftover boiled potatoes, use them to create a more substantial green salad, or to make low-fat home fries or hash browns.

Radishes

Radishes are root vegetables that resemble beets or turnips in appearance and texture. But their flavor is distinctive, ranging from the juicy crispness of the familiar red globe radish to the sharp bite of the turnip-shaped black radish. Like their relatives broccoli, cabbage, and kale, radishes are cruciferous vegetables that offer cancer-protecting potential. They were first cultivated thousands of years ago in China, then in Egypt and Greece (where the vegetable was so highly regarded that gold replicas were made of it). Since then, many varieties have been developed in a number of shapes, sizes, and colors.

In the United States, radishes are usually eaten raw; however, they can be added to cooked dishes such as soups, or heated and served as a whole vegetable, or pickled. As with many other root vegetables, their green tops are edible and lend a peppery taste to salads. While radishes are not outstanding nutritionally, they are a good source of vitamin C. Very low in calories, they make a perfect snacking food.

VARIETIES Growers classify radishes by shape—round, oval, oblong, and long are the most common. Some markets label them by color—red, white, and black ones are the most frequently displayed.

Black radishes Turniplike in size and shape (about 8 inches long), these have dull black or dark brown skin. When peeled, their flesh is white, quite pungent, and drier than other radishes. "Black Spanish" is the name for commercially grown black radishes, which are available in round and long varieties.

California mammoth whites A larger variety than the white icicles, these radishes have oblong-shaped roots about 8 inches long; their flesh is slightly pungent.

Daikons Native to Asia, these are very large carrot-shaped radishes (up to 18 inches long and

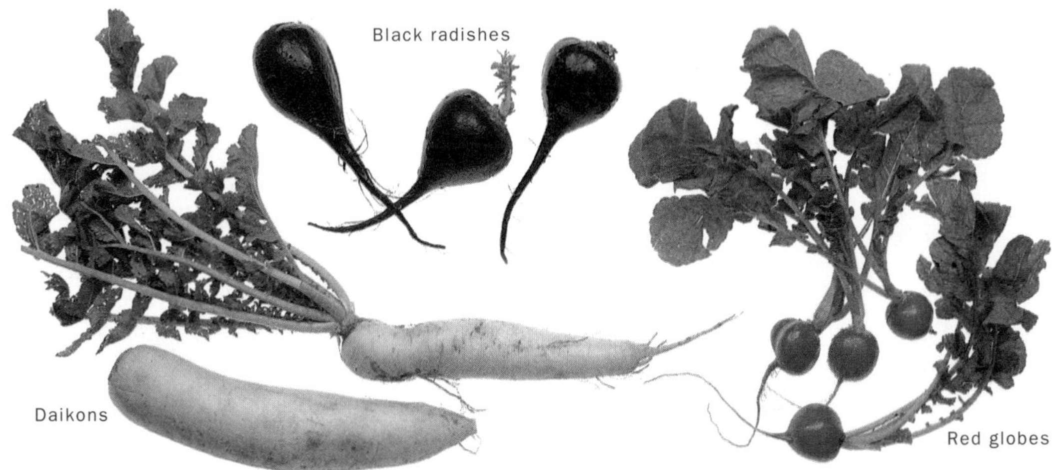

weighing 1 to 2 pounds). Also called Japanese or oriental radishes, domestic daikons have a white flesh that is juicy and a bit hotter than that of red radishes but milder than that of black ones.

Red globe Americans are probably most familiar with these small round or oval-shaped "button" red radishes. They range from about 1 to 4 inches in diameter and have solid, crisp flesh.

White icicles Long (up to half a foot) and tapered, these have a white flesh that is milder than that of red radishes.

AVAILABILITY Red and white radishes are sold year round; their supplies are most plentiful during the spring months. The biggest crops come from California and Florida, but most states grow them. Black radishes, which have a longer shelf life, are at their peak in winter and early spring. Daikons are most flavorful in fall and winter.

SHOPPING TIPS Although red globe radishes can grow to 4 or 5 inches in diameter, the ones you'll find in the produce bin will probably be closer to the size of a ping-pong ball—about 1 to 1½ inches in diameter. Much larger than that, red radishes are likely to be pithy. Radishes with their leaves intact are usually tied in bunches, while topped radishes are sold in plastic bags. If the leaves are attached, they should be crisp and green. Look for well-shaped radishes with good color. Whether red or white, the roots should be hard and solid, with a smooth, unblemished surface. Check bagged radishes to make sure they are free of mold.

Black radishes (often sold in Russian or Polish neighborhoods) should be solid, heavy, and free of cracks. Daikons, found at Asian markets and many supermarkets, should be evenly shaped and firm, with a glossy, almost translucent sheen.

STORAGE If you've bought radishes with their leaves attached, remove the tops unless you'll be serving them the same day (leaf-topped radishes are handsome on a crudité platter). Radishes will not keep as well with their tops left on. The leaves, if fresh and green, can be cooked like other greens or used in soups. Place radishes in plastic bags if they are not already packaged. Both red radishes and daikons will keep for up to two weeks in the refrigerator. Black radishes can be stored for months if they remain dry; store them in perforated plastic bags in the refrigerator.

PREPARATION Scrub the radishes and trim off the stem end and tip. Since it is their skin that contains most of the enzymes that form the mustard oils responsible for their pungency, you may want to peel the radishes. However, red globe and white icicle radishes are rarely hot enough to warrant paring (and it's a shame to remove the globes' cherry red skin). Daikons have a very thin skin that can be removed with a vegetable peeler, if you wish. Black radishes should be well scrubbed; whether you peel them or not depends on the thickness of the skin. If it is thin, leave it on; the dark color provides a striking contrast with the white flesh.

HORSERADISH

A relative of the radish, horseradish is a large cylindrical root with thin, light brown skin and white flesh. The root is commonly grated and eaten raw as a condiment. Though its pungency complements meat, poultry, and vegetables, it is used far less often than mustard or ketchup. The strong bite of horseradish (it is also known as German mustard) comes from mustard oils that form when the vegetable's tissues are cut. Like other radishes, horseradish is a cruciferous vegetable, and so may have cancer-protecting properties. It's also a good source of vitamin C. Usually, however, it is eaten in small quantities.

Commercially prepared horseradish is bottled with vinegar and salt; the sodium content, though, is fairly low. Red horseradish also has beet juice added. Alternatively, you can buy fresh horseradish and make your own condiment (be advised that fresh horseradish is considerably more pungent than prepared versions). It is most widely available in the spring (to coincide with the Jewish holiday of Passover, when it is used as part of the celebratory meal). Choose firm roots with no soft spots; they will keep in the refrigerator for up to a week when stored in a plastic bag. Before grating the roots, scrub them and scrape away the outer skin.

While homemade or bottled horseradish has virtually no fat, the store-bought sauce contains mayonnaise and, therefore, is high in fat and calories. For a healthier spread, blend horseradish with yogurt or stir it into applesauce, to make a traditional Austrian accompaniment to meat.

Small radishes can be served whole, raw, or cooked; black radishes and daikons, which are larger and sharper, are usually cut up or grated.

Boiling Cooked black radishes can be eaten like turnips. When serving them as dippers or in salads, boil them until barely tender. The heat will tame their rather harsh flavor. Wash and trim them before; peel if desired (or peel off thin strips of the skin to make a striking black-and-white pattern). For red globes, boil ½ inch of water, then add the sliced radishes, cover and simmer until tender, adding more water if neccessary. *Cooking times:* for black radishes, 15 to 30 minutes; for red globes, 5 to 10 minutes.

Microwaving Place ½ pound of sliced radishes in a microwavable dish with 1 tablespoon of water or broth. Cover and cook until tender. *Cooking time:* 4 minutes.

Steaming People who find raw radishes too sharp may enjoy the milder taste of steamed radishes, served as an edible garnish or a vegetable side dish. The flesh of steamed red radishes will turn pink. Place whole radishes in a vegetable steamer and cook over boiling water until barely tender. Shredded daikon can also be steamed, alone or with shredded carrots, then dressed with a vinaigrette. *Cooking times:* for whole radishes in a steamer, 8 to 12 minutes; for shredded daikon, 5 minutes.

Stir-frying Sliced radishes or thin strips of daikon combine well with other vegetables and meat in stir-fries. Be careful not to overcook the radishes so that they retain most of their crispness. *Cooking time:* 3 to 5 minutes.

SERVING SUGGESTIONS Whole red radishes make an ideal edible garnish, whether trimmed, with their tops on, or carved into "roses." Radish slices, with their crisp white interior and scarlet edge, bring color and flavor to a tossed salad or crudité platter. Raw red or white radishes, or daikons, can be served in many of the same ways as cucumbers (see page 90); yogurt dressings and sweet-and-sour marinades make excellent radish accompaniments.

Combine grated daikon and carrots (raw or

RADISHES 3½ oz raw (1 cup sliced)			
Calories	17	Fat	<1 g
Protein	1 g	Saturated Fat	<1 g
Carbohydrate	4 g	Cholesterol	0 mg
Dietary Fiber	Low	Sodium	24 mg

KEY NUTRIENTS		% RDA Men	% RDA Women
Vitamin C	23 mg	38%	38%
Folacin	27 mcg	14%	15%

S=40% or more soluble N/A=Not Applicable N=Not Available

steamed) for an attractive slaw, using a dressing made with a small amount of dark sesame oil; sprinkle the salad with sesame seeds and fresh coriander. Toss finely sliced radishes or daikon with orange sections and a little lemon juice and salt. In Japan, finely chopped or grated daikon is used as a condiment; serve with broiled fish or chicken, or mix it with yogurt or lemon juice to make a zesty salad dressing.

Whole radishes can also be steamed and then glazed with orange juice, like carrots. Or, try simmering daikon slices in stock. You can also substitute radishes for turnips in many recipes; depending on the type you choose, the flavor will range from mild to hot. Like turnips, daikon can be used to flavor vegetable soups and stews: Cut it into good-sized chunks and cook just until crisp-tender. They offer contrast with the more tender carrots or potatoes. If you are looking for a simple way to enliven chicken or beef broth, just add julienne strips or thinly sliced radishes during the last 10 minutes of cooking time.

Radishes that mature in the hot summer months are likely to have more of a bite than those harvested in the cooler spring or fall months.

Although black radishes are too strongly flavored to eat by themselves, if you shred them or slice them thin they will provide a spicy accent to slaws and salads.

Scallions

Though they look like skinny leeks (an onion relative), scallions are true onions—just very immature ones. Mature dry onions are allowed to grow a well-developed bulb, but scallions are pulled from the ground while their tops are still green and before a significant bulb has formed. (Strictly speaking, scallions are bulbless, while green onions are harvested at the miniature bulb stage. But from a consumer's viewpoint, the two types are nearly identical.) Like their dry-skinned counterparts, scallions can be eaten cooked or raw, and are valued for their savory flavor, which is characteristically milder than that of many other onions. (In some countries, such as China, scallions are the most popular form of onion.) Nutritionally, they have a distinct advantage over other onions: Their green tops, which can be enjoyed along with the white part, provide about five times more vitamin C, ounce for ounce, than full grown onions.

AVAILABILITY Scallions are readily available year round, with quantities peaking somewhat in the early summer. The biggest suppliers are California, Arizona, New Jersey, and Texas, but scallions are grown in more than thirty states.

SHOPPING TIPS Look for green, crisp tops and clean, white bottoms. As a rule, the more slender the bottoms are, the sweeter the scallions.

STORAGE Compared to dry onions, scallions are quite perishable: Store them in the refrigerator in a tightly closed plastic bag and use them within three days; otherwise, the tops begin to wilt.

Chives are also a member of the onion family; like scallions, they bear hollow green shoots—though these are much thinner and more grasslike than the green tops on scallions. No usable bulb is formed, so only the green portion is used, usually as a seasoning or garnish.

PREPARATION First, cut away any wilted parts from the green ends and trim off the tip of the white root. Both the white and green portions can be used as seasonings or salad ingredients, sliced or chopped, according to the size you need.

SERVING SUGGESTIONS Scallions are used primarily to enhance foods. They have an oniony flavor that's not overly assertive (though the flavor of raw scallions becomes stronger if a prepared dish is left to stand for any length of time). The chopped greens can be substituted for chives in most dishes, should the latter be unavailable. For example, add coarsely chopped scallions to garnish tuna or potato salad, or stir them into low-fat cottage cheese to create a flavorful, low-calorie toast or bagel spread. Finely chopped scallions blended into low-fat cream cheese or nonfat plain yogurt also make an excellent dip for raw vegetables.

For a savory touch, you can mix scallions with freshly cooked rice or other grains; chopped, the bright, fresh-tasting greens are a wonderful seasoning for tomato-sauced pasta dishes, soups, and omelettes. Or, try preparing an old-fashioned Irish dish called "champ," which is a combination of potatoes and scallions—in roughly a three-to-one ratio. Boil the potatoes, then cut up the scallions and simmer in milk (use low-fat or skim milk). Mash the two ingredients together until the mixture is uniformly green and savory.

Because they cook quickly, scallions work particularly well in stir-fry dishes. Trim off the leaves at the thicker portion near the white end and slice the scallions on the diagonal into 1-inch lengths; then cook until just crisp-tender—no more than 4 to 5 minutes. Plump scallions can also be braised like leeks and served as a side dish.

SCALLIONS 3½ oz raw (1 cup chopped)

Calories	32	Fat	<1 g
Protein	2 g	Saturated Fat	<1 g
Carbohydrate	7 g	Cholesterol	0 mg
Dietary Fiber	Low	Sodium	16 mg

KEY NUTRIENTS		%RDA Men	%RDA Women
Vitamin A	385 IU	8%	10%
Vitamin C	19 mg	32%	32%
Folacin	64 mcg	32%	36%
Iron	1 mg	10%	7%

S=40% or more soluble N/A=Not Applicable N=Not Available

Spinach

Make no mistake about it, spinach is good for you. It is exceptionally high in beta carotene and is rich in other vitamins and minerals, particularly folacin; it also contains more protein than most vegetables. (Although the protein is incomplete—spinach and other leafy green vegetables are low in the amino acid methionine—it is complemented by the protein in cereal grains.) However, spinach is not the body builder many people may think it is (thanks, in large part, to the cartoon character Popeye). The vegetable is not a miracle food and eating a lot of it (or any other food) won't make anyone stronger. In fact, some of the minerals spinach is highest in—iron and calcium in particular—cannot be completely used by the body because the vegetable also contains a chemical called oxalic acid that, when combined with these minerals, limits their absorption by the body. Hence, as a vegetarian source for iron and calcium, there are better choices than spinach—turnip greens and broccoli, for example, have significantly more available mineral content.

Spinach's value stems from its other nutrients, and from the fact that it tastes good raw or cooked. It can be served in salads, in soups, as a bed for meat and fish dishes, in combination with other vegetables, or as a side dish on its own. No one knows when the vegetable was first cultivated in the United States, but seed catalogues from 1806 mention three varieties. By the nineteenth century, spinach was an established part of the national cuisine, though not necessarily a favorite dish, since cooks customarily boiled it to a flavorless, gray-green mush. Fortunately, more appealing ways of preparing spinach, and the recognition that it can blend well with other foods, have made this vegetable more widely appreciated.

Although frozen spinach may be less flavorful than cooked fresh spinach, the unsauced frozen form is an acceptable substitute in cooked dishes, and it can undeniably save a great deal of time in preparation.

VARIETIES There are three basic types of spinach. Savoy has crinkly, curly leaves with a dark green color; it is the type sold in fresh bunches at most markets. Flat or smooth-leaf spinach has unwrinkled, spade-shaped leaves that are easier to clean than savoy; varieties of this type are generally used for canned and frozen spinach as well as soups, baby foods, and other processed foods. Increasingly popular are semi-savoy varieties, which have slightly crinkled leaves. These offer some of the texture of savoy, but are not as difficult to clean; they are cultivated for both the fresh market and for processing.

AVAILABILITY Fresh spinach is readily available all year. The major suppliers are California and Texas, where spinach grows best during the mild winter months.

SHOPPING TIPS Fresh spinach is sold both loose and in bags, which usually hold about 10 ounces.

Spinach

Loose spinach is easier to evaluate for quality, since you can examine each leaf individually. Select small spinach leaves with good green color and a crisp, springy texture; reject wilted, crushed, or bruised leaves, and those with yellow spots or insect damage. Fresh spinach should smell sweet, never sour or musty. Look for stems that are fairly thin; coarse, thick ones indicate overgrown spinach, which may be leathery and bitter. In addition, thick stems mean more waste for the consumer, who is paying for the vegetable by the pound.

IS SPINACH A GOOD SOURCE OF IRON?

Spinach (as well as related foods such as beet greens and Swiss chard) contains a chemical called oxalic acid, which combines with the iron and calcium in spinach, limiting the amount of these minerals the body can absorb. As a result, roughly 53 percent of the iron and only 5 percent of the apparently rich supply of calcium remain available as a usable nutrient, though how much of these minerals an individual will absorb depends on many factors, such as the amount of fiber in the diet and the person's need for a particular nutrient. This effect of oxalic acid has led to claims that eating moderate amounts of spinach interferes with the absorption of calcium generally, not only from spinach but from any other calcium-containing foods you eat during the day. However, various studies indicate that an individual would have to eat a massive amount of spinach for any interference from oxalic acid to become a serious nutritional problem.

Loose spinach usually does have more stem on it than bagged, but the latter also needs to be stemmed. Despite having gone through a preliminary washing prior to being packaged, bagged spinach still must be carefully rinsed to clean away sand and grit. And if you choose loose spinach carefully, you'll make up in quality what little you sacrifice in convenience. If only bagged spinach is available where you shop, check whether the contents seem resilient when you squeeze the bag.

STORAGE Leave packaged spinach in its cellophane bag, or pack it loosely in a plastic bag and store in the refrigerator crisper. Fresh spinach will keep for three to four days.

PREPARATION A bit of grit in a bowl of raw or cooked spinach has probably deterred many a would-be spinach lover. Fresh spinach—especially the curly savoy type—requires careful washing. (Don't, however, wash spinach before storing it for any length of time: After a day or so, it will begin to wilt and decay.) Trim off any roots, separate the leaves, and drop them into a large bowl of cool water; agitate them gently with your hands. Lift out the leaves, letting the sand and grit settle, then empty and refill the bowl and repeat the process until the leaves are clean. Pinch off the stems and also the midribs (the part of the stem that extends into the leaf), if they are thick and tough. You can easily stem spinach by folding each leaf in half, vein-side out, and pulling up on the stem as you hold the folded leaf closed.

If you want very crisp spinach for a salad, dry it in a salad spinner or shake it dry in a colander, then wrap it in paper towels and refrigerate for no longer than a few hours. Spinach that is to be cooked need not be dried; in fact, there is usually just enough water clinging to freshly washed leaves so that they can be steamed without additional cooking liquid.

If the leaves are small, leave them whole; tear larger leaves into smaller pieces for salad, or chop them for cooking.

Blanching To quick-cook spinach, or to prepare it for sautéing, braising, or stuffing, drop the leaves into a large pot of boiling water and cook just until wilted. Drain and squeeze out excess moisture (cool under cold water if not serving immediately or continuing with another cooking process). *Cooking time:* 2 to 5 minutes.

Microwaving This method is a good substitute for blanching, as a preliminary step before sautéing or braising greens. Place ½ pound of spinach (washed but not dried) in a microwavable dish; cover loosely and cook until tender. *Cooking time:* 4 to 7 minutes.

ANOTHER TYPE OF SPINACH

In many markets today you will find New Zealand spinach for sale. Is it a new variety? Actually, it's not a true spinach, but a member of a different botanical family. Native to New Zealand, Australia, and Japan, it is now grown in many parts of the world where warm weather prevails. It has a less astringent taste than spinach and is good eaten raw in salads. Nutritionally, it is comparable to spinach in its vitamin C content, but contains slightly less beta carotene, providing 2 milligrams in 3½ ounces, raw. Like spinach, however, New Zealand spinach contains oxalic acid, which makes its calcium and iron less available for absorption by the body.

Sautéing If the spinach is blanched first, it can be sautéed quickly in a small amount of oil. If you use a nonstick pan, one teaspoon of oil should be sufficient for 3 cups of chopped spinach. In addition, spinach can be sautéed in stock, if you are careful to stir and toss the leaves constantly; be prepared to add more stock to the pan as it evaporates. *Cooking time:* 3 to 15 minutes.

Steaming Wash, but do not dry, the spinach, allowing some moisture to lightly cling to the leaves. *Cooking time:* 5 to 10 minutes.

SERVING SUGGESTIONS Spinach salad—traditionally made with bacon and hard-boiled eggs—has become an American classic. For a healthier salad, omit the bacon and eggs, and substitute sliced mushrooms or other vegetables that have already been sautéed in the dressing you plan to use for the salad. The vegetables and dressing can be added while warm, for a slightly "wilted" salad, or chilled first, then tossed with the leaves for a crisp salad. Thin slices of red onion or orange or grapefruit sections will provide color and texture, as will thin slices of steamed cauliflower, tomato quarters, slivered red bell pepper, or marinated green, wax, or shell beans.

SPINACH 3½ oz raw (2 cups chopped)

Calories	22	Fat	<1 g
Protein	3 g	Saturated Fat	<1 g
Carbohydrate	4 g	Cholesterol	0 g
Dietary Fiber	Low	Sodium	79 mg

KEY NUTRIENTS		% RDA Men	% RDA Women
Vitamin A	6715 IU	134%	168%
Vitamin B_6	0.2 mg	10%	12%
Beta Carotene	4 mg	N/A	N/A
Vitamin C	28 mg	47%	47%
Calcium	99 mg	12%	12%
Vitamin E	2 mg	20%	25%
Folacin	194 mcg	97%	108%
Iron	3 mg	30%	20%
Magnesium	79 mg	26%	28%
Manganese	0.9 mg	N/A	N/A
Potassium	558 mg	N/A	N/A
Riboflavin	0.2 mg	12%	15%

S=40% or more soluble N/A=Not Applicable N=Not Available

Serve cooked spinach whole, chop it by hand, or purée it in a food processor or blender (squeeze it dry before puréeing). Cooked spinach is even more appetizing, seasoned with lemon juice and zest, or vinegar, soy sauce, horseradish, sautéed garlic, or a sprinkling of nutmeg. Stir yogurt into chopped or puréed spinach for a low-fat version of "creamed" spinach, or flavor the spinach with tomato sauce. These mixtures can also be used as a filling for mushroom caps or a topping for baked potatoes.

Spinach soufflé may sound healthy, but when it is made with whole milk, butter, eggs, and Gruyère or Parmesan cheese (the common ingredients), the result is a high-fat dish. A 3½-ounce serving (about ¾ cup) gets 75 percent of its calories from fat and supplies 135 milligrams of cholesterol.

As a side dish, try steaming spinach, then stir-frying it along with garlic, onion, and chopped red bell pepper. Use blanched spinach leaves as wrappers for soft light fillings, such as cooked mushrooms.

Cooked spinach can be fashioned into a bed for fish fillets or chicken breasts: Steam the spinach (and stir-fry, if desired), steam or poach the fish or chicken, then arrange the spinach on the bottom of a baking dish and place the fish or chicken on top. Sprinkle with breadcrumbs and grated Parmesan, and broil until browned. You can also add spinach leaves to vegetable soups or broth just before serving, so they barely wilt. Or, stir chopped spinach (frozen can be substituted) into cooked rice.

For a variation on a traditional Japanese salad, squeeze blanched spinach leaves dry, chop them, and toss with a dressing made of soy sauce, dark sesame oil, and a pinch of sugar; sprinkle with toasted sesame seeds.

Sprouts

Sprouts have arrived. People may still joke about them as typifying "health" foods, but over the past decade these crisp tendrils have become a common sight at salad bars and in the produce sections of supermarkets. Their culinary appeal—long appreciated in Asian countries—lies in the refined crunchiness they add to dishes, backed up by a fresh, delicate flavor that can be enjoyed whether the sprouts are cooked or eaten raw. At the same time, sprouts continue to be touted as a wonder food that contains concentrated sources of essential nutrients. Do they live up to their reputation?

Probably the most familiar sprouts are those of alfalfa and mung bean seeds, but many food plants—ranging from lentil and soybean to watercress, radish, sunflower, and mustard—have seeds that, when moistened, will germinate to yield edible shoots. This growth from seed to sprout is accompanied by changes in nutritional value. Most of the carbohydrate and fat in the seed is utilized for growth. Water content increases dramatically, as does the concentration of vitamin C (by 300 to 500 percent). However, since the vitamin C content of seeds is relatively low, the increase makes sprouts a good but not out-

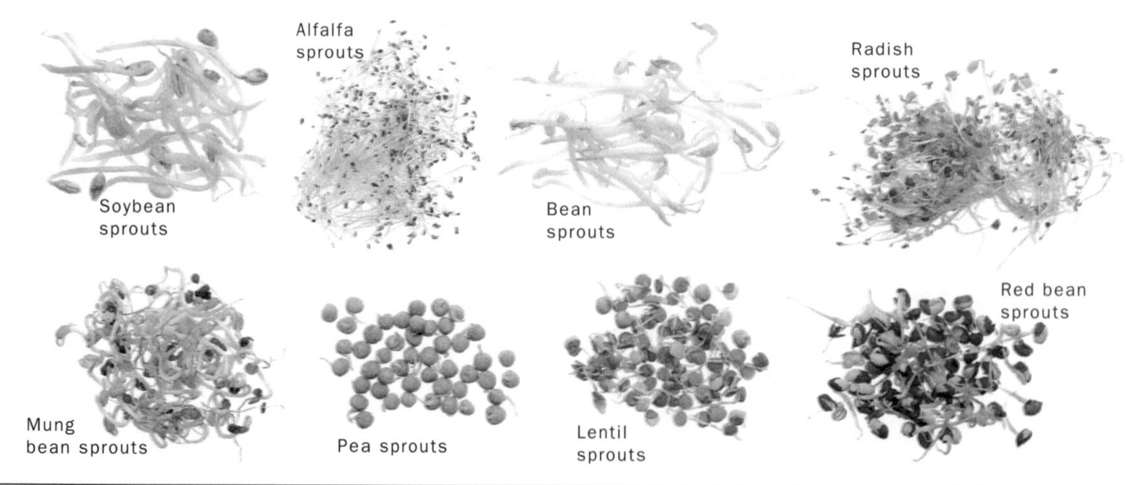

GROWING YOUR OWN SPROUTS

Growing sprouts is not difficult. Almost any seed or bean can be sprouted; just make sure the ones you choose are intended to be eaten. (Seeds to be planted are often treated with fungicides.) In addition to the familiar alfalfa, mung bean, and radish sprouts, try other seeds, grains, and beans for variety. For instance, sunflower seeds, lentils, buckwheat, mustard seed, and Chinese cabbage seed work well.

1. Rinse the beans, seeds, or grains thoroughly and place them in a clean quart-sized glass jar. (A quart jar is large enough to accommodate the sprouts from ⅓ cup of most seeds, beans, or grains.) Fill the jar three-quarters full with tepid water. Cover the mouth of the jar with cheesecloth and secure with a heavy rubber band. Soak, unrefrigerated, overnight.

2. Next morning, drain the beans, seeds, or grains well and rinse with fresh water. Drain well once again, and place the jar lying on its side in a dark area.

3. Rinse and drain the beans, seeds, or grains twice a day, returning the jar to the dark place after each rinsing. Sprouting times vary, but most are ready in two to three days. To turn the sprouts green, place them in indirect sunlight on the last growing day.

standing source of this vitamin compared to most other vegetables. The same process holds true for other nutrients. Sprouts provide some B vitamins and iron, but their overall mineral content is modest. And while some sprouts do contain exceptional amounts of beta carotene—sprouted oats, for example—others have very little.

What happens to protein when a seed germinates is somewhat more complicated. While the protein content remains relatively the same when you compare a sprout to the seed it came from, *by weight* a sprout contributes less protein than the seed since much of its weight is water. For example, 3½ ounces of raw mung bean sprouts (about one cup) provide 5 percent of the RDA for protein for the average man and 6 percent for the average woman, as compared to 13 percent of the protein RDA for men and 16 percent for women in the same amount of beans.

But if sprouts aren't nutritional superstars, they, nevertheless, are a filling, low-calorie food (due to their high water content) that will provide a wholesome and delicious component to your diet. Because they are young—just a few days from the seed stage—sprouts always taste tender and sweet. They have another distinctive feature: You can grow them yourself at any time of the year.

VARIETIES Each kind of sprout has its own shape, taste, and texture. Here are some of the more common types you're likely to find at supermarkets or greengrocers:

Adzuki bean These very sweet lentil-shaped beans form fine, grasslike sprouts, with a nutty taste and texture. Add them to stir-fries or eat them raw.

Alfalfa These threadlike white sprouts, with tiny green tops and a mild, nutty flavor, are a favorite in salads and sandwiches. They are often shipped in the containers in which they have been grown, and then are packaged in plastic bags or boxes by distributors.

Clover An alfalfa sprout look-alike, most clover sprouts are produced from red clover; these tiny seeds resemble poppy seeds.

Daikon radish Often marketed as "kaiware," these upright sprouts have silky stems, leafy tops, and a peppery-hot taste. They add tang to salads, sandwiches, and cooked dishes.

Mung bean Larger and crunchier than alfalfas, with a blander flavor, these thick white sprouts are a staple in oriental dishes and are excellent in stir-fries, soups, and salads.

Soybean More strongly flavored than mung bean sprouts, and a rich source of protein, soy

COMPARING SPROUTS (1 cup raw)

TYPE	Weight (grams)	Calories	Protein (g)	Vitamin C (mg)	Niacin (mg)	Folacin (mcg)	Riboflavin (mg)
Alfalfa	33	10	1	3	0.2	12	0.04
Kidney bean	184	53	8	71	5	108	0.5
Mung bean	104	31	3	14	0.8	63	0.1
Navy bean	104	70	6	20	1	137	0.2
Radish	38	16	1	11	1	36	0.03
Wheat	108	214	8	3	3	41	0.2

bean sprouts are used in salads and casseroles. Soybean sprouts contain small amounts of toxins that can be harmful, if eaten in large quantities. To prevent complications, cook sprouts for at least five minutes. If you consume them infrequently, there's no need to cook them.

Sunflower These are mildly flavored, like alfalfas, but much crunchier.

AVAILABILITY Since sprouts grow indoors hydroponically—that is, in water—they are available year-round.

SHOPPING TIPS The best way to get ultrafresh sprouts is to grow your own. It's not difficult, however, to tell whether those you find in your market are in prime condition. Sprouts are sold loose (sometimes immersed in water), in plastic bags, or in clear plastic boxes (often containing the pad of absorbent material on which the seeds were sprouted). In each case, you can clearly see and evaluate the quality of the sprouts. They should be moist and crisp, and should look and smell clean; watch out for sliminess, discoloration, mold, or a sour smell. The shorter the sprout, the younger it is, and thus the more tender it will be.

Mung bean sprouts may have their split seed cases still attached; these will wash away when you rinse the sprouts. If you buy mung bean sprouts from an open, water-filled container (as they are displayed in many Asian markets), be sure that a serving implement is provided and that the sprouts are not scooped out by hand.

STORAGE Refrigerate sprouts in the container or loosely packed in plastic bags; tightly packed sprouts will be crushed and begin to decay quickly. Do not wash them before storing; plan to keep bagged sprouts for no more than three days. Boxed sprouts will stay for four to five days; snip the sprouts as needed, leaving the tangle of roots in the box. Check your stored sprouts frequently and be sure to remove any that have become slimy or discolored.

PREPARATION Sprouts sealed in plastic bags or boxes are sold clean and need no additional washing. Those that are available in bulk, however, may need to be rinsed before using. Any that seem slightly wilted can be revived by a 10-minute soaking in ice water; pat them dry with paper towels before using. Rinse mung bean sprouts in a bowl of water, stirring them gently with your hand, and discard the seed casings, which will float to the top.

Drain canned mung bean sprouts and rinse them in cold water to remove some of the sodium in the packing liquid and to freshen their flavor.

Slender leafy sprouts, such as alfalfa and radish sprouts, are tastiest when eaten raw, but sturdy mung bean sprouts are also delicious stir-fried for 2 to 3 minutes. The finer sprouts can be used in stir-fries, but should not be added until the last

30 seconds of cooking time. The brief heating will help to preserve their crispness.

SERVING SUGGESTIONS Sprouts make an unusual edible garnish as well as a crunchy addition to any green salad; they can also be substituted for watercress in many recipes. To avoid having tiny sprouts practically disappear in leafy tossed salads, pinch off bunches of sprouts and scatter them over the salad just before serving.

The fine texture of grated salads and slaws marries well with any type of sprout: Try mixing sweet and hot varieties for a more interesting flavor. Tiny sprouts, such as alfalfa or radish, are best when they are not overwhelmed by heavy, strong-flavored dressings; however, tart, citrusy flavors, as well as those containing ginger and sesame, complement them nicely. Mung beans are particularly good when tossed with a zesty soy sauce-based dressing.

Use a handful of feathery sprouts as a bed on which to serve hot or cold cooked foods or hearty salads, or include spicy sprouts in cheese or chicken sandwiches. Prepare a California favorite: Arrange sliced avocado and sprouts on whole-grain bread. Or, tuck sprouts into pita pockets with a vegetable or hummus filling. For a finishing touch, toss sprouts into broths or soups just before serving, or sprinkle them over casseroles after baking.

Stir-fry mung bean sprouts with summer squash, scallions, soy sauce, and ginger.

While any bean can be sprouted, alfalfa and mung bean sprouts are the most common commercially sold types.

MUNG BEAN SPROUTS 3½ oz raw (1 cup)

Calories	30	Fat	<1 g
Protein	3 g	Saturated Fat	<1 g
Carbohydrate	6 g	Cholesterol	0 mg
Dietary Fiber	Low	Sodium	6 mg

KEY NUTRIENTS		% RDA Men	% RDA Women
Vitamin C	13 mg	22%	22%
Copper	0.2 mg	N/A	N/A
Folacin	61 mcg	31%	34%

S=40% or more soluble N/A=Not Applicable N=Not Available

ALFALFA SPROUTS 3½ oz raw (3 cups)

Calories	29	Fat	1 g
Protein	4 g	Saturated Fat	1 g
Carbohydrate	4 g	Cholesterol	0 mg
Dietary Fiber	Low	Sodium	6 mg

KEY NUTRIENTS		% RDA Men	% RDA Women
Vitamin C	8 mg	13%	13%
Copper	0.2 mg	N/A	N/A
Folacin	36 mcg	18%	20%
Iron	1 mg	10%	6%
Magnesium	27 mg	8%	10%
Manganese	0,2 mg	N/A	N/A

S=40% or more soluble N/A=Not Applicable N=Not Available

Squash (Summer)

Squashes are gourds—fleshy vegetables protected by a rind—that belong to the Cucurbitaceae family, which also includes melons and cucumbers. Although some grow on vines and others on bushes, all are commonly divided into one of two main groups, summer squashes and winter squashes. Once considered seasonal vegetables, today both types can be found in markets throughout much of the year. A more accurate distinction between the two is that summer squashes, with their soft shells and tender, light-colored flesh, are picked while immature; winter squashes, with their hard shells and darker, tougher flesh and seeds, are not harvested until maturity.

Like corn and beans, squash is a notably American food. It sustained Native Americans for some five thousand years and then helped nourish the early European settlers, who quickly made the vegetable a mainstay of their diet. New England colonists adapted the word *squash* from several Native American names for the vegetable, all of which meant "something eaten raw" (presumably referring to summer squashes, though both Native Americans and colonists also ate squash cooked.) Two former presidents, George Washington and Thomas Jefferson, were enthusiastic squash growers. In the nineteenth century, merchant seamen returned from other parts of the Americas with many new varieties; squashes continue to be available in a great assortment of sizes, shapes, and colors, such as white, yellow, orange, green-brown, gray, and even light blue.

Summer squashes—which are designated botanically as *Cucurbita pepo*—are more than 95 percent water, and so offer only a moderate amount of nutrients. The high water content, however, means that they are very low in calories (about 19 per cup of raw sliced squash). In addition, they are inexpensive and can be eaten raw or cooked. Their mild, refreshing flavor and satisfying texture make them suitable for inclusion in many different dishes.

VARIETIES The most popular summer squash in the United States is the familiar and prolific green zucchini—entire cookbooks have been devoted to it. But it is only one among several common types of summer squash, which vary mainly in shape and color. All are similar enough in flavor and texture to be interchangeable in recipes.

Chayote Although best known in the South and Southwest, chayote (chy-*o*-tay, to rhyme with coyote) is becoming increasingly popular elsewhere in the country. This pale or dark green (or white) pear-shaped summer squash is also called mirliton, vegetable pear, and christophene. Unlike other summer squashes, it has a large, central seed and a fairly thick, deeply ridged skin. It also requires a longer cooking time.

Patty pan (also called cymling or scallop) This greenish white, disk-shaped squash is convex at both its top and bottom, with a scalloped edge. Its flesh is white and quite succulent. Yellow patty pan squash (such as Sunburst) is similar but more cup-shaped; scallopini is the name of a smaller green-scalloped version.

Yellow crookneck This squash tapers from a bulbous blossom end to a curved, narrow stem end. Its pale yellow skin has a slightly pebbled texture and its flesh is yellow.

Yellow straightneck Almost a twin of crookneck, this squash forms a tapering cylinder without a curved neck. Its skin may be pebbled like crookneck's, or smooth, while the flesh is paler.

Zucchini The shape of a zucchini resembles a lightly ridged cucumber; its skin is medium to deep green, with paler flecks or stripes. Golden zucchini, such as Gold Rush, is about the same size and shape, but has a deep golden yellow skin and a dark green stem; its flavor is sweeter than that of green zucchini. Another variety known as

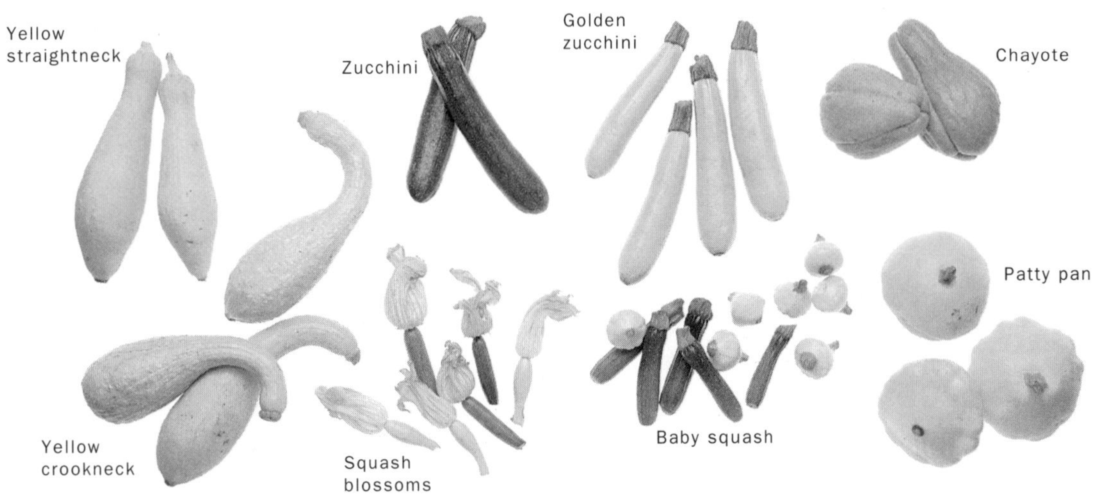

Italian squash, or cocozelle, is shorter and blunter, with striped skin.

AVAILABILITY Summer squash is most plentiful from May to August, but it is generally available year-round. Chayote's peak season runs from October through April.

SQUASH BLOSSOMS

Yellow-orange flowers appear first on the vines that produce squash. These blossoms are not only edible but are considered a delicacy by many. They are also very low in calories and a good source of beta carotene, vitamin C and potassium.

Although the flowers of any type of squash can be eaten (their flavor faintly resembles that of squash), the most frequently consumed are zucchini blossoms. Unfortunately, they are usually served battered and deep fried, which adds fat and calories. More healthful ways of preparing them include: sautéed in a small amount of oil, stuffed with a low-fat filling and then briefly sautéed, or steamed lightly.

SHOPPING TIPS Summer squashes can grow quite large (home gardeners often discover baseball-bat-sized zucchini hidden under the plant's large leaves), but when allowed to do so, they have coarse, stringy flesh and large seeds. They taste best when small- to medium-sized—not more than 7 inches long (patty pan squash should be no more than 4 inches across). Choose squashes that are also firm and fairly heavy for their size; otherwise, they may be dry and cottony within. Farmers' markets and greengrocers sometimes offer baby summer squashes, just 1 to 2 inches long; these are particularly tender and sweet.

The skin of summer squashes is thin and fragile—delicate enough to puncture with a fingernail. Unfortunately, some shoppers do just this—they prick the skin to test for tenderness, leaving the squash susceptible to decay. Look for squashes with sound, glossy exteriors; avoid those with skins showing nicks, pits, bruises, or soft spots. The squashes should be plump (not shriveled), the stem ends fresh and green. Color should be uniform and bright.

STORAGE Place summer squash in plastic bags and store in the refrigerator crisper. It should keep for up to a week. Thicker-skinned chayote will stay for two weeks or longer.

PREPARATION Wash squash well and trim the ends. Summer squash need not be peeled or seeded unless it is oversized and has a thick skin or large seeds. Chayote is the exception; unless it is very small, the skin is quite tough. Peel it with a vegetable peeler, using a sharp paring knife to remove the skin from the deep ridges. If cooking chayote whole, you can slip off the skin after cooking. When peeled, chayote exudes a sticky liquid that may burn or even numb the skin, so peel the vegetable under cold running water. Halve the chayote and remove the seed; it can be cooked with the squash, as it has a pleasant almondlike flavor.

To get the beta carotene value from summer squashes, you must eat them with their skins; the flesh has no beta carotene.

Squash can be prepared in various ways when used as a side dish or added to other recipes. For example, zucchini or yellow straightneck can be easily cut into julienne strips, or, if first halved lengthwise, cut into near half-round slices. You can also make squash "boats" to hold a filling—slice cylindrical squash and chayote in half lengthwise, then scoop out the seeds and some of the pulp, leaving a shell. To stuff patty pan squash, cut a small "lid" from the top, then scoop out some of the flesh. A melon baller works well for this purpose.

Because squash is mostly water, it will exude a lot of liquid during cooking. If you want to prevent a cooked dish containing the vegetable from becoming "waterlogged," salt the squash before heating it. Follow the procedure given for salting eggplant on page 92, rinsing and draining the squash well after salting. Blanching is as effective as salting, and is recommended for anyone on a sodium-restricted diet. Drop whole squash into boiling water and cook for 2 to 8 minutes (depending on size), until you can easily pierce it with the tip of a sharp knife. (Chill in ice water if you are planning to cook the squash later.) Then halve, slice, or chop the squash, as required.

Baking Place squashes, whole, sliced, or halved lengthwise (for cylindrical squashes) or crosswise (for patty pan squash), in a baking pan. Add a few spoonfuls of liquid (broth, vegetable or tomato juice, or water) and cover. Flavor the squash with chopped onion and garlic and herbs, or layer it with onion slices. Or, top halved or sliced squash with breadcrumbs (or a mixture of breadcrumbs and grated hard cheese) and bake uncovered; broil after baking to crisp the topping. *Cooking time:* 30 to 35 minutes in a 350° oven.

COMPARING SUMMER SQUASH
3½ ounces raw (¾ cup sliced)

	Calories	Vitamin C (mg)
Patty pan	18	18
Yellow crookneck	19	8
Yellow straightneck	19	8
Zucchini	14	9

Boiling Use this method for larger squash: Drop whole squash into boiling water and cook until tender. To shorten their cooking time, you can also boil hollowed-out squash halves prior to baking them. *Cooking times:* for whole squash, 10 to 15 minutes; for halves, 5 minutes.

Microwaving Cut squash into ¼-inch slices, then arrange in a microwavable baking dish. Add three tablespoons of water, cover, and cook until tender. Stir the squash when halfway through. *Cooking time:* 4 to 7 minutes.

Sautéing Slices or chunks of squash (or grated squash) can be sautéed in stock or a mixture of stock and a little oil. Blanch or salt the squash first, if desired. Use a nonstick skillet, if possible, and toss frequently to keep the squash from browning. *Cooking times:* for summer squash, 3 to 6 minutes; for chayote, 6 to 8 minutes.

Steaming Summer squash can be steamed whole, sliced, or diced, in a vegetable steamer. Cut chayote into thin slices to speed cooking. *Cooking times:* for whole summer squash, 10 to 12 minutes; for halves or slices, 3 to 5 minutes; for chayote halves, 35 to 40 minutes; and for slices, 18 to 22 minutes.

Stir-frying The delicate flavor and texture of

summer squash are best preserved by stir-frying alone or with other mild-flavored vegetables, such as green beans, mushrooms, or corn. Be sure to keep stirring and tossing the slices in the skillet or wok so that they cook quickly—before they can release all their juices and turn the dish watery. *Cooking time:* 4 to 5 minutes.

SERVING SUGGESTIONS Summer squash is a vegetable whose versatility is based on its rather unassuming flavor. All summer squashes are similar in taste and texture; try cooking several varieties—green, yellow and white—together to produce a colorful dish. Then season the squash with herbs (dill, basil, thyme, mint, tarragon, parsley, marjoram, or oregano) or spices (cumin, curry powder, or black pepper).

Three and a half ounces of battered and fried zucchini sticks may have as many as 210 calories—47 percent of them coming from fat. Compare that to the 14 calories—and virtually no fat—in the same amount of raw zucchini.

Raw or steamed squash slices or sticks can be used to enhance a tossed salad; while grated raw or steamed squash can be added to a cabbage slaw or served on its own, tossed with vinaigrette and fresh herbs.

Zucchini marries well with fresh tomatoes, tomato sauce, or spaghetti sauce; such combinations make tasty toppings for pasta. Zucchini and yellow squash can be cut into narrow ribbons with a vegetable peeler; blanch, then combine them with regular or spinach fettuccine to make an attractive pasta dish. Sauté zucchini with tomatoes, red, green, and yellow bell pepper strips, onions, shallots, or garlic for an appetizing side dish.

Top halved summer squash with tomato sauce, or with a "cream sauce" made of puréed cottage cheese and herbs. Then sprinkle a little grated cheese over each half and broil or bake until the topping is hot and bubbly. Stuff summer squash "boats" with meat, seafood, vegetable, or grain fillings and bake. The squash boats, or bowls, can also be boiled until tender, then served as containers for stew or hot cooked grains; or, they can be left to cool and be used as holders for mixtures of chilled cooked vegetables. In South America, chayote is prepared like a baked apple. It is filled with raisins, nuts, and brown sugar, then baked and served as dessert.

Include summer squash in ratatouille and in other eggplant recipes (see page 94). Thread skewers with large chunks of squash and other vegetables, or alternate with turkey chunks, and broil. Add smaller chunks of squash to vegetable soups, fish chowders, or beef stews; or, combine the squash chunks with other summer produce—bell peppers, tomatoes, eggplant, corn, snap beans—in a vegetable chowder.

Well-drained, grated summer squash can be mixed in with grated potatoes to make potato pancakes, or can be cooked alone to create more delicate pancakes. These can be served with a zesty tomato sauce. Grated summer squash is often added to quick bread, muffin, and cake batter; it can also be substituted for some or all of the carrots in carrot cake.

ZUCCHINI 3½ oz raw (¾ cup sliced)

Calories	14	Fat	<1 g
Protein	1 g	Saturated Fat	<1 g
Carbohydrate	3 g	Cholesterol	0 mg
Dietary Fiber	Low	Sodium	3 mg

KEY NUTRIENTS		% RDA Men	% RDA Women
Vitamin C	9 mg	15%	15%
Folacin	22 mcg	11%	12%

S=40% or more soluble N/A=Not Applicable N=Not Available

Squash (Winter)

In contrast to the tender young summer squashes, the many varieties of winter squash are all harvested at a mature stage, when their shells (and usually their seeds) have grown hard and inedible. Because of these protective shells, winter squashes (all members of the gourd family) have a much longer storage life than their summer counterparts—some can keep for three months at home, longer in a commercial facility. Harvested in the fall, for example, they can be stored throughout the winter in a cool, dry place (which is the principal reason that colonial Americans adopted winter squashes as a staple). However, winter squashes are no longer bound to a particular season. Today, the term simply refers to hard-shelled varieties that keep well (as compared to summer squashes, such as zucchini, that do not).

The yellow or orange flesh of winter squashes is darker than that of summer varieties, and it is more nutritious, richer in complex carbohydrates and, in many cases, beta carotene. Some types—such as Hubbard and butternut—contain enough beta carotene to supply more than 100 percent of the RDA for vitamin A in a 3½-ounce serving.

Winter squashes are almost always cooked, but only the flesh is eaten—the seeds, which are high in protein and fat, are usually discarded (although some, such as pumpkin seeds, can be eaten if toasted and husked).

VARIETIES Winter squashes vary greatly in size—from small acorn squashes to Hubbards, weighing 15 pounds or more, and pumpkins that can reach 200 pounds. They also exhibit a greater array of flavors and textures than summer squashes. Still, most varieties can be substituted for one another in recipes, even in pumpkin pie. The only exception is spaghetti squash, with its uniquely textured flesh. Hundreds of varieties of winter squash are grown, though many are sold only at farm stands or specialty greengrocers. The three most popular winter squashes are acorn, butternut, and Hubbard; the others listed below are less common varieties that are becoming more widely available.

Acorn Excellent for baking, this acorn-shaped squash, which tapers at one end, measures about six inches long. Its deeply ridged skin is dark green with orange markings. A new variety, Golden Acorn, is a glowing pumpkin color; another variety, sometimes called Table Queen, is white. All have yellow-orange flesh. Unlike most other winter squashes, acorns do not contain much beta carotene. However, they are a good source of calcium: A cup of baked acorn squash (about 7 ounces) supplies 90 milligrams of calcium—11 percent of the RDA—and has just over 100 calories.

Banana This large cylindrical squash (one type weighs up to 30 pounds) has thick skin, which ranges in color from pale yellow to ivory, and a finely textured orange flesh.

Buttercup So named because of its turbanlike cap at the blossom end (opposite the stem end), buttercup has a squat shape. Its dark green skin is punctuated with lighter green stripes. The orange flesh is sweet but somewhat dry.

Butternut Weighing 2 to 4 pounds, this elongated bell-shaped squash has a tan rind; its deep orange flesh has a mildly sweet flavor. The skin is

COMPARING WINTER SQUASHES
3½ ounces raw (1 cup cubed)

	Calories	Beta Carotene (mg)	Vitamin C (mg)
Acorn	40	0.2	11
Butternut	45	5	21
Hubbard	40	3	11
Pumpkin, fresh	26	1	9
Spaghetti	33	trace	2

PREPARING SPAGHETTI SQUASH

When cooked, the flesh of spaghetti squash can be pulled apart to form slender strands that resemble spaghetti. In addition to a low calorie count—an 8-ounce serving contains only about 75 calories—spaghetti squash has a crunchy texture that makes it a particularly satisfying vegetable to eat.

Choose spaghetti squash as you would any other winter squash; it can be stored for up to two months. Spaghetti squash can be cooked whole, or halved.

•To bake whole, pierce the shell of the squash several times with a fork, then place it in a baking pan. Bake in a 350° oven for 1 hour to 1 hour and 45 minutes, or until the squash gives when squeezed (protect your hand with a potholder).

•To boil whole, pierce the squash with a fork, place it in a large pot of boiling water, and simmer, covered, for 30 to 45 minutes, or until tender when pricked.

•You can microwave a whole spaghetti squash, but be sure to pierce it with a fork several times, or it may explode. Microwave the squash for 6 to 7 minutes, then turn it over and cook for 6 to 7 minutes more; let stand for 5 minutes before serving.

•To cook squash halves (a time-saver), cut the raw squash lengthwise (not crosswise) through the middle; then, you will get the full spaghettilike length of the strands when you scoop them out. Place the halves, cut-side up, in a pot and add 2 inches of boiling water. Cover and simmer until tender, adding more water, if necessary. This method is, in effect, steaming—the water should remain below the cut edge of the squash, so that the flesh cooks by steam. You can also cook spaghetti squash halves, cut-side down, in a vegetable steamer.

When cool enough to handle, cut the squash in half crosswise if it was cooked whole. Scoop out the seeds and fibers. Then take a fork and begin to scrape at the squash flesh. As you tease it apart, the flesh will separate into pastalike strands. Continue scraping down to the shell, transferring the forkfuls of strands to a pot to keep them warm as you remove them.

Serve spaghetti squash with your favorite pasta sauce (see page 344 for some low-fat pasta toppings) or chill the crunchy strands and toss them with a light vinaigrette dressing, fresh herbs, and, perhaps, chunks of fresh tomato to make a dish similar to a light pasta salad.

softer than the acorn or Hubbard, and thus is easier to cut and prepare.

Calabaza Generally, this large squash is bright orange, but it can be found with green, yellow, or cream-colored skin. Sweet and moist when cooked, it's most often sold in portions.

Delicata Also called Bohemian squash, the 1- to 2-pound oblong delicata has cream-colored skin with stripes that vary in color from green to orange. Its flesh is yellow and sweet.

Golden Nugget This orange-skinned, mildly sweet-tasting squash resembles a miniature pumpkin. With only enough flesh for one serving, it tastes best when baked whole or in halves, like acorn squash.

Hubbard Hubbards are an old, extensive group of squashes that are usually plump in the middle and more tapered at the neck. Their bumpy skin varies in color from dark green to light blue to orange. Over the years, the popularity of Hubbards has diminished because of their size—the smallest weigh 5 pounds, the largest about 15 pounds. In the supermarket, they may be sold precut.

Spaghetti Also called vegetable spaghetti, this oval-shaped yellow squash is a relative newcomer and a novel one: When cooked, its flesh forms spaghettilike strands. It has a mild taste and crisp texture, but requires more time and care to prepare than other squashes (see box above).

Sweet Dumpling Like the Golden Nugget, this small squash serves only one person, and can

Golden Acorn
Table Queen
Pumpkin
Spaghetti
Acorn
Delicata
Banana
Turban
Sweet Dumpling
Butternut
Buttercup
Golden Nugget
Hubbard

be cooked whole. The skin is light colored, usually with dark green stripes.

Turban An orange base and bright stripes in several colors distinguish this turban-shaped squash, which is capped with a knob similar to that on buttercup squash. It is valued more for its use as a table decoration than for its taste.

Pumpkin About 99 percent of the pumpkins marketed domestically are used as jack-o'-lanterns at Halloween. But these deep orange pumpkins—most of which belong to a variety called Connecticut Field—are too stringy to eat, and often too large. (They can easily grow to 20 pounds, and the very largest can exceed 200 pounds.) For pie filling and other cooking needs, sugar pumpkins—a smaller, sweeter variety with close-grained flesh—are much better. There are also several miniature varieties that can be eaten fresh. However, most people prefer canned pumpkin, which tastes as good as fresh.

AVAILABILITY Some winter squashes, particularly acorn, are in good supply year-round. But most are at their peak beginning in late summer and continuing on throughout the fall and winter; they become scarce in spring. Fresh pumpkins are available only in the fall and early winter.

SHOPPING TIPS The size you buy will depend on your needs. There is no such thing as an "overgrown" winter squash; and the longer the squash grows, the sweeter it will be. However, after picking, squash may be damaged by poor storage. Clues to good quality are a smooth, dry rind, free of cracks or soft spots. Moreover, the rind should be dull; a shiny rind indicates that the squash was picked too early, and will not have the full sweetness of a mature specimen.

Deep color is also a sign of a good winter squash. Green acorn squash may have splashes of orange, but avoid any that has orange on more than half its surface; butternut squash should be uniformly tan, with no tinge of green; pumpkin should have a rich orange color. A winter squash should feel heavy for its size. If possible, choose squash with their stems attached, as these are also indicators of quality: The stems should be rounded and dry, not collapsed, blackened, or moist.

Some very large squash, such as calabaza, banana, or Hubbard, are sold cut into quarters or chunks and wrapped in plastic. When buying cut squash, look for good interior color and fine-grained flesh.

STORAGE Winter squash is one of the best-keeping vegetables. Uncut squash should keep for three months or longer in a cool, dry place; pumpkins will keep for about one month. Storage below 50° (as in the refrigerator) will cause squash to deteriorate more quickly, but refrigerator storage is acceptable for a week or two. Cut squash will stay for up to a week if tightly wrapped and refrigerated.

Winter squash that is stored has more carotene—and therefore more vitamin A value—than freshly picked squash. The same could be said for all carotene-containing vegetables, except that most deteriorate before the increase in carotene occurs.

PREPARATION Rinse off any dirt before using. The hard shell of some types of winter squash can prove challenging to cut: Use a heavy chef's knife or a cleaver, especially for larger squash. First, make a shallow cut in the skin to use as a guide to prevent the knife blade from slipping. Then place the blade in the cut and tap the base of the knife (near the handle) with your fist (or, if necessary, with a mallet or rolling pin) until the squash is cut through. Scoop out the seeds and fibers and cut the squash into smaller chunks, if desired. Small, very hard-shelled squash, such as Golden Nugget, may be impossible to split before cooking; bake or steam them whole. To bake a pumpkin whole, cut a lid off the top, then use a tablespoon to scrape out the seeds and strings.

If peeled chunks of squash are required, cut the squash into pieces, then peel them with a sturdy, sharp paring knife. Very hard-shelled squash is much easier to peel after cooking.

Baking This method brings out the sweetness in winter squash, caramelizing some of its sugars—and best conserves its beta carotene content. Bake halved squash and serve plain, or bake, then fill with a stuffing and return to the oven until the stuffing is heated through (10 to 15 minutes). You can also bake squash halves, then scoop out and mash the flesh with your favorite seasonings; spoon the mashed squash back into the shells (sprinkle with grated cheese, breadcrumbs, chopped nuts, or sesame seeds, if desired) and return to the oven until heated through.

To bake, halve small squash lengthwise and scoop out the seeds and strings (squash can also be seeded after baking). Cut large squash into serving-sized pieces. Place the squash, cut-side down, in a foil-lined baking pan (its sugary juices may burn onto the pan). Pour about 1/4 inch of water into the pan, cover with foil, and bake in a 350° to 400° oven until the squash is tender when pierced with a knife or toothpick. Halfway through baking, the squash halves (or pieces) may be turned, cut-side up, brushed with a little melted butter or oil, and sprinkled with brown sugar and spices. *Cooking times:* for squash halves or whole small pumpkins, 40 to 45 minutes; for cut-up squash, 15 to 25 minutes; for cut-up pumpkin, 40 minutes.

Boiling Although this method is faster than steaming, boiling water will dilute the flavor of the squash slightly. Place peeled squash pieces in a small amount of boiling water and cook until tender. Drain well. *Cooking times:* for squash, 5 minutes; for pumpkin, 8 to 12 minutes.

Microwaving Arrange squash halves, cut-side up, in a shallow microwavable dish, cover, and cook until tender, rotating the dish halfway through the cooking time. Or, place large chunks of any winter squash in a shallow microwavable dish, cover, and cook until tender. Let stand for 5 minutes after cooking. *Cooking time:* for squash halves, 7 to 10 minutes; for chunks, 8 minutes.

Sautéing Grated or peeled, diced squash can be sautéed in broth, or in a combination of broth and oil. Use a nonstick skillet, if possible. Grated squash is best if it is cooked just to the point where it is still slightly crunchy. *Cooking time:* 8 to 15 minutes.

Steaming Place seeded squash halves, cut-side down, in a vegetable steamer and cook over boiling water until tender. Or, cook peeled chunks or slices of squash in the steamer. *Cooking time:* 15 to 20 minutes.

SERVING SUGGESTIONS Baked or steamed winter squash is delicious mashed or puréed, like sweet potatoes. To enhance its natural sweetness, combine the squash with any of the following: baked or steamed pears or apples (or applesauce); bananas; chopped cranberries; lemon, lime, or orange juice; almond or vanilla extract; fresh or powdered ginger; curry powder; cinnamon; nutmeg; mace; cardamom; cloves; allspice or pumpkin pie spice; brown sugar; maple sugar; or honey. For a savory side dish, mash the cooked squash with sautéed onions or garlic and herbs, or combine chunks of squash with cooked corn, tomatoes, and bell peppers.

HEALTHY PUMPKIN PIE

Pumpkin pie is traditionally made by combining the pumpkin with heavy cream and whole eggs. When placed in a standard pie crust, a slice (1/8 of a 9-inch pie) gets about 49 percent of its calories from fat. By substituting evaporated skim milk for the cream and 3 egg whites for every 2 whole eggs, you'll cut the fat to 26 percent of the calories, though the calorie count remains about the same, 240 per slice. Use a graham cracker crust and you'll cut the fat—and calories—even further.

Squash purée can also be prepared and frozen for future use in soups, baked goods, and other recipes. Steam or bake squash, then cool, peel, and purée; you can mash the squash with a potato masher, put it through a food mill, or purée it

BUTTERNUT SQUASH	3½ oz raw (1 cup cubed)		
Calories	45	Fat	<1 g
Protein	1 g	Saturated Fat	<1 g
Carbohydrate	12 g	Cholesterol	0 mg
Dietary Fiber	Low	Sodium	4 mg

KEY NUTRIENTS		% RDA Men	% RDA Women
Vitamin A	7800 IU	156%	195%
Vitamin B_6	0.2 mg	10%	13%
Beta Carotene	5 mg	N/A	N/A
Vitamin C	21 mg	35%	35%
Folacin	27 mcg	14%	15%
Magnesium	34 mg	10%	12%
Manganese	0.2 mg	N/A	N/A
Potassium	352 mg	N/A	N/A

S=S40% or more soluble N/A=Not Applicable N=Not Available

in a blender or food processor. (Because pumpkin can be very watery, the pieces should be well drained after cooking, and the purée drained again before storing.) Pack the squash purée into freezer containers; it will keep for up to a year. For soup, thaw the purée and thin with chicken or vegetable broth. Season to taste and garnish with chopped chives, a dollop of yogurt, or a sprinkling of nutmeg.

Just before baking chunks of squash, drizzle orange or apple juice over them. Or, toss chunks of squash with fruit juice and raisins or pineapple chunks and bake. You can also bake stuffed squash halves; try a savory vegetable and grain or breadcrumb filling, or a sweet mixture of chopped fresh and dried fruits and nuts. Use whole small steamed or baked squashes (or even good-sized pumpkins) as serving bowls for soups or stews: Scoop out the flesh after baking and use it in the soup, or mash it and reserve for a subsequent meal.

Substitute any type of cooked, mashed winter squash for canned pumpkin in soup, pie, cookie, or quick bread recipes.

Butternut squash, highlighted above, left, is one of the most popular and most nutritious winter squashes.

Sunchokes (Jerusalem Artichokes)

Once strictly a specialty food, this native American vegetable is becoming more widely available in markets everywhere. "Jerusalem artichoke" has been its common name since the seventeenth century, but it has recently been dubbed "sunchoke," which is certainly more appropriate. The plant has no connection to either Jerusalem or artichokes, but is, in fact, a type of sunflower. Then why is it called Jerusalem artichoke? One conjecture is that the French explorer Champlain sampled the vegetable in the early 1600s in Massachusetts, where it was cultivated by Native Americans, and he likened its taste to that of an artichoke. Some years later, after the "chokes" had been introduced to Europe, the English added *Jerusalem*—perhaps a corruption of *girasole* (an Italian word that means "turning to the sun," which the plant does during the day) or the mispronunciation of Terneuzen, a Dutch town that may have supplied the English with some of its first samples.

The sunchoke is actually a tuber, or underground stem, that resembles a small nubby potato or a piece of gingerroot. But it has a sweet, almost nutty taste and a crisp texture that is quite distinctive. A versatile vegetable, it can be eaten raw or cooked, and added to all manner of dishes. Like potatoes and other tubers, the sunchoke stores carbohydrates, but most of them are in the form of inulin, a sugar that can sometimes cause flatulence. (If you have never sampled sunchoke, you should eat it in small amounts until you are able to determine how your body will react to it.) The vegetable is also an incomparable source of iron, almost on a par with meats, yet without any fat content.

Sunchokes contain more than three times as much iron as an equal serving of broccoli, and more than twice as much as a similar serving of globe artichokes or potatoes with skin.

AVAILABILITY Sunchokes can be found in markets at any time of the year, but they are most plentiful (and at their best) from late fall through early spring.

SHOPPING TIPS Sunchokes are sold loose or packed in one-pound plastic bags. Look for clean, firm tubers with unblemished skin, which may be as glossy and tan as the skin of gingerroot, or a mat brown. They should not show a greenish tinge or any sign of sprouting or mold. Choose the least knobby tubers, and be sure they are not limp or spongy. If you're planning to cook them whole, choose sunchokes of similar size.

STORAGE Wrap sunchokes in a plastic bag, seal, and store in the refrigerator crisper. They will keep for up to two weeks. If you have a cool, dark storage place, such as a dry cellar, they can also be kept there.

PREPARATION Scrub sunchokes well with a vegetable brush. It's better not to peel them, as much of their nutrient value lies just beneath their thin, edible skin. If you choose to do so, however, use a vegetable peeler. Should the small areas of skin around the knobby portions prove difficult to remove, just leave them on. (Immediately immerse peeled or cut-up sunchokes in cold water acidulated with lemon juice or vinegar, or their flesh will discolor.) If you are boiling or blanching the tubers, you may remove the skin after cooking; it will peel or rub off easily. Do be aware, however, that when cooked unpeeled, the flesh of sunchokes will darken because of their iron content.

Sunchokes can be prepared and served in many of the same ways as potatoes—and can be used in place of parsnips and turnips in some recipes. Whatever cooking method you choose, check frequently for doneness; sunchokes can turn mushy in seconds once they reach the point of tenderness. Don't cook sunchokes in aluminum or iron pans, as their white flesh will darken.

Baking Sunchokes are delicious baked. Place whole tubers in a baking pan, brush lightly with oil, and bake in a 350° oven until tender. Or parboil sliced sunchokes for faster baking. *Cooking times:* for whole, 30 to 60 minutes; for sliced, parboiled, 25 to 30 minutes.

Blanching Sunchokes can be briefly blanched before cooking further by another method such as sautéing. Drop whole sunchokes in a large pot of boiling water, cook just until crisp-tender, and

Sunchokes

SUNCHOKES $3\frac{1}{2}$ oz raw ($\frac{3}{4}$ cup sliced)			
Calories	76	Fat	<1 g
Protein	2 g	Saturated Fat	<1 g
Carbohydrate	17 g	Cholesterol	0 mg
Dietary Fiber	High	Sodium	4 mg

KEY NUTRIENTS		% RDA Men	Women
Iron	3 mg	30%	20%
Phosphorus	78 mg	10%	10%
Potassium	429 mg	N/A	N/A
Thiamin	0.2 mg	13%	18%

S=40% or more soluble N/A=Not Applicable N=Not Available

cool in ice water. *Cooking time:* 3 to 5 minutes.

Boiling Drop whole sunchokes into a large pot of boiling water, or place sliced tubers in a skillet of water. Cook until they feel tender when pierced with the tip of a knife. *Cooking times:* for whole, 10 to 20 minutes, depending on size; for sliced, 5 to 10 minutes.

Braising Sauté cut-up, blanched sunchokes with herbs, garlic, onions, or other vegetables, then add wine or broth to cover. Simmer, covered, over low heat until the sunchokes are tender. If necessary, uncover toward the end of the cooking time to allow the liquid to reduce. *Cooking time:* 20 to 30 minutes.

Sautéing Blanched sunchokes sauté quickly to a pleasant al dente consistency. First, cut the sunchokes into bite-sized pieces and blanch them. After blanching, sauté them in a small amount of vegetable oil, along with onions and other vegetables. *Cooking time:* 3 to 4 minutes.

Steaming Place whole or sliced sunchokes in a vegetable steamer and cook until tender. *Cooking times:* for whole, 15 to 20 minutes; for sliced, 5 to 10 minutes.

Stir-frying Sunchokes make a perfect substitute for water chestnuts in meat, poultry, or vegetable stir-fries. Slice the tubers and add for the last 2 minutes of cooking time.

SERVING SUGGESTIONS When serving cooked sunchokes alone, top them with lots of chopped parsley or other fresh herbs. Sliced, blanched sunchokes will add crisp texture to most cooked vegetables. Mash or purée cooked sunchokes alone or with white or sweet potatoes, turnips, parsnips, or carrots. Glaze cooked sunchokes as you would carrots.

Braise sunchokes with potatoes, carrots, celery, or tomatoes. To make a delicious soup, braise sunchokes with potatoes, onions, and celery, but use plenty of stock; when the vegetables are tender, purée the mixture. Add milk to the purée for a thick, creamy soup; serve hot or cold.

Marinate sliced, boiled sunchokes in a vinaigrette and serve as a salad or condiment. Or, mix peeled, boiled sunchokes into your favorite potato salad.

Raw sunchokes are prized for their fresh flavor and crisp texture. Shred them and add to a slaw, or slice very thinly into a tossed salad. You can pickle thin slices or strips of sunchoke in the leftover brine from commercial pickles and serve them as part of a crudité platter.

Sweet Potatoes

Many people eat sweet potatoes only on Thanksgiving—a pity, since these tuberous roots are among the most nutritious foods in the vegetable kingdom. They also possess an intense natural sweetness, which is produced by an enzyme in the potato that converts most of its starches to sugars as the potato matures. This sweetness continues to increase during storage, and when the potato is cooked.

The sweet potato is not related to the white potato, but is a member of the morning glory family; the resemblance is evident in the leafy vines that can be grown from sweet potato cuttings. A native American plant, it was carried to Europe by Columbus (and to Asia by other explorers) and was widely cultivated in colonial America, where it often provided the chief means of sustenance for early homesteaders and for soldiers during the Revolutionary War. As one colonial physician put it, the sweet potato was the "vegetable indispensable."

Moist orange-fleshed varieties of sweet potato dominate the market, but you can also find dry yellow-fleshed types. The former are usually plumper in shape and somewhat sweeter than the latter. Moist-fleshed potatoes are often incorrectly called "yams." True yams (botanical family Dioscoreaceae) are large (up to 100 pounds), starchy roots grown in Africa and Asia; they are seldom available in this country. However, common usage has made the term "yams" acceptable when referring to sweet potatoes.

Because of its rich flavor, the sweet potato's reputation is, unfairly, that of a caloric treat. In reality, a 5-inch baked sweet potato contains only about 120 calories—no more than a white potato.

Sweet potatoes are also sold canned or frozen. The canned potatoes are usually packed in heavy syrup—"candied"—although some processors also pack them in water. Canned sweet potatoes are substantially lower in beta carotene, vitamin C, and B vitamins than fresh ones. A baked frozen sweet potato contains approximately 50 percent less vitamin C and about 25 percent less beta carotene than a fresh sweet potato baked in its skin.

AVAILABILITY Sweet potatoes, which are grown largely in California, Louisiana, and New Jersey, are sold throughout the year, but the greatest supplies are available in the fall and early winter. Many stores feature sweet potatoes around Thanksgiving and Christmas.

SHOPPING TIPS Look for potatoes that are heavy for their size. Avoid any that are not smooth, hard, and free of bruises or decay, which may appear as shriveled or sunken areas or black spots. Even if cut away, a decayed spot may have already imparted an unpleasant flavor to the entire potato. Check the tips, where decay usually begins. Buy similar-sized potatoes if you plan to cook them whole.

STORAGE Sweet potatoes are subject to rapid spoilage; to help preserve them, growers cure them, that is, they store them at a high temperature and humidity for about 10 days before sending them to market. This process also enhances their natural sweetness. After purchase, sweet potatoes should be kept in a cool (55° to 60°), dry place, such as a cellar, pantry, or garage—never in the refrigerator, where they may develop a hard core and an "off" taste. Sweet potatoes will keep for a month or longer if stored at 55°; at normal room temperature, they should be used within a week of purchase.

Handle the potatoes gently: Despite their rugged appearance, their skin is quite thin and easily damaged. Sweet potatoes may be some-

what dirty, especially if bought at a farmstand or a farmers' market. You should brush off any excess dirt before storing, but don't wash the potatoes until you are ready to cook them, as the moisture will hasten spoilage.

Cooked sliced or mashed sweet potatoes can be frozen; add a little lemon juice to keep them from darkening and pack them into freezer containers.

PREPARATION Moist- and dry-fleshed sweet potatoes are interchangeable in recipes. Try not to combine the two types in a single dish, however, as their differing textures and cooking times may affect the outcome of the recipe. (Moist-fleshed varieties take longer to cook than dry-fleshed, and will be done at the upper ends of the ranges given in cooking times below.) Scrub the potatoes under cold running water before cooking.

Baking Wash (but don't peel) the sweet potatoes and then pierce them with a fork before baking to let the steam escape. To speed clean-up, place the potatoes on a foil-lined baking sheet to catch the sticky juices that ooze from them as they bake. *Cooking time:* 30 to 60 minutes in a 400° oven, depending on size.

Boiling If you cook the potatoes whole, there's no need to peel them first; the thin skins will slip off easily when the potatoes are done, leaving most of the nutrients intact. The skin is edible, however, and supplies additional dietary fiber. *Cooking times:* for whole potatoes, 15 to 35 minutes; for chunks, 10 to 15 minutes.

Microwaving Wash the potato and pierce it several times with a fork, then place it on a paper towel. Let stand for 3 minutes after cooking. *Cooking times:* for two medium potatoes, 5 to 9 minutes; for four, 10 to 13 minutes.

SERVING SUGGESTIONS With its naturally creamy texture and sweet taste, this vegetable seldom requires the quantities of butter, sugar, or cream called for in many traditional recipes. To enhance the flavor of sweet potatoes without adding a lot of calories, slice cooked sweet potatoes and place them in a saucepan with a little apple juice or cider; cook over low heat until the liquid forms a shiny glaze. Or, whip the cooked potatoes with some orange peel, orange juice, or pineapple juice, then season with nutmeg, cinnamon, and ginger.

SWEET POTATO 3½ oz (¾ sweet potato)			
Calories	105	Fat	<1 g
Protein	2 g	Saturated Fat	<1 g
Carbohydrate	24 g	Cholesterol	0 mg
Dietary Fiber	Medium (S)	Sodium	13 mg

KEY NUTRIENTS		% RDA Men	% RDA Women
Vitamin A	20,063 IU	401%	502%
Vitamin B_6	0.3 mg	15%	19%
Beta Carotene	12 mg	N/A	N/A
Vitamin C	23 mg	38%	38%
Copper	0.2 mg	N/A	N/A
Manganese	0.4 mg	N/A	N/A

S=40% or more soluble N/A=Not Applicable N=Not Available

Sweet potatoes can also be used in many of the same ways as white potatoes. To make a sweet potato salad, for example, slice or cube cooked potatoes and toss them with a sweet vinaigrette (add some fruit juice or honey to your favorite recipe) or with low-fat yogurt flavored with lemon juice and herbs. Then add diced celery, red or green bell pepper, chopped scallions, or thinly sliced onions. Sweet potatoes also work well in stews. They make handsome additions to stir-fries; just cut them into thin sticks so they will cook quickly. Sweet potatoes also taste good cold; save leftovers (they keep for up to five days refrigerated) to make a healthy snack.

Tomatoes

Although botanically a fruit—specifically, a berry—the tomato is prepared and served as a vegetable. (As the result of a tariff dispute, it was officially proclaimed a vegetable in 1893 by the Supreme Court of the United States.) A member of the nightshade family—which includes deadly nightshade as well as potatoes, bell peppers, and eggplant—the tomato is a native South American plant that was brought to Europe by Spanish explorers in the sixteenth century. Europeans, however, believed it to be poisonous and used it only as an ornamental houseplant. Not until the nineteenth century was the tomato widely accepted as a food, and even then it was customarily cooked for hours to neutralize its "poisons." Only in the second half of the century were raw or lightly cooked tomatoes consumed by Europeans or Americans.

In this century, tomatoes have become the third most-popular vegetable eaten by Americans—second (behind potatoes) if you include processed tomato products such as tomato juice and sauce. A major reason for their widespread consumption is that tomatoes combine well with many other foods—poultry, meats, fish, rice, pasta, and most other vegetables. While tomatoes are not as high in nutrients as some other vegetables, they are the leading vegetable source of vitamin C in the American diet because of the quantities we eat. They also provide some beta carotene. Tomato products can further concentrate these nutrients: A cup of tomato purée, for example, contains enough beta carotene to provide about half the RDA for vitamin A.

VARIETIES There are thousands of tomato varieties, but those usually available in stores fall into one of three distinct categories:

Cherry tomatoes Round and bite-sized, these tomatoes are often served in salads and as garnishes. Their skin may be red or yellow.

Plum tomatoes Also known as Italian or Roma tomatoes, these are small and egg-shaped. In general, they are meatier and less juicy than slicing tomatoes, and so are ideal for making sauces and adding to other cooked foods.

Slicing (round) tomatoes These large, rounded varieties include round globe types commonly found in most supermarkets as well as the flatter beefsteak tomatoes prized by home gardeners. A variety called "Sunny" is the most widely grown commercially in the United States.

Other varieties include yellow or orange tomatoes, which are sometimes advertised as "low-acid" tomatoes. They are in fact not lower in acid than other tomatoes, but higher in sugar, which produces a very mild, sweet flavor. Tiny red and yellow pear tomatoes are particularly sweet; they

are excellent tossed in salads and used as garnishes or crudités.

Tomatoes are also differentiated according to how they are grown. Although the majority are planted in fields, they are also grown under glass—either in soil or water (hydroponically)—in almost every state. In fact, in the United States, the tomato is the most popular greenhouse vegetable. It is relatively easy to distinguish greenhouse tomatoes by their appearance. Because their environment is protected, they are usually smoother and more uniform than field-grown varieties, and they are often sold with part of the stem and leaves still attached. Many people believe that greenhouse tomatoes have a better flavor; generally, they are more expensive.

Sun-dried tomatoes are dehydrated to preserve them and intensify their flavor. Before being used, they are often reconstituted in liquid, primarily oil. Indeed, sun-dried tomatoes are frequently sold packed in olive oil. It is better to buy them dehydrated and reconstitute them by soaking in boiling water. They will taste fine, and you will avoid the extra calories and fat.

AVAILABILITY During the last hundred years, tomatoes have been bred for hardiness in a variety of climates, and today commercial crops are cultivated in every state. Local growers supply tomatoes to every region of the country in season, mainly summer to fall. Out of season, most tomatoes in the United States are shipped from Florida (which produces about 45 percent of the total U.S. supply) or California, with the bulk of the crop harvested between October and June. A large proportion are also imported from Mexico, primarily from January to May. Of course, many of the tomatoes Americans eat are home grown. (The tomato is the number-one vegetable favored by backyard gardeners.)

SHOPPING TIPS As a basic rule, never buy tomatoes from a refrigerated case; the cold damages them (see box on page 178). Tomatoes displayed loose are easier to evaluate than those that are packed in boxes. Look for plump, heavy tomatoes with smooth skins. They should be free of bruises, blemishes, or deep cracks, although fine cracks at the stem ends of ripe tomatoes do not affect flavor. If greenhouse tomatoes still have their leaves, check that they are fresh and green.

Ripe tomatoes are fragrant, but even mature green ones should have a mild fragrance that promises future ripeness. If they have no aroma at

THOSE PALE WINTER TOMATOES

The tomatoes available during the winter months oftentimes bear little resemblance to their in-season counterparts: They may be pale red or streaky greenish-pink in color, rock hard, and taste much blander. Year-round demand has led growers and breeders to develop thicker-skinned hardy varieties that can withstand the rigors of shipping long distances. Because of this, and because of the way these tomatoes are handled on their way to the market, their taste, texture, and juiciness often suffer in comparison to tomatoes available in peak season. Still, it's possible to get a winter tomato with decent flavor in the off-season if a few criteria have been met.

The picking stage

To increase their durability, tomatoes are picked when they are still green—a stage referred to as "mature green"—or just when they begin to show a spot of pink at the blossom end, a stage known as "breaker." Tomatoes at either stage are fully developed, they just haven't begun the ripening process.

To speed along the ripening process of mature green and breaker stage tomatoes, growers and shippers often spray them with ethylene gas. Though it sounds like a synthetic creation, ethylene is the same organic compound (actually a ripening hormone) produced naturally by many fruits—oranges, bananas, honeydew melons—as well as by tomatoes. Left on the vine, a tomato will produce its own ethylene, but the external application of ethylene gas is used to initiate and promote the ripening process. Since not all tomatoes in a crop develop at the same rate, it is inevitable that some will be picked too early, and you may occasionally get a tomato that, although it turns completely red, never develops a palatable flavor or texture. But if handled properly these tomatoes have the potential to develop good flavor and juicy texture. A study by the USDA has found that artificial exposure to ethylene has little if any effect on a tomato's nutritional value. Another study at the University of Georgia that compared tomatoes left on the vine to ripen to those treated with ethylene found that treated tomatoes have the same "sensory attributes and post-harvest quality" and only minor differences in taste and texture.

Are "vine ripened" better?

The term "vine ripe" has no standard definition and can be misleading, as it covers a wide range of ripening stages. It usually refers to tomatoes that have been picked at the breaker stage, but tomatoes picked at any time can carry the label. Generally, tomatoes shipped to nearby markets are picked at a greater degree of ripeness than tomatoes shipped across the country. And since most greenhouse tomatoes are grown close to their market, they are also likely to be left on the vine a bit longer. However, as long as a tomato is handled properly, where it ripens should make little difference in ultimate flavor and texture.

Temperature: the crucial factor

To help ensure that the tomatoes you buy will at least taste adequate, don't buy any that have been refrigerated. Exposure to temperatures under 55° during growth or after harvest prevents a tomato from ripening satisfactorily. Unfortunately, shippers and retailers sometimes keep tomatoes with other vegetables, like lettuce or broccoli, under refrigeration, destroying their ripening potential. It's difficult to identify a tomato damaged by the cold until you get it home and slice it—the skin pulls away easily from the flesh, and the tomatoes will be mealy and virtually tasteless. Ask the produce manager of the supermarket what conditions the tomatoes were shipped and stored under, and avoid buying tomatoes held in refrigerated cases. Another key to flavor is to buy tomatoes slightly under-ripe, and let them ripen at room temperature for a few days.

all, the tomatoes were probably picked when immature, and will never ripen. Salmon pink tomatoes that feel firm are fine, but give them a few days to ripen. Fully ripe tomatoes are soft and yielding to the touch; buy them only if you plan to use them immediately. Overripe tomatoes, provided they are not moldy or rotting, are perfect for making sauce.

Choose whatever size tomatoes are appropriate for your intended use; size has no bearing on the vegetable's flavor, texture, or quality. Large tomatoes weigh about ½ pound each; there are three to four medium-sized tomatoes to a pound.

STORAGE Room temperature (above 55°) is best for storing tomatoes; don't refrigerate them. Place less-than-ripe tomatoes in a paper bag with an apple or banana; the ethylene gas given off by the fruit will hasten the ripening process. Keep the tomatoes out of sunlight—they will overheat and ripen unevenly—and arrange them, stem-side up, to prevent bruising. Once the tomatoes are red and yield to the touch, they will keep for a day or two at room temperature. Should you need to hold them longer, refrigerate them; if they'll fit, place them in the butter compartment, which is the warmest part of the refrigerator. For full flavor, let the tomatoes come back to room temperature before you serve them.

Chopped tomatoes may be frozen for use in sauces or other cooked dishes. Tomato sauce also freezes well. When you have a plentiful supply of perfectly ripe or overripe tomatoes, cook a batch of a basic sauce and freeze it for later use; use individual containers that hold the right amount of sauce for one meal.

PREPARATION Wash tomatoes gently in cold water before serving them. To cut tomato slices for a salad or sandwich, stand the tomato upright and cut from top to bottom—the slices will retain their juices better than slices cut from side to side. Add sliced tomatoes to salads and sandwiches at the last minute because they begin to release their juices as soon as they are cut; contact with salty condiments or dressings will draw out more juice.

To remove excessive seeds or juice, cut the tomato in half crosswise, then hold each half, cut-side down, and squeeze it gently (you can sieve the juice and drink it). If you need very well drained tomato halves (for a stuffed tomato recipe, for instance), salt them lightly, then place them, with the cut side down, on several layers of paper towel.

When a recipe calls for peeled tomatoes, drop them into a pot of boiling water and blanch for 15 to 30 seconds (the harder the tomato, the more time it requires). Remove the tomatoes from the pot with a slotted spoon and cool them briefly under cold running water. The skin can then be rubbed off easily, using a paring knife. You can also spear tomatoes individually on a cooking fork and turn them slowly over a gas flame until the skin splits and can be pulled off. Or, you can loosen the peel in a microwave oven by heating it for 15 seconds on high power.

For cooked dishes, you can prepare tomatoes in a variety of quick, easy ways:

Baking Prepare tomatoes as for broiling, then bake instead. For stuffed tomatoes, halve firm tomatoes, drain them, and scoop out the pulp (reserve it for use in the stuffing, if you wish). Salt and drain the halves, then fill them with a stuffing, such as cooked rice, pasta, grains, cooked corn, peas or other vegetables, or a bread or breadcrumb stuffing. Do not overcook the tomatoes, or they will split and fall apart. *Cooking time:* 8 to 15 minutes in a 400° oven.

Broiling Broiled tomato halves are delicious served on their own or as a low-fat accompaniment to meat or poultry. Halve firm tomatoes and place, cut-side up, on a broiler pan. Sprinkle with breadcrumbs, herbs, and a little grated cheese and broil. *Cooking time:* 5 minutes.

Sautéing Use sautéed cherry tomatoes to lend color to a simple main dish. Pierce each tomato with a pin (to prevent bursting) and sauté them in a little oil. Toss with chopped fresh herbs. Halved

TOMATO PRODUCTS

Tomatoes are sold in myriad forms other than fresh. In fact, for every pound of fresh tomatoes consumed, Americans eat about 3 pounds of processed tomatoes. Below are the ways you'll see tomatoes packaged on your supermarket shelf:

Canned tomatoes: **These are available in two forms: either as mature whole tomatoes that have been peeled and cored, or as diced tomatoes sometimes labeled "crushed." Canned tomatoes may be designated "solid pack," which means no liquid has been added, or they may be packed in tomato juice, purée, or paste; the label indicates the packing medium. Sometimes calcium pectate is added to help canned tomatoes stay firm; as a result, this additive contributes a small amount of calcium to the diet. Salt or other flavorings, such as bay leaf, may also be included. It is best to choose "no salt added" brands, however, since canned tomatoes with added salt may have twelve times the sodium of unsalted. If other vegetables and seasonings are mixed in—such as onion, green pepper, or celery—the tomatoes are labeled stewed.**

Tomato purée: **A concentrated form of tomato juice and tomato pulp, it is available in cans and sometimes in aseptic packaging. Purée has the consistency of a thick tomato sauce, and may contain salt.**

Tomato sauce: **This product is the same as tomato purée, except that the sauce has been seasoned. It is available canned or jarred. Be sure to read labels; some brands have whopping amounts of fat and sodium added. One popular brand of marinara sauce gets 40 percent of its calories from fat and contains nearly 800 milligrams of sodium per ½ cup serving. Brands with added meat can be even higher in fat.**

Tomato paste: **This very concentrated form is sold in cans or in tubes. By law, tomato paste must be concentrated to more than 24 percent solids (compared to 8 to 24 percent for tomato purée). The nutrients are densely packed in tomato paste as well; a cup of paste has twice as much beta carotene and 25 percent more vitamin C than the same amount of tomato purée, although smaller amounts of tomato paste are generally used.**

plum tomatoes can be cooked the same way. Thick slices of green tomatoes (or firm ripe tomatoes), dredged in flour, oatmeal, or cornmeal, can also be sautéed until lightly browned and tender. *Cooking time:* 1 to 2 minutes.

Stewing Skin and seed tomatoes, then place them in a pan with a little water, broth, or tomato juice. Cover and cook until the tomatoes are softened. Season to taste with salt, pepper, a pinch of sugar, if necessary, and fresh or dried herbs, such as basil, oregano, tarragon, or dill. *Cooking time:* 10 minutes.

SERVING SUGGESTIONS One of the best ways to enjoy fresh tomatoes is to slice and layer them on a plate topped with fresh basil leaves. Or, arrange them on dense whole-wheat bread or French bread that has been spread with mustard and sprinkled with pepper. For salads, use either tomato quarters, which retain more juice than flat slices, or whole or halved cherry tomatoes. The latter also make wonderful crudités. You can even concoct a low-fat, low-calorie salad dressing by puréeing a fresh tomato, then blending in some vinegar and herbs and spices to taste.

The iron content in a cup of tomato sauce increases from 6 to 100 milligrams or more when it's simmered in a cast-iron pot for a few hours.

For a basic cooked tomato sauce, sauté a chopped onion and a few chopped cloves of garlic in olive oil. Add 3 cups of chopped tomatoes (peeled and seeded before chopping), bring to a boil, and then simmer for about 30 minutes, or until thickened. Season to taste; many cooks like to use basil and oregano, which are traditional Italian seasonings.

Raw tomatoes can be turned into a Mexican-style salsa. This piquant sauce can be offered alongside grilled meat, poultry or fish, or used as a dip for raw vegetables or to top baked potatoes: Just mix chopped ripe tomatoes with some minced onion, garlic, and chopped fresh cilantro or parsley. Add lime juice and chopped hot peppers (or a few drops of hot pepper sauce) to taste. Let stand for a few minutes and serve at room temperature.

As an alternative to making a tomato sauce for pasta dishes, try tossing coarsely chopped tomatoes with pasta or alternate layers of well-drained, sliced tomatoes with pasta in a casserole. Tomato wedges can enhance the flavor of stir-fried dishes; add the tomatoes at the last minute, though, since they won't remain firm very long with such intense heat.

Tomatoes also combine well with other vegetables. Add juicy ripe tomatoes (or canned varieties) to perk up vegetables such as eggplant or zucchini; toss cooked, chopped tomatoes with cooked corn kernels; sauté or grill thick tomato slices with bell pepper strips; or layer diced tomatoes with green beans and chopped onions and bake them in a casserole. Chopped or diced tomatoes also nicely complement hearty dishes made with dried beans, lentils, or rice.

TOMATO 3½ oz raw (¾ tomato)			
Calories	21	Fat	<1 g
Protein	1 g	Saturated Fat	<1 g
Carbohydrate	5 g	Cholesterol	0 mg
Dietary Fiber	Low	Sodium	9 mg

KEY NUTRIENTS		% RDA Men	% RDA Women
Vitamin A	623 IU	12%	16%
Vitamin C	19 mg	32%	32%
Vitamin E	1 mg	10%	13%

S=40% or more soluble N/A=Not Applicable N=Not Available

Turnips and Rutabagas

Like cabbage, to which it is related, the turnip has long been thought of as "plain folks" food. It is economical; it grows well in poor soil; it keeps well; and it supplies complex carbohydrates. One of the cruciferous vegetables in the *Brassica* genus, it can be cultivated for its root—which is a good source of complex carbohydrates—as well as for its greens, which are rich in vitamins and minerals (see page 104). Turnips come in an astonishing range of shapes and sizes, depending on the age and variety—some have weighed 40 to 50 pounds, others are the size of a golf ball. The flesh can be white or yellow, but most commercial turnips have white flesh.

Rutabagas look similar to turnips, but are a separate botanical species that probably evolved from a cross between a turnip and a wild cabbage. Rutabagas are larger and rounder than turnips (the vegetable's name comes from the Swedish word *rotabagge,* meaning "round root"). They have a firmer flesh, which is usually yellow, and a stronger, sweeter flavor. They also contain more beta carotene and vitamin C than turnips (which have no beta carotene at all) and less water (which allows them to store somewhat better).

Of the two, turnips (*Brassica rapa*) have a much older history. They were eaten by the Romans as well as by the peoples of Europe during the Middle Ages; eventually, they were brought to America by both French and English colonists.

They are especially appreciated in the South. Rutabagas (*Brassica napus*) are comparatively new—the first record of them is from the seventeenth century, when they were used as both food and animal fodder in southern Europe. In England, they were referred to as "turnip-rooted cabbages," and their popularity in Scandinavia eventually earned them the name of Swedish turnips, or "swedes" (Europeans still use this term). Americans were growing rutabagas as early as 1806. Warm temperatures (above 75°) can damage rutabagas, and, as a result, they are planted chiefly in northern states and in Canada, while turnips are found in every state.

Like other cruciferous vegetables, turnips and rutabagas can become more strongly flavored when cooked. However, the odors from both vegetables are quite mild compared to, say, Brussels sprouts and cabbages, and you will find that when turnips and rutabagas are well prepared, their sweet, somewhat peppery flesh makes them excellent side dishes as well as tasty additions to salads, soups, and stews.

AVAILABILITY Turnips and rutabagas are available all year, in part because they store well—up to four months or more at 32° in commercial storage. Supplies peak in the fall and winter months, when the bulk of both crops is harvested. California, Colorado, and Indiana are among the leading turnip producers; most of the domestic rutabaga supply is imported from Canada.

SHOPPING TIPS Despite their resemblance in flavor and texture, turnips and rutabagas differ in appearance.

The turnips you'll find in the supermarket may range from roughly the size of a golf ball to that of a baseball. More or less smoothly spherical or top-shaped, the most common varieties have a creamy white skin that shades to purple or reddish pink or green at the top. (The top of the root develops above the ground, and exposure to sunlight causes it to become pigmented while the lower part, buried in earth, does not.) Other turnip varieties, however, are completely white from top to tip.

Newly harvested turnips are sometimes sold in bunches with their leaves; these should be crisp and green. If in good condition, the leaves can be cooked and eaten. Topped turnips (with the greens cut off) are frequently sold in plastic bags. Leaf scars at the stem end of topped turnips should be few. The turnips themselves should always be firm and heavy for their size, with a minimum of fibrous root hairs at the bottom. Their surface should be smooth, not shriveled or bruised. Although gardeners once prided themselves on producing massive turnips of 30 pounds or more, small ones are sweeter and more tender than large ones, which may be bitter and pithy. Bunched turnips are usually about 2 inches in diameter, topped turnips about 3 inches.

Rutabagas are considerably larger than turnips.

Their skin is tan, with a dark purple band at their crown, and they have a rather lumpy, irregular shape. They are almost always trimmed of their taproots and tops, and are often coated with a thick layer of clear wax to prevent moisture loss. The skin visible through the wax should be free of major scars and bruises. Watch out for mold on the surface of the wax. Rutabagas should feel firm and solid, never spongy. For sweetest flavor, choose smallish rutabagas, about 4 inches in diameter.

STORAGE Both turnips and rutabagas keep well. Cut off turnip greens and bag them separately for storage (they keep for just a few days). Place the roots in plastic bags and store them in the refrigerator crisper. Turnips will keep for about a week. Rutabagas can be stored in the refrigerator for two weeks or more, or at room temperature for about a week.

PREPARATION Both turnips and rutabagas can be eaten raw, but large ones may be strongly flavored; you can reduce their assertive taste somewhat by blanching them in boiling water for about 5 minutes before baking, braising, or stir-frying. And to keep the flavor mild, don't overcook these vegetables.

Avoid cooking turnips in aluminum or iron pots, as their flesh may darken. However, this discoloration isn't a problem with rutabagas, which have more stable pigments.

Turnips are usually peeled before cooking (or using raw), although very young, fresh turnips need not be. A vegetable peeler will remove the thinnest possible layer of skin. First, trim a slice from the top and bottom of each turnip and halve the vegetable around the "equator." Then peel and slice, dice or cut into julienne strips, as required.

The wax applied to rutabagas must be peeled (along with the skin) before cooking. It's easier to peel rutabagas if you quarter them first. A sharp paring knife is better for this purpose than a vegetable peeler.

Baking/roasting Place ¼-inch-thick slices of rutabaga or turnip in a shallow baking dish and sprinkle with a few tablespoons of water. Cover and bake in a 350° oven until tender. Sliced onions can be layered with the rutabagas for additional flavor. Quartered turnips or rutabagas can be roasted alongside meat or poultry. *Cooking times:* for turnips, 30 to 45 minutes; for rutabagas, 50 to 60 minutes.

Boiling Drop whole turnips or rutabagas into a pot of boiling water, cover, and cook just until tender. Uncover the pot occasionally during cooking to allow the gases to escape and to ensure a delicate flavor. If a little sugar is added to the water, it will sweeten the taste of either vegetable. Cook thick slices of turnip or rutabaga in a skillet with an inch of boiling water; blanch julienne turnips or rutabagas in boiling water for just 1 to 2 minutes. *Cooking times:* for whole turnips, 20 to 30 minutes; for sliced or diced turnips, 6 to 8 minutes; for whole rutabagas, 25 to 35 minutes; for sliced rutabagas, 7 to 10 minutes.

Braising Place sliced or cubed turnips or rutabagas in a heavy skillet. Add enough stock to cover the bottom of the pan, cover, and simmer until tender. Uncover the pan and continue to cook until the liquid is reduced; serve as a sauce. *Cooking times*: for turnips, 10 to 12 minutes; for rutabagas, 15 to 20 minutes.

Microwaving Place a pound of cubed turnips or rutabagas in a microwaveable baking dish, add 3 tablespoons of liquid, cover, and cook until tender. Stir halfway through cooking time; let stand 3 minutes after removing them from the microwave. *Cooking time:* 7 to 9 minutes.

Steaming Whole turnips or cut-up turnips or rutabagas can be steamed over boiling water, then cooked until just tender. *Cooking times:* for whole medium-sized turnips, 20 to 25 minutes; for cut-up turnips, 12 to 15 minutes; for cut-up rutabagas, 25 to 35 minutes.

Stir-frying Stir-fry thinly sliced turnips or rutabagas until they are crisp-tender. *Cooking time:* 6 to 7 minutes.

TURNIPS 3½ oz raw (¾ cup cubed)			
Calories	27	Fat	<1 g
Protein	1 g	Saturated Fat	<1 g
Carbohydrate	6 g	Cholesterol	0 mg
Dietary Fiber	Low	Sodium	67 mg

KEY NUTRIENTS		% RDA Men	Women
Vitamin C	21 mg	35%	35%

S=40% or more soluble N/A=Not Applicable N=Not Available

RUTABAGAS 3½ oz raw (¾ cup cubed)			
Calories	36	Fat	<1 g
Protein	1 g	Saturated Fat	<1 g
Carbohydrate	8 g	Cholesterol	0 mg
Dietary Fiber	Low	Sodium	20 mg

KEY NUTRIENTS		% RDA Men	Women
Vitamin C	25 mg	42%	42%
Folacin	21 mcg	11%	12%
Potassium	337 mg	N/A	N/A

S=40% or more soluble N/A=Not Applicable N=Not Available

SERVING SUGGESTIONS The delicate flavor of turnips marries well with many ingredients. Rutabagas' bolder taste complements strong-flavored foods, such as pork, duck, and ham, or highly spiced dishes.

Mashed or puréed turnips or rutabagas can be served like mashed potatoes. And either vegetable is delicious when combined with mashed potatoes (in equal portions) and topped with chopped scallions or chives. Rutabagas or turnips make flavorful additions to many soups and stews, and they can be used as the basis for a hearty chowder, along with potatoes, carrots, celery, and other vegetables.

Rutabagas can be treated like sweet potatoes, sweetened or glazed with honey or brown sugar. Sweet spices, such as ground ginger and cloves, go well with both rutabagas and turnips. Orange and lemon juice and zest, fresh ginger, black pepper, basil, and dill are also excellent seasonings for these vegetables.

Raw grated turnips and rutabagas make an interesting bicolored coleslaw on their own and will contribute a refreshing flavor and texture to a favorite recipe for cabbage slaw. Consider including thin slices of young, sweet turnips or rutabagas when you next serve crudités.

Water Chestnuts

Anyone who has eaten in a Chinese restaurant is probably familiar with water chestnuts: Their crisp white flesh has a mildly sweet flavor and a crunchy texture that is actually closer to apples than to any kind of nut. In their fresh form, they do look like chestnuts, but they are not nuts. When added to dishes, they contribute hardly any fat.

There are two distinct plants, unrelated to each other, that carry the name water chestnut; the one we eat is often referred to as the Chinese water chestnut (its botanical name is *Eleocharis dulcis*). Some sources classify this vegetable as a tuber, but it is technically a corm—the swollen tip of an underground stem that, like a tuber, stores carbohydrates for the plant's growth. The water chestnut grows underwater in mud. It has brown or black scalelike leaves and and closely resembles a small, muddy tulip bulb.

Nearly all of the water chestnuts marketed in the United States come in canned form, so they are most commonly seen only after their outer wrapping has been removed. Although fresh ones need to be peeled and cleaned, they are tastier

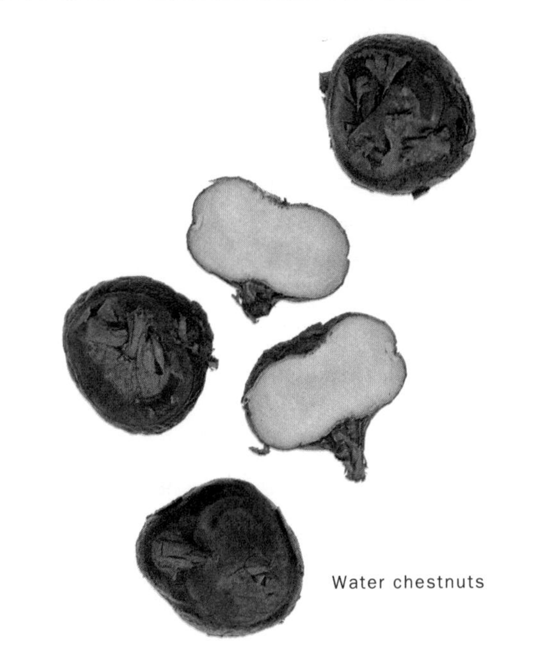
Water chestnuts

than canned chestnuts and hold up especially well under cooking, gaining in sweetness while losing none of their crunch.

AVAILABILITY Fresh water chestnuts are sold primarily in Asian food markets. Though available year round, they are most plentiful from early summer through late fall. The majority are imported from China or Japan, but they have recently been cultivated in the southeastern United States.

SHOPPING TIPS Fresh water chestnuts look sooty (they should not have been washed), but should be smooth, except for a few leaf scales. In addition, they should be rock hard and completely free of soft spots. Buy a few more than you think you will need; water chestnuts are very perishable, and, despite careful shopping, you may find a few bad ones in the batch you bring home.

STORAGE Keep water chestnuts cool, or they will sprout. Store them, unwashed and unpeeled, in a loosely closed paper or plastic bag in the refrigerator crisper. Or, refrigerate them, unwashed and unpeeled, in a loosely covered bowl or jar of water. Either way, they will keep for up to two weeks.

PREPARATION Fresh water chestnuts can be used raw in recipes, but they are sweeter and denser if they have first been briefly boiled or steamed. If they are to be subsequently cooked by another method—added to a stir-fry or sautéed, for instance—use the shorter cooking times indicated below. Steam or boil them a bit longer if no further cooking is planned—for example, if added to salads.

Wash the chestnuts and scrub them with a vegetable brush. Peel them with a sharp paring knife and cut out any bruises. To prevent discoloration, place each chestnut in cold water as it is peeled. If any of the chestnuts seem decayed, sniff them: A pronounced sour smell means they should be discarded. Halve, quarter, slice or cut into julienne strips before cooking.

Blanching canned water chestnuts for about 15 seconds will freshen their flavor. After blanching, drain them and cool in ice water.

Boiling Drop the water chestnuts into a large pot of boiling water. Return the water to a boil and cook until crisp-tender. If not serving immediately, drain the water chestnuts and cool in a bowl of ice water. *Cooking time:* 5 to 10 minutes.

WATER CHESTNUTS 3½ oz raw (¾ cup sliced)			
Calories	106	Fat	<1 g
Protein	1 g	Saturated Fat	<1 g
Carbohydrate	24 g	Cholesterol	0 mg
Dietary Fiber	Medium	Sodium	14 mg

KEY NUTRIENTS		% RDA Men	% RDA Women
Vitamin B_6	0.3 mg	15%	19%
Copper	0.3 mg	N/A	N/A
Manganese	0.3 mg	N/A	N/A
Potassium	584 mg	N/A	N/A
Riboflavin	0.2 mg	12%	15%

S=40% or more soluble N/A=Not Applicable N=Not Available

Steaming Place the water chestnuts in a steamer basket and cook over boiling water. *Cooking time:* 8 to 15 minutes.

Stir-frying Whether using fresh or canned water chestnuts, stir-fry with other ingredients just until heated through. (If they are cooked longer, they will lose their refreshing crispness and turn mushy.)

SERVING SUGGESTIONS Satisfyingly crisp and low in calories, water chestnuts are an ideal snack or appetizer. They make a good foil for spicy or salty foods, such as salsa, or smoked turkey or ham, and also go well with creamy dips made with low-fat yogurt or "light" cream cheese.

Sliced water chestnuts will enhance almost any mixed salad; they're especially tasty when served with an Asian-inspired dressing made with soy sauce, fresh ginger, and/or rice vinegar, or with a citrusy dressing. Chopped water chestnuts provide interesting texture to chicken or tuna salad, quartered water chestnuts to fruit salads.

Water chestnuts can be substituted for almonds in some cooked recipes, to reduce the fat content; try slivered water chestnuts as a topping for steamed green beans or broccoli. You can also float thin slices of water chestnut in broth. For an unusual poultry stuffing, combine chopped water chestnuts with cooked brown rice, celery, and onions, then season with fresh ginger.

Chapter 3

FRUITS

Most people like fruit—contrary to the nutritional myth that says anything fun to eat can't be good for you. There are two traits shared by most fruits that make them so appealing: They taste sweet, yet are relatively low in calories. Not only do fruits make excellent snack foods and desserts; they also add sweetness (along with vitamins and minerals) to prepared dishes. A combination of sugars—fructose, glucose, and sucrose—are present in fruits in varying proportions. Fructose is often considered the principal fruit sugar, and it is the sweetest, but sucrose is the main sugar in some fruit, such as oranges, melons, and peaches. What keeps the calorie content of fruit low is water, which makes up 80 to 95 percent of most fruits and gives them their refreshing juiciness.

Fiber is another benefit that fruits provide. The characteristic textures of different fruits—the crispness of apples, the graininess of certain pears, the chewiness of dates and figs—are partly due to insoluble fibers. In most fruits, particularly apples and citrus fruits, some of the fiber takes the form of pectin, the soluble fiber that may help lower cholesterol levels and stabilize blood sugar. With few exceptions—most notably avocados—fruits are nearly free of fat, and they contain no cholesterol.

Fruits supply some minerals—among them potassium (in bananas, pears, and oranges, three of the most popular fruits); iron (in various berries and dried fruits); and even small amounts of calcium and magnesium. But the chief contribution fruits make to our diet is vitamins, particularly vitamin C and beta carotene, the precursor of vitamin A. Citrus fruits, berries, and melons are all good sources of vitamin C, as are a number of tropical fruits, such as kiwi fruit and papaya. Yellow and orange fruits like apricots, cantaloupes, peaches, nectarines, and mangoes are the best sources of beta carotene.

Modern methods for harvesting, shipping, and storing fruit have made these fresh foods more widely available than ever. At the same time, fruits are often picked before they are ripe, and may be offered for sale when they are not at their best. Some

fruits are bred more for appearance and their ability to ship and store well than for flavor. Fortunately, you can learn to recognize when prime fruits are at their peak, and the following pages will also show you how to home-ripen and store individual varieties for maximum eating pleasure.

TYPES OF FRUITS

All fruits develop from a plant's flower—actually from the ovary, the flower's female tissue. Most fruits are simply the matured and thickened ovary, including its seeds, though in many instances the ovary is surrounded by a fleshy layer of adjacent tissue—the fruit's pulp—and enclosed by a protective skin. Beyond this basic arrangement, of course, there are enormous differences in the structure of various fruits: Just think of a pineapple compared to a grape. Moreover, some plants—such as tomatoes and peppers—are nonsweet fruits that we treat as vegetables, while others—rhubarb, for example—are botanically classified as vegetables but used as fruits. Indeed, fruits are so diverse that they don't all fit neatly into categories, botanical or otherwise. However, it is possible to loosely organize the most familiar fruits based on some of their shared characteristics.

Apples and pears, which are known botanically as pomes, have firm, moist flesh surrounding a central seedy core. Though not especially high in vitamins, they rank as some of the best sources of dietary fiber.

Apricots, peaches, nectarines, and plums are drupes, or fruits with a single stone or pit. Sweet, juicy, and comparatively fragile, they supply both beta carotene and vitamin C, along with some potassium and fiber. *Cherries* are also drupes, but with fewer nutrients per ounce than their larger cousins.

Berries have seeds embedded in succulent layers of flesh. As a botanical group, they embrace a wide range of fruits, from dates to grapes, as well as eggplants, peppers, and tomatoes. But the plants we conventionally think of as berries are small, juicy round-

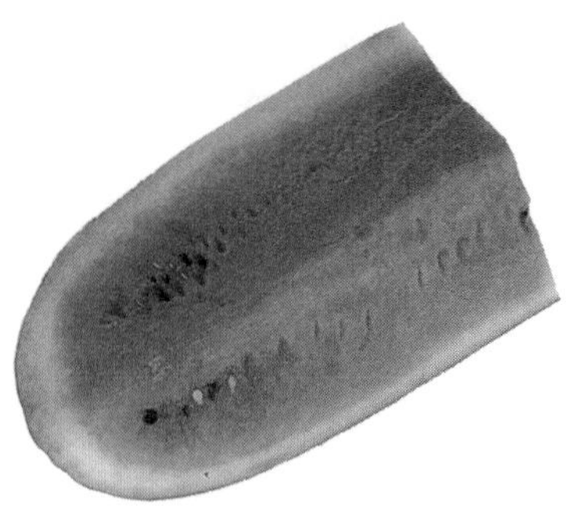

ed fruits that range in taste from sweet to sour. Berries supply varying amounts of vitamin C, and many are a surprisingly good source of fiber.

Citrus fruits—oranges, mandarins, grapefruit, lemons, and limes—are multi-sectioned, warm-weather fruits best known for their vitamin C content. Oranges and grapefruit also provide fair amounts of dietary fiber.

Melons are usually divided into two classes, watermelons and muskmelons (which include cantaloupe, honeydew, casaba, and many others). Vitamin C is the principal nutrient supplied by these exceptionally juicy fruits, though orange-fleshed melons provide beta carotene as well.

Many other fruits don't lend themselves to simple classification. Bananas, for example, are botanically lumped with berries, but are quite distinct in shape and texture. A papaya, too, is a berry, though it weighs up to 2 pounds. Pineapples are multiple fruits; each one develops from dozens of separate flowers that are discernible as "eyes" on the rough skin and yellow flesh. And many tropical fruits, from mangoes and avocados to some of the truly exotic examples covered in Chapter 4, are singular varieties that boast unique flavors and textures.

RIPENING AND FRESHNESS

With many vegetables, "ripeness" often means they are beyond the point of freshness. Summer squashes, lettuce, and cucumbers, for example, are not palatable if truly ripe. With fruits, on the other hand, ripeness is the key to enjoying them. As most fruits reach the final stage of maturity, several important changes occur that make them delectable as well as nutritious. The fruit softens, its color changes, the vitamin content increases, acidic content decreases, and the starch changes to sugar, giving the fruit a mild, sweet flavor and aroma. These changes are brought about by various enzymes that can continue to act on the fruit even after harvesting—though the degree of ripening depends on

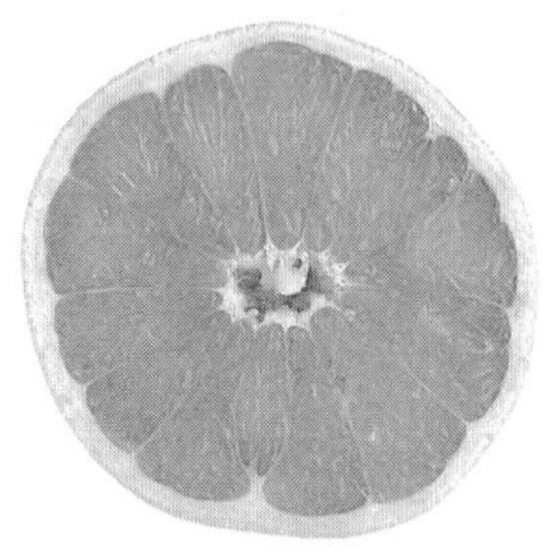

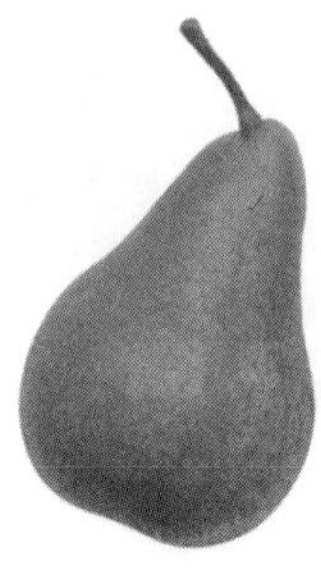

the particular fruit. Melons and citrus fruits, for example, won't get any sweeter after they are picked, while bananas and peaches ripen very nicely after picking. Still other fruits, such as avocados and pears, must be picked before they can begin to ripen. If the ripening action of the enzymes continues for too long, however, the fruit decays: Flavor and texture deteriorate, the flesh turns brown, and the vitamin content drops.

In order to withstand the rigors of shipping and distribution, many fruits are harvested while still in a firm, underripe stage. Some fruits are then allowed to ripen on their own in storage, but others are treated with ethylene gas. Fruits give off this gas during normal ripening, and for many years growers and distributors have introduced ethylene gas into storage rooms to speed up the ripening of certain fruits, reducing the time by as much as 50 percent. Ethylene can stimulate pigment change in a fruit—bringing out the yellow in bananas or the golden brown in pineapples—and will help soften and sweeten firm tropical fruits as well as certain varieties of apples and pears that need to be ripened quickly to meet market demand. Ethylene is completely safe, and it does not affect a fruit's vitamin content. By the time you buy the fruit, all traces of the gas are gone.

Cold temperatures can slow the ripening process and also stave off the growth of microbes, the other principal cause of spoilage. Some fruits are held after harvesting in controlled atmosphere (CA) storage, in which oxygen levels are significantly reduced, a change that greatly prolongs the life of the fruit. CA storage, combined with modern shipping methods, makes apples, pears, and citrus fruits available all year. Other fresh fruits, particularly berries and many tropical fruits, are seasonal—though the season for many fruits is being extended by imports, which nearly doubled between 1970 and 1989.

CANNED AND FROZEN

Canning is the most common way to preserve whole fruits, making them available out of season. A few fruits, most notably berries and cherries, are frozen. Most frozen fruits are

processed without cooking, and so there is little if any nutrient loss. Canned fruits, on the other hand, lose varying amounts of vitamin C and beta carotene. However, the vitamin loss is not as substantial as it is with vegetables (because fruits are processed at lower temperatures). In addition, people usually consume the juices that are canned along with the fruit, so the nutrients dissolved in them aren't really lost. It is true that canned fruits are often packed in heavy syrup, which can more than double the calories. (For example, a cup of raw sliced peaches has 75 calories, as compared to 190 when the slices are canned and packed in syrup.) Fortunately, canned fruits are available packed in water or in unsweetened juice; in the latter form, the nutrients are retained, and the caloric increase is far smaller. (When packed in juice, the cup of peaches has only 110 calories.)

DRIED FRUITS

Another way to preserve fruit is by drying, either in the sun or with heated air. This process turns such fruits as apples, apricots, bananas, dates, figs, grapes (raisins), peaches, pineapples, and plums (prunes) into concentrated packages of nutrients. Drying reduces the fruit's water content, usually from about 80 percent to between 15 and 25 percent. Consequently, the proportion of minerals and vitamins is substantially increased—especially iron, copper, potassium, and beta carotene (though vitamin C is sometimes lost). Dried fruit is also a compact source of dietary fiber. The catch is that drying also concentrates the sugars and calories, so that, in return for the high vitamin and mineral content, you are getting a snack food that can be as as calorie-laden as many kinds of cookies.

Some light-colored dried fruits—apples, peaches, pears, apricots, and golden raisins—have sulfite preservatives added to them to keep them from turning brown; this treatment also helps minimize any loss of vitamin C and beta carotene. But these preservatives can produce allergic reactions, sometimes severe ones, in certain people, especially asthmatics. Manufacturers are required to list the preservatives—usually sulfur

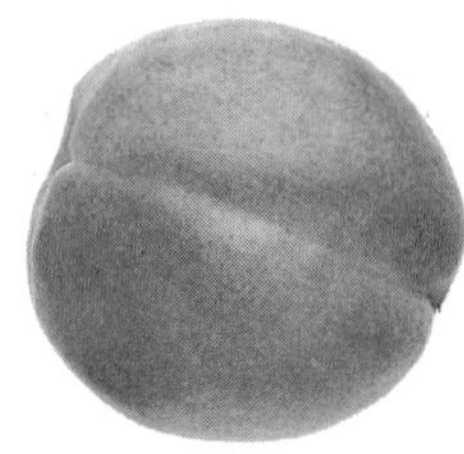

dioxide—clearly on packages, shipping containers, and bulk bins. Sulfite-sensitive people should be sure to check labels. Fortunately, there are some sulfite-free, light-colored fruits available, usually labeled as such.

JUICES

The next best thing to whole fruits is their juice. Most of their nutrients are retained, though not their fiber. All citrus juices are high in vitamin C, containing up to twice the RDA in an 8-ounce glass. Potassium is also abundant in nearly all fruit juices. Fresh-squeezed juice usually has the highest vitamin C content, followed by canned or frozen (which retain their vitamin C for months). Since vitamin C deteriorates when in contact with oxygen, chilled cartons and refrigerated mini-boxes, which are permeable to air, retain the least vitamin C. If the "sell-by" date on a juice carton is close or has passed, there may be significant loss of vitamin C—and of flavor. To protect the vitamin C from air, keep all juices refrigerated in tightly closed glass containers.

When buying juice, watch the wording on labels. Beverages labeled "juice" must be 100 percent juice, but "juice blends," fruit "punches" or "drinks," and "juice cocktails" usually contain little fruit juice—the rest being water and sugar. In some cases, these products cost more than real juice, so you're paying a lot for water. If you want diluted fruit juice, you're better off mixing real juice with water or seltzer.

PEELING AND OTHER TIPS

As is also true of vegetables, the peel of fruit tends to be relatively rich in nutrients. (It's not true, though, that nutrients are heavily concentrated in the peel; if you ate only the peel, you'd be shortchanging yourself considerably.) Not everyone likes to eat peels, of course, and the peel on some fruit is inedible, but many popular fruits—such as apples, peaches, and pears—have a peel that is tasty and nutritious. Yet these fruits are often

waxed before shipping to improve their appearance and retard spoilage. While the waxes themselves are safe, they have been shown to seal in residues of fungicides or pesticides. While the Food and Drug Administration (FDA) has found what it considers unsafe residue levels in less than 1 percent of some 5400 samples of domestic and imported fruit, there isn't any sound way to evaluate a particular piece of produce.

To minimize chemical residues, the same measures that apply to vegetables apply to fruit (see pages 45-47). It's especially important to scrub fruit thoroughly. Check with the produce manager to see if fruit has been waxed, and if so, peel it before eating it. And remember that fruit doesn't have to look perfect to be good. Melon, citrus fruit, and even apples or pears can have minor blemishes or colors that aren't ideal and still taste quite delicious, while picture-perfect fruit may turn out to be mealy and practically flavorless. To be assured that fruits are at their best, select them during their peak season, if possible, and at the proper stage of ripeness. The entries that follow describe how to choose, home-ripen, store, and serve fresh fruit for maximum eating pleasure.

Apples

It seems that most Americans enjoy eating apples: U.S. per capita consumption of apples (and processed apple products) is about 120 apples (roughly 40 pounds) per year. The apple may not be the nutritional standout of the fruit bowl—an orange or a banana, for instance, is richer in vitamins and minerals—but if an apple is eaten as one of the recommended two to four servings of fruit a day, it will provide you with respectable amounts of soluble and insoluble fiber, some vitamin C and beta carotene (if you eat the peel), and potassium and boron. The fruit is fibrous, juicy, and nonsticky, making it a good tooth-cleaner and gum stimulator. Apples are also widely available, and they store well compared to many other fruits.

THE FIBER IN APPLES

Apples are a good source of dietary fiber, with the edible portion of a 5-ounce apple supplying 17 percent of the minimum amount of fiber experts say should be consumed daily. About 81 percent of the fiber is soluble; most of it is presumed to be a type called pectin. Studies indicate that pectin and other soluble fibers are effective in lowering cholesterol levels.

A member of the rose family, the apple has a compartmented core and is thus classified as a pome fruit (the Latin word *pome* means "apple"). Fossil remains have shown that apples were gathered and stored five thousand years ago, and it is likely that they were already being cultivated in Neolithic times.

The Egyptians and the Romans grew apples, and invading Roman legions introduced them to Britain, where they are still prized today. The early colonists brought apples to America from their home country, establishing the orchards in Massachusetts and Virginia that became the foundation for most of the apples grown in the United States today.

Although apples can be grown almost anywhere in the continental United States, commercial apple growing is concentrated in the northern states, as the trees require a period of cold weather in order to flower and fruit properly. Washington, Michigan, and New York are the top producers. About half of the domestic crop is processed into applesauce, jellies, juice, and other apple products.

Of the apples cultivated for the fresh market, about half are preserved by a process known as "controlled atmosphere" (or CA) storage, which was developed in the 1940s. CA storage ensures that apples stay in good condition three to six times as long as normal cold storage, and it is because of this process that apples are now available year round. The controlled atmosphere requires a temperature of around 30°, high humidity, and a specific mixture of oxygen, carbon dioxide, nitrogen, and other gases. Some varieties, such as Delicious, McIntosh, and Rome Beauty, fare better than others in CA storage.

VARIETIES There are about seventy-five hundred varieties of apples grown all over the world, and twenty-five hundred in the United States alone. You won't encounter most of these, but it's helpful to be familiar with the more popular varieties, since some are best for eating, others are better for cooking and baking, while still others are suited to more than one purpose.

Eight favorites

Just sixteen varieties account for 90 percent of the domestic apple production—and eight of them make up 80 percent. These leading varieties not only have an appealing taste, but also ship and store well. In addition, they are more resistant to disease than other varieties. Unless otherwise noted, they are available nationwide.

Golden Delicious Despite its resemblance to the

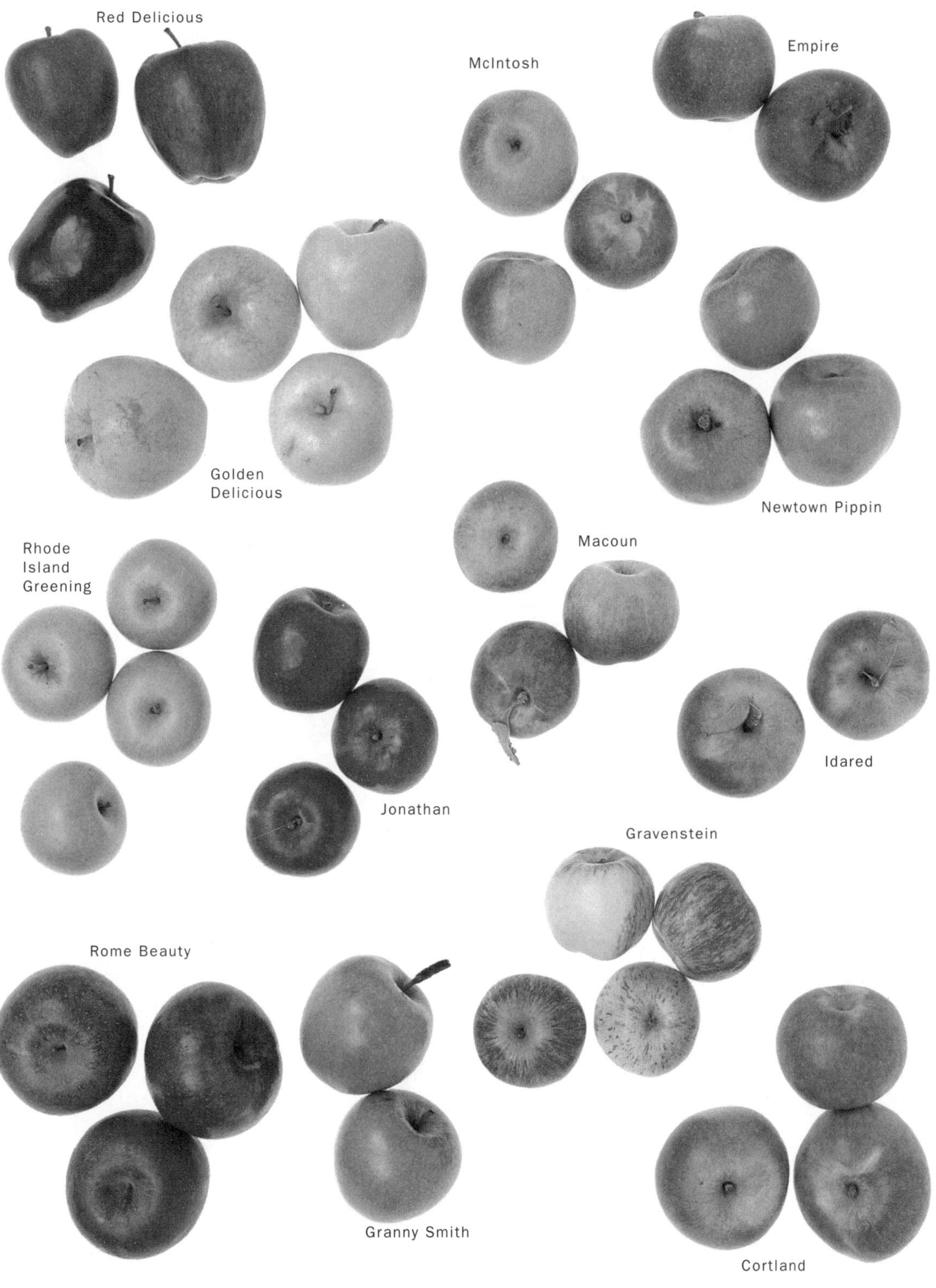
Red Delicious
McIntosh
Empire
Golden Delicious
Newtown Pippin
Rhode Island Greening
Macoun
Jonathan
Idared
Gravenstein
Rome Beauty
Granny Smith
Cortland

Red Delicious apple in shape and flavor, the Golden Delicious is an entirely separate variety. It is also an all-purpose apple, suitable for baking, eating raw, using in pies, and making applesauce. Its freckled, golden yellow skin is distinctive, as is the fact that its flesh, when sliced, doesn't darken as readily as that of other apples—a virtue that makes it a worthy ingredient in salads. *Season:* Year-round.

Granny Smith This pale green apple is originally from Australia, but is now widely grown on the West Coast. It is an all-purpose variety, with a crisp texture and tart flavor. *Season:* Year-round.

Jonathan Deep red with yellow undertones, this small- to medium-sized apple, with juicy, firm yellow flesh, is available primarily in the East and Midwest. Use it for eating or baking pies or making applesauce; however, it's not a good choice for baking whole because it loses its shape. *Season:* September through spring.

McIntosh A green-red apple from the East and Midwest, the McIntosh is a parent variety of many other apples, such as Cortland and Empire. It is very juicy, with a slightly tart flavor. Although it is excellent raw or cooked, the exceptionally smooth texture of the cooked apple may not appeal to some people. McIntoshes bruise more easily than other apples and should be handled with care. *Season:* September through spring.

Red Delicious This familiar bright red apple (which may have yellow undertones) is the most popular variety in the United States, accounting for almost one-half of the domestic crop. It has thin but tough skin, and crisp, juicy, sweet-tasting flesh. Red Delicious is best eaten raw or in salads; when cooked, it disintegrates and loses most of its flavor. *Season:* Year-round.

Rome Beauty A favorite for baking, the red or red-striped Rome Beauty holds its spherical shape well during cooking, which also brings out its flavor. Eaten raw, however, it tastes rather bland and mealy. *Season:* October through July.

Stayman This is a good all-purpose apple, with purplish red skin and white flesh that is mildly tart and juicy. It is available in the Middle Atlantic states. *Season:* September through spring.

York Also known as York Imperial, this variety—which is available in the Middle Atlantic and southeastern states—has a lopsided shape and pinkish red skin, often dotted with pale spots (which don't affect the quality of the fruit). The flesh is yellow and moderately juicy. Yorks are good baking apples, holding their shape and flavor—they are neither too tart nor too sweet—when cooked. *Season:* October through spring.

The seeds of apples—like those of other members of the same botanical family, such as apricots and peaches—contain a minute amount of the deadly poison cyanide. This fact shouldn't cause concern, however, because you would have to eat hundreds of seeds to suffer any ill effects. Still, it's wise to avoid swallowing apple seeds.

Other flavorful varieties

The following apples are produced in relatively small quantities, and they turn up in different parts of the country. Some are newly developed varieties, others are once-popular types that are no longer highly marketable, and still others are regional favorites.

Cortland This large apple has deep purplish-red skin, and snow-white flesh that resists browning. Available primarily in the East and Midwest, the Cortland is good for eating raw and also baking in pies. *Season:* September through spring.

Crispin Also known as Mutsu, the Crispin is a large green apple developed from crossing a Golden Delicious with a Japanese apple called Indo. Grown extensively in New York State, it is an all-purpose variety, with a firm texture and sweet flavor. *Season:* Year-round.

Empire This is another relatively new variety from New York State, the result of crossing the McIntosh with the Red Delicious. The deep red skin is rather thick, but the crisp texture and sweet-tart taste make the Empire ideal for eating fresh. *Season:* September through spring.

Gravenstein This distinctively red-striped apple is used primarily to make commercial applesauce, but it is occasionally sold fresh on the West Coast. Moderately tart, it is an all-purpose apple that is perfect for homemade applesauce. *Season:* Late summer through early fall.

Anyone who's ever bobbed for apples knows that they float. Twenty to 25 percent of the volume of raw apples is made up of air located between the cells of the fruit. When apples are cooked, these cells collapse and the air between them is forced out, which partially explains the softer texture of cooked apples.

Idared This all-purpose apple, red-skinned and with a mild flavor, is a favorite in the Northeast and parts of the Midwest. *Season:* September through early spring.

Macoun Tart and juicy, the red-green Macoun is excellent eaten raw, but it arrives late in the year and doesn't keep well. *Season:* September through November.

Newtown Pippin A tart green apple available on the West Coast, this variety is generally used as a cooking apple, but is also suitable for eating fresh. *Season:* September through February.

Northern Spy Produced in Michigan, New York, and parts of New England, this large red-green apple has firm yellow flesh and a tart flavor, making it suitable for pies or for snacking. *Season:* Late fall through early winter.

Rhode Island Greening Though it isn't widely available, many apple fanciers consider this East Coast green apple the best choice for pies. *Season:* October through November.

Winesap As its name suggests, this all-purpose apple—one of the oldest varieties in the United States—has a tangy winelike flavor. The flesh is firm and juicy, the skin is a deep red-purple. Winesaps are frequently used to make cider. *Season:* October through July.

SHOPPING TIPS Never buy apples that have not been kept cold, since they can become overripe and mealy in as little as two to three days, and will also turn brown near the core. After January, almost any apple you buy will probably have been stored in CA after harvesting: Although CA storage slows aging, it does not stop it, and CA-stored apples, once removed from their controlled environment, begin to deteriorate just as quickly as fresh apples do.

Apples should be firm to hard—if you can dent one with your fingers, it will make disappointing eating. Large apples are more likely to be overripe than smaller ones, so pay extra attention to firmness when buying them.

Apples should also be well colored for their variety. The skins should be tight, unbroken, and unblemished, although brown freckles or streaks (russeting) are characteristic of some varieties, such as Golden Delicious, and do not affect taste.

STORAGE Cold temperatures keep apples in "suspended animation," preventing them from ripening further after they are picked. Since most apples are picked at peak ripeness, additional "ripening" actually means "decaying"—and this process is speeded up tenfold when the fruit is left at room temperature rather than refrigerated. Whether an apple is freshly picked or has emerged from months of cold storage, it must be kept cold or its flesh will degenerate into mushiness. Place apples in plastic bags and keep them in the refrigerator crisper. If they were in good condition when you bought them, apples should keep for up to six weeks in the refrigerator. Check them often and remove any decayed apples, since one rotten apple can indeed spoil the whole bushel.

PREPARATION Wash apples before using them peeled or unpeeled. If the fruit is waxed, peel the skin before eating. Use a vegetable peeler or a sharp paring knife to peel apples, and remove the thinnest possible layer of skin.

Core apples by quartering them and cutting out the semicircular wedge that contains the seeds;

or, core whole apples with an apple corer, an inexpensive utensil consisting of a pointed metal tube affixed to a handle. Insert the tube into either end of the apple, push the corer through, then draw it out again; the core will stay in the tube.

To prevent browning, rub the cut surfaces of apples with a mixture of lemon juice and water, or drop sliced or peeled apples into cold water as you work.

Although fresh apples are delicious, the mellow, tender quality they take on during cooking is equally good.

Baking Cut cone-shaped "caps" from the tops of unpeeled apples and remove the cores. Pare a ribbon of peel from around the "equator" of each, to keep the skin from splitting as it swells in cooking. Fill the apples as desired (see Serving Suggestions), replace the caps, and set the apples in a baking pan. Pour some apple juice, cider, or water into the pan to keep the apples from drying out. Cover and bake in a 350° oven for 30 minutes, then uncover and bake until fully tender. *Cooking time:* about 60 minutes.

Microwaving Bake apples in the microwave for a quick breakfast, snack, or dessert. Place cored apples, stuffed if desired, in custard cups and pour a tablespoon of water or cider over each. Cover the apples with waxed paper and cook until tender. *Cooking times:* for two apples, 4 minutes; for four apples, 8 minutes.

Sautéing For a colorful accompaniment to poultry, beef, veal, or pork, sauté unpeeled apple slices, using an assortment of red, yellow, and green varieties. Core and slice the apples, then sauté in apple cider or apple juice; add just a touch of butter for flavor. Sauté shredded cabbage along with the apples for a German-style side dish. *Cooking time:* 3 to 5 minutes.

Apple butter Apple butter is a jamlike condiment that contains spices, such as cinnamon and allspice, and sometimes sugar. Despite its name, this butter contains no fat. For an easy homemade version, prepare homemade applesauce (see below), then continue cooking over low heat, stirring frequently, until very thick and smooth. Season as for applesauce.

Applesauce Commercial applesauce with added sugar can contain as much as 77 percent more calories than unsweetened varieties. One way to control the added sugar is to make your own applesauce. It is simple to prepare and it freezes well; you can make quarts of it at a time. Core peeled or unpeeled apples (unpeeled red apples produce rosy applesauce, but the sauce must be passed through a food mill after cooking). Cut the apples into slices or chunks and add them to a pan with just a little water, apple juice, or cider—about ⅓ cup to 3 pounds of apples. (You need only enough liquid to prevent the apples from sticking to the pan until they have begun to render their juices.) Bring to a boil, cover, and simmer, stirring occasionally, until the apples are soft. (If using unpeeled apples, put them through a food mill at this point to remove the peels.) Mash the apples—leave them slightly chunky, if you like—then taste and add sugar, honey, or maple syrup, if necessary; many varieties of apples require no sweetening. Flavor the sauce with spices (cinnamon, nutmeg, allspice, or ginger), vanilla or almond extract or lemon zest, and cook for another minute or so to blend the flavors. *Cooking time:* about 15 minutes.

You can also make applesauce in the microwave: Place peeled, sliced apples in a microwavable baking dish, cover with plastic wrap, and cook until tender. Remove apples from the microwave, mash, sweeten, and season them. *Cooking time:* 20 minutes.

SERVING SUGGESTIONS Serve sliced apples for dessert, with a sprinkling of either cinnamon or crushed walnuts, or with a small wedge of sharp cheddar or blue cheese. Offer apple slices or rounds with sweet or savory dips, and add thin apple slices to mixed green or spinach salads. Make an updated version of a Waldorf salad with unpeeled apple chunks, walnuts, celery, and a yogurt-apple juice dressing instead of mayonnaise; add chunks of chicken for a heartier dish.

If you love melted cheese sandwiches, cut the fat and boost the flavor by substituting thick apple slices or grated apple for some of the cheese. Add grated apple to a peanut-butter sandwich. Lend zest and texture to tuna or chicken salad by tossing in some chopped apple. Stir chopped apple, raisins, and almonds into rice for a pilaf to accompany roast chicken. Or, use chopped apple to make a tangy, moist stuffing. Grate apples into meatloaf or meatball mixtures to enhance flavor and moistness.

Apple juice and cider contain virtually no vitamin C, unless it has been added in processing. Products with added vitamin C provide anywhere from 95 to 160 percent of the RDA for this vitamin in an 8-ounce glass. If vitamin C has been added, it will be listed on the label.

Sweet, warm spices, such as cinnamon, cloves, nutmeg, mace, allspice, ginger, or premixed apple-pie spice (which is a blend of several of these), are natural partners for cooked apples. If the applesauce or apples you're cooking with taste insipid, perk up their flavor with a little lemon juice and/or vanilla extract. Be creative the next time you make applesauce; include fruits and nuts, such as cranberries, blueberries, chopped pecans, or almonds.

Use hot applesauce as a waffle or pancake topping or as a spread on toast. Stir applesauce or apple butter into cottage cheese and eat it with crackers or on thickly sliced whole wheat toast. Serve hot chunky applesauce for dessert, with a sprinkling of crisp cereal, or ladle it over plain cake or a scoop of ice milk. Apple butter is a delicious spread for bread and a tasty addition to yogurt or cottage cheese.

APPLES 3½ oz raw (1 cup sliced)

Calories	59	Fat	<1 g
Protein	19 g	Saturated Fat	<1 g
Carbohydrate	15 g	Cholesterol	0 mg
Dietary Fiber	Low (S)	Sodium	0 mg

KEY NUTRIENTS		% RDA Men	% RDA Women
Vitamin C	6 mg	10%	10%

S=40% or more soluble N/A=Not Applicable N=Not Available

Glaze meat or poultry with applesauce, but make it sweet and hot by mixing in some mustard, a touch of vinegar, or curry powder. Blend prepared horseradish into applesauce for an unusual condiment for beef.

Chopped dried fruits (raisins, dates or figs, for instance) and nuts (such as pecans or almonds) are wonderful in a baked apple; so is chopped pineapple. Fill baked apples with leftover cooked rice, sweetened and spiced. Baked apples can also be served for breakfast—hot or cold—topped with yogurt and a sprinkling of crunchy cereal.

Apricots

Fresh apricots, which are among the first fruits of summer, are notable for their fragrance, delicate flavor, and velvety surface. Nutritionally, these fragile peachlike fruits (they are a peach relative) contain impressive amounts of beta carotene—one apricot, weighing a little over an ounce, contains enough beta carotene to supply 18 percent of the RDA for vitamin A. They are also a good source of vitamin C, iron, and potassium. In fact, NASA officials made them a key part of the astronauts' diet on a number of space flights, including the Apollo moon mission.

Apricots

Apricots originated in China about four thousand years ago and were transplanted throughout Asia and Europe. The Spanish brought them to California in the late 1700s. Today, California supplies more than 90 percent of the domestic crop. Only about 16 percent of these apricots are sold fresh during a relatively short growing season of about ten weeks. About half the apricot crop is canned, and consequently, is somewhat less nutritious than fresh: Apricots packed in light syrup have double the calories and half the beta carotene and vitamin C of fresh. Juice-packed canned apricots can be substituted for fresh in most instances.

There are approximately a dozen varieties of apricots: All are similar in taste, but differ somewhat in size and color (which ranges from yellow to deep orange). Blenheim, Tilton, Patterson, and Castlebrite are among the better-known varieties.

AVAILABILITY Domestic apricots are available from mid-May through mid-August. Imports from Chile and New Zealand appear in markets in December and January.

SHOPPING TIPS Fully-ripe apricots ship poorly, so unless you live near an apricot-growing region, you may have a difficult time finding any ripe ones. Fruits at this stage of maturity are soft to the touch and brimming with juice. You should eat them as soon as possible, as they will not keep. Apricots that still need a day or two of ripening at room temperature should be plump, firm, and orange-gold in color. Don't buy hard fruits that are tinged with green—they will never develop full flavor.

Even when not fully ripe, apricots should yield to gentle pressure and exude a perfumy fragrance; their skin should be smooth and velvety. Avoid any that have shriveled skin or bruises; however, minor blemishes that do not break the skin will not affect the flavor.

STORAGE If you buy apricots that are not quite ripe, store them in a paper bag at room temperature, away from heat or direct sunlight, for two to three days. Once ripe, they may be stored in the refrigerator in a plastic bag, where they will keep a day or two at most. Don't wash the fruits until you're ready to eat them.

APRICOT NECTAR

Try apricot nectar—the juice of fresh apricots—for a refreshing change from the old standbys, orange and apple juice. The nectar's chief advantage is its substantial beta carotene content; a cup contains 2 milligrams of beta carotene. (A cup of fresh-squeezed orange juice, for example, contains less than half a milligram.) The nectar is only slightly higher in calories than orange juice, and while not naturally high in vitamin C, it is usually available fortified with this vitamin; a cup offers 228 percent of the RDA. Like fresh apricots, nectar is also a good source of potassium.

PREPARATION Rinse apricots under cold running water before using them. Ripe apricots are soft and delicate, so if you need to peel them for a recipe, do so carefully. Place the fruits in boiling water for 15 to 20 seconds, then remove them and

DRIED APRICOTS

In their dried form, apricots are a concentrated source of nutrients. Three and a half ounces of dried apricots (about twenty-nine halves) provide 4 milligrams of beta carotene, 47 percent of the RDA for iron for men (31 percent for women), and 16 percent of the niacin for men (20 percent for women). The same amount also contains 1378 milligrams of potassium, nearly 8 grams of dietary fiber, and some calcium. When fresh apricots are dried, their vitamin C content is greatly reduced, and their calorie content is increased dramatically. (Three and a half ounces of dried apricots have 238 calories, while the same amount of fresh ones have only 48 calories.)

Dried apricots are over 40 percent sugar; they are chewy and will stick to your teeth, encouraging the development of cavities. You should brush your teeth or, at least, rinse your mouth soon after eating the fruits.

Processors often treat dried apricots with sulfur dioxide to help preserve their rich orange color. Sulfites, however, can cause severe allergic reactions in people who are sensitive to them. Whenever they are used, government regulations stipulate that they be listed on the label or package. Unsulfured apricots can usually be obtained in health-food stores; they are brown, not orange.

cool them under cold water. Use a knife to pull away their skin; it should slip right off. To halve apricots, cut down to the pit around the longitudinal seam and twist the two halves to separate them; discard the pit. Dip peeled or cut-up apricots into diluted lemon juice to keep them from browning.

When cooking fresh apricots, it is important to heat them only briefly, or they will lose their flavor.

Broiling/grilling Apricots prepared by this method make a delicious accompaniment to chicken cooked on the grill; they can also be served as a dessert at a barbecue or picnic. Thread whole or halved fresh apricots on skewers, brush with honey, and grill until tender. Or, oven-broil apricot halves, cut-side up, 4 to 5 inches from the heat. *Cooking time:* 7 to 10 minutes.

Poaching Place apricots—peeled or unpeeled, whole or halved—in barely simmering fruit juice, cover, and cook until tender. Add whole cloves or a cinnamon stick to the liquid for extra flavor. Once the apricots are poached, the liquid can be cooked down to produce a sauce. *Cooking time:* 6 to 8 minutes.

Reconstituting dried apricots Serve dried apricots for breakfast or dessert, at any time of year. Simmer them in a small amount of water, wine, or fruit juice until tender. *Cooking time:* 15 minutes.

SERVING SUGGESTIONS The delicate flavor of fresh apricots is best appreciated by eating them raw, preferably at room temperature. These fruits can also be used in any recipe that calls for nectarines or fresh, frozen, or canned peaches. Cinnamon, cloves, cardamom, and almond nicely complement apricots.

Combine fresh or canned apricots with hot peppers, lime juice, chopped onion, and ground cumin for an imaginative version of fruit salsa to serve alongside chicken or fish. Or, add sliced fresh or canned apricots to chicken salad.

APRICOTS 3½ oz raw (3 apricots)

Calories	48	Fat	<1 g
Protein	1 g	Saturated Fat	<1 g
Carbohydrate	11 g	Cholesterol	0 mg
Dietary Fiber	Medium (S)	Sodium	1 mg

KEY NUTRIENTS		% RDA Men	% RDA Women
Vitamin A	2612 IU	52%	65%
Beta Carotene	2 mg	N/A	N/A
Vitamin C	10 mg	17%	17%

S=40% or more soluble N/A=Not Applicable N=Not Available

Stir chopped fresh apricots into yogurt or incorporate them in quick bread or muffin batters for a more interesting texture. If you have lots of ripe apricots on hand, you can make your own nectar by puréeing the peeled fruit in a food processor or blender.

Dried apricots are often stewed—alone or with other dried fruits—and served for breakfast or as a side dish, or cooked along with roasted chicken or lamb. They can also be mixed into a rice or bread stuffing for poultry, or added to rice or bulgur pilaf or couscous. Reconstitute dried apricots, purée them, then spoon the sauce over plain cake or frozen yogurt. Chopped dried apricots are a popular ingredient in cookies, coffee cakes, and quick breads.

Avocados

A smooth, buttery texture and a mild, nutty flavor are the hallmarks of the avocado, a tropical fruit that is often considered a "vegetable fruit" because of its unique flavor and the ways in which it can be used. Outwardly, it looks so much like a leathery pear that it is sometimes called an "alligator pear" or a "butter pear." But unlike a pear, or any other fruit except olives, the avocado is exceptionally high in fat. In addition, whereas most other fruits tend to gain sugar, the sugar content of the avocado decreases as it ripens. (When the avocado is used in desserts, sugar is often mashed into it.) However, it does contain more beta carotene than many other fruits—including apples, bananas, and grapefruit—and it is high in potassium: Ounce for ounce, the avocado supplies 60 percent more potassium than a banana. It is also a fair source of dietary fiber.

Avocados are native to Central America, and were first cultivated in the United States in the mid-1800s in Florida and California. These are still the only areas where domestic avocado production has thrived. Today, California alone produces nearly 90 percent of the domestic crop, and the two states together provide a year-round supply that adds up to the world's largest commercial production.

VARIETIES Together, California and Florida grow some two dozen commercial varieties, ranging in size from a few ounces to several pounds, and in color from dark green to bright green to black. The varieties produced by each state depend on the soil and weather conditions specific to that area, and so they don't adapt well (or at all) to growing elsewhere. The most popular California variety (about 90 percent of the state's production) is the Hass, which weighs about half a pound and has a thick, pebbled skin that changes from green to purplish black as the fruit ripens. Fuerte, another popular California variety, which can weigh up to a pound, has a more pronounced pear shape, a milder flavor, and a thinner, smoother skin than the Hass. Other smooth-skinned types of California avocados are Bacon and Zutano.

Ounce for ounce, Florida avocado varieties have about half the fat and two-thirds the calories of the varieties grown in California.

Florida avocados are larger than those from California and less costly; they also contain less fat and fewer calories. Their texture is not as rich or creamy, and they are slightly more perishable. Booth, Lula, and Waldin are the leading varieties.

AVAILABILITY Avocados can be found in markets throughout the year. California and Florida ship different varieties, according to season: Hass, for example, is available year round; Fuerte, Bacon, and Zutano are in good supply during the fall and winter. Generally, California avocados are at a peak in spring and summer, while Florida's season extends from June through March, with its peak in October.

THE FAT STORY

No doubt about it, avocados are high in fat—especially when compared to other fruits and vegetables. They derive between 71 and 88 percent of their calories from fat (depending on whether it's a Florida or California avocado—Florida's fat content is lower). But the fat is mostly monounsaturated—the same type that is found in olive oil—which has been shown in studies to lower blood cholesterol. And, of course, like all fruits and vegetables, avocados contain no cholesterol.

Despite its positive features, you should not eat an avocado every day, unless you don't have to worry about calories. Still, avocados can easily fit into a diet that derives the recommended 30 percent of its calories from fat. Three and a half ounces of avocado have less fat than a salad with 2 tablespoons of Italian dressing, a cup of potato salad made with mayonnaise, or a 3½-ounce hamburger made with lean ground beef.

SHOPPING TIPS Many markets sell avocados while they're still hard and unripe, so you will have to allow them a few days at room temperature to soften. To choose a good avocado, select a heavy fruit with an unblemished, unbroken skin. Pick it up and squeeze it gently between your hands: The fruit should yield to gentle pressure. If your fingers leave a dent, however, it means that the avocado is overripe. (A *slightly* overripe avocado will be too soft for slicing but fine for mashing; however, a *very* overripe one will have unusable, blackened flesh.)

Most avocado varieties stay green even when ripe, taking on a slight yellowing tinge, but Hass avocados turn purplish black as they soften.

STORAGE Ripe avocados will keep in the refrigerator for four to five days; however, longer storage at cold temperatures will cause discoloration of the flesh and unpleasant changes in the flavor. Don't store unripe avocados in the refrigerator, as they will never ripen properly. Unripe fruits should be left at room temperature until softened—a process that takes three to six days; quicker ripening can be achieved by placing the avocados in a loosely closed paper bag with a tomato.

PREPARATION To halve and pit an avocado, run a knife lengthwise around the fruit, then twist the two halves to separate them. Strike the pit with the blade of a heavy knife, then twist it as if you're turning a screw; the pit will loosen so you can lift it out. Or, pry out the pit with the tip of a teaspoon. Place the halves face down and peel off the skin (if it doesn't slip off like a banana skin, help it along with a paring knife), or use a spoon or a melon baller to scoop out the flesh. To cut avocado rings, cut the fruit crosswise around the middle, remove the pit, and cut crosswise slices.

WHEN AVOCADOS RIPEN

Unlike most other fruits, an avocado won't start to ripen until it is cut from the tree—the leaves supply a hormone to the fruit that inhibits the production of ethylene, the chemical substance that causes fruit to ripen. Once the fruit is harvested, the supply of the hormone is cut off. The delay in ripening is a boon to growers, who can leave avocados on the tree (for up to seven months) if market conditions aren't favorable when the fruit is first ready to harvest. It also explains why the avocados at your produce counter are likely to be hard, and will need a few extra days to become fully ripe.

Once cut or peeled, avocado flesh will discolor; this browning has no affect on flavor, but it makes the avocado look less appetizing. Rub or sprinkle the flesh with lemon or lime juice as soon as you cut it, and add citrus juice to mashed avocado to prevent it from darkening rapidly. When storing mashed avocado or guacamole, place a sheet of heavy-duty plastic wrap directly on the surface of the mixture and press out any air bubbles; this cover will also help forestall the inevitable browning of the flesh. Or, leave the pit embedded in a cut avocado half; it will slow down the discoloration of the area surrounding it (because it prevents oxygen from reaching there). The widely held belief that a pit left in a bowl of guacamole will keep the mixture green is a myth; however, the acid ingredients in guacamole—tomatoes and citrus juice—will delay the discoloration for at least an hour or so.

AVOCADO, California 3½ oz raw (⅔ avocado)

Calories	177	Fat	17 g
Protein	2 g	Saturated Fat	3 g
Carbohydrate	7 g	Cholesterol	0 mg
Dietary Fiber	High	Sodium	12 mg

KEY NUTRIENTS		% RDA Men	% RDA Women
Vitamin A	612 IU	12%	15%
Vitamin B_6	0.3 mg	15%	19%
Vitamin C	8 mg	13%	13%
Copper	0.3 mg	N/A	N/A
Vitamin E	1 mg	13%	10%
Folacin	66 mcg	33%	37%
Iron	1 mg	10%	7%
Magnesium	41 mg	12%	15%
Manganese	0.2 mg	N/A	N/A
Niacin	2 mg	10%	13%
Potassium	634 mg	N/A	N/A
Thiamin	0.1 mg	7%	10%

S=40% or more soluble N/A=Not Applicable N=Not Available

AVOCADO, Florida 3½ oz raw (⅔ avocado)

Calories	112	Fat	9 g
Protein	2 g	Saturated Fat	2 g
Carbohydrate	9 g	Cholesterol	0 mg
Dietary Fiber	High	Sodium	5 mg

KEY NUTRIENTS		% RDA Men	% RDA Women
Vitamin B_6	0.3	15%	9%
Vitamin C	8 mg	13%	13%
Copper	0.3	N/A	N/A
Folacin	53 mcg	27%	29%
Magnesium	34 mg	10%	12%
Niacin	2 mg	10%	13%
Potassium	488 mg	N/A	N/A

S=40% or more soluble N/A=Not Applicable N=Not Available

SERVING SUGGESTIONS Since avocados are high in fat—the edible portion of an 8-ounce California avocado contains about 30 grams of fat—they should be used judiciously, preferably in combination with low-fat foods. For a substantial green salad, toss in avocado chunks, as well as grapefruit slices. Or, slice avocado into turkey, tuna, salmon, shrimp, cold rice, or pasta salad; then heighten its flavor with Mexican seasonings, such as chilies, cumin, lime juice and fresh coriander. Use avocados in fruit salads or cut them in half and stuff them with cold salad fillings.

Mashed avocado (or guacamole) makes a buttery, flavorful, lower-fat substitute for mayonnaise on sandwiches. Guacamole is easy to make:

Mash an avocado and blend it with finely chopped tomato, onion, garlic, lemon or lime juice, and hot pepper sauce; add chopped fresh coriander, if available. Serve guacamole with vegetable dippers and oven-baked tortilla triangles rather than high-fat, packaged tortilla chips.

The combination of avocado and sprouts in a sandwich—a California specialty—works well: The crunchy, spicy sprouts set off the creamy, mellow avocado to advantage. Add other chopped vegetables, toss with a yogurt dressing or vinaigrette, and pack into pita pockets. Avocado is also delicious in chicken or turkey sandwiches.

A summery cold avocado soup requires no cooking: Just purée avocados in a blender or food processor with chicken broth, lemon juice, and plain yogurt. Add chopped onion or garlic, if you like, and season to taste.

Avocados are usually eaten raw; they develop a bitter flavor when cooked over high heat. Once cooked foods have been removed from the heat, however, avocados can be used to complement them. Fan avocado slices atop broiled chicken breasts, toss avocado chunks with hot pasta, or add avocado cubes to a bowl of chicken soup.

The fruit's creamy texture can also be enjoyed in desserts. Purée peeled avocados with sugar and some lemon juice for an instant, cholesterol-free mousse or, drizzle honey and sprinkle chopped fresh mint over avocado halves.

Bananas

If you were to design an ideal food, you might arrive at the banana—a fruit that was among the first plants to be cultivated and that has been a staple for thousands of years. Bananas have a peel that comes off easily and neatly; they ripen best after they have been picked; they can be chosen (and consumed) at several stages of ripeness; they are in generous supply all year; they are inexpensive; and they can be easily digested by virtually everyone, including infants and elderly people. All of these attributes explain why bananas have become the most popular fresh fruit in the United States: Americans consume about 25 pounds per person, on average, each year. Yet bananas are not a commercial crop in the United States; they are cultivated in tropical regions, most prolifically in Central and South America, and are shipped to northern ports on a grand scale. Banana prices remain moderate, however, because of abundant supplies, intense competition among growers, and cheap land and labor.

Nutritionally, bananas have a great deal to offer. Since they contain less water than most other fruits, their carbohydrate content, by weight, is higher—which is one of the reasons that bananas have become the snack of choice for endurance athletes. Besides helping to replenish the body's store of carbohydrates, bananas provide substantial amounts of potassium, a mineral that is lost during bouts of physical activity, yet is vital for controlling the body's fluid balance. Potassium also works to regulate heartbeat and blood pressure, and, in older people, may help to reduce the risk of fatal stroke.

Bananas have more potassium by weight than practically any other fruit, except avocados (which have a great deal more fat).

VARIETIES The familiar yellow banana sold in U.S. supermarkets is usually the Cavendish variety. In specialty stores, urban supermarkets, and

in Hispanic neighborhoods, you can sometimes find a number of more exotic varieties that offer different tastes and textures. These include manzano (also called apple or finger bananas), which are finger sized and turn black when ripe; Saba and Brazilian, which are straight, medium sized, and somewhat tart; red bananas, which are sweet tasting, and turn purplish red as they ripen; and plantains, which are large, starchy fruits that are usually cooked (see box on page 207).

AVAILABILITY Yellow bananas are in good supply all year; exotic varieties are more seasonal.

SHOPPING TIPS The taste and texture of a banana is directly related to its stage of ripeness. The carbohydrates in green bananas are primarily starches that convert to sugar as the fruits ripen and turn yellow. Very green bananas are hard and have an astringent taste, whereas fully ripened yellow bananas are soft, sweet, and creamy. For eating out of hand, bananas that are yellow and flecked with brown spots will be at their peak flavor, but many people prefer the texture and less-sweet taste of bananas that have yellow jackets and green tips. There's no harm in eating a less-than-ripe banana, except that if it is very green, it may be hard to digest.

Choose bananas according to how—and when—you'll eat them. If you prefer fully ripe, brown-flecked bananas, and the store carries only greenish ones, you'll need to shop several days in advance of the time you plan to eat the fruit. If you prefer bananas just yellow, a day or two will suffice to ripen greenish ones. Don't buy any that have a dull, grayish cast; these may have been stored at very cold temperatures, and will not ripen properly.

Bananas should be plump, firm, and bright colored. Look for unblemished fruit: Occasional brown spots on the skin are normal, but sunken, moist-looking dark areas will likely show up as bruises on the fruit. Bananas should have their stem ends and skins intact: A split skin or stem may become an entry point for contamination. There's no quality difference between small and large fruit, so you can choose the "portion size" you prefer. Bananas bruise easily, so handle them with care.

STORAGE Bananas that require further ripening should be left at room temperature, but away from heat or direct sun. To speed ripening, place them in a plastic or paper bag; you can also put an apple in the bag with the bananas to hasten the process (the apple, however, will overripen to a mealy mush). Once ripened to your liking, bananas can be held at room temperature for about a day or two. Then, you can store them in the refrigerator to slow down ripening; although the skins will turn dark, the fruits will remain perfectly edible. You can keep refrigerated bananas for up to two weeks. You should never refrigerate unripe bananas, however: The exposure to cold interrupts their ripening cycle, and it will not resume even if the fruits are returned to room temperature.

You can salvage an overabundance of overripe bananas by peeling them, wrapping them whole or in chunks in plastic wrap, and freezing them. Eat them frozen (a sweet treat in summer) or thaw them and use in baking.

PREPARATION When peeling and slicing bananas that you won't be serving immediately, dip them into lemon, lime, or orange juice to slow browning.

Heating enhances this aromatic fruit, making it taste and smell even sweeter—suitable for serving as a dessert, or as a side dish to accompany chicken or fish. Bananas are tender and require very little cooking time; however, green-tipped varieties are best for cooking, as they tend to hold their shape better.

Baking Halve bananas lengthwise, but do not peel them. Place in a baking dish, brush with orange or other fruit juice and a little honey, if desired, and bake until hot and tender. *Cooking time:* about 15 minutes.

A TREE THAT'S NOT A TREE

Despite their elongated shape and distinctive packaging, bananas are actually a type of berry, and banana "trees" are really huge plants botanically classified as herbs. The plants can grow anywhere from 15 to 30 feet high, and have a slender "trunk" made up of tightly wrapped layers of leaves—making them the largest plants in the world without a woody stem. Yet some varieties are very fragile; a strong wind can wipe out a growing field in minutes.

Each plant consists of huge leaves—so large that they are used to thatch roofs and make umbrellas in some parts of the tropics. The plant develops a single stem and bud that sustains rows of tiny flowers, each one of which becomes an individual banana, called a "finger." The bananas, which form into clusters of ten to twenty, called "hands," grow out and upward so that they appear to be upside down. A plant produces seven to nine hands.

Grilling/broiling For an unusual but delicious dessert at a barbecue, serve grilled bananas.

PLANTAINS

Resembling large, fat, green bananas, plantains are banana relatives that have a high starch content; they are cooked and served like vegetables. When allowed to ripen, some varieties go through the same color changes as bananas, but they won't become as sweet. Nutritionally, they are similar to bananas. They are a good source of potassium and vitamin C. Plantains are higher in beta carotene, however, with 3½ ounces, cooked, containing enough to provide 18 percent of the RDA for vitamin A, compared to 2 percent in the same amount of raw bananas.

Plantains are usually available in Hispanic markets—where they may be labeled *platanos*—or urban supermarkets. They may appear bruised, but as long as they are firm and their skin is intact, they are fine to eat. You can use them as you would potatoes—either as a side dish or as an addition to soups and stews. Traditionally, plantains are fried, but this method will increase their fat content considerably. Instead, try baking green plantains in their skins—first, perforate the skin with a fork, then bake in a 400° oven until a fork will easily pierce the flesh (about 40 minutes). Or, add peeled, sliced plantains to stir-fries, soups, or stews.

Thread banana chunks on skewers and cook over the coals; or, place unpeeled fruit, halved lengthwise, directly on the grill until heated through. Indoors, place halved bananas, cut-side up, under the broiler. *Cooking time:* about 5 minutes.

SERVING SUGGESTIONS Start your day with bananas: Slice them onto hot or cold cereal, stir them into yogurt, or use them to top hot toast, waffles, or pancakes. Use them in a mixed fruit salad, but don't add until just before serving. Ripe bananas are one of the best fruits to use in a blender drink: Whirl them with yogurt or skim milk and other fruits or juices (try strawberries or pineapple juice), for a thick breakfast shake. If you have overripe bananas, mash and add them to your favorite muffin or quick bread recipe. (Citrus juices and spices such as cinnamon, nutmeg, and vanilla are excellent for flavoring dishes made with bananas.)

Bananas are always a good dessert or snack choice. Place grilled banana chunks between graham crackers or, for a rich-tasting topping, whip soft, ripe bananas with ice-cold evaporated skim milk. Chunks of banana, frozen until firm, also make a satisfying dessert. To prepare a special ice-creamlike treat, purée frozen bananas with a bit of skim milk in a blender or food processor.

BANANA 3½ oz raw (1 banana)			
Calories	92	Fat	<1 g
Protein	1 g	Saturated Fat	<1 g
Carbohydrate	23	Cholesterol	0 mg
Dietary Fiber	Low	Sodium	1 mg

KEY NUTRIENTS		% RDA Men	% RDA Women
Vitamin B_6	0.6 mg	30%	37%
Vitamin C	9 mg	15%	15%
Folacin	19 mcg	10%	11%
Potassium	396 mg	N/A	N/A
Magnesium	29 mg	8%	10%

S=40% or more soluble N/A=Not Applicable N=Not Available

Berries

Berries are fun to eat. They're small, juicy, and low in calories. (The various types range from about 50 to 70 calories per cup, so don't worry about overindulging.) Many berries are sufficiently sweet for eating raw; others can be cooked and sweetened to make compotes, relishes, and preserves. Among the first people to appreciate these succulent fruits were Native Americans, who ate them, cooked them, dried them for adding to winter soups and stews, and also used them as medicines, dyes, and food preservatives. Colonists, dating back to the Pilgrims, quickly developed a taste for the many varieties growing wild in woods and fields throughout the United States. Today, wild varieties are still gathered with enthusiasm, but most of the berries in stores are from cultivated acreage; each year these supplies increase, not only from domestic sources but also from growers in Europe and New Zealand.

The chief nutrients found in berries are vitamin C and potassium (in varying proportions, depending on the type of berry), and fiber is in relatively good supply, too. Commercially canned berries, however, almost always contain added sugar, which can double or triple the calorie count. The sugar in store-bought cranberry sauce, for example, increases the calories to 209 per half cup (compared to 27 calories for the same amount of chopped raw fruit). In addition, dur-

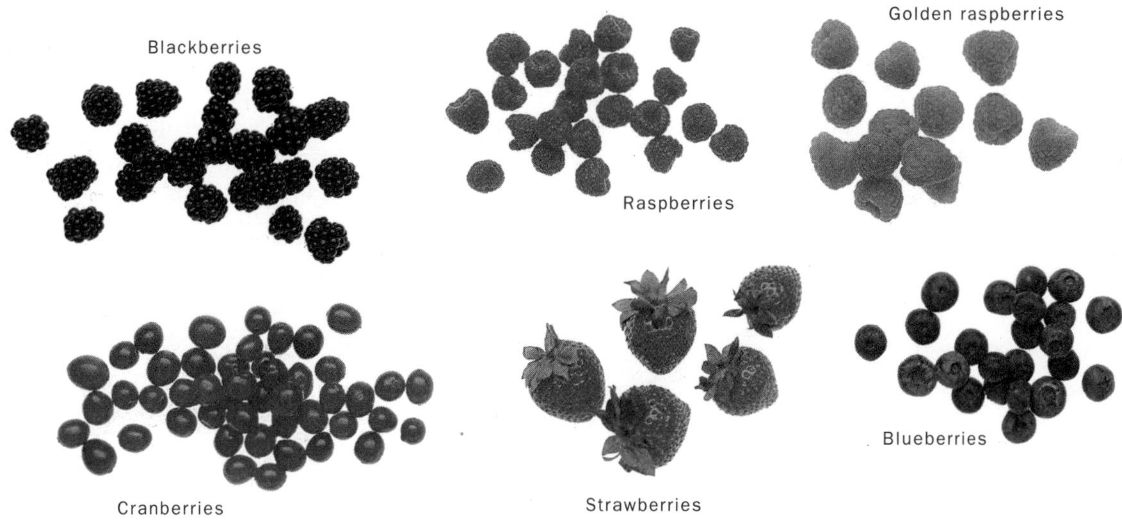

ing canning the berries are heated, which significantly reduces their vitamin C content.

Cranberries, raspberries, strawberries, and loganberries contain ellagic acid, a natural substance that preliminary research suggests may help to prevent certain types of cancer. Ellagic acid doesn't seem to break down when food is cooked, and so a fair amount can be found in processed foods, such as berry preserves and pies.

VARIETIES The principal types of berries available commercially differ in size, color, season, and nutrient content, but especially in regard to how sweet or sour they are. They include smooth-skinned varieties such as cranberries, blueberries, and gooseberries; others that have fleshy segments, such as blackberries and raspberries; and the strawberry, which is known as a "false" fruit because it grows from the base rather than from the ovary of a flower, and so is not a true berry.

Blackberries True blackberries, which taste tart to relatively sweet, outwardly resemble raspberries, but they are longer, firmer, and have a black to purplish black color. (The blacker the color, the riper—and sweeter—the berry.) One type of blackberry grows on brambles, another (sometimes called a dewberry) on trailing vines. Berry growers have also developed some hybrid varieties that are mostly cultivated on the West Coast. These include boysenberries (maroon and tart); loganberries (large, dark red, and very tart); and ollalieberries (shiny black and sweet to tart). The tarter berries are used in pies and jams. *Season:* May through September, with the peak season occurring in June and July.

Blueberries Excellent raw or cooked, blueberries can be eaten by the handful or added to cereal, muffin and pancake recipes, fruit salads, and yogurt. They are also an excellent source of fiber. Cultivated varieties are three to four times larger than their wild cousins. They have a powdery gloss, which is a natural protective coating, on their dark blue skins. Blueberries also store longer than most other berries—up to five days fresh and for months when frozen. *Season:* May through September.

Canned cranberry sauce has 86 percent less vitamin C than an equal amount of fresh cranberries, and more than three times the calories.

Cranberries Too tart to eat raw, glossy red cranberries are made into sauces, relishes, pies, and preserves. Only about 10 percent of the commercial crop is sold fresh; the rest is used either in juice or canned cranberry sauce. Like blueberries, the wild cranberries favored by early settlers have been largely replaced by cultivated varieties that are larger, glossier, and more flavorful. (There are four major varieties that vary somewhat in size and color, but all taste virtually the same.) Cranberries also store well (about a month in the refrigerator, a year in the freezer). *Season:* September through December.

Currants These small berries grow on vines in clusters, like grapes. Only red and white currants are grown domestically (Europeans also cultivate a black variety), and these have an intense tartness that makes them well-suited for jams and jellies. The supply of fresh currants is quite limited. *Season:* July through early August.

Gooseberries Closely related to currants, gooseberries are very tart grapelike fruits that turn from pale green to amber as they ripen. Most are used for pies and preserves, though a bright yellow Peruvian variety, known as Yellow Cape, is sweet enough for eating raw. *Season:* May through August, supplemented by a small supply of imports from October through December.

Raspberries These are the most expensive and most fragile berries, and their supply is extremely limited. A bramble fruit like blackberries, raspberries have a delicate structure with a hollow core, so that they have to be handled very gently and eaten as soon as possible. (Once they reach market, they have a shelf life of a day or two.) Most cultivated raspberries are red, but there are also varieties in yellow, apricot, amber, and purple (or "black")—all similar in flavor and texture. In the northeastern states local varieties are available from midsummer to late summer, but the bulk of this fresh fruit comes from California. *Season:* June through October. Chilean imports may be available at other times of the year.

Strawberries These are the most popular berries and they also contain more vitamin C than other members of the berry family—½ cup provides 70 percent of the RDA. In addition, the half cup supplies more fiber than a slice of whole wheat bread. Strawberries are also the most plentiful berry: Some seventy varieties are produced commercially, mostly in California and Florida (though they are grown in all fifty states). Oversized strawberries are no longer less tasty, as was often the case some years ago; new varieties are bred to be large without sacrificing flavor. *Season:* Year round, with the peak from April through July. Supplies diminish significantly from October through January.

Some people have an allergic reaction to strawberries—they break out in hives. The substance in the fruit that causes the reaction is unknown, but it appears to make body cells release histamine, which causes the hives. Antihistamines can control the hives, but people who have this reaction to strawberries are advised to avoid them altogether.

SHOPPING TIPS For best flavor, buy berries when they're in season where you live; they'll undoubtedly be riper, tastier, and less expensive than berries that are flown in from distant regions "out of season." Also, the closer the berries are to the market, the less damage they're likely to suffer in transit.

Choose berries very carefully; they are often packed in opaque boxes that may conceal inferior fruit beneath a display of perfect specimens on top. If the box is cellophane wrapped, your best bet is to examine the berries you can see, and check the box for dampness or stains, which indicate that the fruit below may be decaying. If the box is not wrapped, you can remove a few of the top berries and peek beneath. Check, too, for twigs or other debris (there shouldn't be any).

All berries should be plump, dry, firm, well shaped and uniformly colored. Don't purchase berries that are withered or crushed. Except for strawberries, none should have caps or stems attached. The caps on strawberries should look fresh and green.

Strawberries should be a bright red: Pale, greenish, or yellowish fruit is unripe and will be hard and sour. Blueberries should be navy blue with a powdery, silver-white "bloom" on their surface; reddish blueberries are unripe, and thus lack the flavor for eating raw (though they are fine for cooking).

Strawberries contain 60 percent more vitamin C by weight than grapefruit and 8 percent more vitamin C than oranges.

Blackberries should be deep purple to black, and should not have any green or white patches. Currants should be firmly attached to their branchlike stems. Cranberries are usually packed in bags, but you can still check them for firmness and good red color; the bag should contain a minimum of pale berries and debris.

STORAGE Berries are among the most perishable of fruits; they can turn soft, mushy, and moldy within 24 hours. When you bring home a box of berries, turn it out and check the fruit. Remove soft, overripe berries for immediate consumption; discard any smashed or moldy berries and gently blot the remainder dry with a paper towel. Return the berries to the box, or, better yet, spread them on a shallow plate or pan and cover with paper towels, then with plastic wrap.

Storage times vary slightly, but most berries should be kept for no longer than two days. Fresh, sound blueberries will keep for about ten days; cranberries will keep for up to two weeks. Raspberries, the most fragile of all, should be used within a day of purchase.

PREPARATION Sort berries again before serving, discarding any bad ones. Rinse the fruit, drain, and gently pat dry. (Frozen berries need not be thawed before using them in recipes, but extra cooking time may be necessary. Commercially frozen berries do not require washing, but home-frozen berries—which should not have been washed previously—should be quickly rinsed under cold water.)

Cranberries and blueberries can be cleaned and sorted by placing them in a basin of cold water; twigs, leaves, and unripe berries are easy to spot because they float to the surface. The process should be done quickly, though—you don't want to soak the berries.

Keep the caps of strawberries intact until after they're rinsed and drained, as the opening left by the removal of the cap will allow the berries to absorb water. Use your fingers, a paring knife, or a pincerlike strawberry huller to take off the caps.

Gooseberries need to have their stems and "tails" removed; currants can be stripped from their stems by slipping a fork over each stem and pushing off the berries.

FREEZING BERRIES

Berries have a short season and are also highly perishable. Fortunately, though, some freeze beautifully, allowing you to enjoy them practically year round. You can buy prepackaged frozen berries, but these may have had sweetener added, which can double their calorie content. Freezing berries yourself is simple. Fresh cranberries can be frozen, unwashed, in their store-bought prepackaged bags for up to a year. As for raspberries and blackberries, wash and drain them thoroughly, then spread them out in a single layer on a cookie sheet. Place the berries in the freezer until they are solidly frozen, and then transfer them to a heavy plastic bag. They'll keep for ten months to a year. Follow the same procedure for blueberries, but do not wash them prior to freezing.

SERVING SUGGESTIONS Sweet-tasting berries and yogurt were made for each other: Simply stir the berries into the yogurt, or layer berries and yogurt on a sliced muffin for a breakfast shortcake. Vanilla yogurt also makes a perfect dip for strawberries. Sweet berries are wonderful scattered on cereal or served in a melon wedge. Add berries to batters for pancakes, waffles, muffins, and quick breads.

Berries will lend flavor and color to fruit salads: Combine strawberries with bananas, blueberries with oranges, raspberries with peaches, or mixed berries with grapes and melon balls. Or, slice strawberries into a colorful salad of spinach and orange segments.

For a delicious blender drink, purée blueberries, raspberries, or strawberries with skim milk, yogurt, or buttermilk; or blend puréed berries with orange, pineapple, or other fruit juice. Prepare a berry spritzer by adding berry purée to sparkling water.

CRANBERRY JUICE AND URINARY TRACT INFECTIONS

Contrary to home health folklore, cranberry juice by itself is not a preventive or a cure for urinary tract infections, which are most commonly caused by *Escherichia coli*, an intestinal bacterium. While cranberry juice may discourage or occasionally kill bacteria, it's not reliable as a preventive and certainly not as a treatment. Cranberry juice is also very high in calories because of the sugar added to make it palatable—140 calories per 8 fluid ounces. Drinking lots of any liquid every day promotes frequent urination and is probably as good for this purpose as downing several glasses of cranberry juice.

Berry sauces can be made in minutes: Gently heat fresh or frozen sweet berries in a small saucepan, then crush some of the berries with a fork so that they release their juices and "melt" into a pourable sauce. Reserve some whole berries and stir them in after you take the pan off the heat. Vanilla extract, grated lemon, or orange zest are often used to heighten the berries' flavor; cinnamon particularly complements blueberries. Add a little sugar to the sauce, if necessary, or sweeten with frozen orange-juice or apple-juice concentrate. You can create interesting sauces by cooking different berries together, or with other fruits, such as the classic combination of strawberries and rhubarb. Stir in cornstarch dissolved in cold water for a thicker sauce.

Although cranberry sauce is traditionally served with Thanksgiving turkey, it goes equally well with other types of poultry and meat at any time of year. Decrease the sugar and calorie content of cranberry sauce by cooking the berries with sweeter fruits, such as apples or pears, or by simmering them in apple juice instead of water (use frozen apple-juice concentrate, undiluted). If you use a standard recipe, start with about half the amount of sugar called for; you will probably be pleased with its refreshingly tart flavor. Cook the berries until they start to pop, then add sweetener and flavor the sauce with orange zest, fresh ginger, or spices. Chopped cranberries can be mixed into poultry stuffings, quick breads, and muffins, too.

For an elegant dessert, pour sparkling wine over ripe strawberries or raspberries. Or, serve strawberries that have been macerated in mild balsamic vinegar—an Italian favorite.

COMPARING BERRIES 3½ ounces raw

	Volume in 3½ ounces	**Calories**	**Vitamin C** (mg)	**Potassium** (mg)
Blackberries	⅔ cup	52	21	196
Blueberries	⅔ cup	56	13	89
Cranberries	1 cup	49	14	71
Currants	1 cup	56	41	275
Gooseberries	⅔ cup	44	28	198
Raspberries	¾ cup	49	25	152
Strawberries	⅔ cup	30	57	166

STRAWBERRIES 3½ oz raw (⅔ cup)			
Calories	30	Fat	<1 g
Protein	1 g	Saturated Fat	<1 g
Carbohydrate	7 g	Cholesterol	0 mg
Dietary Fiber	Low	Sodium	1 mg

KEY NUTRIENTS		% RDA Men	Women
Vitamin C	57 mg	95%	95%
Folacin	18 mcg	9%	10%
Manganese	0.3 mg	N/A	N/A

S=40% or more soluble N/A=Not Applicable N=Not Available

Gooseberries and currants are commonly used in cooked desserts or used to create tangy sauces, relishes, or preserves. Some people, however, enjoy the sweet-tart flavor of the raw berries, and eat them "as is."

Berries work well with main dishes, too. For example, try raspberry purée on baked chicken breasts, or gooseberry sauce on fish, such as mackerel (the English enjoy the latter combination; they find that the berry's tartness nicely cuts the oiliness of the fish).

Strawberries—the berries with the most vitamin C—are profiled above left. Potassium and vitamin C content for other berries are compared in the chart on page 212.

Cherries

Compact, juicy, and colorful, sweet cherries are among the best foods for snacking and desserts. They require hardly any preparation, yet a cup of cherries has only 104 calories, and comes packed with nutrients. True, they do have pits—cherries are drupes, or stone fruits, related to plums and more distantly to peaches and nectarines—and these can be annoying in so small a package. Their only other shortcoming is their brief season, which lasts less than three months. But during that time, they are in abundant supply. Cherries are grown successfully in commercial quantities in only twenty countries, and the United States is one of the leading producers. Current levels stand at about sixty thousand tons, but that is increasing 2 to 5 percent each year. Seventy percent of the cherries produced in the United States come from four states: Washington, Oregon, Idaho, and Utah.

VARIETIES There are two main types of cultivated cherries, sweet and sour. Most commercially grown sour varieties—such as Montmorency, the best known—are canned or frozen for use as pie fillings or sauces. They come from eastern and midwestern states, and during the summer you may find local harvests of fresh sour cherries at farmers' markets and roadside stands.

Sour cherries are lower in calories and higher in vitamin C and beta carotene than sweet cherries. Three and a half ounces supply 17 percent of the RDA for vitamin C and enough beta carotene to provide 26 percent of the RDA for vitamin A, compared with 12 percent and 2 percent, respectively, for the same amount of sweet cherries.

Sweet cherries are cultivated in far greater numbers. There are many commercial varieties, but the leader is the Bing, a large, round, extra-sweet cherry with purple-red flesh and a deep red skin that verges on black when fully ripe. The second most popular variety is the Lambert, a smaller, heart-shaped red cherry similar in taste

and texture to the Bing. Other red- or dark-skinned varieties include the Van, Chapman, Larian, and Black Republican.

The Rainer, a sweet cherry with yellow or pinkish skin, is produced in limited quantities and is milder and sweeter than the Bing. Another light-skinned variety, the Royal Ann, is often canned or made into maraschino cherries.

AVAILABILITY Bing cherries are usually available from the end of May through early August, with their peak in June and July. Lamberts, Vans, and other Bing look-alikes appear in markets until mid-August. Keep in mind that the varieties appearing earliest and latest in the season are softer and less sweet than Bings. Any fresh cherries sold after August probably come from cold storage. Small quantities of sweet cherries are imported from New Zealand during the winter months.

SHOPPING TIPS Buy cherries that have been kept cool and moist, as flavor and texture both suffer at warm temperatures. Take a few cherries at a time in your hand and select only the best. If circumstances allow, taste one. Good cherries should be large (an inch or more in diameter), glossy, plump, hard, and dark colored for their variety (good Bing cherries, for example, range from a purplish-mahogany color to nearly black). Reject undersized fruits or those that are soft or flabby. Sweet cherries should crackle when you bite into them.

Check carefully for bruises or cuts on the dark surface, and toss back cherries that are sticky through juice leakage. If you find many damaged fruits, consider shopping elsewhere, as a number of spoiled cherries in a bin will start the others on the road to decay.

The stems should be fresh and green; avoid cherries without stems, as the resulting skin break presents an opportunity for decay to begin. Darkened stems are a sign of either old age or poor storage conditions.

Sour cherries sold fresh should be plump, firm, and a bright scarlet color.

STORAGE Loosely pack (to minimize bruising) unwashed cherries in plastic bags, or pour them into a shallow pan in a single layer and cover with plastic wrap. Store them in the refrigerator. Fresh cherries in good condition should keep for up to a week, but check them occasionally and remove any that have begun to go bad.

You can extend the cherry season by freezing them. Rinse and drain the cherries thoroughly, then spread them out in a single layer on a cookie sheet and freeze. Once frozen, transfer the cherries to a heavy plastic bag. They'll keep for up to a year.

PREPARATION When serving fresh cherries, simply rinse them under cold water and drain; they're most attractive with the stems intact. To pit cherries for cooking, halve them with a paring knife and pry out the pit with the tip of the knife, or use an inexpensive cherry pitter (found in any kitchenware shop), which works like a hole punch. A partially unbent paper clip (or an old-fashioned V-shaped hairpin, if you can find one) will also do the job.

If cooked for just a few minutes, sweet cherries retain their firm texture, and their flavor mellows. Try poaching them—this gentle cooking method preserves their texture. Stem and pit the cherries, then drop them into a small amount of simmering water or a combination of water and wine (about 1 cup of liquid per 2 cups of cherries) and cook until the fruit is slightly softened and heated through—about 1 to 3 minutes. Sweeten to taste and thicken the liquid with cornstarch or arrowroot, if desired.

CHERRIES, sweet 3½ oz raw (⅔ cup)			
Calories	72	Fat	1 g
Protein	1 g	Saturated Fat	<1 g
Carbohydrate	17 g	Cholesterol	0 mg
Dietary Fiber	Low (S)	Sodium	0 mg

KEY NUTRIENTS		% RDA Men	% RDA Women
Vitamin C	7 mg	12%	12%

S=40% or more soluble N/A=Not Applicable N=Not Available

SERVING SUGGESTIONS An unadorned bowl of perfect sweet cherries makes an inviting presentation. Some people prefer cherries chilled, while others find them sweetest at room temperature. Cherries are a treat in packed lunches, but should be kept cool so they're still firm and appetizing at lunchtime.

Sweet cherries combine well with other fruits, adding a luxurious touch to mixed fruit salads; try them with pineapple and bananas. (Add the cherries at the last minute to avoid having their color "run" into the other ingredients.) Replace strawberries with halved cherries in a low-fat shortcake made with angel food cake and vanilla yogurt. Stir pitted cherry pieces into plain yogurt, or scatter them over ice milk or frozen yogurt. Combine pitted cherries with yogurt or ice milk in a blender or food processor for a satisfying breakfast shake.

Spiced cooked cherries make a delicious dessert or breakfast dish, and a tempting accompaniment to meat or poultry (instead of apple or cranberry sauce). Poached cherries can also be used as a sauce for broiled chicken or as a topping for waffles or pancakes. The flavor of cherries can be further enhanced by a few drops of almond extract, some slivers of orange or lemon zest, or a sprinkle of cinnamon.

Chilled cherry soup, a favorite in Europe, provides a refreshing summer appetizer, lunch or dessert: To make a simple version, cook pitted sweet or sour cherries in a combination of water and fruit juice or wine (or use almond-flavored tea, for an unusual variation). Use 2 cups of liquid per 1 cup of fruit. Simmer until the fruit is soft, then purée the fruit and liquid, sweeten to taste, and serve well chilled, topped with a dollop of plain yogurt.

If you have lots of cherries on hand (especially if they're slightly past their prime), enjoy them in muffins, waffles, or pancakes.

Sour cherries, traditionally used in pies, are too tart to eat uncooked, and always require some sweetening; try reducing the amount of sugar called for in old-fashioned pie recipes so that you can more fully appreciate the pleasant tart-sweet flavor of the fruit.

Dates

Dates are among the sweetest of fruits: Up to 70 percent of their weight may be sugar. In the dry, desertlike regions of North Africa and the Middle East, where dates have been cultivated for more than four thousand years, they provide an important source of carbohydrates. Crowning the tops of towering palm trees, dates grow in heavy clusters of oblong brown fruits—as many as two hundred in a cluster that weighs up to 25 pounds. About three-quarters of the world's date crop is grown in the Middle East, but much of the United States' supply comes from California and Arizona, where date orchards—called gardens in the industry—were introduced in the early 1900s. Until recently, fresh dates were usually marketed with pits, but they are now sold pitted as well, which has helped to make them more popular.

Unlike most fruits, dates contain almost no vitamin C. However, they are high in potassium and dietary fiber, and are a good source of iron.

VARIETIES Dates are classified into three categories—soft, semisoft, and dry—according to the softness of the fruit. (Dry varieties are not dates that have been deliberately dehydrated, as is the case with other kinds of dried fruits; they simply contain relatively little moisture when ripe.) The variety most often available—it accounts for 95 percent of U.S. production—is Deglet Noor, a semisoft date with firm flesh. Two other popular semisoft varieties are Zahidi and Medjool; Barhi is a very soft date. You're more likely to find dry varieties in health-food stores.

AVAILABILITY Dates are harvested in late fall and early winter, but because they store well, they are available throughout the year.

SHOPPING TIPS Dates are sold in both fresh and dried form. It isn't always easy to tell the difference between the two, since fresh dates may appear somewhat wrinkled, and both types are usually packaged in cellophane or plastic containers. The dates that are commonly available in stores are fresh or partially dried, and do not contain any preservatives.

Ounce for ounce, dates supply 260 percent more potassium than oranges, and 64 percent more potassium than bananas. However, they also contain about 60 percent more calories.

Both fresh and dried dates should be smooth skinned, glossy, and plump; they should not be broken, cracked, dry, or shriveled (although they may be slightly wrinkled). Avoid those that smell sour or have crystallized sugar on their surface. Dried dates should not be rock hard.

STORAGE Deglet Noor and other semisoft varieties store best in the refrigerator, where they will keep for up to eight months if placed in airtight plastic bags or containers. Dates refrigerated in this manner will be protected from the odors of other foods, which they readily absorb. Even at room temperature, they can be held for a month or more.

Dried dates keep extremely well, since they are often pasteurized to inhibit mold growth. They can stay for up to a year in the refrigerator, or five years in the freezer.

DATES 3½ oz raw (12 dates)			
Calories	275	Fat	<1 g
Protein	2 g	Saturated Fat	<1 g
Carbohydrate	74 g	Cholesterol	0 mg
Dietary Fiber	High	Sodium	3 mg

KEY NUTRIENTS		% RDA Men	% RDA Women
Vitamin B_6	0.2	10%	12%
Copper	0.3 mg	N/A	N/A
Iron	1 mg	10%	6%
Magnesium	35 mg	10%	13%
Manganese	0.3 mg	N/A	N/A
Niacin	2 mg	10%	13%

S=40% or more soluble N/A=Not Applicable N=Not Available

THE CHINESE DATE

The Chinese date, or jujube (not to be confused with the chewy jelly candy of that name), is neither a variety of date, nor a member of the same botanical family. It does, however, strongly resemble a true date in color and texture, and is used in much the same way.

Unlike true dates, fresh Chinese dates are an excellent source of vitamin C, providing 115 percent of the RDA in 3½ ounces, and some potassium, too. In their dried form, they are even richer in potassium; 3½ ounces supplies 10 percent of the RDA for calcium and 18 percent of the RDA for iron for men (12 percent for women). However, dried fruits contain significantly more calories than fresh ones and considerably less vitamin C, providing only 22 percent of the RDA.

PREPARATION Dates sold as pitted may occasionally contain a pit; the labels on their packages often carry warnings as to this possibility. Check each date before you eat it.

To prepare unpitted dates for eating or cooking, slit each date open and push out the pit. To chop dates, either snip them with scissors or cut them with a knife. In either case, dip the blades into water frequently to keep them from sticking. For easier slicing, separate dates and place them in the freezer for an hour to firm them.

If dried dates seem excessively dry, you can plump them by soaking them in hot water or juice for about 15 minutes.

SERVING SUGGESTIONS Dates are as sweet as candy, and so can be enjoyed on their own. They're also delicious stuffed—with a whole almond, for example, or a dab of cottage cheese mixed with orange zest.

Chopped dates will add flavor and texture to hot or cold cereal, yogurt, rice or noodle puddings, muffins or cookies; they can also be substituted for raisins in most recipes. If you're a peanut butter fan, try stirring some chopped dates into the spread. In the Middle East, they are often mixed into poultry stuffings and pilafs, or served as a topping on cooked carrots or winter squash. In North Africa, dates are a common ingredient in lamb stews; consider using them in baked or sautéed chicken dishes.

Figs

One of our oldest fruits, the fig has been cultivated for centuries in warm, semi-arid climates, similar or identical to the environments in which dates are grown. Like dates, figs are noted for their sweetness and soft texture—they consist of a pliable skin enclosing a sweet, even softer, fleshy interior filled with edible seeds. Fresh figs have an incomparable taste, but they also have about the shortest life-span of any fruit on the market: Once they are harvested, they last only about a week. As a consequence, about 90 percent of the world's fig harvest is dried. Even though dried figs do not have the texture of fresh, they offer a surprisingly dense nutritional package. Most notably, they boast an impressive amount of dietary fiber—about 9 grams in 3½ ounces. Dried figs are also a good source of certain minerals, especially potassium, iron, and calcium.

By weight, dried figs provide 17 percent more calcium than skim milk, but also 629 percent more calories.

Of course, dried figs are higher in calories than fresh, and the bulk of their calories—about 60 percent—is derived from natural sugar. But they are undoubtedly one of the best snacking and dessert foods available.

VARIETIES Today, nearly all domestic figs are produced in California. They were first introduced there by Spaniards in the mid-1700s. The major varieties of fresh fig (which are also sold dried) are Black Mission (black or purple skin and pink flesh) and Kadota (greenish yellow skin and purple flesh). Calimyrna, a large greenish-yellow fig when fresh, is the most popular dried variety. It was developed from the Smyrna fig, a Turkish variety that is commonly imported in its dried state. Brown Turkey (purplish skin and red flesh) is sold fresh, as well as dried. The principal variety used in making fig bars and fig paste is the Adriatic, which has light green skin and pale pink flesh.

AVAILABILITY Each of the different fresh varieties is available at a different period from June through September. Dried figs are plentiful year round.

A UNIQUE POLLINATION

Unlike Mission and other types of figs, the Calimyrna fig—the most popular dried fig—is not self pollinating and relies on an unusual method of pollination to produce mature edible fruit. Early growers of the Calimyrna were puzzled because the fruit would drop off the tree before maturing. Eventually, a researcher discovered that Calimyrna figs would remain on the trees if they received the pollen from an inedible fig called the caprifig. Each caprifig has a colony of small fig wasps, called *Blastophaga*, living inside it. When the wasp larvae mature and break out of each caprifig, they search for another fig to serve as a nest in order to reproduce. Calimyrna growers intervene just prior to this point and place baskets of caprifigs in their orchards. Female wasps then work their way into the Calimyrna figs, carrying a few grains of caprifig pollen on their wings and bodies. Once inside, the wasps discover that the structure of the Calimyrna figs is not suitable for laying eggs and they depart, leaving the pollen behind.

SHOPPING TIPS A "fancy" produce item, fresh figs are packed carefully and thus should be in good condition when displayed in your market. Color differs with variety, but healthy figs will always have a rich color; ripe Mission figs, for example, will be nearly black. Look for shapely, plump figs with unbruised, unbroken skins and a mild fragrance; sour-smelling figs indicate spoilage. They should be just soft to the touch, but not mushy. If the figs seem somewhat shriveled, as if they are beginning to dry, they will be

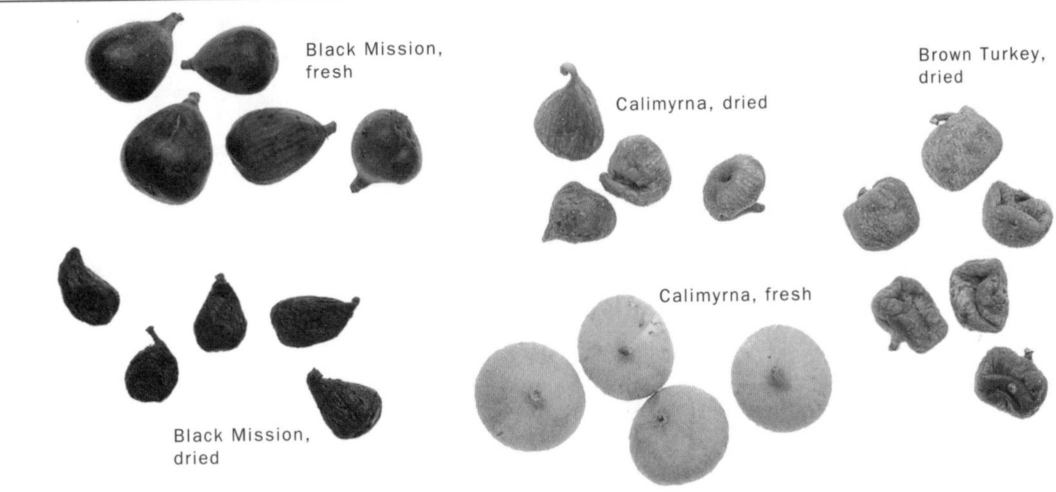

particularly sweet. Size is not an indicator of quality, but you'll probably want to choose uniformly sized fruits if you are planning to serve them as individual portions for dessert.

When buying packages of dried figs, check for unbroken wrapping; the figs should give slightly when gently squeezed through the package. Watch out for moldy or sour-smelling dried figs. String figs are imported from Greece from October through December. They should be firm and clean.

STORAGE To ripen slightly underripe figs, place them on a plate at room temperature, away from sunlight, and turn them frequently. Keep ripe fresh figs in the refrigerator. They bruise easily, so arrange them on a shallow dish that has been lined with a paper towel, to keep them from getting crushed. Cover the dish with plastic wrap and store the figs for no longer than two to three days.

Dried figs can be stored at cool room temperature or in the refrigerator; just be sure that they are well wrapped after opening so that they do not become too dry and hard. Dried figs should keep for several months. They can also be frozen, then thawed at room temperature.

PREPARATION Wash fresh figs and remove the hard portion of the stem end. Halve or quarter the fruit. Thick-skinned Calimyrna figs are usually peeled; Mission figs do not need to be, as they have thin, edible skins.

Placing dried figs in the freezer for an hour will make them easier to slice. When chopping dried figs, dip the knife into hot water from time to time, to prevent the fruit from sticking to it. Before using chopped figs in batters and doughs, toss the pieces with a little flour to keep them from sinking to the bottom of the baked goods.

Baking Fresh figs are usually eaten raw, but they can also be baked and served for dessert. Pierce them a few times with a fork, place them in a baking pan, and sprinkle with fruit juice to keep them moist. *Cooking time:* about 20 minutes in a 300° oven.

Reconstituting dried figs If you like dried figs plumped, simmer them in boiling water, wine, or fruit juice for 2 minutes; add a drop of almond extract to enhance their flavor.

SERVING SUGGESTIONS The flavor and fragrance of fresh figs are best at room temperature. Simply quarter the figs lengthwise and lay them on a plate. A sprinkling of orange or lemon juice will heighten their flavor. Or, wrap a thin slice of prosciutto around a fresh fig. This classic appetizer combination is a reasonable indulgence, since one slice of the Italian-style ham has about

30 calories and 2 grams of fat. Figs also work well with walnuts or almonds, or with a dollop of sweetened and spiced part-skim ricotta cheese.

Use dried figs in recipes that call for apricots, dates, or other dried fruits. Try them in whole wheat muffins, cookies, and cake fillings. Stir chopped dried figs into low-fat cream cheese and spread on pumpernickel bread, or mix figs into cottage cheese and serve with crackers. Sweeten cooked cereal by adding chopped figs during the last minute of cooking time.

Fig bars are one of the healthiest cookie choices, since they are low in fat and provide some fiber. Two fig bar cookies have 100 calories, with 18 percent of the calories coming from fat.

Chopped dried figs (either plumped or as-is) provide interesting texture to fresh fruit salads; combine them with bananas or berries. For a special vegetable side dish, sprinkle chopped dried figs over baked sweet potatoes or winter squash, or stir the figs into mashed sweet potatoes or squash. Thread skewers with fresh or dried figs and grill with kebabs, or offer them on their own as a barbecue dessert. You'll find that dried figs, plumped in wine and then heated, marry well with poultry or pork.

FIGS, dried 3½ oz (5 figs)

Calories	255	Fat	1 g
Protein	3 g	Saturated Fat	<1 g
Carbohydrate	65 g	Cholesterol	0 mg
Dietary Fiber	High (S)	Sodium	11 mg

KEY NUTRIENTS		% RDA Men	% RDA Women
Vitamin B_6	0.2 mg	10%	13%
Calcium	144 mg	18%	18%
Copper	0.3 mg	N/A	N/A
Iron	2 mg	20%	13%
Magnesium	59 mg	17%	21%
Manganese	0.4 mg	N/A	N/A
Potassium	712 mg	N/A	N/A

S=40% or more soluble N/A=Not Applicable N=Not Available

FIGS, fresh 3½ oz raw (2 medium figs)

Calories	74	Fat	<1 g
Protein	1 g	Saturated Fat	<1 g
Carbohydrate	19 g	Cholesterol	0 mg
Dietary Fiber	Low (S)	Sodium	1 mg

S=40% or more soluble N/A=Not Applicable N=Not Available

Grapefruit

Grapefruit provides a variety of important nutrients in one convenient package. It has an ample supply of pectin, the soluble fiber that is effective in lowering cholesterol levels, and of potassium, which is important in controlling blood pressure. This familiar member of the citrus family is even more highly valued as a source of vitamin C: One half of a medium-sized grapefruit—a typical serving for breakfast—supplies 41 milligrams, or nearly 69 percent of the RDA. In addition, the pink or red varieties contain beta carotene—an antioxidant nutrient that may help prevent cancer. These attributes, along with its refreshing tart flavor, juicy texture, and low calorie count, have made grapefruit a popular breakfast food and salad ingredient.

Grapefruit probably developed from a cross between an orange and a shaddock, a citrus fruit with thick skin, many seeds, almost no juice, and a very sour taste. But skillful growers dramatically improved the flavor and texture of grapefruit, beginning with the development of seedless varieties nearly a century ago. The result is a citrus fruit that combines tanginess and sweetness. Indigenous to the West Indies, grapefruit became well established in Florida in the early 1800s: Today, 80 percent of the domestic crop and half of the world's production is shipped from that state.

GRAPEFRUIT AND DIETING

Grapefruit is a popular "diet" food; some people believe that it can burn away fat. But the fact is no food can cause fat to be burned away. Dozens of diets based on eating vast quantities of grapefruit have been in circulation over the years, and all claim that the fruit contains an enzyme that digests fats and so burns them away. However, there are no known enzymes that will increase the rate at which the body burns fat.

Grapefruit is filling, tasty, low in calories, and virtually fat-free; it is an excellent food for those concerned about their calorie and fat intake. But there is nothing in grapefruit that will digest calories or diminish appetite.

VARIETIES Grapefruit comes in white (actually yellow), pink, and red varieties—colors that refer to the flesh. All three types are similar in taste and texture. The varieties that have seeds are often used for making grapefruit juice. The most popular variety for eating is a white-fleshed grapefruit called Marsh Seedless, from which pink and red fruits (known as Pink Seedless and Ruby Red Seedless) have been developed. A number of newer red and pink varieties, such as Star Ruby (a seedless grapefruit with a blush three times redder than Ruby Red) are grown in Texas, California, and Arizona—the other grapefruit-growing states—as well as Florida.

White grapefruit

Both pink and red grapefruit are fair sources of beta carotene—enough to supply 5 and 12 percent, respectively, of the RDA for vitamin A. White grapefruit, on the other hand, has only a negligible amount.

AVAILABILITY Grapefruit is available year round, with the peak season extending from January through June.

SHOPPING TIPS Since grapefruit is not picked until fully ripe, you never have to worry about getting a "green" one. Under certain growing conditions, the lemon yellow skin may revert to green after it is ripe, but the fruit will lose none of its tangy sweetness.

Look for round, smooth fruits that are heavy for their size (they will be juicy). Coarse-skinned grapefruits or those that are puffy, soft, or pointed at one end are inferior; glossy fruits with slightly flattened ends are preferable. Gray-brown "russeting" or other skin defects are superficial and do not affect quality. At room temperature, you may be able to detect a mildly sweet fragrance, but it will not be apparent if the fruit is chilled.

STORAGE Grapefruits can be left at room temperature for a week, and are juiciest when slightly warm rather than chilled. For longer storage, they should be held in the refrigerator crisper, where they will keep for six to eight weeks. Leave them at room temperature for a while before you juice them or eat them.

PREPARATION Rinse grapefruits before cutting them. For serving from the "shell," halve grapefruit crosswise. Use a grapefruit spoon with a serrated tip to scoop out the sections, or prepare the fruit using a sharp paring knife or a curved-blade grapefruit knife, running it between each segment of flesh and the membrane "dividers." (Grapefruits, like other citrus fruits, may be called "seedless" if they contain no more than five seeds, so don't be surprised if you have to remove a few seeds.

You can also peel a grapefruit as you would an orange; use your hands or pare the skin with a sharp knife: Slice a disk of peel from the top, then pare slices downward around the fruit; or, pare the skin in a spiral, as you would an apple. Then pull apart the segments with your hands and, if desired, remove the membranes from each segment.

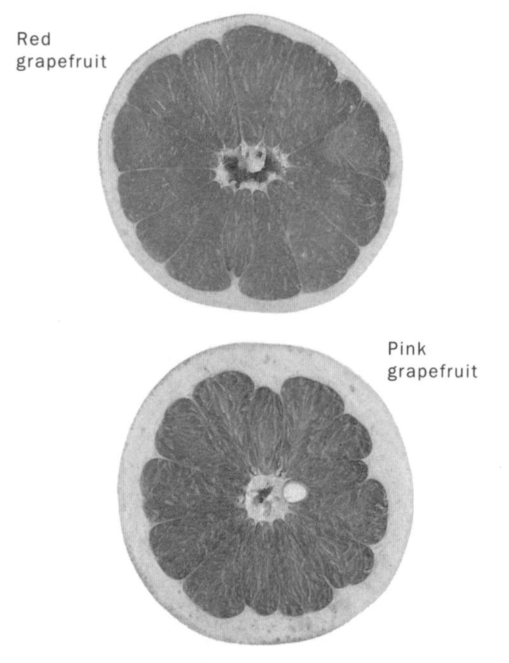

SERVING SUGGESTIONS Many people enjoy eating grapefruit at room temperature; some favor it chilled; others prefer the fruit heated briefly under the broiler. You can sweeten grapefruit halves with a sprinkling of brown sugar or a drizzling of maple syrup or honey. Or, add chopped fresh mint leaves, spices, and almond or vanilla extract just before serving to accent the fruit's flavor. Grapefruit shells make attractive fruit cups: Remove the grapefruit segments, mix them with other fruits—berries, bananas, grapes, oranges, or melon—for a refreshing first course or dessert. For extra color, combine pink, red, and white grapefruit segments in each serving.

Like the fresh fruit, grapefruit juice is a good source of vitamin C, with an 8-ounce glass (made from concentrate) supplying 139 percent of the RDA (canned grapefruit juice provides 112 percent of the RDA; fresh-squeezed juice offers 157 percent). When you choose the juice over the fruit, however, you miss out on the benefits of fiber.

Grapefruit can be used in a number of salad combinations . Tart, juicy segments complement shrimp, crab meat, chicken, and avocado. Slice grapefruit into green salads or add chopped grapefruit to tuna or salmon salad; like lemon juice, it "freshens" the taste of canned fish. Prepare a grapefruit-juice vinaigrette for a seafood, spinach, chicory, or endive salad.

Substitute fresh grapefruit juice in beverages more commonly made with oranges or lemons—for example, blend cranberry juice with grapefruit juice or concoct a not-too-sweet fruit soda, using fresh-squeezed grapefruit juice and seltzer.

GRAPEFRUIT 3½ oz raw (⅔ grapefruit)			
Calories	30	Fat	<1 g
Protein	1 g	Saturated Fat	<1 g
Carbohydrate	8 g	Cholesterol	0 mg
Dietary Fiber	Low (S)	Sodium	0 mg

KEY NUTRIENTS		% RDA Men	% RDA Women
Vitamin C	37 mg	62%	62%

S=40% or more soluble N/A=Not Applicable N=Not Available

Grapes

Grapes can grow in almost every type of climate, and while they do particularly well in regions like the Mediterranean (where they have long been established), they are now cultivated on six continents. They are enjoyed in several widely popular ways—served as a fresh fruit, preserved or canned in jellies and jams, dried into raisins, and crushed for making juice or wine.

Grapes are not notable for their nutrient content—the table grapes that we eat fresh have only low to moderate amounts of vitamins and minerals. But some varieties are good sources of vitamin C. Their juiciness and natural sweetness, combined with a low calorie count, make them an excellent snack and dessert food.

The grape is one of the oldest cultivated fruits: Fossils indicate that the cultivation, or at least the consumption, of grapes goes back to early times, perhaps to the Neolithic era. Hieroglyphics show that Egyptians were involved in grape and wine production, and the early Romans were known to have developed new varieties. And, of course, the grape is mentioned in the Old Testament as the "fruit of the vine."

Today, even though modern equipment is employed in certain aspects of grape growing, much of viticulture (as grape-growing is called) is still done by hand. Grapes grow on woody vines that are not raised from seeds, but are propagated from cuttings or grafted onto existing rootstocks. The vining plants must be staked or trellised as they grow, to support the heavy bunches of fruit. Leaves and shoots are pruned from the vines and, depending on the variety, the flower clusters or the berries themselves must be thinned by hand to improve the quality of the fruit. Grapes develop sugar as they ripen, but will become no sweeter once picked, so timing the harvest is of the utmost importance. And to ensure that they reach the consumer in full, handsome clusters, table grapes are harvested by hand (although grapes intended for processing can be shaken from the vines with mechanical pickers).

You might think that red and purple grapes would be high in beta carotene, but their color comes from anthocyanin pigments, not carotene.

VARIETIES There are two basic types of grapes, American and European. Today, both are grown in the United States, but the European grapes are certainly more popular and versatile. Seeded varieties are thought to have better flavor than seedless, but Americans—who tend to eat grapes as a snack rather than as a proper dessert—seem to prefer the convenience of seedless grapes. The list that follows covers the major (and a few minor) varieties of grapes, both seeded and seedless, grown in this country.

European varieties

Our familiar table grapes are derived from a single European species, *Vitis vinifera.* Varieties of vinifera grapes were grown by the ancients, and now are made into the world's great wines and dried to produce raisins. They have relatively thin skins that adhere closely to their flesh; when seeds are present, they can be slipped out of the pulp quite easily (some varieties are seedless). It is believed that Spanish missionaries moving north from Mexico established vineyards in California in the late eighteenth century, and by 1860 commercial cultivation of several varieties was established there.

Today, California produces about 97 percent of all European varieties of grapes in the United States (the other 3 percent comes from Arizona). Although a large proportion of the California crop is used for winemaking and raisins, the remainder is sufficient to provide a bountiful supply of fresh fruit for American tables during the

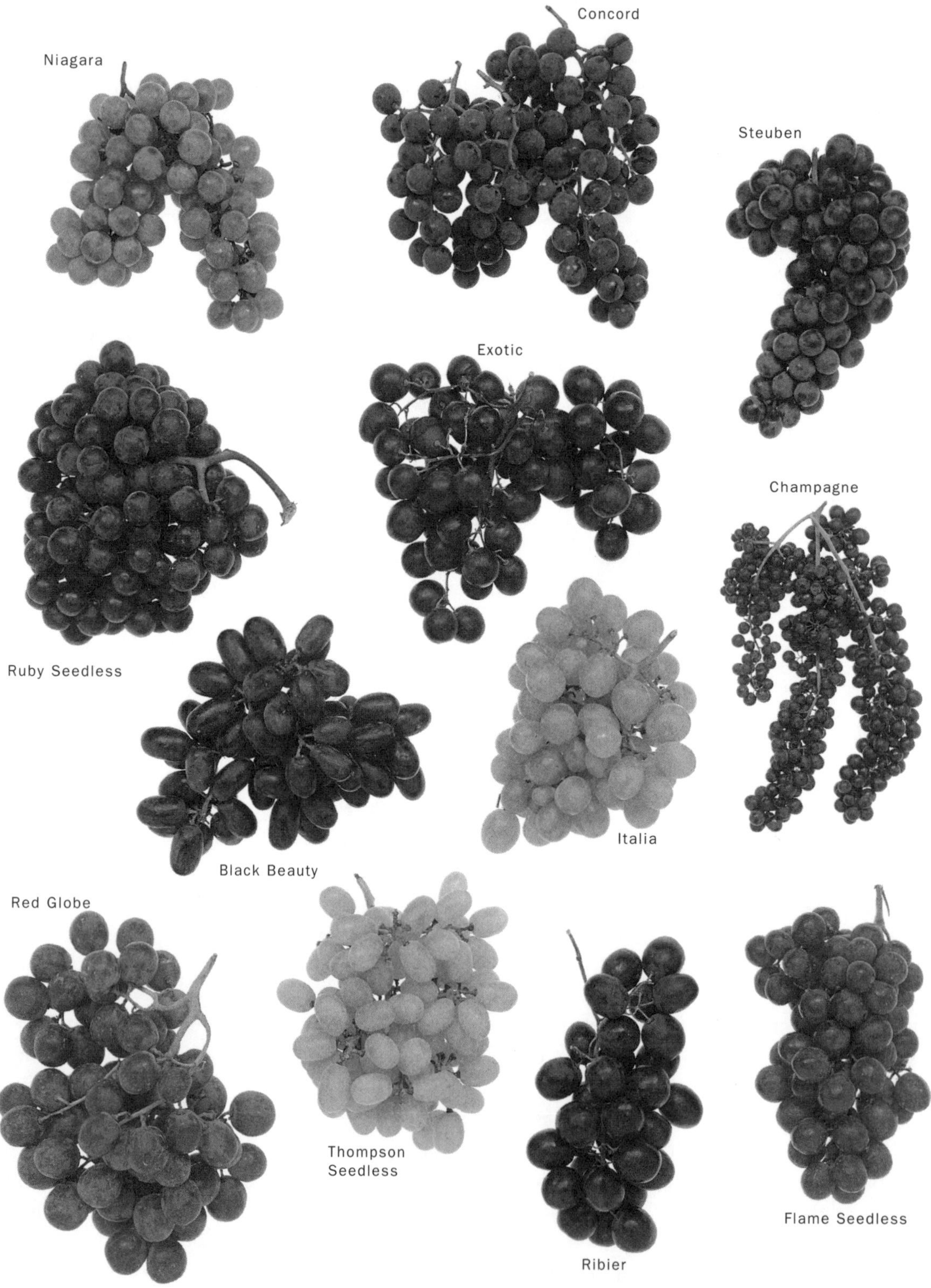
Concord
Niagara
Steuben
Exotic
Champagne
Ruby Seedless
Italia
Black Beauty
Red Globe
Thompson
Seedless
Flame Seedless
Ribier

greater part of the year. The major varieties are harvested in different seasons, and the period of market availability for some types is extended by imported grapes from Chile and Mexico.

***Black Beauty* (*Beauty Seedless*)** These are the only seedless black grapes. They are spicy and sweet, resembling Concords in flavor. *Season:* late May to early July.

Calmeria These are pale green oval fruits. They have a mildly sweet flavor, comparatively thick skin, and a few small seeds. The grapes are so elongated that they are sometimes called Lady Finger grapes. *Season:* January and February.

Cardinal A cross between the Flame Tokay and the Ribier, these large, dark red grapes have a pearly gray finish, a full, fruity flavor, and few seeds. *Season:* mid-May through mid-August.

***Champagne* (*Black Corinth*)** The grapes from which dried currants are made, these are tiny, purple seedless fruits with a deliciously winy sweetness. They are available primarily at gourmet produce markets. *Season:* September and October.

Emperor Second only to Thompson Seedless in quantity grown, these small-seeded red grapes may vary in color from red-violet to deep purple. Their flavor is mild and somewhat cherrylike (they have a lower sugar content than many table grapes). Thick-skinned Emperors are good shippers and stand up well to consumer handling; their large size and full, round shape make them popular for holiday tables. They also store well, lengthening their period of availability. *Season:* California-grown Emperors are on the market from August through March; Chilean imports are available in March and April.

Exotic These blue-black grapes are seeded and firm-fleshed, and resemble the Ribiers. *Season:* June through August.

Flame Seedless Round, deep red, and seedless, these grapes, a relatively new variety, are sweet-tart and crunchy. *Season:* mid-June through September; Chilean imports are available from December through April.

***Italia* (*Italia Muscat*)** This variety has taken the place of the older Muscat varieties, which today are mainly used for making wine. Muscats are large, greenish gold seeded grapes with a winy sweetness and fragrance; the Italias have a milder flavor than the older varieties. *Season:* August to November.

GRAPE JUICE

Grape juice is made by crushing grapes. If the juice is purple, its color comes from the skin, which is included in the processing. Virtually any type of grape can be used to make juice, but Concord grapes are the main variety used. Because of its high sugar content, grape juice has more calories than other fruit juices. An 8-ounce glass has 128 to 155 calories (depending on whether it is bottled juice or made from concentrate), compared with 100 calories in grapefruit juice or 110 calories in orange juice. Grape juice contains virtually no vitamin C, unless it is added in processing; in that case, an 8-ounce glass would supply 100% of the RDA.

When buying grape juice—or any fruit juice—check the wording on the label. If it is simply called "grape juice," it must be 100 percent juice. Grape "drinks," "beverages," "punches," or "blends" usually contain little fruit juice; they are mainly a mixture of water and sugar, such as corn syrup. These products are not necessarily bad for you, but they may be a waste of money. Sometimes, they cost more than real grape juice. If you find grape juice too sweet, dilute it with water or seltzer. Then you'll reduce the calories and you'll know what you're drinking.

Perlette Seedless These round, crisp green grapes, which have a frosty white "bloom" on their surface, are the first arrivals from California each year. They are also imported from Mexico in the early summer. *Season:* May into early July.

Queen These large, firm grapes are rusty red in color and have a mildly sweet flavor. *Season:* August and September.

Red Globe These very large red grapes have a crisp texture and large seeds. The flavor is quite delicate. *Season:* September through January.

Red Malaga Ranging in color from pinkish red to purple, these grapes are crisp and mildly sweet. Their rather thick skins make them good shippers. *Season:* July through September.

Ribier These large, blue-black grapes, which grow in generous bunches, have tender skins. They are sweeter than the look-alike Exotic, and arrive at market later in the summer. Chilean imports augment the supply during the winter. *Season:* August through February.

Ruby Seedless These deep red oval grapes are sweet and juicy. *Season:* late August through January; Chilean imports are available from January through May.

Thompson Seedless These oval, amber green grapes are the most popular fresh variety grown in the United States (and also the foremost variety used for processing into raisins). *Season:* June through November; Chilean imports are available from December through April.

Tokay (Flame Tokay) A sweeter version of the Flame Seedless, these grapes have large, elongated, crunchy orange-red berries. *Season:* August through December.

American varieties

Two species native to the United States are *Vitis labrusca* and *Vitis rotundita.* Labrusca grapes are the ones that Viking explorer Leif Ericson found growing so abundantly on the east coast of North America, which resulted in his naming the newfound territory "Vinland." Later settlers tried and failed to establish European grapes (for winemaking) in the eastern United States; in the late eighteenth century Easterners started to domesticate native varieties, which were obviously well suited to the local climate. Today, labrusca are the primary type of American grapes grown.

American varieties are sometimes called slipskin grapes, as their skins separate readily from the flesh; their seeds are tightly embedded in the pulp. The most familiar American variety is the Concord, a typical labrusca grape, with a thick skin and a heady, sweet aroma that surpasses its bland-to-sour flavor. This variety originated in the 1840s near the Massachusetts town whose name it bears. Another fairly well-known American variety is the Catawba, discovered in the 1820s in Maryland and used for making wine.

Although they can be grown in many parts of the country, commercial production of American varieties is still concentrated in the East: New York State is the major grower. Pennsylvania, Michigan, Arkansas, and the state of Washington also produce some American grapes. Nearly all of the crop is processed into jam, jelly, juice, wine, and other food products; cream of tartar, an ingredient in some types of baking powder, is made from Concord grapes. A small quantity of these grapes reach the market as table grapes, but since they do not ship well, they are generally sold locally.

All American grape varieties ripen in the fall and are available only in September and October.

Concord The major variety of American grape, large, round Concord grapes are blue-black with a powdery bloom, sweet-tart flavor, and perfumy fragrance. They are most commonly used in grape preserves and juice.

Delaware These small, pinkish-red grapes have a more tender skin than other American varieties. They are sweet and juicy.

Niagara These large, amber-colored grapes have a grayish bloom. Niagaras may be either round or egg-shaped. They are somewhat coarse-fleshed, and are less sweet than most other American varieties.

Steuben These blue-black grapes are similar to the Concord, but have less of a winy flavor.

SHOPPING TIPS Because they are thin-skinned and easily damaged, grapes should be displayed no more than two bunches deep, and under refrigeration. The bunches may be wrapped in tissue paper, or enclosed in perforated plastic bags. Loose bunches are easiest to evaluate, but the wrapped grapes are better protected from damage caused by customer handling.

Grapes are not picked and shipped until ripe, so unripe grapes are not usually a problem for the consumer. You can, however, use color as a guide to the sweetest fruit. Green grapes should tend toward a translucent yellow-green rather than an opaque grass green; all fruit on a bunch of red grapes should be predominantly crimson; and blue grapes should be darkly hued, almost black. Once they have been picked, grapes will not ripen further: If you spot a bunch with many underdeveloped, very green fruits, leave it in the store.

A bunch of grapes in the market should look as inviting as those in a still-life painting: plump fruit with a silvery white "bloom," tightly attached to moist, flexible stems (except Emperor grapes, which should have brown, woody stems). The powdery bloom, more visible on dark-colored grapes than on pale ones, is an important sign of freshness; it fades with time and handling. Avoid wrinkled, sticky, or discolored grapes on withered, brown, limp, or brittle stems.

STORAGE Before storing grapes at home, remove any spoiled fruit. Place unwashed grapes in a plastic bag and store them in the refrigerator. They should keep for about a week.

PREPARATION Wash grapes under cold water just before serving and remove any damaged fruit. Leave the bunch whole, or divide it into smaller branches for serving.

If your recipe requires peeled grapes, you'll find that American (slipskin) varieties readily slip out of their skins. European grapes are easier to peel if you drop them into boiling water for a few seconds; immediately drain and cool them in ice water. If seeding is required, halve each grape and pick out the seeds with the tip of the knife.

SERVING SUGGESTIONS A handsome bunch of chilled grapes makes an unbeatable dessert; combine several different varieties in a fruit bowl for a colorful presentation. A mixture of seedless or seeded grapes will enhance a mixed fruit salad or a gelatin mold. For a nourishing snack, stir halved grapes into low-fat yogurt.

Frozen grapes are a fun, refreshing, hot-weather snack. Pull grapes from their stems, place them on a plate or tray, and freeze until hard. (Like other small food items, grapes are not recommended for children under the age of two or three, as they can choke on the fruit.)

If you've eaten chicken or sole Véronique, you know how well green grapes complement poultry or mild-flavored fish, especially when cooked in wine. Just before serving, grapes are added to the pan and sautéed or simmered until heated through. Seedless or seeded grapes are also delicious in chunky chicken salad, pasta or grain salads, and coleslaw, and small bunches of grapes create a handsome garnish for a platter of meat or poultry.

Grape juice, one of the sweetest fruit juices, is tasty in combination with more tart juices, such as lemon or grapefruit. Grape lemonade is an excellent thirst quencher, served hot or cold. Grape juice brings sweetness and a distinct fruit flavor to cooked dishes, too: Use frozen grape-juice concentrate or bottled grape juice for cooking cranberries or other fresh fruits; for poaching dried fruit, chicken, or fish, and for making sauces and baked goods. But use white grape juice with light-colored foods, as purple grape juice will turn your muffins or sauce an unappetizing blue.

GRAPES 3½ oz raw (20 grapes)			
Calories	71	Fat	<1 g
Protein	1 g	Saturated Fat	<1 g
Carbohydrate	18 g	Cholesterol	0 mg
Dietary Fiber	Low	Sodium	2 mg

KEY NUTRIENTS		%RDA Men	%RDA Women
Vitamin C	11 mg	18%	18%

S=40% or more soluble N/A=Not Applicable N=Not Available

Kiwi Fruit

On the outside, a kiwi fruit looks like a fuzzy brown egg—appropriate, since it is named after a fuzzy flightless brown bird. Once considered an exotic specialty item, kiwi fruit has become immensely popular during the past decade, and deservedly so. When you cut (or bite) through its thin brown skin, which is covered with a downy fuzz, you reach velvety bright green flesh sprinkled with a ring of tiny, edible black seeds. The taste of kiwi fruit, which varies from sweet to tart, has been compared to a combination of other fruits, such as strawberries, nectarines, and melons. Kiwi fruit blends well with other fruits and makes a striking garnish, but it is also highly satisfying (and nutritious) eaten on its own. Ounce for ounce, it is higher in vitamin C than most other fruits and is an excellent source of potassium.

One large kiwi fruit has more vitamin C than a cup of strawberries, a medium-sized orange, or half a grapefruit.

The kiwi fruit was a much-appreciated treat in ancient China, and was introduced into New Zealand in 1906, where it was called "Chinese gooseberry" (though it isn't related to the green gooseberry). Years later, as foreign demand for the fruit increased, New Zealanders re-named it for their national treasure, the kiwi bird. Today, kiwi fruit is also a commercial crop in California; since New Zealand and California have opposite growing seasons, a year-round supply is available. (The fruit keeps well for up to 10 months in cold storage, allowing it to be brought to market for several months after it is harvested.) Both New Zealand and California produce one principal variety, the Hayward.

AVAILABILITY California kiwi fruit is available from November through May; the New Zealand supply is at its peak from June to October. Chile provides additional fruit from May through July.

SHOPPING TIPS For the sweetest, fullest flavor, choose plump, fragrant kiwi fruit that yield to gentle pressure, like ripe peaches. Unripe fruit has a hard core and a tart, astringent taste. If only firm kiwis are available, ripen them for a few days before eating them. Reject shriveled or mushy fruits, or those with bruises or wet spots.

Two large kiwi fruits supply one and a half times as much potassium as an average-sized banana and almost as much dietary fiber as a cup of bran flakes.

STORAGE To ripen firm kiwis, leave them at room temperature, but away from heat or direct sunlight, for a few days to a week. Hasten ripening by placing them in a paper bag with an apple, pear, or banana. Once a kiwi fruit is ripe, however, store it far from other fruits, as it is very sensitive to the ethylene gas they emit, and tends to

Kiwi Fruit

KIWI FRUIT 3½ oz raw (1 large kiwi fruit)			
Calories	61	Fat	<1 g
Protein	1 g	Saturated Fat	<1 g
Carbohydrate	15 g	Cholesterol	0 mg
Dietary Fiber	Medium	Sodium	5 mg

KEY NUTRIENTS		% RDA Men	% RDA Women
Vitamin C	98 mg	163%	163%
Magnesium	30 mg	9%	11%

S=40% or more soluble N/A=Not Applicable N=Not Available

overripen even in the refrigerator. Ripe kiwis should keep for about one to two weeks.

PREPARATION Kiwi fruit can be peeled with a vegetable peeler or sharp paring knife; peeling is easier if the ends of the fruit are cut off first. To eat the fruit with a spoon, cut it in halve crosswise or lengthwise and scoop out the flesh. If the peachlike fuzz is rubbed off, the fruit can be eaten whole, skin and all.

SERVING SUGGESTIONS Kiwi slices, which are patterned with an oval of tiny black seeds, make an attractive edible garnish for plate or platter. Use kiwi fruit in shrimp or turkey salad; its delicate flavor is especially pleasing in combination with smoked turkey or chicken. The kiwi fruit's jade green flesh and its light, crunchy texture will brighten any fruit salad; for an appetizing color contrast, combine kiwi fruit with watermelon or cantaloupe. They are also attractive mixed with tropical fruits, such as mangoes or papayas. Or, slice a kiwi into a conventional green salad as you would an orange or grapefruit: The fruit provides a welcome contrast to slightly bitter greens, such as watercress or endive.

For a potassium-rich breakfast, top cold cereal with banana and kiwi-fruit "wheels." Or, serve halved kiwi fruit instead of oranges or grapefruit. The fruit makes a wonderful lunchtime snack.

For a refreshing beverage, purée kiwi fruit and blend the juice with orange or pineapple juice; garnish with kiwi fruit slices. The purée can also be served over fruit salad or angel food cake.

THE TENDERIZING ENZYME

An enzyme present in kiwi fruit, called actinidin, makes the fruit a good meat tenderizer. Fresh kiwi fruit can be puréed and used as a marinade for beef, poultry, or pork. Or, you can simply cut the fruit in half and rub it over the meat before cooking; the meat will be tenderized without taking on the kiwi fruit's distinct flavor. Let stand about 30 minutes before cooking.

Actinidin affects other dishes prepared with the fruit. For example, it prevents gelatin from setting; if you want to add kiwi fruit to gelatin, you should first briefly cook the fruit, which deactivates the enzyme. Similarly, kiwi fruit must be cooked before it is added to foods containing dairy products such as ice cream or yogurt, to which it will impart an off-flavor.

The flavor and texture of this fruit is too delicate to stand up to more than a few minutes' cooking. It should, however, be poached very briefly before adding it to gelatin mixtures.

Lemons and Limes

While rarely consumed on their own, lemons and limes make a major contribution to the flavors of many of the foods we eat. Although you wouldn't choose either of these tart citrus fruits for a snack, you might well squeeze some lime juice over a fish filet, add a wedge of lemon to your tea, or grate some flavorful lemon or lime zest into your favorite cookie dough. These flavor-packed fruits are also loaded with vitamin C: In fact, eaten in sufficient quantities, they protect against scurvy, a disease caused by a vitamin C deficiency. In the eighteenth century, the British navy ordered ships going on long journeys to carry limes for their crew (hence the nickname "limeys" for British sailors), even though, at the time, it was not understood exactly how the fruit prevented scurvy. During the California Gold Rush, the disease was so rampant, and fresh produce so scarce, that miners were willing to pay a dollar for a lemon. But it wasn't until vitamin C was discovered in 1932 that scientists understood that it was this vitamin, not the fresh fruit itself, that protected against the disease.

Lemon juice is a good flavoring to use in place of salt. The acid contained in the juice stimulates the taste buds, and the sour flavor probably masks the need for a salty taste.

Aside from supplying substantial amounts of vitamin C, the main benefits of these fruits relate to their seasoning potential. Tart, refreshing lemon juice and sweeter, tangy lime juice and their zests can help you cut down on the amount of salt you add to dishes you prepare; they also enhance the flavor of foods such as rice, potatoes, salads, and cooked vegetables—while adding no fat and negligible calories.

Lemons and limes probably originated on the Indian subcontinent, and depictions of lemons were found in second- and third-century Roman mosaics. It seems likely that both lemons and limes were popularized in Europe at the time of the Crusades, and Columbus may have brought the seeds of both fruits to the New World on one of his voyages. Citrus fruits, including lemons and limes, were established in what is now Florida by the sixteenth century.

Lemons and limes are tropical plants, and, not surprisingly, their growing region in the United States is restricted; only southern Florida and the Southwest have climates hospitable to these fruits. The commercial lemon and lime industry in Florida began around 1880, then declined after a damaging freeze in the 1890s. Lime growing revived there after World War I and increased in the decades that followed; today, south Florida is the source of more than 85 percent of North American limes. Southern California also produces a very small lime crop. Almost all the lemons cultivated in the United States (and nearly a third of all lemons in the world) come from southern California. The industry was established there during the Gold Rush, when lemon trees were planted to offset the shortages of fresh fruits and vegetables. Arizona ranks second to California in lemon production.

Frozen and bottled lemon and lime juice, though not as flavorful (or nutritious) as the fresh-squeezed equivalents, can be useful pantry staples; however, the fresh fruits keep well, so you should always have some on hand.

VARIETIES There are two basic types of lemons and limes—acid and sweet—but only acidic types are grown commercially. (The sweet types are grown by home gardeners as ornamental fruit.) The types of lemons and limes differ somewhat in size, shape, and thickness of peel, but the different varieties are basically alike.

Lemons The bulk of lemons are either Eurekas or Lisbons. Eureka lemons are distinguished by a short neck at the stem end; Lisbons have no distinct neck, but the blossom end tapers to a pointed nipple. Eurekas may have a few seeds and a somewhat pitted skin, while Lisbons are commonly seedless, with smoother skin. Both types have medium-thick skins and are abundantly juicy. (Florida-grown lemons are likely to be Lisbon-type fruits called "Bearss"—with two s's.)

Lemon and lime peel contain an oil, known as limonene, that can cause skin irritation in sensitive people. In addition, the peels of limes contain psoralens, substances that are photosensitizers, and these can make skin sensitive to light.

Limes Most limes are a Tahitian strain (they are believed to have originated on that island) that comes in two similar varieties: Persian limes, which are egg-sized, oval fruits cultivated in Florida; and a Bearss variety, which is a smaller, seedless California-grown lime. Both are greenish yellow when fully mature, but are sold at the green stage for better flavor.

Key limes are smaller and rounder, with a higher acid content. Grown only in southern Florida, they are best known as an ingredient in Key lime pie. A small number of Key limes are sold commercially, and their juice is bottled and may be found in some gourmet shops.

AVAILABILITY Lemons are harvested year round, with slight seasonal peaks in May, June, and August. Limes are also available throughout the year, with supplies most plentiful from May through October.

SHOPPING TIPS These fruits should be firm, glossy, and bright—beautiful enough to be treated as ornaments for your kitchen. Lemons should be bright yellow, not greenish, and limes should be dark green. (Limes turn from green to yellow as they ripen, but it's the immature fruits that have the desirably tart juice; yellowish limes have an insipid flavor.)

A very coarse exterior may indicate an excessively thick skin, which in turn may mean less flesh and juice (large lemons are likely to be thick skinned); heavy fruits with fine-grained skin are juiciest. Avoid both hard, shriveled lemons and limes as well as spongy, soft ones.

STORAGE If you are planning to use lemons quickly, you can leave them in a basket at room temperature; they will keep for about two weeks without refrigeration. Limes are more perishable and should be refrigerated immediately. Both lemons and limes stored in a plastic bag in the refrigerator crisper will keep for up to six weeks.

If you have extra lemons or limes on hand and want to save them before they spoil, squeeze the juice into an ice-cube tray, then transfer the frozen juice cubes to a plastic bag.

PREPARATION To get the most juice from a lemon or lime, the fruit should be at room temperature or warmer; if need be, place it in hot water or a low oven for a few minutes to warm it, or microwave it for 30 seconds. Then roll the fruit under your palm on the countertop until it feels softened.

There are lots of gadgets for juicing citrus fruits—juicers onto which you press the fruit, reamers you twist into the fruit—but it's simplest to halve the fruit and squeeze it in your hand, using your fingers to hold back the seeds. If you don't need all the juice at once, you can pierce the fruit with a toothpick and squeeze the juice from the opening; "reseal" the fruit by reinserting the toothpick. If you like gadgets, you can purchase a lemon "spigot"—twist it into the fruit, and soon the juice will pour out through the spout, which can be recapped until more juice is needed.

A large lemon will yield about 3 to 4 tablespoons of juice and 2 to 3 teaspoons of zest; a large lime will provide 2 to 3 tablespoons of juice and 1 to 2 teaspoons of zest.

One tablespoon of grated lemon peel provides 13 percent of the RDA for vitamin C.

Recipes often call for lemon or lime zest—the flavorful colored part of the peel. When grating or paring the zest from a lemon or lime, be careful not to remove any of the bitter white pith along with it. Scrub the fruit, then use the fine side of a hand grater, a special zesting tool, a sharp paring knife, or a vegetable peeler to remove the zest.

SERVING SUGGESTIONS Marinate meat or chicken in lemon or lime juice to tenderize and flavor it; sauté chicken or veal cutlets with lemon slices and lemon juice. Stuff a roasting chicken with lemon halves and herbs. To enliven chicken broth, tomato soup, clam chowder, or beef stew, add a little lemon juice just before serving.

LEMON 3½ oz raw (1 medium lemon)

Calories	29	Fat	<1 g
Protein	1 g	Saturated Fat	<1 g
Carbohydrate	9 g	Cholesterol	0 mg
Dietary Fiber	N	Sodium	2 mg

KEY NUTRIENTS		% RDA Men	% RDA Women
Vitamin C	53 mg	88%	88%

S=40% or more soluble N/A=Not Applicable N=Not Available

LIMES 3½ oz raw (1½ limes)

Calories	30	Fat	<1 g
Protein	1 g	Saturated Fat	<1 g
Carbohydrate	11 g	Cholesterol	0 mg
Dietary Fiber	N	Sodium	2 mg

KEY NUTRIENTS		% RDA Men	% RDA Women
Vitamin C	29 mg	48%	48%

S=40% or more soluble N/A=Not Applicable N=Not Available

Use lemon or lime juice instead of vinegar in salad dressings, and substitute these tart juices for vinegar in other recipes. The acid in citrus juice keeps fruits from browning; sprinkle some on cut-up bananas, apples, peaches, avocados, and other fruits that are prone to discoloration.

A wedge of lemon or lime, a squeeze of juice, or a sprinkling of zest freshens the flavor of many other foods. Juice and zest will enhance mixed fruit salads, cranberry sauce or applesauce, melons, and berries; serve citrus wedges with fish and shellfish; sprinkle cooked green vegetables with juice; or stir zest and herbs into yogurt for a savory dip.

Although both lemon juice and lime juice require considerable sweetening when served on their own as a beverage, they add a delicious accent to other juices, such as orange, pineapple, or tomato. Try blending equal amounts of lemon juice and ice tea; in cold weather, treat yourself to hot lemonade or limeade with honey; either makes a comforting drink for a sore throat.

Mangoes

Many Americans still consider the mango an exotic fruit, and certainly it isn't as popular in the United States as it is in the tropics, where the fruit is as widely consumed as the apple is in North America. Mangoes originated in Southeast Asia or India, and India is still the primary producer (it grows more mangoes than all its other fruits combined). Latin American countries and the Caribbean Islands are also avid consumers of this luscious fruit. It has smooth skin and orange-yellow flesh that is rich in beta carotene. When ripe, the flesh is soft and exceptionally juicy, to the point where eating a mango can be a fairly messy business. But the taste is matchless—somewhat like a mix of peach and pineapple, only sweeter than either.

Mangoes have slightly more beta carotene than an equal serving of apricots or cantaloupe, the other leading—and more familiar—fruit sources of beta carotene.

VARIETIES Mangoes come in hundreds of varieties and a range of shapes and sizes, from plum-sized fruits to those weighing four pounds or more. The varieties grown commercially, however, are round, oval, or kidney shaped, and are about the size of a small melon or large avocado. Though there are differences in color according to variety, most mangoes start off green and develop patches of gold, yellow, or red as they ripen. Much of the United States supply is imported from Mexico, Central America, and Haiti; about 10 percent of the commercial crop is grown in Florida.

In the market, mangoes aren't usually identified by their varietal names, but it's worth asking the produce manager what's available in order to take advantage of the differences in taste and texture. Three of the better-tasting varieties are Haden, Kent, and Keitt, all of which have richly flavored, exceptionally smooth flesh. (These are grown in Mexico and Central America, as well as Florida.) The most common variety, Tommy Atkins, is an oval-shaped fruit that is more fibrous and has a blander taste. The Francine, from Haiti, is a completely green S-shaped mango that is available late in the season.

AVAILABILITY Some mangoes are available as early as January, but those that come on the market later are generally of better quality. Mexican mangoes are plentiful from April through September, and Florida mangoes are in good supply from May through August, usually peaking in June and July.

SHOPPING TIPS The size of a mango depends on the variety; it is not an indicator of quality or ripeness. A ripe mango will yield to slight pressure when held between your hands. The skin should show a blush of either yellow-orange or red, which will increase in area as the fruit ripens.

Mangoes

(A Keitt mango may remain totally green with just the slightest trace of yellow even when fully ripe, so check for softness and fragrance instead of color.) A completely greenish-gray skin indicates a mango that will not ripen properly.

A perfectly ripe mango will have an intense, flowery fragrance; it should not smell fermented or have overtones of turpentine. Black speckles on the skin are characteristic of this fruit as it ripens, but an overabundance of black spots on a ripe mango may indicate damage to the flesh beneath. A loose or shriveled skin is also a sign of a mango past its prime.

STORAGE Leave underripe mangoes at cool room temperature for a few days to soften and sweeten—very warm temperatures can cause an off-flavor to develop. Place two mangoes in a plastic or paper bag to speed ripening. Ripe fruits will keep in a plastic bag in the refrigerator for two to three days.

EATING A MANGO

In addition to being extremely juicy, the flesh of a mango clings tightly to a large flat pit. As a result, eating a mango can require more effort—and create more of a mess—than other pitted fruits. The most direct way to enjoy a mango is to peel it and eat it like a peach, nibbling off every last bit of flesh adhering to the pit. However, you'll need plenty of napkins to sop up the juice that will inevitably run down your chin. A neater approach is to vertically slice through a mango on either side of the pit. In the tropics, a common technique is to roll a very ripe mango back and forth on a tabletop; when the pulp is softened, cut off the tip of the stem end and suck on the mango to draw out the pulp. (Do not attempt this method with an *unripe* mango, since it contains a substance that can cause an allergic skin reaction.)

PREPARATION Although it resembles an avocado, a mango is much trickier to pit and slice. For flatter types of mangoes, hold the fruit with one of the ends pointing toward you and make a slice vertically down either side of the stem (and pit), creating two near-halves; a band of fruit will remain around the pit. Use a paring knife to carefully loosen each half-fruit from its thick skin, then slice it. (Or, without peeling the fruit, score the flesh of each half into cubes, being careful not to slice through the skin; then turn the fruit inside-out so the cut side pops outward, and slice the cubes off the skin.) Cut away the band of fruit left around the pit, then peel off the skin.

To slice a rounder mango, concentrate on one side of the fruit at a time: Hold the mango in your hand and score the skin into four lengthwise portions, then peel each quarter section like a banana. After peeling, slice the flesh where you scored it, then run the knife under it to free it from the pit; carefully remove the flesh. Treat the other side of the fruit the same way.

SERVING SUGGESTIONS Mangoes, which are best eaten slightly chilled, make a wonderful breakfast food. They can be served alone (add a lemon or lime wedge to bring out their flavor) or combined in a tropical fruit salad with papayas, bananas, and a sprinkling of coconut. Diced or sliced, scatter the pieces over waffles or pancakes. Or, make a breakfast shake by mixing mango with yogurt and ice cubes in a blender or food processor.

For a simple but delicious dessert, arrange slices of mango over plain or frozen yogurt or ice milk.

MANGO 3½ oz raw (½ mango)

Calories	65	Fat	<1 g
Protein	1 g	Saturated Fat	<1 g
Carbohydrate	17 g	Cholesterol	0 mg
Dietary Fiber	Low	Sodium	2 mg

KEY NUTRIENTS		% RDA Men	% RDA Women
Vitamin A	3894 IU	78%	97%
Beta Carotene	2 mg	N/A	N/A
Vitamin C	28 mg	46%	46%
Vitamin E	1 mg	10%	13%

S=40% or more soluble N/A=Not Applicable N=Not Available

Or, purée some ripe mangoes in a blender or food processor and use as a dessert sauce over other fruits, rice pudding, or angel food cake. Slightly underripe mangoes are suitable for cooking. They can be treated like apples or peaches, and used to make a crisp or a brown Betty.

Mangoes also nicely complement meat and fish dishes. Serve bright orange mango purée over grilled or sautéd chicken or pork, or garnish broiled or roasted meat, poultry, or fish with fresh mango slices. If you wish, add the slices during the last few minutes of cooking to heat them through.

Firm, ripe mangoes are an important ingredient in Indian chutneys, which are traditionally served with savory foods. The mangoes are chopped and simmered with sweet, sour, hot, and spicy ingredients (such as brown sugar, vinegar, hot peppers and ginger), as well as with other fruits, such as raisins.

Melons

Although it doesn't seem as though a honeydew melon and a Hubbard squash have much in common, the two belong to the same botanical family. Melons, squashes, and cucumbers are members of the Cucurbitaceae, or gourd family; they all grow on vines. Except for watermelons, all melons resemble winter squashes in structure—they have a thick flesh with a central seed-filled cavity. Watermelon bears more resemblance to a cucumber, with its seeds dispersed in a radial pattern throughout its flesh. The principal difference between melons and squashes is the way they are used. While squashes are treated as vegetables, melons are considered fruits—sweet and juicy.

Melons rank somewhere between summer and winter squashes in terms of nutritiousness. They resemble summer squashes in their high water content and low calorie count, but approach winter squashes in their nutrient value. Melons are a good source of potassium and vitamin C, and—like pumpkin or butternut squash—the orange-fleshed varieties have exceptional amounts of beta carotene.

Most melons originated in the Near East, and from there spread throughout Europe. The ancient Egyptians enjoyed muskmelons (the melons called cantaloupes in the United States), as did the ancient Romans, and it was during the Roman Empire that melons were introduced into Europe. But melons were not well known in northern Europe until the fifteenth century, when they became hugely popular at the French royal court. Melon seeds were carried to America by Columbus, and later Spanish explorers cultivated muskmelons in what is now California.

Watermelon originally came from Africa; while there is some evidence that it is also indigenous to North America, watermelon seeds were brought to America by European colonists and with the slave trade. Honeydew melon may also have originated in Africa, but the varieties that we eat today were developed around the turn of the century from a French strain called the Antibes White melon.

VARIETIES Although cantaloupe, watermelon, and honeydew are the best-known melons, your supermarket or local farm stand may have other varieties for sale. Most of these melons are grown in the United States, but imports from Central America, New Zealand, and Chile augment domestic supplies in some seasons. California, Arizona, and Texas provide the majority of sweet melons, such as cantaloupe, Persian, and honeydew; Florida, Texas, California, and Georgia furnish the bulk of the watermelon crop.

Cantaloupe The melon we call cantaloupe—which is the most popular melon in the United States—is actually a muskmelon. True cantaloupe comes from Europe and has a rough, warty surface quite unlike the netted rind of our familiar fruit. The khaki-colored skin of an American cantaloupe has green undertones that ripen to yellow or cream. The orange color of its flesh comes from beta carotene; in fact, cantaloupe has more beta carotene than any of the other melons. *Season:* Available year round, with its peak season from June through August.

Casaba Pale yellow when ripe, this large melon has deep wrinkles that gather at the stem end. The flesh is white and sweet. Skin color is the best clue to ripeness when choosing a whole casaba. Unlike most other melons, it has no aroma. *Season:* July through December; however, casabas are at their best in the fall.

Crenshaw A hybrid between a casaba and a Persian melon, the oblong crenshaw—which can weigh up to 10 pounds—has a buttercup yellow rind and dense salmon-colored flesh. The flavor is both sweet and spicy. *Season:* July through October, with the peak season occurring from August through September.

Honeydew This large melon—averaging 5 to 6 pounds—has a creamy white or yellow-green rind that ripens to creamy yellow. The flesh is pale green, although there is a variety of honeydew that has orange flesh and a salmon-colored rind. When ripe, the honeydew is the sweetest of all the melons. *Season:* Year round, but they are best from June through October.

Juan Canary As the name suggests, this melon is canary yellow when ripe. It is oblong in shape and has white flesh tinged with pink around the seed cavity. *Season:* July through November.

Persian This melon resembles cantaloupe, except that it is slightly larger, the rind is greener, and the netting is finer. *Season:* June through November, with the peak season in August and September.

Santa Claus Also called Christmas melon (because it peaks in December), this late-season variety resembles a small watermelon with green and gold stripes. About a foot long, it has crisp flesh, but is not as sweet as other melons. *Season:* September through December.

Sharlyn A sweet melon with a netted greenish-orange rind and white flesh. Sharlyn tastes like a cross between cantaloupe and honeydew. *Season:* varies.

Watermelon There are more than fifty varieties of watermelon. Generally, they are divided into "picnic" and "ice-box" varieties. Picnic types usually weigh 12 to 50 pounds and are round, oblong, or oval shaped. Ice-box varieties—designed to fit a into refrigerator—weigh 5 to 10 pounds and are round or oval. Most watermelons have familiar red flesh, but there are orange- and yellow-fleshed varieties. There is little difference in taste among the three types. There are also seedless varieties (which have been in existence for about fifty years). Watermelons are about 92 percent water and 8 percent sugar. *Season:* March through October (though most are sold during the summer months).

SHOPPING TIPS Since melons have no starch reserves to convert to sugar, they will not ripen further once they have left the vine. Growers pick melons when they are ripe but still firm, to protect them during shipping. Invariably, some melons are picked too early, so it is important to know the characteristics of a ripe melon.

Unless a melon is cut, the only clue to ripeness is the condition of the rind. Furthermore, since each melon has its own characteristics, there are only a few general rules that apply to all melons. They should be regularly shaped—symmetrically round, oval, or oblong—and free of cracks, soft spots, or dark bruises. While ripe melons may be

Casaba
Persian melon
Santa Claus
Juan Canary
Crenshaw
Cantaloupe
Yellow watermelon
Sharlyn
Honeydew
Orange honeydew
Red watermelon

firm, slight softness is a good sign, though melons should not be spongy or "soggy." Look for a clean, smooth break at the stem end, rather than a broken bit of stem; casabas and watermelons, however, may show bits of stem. A full, fruity fragrance is a clue to the maturity of most melons, but there may be no sweet odor if the melons have been chilled, and some melons have no aroma even when ripe. Traditional methods such as thumping and shaking are not accurate indicators of ripeness.

Watermelon seeds are edible. In China, for example, they are often roasted, salted, and eaten like popcorn. However, as is true of most seeds and nuts, watermelon seeds are high in fat calories. Three and a half ounces contains 536 calories—67 percent of them from fat.

Cantaloupe should be slightly golden—not a dull green—under their netting, which should cover the whole rind; reject those with slick spots, which indicate major breaks in the netting. The stem end should have a slight indentation (called a "full slip") if the melon was picked at the proper stage. The blossom end will be slightly soft if the melon is ready to eat and, unless the fruit is chilled, a flowery fragrance will be apparent. Cantaloupes may be football shaped or spherical, and while it's natural for the melon to be slightly bleached on one side from lying on the ground as it grew, it should not be flattened or lopsided.

Casabas may have a bit of stem still attached; choose one with a deeply furrowed rind that is golden yellow, not green. Crenshaws should also be yellow, not green (although late in the season—November and December—even ripe crenshaws will show quite a bit of green). The ribbing should be light, not excessively coarse. Choose a large specimen (5 pounds or more) for best flavor. When ripe, both of these melons will be a little springy at the blossom end.

Honeydews should be a pale, creamy yellow, not a harsh greenish white; tiny freckles on the skin are a sign of sweetness. The melon should have a soft velvety surface and the blossom end should be slightly soft and fragrant. Choose a large melon for best flavor. Persian melons are particularly susceptible to bruising, so watch out for soft or dark patches, sunken spots, or discolored areas of rind.

Watermelons are sold whole, or cut into halves, quarters, or smaller pieces. Skin color ranges from deep green to gray, solid to streaked or dappled; look for a melon with a rind that is neither very shiny nor very dull, but showing a waxy "bloom." The underside should be yellowish- rather than greenish-white. If the stem is still attached, it should look dry and brown; if the stem is green, the melon was picked too soon, and if it has fallen off, the fruit may be overripe.

Of course, if your market sells cut melons, the fruit should be perfect for immediate consumption, as it will not improve once it is cut. With cut melons, you can check the color and texture of the flesh, and usually smell the delectable fragrance of a ripe melon even through the tight plastic wrapping.

Cut watermelon should have dense, firm flesh that is well colored for its type, with dark seeds. White seeds are a sign of immaturity (seedless varieties may contain a few small white seeds). If the piece of melon has seeds that have begun to separate from the flesh, white streaks, or large cracks in the flesh, don't buy it.

STORAGE You can improve the eating quality of firm, uncut melons by leaving them at room temperature for a two to four days; the fruit will not become sweeter, but it will turn softer and juicier. If during that time the fruit has not reached its peak ripeness, it was picked immature and will not be worth eating. Once ripened (or cut), melons should be refrigerated and used within about two days. Enclose them in plastic bags to protect other produce in the refrigerator from the ethylene gas that the melons give off. Ripe melons are also very fragrant, and the aroma of a cut melon can penetrate other foods.

COMPARING MELONS 3½ ounces raw (about ⅔ cup, cubed)

	Calories	Vitamin C (mg)	Beta Carotene (mg)	Potassium (mg)
Cantaloupe	35	42	2	309
Casaba	26	16	trace	210
Honeydew	35	25	trace	271
Watermelon	32	10	0.2	116

An uncut watermelon can, if necessary, be stored at room temperature for up to a week, but in summer, when room temperatures can be quite high, the fruit should be refrigerated or kept on ice. It takes 8 to 12 hours to chill a whole watermelon thoroughly. Cut watermelon should be tightly wrapped in plastic and refrigerated for no more than four days.

PREPARATION With the exception of watermelon, the preparation is the same for all melons. Simply cut the melon open and remove the seeds and strings. It can be served in many attractive ways: cut into halves, quarters, wedges or cubes; or the flesh can be scooped out with a melon baller. For the simplest, least messy way to eat it, halve the watermelon lengthwise and seed it, then cut it crosswise into wedges. Slide a knife between the rind and flesh to remove the rind; leave the wedges whole or cut each one into bite-sized pieces.

For melon rings, cut melons into thick crosswise slices, scrape out the seeds, and remove the rind, if desired. Place the melon ring on a plate and fill the center with cottage cheese or salad.

Use a large, heavy knife to cut a whole watermelon into thick slices or wedges, or else remove the flesh with a melon baller. Seed melon chunks or balls with the tip of a knife.

SERVING SUGGESTIONS The flavor of most melons will be enhanced by a squeeze of lemon or lime juice; some people prefer the fruit with a sprinkling of salt or a little chopped fresh mint. Serve melons slightly chilled; if they are very cold, you'll miss their full fragrance. The one exception is watermelon, which is at its best served icy cold.

Melon-based fruit salads—for breakfasts, appetizers, or desserts—are subject to nearly endless variations. Mix different types of melon or combine with raspberries, blueberries, strawberries, bananas, pineapple, or oranges; then flavor this colorful mixture with fruit juice or liqueur. For a side-dish salad to serve with meals, toss melon with watercress or cilantro and sliced water chestnuts or jicama.

To prepare a decorative party dessert, use a melon baller to scoop out different varieties of melon, then heap the balls into hollowed-out melon shells with same-sized balls of sherbet. Or, freeze the melon balls and use as a frozen dessert. Thread a mixture of cubes or balls of cantaloupe, honeydew, and watermelon, onto wooden skewers and pack in your picnic basket. If you prefer, macerate the melon kebabs in fruit juice or liqueur for more interesting flavor. Skewered

CANTALOUPE 3½ oz raw (⅔ cup cubed)

Calories	35	Fat	<1 g
Protein	1 g	Saturated Fat	<1 g
Carbohydrate	8 g	Cholesterol	0 mg
Dietary Fiber	Low	Sodium	9 mg

KEY NUTRIENTS		%RDA Men	%RDA Women
Vitamin A	3224 IU	64%	81%
Beta Carotene	2 mg	N/A	N/A
Vitamin C	42 mg	70%	70%
Potassium	309 mg	N/A	N/A

S=40% or more soluble N/A=Not Applicable N=Not Available

melon slices can also be grilled and served as a side dish or dessert at a barbecue meal.

Melon halves or wedges make appealing containers for other foods. Serve cold cereal, cottage cheese, or yogurt in a melon bowl; heap shrimp, chicken, or tuna salad in melon "boats."

For a simple yet elegant hot-weather soup, purée melon pieces in a blender or food processor with white wine or orange juice. Season to taste, chill thoroughly, and serve in hollowed-out melon shells.

If you're in need of a refreshing drink during the hot days of summer, mix puréed melon pulp with fruit juice or seltzer; for an extra-special treat, make yourself a melon sorbet.

Cantaloupe, the melon highest in beta carotene and potassium, is highlighted on page 239.

Nectarines

In many people's minds, nectarines are simply peaches without fuzz—an understandable association, given that the two fruits are nearly alike in size, texture, and color. Nectarines, however, are generally sweeter than peaches. Botanically, the nectarine is classified as a subspecies of the peach, but it is more accurate to describe each fruit as a genetic variant of the other, akin to first cousins.

Despite their similarity, nectarines (their name is probably derived from *nektar,* the Greek word for "drink of the gods") have been distinguished from peaches and other pitted fruits for hundreds of years. Judging from historical references, early nectarine varieties were small and white-fleshed, with skins that could be green, red, or yellow. Today's modern cross-breeding techniques, in which nectarine varieties are cross bred with one another as well as with peaches, have yielded larger, peachlike nectarines with gold and crimson skin and yellow flesh.

VARIETIES There are more than 150 nectarine varieties that differ slightly in size, shape, taste, texture, and skin coloring (which ranges from golden yellow with a red blush to almost entirely red). The fruit may be clingstone or freestone (a classification indicating how tightly the flesh clings to the pit). No single variety is superior in all respects, but the most popular varieties—among them Fantasia, Summer Grand, Royal Giant, and May Grand—are all equally desirable.

AVAILABILITY Nectarines are available throughout the summer, reaching their peak in July and August. About 98 percent of the domestic crop is grown in California, though the nectarines produced in southern and eastern states are of excellent quality. Smaller quantities imported from South America or the Middle East come on the market in winter and early spring; these generally aren't as sweet because they are picked at an earlier stage. (Once a mature nectarine is picked, it won't get much sweeter; it does, however, become juicier and softer at room temperature.)

SHOPPING TIPS Select bright, well-rounded nectarines with shades of deep yellow under a red blush. Ripe fruit should yield to gentle pressure, particularly along the seam, and should have a sweet fragrance. If you select brightly colored fruits that are firm or moderately hard, they will ripen within two or three days at room temperature. Avoid fruits that are rock hard or greenish—

Nectarines

signs that the fruit was picked too soon and won't ripen properly. Also pass up fruits that are mushy or have shriveled skins, both signs of decay. Sometimes the skin of a nectarine may look stained, as though the blush has spread out in an irregular pattern under the skin, but this doesn't affect taste or texture. Moreover, a rosy blush doesn't indicate the degree of ripeness, but is simply a characteristic of the variety.

STORAGE Allow hard nectarines to ripen by storing them for two to three days at room temperature in a loosely closed paper bag, away from sunlight. Once the fruit gives slightly to gentle pressure, it's ready to eat. You can keep it fresh for another three to five days by storing it in the refrigerator crisper.

PREPARATION Before eating a nectarine whole, wash the fruit thoroughly in cold running water; if refrigerated, let it warm to room temperature for optimum flavor. Since the flesh of a fresh nectarine darkens when exposed to air, don't slice it until you are ready to use the fruit. You can preserve its color temporarily by dipping the slices in a cup of water to which you've already added a tablespoon of lemon juice, or by simply tossing them with lemon juice.

To peel nectarines, blanch them first by dropping them into boiling water for a minute, then cooling them in ice water; the skins will slip off easily. Rub the peeled fruits with lemon juice to keep them from darkening.

Cooking softens nectarines and enhances their sweetness. It can also salvage slightly underripe fruit that's not satisfactory for eating raw.

Baking Place peeled, halved, pitted nectarines cut-side up in a baking pan; brush with citrus juice to prevent browning. Sprinkle with sugar or drizzle with honey if they are less than perfectly ripe. Bake in a 325° oven until tender and heated through. *Cooking time:* about 25 minutes.

Grilling/broiling Place peeled, halved, pitted nectarines on the grill or under the broiler; brush with fruit juice and cook until heated through. For oven broiling, the fruit may be sprinkled with brown sugar, which will caramelize under the broiler. *Cooking time:* 4 to 8 minutes.

Poaching Immerse nectarine halves, quarters, or slices in simmering fruit juice or wine and cook until tender. *Cooking time:* 5 to 7 minutes.

SERVING SUGGESTIONS You can substitute nectarines in any dish that calls for peaches or apricots. Whether as an addition or as the main ingredient, they bring color and flavor to fruit salads, salsas, and chutneys.

Nectarines are a welcome breakfast treat; slice them and top with yogurt and crunchy cereal. If you want a refreshing drink, purée ripe nectarines with skim milk for a breakfast shake or blend them with orange juice for a beverage. Use sliced or chopped nectarines, raw or cooked, as a topping for waffles, pancakes, or French toast.

NECTARINE 3½ oz raw (¾ nectarine)			
Calories	49	Fat	<1 g
Protein	1 g	Saturated Fat	<1 g
Carbohydrate	12 g	Cholesterol	0 mg
Dietary Fiber	Low (S)	Sodium	0 mg

KEY NUTRIENTS		%RDA Men	%RDA Women
Vitamin A	736 IU	15%	18%

S=40% or more soluble N/A=Not Applicable N=Not Available

Flavor cut-up fresh nectarines, or the poached or baked fruit, with almond extract, cloves, cinnamon, or ground or crystallized ginger. Then combine them with blackberries or pitted sweet cherries to create a tempting fruit salad.

Baked nectarine halves make an appetizing accompaniment to baked chicken or ham, as well as a delicious dessert. Grill nectarine halves and offer them with barbecued meat or poultry, or serve them for dessert. When sautéing chicken breasts, veal scallops, or pork chops, add nectarine slices to the pan for the last few minutes of cooking, then spoon the fruit over the meat at serving time.

Oranges and Mandarins

More than any other fruit, the orange is associated with—and valued for—its vitamin C content. It is, in fact, the primary source of vitamin C for the majority of Americans. But oranges and their relatives, mandarins, have more to offer nutritionally than just this one nutrient. A small orange (about 5 ounces) or tangerine (about 3 ounces) contain generous levels of folacin as well as modest amounts of calcium, potassium, thiamin, niacin, and magnesium. And compared to other citrus fruits, oranges and mandarins have a broader range of uses: They can be added to various cooked or cold dishes, or eaten as snacks.

Americans consume most of their oranges in the form of juice, which provides 60 percent of their daily vitamin C intake. An 8-ounce serving of orange juice has about twice the RDA for vitamin C, along with substantial amounts of potassium and folacin. You won't get as much vitamin C from eating the whole fruit, but a small orange (about 5 ounces of orange sections) still provides 126 percent of the RDA for vitamin C, along with about 3 grams of dietary fiber, which is not available in the juice.

Orange trees (and orange hybrids such as tangerines and tangelos) are semitropical evergreens, and like other citrus fruits, oranges probably originated in Southeast Asia. Nowadays, we take oranges for granted (next to apples and bananas, oranges are the most popular fruit in this country), but at one time they were expensive and rarely found in northern countries. Columbus and other European explorers brought orange seeds and seedlings with them to the New World, and by the 1820s, when Florida became a U.S. territory, there were thriving orange groves in St. Augustine. Florida-grown oranges were being shipped north in impressive quantities by the end of the Civil War, but a severe freeze in the winter of 1894-1895 threatened the survival of the industry. By 1910, the orange crop was reestablished and Florida was on its way to its current status as the number-one citrus-growing state.

In the 1940s, scientists developed frozen orange-juice concentrate, which led to the orange becoming the chief fruit crop in the United States. Today, Florida produces about 70 percent of the country's oranges, and about 90 percent of the crop is processed into juice. California and Arizona are the other two states where oranges are extensively cultivated. Their oranges, however, have thicker skins than Florida fruits, a characteristic that helps to protect them against the drier climates of the West.

VARIETIES Oranges and their relatives on the market fall into two groups, oranges and man-

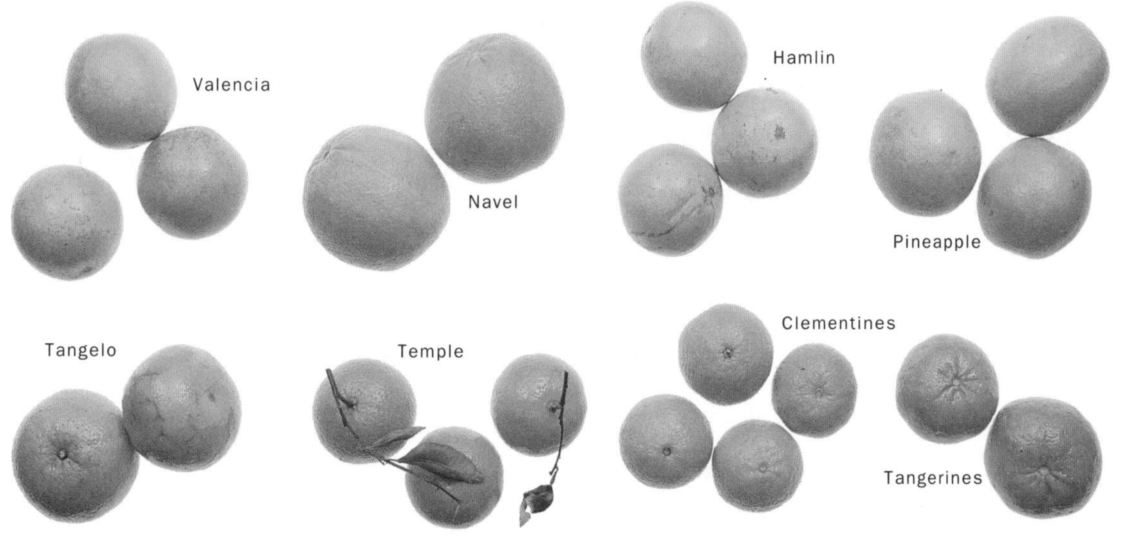

darins, and there are varieties within each of these. Here is a list of the most common ones.

Oranges

There are two types of oranges, sweet and sour. Only sweet oranges are grown commercially in the United States, and those you are most likely to find include:

Blood The blood-red color of their flesh and juice gives these sweet, juicy oranges their name. Mostly imported from Mediterranean countries, blood oranges are small- to medium-sized fruits, with smooth or pitted skin that is sometimes tinged with red. The red color comes from anthocyanin pigments, not carotene, so this variety is not a better source of beta carotene than any other orange. *Season:* March through May.

Hamlin One of the earliest-maturing oranges, Hamlins are grown primarily in Florida. Although they are practically seedless, their flesh is rather pulpy; they are better for juicing than for eating. Small in size, Hamlins have a very thin skin. *Season:* October through December.

Jaffa These oranges are imported from Israel. They are similar to Valencias, but have a sweeter flavor. *Season:* mid-December through mid-February.

Navel These large, thick-skinned oranges are easily identified by the "belly-button" scar located at their blossom end. Navels are seedless, almost effortlessly peeled, and easily segmented—qualities that, along with their sweet-tart flavor, make them excellent eating oranges. California navels are somewhat more flavorful than those grown in Florida. They can be used for juice, but they should be squeezed as needed because the juice turns bitter over time, even when it is refrigerated. Navel oranges are somewhat higher in vitamin C, by weight, than Valencias; a 3½-ounce serving of California navel orange provides 95 percent of the RDA for vitamin C, versus 82 percent supplied by the same amount of California Valencia. *Season:* November through April.

Pineapple Similar to Hamlins in appearance, these oranges—named for their aromatic quality—are seedy but very flavorful and juicy; though best for juicing, they are good for eating if you don't mind the seeds. *Season:* December through February.

Valencia These are the most widely grown oranges; they account for about half the crop produced each year. Medium- to large-sized, Valencias have a smooth, thin skin and an oval or round shape. They are dual purpose oranges, because they can either be eaten whole or squeezed for juice. Florida Valencias, which are available in the middle of the orange season, are considered the best juice oranges. *Season:* March through June.

Both eating and juice oranges tend to be sweet varieties. Less familiar are sour oranges, of which the Seville is the most common type. It is grown mostly in Spain and used primarily for making marmalade and orange liqueurs.

Mandarins

This term is used to refer to the group of citrus fruits that have a loose, easily peeled "zipper" skin, with red undertones. The carpels, or sections, of mandarins separate more easily than those of oranges. Those you're most likely to find in the market are:

Clementine Also called Algerian tangerines, these small, sweet-tasting fruits are seedless. The membranes covering the carpels are thinner than in other tangerines, and the texture of the fruit is very delicate. Most clementines are imported from North Africa and Spain. *Season:* November through April.

Tangelo This fruit is the result of a cross between a tangerine and a grapefruit or pomelo (a large citrus fruit that is related to the grapefruit); the name is a combination of tangerine and pomelo. Tangelos look like large oranges; the most popular variety, Minneola, has a distinct knoblike projection on the stem end. Although they are closer to tangerines than to grapefruits in flavor, they have a taste all their own. *Season:* November through February.

Tangerine The names mandarin and tangerine are often used interchangeably in the United States, but a tangerine is actually a subgroup of mandarin orange. The flavor is distinctive and slightly tart. Tangerines are somewhat flat at the ends and have deep orange, loose-fitting, pebbly skin. Honey tangerines, which were originally called Murcotts, have deep orange flesh, but their skins are more green than orange. They are very sweet, as their name suggests. *Season:* November through January.

Temple Sometimes also called a Royal mandarin, this fruit is a tangor, which is a cross between a tangerine and an orange. Temples resemble overgrown tangerines and have many seeds. They are very sweet and juicy, and their flavor is similar to that of an orange. *Season:* January through March.

SHOPPING TIPS The different varieties of oranges and mandarins will be at their best during the midpoint of their growing seasons (noted above). Choose oranges that are firm, heavy for their size (they will be juiciest), and evenly shaped. The skin should be smooth rather than deeply pitted, although juice oranges are generally smoother than navels. Thin-skinned oranges are juicier than thick-skinned specimens, and small- to medium-sized fruits are sweeter than the largest oranges. There's no need to worry about ripeness—oranges are always picked when they are ripe.

Skin color is not a good guide to quality: Some oranges are artificially colored, while others may show traces of green although they are ripe. Superficial brown streaks will not affect the flavor or texture of the fruit, but oranges that have serious bruises or soft spots, or feel spongy, should be avoided.

Mandarins, with their loose-fitting skins, will feel soft and puffy compared to oranges, but should be heavy for their size; otherwise, they are likely to be pithy and dry. Choose fruits with glossy, deep orange skins, but disregard small green patches near the stems.

STORAGE Oranges keep for up to two weeks in the refrigerator. But oranges store almost as well at room temperature, retaining nearly all of their vitamin content even after two weeks. (They will also yield more juice at room temperature.) Their sturdy peel protects them and they require no fur-

ORANGE ORANGES

The color of an orange depends on the climate where it was grown. In tropical climates, like Florida's—where the days and nights are warm—fully mature oranges can remain slightly green. In more temperate areas, like California, where the days are warm and the nights cool, oranges turn their familiar orange color. Thus, Florida oranges are more likely than California oranges to be tinged with green on the outside.

Two other factors can contribute to the color of an orange peel. The first is a phenomenon known as "regreening." Chlorophyll is produced by an orange tree to feed its blossoms. Since the tree can bear both blossoms and fruit at the same time, sometimes the already mature fruit receives some of this chlorophyll, which gives its skin a greenish tinge. Such oranges are extra ripe and often sweeter.

The second factor is that some orange producers use a harmless vegetable dye to enhance the appearance of mature green oranges. (By law, however, growers are not allowed to give the oranges a better color than they would develop naturally.) According to FDA regulations, oranges treated in this manner must be stamped "Color Added" on the containers they are shipped in or must have a sign affixed to the crate declaring this fact. Only oranges that are produced in Florida are dyed in this manner, however; California and Arizona state laws prohibit adding color to citrus fruits.

Whatever the color of the skin, only fully developed, mature oranges are picked. Growers do not depend solely on the color of the skin to judge ripeness, but harvest fruit based on characteristics such as the ratio of juice solids to acid content of the juice. The point at which an orange is considered mature is regulated by state laws and strictly enforced.

ther wrapping. In fact, if oranges are placed in unperforated plastic bags the moisture trapped inside may encourage mold growth.

Tangerines and other mandarins should be refrigerated; they will keep for just a few days.

The white membrane under the skin of an orange—called the albedo—holds more vitamin C than the flesh. It also contains much of the pectin, the type of soluble fiber thought to help lower cholesterol levels.

PREPARATION Halve unpeeled oranges crosswise for juicing, or halve them either crosswise or lengthwise and then cut each half into thirds, for a juicy snack to be eaten from the peel. For garnishing, halve an orange lengthwise, then cut each half crosswise into slices.

Navel oranges and mandarins peel easily if you insert your finger into the opening and pull back the peel. To peel other types of oranges, cut a disk of peel from the top, then cut slices of peel longitudinally from top to bottom. Finally, cut the remaining peel from the bottom. Or, peel spiral-fashion (as you would an apple) after removing a slice from the top. Separate the orange segments by cutting between the membrane and flesh with a sharp knife. Work over a bowl to catch the juices. For orange "cartwheels," just slice the peeled fruit crosswise.

To prepare mandarins for use in fruit salad or cooked dishes, peel the fruit, separate the segments, and then pull off the membrane from each segment, if desired. Remove and discard the pits, which may be many or few depending on the variety.

If you need orange zest—the flavorful colored part of the peel—use the fine side of a hand grater, a special zesting tool, a sharp paring knife, or a vegetable peeler to remove the zest from a scrubbed orange. Try not to scrape any of the bitter white pith from the fruit along with the colored part of the peel. Check that the oranges you use for zest are not artificially colored or waxed.

Two to four medium-sized oranges will yield

about a cup of juice; one medium-sized orange will yield about 4 teaspoons of grated zest.

SERVING SUGGESTIONS Serve halved oranges instead of grapefruit at breakfast, or mix a fruit salad of oranges or mandarins, banana slices, grapefruit segments, and blueberries. Offer tangerine or orange segments with a yogurt dip. Diminutive clementines make an ideal lunchbox dessert for children: The fruit comes in its own "package" and is sweet, seedless, and easy to peel.

PRESERVING VITAMIN C

The vitamin C in orange juice is relatively stable. According to a study by the USDA, orange juice retains about 90 percent of its vitamin C after a week under typical home refrigerator conditions, and over 66 percent after two weeks. Still, improper handling of orange juice can significantly decrease its vitamin C content. To get the most vitamin C from your orange juice, follow these steps:

- **Check the freshness date, if the juice has one.**
- **Keep orange juice cold.**
- **Store juice made from frozen concentrate in glass jars with screw tops rather than in plastic jugs or uncovered pitchers.**
- **If not drinking fresh-squeezed juice immediately, store it in the refrigerator in a glass container with a screw top; it will keep for up to 24 hours without suffering any serious loss of vitamin C. Remember, though, that the flavor of fresh-squeezed juice will change if it's stored for any length of time.**

With the help of a blender or food processor, prepare breakfast drinks: Combine fresh-squeezed orange or tangerine juice with strawberries or raspberries, peaches, bananas, pineapple, or pineapple or cranberry juice. Use orange juice to keep sliced apples, bananas, and other fruits from browning, and to add unexpected flavor. Rather than buying fruit-flavored gelatins, make your own sparkling desserts with a mixture

ORANGE 3½ oz raw (¾ orange)

Calories	47	Fat	<1 g
Protein	1 g	Saturated Fat	<1 g
Carbohydrate	12 g	Cholesterol	0 mg
Dietary Fiber	Low (S)	Sodium	0 mg

KEY NUTRIENTS		% RDA Men	% RDA Women
Vitamin C	53 mg	89%	89%
Folacin	30 mcg	15%	17%

S=40% or more soluble N/A=Not Applicable N=Not Available

of unflavored gelatin and fresh orange or tangerine juice; include pieces of fruit in the mold.

Marinate meat, fish, or poultry in orange juice or with chopped oranges. Add orange juice and zest to a chicken, veal, or pork sauté, or stir-fry meat, then add orange segments or slices for the last five minutes of cooking time. Oranges nicely complement shrimp and other shellfish, and they provide an excellent foil for rich, fatty fish, like snapper or bluefish. Cook white or brown rice in a combination of orange juice and water (or broth), and add a pinch of orange zest; serve it as a side dish for poultry or lamb.

Orange slices are usually tossed into spinach salad, but they're equally appealing when mixed with other greens or added to chicken or turkey salad. The combination of oranges and thinly sliced red onions, dressed with a tart vinaigrette, makes a lively counterpoint to spicy foods. Oranges and orange juice will also enhance any vegetable dish made with sweet potatoes, winter squash, or beets.

Use ruby-colored blood oranges as a dramatic accent in fruit salad or as a garnish for platters and desserts. Offer guests glasses of chilled blood orange juice at a summer luncheon.

A nutritional profile of an average orange is presented above. Mandarins are similar to oranges in nutrient value, except that they have about 43 percent less vitamin C.

Papayas

The romance and lure of the tropics is part of the papaya's appeal, even though this fruit is no longer the exotic import that it once was. Today, papayas are relatively easy to buy in this country, and that is indeed fortunate for the consumer. They are not only sweet and refreshing, but an excellent source of vitamin C. The cultivated papaya is a melonlike fruit with yellow-orange flesh enclosed in skin that ranges in color from green to orange to rose.

At the papaya's center is an oblong cavity containing dozens of small black seeds. The fruit, which grows in groups at the top of a palmlike tree, can weigh from half a pound to 20 pounds. It can be round, pear-shaped, or elongated like a banana, depending upon the particular strain of fruit. The papaya is sometimes referred to as a papaw, but that is a misnomer, as the papaw is a separate fruit that belongs to an unrelated botanical family and has a different taste and texture (it's creamier and more pungent than the papaya).

Exactly where the papaya originated is unknown. It is probably native to the Americas, but it has been introduced into other continents and grows profusely throughout the world's tropical regions. Most of the domestic papayas come from Hawaii, where they have been extensively cultivated since the 1920s, but smaller quantities from Florida, California, Mexico, Puerto Rico, and Central and South American countries are becoming increasingly available.

Solo papayas

Mexican-type papayas

VARIETIES The papayas that most frequently appear on the market are the Solo varieties grown in Hawaii. These fruits are pear shaped, about 6 inches long, and weigh roughly a pound each. They have green-yellow skin and their flesh can be bright golden or pinkish.

Mexican varieties are not as common—you may be able to find them in Hispanic markets. They are much larger than the Solo types—reaching lengths of 2 feet and weighing 10 pounds or more—and are not as sweet.

PAPAYA SEEDS

Most people scoop out the papaya seeds and discard them, but they are edible. These glossy black seeds resemble peppercorns and have a spicy, pepperlike flavor. Rinse the seeds well and use them as a garnish, like capers; or dry them and grind them in a blender or food processor to the consistency of coarse ground pepper for use as a seasoning.

AVAILABILITY Since papaya trees produce fruit through all seasons, a good supply is available year round. There is a peak in early summer and again in the fall.

SHOPPING TIPS Papayas are picked when firm-ripe to help them survive long-distance shipping; those in the market are likely to be partially ripe. Papayas turn from green to yellow-orange as they ripen, so you should choose fruits that are at least half yellow; the color change begins at the bottom and progresses toward the stem end. Papayas that are completely green with no tinge of yellow have been picked too soon and may never ripen properly.

Fully ripe papayas are three-quarters to totally yellow or yellow-orange; they will give slightly when pressed gently between your palms, but should not be soft and mushy at the stem end. The skin should be smooth, unbruised, and unshriveled, but light, superficial blemishes may be disregarded. Uncut papayas have no aroma; cut papayas should smell fragrant and sweet, not harsh or fermented.

PAPAIN—A MEAT TENDERIZER

Papaya contains an enzyme called papain that breaks down protein, and thus is responsible for the fruit's role as a good meat tenderizer. Only unripe papayas and the leaves of the papaya tree have papain; ripe papaya holds very little. Cooks in the Caribbean Islands wrap meats in papaya leaves before baking or grilling, and they also marinate stew meats and poultry with chunks of unripe papaya before cooking to tenderize the meat. Papain is also extracted from papaya, dried to a powder, and sold as a meat tenderizer. Simply sprinkling the powder on the surface of the meat, however, will not produce the desired effect; the meat must be pierced all over with a fork or skewer to allow the tenderizer to penetrate it.

STORAGE A papaya that is one-quarter to one-third yellow will ripen in two to four days if left at room temperature; place it in a paper bag with a banana for faster ripening. Transfer ripe papayas to a plastic bag and store in the refrigerator. They will keep for up to a week, but the delicate flavor fades with time, so use them within a day or two, if possible.

PAPAYA 3½ oz raw (⅓ papaya)

Calories	39	Fat	<1 g
Protein	1 g	Saturated Fat	<1 g
Carbohydrate	10 g	Cholesterol	0 mg
Dietary Fiber	Low (S)	Sodium	3 mg

KEY NUTRIENTS		% RDA Men	Women
Vitamin C	62 mg	103%	103%
Folacin	38 mcg	19%	21%

S=40% or more soluble N/A=Not Applicable N=Not Available

PREPARATION Wash the papaya, then cut it in half lengthwise and scoop out the seeds. Save them for cooking, if desired. Or, pare a whole or halved papaya with a paring knife or vegetable peeler and cut the flesh into wedges, slices, or dice. A melon baller is handy for scooping out the flesh.

Don't use uncooked papaya in gelatin molds, as the enzymes it contains will prevent the mixture from gelling.

Baking Bake unripe papaya halves as you would winter squash or pumpkin, or use them for chutney (see Mangoes, page 233). Sweet, ripe papaya halves can also be baked with a sprinkling of sugar and served with a dollop of yogurt for a very special dessert. *Cooking time:* about 25 minutes in a 325° oven.

SERVING SUGGESTIONS Fresh papaya is often served with a wedge of lemon or lime, but offset its sweet flavor with a dash of cayenne pepper, for a change. Prepare a colorful fruit salad with papaya, honeydew melon, and strawberries or blackberries. Like melon, which it resembles in texture, papaya makes a fine appetizer when paired with a thin slice of smoked turkey, smoked salmon, or prosciutto. A halved papaya can be used as a delectable serving bowl for various fillings: cottage cheese, fruit, tuna, crab, shrimp, or chicken salad. Or, for a quick dessert, add a scoop of sherbet or yogurt to the hollowed-out shell. Purée this versatile fruit and use it as a sauce, as a drink ingredient (combine it with pineapple or bananas), or as a low-fat dressing for fruit or vegetable salad.

Papaya purée makes a tasty sauce for poultry or pork. Serve meat, poultry, or fish with fragrant papaya slices (instead of applesauce). Grill papaya quarters when you're barbecuing chicken, or thread large cubes of the fruit with meat when grilling kebabs.

Peaches

With their juicy flesh that ranges from white to intensely yellow, and their sweet flavor, it is not surprising that peaches are the third most popular fruit grown in the United States, right behind apples and oranges. Whether fresh, frozen, or canned, they can be used in a variety of ways—eaten on their own as a snack, or added to salads, desserts, cereals, and cooked dishes. Furthermore, they provide a good amount of vitamin C.

FUZZLESS PEACHES?

You may remember the fuzzy beard that was present on the skin of peaches not so long ago. Today's peaches have no fuzz, but it's not because growers have developed "fuzzless" varieties. Most people don't like the fuzz, so commercially grown peaches are mechanically brushed after harvest to remove most of it. You may still find fuzzy peaches at farmers' markets and roadside stands.

Early explorers and settlers planted peaches up and down the eastern seaboard, establishing the fruit so firmly in the United States that some botanists in the mid-1700s assumed that the peach was native to America. (It probably originated in China and was introduced into the Middle East and Europe centuries before Spanish explorers brought it to the New World.) Commercial growers began cultivating peaches in the early 1800s, and the fruit has been thriving in the United States ever since.

VARIETIES Georgia is known as the Peach State, and for many years a favorite Georgia variety, the Elberta, was the country's quintessential peach. But peaches are now grown commercially in more than 30 states, and California has become the largest producer.

Dozens of new varieties have been developed since the Elberta's heyday; these are larger and firmer, but the differences among them are relatively minor. Though some have white flesh, growers seem to have emphasized the yellow-flesh varieties, with names such as Elegant Lady, June Lady, Flavorcrest, and Red Top.

Older standards, such as Elberta, Hale, and Rio Oso Gem, which can have a tender, "melting" texture, are much more likely to be found at either farmers' markets or roadside fruit stands than in supermarkets.

Like plums, to which they are related, peaches are primarily classified as either freestone or clingstone; a few varieties fall in between and are referred to as semifreestone. Nearly all the varieties that are sold fresh are freestone—the flesh slips easily off the pit. They are softer and juicier than clingstone varieties, which are generally used for canned fruit.

AVAILABILITY The domestic peach season extends from April through October, with the peak in July and August. Peaches imported from Mexico, Chile, and New Zealand are available from November through April.

Peaches

SHOPPING TIPS When you buy local peaches in summer, you'll undoubtedly find softer, sweeter, more fragrant fruit than you'll ever encounter in your supermarket during other seasons. (Peaches don't get any sweeter after they have been harvested, though fruit will become softer and juicier as it matures.)

Whenever you buy peaches, look for skins that show a background color of yellow or warm cream—the amount of pink or red "blush" on their cheeks depends on the variety, and is not a reliable indicator of ripeness. Undertones of green, however, mean that the peaches were picked too soon and will not be sweet. Look for plump, medium- to large-sized peaches with unwrinkled skins.

Avoid the rock-hard fruits and choose those that yield slightly to pressure along the seam, even if they may otherwise be fairly firm. Peaches such as these will soften if kept at room temperature for a few days. Once peaches are picked, their sweetness will not increase, so choose fruits that are mildly fragrant.

For immediate eating pleasure, especially when buying locally grown peaches, choose soft, perfumy fruit, but watch out for dark-colored, mushy, bruised peaches that are overripe and beginning to spoil. Tan circles or spots on the skin are early signs of decay.

STORAGE If you bring home firm peaches, leave them at room temperature for a few days to soften; place them in a paper bag to encourage the process. Store ripe peaches in the refrigerator crisper if you are not going to eat them within a day. They should keep for three to five days.

PREPARATION Serve peaches chilled or at room temperature, as you prefer. Wash them before eating or cooking them. To halve a freestone peach, cut it along the seam right down to the stone, and then twist the halves apart. Lift out the stone with the tip of a paring knife. Slice or quarter the flesh of a clingstone peach by making cuts into the fruit, then lifting each section off the stone.

To peel peaches, place them in a pot of boiling water; remove them after about a minute and cool in a bowl of ice water. Then pull or rub off the peel, using your fingers or a paring knife. Peeled or cut peaches will turn brown if exposed to air, so rub peeled fruit with lemon or orange juice or dip slices into the fruit juice.

Although most people prefer to eat a juicy ripe peach fresh, the fruit can be cooked to make old-fashioned desserts or a delicious side dish for meat or poultry. Unsweetened frozen and juice-pack canned peaches are acceptable substitutes for fresh peaches in cooking.

Baking Place peeled, halved, pitted peaches, cut side up, in a baking pan; brush with lemon, orange, or other citrus juice to prevent browning and add flavor, then sprinkle with brown sugar, if desired. Bake in a 325° oven until hot, and tender when pierced with a knife. *Cooking time:* about 25 minutes.

Grilling/broiling Place peeled, halved, pitted peaches on the grill or under the broiler; brush with lemon or orange juice and cook until heated through. *Cooking time:* 6 to 8 minutes.

Poaching Immerse peach halves, quarters, or slices in simmering fruit juice or wine and cook until tender. *Cooking times:* for slices, 3 minutes; for halves and quarters, 3 to 7 minutes.

PEACHES 3½ oz raw (1¾ peach)			
Calories	43	Fat	<1 g
Protein	1 g	Saturated Fat	<1 g
Carbohydrate	11 g	Cholesterol	0 mg
Dietary Fiber	Low	Sodium	0 mg

KEY NUTRIENTS		% RDA Men	% RDA Women
Vitamin A	535 IU	11%	13%
Vitamin C	7 mg	12%	12%

S=40% or more soluble N/A=Not Applicable N=Not Available

SERVING SUGGESTIONS For your first meal of the day, scatter peach slices over cold cereal, or make a breakfast (or dessert) parfait by layering peaches, low-fat yogurt and crunchy cereal in a tall glass. Add chopped fresh, frozen, or canned peaches to waffle batter, or use them as a topping for waffles or pancakes. Arrange thin, peeled peach slices on hot toast that has been spread with a little low-fat cream cheese; dust with cinnamon and serve immediately.

Peaches are an excellent dessert fruit: They can be poached, broiled, grilled, or baked, then flavored with almond extract or almond liqueur, or with spices such as nutmeg, cloves, cinnamon, mace, or fresh or ground ginger. For a colorful fruit salad, combine peaches with blueberries, raspberries, or strawberries. Or, serve peaches and "cream"—but make it low-fat yogurt, plain or lightly sweetened, and flavor it with almond extract or grated lemon zest. Macerate peeled peaches in red or white, still or sparkling wine. To approximate the famous dessert called Peach Melba, top a scoop of vanilla frozen yogurt with poached peach slices and pour a sauce of puréed raspberries over the top.

Use baked peach halves filled with cranberry sauce as a garnish for roast poultry, or serve grilled peach halves with barbecued chicken. Bake, broil, or sauté peach slices along with chicken, adding them during the last few minutes of cooking, or make a sweet-savory peach sauce: Sauté some onions in chicken broth and wine, then add chopped peaches and cook until very tender. Purée the mixture in a blender or food processor and serve over poultry.

Pears

Immensely popular, pears are also easily recognizable—the adjective "pear-shaped" has become a part of our modern vocabulary. First cultivated some four thousand years ago, pears are now grown in temperate regions all over the world, so enthusiastically that some five thousand varieties have been developed. In the United States, the pear is almost as much a national favorite as the apple, to which it is related—both are members of the rose family, and both are pome fruits (those with a distinct seeded core). When eaten with their skin, pears are a good source of dietary fiber, providing slightly more than an equivalent amount of apples. Still, pears are not consumed in the same quantities as apples, probably because they are not quite as hardy. They quickly become mealy if left to ripen on the tree, and they have a much shorter storage life than apples.

Pear trees were brought to North America by early colonists, who used cuttings from European stock. Though pear trees have a long life-span (seventy-five to one hundred years), most of the original ones planted here were killed by a disease called fire blight; it is still prevalent enough in the northeastern part of the country to limit com-

mercial cultivation there. The blight proved to be less severe in the Pacific Coast regions, and today 98 percent of the domestic pear crop is grown in California, Oregon, and Washington.

Pears, like bananas, are seldom tree ripened. Growers pick pears when they are mature but still green and firm, allowing them to ripen in the marketplace and at home. If left to ripen on the tree, the flesh will become mealy. As pears ripen, their starch converts to sugar and their flesh gets sweeter, juicier, and softer—an almost melting texture that led Europeans to nickname some of the most smoothly fleshed varieties "butter fruit."

VARIETIES While there are countless pear varieties, only four principal varieties and a handful of specialty types are available in most areas of the country. Bartletts appear in summer, the others reach the market in fall and winter (though a number of varieties are imported when their domestic counterparts are out of season). Each type has a distinct shape and color, with more subtle differences in flavor and texture.

Anjou The most abundant (and least expensive) winter pear, the Anjou is oval shaped, somewhat stubby, with smooth yellow-green skin and creamy flesh that has a slightly blander taste than the other leading varieties.

Bartlett The leading summer pear and the most popular variety, the Bartlett accounts for 65 percent or more of commercial production. It is also the principal pear for canning and the only variety sold dried. Large and juicy, a ripening Bartlett turns from dark green to golden yellow (often with a rosy blush); growers have also developed a red-skinned strain.

Bosc A firm, almost crunchy pear, the Bosc has a long, tapering neck and rough, reddish brown skin. It holds its shape well when cooked, and so is good for baking and poaching.

Most of the vitamin C in pears is concentrated in the skin. Canned pears are low in vitamin C not only because the canning process destroys this vitamin, but because the pears are peeled.

Comice This pear has the reputation of being the sweetest and most flavorful. The Comice is favored as a dessert pear and is likely to be the type included in gift boxes and fruit baskets. It has a squat shape and a dull green skin that may show light blemishes and discolorations (which do not affect the flavor).

Among the lesser-known domestic varieties are Seckel, the smallest pear variety and very sweet, which makes it ideal for snacking; Winter Nellis, a spring pear with a squat shape, dull green skin, and firm flesh that is excellent for baking; Clapp, a juicy, sweet pear with green-yellow blushed skin; and Forelle, a small, bell-shaped snacking variety, with golden yellow skin and freckles that turn bright red during ripening. Also available are Asian pears (see page 254), which are apple-shaped and crisp-tasting. They are in limited supply, and so can be quite expensive.

AVAILABILITY August through October is the height of the pear season, though one or another variety (supplemented by imports from Latin America, New Zealand, and Australia) is available year round. Bartlett pears are on the market from July through December; Anjou and Bosc pears from October through May; and Comice from October through December. Imported Bosc pears and a Bartlett-like variety called Packham are for sale from March through July.

SHOPPING TIPS In general, pears should look relatively unblemished and well-colored, but in some varieties full color will not develop until the fruit ripens. Bartletts turn pale yellow but may or may not develop their characteristic blush when they're ready to serve, while Anjous stay completely green when fully ripe. Russetting—a brown network or speckling on the skin—is common on many types of pears and may indicate superior flavor.

The canning process sometimes gives pears a pinkish tinge. This is because pears contain colorless chemical compounds called proanthocyanins that, when heated in the presence of acid and oxygen, form anthocyanins, the pigments responsible for the color of some red fruits and vegetables (such as beets).

Since they are always picked unripe, pears are a "plan ahead" fruit; they will usually be quite hard in the market and need additional ripening at home to soften and attain their best flavor. Some stores offer ripe or near-ripe pears, but unless these are individually wrapped and displayed just one or two deep, they are likely to be bruised by their own weight or by customer "testing." If you find ripe, undamaged pears, handle them carefully until you get them safely home. Ripe pears will give to gentle pressure at the stem end, depending on the particular variety: Crisp Bosc pears and firm Anjous never get as softly melting or as fragrant as Bartlett or Comice pears. Watch out for pears that are soft at the blossom end (the bottom), shriveled at the stem end, or those that show nicks or dark, soft spots. Small surface blemishes can be ignored.

STORAGE You can handle the ripening of pears in two ways: Ripen them at room temperature first, then refrigerate them for no longer than a day or two before eating them. Or, refrigerate the pears until you're ready to ripen them—the cold will slow, but not stop, the ripening process. Remove the pears from the refrigerator several days before you plan to eat them, and let them ripen at room temperature.

To speed ripening, place the pears in a paper or perforated plastic bag and remember to turn them occasionally to ensure more even ripening. The process will take from three to seven days. Never store pears—either in or out of the refrigerator—in sealed plastic bags; the lack of oxygen will cause the fruit to brown at the core. Check the fruit often and refrigerate it (or eat it) as soon as it yields to gentle pressure.

PREPARATION When eaten raw with their skins—the skin contains most of the vitamin C and some of the fiber—pears need only to be washed (and sliced, if you like). For other purposes, either core the pears with an apple corer from either end, or halve the fruit lengthwise and scoop out the core with a teaspoon or a melon baller. Peel very thinly with a paring knife or vegetable peeler, if necessary, and coat the peeled or cut pears with lemon juice to keep them from darkening.

Pears respond well to cooking, turning even more mellow and creamy. The cooking time will vary with the type and degree of ripeness of the pear; slightly underripe fruit will hold its shape better for poaching or baking than fully ripe, sweet fruit, which can be used for making pear sauce or purée.

Baking Bartletts and Boscs both hold their shape well during cooking. Core the unpeeled fruit from the stem end or the blossom end, then cut a thin slice from the bottom so the pears will stand without toppling. Or, halve the pears lengthwise and core them. Stuff the pears, if desired, and place them in a baking dish with a small amount of liquid. Cover with foil and bake in a 325° oven until tender, basting occasionally with the pan juices. *Cooking time:* 40 to 60 minutes in a 325° oven.

Poaching Pears may be poached in water, fruit juice, or wine; red wine or cranberry juice will tint them a deep rose color. Add whole cloves, cinnamon sticks, or ground spices to the cooking liquid. To poach, rub peeled, cored whole pears with lemon juice, then place them in simmering liquid and cook, partially covered, until tender when pierced with a knife. Turn the pears once during cooking and baste them occasionally with the cooking liquid. *Cooking time:* 15 to 20 minutes.

Sautéing For a sweet and spicy side dish, sauté unpeeled pear slices in fruit juice or stock; season with cinnamon, ginger, or curry powder. *Cooking time:* 2 to 5 minutes.

Pear nectar is sold canned or bottled in many markets. Its high sugar content makes it higher in calories than most fruit juices (150 calories per cup, compared to 116 in apple juice and 110 in orange juice). Fortified with vitamin C, a cup supplies over 100 percent of the RDA; unfortified brands contain very little vitamin C.

SERVING SUGGESTIONS Fresh pears are at their best at cool room temperature—if they are too cold, they will lack their full, sweet aroma; if they are too warm, their crisp, refreshing texture suffers. Serve the fruit whole for dessert or a snack, or stir chopped ripe pear into hot cereal or vanilla yogurt for breakfast. Add mellow pear slices to a chicken sandwich. Fan pear slices over a green salad, then sprinkle with crumbled blue cheese. Use pears instead of apples in a Waldorf salad made with a yogurt dressing.

ASIAN PEARS

An Asian pear—also called Chinese or Oriental pear, Nashi, or apple pear—looks very much like a cross between an apple and a pear, but it is a true pear. It has the round shape of an apple (though sometimes they are lopsided), and its texture and flavor—crisp, firm, juicy, and sweet—is like that of an apple. But its coloring is yellow-green or russet, and it has a more mellow flavor than either an apple or any European pear variety. The most popular variety of Asian pear is the Twentieth Century, which has thin yellow-green skin. Unlike European pears, ripe Asian pears do not yield to gentle pressure; the best indicator of ripeness is a sweet aroma. Most Asian pears are sold ready to eat, and they store very well even when ripe, keeping for a week at room temperature or up to three months refrigerated.

For a tasty low-fat dessert or snack, fill the hollows of halved, cored pears with a tablespoon of low-fat cream cheese blended with chopped figs, or spoon some yogurt onto each pear half. Brie and camembert—both are slightly lower in fat than blue cheese—are also delicious with pears. Rich blue cheese, such as Roquefort or Stilton, should be saved for an occasional treat, but it's at its best when eaten with ripe pears. Simply slice the pears and serve them with slivers of cheese, or soften the cheese and spread a very thin layer on pear halves.

Cooked pears are enhanced by warm spices, such as cinnamon, nutmeg, cloves, and allspice. Sweeten poached or baked pears with brown sugar or spike them with a touch of rum, or marinate peeled, quartered pears in orange juice and orange-flavored liqueur. Sauté pear slices in fruit juice and use as a topping for frozen yogurt or ice milk. Or, arrange sliced sautéed pears on thick slices of whole wheat toast, sprinkle with grated Parmesan or Asiago cheese, and broil until golden. Serve poached pears with a sauce of puréed raspberries or strawberries.

For baking, stuff pears with raisins, chopped dried figs or dates, brown sugar, and spices such as cinnamon or nutmeg. Serve the baked pears with a dollop of low-fat yogurt. Bake pears and apples together, then halve the fruits through the stem end and place an apple half and a pear half on each plate. For a savory main-dish accompaniment, halve pears lengthwise and sprinkle with Parmesan before baking.

Make pear sauce as you would applesauce (see Apples, page 198), or combine the two fruits. Pears will usually take longer to cook, so chop them more finely than you do the apples and simmer them for 10 to 15 minutes before adding the apples to the pot. Crush the cooked fruit with a potato masher. For a thick, spreadable fruit butter, reduce the sauce until very thick. If you use sweet, ripe pears, the sauce will require no sugar; accent the flavor with lemon juice or zest and vanilla extract.

Grainy-fleshed pears, such as Boscs or Seckels, which have a high lignin content, will never cook down as soft as buttery Bartletts or Comices. If you make the sauce with these coarser-fleshed pears, purée the fruit in a food processor or blender after cooking for a smoother result.

PEAR 3½ oz raw (⅔ large pear)			
Calories	59	Fat	<1 g
Protein	1 g	Saturated Fat	<1 g
Carbohydrate	15 g	Cholesterol	0 mg
Dietary Fiber	Low	Sodium	0 mg

S=40% or more soluble N/A=Not Applicable N=Not Available

Persimmons

The persimmon, with its beautiful, brilliant orange-red glossy skin, arrives in markets just as summer is ending. Nevertheless, it hasn't become as popular in the United States as it has in Japan, where the fruit is widely cultivated and as eagerly consumed as oranges are in the West. Though there are native persimmon trees in the United States, the varieties that Americans eat were brought here from Japan in the late nineteenth century (and are now grown mainly in California). Persimmons are well worth trying not only for their exceptional flavor but also for their vitamin C, beta carotene, and potassium content.

There are two types of persimmons: astringent and nonastringent. As novice persimmon eaters often belatedly discover, the astringent persimmon has two personalities. When ripe, it possesses a rich, sweet, spicy flavor. The unripened fruit, however, tastes so bitter that biting into it causes the mouth to pucker. The astringency is due to the presence of tannins, a group of chemicals that occur in tea, red wine, and in a few other fruits, such as peaches and dates, before they ripen—though the quantity in a persimmon is much greater. As the fruit ripens and softens, the tannins become inert and the astringency disappears.

VARIETIES Of the hundreds of varieties cultivated in the United States, there are only two of commercial importance. Hachiya, which makes up about 90 percent of the commercial crop, is an acorn-shaped persimmon that is astringent until it's soft-ripe. Fuyu, which is popular in Japan and becoming increasingly available in the United States, has the same bright color, but is a smaller, flatter, nonastringent variety that can be eaten while still firm.

AVAILABILITY Persimmons are available in September and peak during November and December. Some markets also carry dried persimmons year round.

SHOPPING TIPS Persimmons are usually tucked into individual egg "nests," rather like egg cartons, for shipping and store display; the fruits are very susceptible to bruising and won't survive careless handling. Persimmons reach their full color while still hard, and they are harvested and shipped in this hard, pre-ripe state. Look for deeply colored fruits, which should be reddish rather than yellowish. Choose persimmons that are glossy, well-rounded, and free of cracks or bruises, with their leaflike sepals still green and firmly attached.

Though persimmons are shipped unripe, your grocer may have some ripe ones to offer. Buy ripe fruits, if you can find them, to eat immediately, and plan to ripen firmer ones at home for later use. Ripe Hachiya persimmons should be completely soft—their thin skins virtually bursting with jellylike, juicy flesh. (In this state of ripeness, they have been compared to water balloons.) Fuyu persimmons, by contrast, are crisp.

STORAGE For good eating, a very firm Fuyu persimmon may need to be put aside for just a day or two. An unripe Hachiya, packed with mouth-puckering tannins, will probably need more time to soften and lose its astringency. There is still some controversy as to the best way to ripen these fruits. You can leave persimmons at room temperature in a paper bag along with an apple, which will produce additional ethylene gas (to hasten the ripening), and turn the fruit occasionally for even ripening. For Hachiya persimmons, however, the process may take a number of weeks.

Another approach for Hachiya persimmons—a modified version of a technique Japanese shippers use—incorporates two ripening principles: One method involves excluding oxygen, causing the persimmons to produce aldehydes, which counteract the astringency of the tannins. The other requires exposing the persimmons to alcohol, encouraging the fruits to produce their own ethylene gas. The kitchen adaptation of this method is quite simple: Stand the fruits in a plastic food-storage container, place a few drops of liquor (brandy or rum, for instance) on each of the leaflike sepals, then cover the container tightly. The fruits will soften considerably as they turn sweeter, so don't expect to be able to slice the persimmons. Fruit treated in this manner may ripen in less than a week.

Freezing is sometimes recommended as an overnight ripening method for persimmons, but while the fruit will emerge from the freezer softened, it will not develop the sweetness that only slow ripening can produce. Even in the freezer, it can still take several weeks for the astringency of

PERSIMMON, Fuyu 3½ oz raw (⅔ persimmon)			
Calories	70	Fat	<1 g
Protein	1 g	Saturated Fat	<1 g
Carbohydrate	19 g	Cholesterol	0 mg
Dietary Fiber	N	Sodium	1 mg

KEY NUTRIENTS		%RDA Men	%RDA Women
Vitamin C	218 mg	363%	363%

S=40% or more soluble N/A=Not Applicable N=Not Available

PERSIMMON, Hachiya 3½ oz raw (⅔ persimmon)			
Calories	70	Fat	<1 g
Protein	1 g	Saturated Fat	<1 g
Carbohydrate	19 g	Cholesterol	0 mg
Dietary Fiber	N	Sodium	1 mg

KEY NUTRIENTS		%RDA Men	%RDA Women
Beta carotene	0.5 mg	N/A	N/A
Vitamin C	35 mg	58%	58%

S=40% or more soluble N/A=Not Applicable N=Not Available

an unripe Hachiya persimmon to diminish.

Ripe persimmons should be placed in a plastic bag, stored in the refrigerator, and used as soon as possible.

If you'd like to cook with persimmons year round, pack the puréed fruit (mixed with a little lemon juice) into small containers and freeze for up to six months.

PREPARATION You can wash a Fuyu persimmon and eat it like an apple, either whole or cut into slices or wedges.They are easy to peel with a paring knife. Pull off the sepals before serving, or cut off the stem end with a cone-shaped "core" of flesh. The thicker-skinned Hachiya can be messy to bite into, and is easier to handle if halved lengthwise and eaten from the skin with a spoon. Some Hachiya persimmons contain a few seeds, which are easily removed.

To scoop out Hachiya persimmons for mashing or puréeing, halve the fruit and scoop out the pulp with a spoon, discarding the stem, skin, and seeds, if any.

SERVING SUGGESTIONS Halved persimmons are used mainly as an appetizer or dessert; serve them with a squeeze of lemon or lime juice, or combine them in a fruit salad with fresh figs, melon slices, or grapes. Serve cut-up persimmons with sweetened yogurt.

For a dessert sauce, press ripe persimmons through a coarse sieve or purée them in a blender or food processor. Ripe persimmon flesh thickens to a consistency similar to whipped cream, and makes a wonderful low-fat topping for angel food cake—or a spoonable dessert on its own.

Although freezing doesn't fully ripen these fruits, it can transform a ripe persimmon into a self-contained cup of persimmon "sorbet." Cut off the pointed tip of the fruit before wrapping and freezing it; if the persimmon freezes quite hard, let it thaw for a few hours in the refrigerator before serving. You can also scoop the frozen persimmon flesh into a blender or food processor and purée it to make a frozen-fruit mousse.

Sliced or chopped, peeled Fuyu persimmons can be substituted for apples in some baked goods; sweet, mashed Hachiya can stand in for applesauce in muffins and cakes. Slice a Fuyu persimmon into a green salad to provide an interesting color contrast and sweet flavor. Mash a Hachiya persimmon and serve it as a sauce accompaniment to meat or poultry.

Pineapples

Among Americans, the sweet taste and lush juiciness of pineapples has made them the most popular tropical fruit next to bananas. Pineapples contain vitamin C and manganese, a trace mineral that is a constituent in certain enzymes involved in metabolizing protein and carbohydrates. Most of the pineapple consumed in the United States is canned (in the form of juice as well as fruit), but fresh pineapple is much more flavorful, and, despite its tough bristly shell, is easy to prepare.

No pineapples are grown in the continental United States. Hawaii is a major producer of fresh and canned fruit, though, increasingly, we get canned pineapple from countries in the Far East. Fresh pineapples are also imported from Mexico and Central America. The fruit probably first grew wild in parts of South America and then spread to the Caribbean, where Columbus encountered it (on the island of Guadaloupe) during a 1493 voyage.

"Pineapple" was derived from *piña,* a name supplied by the Spanish, who thought the fruit resembled a pine cone. By 1600, early European explorers had carried pineapples as far as China and the Philippines, and in the eighteenth century it was introduced into the Hawaiian Islands, eventually becoming their principal fruit crop. Hawaiian pineapple producers were the first to can the fruit.

Like melons, pineapples have no built-in reserves of starch that convert to sugar—the starch is stored in the stem of the plant rather than in the fruit itself. Just before the fruit ripens completely, the starch converts to sugar and enters the fruit. Once the fruit has been harvested, it won't get any sweeter, so growers ripen pineapples on the plant to a point where they are almost fully ripe, with a high sugar content and plenty of juice. (If too ripe, the fruit may spoil before it gets to market.) After harvesting, the pineapples are shipped to market as quickly as possible, arriving within two to three days.

VARIETIES Three varieties dominate the market. Smooth Cayenne, a cone-shaped Hawaiian pineapple that weighs 3 to 5 pounds, is the most popular (and is considered by many to be the best tasting). It is widely marketed both fresh and canned; Smooth Cayennes for the fresh market are also grown in Mexico and Central America. Next in popularity is Red Spanish, which is similar in weight to Smooth Cayenne but has a squarish shape, and a tougher shell that protects it better during shipping. Grown in the Caribbean, most are sold fresh. Sugar Loaf is a large pineapple—it weighs from 5 to 10 pounds—that is brought in from Mexico, mostly in fresh form.

AVAILABILITY Pineapples are available year round, with supplies peaking from March through June.

Pineapple juice is available in bottles or as frozen concentrate. Per cup, it has 130 calories and provides 50 percent of the RDA for vitamin C.

SHOPPING TIPS Since you can't ripen a pineapple at home, it's important to choose one in prime condition. But most of the traditional "secrets" to selecting this fruit are, in fact, unreliable. Don't bother trying to judge the fruit by its color, thumping it to test its "soundness," or pulling a crown leaf to see how loose it is.

Your best guide to quality is a label or tag indicating that the pineapple was jet-shipped from Hawaii. These pineapples are more likely to be in prime condition (and also more expensive) than those brought in by truck or boat from Latin America. Pineapples grown in Central America are often picked too green, which means they may be fibrous and not very sweet.

Pineapple

A large pineapple will have a greater proportion of edible flesh to rind and core, but small and medium-sized pineapples can still be delicious. The fruit should be firm and plump, as well as heavy for its size, with fresh-looking green leaves. Look out for bruises or soft spots, especially at the base. A good pineapple should be fragrant, but if the fruit is cold, the aroma may not be apparent. Never buy a pineapple with a sour or fermented smell.

STORAGE Although it will not increase in sweetness, a pineapple will get somewhat softer and juicier if it is left at room temperature for a day or two before serving. After ripening, it can be refrigerated for three to five days—no longer, or the fruit may be damaged by the cold. Refrigerate the pineapple in a plastic bag to help conserve its moisture content. Cut-up pineapple, if it is stored in an airtight container, will keep for about a week.

PREPARATION Some stores have pineapple coring and shelling devices in their produce department to simplify the preparation of this fruit. If you take advantage of this convenience, you may lose some of the fruit you're paying for, as the device cannot be adjusted to the size of the individual fruit and may remove more flesh than necessary. There are also pineapple-cutting gadgets available for home use: First, cut off the top of the pineapple, then press the cutter over the fruit to core it and divide it into wedges.

To cut pineapple into chunks, wash the fruit and twist or cut off the leafy crown (or leave it on for a more decorative serving). Using a large, heavy knife, halve the fruit lengthwise from bottom to top, then cut the two halves in half again to form quarters. Slice out the section of core from the top of each wedge-shaped quarter, then slide a knife (preferably a curved one) between the flesh and rind to free the flesh. Cut the wedge of fruit as required for your recipe. For a serving "boat," replace the flesh on the rind and then make crosswise cuts to divide the fruit into bite-sized pieces.

ENZYME ACTION

Fresh pineapple contains an enzyme called bromelain, which digests protein. The fresh fruit is never used in gelatin molds because the bromelain would break down the protein in the gelatin and prevent it from setting. (Heating pineapple to the boiling point, however, inactivates the enzyme, so canned pineapple can be safely substituted.) Fresh pineapple should not be mixed with yogurt or cottage cheese until just before serving, or the bromelain will begin to digest the protein in these foods, too, changing their flavor and consistency.

You can use pineapple to tenderize meats and poultry by including the fresh fruit (shredded, puréed, or juiced) in marinades.

There are two methods for cutting round slices. It's easiest to cut off the top and bottom of the pineapple, then cut the unpeeled fruit into slices

PINEAPPLE 3½ oz raw (⅔ cup diced)			
Calories	49	Fat	<1 g
Protein	<1 g	Saturated Fat	<1 g
Carbohydrate	12 g	Cholesterol	0 mg
Dietary Fiber	Low	Sodium	1 mg

KEY NUTRIENTS		% RDA Men	% RDA Women
Vitamin C	15 mg	25%	25%
Manganese	2 mg	N/A	N/A

S=40% or more soluble N/A=Not Applicable N=Not Available

and pare and core each one individually. To peel the pineapple first, cut off the top and bottom, then stand the fruit on a cutting board and cut downward to remove the rind in wide strips; the "eyes" will remain intact. With a paring knife, follow the diagonal pattern made by the eyes, cutting spiraling grooves to remove them. Then cut the pineapple crosswise into slices and cut the core from each slice.

SERVING SUGGESTIONS Pineapple slices on the quarter shell make a festive breakfast or dessert. For a finishing touch, stick a toothpick into each slice and top it with a pitted cherry or a strawberry. Combine pineapple chunks with bananas, oranges, mangoes, papayas, or kiwi fruit for a mouth-watering tropical fruit salad. Strawberries and raspberries also work well with pineapple. Stir diced pineapple into plain yogurt for a breakfast treat, or offer the fruit with a scoop of lemon sorbet for a refreshing dessert.

When serving pineapple on its own, add mint, cardamom, cloves, fresh or ground ginger, rum or rum flavoring, orange juice or orange liqueur for a contrast of flavors. If a fresh pineapple is not as sweet as you'd hoped, you can salvage it by cutting it into thick slices, sprinkling it with a little brown sugar, and broiling it until hot.

Use the fruit or its juice to sweeten vegetables, particularly winter squashes or sweet potatoes, or to enhance meat or fish recipes. Bake pineapple slices with chicken or pork, or try pineapple in a hot and spicy chicken sauté made with hot peppers or chili powder—a Caribbean favorite. Toss fresh or canned pineapple chunks into a Chinese-style chicken or shrimp stir-fry, or add them to curry dishes.

Serve pineapple chunks as an accompaniment to a vinaigrette-dressed chicken or turkey salad. If using fresh pineapple, mix in just before serving. Don't let the meat sit in the fresh pineapple for longer than 10 minutes, otherwise the bromelain will break down *all* the connective tissue and the meat will turn to mush.

Pineapple also grills nicely: Thread chunks on skewers, alternating them with other fruits or with chicken or seafood, and grill; or, place thick slices on the grill and cook until hot and beginning to brown (about 20 minutes).

Plums

Anyone who likes plums has an abundance of choices—there are more than 140 varieties of this colorful fruit sold fresh in the United States. The plum is a drupe—a pitted fruit—related to the nectarine, peach, and apricot, but it is far more diverse than its relatives, coming in a wider range of shapes, sizes, and, especially, skin colors. Its flavors also vary from extremely sweet to quite tart. Some plum varieties are specifically bred so that they can be dried and still retain their sweetness, and these are used for making prunes (see page 263). The varieties that

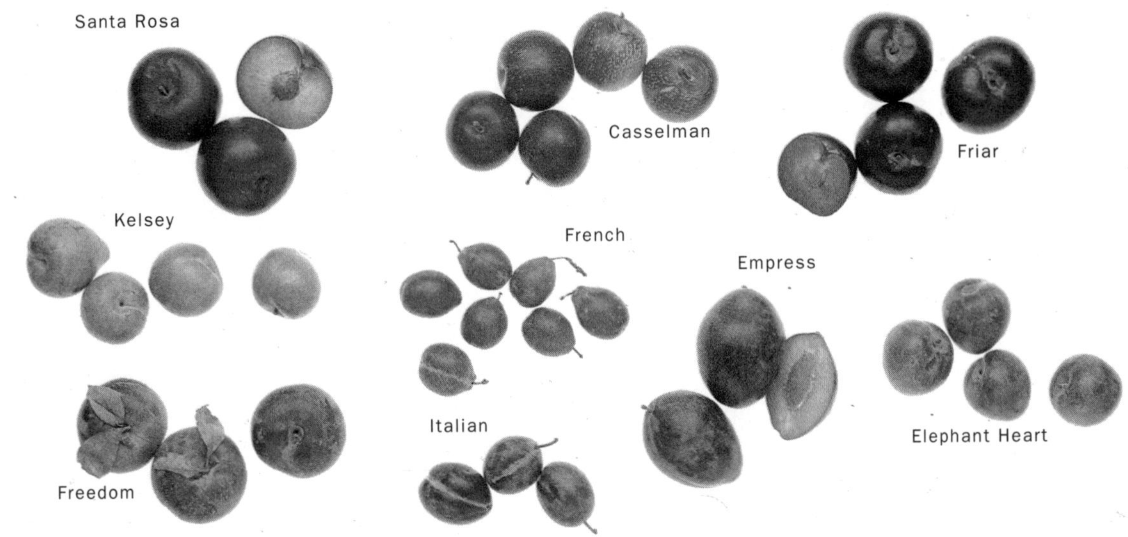

we call plums are mainly eaten fresh, but they are also canned or processed into jams and jellies.

Plums are native to a number of temperate regions around the world, including North America. Early colonists brought European varieties with them, forgoing native American plums, which have never been produced commercially in any quantity.

In the late nineteenth century, dozens of varieties from Europe and Asia were assiduously cultivated in America, primarily in California. One of the most influential plum breeders was the famed horticulturalist Luther Burbank, who in 1907 developed a variety called Santa Rosa, which now accounts for about one-third of the total domestic crop.

VARIETIES About twenty varieties dominate the commercial supply of plums, and most are either Japanese or European varieties. Japanese are the nonprune plums. (They are also known as salicina plums, after their Latin name, *Prunus salicina*.) Originally from China, these plums were introduced into Japan some three hundred years ago, and were eventually brought from there to the United States. Most varieties have yellow or reddish flesh that is quite juicy and skin colors that range from crimson to black-red (but never purple). They are also clingstone fruits—that is, their flesh clings to the pit. Santa Rosa and Red Beaut are two of the more popular varieties; others include El Dorado, Freedom, French, Friar, Nubiana, Queen Rosa, Casselman, Laroda, and Simka. Elephant Heart is a large red-fleshed variety that is good for cooking; Wickson and Kelsey are green-skinned Japanese plums (which may be marketed as greengage plums) that turn yellow or bronze as they ripen.

European-type plums, or *Prunica domestica*, are smaller, denser, and less juicy than Japanese varieties; their skin color is always blue or purple; and their pits are usually freestone, meaning they separate easily from the flesh. The flesh is a golden yellow color. These are the plums made into prunes; a few varieties are sold fresh and are called fresh prunes, or purple plums. Among the better-known varieties are Italian, President, Empress, Stanley, and Tragedy. The bulk of European plums are grown in the Pacific Northwest, but some varieties are successfully cultivated in eastern states. European plums generally lack the flavor of Japanese varieties, and so are better suited for baking or stewing. Damson plums are a small, tart European-type variety used mainly for preserves.

AVAILABILITY The domestic plum season extends from May through October, with Japanese types coming on the market first and peaking in August, followed by European varieties in the fall.

Some varieties of plums are native to North America. The most familiar of these types is the sloe, used to flavor sloe gin.

SHOPPING TIPS Plums should be plump and well colored for their variety. If the fruit yields to gentle pressure, it is ready to eat; however, you can buy plums that are fairly firm but not rock hard and let them soften at home. They will not, however, increase in sweetness. Ripe plums will be slightly soft at the stem and tip, but watch out for shriveled skin, mushy spots, or breaks in the skin.

STORAGE To soften hard plums, place several in a loosely closed paper bag and leave them at room temperature for a day or two; when softened, transfer them to the refrigerator. Ripe plums can be refrigerated for up to three days.

PREPARATION Wash plums before eating or cooking them. They'll be juiciest (and to most palates taste sweetest) at room temperature. To pit Italian plums and other freestone types, cut the fruit in half, twist the halves apart, and lift out the pit. To slice or quarter clingstone plums, use a sharp paring knife and cut through the flesh toward the pit.

Japanese plums are most commonly eaten raw, although they can be poached. European plums are better for cooking as they are easier to pit and their firmer, drier flesh holds up well when it is heated.

Cooked plums are usually eaten with the skins on, but if you need to peel them, first blanch them in boiling water for about 30 seconds.

Baking Place halved, pitted plums in a baking dish and sprinkle with sugar and spices to taste. Add a few spoonfuls of fruit juice and cover. Cook until tender; check during baking and add more liquid, if necessary. *Cooking time:* about 20 minutes in a 400° oven.

Poaching Plums can be cooked whole (prick them with a fork first), halved, or sliced. For serving whole, cook the fruit unpeeled to preserve its shape. Place the fruit in simmering juice, wine, or a mixture of water and sugar, and cook until tender. *Cooking time:* 3 to 8 minutes (European plums cook much faster than Japanese plums).

SERVING SUGGESTIONS Take advantage of the many colors available among the different varieties and arrange a sampling in a serving bowl, or make a multicolored plum salad. Prepare a rainbow plum parfait: Coarsely chop different-colored plums and layer them in a goblet with low-fat vanilla yogurt and cereal or wheat germ. Select some blue-black Friars, ruby-skinned Larodas, jade green Kelseys and frosty purple Italian prune plums.

For a satisfying breakfast dish, try baked plums served cold with a dollop of low-fat yogurt.

The traditional English Christmas plum pudding contains currants and raisins, but no plums.

A fresh plum purée—lightly sweetened and flavored with lemon juice, almond extract, and spices (try for instance, cinnamon, nutmeg, and fresh or ground ginger)—makes a delicious sauce to pour over cake or frozen desserts. Purée peeled or canned plums and use as the main ingredient in a sorbet with port wine. Or, cook peeled plums in fruit juice with spices, then purée for a fruit soup.

PLUMS 3½ oz raw (⅔ cup sliced)			
Calories	55	Fat	<1 g
Protein	1 g	Saturated Fat	<1 g
Carbohydrate	13 g	Cholesterol	0 mg
Dietary Fiber	Low (S)	Sodium	0 mg

KEY NUTRIENTS		%RDA Men	%RDA Women
Vitamin C	10 mg	16%	16%

S=40% or more soluble N/A=Not Applicable N=Not Available

Chopped plums add sweetness to muffins, quick bread or coffee cake, while sliced plums bring new color and texture to a variety of salads.

Chinese plum sauce, also known as duck sauce, is a sweet-and-tart blend of plums, apricots, and sugar, seasoned with hot peppers and vinegar. Available in jars at most supermarkets, it is used as a condiment for dipping egg rolls and as a sauce and marinade for poultry. For a fresh version, purée plums (and apricots, if you like) in a blender or food processor with a clove of garlic and add sugar, soy sauce, and grated fresh ginger to taste. For a thick sauce, add a few teaspoonfuls of cornstarch and heat the mixture until thickened. Cooked, puréed plums can also be the basis of a plum sauce; simmer fresh or canned plums in water just until they burst, then purée them. Skewer pitted plum halves with vegetables and chicken chunks and grill; the spicy plum sauce can serve as a basting or dipping sauce for the kebabs.

Prunes

Prunes are dried plums, but not just any plums. The two fruits are identical botanically—the Latin word for plum is *prunus*—and a century ago the terms prune and plum were often used interchangeably. But today we make a distinction between prunes and plums. Compared to plums that are marketed fresh, the varieties that make satisfactory prunes generally have firmer flesh, more sugar, and a higher acid content—traits that make it possible for the fruits to be dried with their pits intact without fermenting. In addition, prunes usually are freestone, while many fresh plum varieties (though not all) are clingstone. (In a category by themselves are fresh, or European prunes, also called purple plums, equally suited for use as a plum or a prune. See page 261.)

The most common variety of plum used for prunes is California French, also known as d'Agen. The variety is a descendant of the first prune plums brought to the United States from France by Louis Pellier, who started a nursery in California in the 1850s. Today about 70 percent of the world's prune supply, and nearly 100 percent of domestic prunes, come from California prune orchards.

The transition from plum to prune is a carefully controlled process. The plums are allowed to mature on the tree until they are fully ripe and have developed their maximum sweetness. Then they are mechanically harvested and dried for 15 to 24 hours under closely monitored conditions of temperature and humidity.

PRUNE JUICE

If you're not fond of whole prunes, an excellent substitute is prune juice, which retains a far higher proportion of the whole fruit's nutrients than the juice made from most other fruits. Prune juice is made by pulverizing dried prunes and dissolving them in hot water. It is a concentrated source of iron—3 milligrams per cup, or 30 percent of the RDA for men, 20 percent for women. A cup of prune juice contains 473 milligrams of potassium, about the same amount as eight pitted prunes. But it is also relatively high in calories—182 calories per cup of prune juice, as compared to 110 calories in a cup of orange juice. To avoid excess calories, don't purchase brands with added sugar; prune juice is sweet enough on its own.

Because the plums lose so much water, about 3 to 4 pounds of the fruit are needed to produce a

Prunes

pound of prunes. After drying, the plums are sorted by size and then stored to await packing, at which point they are given a hot-water bath to moisturize them.

As with other dried fruits, the drying process concentrates the nutrients in prunes. First and foremost, they are a high-fiber food: Ounce for ounce, prunes contain more fiber than dried beans and most other fruits and vegetables. Over half of this fiber is of the soluble type that studies have linked to lowered blood-cholesterol levels. Prunes are also rich in beta carotene and are a good source of B vitamins, nonheme iron, and potassium.

The drying process concentrates the sugar content as well, which makes whole or pitted prunes a good snacking food. (Of course, the calorie count also increases—prunes contain more than four times the calories, by weight, that plums do.) Beware, though, of "health snacks," such as trail mixes and granola bars, that emphasize prunes as an ingredient: Frequently, the prunes are mixed in with high-fat ingredients, such as nuts and coconut chips.

Diced prunes, prune paste, and prune bits are used in prepared foods, particularly baked goods, to enhance taste and texture (though the quantity may not be sufficient to offer much nutritional value).

SHOPPING TIPS Be sure the package of prunes is tightly sealed to ensure cleanliness and moistness. Some prunes come vacuum-packed in cans, which keep them extra-moist. Buy small or large fruit, as you prefer; size has no relation to flavor or quality. If you don't mind pitting them when snacking or cooking, whole prunes are less expensive than pitted ones.

STORAGE After opening the package, reseal it as tightly as possible or transfer the prunes to an airtight container. Store them in a cool, dry place or in the refrigerator for up to six months.

PREPARATION You can pit prunes by slitting them open with a knife and pushing out the pits. (If you are cooking the prunes alone, pit them after they have been heated.) Pitted prunes are ready to use directly from the package, but be sure to check for the occasional pit in pitted prunes;

PRUNES 3½ oz raw (12 prunes)			
Calories	239	Fat	<1 g
Protein	3 g	Saturated Fat	<1 g
Carbohydrate	63 g	Cholesterol	0 mg
Dietary Fiber	High (S)	Sodium	4 mg

KEY NUTRIENTS		% RDA Men	% RDA Women
Vitamin A	1987 IU	40%	50%
Vitamin B_6	0.3 mg	15%	19%
Beta Carotene	1 mg	N/A	N/A
Copper	0.4 mg	N/A	N/A
Vitamin E	3 mg	30%	38%
Iron	3 mg	30%	20%
Magnesium	45 mg	13%	16%
Manganese	0.2 mg	N/A	N/A
Niacin	2 mg	10%	13%
Phosphorus	79 mg	10%	10%
Potassium	745 mg	N/A	N/A
Riboflavin	0.2 mg	12%	15%

S=40% or more soluble N/A=Not Applicable N=Not Available

the mechanical process is not foolproof.

Cutting, chipping, or dicing prunes can be tedious work because the knife quickly becomes sticky. To make the job easier, use kitchen scissors and dip the blades into warm water between cuts to keep them clean.

Reconstituting prunes To plump prunes, measure the fruit and combine it with an equal amount of liquid in a small saucepan. Simmer, but don't boil the prunes, or the skins may split. *Cooking time:* 7 to 10 minutes.

To soften prunes in the microwave, sprinkle them with fruit juice, cover, and cook at 100 percent power. *Cooking time:* 2 minutes.

To plump the fruit overnight, place the prunes in a heatproof bowl and add boiling liquid to cover. Cover the bowl and refrigerate until needed. You can drink the liquid (or use it in your recipe) as well as eat the prunes; the liquid will contain some of the sugars from the fruit.

SERVING SUGGESTIONS Prunes are a handy portable snack, straight from the package or mixed with other dried fruits. But there are other ways to incorporate them into your diet. Chop or dice them into muffin or pancake batter, or stir them into hot cereal. Plump them in orange or apple juice, and flavor with cinnamon, cloves, citrus zest, or vanilla extract. Or, create a mixed fruit compote with other dried or fresh fruits.

Plumped prunes can be made into a shake by puréeing the prunes (with the cooking liquid) with skim milk and spices. For a rich-tasting, fat-free dessert, plump prunes in red wine, port, or Marsala and serve with a dollop of sweetened, spiced non-fat yogurt.

Pitted prunes are delicious braised with poultry, beef, lamb or pork, or added to stews for the last 15 minutes of cooking time. The French often cook prunes in Armagnac (a type of brandy) and offer them as a side dish with meat or poultry. You can also include chopped prunes in bread stuffings for poultry, or mix them into mashed sweet potatoes or winter squashes. And chopped prunes can readily take the place of raisins in your favorite recipes.

Prune juice is so sweet it can be substituted for sugar in drinks, sauces, and fruit salads. In cold weather, serve hot prune juice with a squeeze of lemon juice and a cinnamon-stick stirrer.

Raisins

Like other dried fruit, raisins are a concentrated source of calories, sugar, and nutrients; they supply iron, potassium, and B vitamins along with a healthy amount of dietary fiber (both soluble and insoluble). The same can be said of currants, which like raisins start out as grapes—the only difference is that currants (don't confuse them with the fresh berries of the same name) are made from a specific type of grape, the Black Corinth.

The first raisins were probably grapes that had dried naturally on the vine, but more than three thousand years ago people were picking grapes and laying them out in the sun to dry—a process that has remained virtually unchanged. (Today, most raisins are still sun-dried, though some are dried in ovens.) Raisins were a precious trade item in the ancient Near East and also highly valued in ancient Rome (where two jars of raisins could be exchanged for a slave). Spanish missionaries brought them to Mexico and California in the eighteenth century, and nearly all the commercially grown raisins in the United States (and about one-half of the total world supply) now come from the San Joaquin valley of California, where the raisin industry began booming in the 1870s after a heat wave dried the grape crop on the vine.

Raisins have almost as much iron, by weight, as cooked dried beans or ground beef. They have 136 percent more iron than raw broccoli and 22 percent more than raw kale.

VARIETIES Most raisins produced in the United States are made from four different types of grapes: Thompson Seedless (which are also the most popular green grapes for fresh consumption), Muscat, Sultana, and Black Corinth. The grapes are dried into the following types of raisins:

Currants Made from small Black Corinth grapes, currants are seedless and very dark in color. These tiny fruits (about one-fourth the size of raisins) are sometimes labeled "Zante Currants," referring to the Greek island where this type of grape first grew.

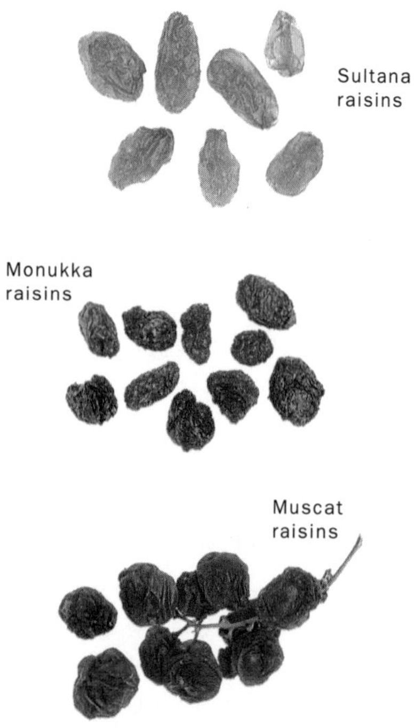

Golden seedless raisins Like natural seedless raisins, these are also Thompson Seedless grapes, but are oven dried to avoid the darkening effect of sunlight. They are also treated with sulfur dioxide to preserve their light color.

Monukka raisins These large, dark, seedless raisins come from the grapes of the same name. They're produced in limited quantities and are mostly available at health-food stores.

Muscat raisins Large, brown, and particularly fruity-tasting, these raisins are made from big, greenish-gold Muscat grapes. Since the grapes contain seeds, the raisins are seeded mechanically, or are sold with seeds. Muscats are considered a specialty item and are mostly used in baking, especially in fruitcakes.

Natural seedless raisins These are sun-dried Thompson Seedless grapes. They account for 95 percent of California raisins. The green grapes naturally develop a dark brown color as they dry in the sun, a process that takes from two to three weeks.

Sultanas The large, yellow-green grapes that are dried into these raisins are particularly flavorful and soft. Sultanas are still more popular in Europe than in the United States, but they can sometimes be purchased in gourmet shops and health-food stores.

Sultana raisins

Monukka raisins

Muscat raisins

AVAILABILITY Boxes and bags of natural and golden raisins are available year round. Muscat raisins, preferred for holiday baking, are usually sold just in the autumn and winter months. Currants may only be found in larger supermarkets. Clusters of raisins still attached to the stem are sometimes displayed in gourmet shops.

SHOPPING TIPS When buying packaged raisins or currants, be sure that the box or bag is tightly sealed. Squeeze and shake the package to see if the fruit is soft—if the raisins rattle inside, they are dried out. When buying raisins in bulk at a

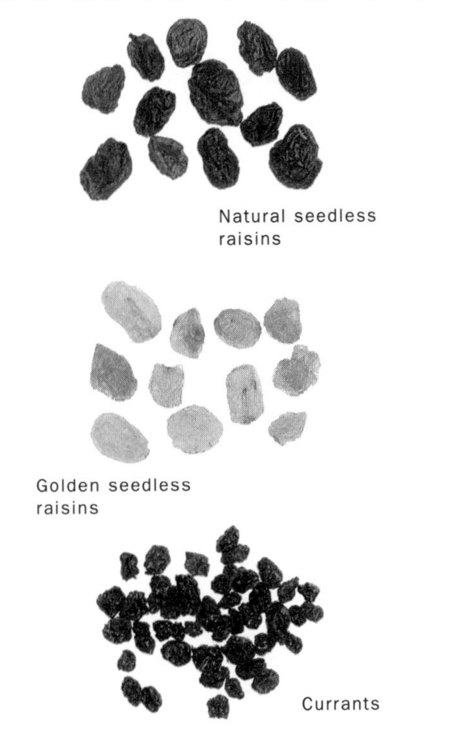

gourmet shop or health-food store, choose moist-looking, clean fruit; don't buy raisins from uncovered bins.

STORAGE Unopened packages of raisins will keep almost indefinitely in the refrigerator. Once opened, reseal the package, excluding as much air as possible, or transfer the raisins to an airtight jar or bag. Proper storage will deter the fruit from drying out and will prevent its sugar from crystallizing on the surface. If refrigerated, the raisins will keep for up to a year; they will stay even longer in the freezer and will thaw quickly at room temperature.

PREPARATION If they've been correctly stored and are not dried out, raisins require no special preparation; however, you may wish to soften them by one of the following methods: To plump raisins for baking, cover them with hot liquid and let stand for 5 minutes. Or, let soak overnight in the refrigerator. To conserve nutrients and flavor, use the least amount of liquid possible and then include it in your recipe.

If raisins have dried out through improper storage, steam them over boiling water for 5 minutes. Or, sprinkle them with liquid, cover, and microwave for 1 minute, then let stand, covered, for 1 minute longer. Raisins that are stuck together in a hard clump will loosen up and separate if they are heated in a 300° oven for a few minutes.

When chopping raisins with a knife or chopper, grease the blade lightly with vegetable oil to keep the fruit from sticking to it. When baking with raisins, dredge them in flour before adding them to the batter or dough to keep them from sinking to the bottom of the pan. Or, mix half the fruit into the batter and sprinkle the rest on top once the mixture is poured into the baking pan.

SERVING SUGGESTIONS Raisins are one of the all-time classic snack foods. You can eat them alone, or make a handy trail mix by combining raisins with other dried fruit, puffed or shredded wheat cereal, popcorn, and sunflower seeds. If you are looking for a treat that is simple to prepare yet flavorful, stir plumped, spiced raisins into yogurt or add raisins and cinnamon to cottage cheese and pack into a pita pocket for a low-fat "Danish."

RAISINS 3½ oz raw (⅔ cup)

Calories	300	Fat	<1 g
Protein	3 g	Saturated Fat	<1 g
Carbohydrate	79 g	Cholesterol	0 mg
Dietary Fiber	High	Sodium	12 mg

KEY NUTRIENTS		%RDA Men	%RDA Women
Vitamin B6	0.2 mg	10%	13%
Copper	0.3 mg	N/A	N/A
Iron	2 mg	20%	13%
Magnesium	33 mg	9%	12%
Manganese	0.3 mg	N/A	N/A
Phosphorus	97 mg	12%	12%
Potassium	751 mg	N/A	N/A
Thiamin	0.2 mg	13%	18%

S=40% or more soluble N/A=Not Applicable N=Not Available

Use raisins in pancakes, quick breads and yeast breads, muffins, cookies, or hot cereal; a mixture of dark and golden raisins will be more visually appealing.

Offset the tart flavor of homemade cranberry sauce with a sprinkling of raisins, mix the fruit with hot applesauce for a simple dessert, or incorporate them into rice pudding. Plump raisins for eating or cooking in fruit juice, wine, brandy, liqueur or rum.

Whole or chopped raisins bring sweetness to bread, rice, or chestnut stuffings for poultry or pork chops, or vegetables such as eggplant and winter squash. The dried fruit also works well with roasted or braised meats or poultry. Sicilian cookery uses raisins and pine nuts in a sauce to accompany fish.

Dark or golden raisins are popular in Indian and Middle Eastern dishes, such as curry, rice pilaf, and couscous. Add them to chicken, carrot, or rice salad, coleslaw, or chutney; toss them with sweet-and-sour cooked cabbage.

To derive the most benefit from the nonheme iron in raisins and currants, cook or serve them with foods containing vitamin C, such as fresh citrus fruits or fruit juices.

Rhubarb

Rhubarb, which looks like a pink celery stalk, is botanically a vegetable, but it is used as a fruit, largely in pies and sauces. (In some areas, it is referred to as "pie plant.") The ancient Chinese cultivated the plant for its roots, which reputedly have medicinal properties, and it didn't gain acceptance as a food in the United States until the late 1700s. The roots and leaves aren't eaten; indeed, the leaves are highly poisonous. At one time, the toxicity was attributed to their exceedingly high levels of oxalic acid, a substance that can interfere with iron and calcium absorption.

A significant amount of calcium is present in rhubarb, but most of it is unavailable to the body, since the plant also contains oxalic acid, which binds calcium. The inedible leaves have more acid than the stalks, but the stalks still hold enough to interfere with calcium absorption.

However, the exact source of the leaf toxin has yet to be determined, since rhubarb stalks also contain significant amounts of oxalic acid (as do a few other foods, such as spinach).

The stalks have an extremely tart flavor. They require sweetening to make them appetizing, which can increase their calorie content considerably. For example, half a cup of frozen, cooked, sweetened rhubarb has 139 calories, as compared to 29 calories in the same amount of unsweetened. But rhubarb can be combined with sweet fruits instead of sugar or honey to cut calories, as explained below.

VARIETIES Rhubarb comes in two main varieties: hothouse-grown (pink or light red stalks, with yellow leaves) and field-grown (dark red stalks, with green leaves). The hothouse variety has a somewhat milder flavor and is less stringy.

AVAILABILITY Field-grown rhubarb appears on the market from April through June or July. Hothouse rhubarb, which is cultivated in California, Oregon, and Michigan, is mainly harvested from January through June, but some

Rhubarb

supermarkets carry it year round. Rhubarb is also available frozen.

SHOPPING TIPS Rhubarb is sold loose and in 1-pound cello bags, like celery. Whichever type is available, choose well-colored, good-sized, straight, firm stalks. If the leaves are attached, they should look fresh and crisp; small leaves usually indicate younger, more tender stalks.

STORAGE If you buy rhubarb stalks with the leaves still attached, cut off the leaves as soon as you get home. *Never eat the leaves, raw or cooked.* Place the stalks in plastic bags and store them in the refrigerator crisper, where they will keep for about a week.

PREPARATION Hothouse rhubarb is ready to cook after it is rinsed and the tops and bottoms of the stalks are trimmed. For stewing or sauce making, cut the stalks into 1- to 2-inch lengths. Mature field-grown rhubarb may need to have the stringy fibers removed: As you cut the stalks, peel the coarse fibers from the back of each piece with a paring knife.

Baking Place cut-up rhubarb in a glass baking dish and sprinkle it with sugar (about 1/2 cup of sugar per pound of rhubarb). Cover tightly and bake in a 300° oven until tender, stirring once. Then taste and add more sugar, if necessary. *Cooking time:* about 30 minutes.

Stewing Rhubarb tastes sweeter after it's cooked, so stew it first, then add sugar or honey to taste. You may use less sweetener than your recipe calls for. Place cut-up rhubarb in a saucepan (don't use aluminum or cast iron) with just enough water to cover (and some lemon or orange zest, if desired). Cover and bring to a boil, then reduce the heat and simmer gently until tender. After cooking, add sugar or honey and cook for another 5 minutes to dissolve it. Initially, try about 1/2 cup of sugar per pound of rhubarb; if you're serving the stewed rhubarb cold, taste it again before serving and add more sugar, if necessary, as sweetness is less intense when food is chilled. *Cooking time:* 6 to 7 minutes.

SERVING SUGGESTIONS When rhubarb is cooked with sweeter fruits, it requires less sweetening. Strawberries and rhubarb make a delicious pie filling, but if you'd prefer to omit the high-fat piecrust, simply stew the two together (add the strawberries about 5 minutes before the rhubarb

RHUBARB 3½ oz raw (¾ cup diced)			
Calories	21	Fat	<1 g
Protein	1 g	Saturated Fat	<1 g
Carbohydrate	5 g	Cholesterol	0 mg
Dietary Fiber	Medium	Sodium	4 mg

KEY NUTRIENTS		% RDA Men	% RDA Women
Vitamin C	8 mg	13%	13%
Calcium	86 mg	11%	11%
Manganese	0.2 mg	N/A	N/A

S=40% or more soluble N/A=Not Applicable N=Not Available

is done) and use the mixture as a topping for angel food cake, gingerbread, or low-fat frozen desserts. Rhubarb-applesauce (or pear sauce) is another tempting blend; to give it a sweet, spicy flavor, add golden raisins and a little grated fresh ginger or ground ginger or cinnamon. Sweeten cooked rhubarb with honey or maple syrup, or with strawberry or raspberry all-fruit preserves.

Stewing rhubarb in orange juice both sweetens it and complements its flavor. Or, cook rhubarb in pineapple juice or with pineapple chunks.

For a low-fat rhubarb "fool"—stewed rhubarb with whipped cream stirred into it—cook the fruit (alone or with a sweeter fruit) in minimal liquid, sweeten it, and then chill it well. Just before serving, stir in some low-fat vanilla yogurt.

Rhubarb sauces marry well with meats and poultry as well as with desserts. Purée stewed, sweetened rhubarb and serve the sauce over veal cutlets, poached chicken breasts, or sliced fruit.

Chapter 4

EXOTIC FRUITS AND VEGETABLES

Interest in unusual fruits and vegetables has risen in the past few years, and many supermarkets and produce stands have begun stocking varieties that you wouldn't have found, or perhaps even heard of, a few years ago. Though not necessarily more nutritious than standbys like potatoes or peaches, these uncommon newcomers can add variety and interest to your diet. They range from high-carbohydrate vegetables such as salsify, which was popular with American cooks of the last century, to hard-to-grow greens like fiddlehead ferns and luscious imported tropical fruits such as guavas and kumquats.

The following guide sorts out some of the more recent arrivals. Most of them aren't really new at all, just unfamiliar to Americans. Because they are uncommon, though, information about their nutritional make-up is in many instances either incomplete or lacking. Therefore, no nutritional profiles accompany these entries; rather, information on any key nutrients is summarized in the text. (Unless noted otherwise, nutritional information is for the food in its raw state).

For variety as well as nutrition and good taste, these foods are well worth trying. Like nearly all fruits and vegetables, they are relatively low in calories and relatively high in vitamins, minerals, and fiber. Many can be eaten raw; most are easy to cook; and the majority are available year round. Some of the larger items often come with labels that offer tips on cooking and handling.

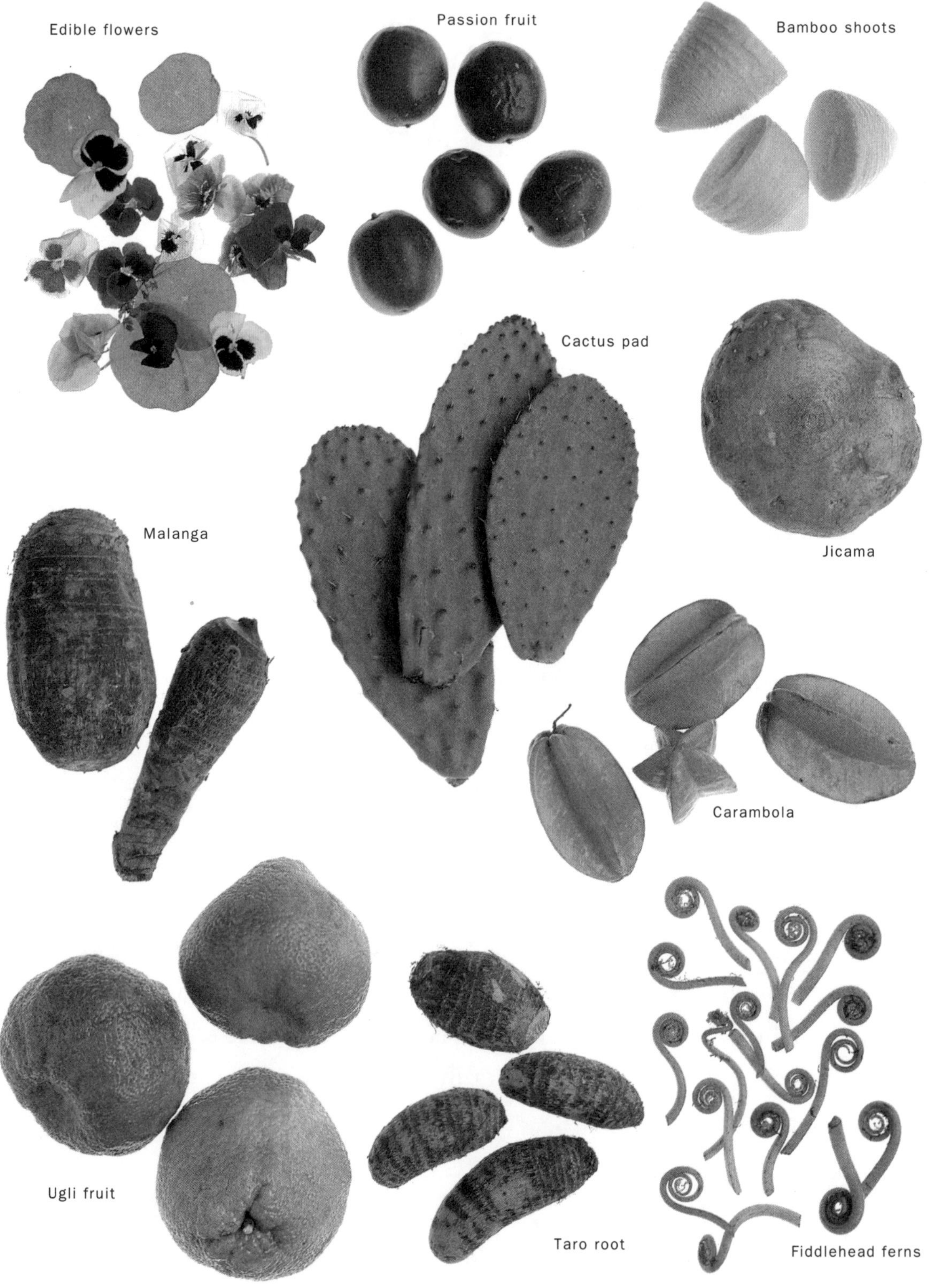
Edible flowers
Passion fruit
Bamboo shoots
Cactus pad
Jicama
Malanga
Carambola
Ugli fruit
Taro root
Fiddlehead ferns

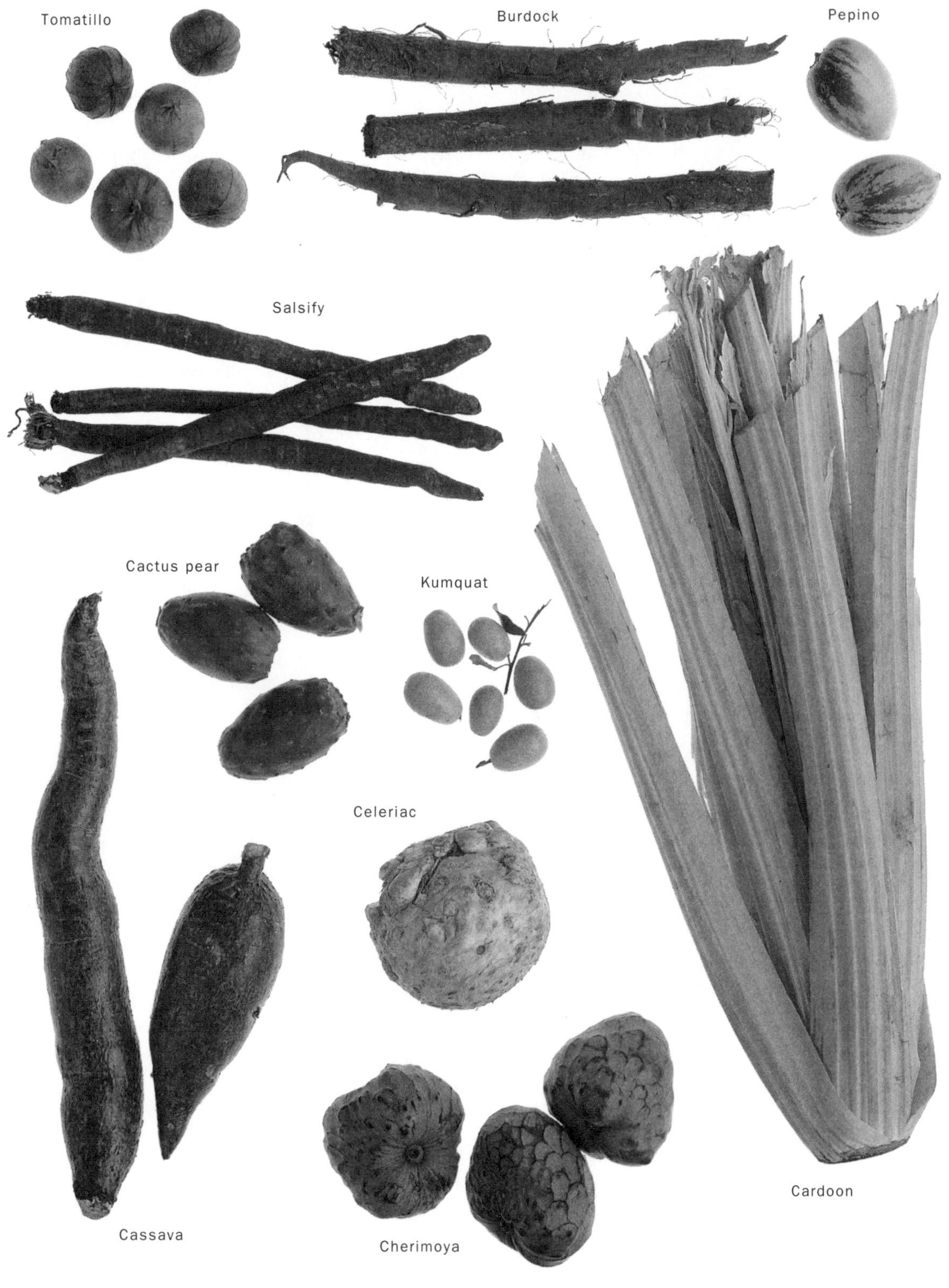
Tomatillo
Burdock
Pepino
Salsify
Cactus pear
Kumquat
Celeriac
Cassava
Cherimoya
Cardoon

Atemoya

This delicious dessert fruit is the result of a cross between a cherimoya (see below) and a sweetsop, or sugar apple. From the outside, an atemoya looks something like an artichoke carved from clay; inside, it has cream-colored flesh with the flavor and texture of a vanilla or fruit custard. Unlike custard, however, the fruit is practically free of fat and sodium, and rich in potassium. Atemoyas are grown in south Florida and are also imported from the West Indies; they are usually available from August through October.

Look for a pale-green fruit that is slightly tender to finger pressure but that has not cracked open (which the fruit often does as it ripens). Keep the atemoya at room temperature for a day or two if it is not already softened and ready to eat when you bring it home. Once it is ripe, you can refrigerate the fruit for a day or two; it tastes best chilled. To serve, cut the atemoya in half through the stem end and scoop out the flesh with a spoon. Or, use cubed atemoya in a fruit salad.

Bamboo shoots

You've probably eaten crisp strips of bamboo shoots in Chinese dishes. They are literally the shoots—the young, sprouting stems—of a bamboo plant, which is a type of grass, and not a tree. Sometimes the shoots are cut when they first appear, but they may also be "hilled"—piled with soil as they grow, which prevents the development of the green pigment chlorophyll so the shoots remain pale. In supermarkets, you can usually find only canned bamboo shoots, which have been peeled and cut into strips. However, Chinese grocery stores often carry the fresh, whole shoots, which are cone-shaped and about 4 inches long.

Canned bamboo shoots, after rinsing, can be added directly to stir-fries; they are precooked and need only to be heated through. Fresh bamboo shoots should be boiled until tender, then husked and cut up; they can be stir-fried or served as you would asparagus.

The fresh shoots are a good source of thiamin, vitamin B_6, and potassium. Canning the shoots, however, strips them of most of their vitamins and minerals.

Breadfruit

The size of a large melon, weighing 2 to 5 pounds, breadfruit (as its name implies) is a starchy, somewhat bland food that is notable for its high carbohydrate content, which is comparable to many vegetables: A 3½-ounce portion (about ¼ of the edible part of a small fruit) contains 27 grams of carbohydrate, which contribute almost 100 percent of the calories. The fruit is also an excellent source of vitamin C, supplying nearly 50 percent of the RDA in 3½ ounces.

Breadfruit has been an important staple for many years in the Pacific islands and the Caribbean. (Captain Bligh of the infamous *Bounty* was en route to Tahiti to get breadfruit trees for the English colonies of St. Vincent and Jamaica when his crew mutinied.) Though it is a tree fruit covered with a scaly green rind, the starchy consistency of its pale-yellow flesh has made it better suited for eating as a vegetable. The flesh resembles that of a potato when unripe, and can be used like a potato at this stage. As breadfruit ripens slightly, it softens, and is creamier and stickier (but still starchy) when cooked. After further ripening, breadfruit turns very soft, but its sweetness never matches that of lusher tropical fruits like the mango and papaya.

Imported from Haiti and the Dominican Republic, breadfruit can be found in grocery stores in West Indian and Caribbean neighborhoods. Choose a hard, firm, evenly-colored specimen. If you want the fruit to reach the soft, creamy stage, ripen it at room temperature until it gives to the touch. You can then refrigerate it for a day (but no longer) if not using it immediately. Breadfruit, like potatoes, can be baked in its skin, or it can be peeled, cut up, and boiled. Ripe breadfruit can be made into a sweetened, baked pudding.

Burdock

Popular in Japan, burdock can be found in Asian grocery stores and some health-food stores. It also grows wild in North America; the plant can be recognized by its very large leaves and spiny burrs (the "cockleburs" that stick to your clothes when you walk through a meadow).

A good source of magnesium, potassium, and folacin, this carrot-like root vegetable is brown-skinned, with white flesh that darkens quickly when cut. The fibrous flesh can be sliced or slivered and used like other root vegetables, in soups, stews and braises. It can also be stir-fried or cooked along with grains.

In the market, look for firm burdock roots. Don't be put off if the outside is dirty or muddy; just wash the root well. If the skin is thin, you need not peel it. Cut the vegetable into chunks, slices or shreds with a sharp, heavy knife. Cook burdock in liquid until tender.

Cactus pad (nopal)

The "leaves" of several varieties of Mexican cactus, cactus pads are eaten as vegetables. Succulent yet crisp, they exude a sticky substance (as okra does) when cooked. Their delicate flavor resembles that of bell peppers or asparagus. Look for *nopales* in Mexican grocery stores and specialty produce markets; choose small, bright-green pads that are resilient, not limp or dry. They will likely be de-spined (or of a spineless variety), but you will still need to trim the "eyes" just in case there are any tiny prickers remaining. A vegetable peeler works well for this. Trim the outside edges of the pads as well. Steaming is one of the best ways to cook cactus pads; they can then be served with lemon juice as a vegetable side dish, or cooled and used in salads. They are good in Mexican and Tex-Mex recipes—with tomatoes, hot peppers, and fresh corn.

Like other dark green vegetables, cactus pads are an excellent source of beta carotene, and are also rich in vitamin C. They supply some iron and B vitamins as well.

Cactus pear (Indian pear, prickly pear, sabra)

The prickly pear cactus grows in many parts of the world, and its large egg-shaped berry—a pinkish- or yellowish-brown fruit covered with spines—is popular in Mexico and the American Southwest, all over the Mediterranean, in South Africa, and in Israel (whose natives are nicknamed "sabras" for their supposed resemblance to cactus fruit: prickly on the outside and sweet on the inside).

Choose cactus pears that are soft but not mushy; let them ripen at room temperature for a few days if they are firm when you buy them, then refrigerate. To eat the juicy flesh, which is full of seeds (edible in some types, too hard to chew in others), you have to get past the prickly skin. Wear rubber gloves, use tongs, or hold the fruit impaled on a fork to protect yourself, then cut off the ends of the fruit, slit it lengthwise in several places, and peel the skin off. You can eat the melony-flavored fruit by itself, or use it in fruit salads or drinks.

Carambola

A ready-made garnish, the golden-yellow carambola, when sliced crosswise, yields perfect five-pointed-star-shaped sections—hence its nickname, star fruit. Its sweet-tart flavor is like a blend of several fruits—plums, pineapple, grapes and lemons. This elliptical, deeply ribbed fruit, 2 to 5 inches long, originated in Southeast Asia but is now grown in Florida.

You'll find carambolas in specialty produce stores and some supermarkets from fall through late winter. Look for shiny, well-shaped fruit. The skin on unripe fruit is green, but ripening at room temperature will turn it a deep, glowing gold and the fruit will develop a fragrant aroma. Slice the unpeeled fruit and remove the seeds; use the slices as a garnish for salads, poultry, desserts or beverages. Carambola slices can also be quickly sautéed and served as a condiment or dessert topping.

Carambola is an excellent source of vitamin C, supplying 35 percent of the RDA in 3½ ounces, which is equal to a small whole fruit or about ⅔ of a cup sliced.

Cardoon

Plants of the thistle family produce the familiar globe artichoke and also the celery-like cardoon. When the thick, silvery stalks are cooked, their flavor is reminiscent of artichokes, but they can also be eaten raw, like fennel or celery. Cardoons have long been popular in Italy, and can often be found in Italian markets in the United States in the winter and early spring. Look for slender, supple but firm stalks; they are velvety gray, not moist-looking and green like celery. Trim the bases and tops of the stalks, then cut them into strips to serve raw or into short pieces or squares for cooking. Cut the base into large chunks. Serve raw cardoon with other crudités and a dip; dress the cooked vegetable with lemon juice or a vinaigrette, and serve it hot or cold.

Like celery, cardoon is very low in calories—only 20 in 3½ ounces (a little over half a cup). For a vegetable, it is rather high in sodium—the half cup contains about 150 milligrams. It also supplies fair amounts of folacin and magnesium.

Cassava

Also called manioc or yuca, this starchy tuber is cultivated in South America (where it originated), Africa, the Caribbean, the South Pacific, and Florida. Cassava is shaped like an elongated potato; it's about a foot long, weighs up to 3 pounds or so, and is covered with a hairy brown bark-like skin enclosing soft dense white flesh. Cooking it not only makes it palatable, but also eliminates a toxic substance that can form in varying amounts in the raw vegetable. Though commonly peeled and cooked like potatoes, cassava can also be dried and ground into flour: Tapioca is a form of cassava flour.

Shop for cassava in Latin American markets, looking for dry, hard, clean roots with perfectly white flesh (grocers often cut them to show the inside). Cassava doesn't keep well, but it may stay fresh for a few days in the refrigerator or in a cool, dry place. To prepare the vegetable, cut it into thick slabs and peel them one at a time with a sharp paring knife. Simmer the chunks for about 20 minutes and serve hot, with a spicy sauce.

Celeriac (celery root)

Closely related to celery, this plant develops a knobby baseball-sized root with a crisp texture and intense celery flavor. (The stalks and leaves are not eaten.) Although not very popular in the United States, celeriac is a favorite vegetable in France and Italy, where it is eaten both raw and cooked. Like celery, this fall and winter vegetable can also be used as a flavoring.

Look for smallish, heavy, firm celeriac roots; although the outside may be dirty, it should be free of deep dents, cuts, or soft spots. If the stems and leaves are attached, they should be fresh and green. No matter how you're cooking celeriac, it needs to be scrubbed well. It can be baked in its skin, then peeled; for other cooking methods the thick skin should be pared off first. Slice or dice celeriac and braise or boil it until tender, or grate it or cut it into thin sticks for serving raw (in salads or as a crudité, with a creamy yogurt dressing or dip). Cooked celeriac and potato complement one another, and the two vegetables are often combined in one dish.

Celeriac, like celery, is low in calories, with about 25 in 3½ ounces (just over half a cup). Vitamin C, potassium, and phosphorus are the key nutrients.

Cherimoya

Sometimes called a custard apple or sherbet fruit, the cherimoya looks like an oversized green pinecone. It is grown in South and Central America and the Caribbean, and recently has been cultivated in California and Florida. The cherimoya is a wonderful dessert fruit, with sweet, juicy custard-like flesh whose flavor echoes that of other fruits—depending on the variety, it may have hints of pineapple, papaya, banana, mango, or strawberry.

Look for cherimoyas in specialty produce stores in winter and early spring: select fruits of any size with uniform yellow-green color, and let them ripen at room temperature until just softened (like a ripe peach) but not mushy, then chill and serve cold. The easiest way to eat this seed-filled fruit is to spoon it from the shell.

Half a medium-size cherimoya has about 250 calories. The fruit is a good source of vitamin C and also supplies some iron.

Edible flowers

As a garnish or a salad ingredient, fresh flowers bring color, fragrance and flavor to a meal. Some, like squash or zucchini blossoms, are large enough to be stuffed and cooked, while others—violets or pansies—simply add eye appeal and sweet scents to festive desserts or platters. Not all flowers are edible; those that are must be acquired from safe sources. If you're going to serve them as food, do not pick flowers from a pesticide-sprayed backyard or exhaust-choked roadside, or buy them from a florist. A gourmet shop or your own unsprayed garden are safe places to get edible flowers. Some farmstands or farmer's markets may offer them, too, and there are also mail-order sources for edible flowers.

Even though the flowers listed here are edible, it's advisable to make them a relatively minor component of the meal—such as a salad garnish. Some flowers (like certain herbs) can have a laxative effect if eaten in quantity.

Among the more common edible flowers are: daisies, nasturtiums (which taste like watercress—the leaves as well as the flowers are eaten), geraniums, lavender, marigolds, pansies, roses, and violets. Herb flowers, such as oregano, thyme and borage, taste much like the herbs themselves. Blossoms from fruit trees—apple, peach, plum, orange and lemon—are also fragrant and delicately flavorful.

Feijoa

This egg-shaped, egg-sized green fruit (it resembles a fuzzless kiwi fruit), native to South America, is grown today in New Zealand and California. Its dense, pale yellow flesh has a slightly gritty texture like that of a bosc pear, with a tart flavor and a strong fragrance. Feijoa can be halved and eaten with a spoon, used in fresh fruit salads or cooked in compotes. (The edible skin may be bitter; if so, peel the fruit before serving.) Look for feijoas in the spring and from fall through early winter. Ripen them at room temperature until they reach the softness of a ripe pear, then refrigerate them for a day or two, if necessary.

Fiddlehead ferns

A spring delicacy, fiddleheads are the young fronds of certain types of ferns. Although the word "fiddlehead" could refer to any fern shoots, only one variety, the ostrich fern, is considered edible. These tightly curled green shoots are picked before their leaves unfurl; gathered from the wild, they are rare and expensive. Once available only in the areas where they grew (Maine is noted for its fiddleheads), the highly perishable greens are now flown in to city markets during their short season. Choose small, bright green, tightly coiled fiddleheads, and use them within a day or two of purchase. Rub off the dry brown coat that some fiddleheads have, then wash the greens and blanch or steam them as you would asparagus.

Grape leaves

Young, tender grape leaves are used as a wrapper for rice and other fillings in Greek and Middle-Eastern cooking. The leaves are also used to wrap some French cheeses, and to protect small game birds from the intense heat of broiling or grilling. Bottled or canned grape leaves are sold in Greek and Middle-Eastern groceries. If you have grapes growing on your property, you can use your own leaves as long as they are unsprayed. Fresh leaves should be blanched or steamed to soften them; canned leaves, usually packed in brine, should be rinsed to reduce their sodium content. One way to enjoy grape leaves is to fill each one with a spoonful of stuffing made from cooked rice, currants or pine nuts, lemon zest, and dill, then fold the leaves around the filling and place them snugly in a pan so they do not unfold. Poach the wrapped rolls in broth, then chill and serve cold.

Guava

Looking something like a smooth-skinned lemon or lime, this native fruit of the Caribbean is available from Florida and California during fall and early winter. The guava crop is small, but if you manage to find fresh guavas in your market, you'll enjoy the sweetness and fragrance of their meaty, bright pink flesh (some varieties have white, yellow, or red flesh).

When shopping for guavas, look for yellow (or faintly greenish-yellow) fruits that are very fragrant and give to gentle pressure; if necessary, ripen at room temperature. Peel and seed the fruit and use it in fruit salads, or scoop out the flesh with a spoon and eat it as is. Slightly underripe guavas can be cooked and puréed as a condiment for meat or poultry, or as a dessert.

Guavas are an excellent source of vitamin C—3½ ounces (one fruit) provides more than three times the RDA. They are also rich in pectin, a form of soluble fiber that may help lower blood cholesterol.

Hearts of palm

This delicate white vegetable comes from palmettos, small palm trees that grow in Florida (there are also some South American palm species). Harvesting the heart, or terminal bud, often kills the plant, so it is an expensive food; for the same reason, some conservationists object to its use. The entire palm heart, weighing 2 to 3 pounds, is sometimes sold fresh in the United States. However, you are much more likely to find canned hearts of palm in supermarkets. These have been stripped of their tough husk and cut into small pieces. The smooth ivory-white cylinders have a velvety, layered flesh. Rinse canned hearts of palm, then slice them crosswise and use them in salads.

Jicama

The growing popularity of Mexican food has popularized this root vegetable in the United States. Jicama is a white-fleshed tuber that can weigh from half a pound to 5 pounds or more. Shaped like a turnip, it has a thin brown skin and crisp, juicy flesh rather like a fine apple. Its bland flavor enables jicama to be used in a variety of ways. You can serve raw slices or sticks sprinkled with lime juice and chili powder, with salsa, or in salads; add slivers to stir-fries (a good substitute for water chestnuts); or boil or bake the jicama like a potato.

Look for hard, unblemished jicama roots that are heavy for their size. Peel the papery skin with a paring knife; store cut pieces of jicama in a container of cold water.

Although jicama can be used in some of the same ways as a potato, it is less starchy and lower in calories (a cup of sliced jicama has about 50 calories). The vegetable is a good source of vitamin C, and also contains some potassium, iron and calcium.

Kumquat

Diminutive, citrus-like fruits that can be eaten skin and all, kumquats are as decorative as they are tasty. The egg-shaped orange fruits are about 1½ inches long, and often come with their shiny dark-green leaves attached. Kumquats are in best supply in the winter, and may be found in supermarkets as well as Asian grocery stores and gourmet markets.

Choose plump, shiny, fully-orange fruits; be sure to wash them before serving, since the skin as well as the pulp is eaten. To mingle the flavors of the sweet rind and tart flesh, squeeze the kumquats between your fingers before biting into the fruit. Add kumquat slices to fruit salad and use the whole or sliced fruit as an edible garnish. You can also use kumquats in cooked dishes that call for oranges.

Kumquat are an excellent source of vitamin C: A 3½-ounce serving (about 5 kumquats) supplies 62 percent of the RDA in only 63 calories.

Longan

These grape- to plum-sized Asian fruits, which are related to lychees, are sometimes called "dragons' eyes," because peeling their thin brown shells reveals a transparent, jellylike fruit with a large, dark seed in its center.

Look for longans in Asian markets in late summer; choose heavy fruits with uncracked shells. Longans are most commonly eaten raw (serve them on their stems, like grapes), but they can also be poached.

Longans are among the richer sources of vitamin C, with 3½ ounces supplying 140 percent of the RDA.

Loquat

This golden-skinned tropical fruit resembles an apricot, but its firm, sweet-tart flesh—which can be orange, yellow, or white—tastes something like plums or cherries. Fresh loquats are usually available only in the summer; although they are grown in the United States (in California, Florida, and Hawaii), they are very perishable when ripe and do not stand up well to shipping.

Choose large loquats that are tender and fragrant. Eat them raw after stemming, peeling and seeding them, or poach them alone or with other fruits; serve over ice milk or with angel food cake. Canned loquats, preserved in sugar syrup, are sold in Asian markets.

Like other yellow-orange fruits, loquats are an excellent source of beta carotene.

Lotus root

Once you've seen slices of lotus root in a dish, there's no mistaking it for anything else. The large, sausage-shaped rhizome of an aquatic plant (commonly known as the water lily), lotus root is pierced with ten air tunnels so that when cut crosswise, the white slices look something like snowflakes—or strangely symmetrical rounds of Swiss cheese. The starchy yet crisp flesh is slightly sweet; it may be sliced or grated to use in salads, stir-fried, or cooked in soups or stews. Thin, lacy slices make a nice garnish. Look for fresh lotus root in Asian markets from July through February.

Lychee (litchee or litchee nut)

Related to longans, lychees sometimes appear on the dessert menu at Chinese restaurants. Once stripped of their nubbly reddish-brown shells, these fruits look like large white grapes, each with a single large, glossy seed within its pale flesh. They have a sweet, flowery fragrance and flavor.

Fresh lychees may be found in Asian markets in the summer months. Select heavy, uncracked fruits with the stems still attached; the redder the shells, the fresher the lychees. Unpeeled, the fruit can be stored for up to three weeks in the refrigerator. Serve whole lychees one at a time (they need to be peeled), or peel several and sprinkle with a little lime or lemon juice to heighten the flavor. They can also be cut up and combined with berries or other soft fruit, or poached. Canned and dried lychees (the latter with a raisin-like texture) are also sold in Asian grocery stores.

Lychees are rich in vitamin C: 3½ ounces (10 fruits) supply more than 100 percent of the RDA.

Malanga

A starchy tropical tuber with a nutlike flavor, malanga is called *yautia* by Puerto Ricans (*malanga* is the Colombian name). It is typically used as a bland foil for spicy side dishes or condiments. Sold in the Latin-food section of some supermarkets and in Latin American grocery stores, malanga can be recognized by its yam-like shape (although it may weigh two pounds or more) and its rough, fuzzy brown skin, which reveals patches of yellowish or pinkish flesh beneath.

Choose a firm, heavy root free of soft spots, and store it at cool room temperature for a day or two, or in the refrigerator crisper for up to a week. Peel malanga and boil, steam, or bake it until tender. Like potatoes, malanga can be served sliced, in chunks, or mashed, with a well-seasoned sauce or as a companion to a flavorful stew. You can also use it to thicken soups.

Monstera

The familiar houseplant called split-leaf philodendron is the source of this unusual fruit. It grows like an elongated pinecone; when ripe, the hexagonal plates on its surface split apart, exposing a creamy, tart-sweet fruit that looks something like a banana, with a pineapple-banana flavor. Monstera, called *ceriman* in Spanish-speaking countries, grows in Florida and California, and is sometimes sold in gourmet produce markets in Northern cities. If you buy it, let it ripen at room temperature; do not eat it until it is fully ripe (when the surface scales fall off), or it will irritate the mouth and throat.

Passion fruit

An egg-shaped tropical fruit that is also called a purple granadilla, the passion fruit has a brittle, wrinkled purple-brown rind enclosing flesh-covered seeds, something like those of a pomegranate (granadilla means "little pomegranate" in Spanish). The seeds are edible, so you can eat the orange pulp straight from the shell, but passion fruit is more commonly sieved and its highly aromatic pulp or juice used as a flavoring for beverages and sauces.

Native to Brazil, passion fruits are now grown in Hawaii, Florida and California; these crops, along with imports from New Zealand, keep passion fruit on the market all year. Choose large, heavy specimens. If the skin is not deeply wrinkled, keep the fruit at room temperature until it is; the leathery rind, however, will not soften much. Ripe passion fruit can be refrigerated for a few days.

Passion fruit has about 97 calories per 3½-ounce serving, which supplies 50 percent of the RDA for vitamin C. It is also a good source of vitamin A, iron, and potassium. And if eaten with the seeds, it is an excellent source of dietary fiber.

Pepino

Its melon-like flavor could fool you about the pepino's place in the plant kingdom: It is a member of the nightshade family, like peppers and tomatoes. The heart-shaped golden fruit is marked with purple stripes or patches. Pepinos, which range from plum-sized to cantaloupe-sized, have fragrant yellow flesh surrounding a central pocket of seeds, like a melon. Pepinos are grown in California and also imported from New Zealand; the growing seasons in these two places put pepinos on the American market from late summer through early winter, then again in the spring.

Choose aromatic fruits (the size does not affect the flavor) that give to gentle finger pressure. Avoid those with greenish undertones; ripen the fruit at room temperature for a few days, if necessary, until it is fully golden-yellow. Serve pepino like melon, with a squeeze of lemon or lime, or use it in fruit salads.

Pomelo

An ancestor of today's grapefruit, the pomelo is a melon-sized, slightly-pear-shaped citrus fruit. It originated in Southeast Asia, and today is grown in China, Japan, and California. Like grapefruit, pomelos are pinkish- or greenish-yellow, with fibrous flesh separated into segments by membranes. Their flavor may range from very tart to very sweet.

Look for pomelos in gourmet produce shops and Asian markets from late fall through mid-winter; select heavy, fragrant fruits and store them in the refrigerator. Serve pomelo as you would grapefruit, but be sure to remove the entire thick layer of white pith; unlike other types of citrus pith, it is inedible.

Like all citrus fruits, pomelos are an excellent vitamin C source, providing more than 100 percent of the RDA in 3½ ounces (about half a cup of sections).

Salsify

"Oyster plant" is an old-fashioned name for this parsnip-like root vegetable, as some people find the flavor reminiscent of oysters. The long, inch-thick roots have tan skin and white flesh. (Scorzonera, a similar root, has brownish-black skin and cream-colored flesh.) Although it is not very common, you'll find this vegetable in some markets in the fall and winter; look for firm, plump unblemished roots and store them in the refrigerator. Cook and serve salsify as you would parsnips (see page 131). After scraping or peeling the roots, place them in acidulated water to keep them from darkening.

Like other root vegetables, salsify's starch turns to sugar during cold storage; it is also sometimes left in the ground over the winter to sweeten (like parsnips). A 3½-ounce serving (about ⅔ cup) has about 82 calories and provides modest amounts of vitamin C, some B vitamins, and potassium.

Sapote

Several quite different fruits have come to be called sapote or sapota. The white sapote, common in tropical markets, is a nearly seedless, orange-sized fruit with a green to yellow skin and mild, creamy-textured white flesh. It has been grown in California since the nineteenth century and also grows in Florida, but it is still scarce in northern markets (though it may become more popular in the next few years). The Florida-grown fruit is marketed in the spring; that from California is available in late summer and fall.

If you are able to buy white sapotes, choose firm ones to ripen at room temperature for a few days; refrigerate them once they are soft. Eat the fruit whole, as you would a plum, or spoon the fruit from its slightly bitter skin; a little lemon or lime juice will enhance the flavor of this fruit.

Seaweed

Consisting of long stems and frondlike leaves, the various types of seaweed, or sea vegetables, are large forms of algae. *Kombu* and *wakame,* popular foods in Japan, are types of kelp, a brown alga; *nori,* used to wrap sushi, and Irish moss (source of carrageenan, which is used as a thickening agent in food products such as cottage cheese and salad dressing) are red algae; sea lettuce is a green alga. The Japanese use *kombu* to make a flavorful broth, while *wakame* is cooked in soups or stir-fried and served over rice. Both *nori* and the laver that the Irish (and Welsh) cook into flat cakes called laverbread are actually the same plant. The Scots collect a type of seaweed called dulse and make soup from it.

Fresh sea vegetables taste rather like greens with an overlay of seawater flavor. Dried sheets or strips of seaweed are commonly sold at Japanese grocery stores and health-food stores. They have a naturally salty flavor from their high mineral content, and are sometimes crumbled or shredded and used as a seasoning rather than served as a vegetable. Dried nori is sometimes toasted over a flame to bring out its flavor before it is used to wrap sushi.

Seaweed is high in fiber, and some varieties are rich in vitamin C and beta carotene. But its greatest claim to fame is as a concentrated source of minerals, including potassium, calcium, magnesium, iron and iodine. (Some types, such as kombu and wakame, are also high in sodium.) However, you have to eat a good-sized serving—not just the tiny amount that's wrapped around sushi—to get any significant benefit.

Tamarillo

This subtropical "tree tomato" is, in fact, related to the tomato (as well as to the potato and eggplant). It looks like an elongated plum, with a purplish-red or crimson skin; its dark orange flesh has a plum-like texture but a bitterish, somewhat astringent flavor. Tamarillos grown in California are available in late fall and winter; in other months, you can find imports from New Zealand.

Look for well-colored fruit that gives just slightly to finger pressure; ripen at room temperature if necessary. They can be served fresh, sliced or puréed as a dessert topping (but will need sweetening); or cooked and eaten (like tomatoes) with savory foods and seasonings. Either way, they must be peeled. Immerse them in boiling water for 3 to 5 minutes, as you would peaches, to loosen the skins.

A half cup of tamarillo supplies about 50 calories. This fruit is a good source of fiber and vitamins A and C.

Taro root

The word taro (as well as dasheen, malanga, and other names) is applied to quite a number of starchy tropical tubers—all of them high-carbohydrate foods that are staples in the Pacific islands, Asia, the Caribbean, Africa, and parts of South America. Taro root's most familiar use is in *poi,* a sticky taro paste eaten in Hawaii. One of the more common forms of taro is a roughly cylindrical brown-skinned root with white or pale purple flesh. You may find it in Spanish or Asian markets, and it may be cut open to display its quality.

Choose a firm taro root with no shriveled or soft spots; store it in a cool, dry place or in the refrigerator crisper for no longer than one week. Taro resembles potatoes in flavor and uses: Boil, bake, or steam it (peeling it before or after cooking) and serve it with flavorful sauce. Be sure to serve it hot, as it becomes very sticky as it cools.

Tomatillo

Its name means "little tomato" in Spanish, and this small, round vegetable-fruit does look like a pearly-skinned cherry tomato. But tomatillos are enclosed in papery brown husks and are almost always used green rather than ripe: Their tart, lemony flavor contributes to Mexican *salsa cruda* and *salsa verde* (a cooked sauce for poultry or enchiladas). Fresh tomatillos can sometimes be found in Latin-American grocery stores: Select hard specimens (like unripe tomatoes) with clean, dry husks; you can refrigerate them in a paper bag for three weeks or longer. Husk, wash, and stem them before using. Canned tomatillos are common in Latin stores, and can be used in many of the same ways as the fresh.

Ugli fruit

This new citrus fruit—bred by crossing a grapefruit with an orange or tangerine—is grapefruit-sized, but loose-skinned like a tangerine, with pinkish-orange flesh that's sweeter than grapefruit and nearly seedless. The skin is thick, rough, and puffy; it may be an even or blotchy greenish-yellow to orange. Ugli fruit originated in Jamaica, but is now grown in Florida. Look for it in specialty produce markets in the winter and early spring. Choose heavy fruit that gives slightly to finger pressure. Use ugli fruit as you would grapefruit or oranges—as a breakfast fruit, and in salads and desserts.

Chapter 5

GRAINS AND GRAIN PRODUCTS

In most countries of the world, grains and grain products—flour, bread, cereal, and pasta—are the chief forms of sustenance. They provide about 50 percent of the world's calories and indirectly contribute much of the other half, since grains are also fed to the animals from which we get meat, eggs, and dairy products. Any number of national dishes—for example, the polenta and pasta of Italy, the kasha of Russia, the couscous of North Africa, the tabbouleh of Lebanon—are made from local grains that have been cooked and then served as a main dish, either on their own or in combination with seasonings or other foods.

Grains are among the best sources of complex carbohydrates, yet despite advice from health professionals to increase complex carbohydrates in the diet, Americans still fall two servings shy of the recommended six to eleven daily servings of grains or grain products. The United States is one of the largest producers of grains, but these healthful foods contribute just 25 percent of the calories in the American diet; more than half of our grain is used for animal feed. By comparison, in countries such as Japan, India, and China, grains (mainly rice) provide about 65 percent of the calories eaten, and in less-developed countries, 80 to 85 percent. The annual per capita consumption of rice in China, for example, stands at 243 pounds; in Japan, it is 169 pounds. In Mexico, corn is the principal food, while in other Latin American countries, rice—often paired with beans—is the basis of most meals.

GRAINS IN THE AMERICAN DIET

Economic conditions are primarily responsible for differences in levels of grain consumption. As a country becomes wealthier, its population can afford to use more of its grain for feeding livestock to provide meat; poorer countries, on the other hand, are almost totally dependent upon their crops to feed people. (The amount of land required for raising enough beef to feed one person can yield enough wheat to feed fifteen people or enough

rice to nourish twenty-four.) This inverse relationship is evident in our own recent past. In 1910, when the average American had fewer material resources, per capita consumption of wheat flour was about 210 pounds. The rate steadily declined as the nation grew wealthier, reaching a low in the early 1970s of about 110 pounds of wheat flour per person. During that same period, meat consumption increased to 170 pounds per person.

Affluent countries also rely more and more on convenience foods. In the case of grain products, many of these are now heavily refined—that is, they have been processed to remove their outer layers, making them easier to chew and quicker to cook. The parts that are discarded, however, contain most of the fiber, B vitamins, and trace minerals found in the whole grain, along with a fair amount of protein. Today, most refined grains are "enriched" with the addition of key nutrients, but this process does not replace all of what has been lost. Moreover, many grain-based convenience foods, from doughnuts and crackers to packaged, frozen side dishes, have fat, sugar, and sodium added to them, further compromising their nutritional wholesomeness. The appeal of convenience foods is that they are either ready to eat or quick to prepare. Whole grains, by contrast, have a reputation for being time consuming to cook. But, in fact, as you will see on the following pages, they are easier and faster to prepare than you might imagine and the results can be quite tasty, too.

Another reason Americans have not embraced whole grains and grain products is that they have a reputation for being fattening. For years, weight-loss diets typically excluded or minimized foods like pasta and bread. Actually, though, grain products are less fattening than the foods emphasized in some of the most popular diets. For example, a 3½-ounce cooked hamburger patty made from lean ground beef has 272 calories and 18 grams of fat—or 60 percent fat calories. The same amount, by weight, of cooked pasta (about ¾ cup) has just 141 calories—and virtually no fat. If a grain dish is high in calories, it's usually because of the fat added to it in the form of butter, cheese, whole milk, or

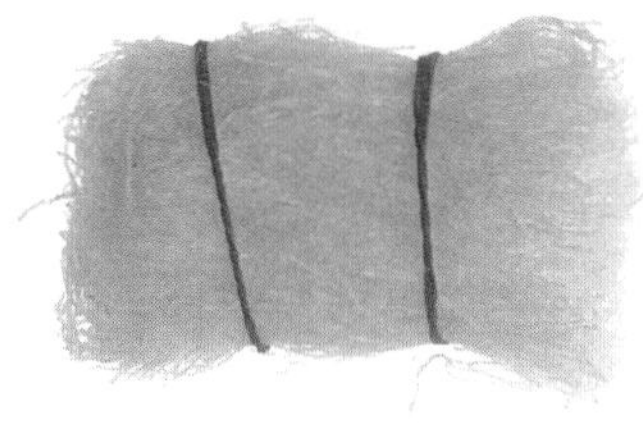

cream sauce. Grains eaten without these fatty ingredients are generally less fattening than most meats and dairy products, which are inherently high in fat.

Even though Americans still don't eat enough grains to supply them with the recommended amounts of complex carbohydrates and dietary fiber, overall grain consumption has risen 17 percent during the past decade. The amount of wheat flour we eat, for example, has increased from 110 pounds in 1972 to 138 pounds today. In 1975, Americans ate 11 pounds of pasta per person, but that figure has grown to over 18 pounds. Even more dramatic are the increases in our levels of oat and rice consumption. Thanks in part to studies linking oat bran to lower cholesterol levels, oat consumption is up 100 percent since the early 1980s. Rice consumption has also increased over 100 percent since the early 1970s.

GRAIN BENEFITS

Between 65 and 90 percent of the calories in grains come from carbohydrates (mostly complex), which should comprise about two-thirds or more of the calories you consume each day. Grains are also rich in both soluble fiber (the kind that lowers blood-cholesterol levels) and insoluble (the kind that helps to prevent constipation and protect against some forms of cancer). People living in areas where unrefined whole grains make up a significant part of the diet are alleged to have a lower incidence of intestinal and bowel problems, such as colon cancer, diverticulosis, and hemorrhoids, than those who live in the industrialized countries of Europe and North America, where grains are a less important component of the diet. Moreover, grains—especially whole grains—and grain products offer significant amounts of B vitamins (riboflavin, thiamin, and niacin), vitamin E, iron, zinc, calcium, selenium, and magnesium.

In addition, grains are an excellent low-fat source of protein—they provide 47 percent of the world's protein intake (though only 16 to 20 percent of the protein con-

sumed in the United States). The protein, however, is incomplete—that is, it is deficient in some essential amino acids that act as "building blocks" for protein in the body. These essential amino acids must be obtained through foods, and most grains are deficient in the amino acid lysine. But it's possible to complete the protein by eating grains with foods that contain complementary proteins, such as legumes, small amounts of meat, poultry, dairy products, eggs, or, in some cases, other grains. A classic example of a dish with complementary proteins is rice and beans. The beans provide the lysine missing from the rice, while the rice contributes methionine, an amino acid missing from the beans. Peanut butter sandwiches, macaroni and cheese, breakfast cereal with milk, and rice and buckwheat in a pilaf (buckwheat is not deficient in lysine) are other examples of food combinations that provide complementary proteins.

WHAT'S IN A GRAIN

Not all grains are botanically related—true grains, such as wheat, rice, oats, rye, millet, corn, triticale, and barley, are members of the grass family, *Gramineae;* other so-called grains, such as amaranth, quinoa, and buckwheat, belong to different botanical families. But the kernels of the different grains all have a similar composition. A kernel is an edible seed composed of three parts—the bran, the endosperm, and the germ, or embryo. Some grains, notably rice, oats, and some varieties of barley, are also covered by an inedible papery sheath called the hull, which must be removed before the grain can be processed or consumed. Within each kernel are the nutrients needed for the embryo to grow until the plant can take root and get nourishment from outside sources.

The bran is the outer covering of the kernel. It makes up only a small portion of the grain but consists of several layers—including the nutrient-rich aleurone—and contains a disproportionate share of nutrients. The bran layers supply 86 percent of the niacin, 43 percent of the riboflavin, and 66 percent of all the minerals in the grain, as well

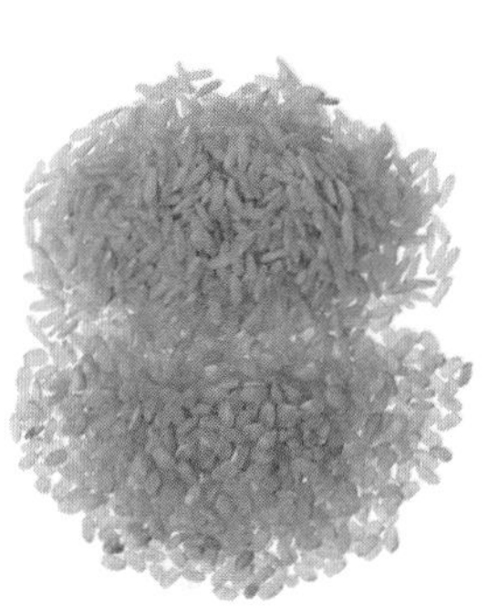

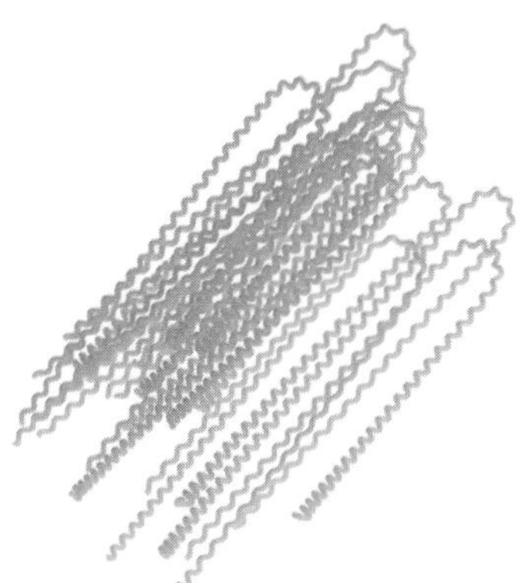

as practically all of the grain's dietary fiber. In some grains—wheat and corn, for example—the fiber is primarily insoluble, while in other grains, such as oats and barley, it is mainly soluble. Whole grains almost always contain the bran, but it is usually stripped away during milling and so is missing from most refined grain products.

The starchy endosperm accounts for about 83 percent of the grain's weight. Most of the protein and carbohydrates are stored in the endosperm, as are some minerals and B vitamins (though less than are in the bran). This layer also has some dietary fiber; for example, about 25 percent of the fiber in wheat is found in the endosperm. In wheat, the endosperm is the part of the grain used to make white flour.

The smallest part of the grain is the germ; it constitutes about 2 percent of the kernel's weight. Located at the base of the kernel, the germ is the part of the seed that if planted would sprout to form a new plant. It contains a good amount of polyunsaturated fat, and, as a consequence, is often removed during milling to prevent grain products from turning rancid. The germ is also relatively rich in vitamin E and the B vitamins, though it has fewer of the latter than are found in the bran or endosperm, and some minerals.

MILLING AND ENRICHMENT

Grains have been milled since they were first cultivated, to make them easier to cook and digest. During milling, the inedible hull and varying amounts of the bran are removed from the grain, and then the grain is ground into smaller granules. For example, barley is milled into three types—hulled, Scotch or pot, and pearled—each with progressively less bran. Similarly, wheat can be milled into cracked wheat (most bran), finely ground cracked wheat, or wheat flour (least bran).

To turn wheat kernels into flour, the seeds are put through an alternating series of high-speed steel rollers and sifters of increasingly finer mesh in order to separate the three parts of the seed. White, or refined, flour consists almost entirely of the ground

endosperm, while whole-wheat flour retains the three constituents, which are recombined after milling.

In the United States, it is the refined grains that are most popular. Sixty-one percent of the bread and rolls we eat are made from white flour, and the pasta we cook is usually made from refined wheat. In addition, the rice is most often white, rather than brown. Admittedly, these are all nourishing foods, but they lack some of the dietary fiber and some of the nutrients found in the whole grain. White flour, for example, can lose up to 80 percent of the vitamins and minerals present in the whole-wheat kernel, and it retains only 25 percent of the fiber.

Today, most of the refined products are enriched—that is, certain nutrients lost during processing are added in amounts that approach their original levels. Some grain products—bread, flour (except whole-wheat flour), and pasta, for example—must meet Federal standards for how much of each nutrient must be added to the product. After milling, white flour, cornmeal, white rice, and semolina (the flourlike product used for pasta) are enriched with thiamin, niacin, and riboflavin, and fortified with iron. Some white wheat flours may also be fortified with calcium. A food is *fortified* with a particular nutrient when the manufacturer has added 10 percent or more of the United States Recommended Dietary Allowance (U.S. RDA) for that nutrient. Thus, white flour has just slightly less of the B vitamins than whole-wheat flour, but more iron.

Enriched grains are more nutritious than unenriched ones, and they also supply the same amount of complex carbohydrates as whole grains. Moreover, refined grains store longer because the natural oils in the bran and germ have been removed, and these oils tend to spoil quickly, especially in warm environments. But from a nutritional vantage point, high-quality whole grains are still superior to refined grains; they contain more dietary fiber as well as a host of trace nutrients, such as zinc and copper, that are removed during milling.

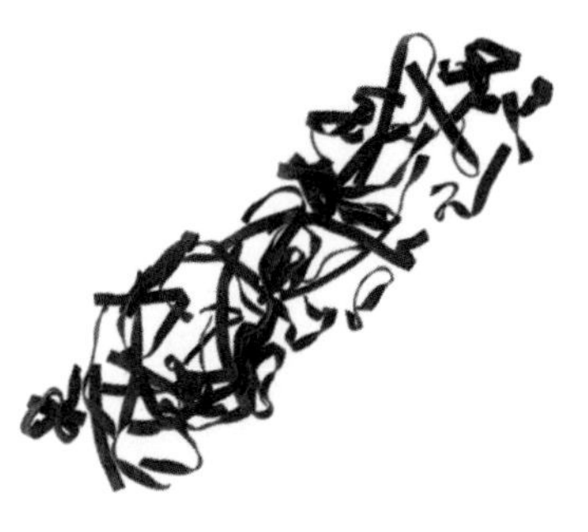

SHOPPING AND STORAGE

Shopping and storage guidelines for whole grains are similar. (The guidelines for grain products are given in the entries.) Most grains are sold in boxes or cellophane bags: Be sure the package is tightly sealed and check for a freshness date. If you buy grains in bulk from bins, try to be sure the store has a good turnover and that the bins are emptied before adding new stock. Grains should be clean and dry, free from chaff or other debris, and smell pleasantly fresh.

Though they have a long shelf life compared to fruits and vegetables, whole grains are subject to spoilage. They contain natural oils that can turn rancid, and they can also fall prey to insect infestation and mold. Therefore, keep grains in tightly closed containers or plastic bags. You can store them at room temperature (except in hot weather) in a dark, dry place for about one month. However, they will keep considerably longer in the refrigerator—at least four to five months. Use moisture-proof containers to prevent them from drying out or getting soggy.

If you freeze grains, they will keep almost indefinitely. The exceptions are oats and oat bran, which are higher in fat than other grains and so can turn rancid after only two or three months in the freezer. Therefore, buy only as much as you will need in that period of time.

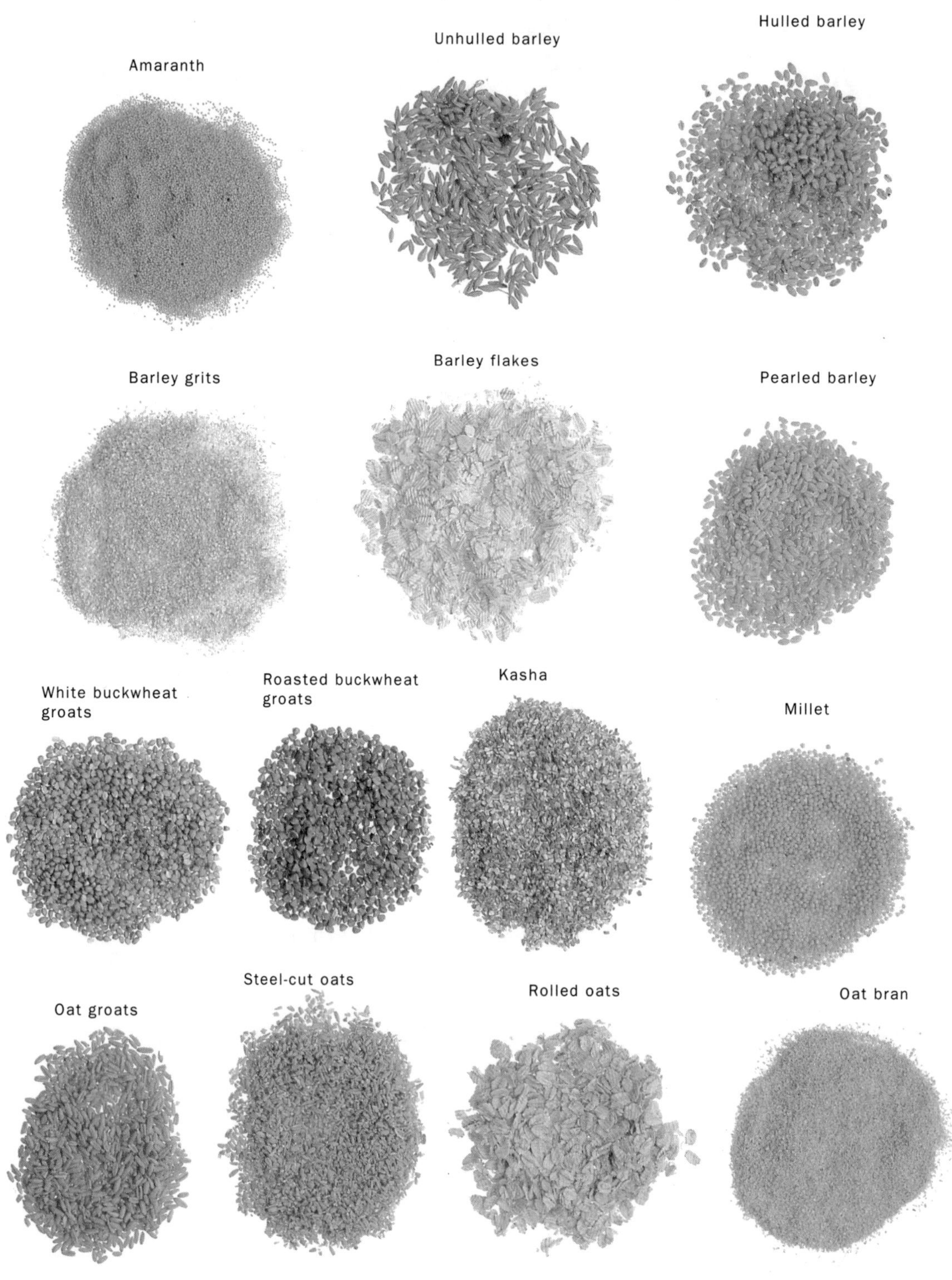
Amaranth
Unhulled barley
Hulled barley
Barley grits
Barley flakes
Pearled barley
White buckwheat groats
Roasted buckwheat groats
Kasha
Millet
Oat groats
Steel-cut oats
Rolled oats
Oat bran

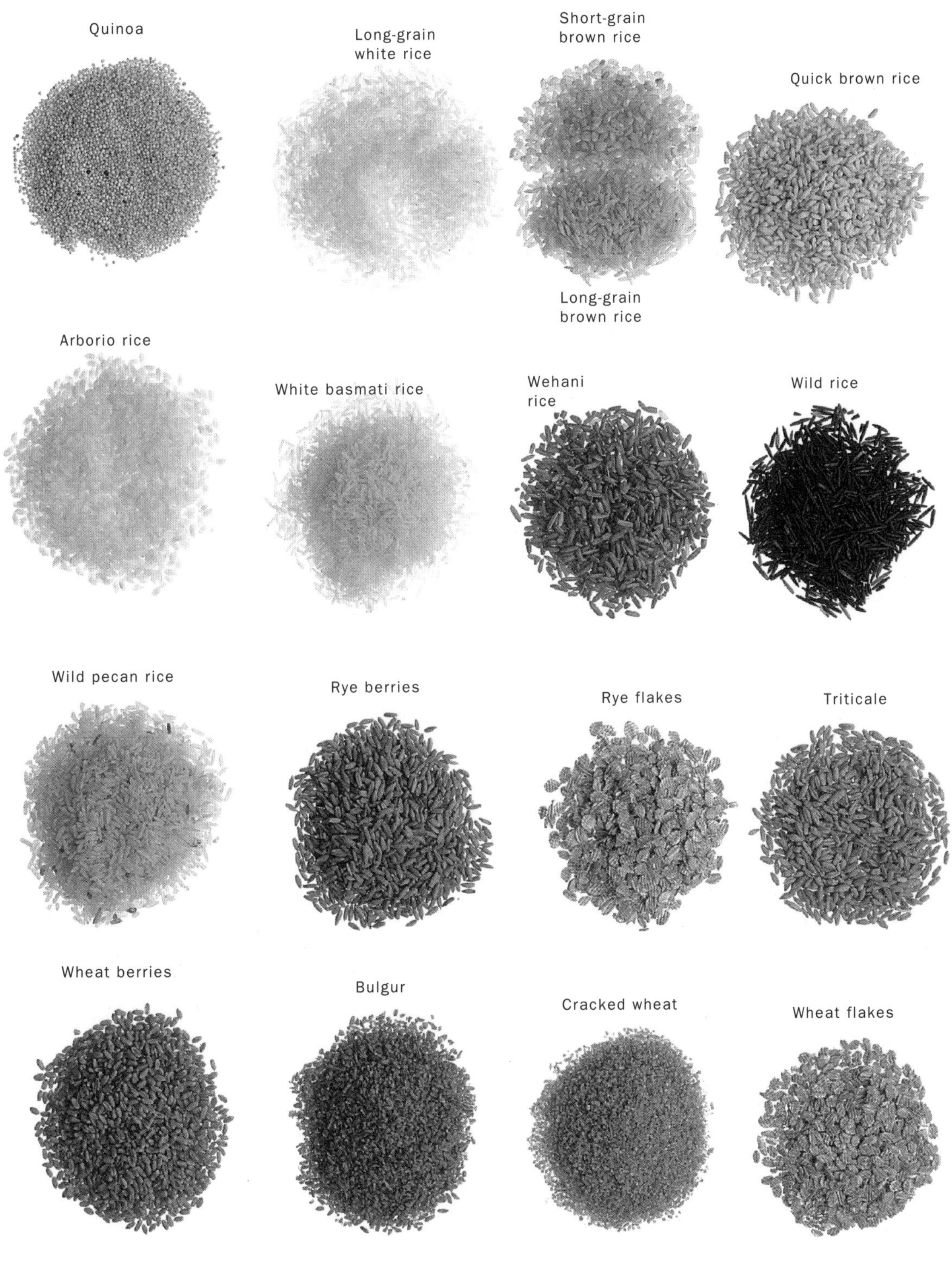
Quinoa
Long-grain white rice
Short-grain brown rice
Quick brown rice
Long-grain brown rice
Arborio rice
White basmati rice
Wehani rice
Wild rice
Wild pecan rice
Rye berries
Rye flakes
Triticale
Wheat berries
Bulgur
Cracked wheat
Wheat flakes

Amaranth

Amaranth has been touted as the miracle grain of the Aztecs, a supergrain, and the grain of the future. Ironically, it is not a true grain at all: The broad-leaved amaranth plant is related to a common garden weed called pigweed and to the tumbleweeds of the Southwestern United States. Its leaves as well as its seeds are usable as food. The "miracle" status of amaranth arises from its protein content and quality. Unlike true grains, amaranth is not deficient in the amino acid lysine, so when it is eaten with wheat, rice, or barley, for example, it provides a complete protein. Amaranth is also notable among the grains for its high calcium, folacin, and magnesium content. Its iron content is especially impressive, providing more than four times the amount in brown rice and twice that in bulgur. Among the grains, only quinoa has more iron.

Amaranth is the only grain that supplies a good amount of calcium. A half cup of the dry seeds (which cooks to 1⅓ cups) has as much calcium as 3 cups of raw broccoli, 1 ounce of blue cheese, or ½ cup of milk.

Amaranth is a tiny grain, each kernel about the size of a poppy seed. There may be as many as 700,000 seeds in 1 pound of the grain. Although the color may range from buff to dark purple, most amaranth sold commercially is pale yellow. Sometimes black seeds are mixed in, which can be very bitter (they are often the seeds of wild pigweed that grows among cultivated amaranth). It's nearly impossible to pick out the black seeds, but their flavor will not dominate that of the paler grains. Amaranth does have a pronounced flavor—a sort of earthy sweetness that might be compared to beets.

An ancient foodstuff, perhaps eight thousand years old, amaranth was "lost" for centuries and was rediscovered only recently in the New World (its cultivation has been promoted since the 1960s by the Food and Agriculture Organization of the United Nations). On this tiny grain turned the fortunes of the ancient Aztec empire; amaranth was not only valued as a dietary staple by the Aztecs, but offered as a royal tribute and used in religious rituals. Cortés, the Spanish conqueror of the Aztecs, outlawed the cultivation of amaranth, effectively starving the Aztecs into submission and destroying their culture. As a direct result of the conquistador's decree, knowledge of amaranth was virtually lost to the Western world for hundreds of years. Sometime after the fifteenth century, however, amaranth was brought to Asia, where it found favor on the Indian subcontinent and in China, which is the largest producer of the grain today. Major crops are also cultivated in Mexico and Central America, and in recent years, the plant has been introduced to wheat-growing regions of the United States, but on a small scale.

Although amaranth's weedlike nature makes it easy to grow, harvesting the grain is labor intensive, so the final product is relatively expensive. It has not yet achieved wide popularity in this country, and at present amaranth products are primarily available in health-food stores or through mail-order sources.

PREPARATION The whole seeds, when simmered, produce a thick, oatmeal-like porridge that has a gelatinous texture many find unpalatable. To make amaranth more appetizing, cook a small proportion (up to 15 percent) of it with another grain (or grains), such as brown rice or buckwheat; follow the cooking instructions for the predominant grain rather than for the amaranth. The seeds can also be baked or steamed. If cooked alone, amaranth benefits from the addition of a strong-flavored cooking liquid, such as beef broth or tomato juice.

Popping The grains can be toasted as you would sesame or poppy seeds; they pop and puff like popcorn. Toast just a tablespoonful of the seeds at a time in a heavy, ungreased skillet, tossing and stirring them over high heat for a few seconds until they pop.

Simmering Use 1½ cups liquid to ½ cup of amaranth. *Cooking time:* about 30 minutes. Makes 1⅓ cups.

Sprouting Follow the instructions for sprouting legumes and seeds on page 159. Amaranth sprouts in four to six days.

SERVING SUGGESTIONS For a tasty breakfast dish or dessert, simmer or bake amaranth along with another grain in apple juice, then serve it with yogurt and fresh fruit.

Broth- or juice-cooked amaranth can be combined, alone or with other grains, with stir-fried or steamed vegetables.

Unlike other grains, amaranth contains some vitamin C; it supplies 7 percent of the RDA in 3½ ounces, dry.

Prepare low-fat "refried" amaranth as an alternative to rice. Stir-fry cooked amaranth in a small amount of sesame oil along with garlic, onion, and red or green bell peppers—or hot peppers.

The gelatinous texture of amaranth makes it an excellent thickener for soups and stews. Add it raw during the last half-hour of cooking time.

Sprouted or popped amaranth seeds are ideal as a garnish or crunchy topping for soups, salads, and casseroles. Popped amaranth can also be used as breading for baked fish or poultry.

AMARANTH 3½ oz dry (½ cup)			
Calories	374	Fat	7 g
Protein	14 g	Saturated Fat	2 g
Carbohydrate	66 g	Cholesterol	0 mg
Dietary Fiber	N	Sodium	21 mg

KEY NUTRIENTS		% RDA Men	% RDA Women
Vitamin B_6	0.2 mg	10%	13%
Calcium	153 mg	19%	19%
Copper	1 mg	N/A	N/A
Folacin	49 mcg	25%	27%
Iron	8 mg	80%	53%
Magnesium	266 mg	76%	95%
Manganese	2 mg	N/A	N/A
Phosphorus	455 mg	57%	57%
Potassium	366 mg	N/A	N/A
Riboflavin	0.2 mg	12%	15%
Zinc	3 mg	20%	25%

S=40% or more soluble N/A=Not Applicable N=Not Available

Barley

Barley was one of the first crops cultivated by man, and has been used as a food and medication—and as a measuring standard and even a form of currency—since biblical times. Today, barley ranks as the fourth most important cereal crop in the world (fifth in the United States), and the United States is the third biggest barley producer. Because it grows well in a range of climatic conditions—from the cold of Scotland to the heat of Ethiopia—it has become a major food staple in many parts of the world. But most of the barley cultivated in this country is not eaten directly as a food; instead, it is either converted into malt for beer production or fed to animals. More flavorful and chewy than white rice, though not as strongly flavored as brown rice, this versatile grain deserves a place in the kitchen of the health-oriented cook.

Like oats, barley is an excellent source of soluble fiber, and so can be effective in lowering cholesterol levels. In its most commonly eaten form, known as pearled barley, the bran is removed and the grain has only about half the iron, manganese, and phosphorus of oats, and 75 percent less thiamin. On the other hand, hulled barley, a form of the grain in which the bran is left intact, is more nutritious, especially in terms of thiamin and dietary fiber.

FORMS OF BARLEY Most of the barley eaten in the United States has been milled to remove the bran. It is possible, however, to find less-refined forms, mostly at health-food stores.

Flakes (flaked barley) Like the rolled oats they resemble, barley flakes are grains that have been flattened. They are usually cooked and offered as a hot cereal, but they can also be mixed into muesli and baked goods.

Grits More similar to bulgur than to corn (hominy) grits, these barley grains have been toasted and cracked into small pieces. They can be cooked and served in place of rice or breakfast cereal, or used in baking.

Hulled barley This form of barley is not as widely available as the other types, but its superior nutrient content makes it worth seeking out (try a health-food store). Because only the outer, inedible hull, and not the bran, is removed, hulled barley is rich in dietary fiber. It also contains more iron and trace minerals than pearled barley—and more than four times the thiamin. The grains are brown, and they take longer to cook than pearled barley. Hulled barley has a pronounced flavor, which makes it an appealing ingredient in hearty, country-style soups and stews.

Pearl (pearled) barley To produce these uniform, ivory-colored granules, the barley grains are scoured six times during milling to completely remove their double outer husk (called the spikelet) and their bran layer. Unfortunately, as with white rice, this process also removes nutrients. The thorough milling, however, shortens the grain's cooking time considerably. Pearl barley comes in fine, medium, and coarse grinds. It has a delicate nutlike taste that readily absorbs the flavors of its companion ingredients in soups, salads, and side dishes. An instant form of pearl barley, called quick barley, cooks even faster because it is precooked by steaming. It is no less nutritious than the regular pearl barley.

Pot barley (Scotch barley) A less-refined version than pearl, pot barley is milled just three times, so that part of the bran layer remains. It is usually added to soups and stews. Although some supermarkets carry this form, it is more likely to be found in health-food stores.

PREPARATION Barley is most often simmered, though it can be baked in a casserole. The chart below gives grain-to-liquid proportions and cooking times for each form of barley.

SERVING SUGGESTIONS Any kind of barley (especially barley flakes or grits) will make a pleasing hot cereal. When using whole barley, cook it in advance to save time and reheat it for a

BARLEY COOKING TIMES

Per ½ Cup Uncooked	**Liquid** (cups)	**Cooking Times**	**Yield** (cups)
Hulled	2	1 hour, 40 minutes	1¼
Pearl	1½	55 minutes	2
Quick	1	10 to 12 minutes (let stand 5 minutes)	1½
Grits	⅓	Let stand 2 to 3 minutes	⅓
Flakes	1½	30 minutes	1

few minutes in the microwave. Serve the cereal with skim milk or yogurt, topped with fresh or dried fruits.

Vary your meals by substituting barley for white or brown rice in both sweet and savory recipes, adjusting the cooking time, if necessary. Barley can also be transformed into a delicious pilaf, risotto, or casserole when steeped or baked in broth with added vegetables and herbs. Combine the grain with beans and vegetables for a protein-rich main dish.

For interesting texture, experiment with barley as a stuffing for poultry or as a filling for vegetables—cabbage rolls, bell peppers, or hollowed-out winter squash.

MALTED BARLEY

Much of the barley grown in the United States is malted; some malted barley is sold as a cereal, but generally it is used to make alcoholic beverages. Malt is made by soaking whole barley seeds—including the husks—for several days under controlled conditions so that it germinates (sprouts). During the soaking, the protein contained in the bran of the barley is converted into enzymes that change the starches to sugars. Then the barley is dried to prevent further sprouting. Theoretically, this process would work with any grain, but barley is well suited to malting because the bran layer is particularly rich in proteins that form many complex enzymes in the sprouting process. The conversion of starch to sugar creates the conditions necessary for fermentation by yeast, which produces alcohol.

Barley is commonly used in soups, either to thicken and fortify them, or to serve as a base. Barley soup or stew, with or without meat, provides a substantial one-dish meal. The variations on barley soup are endless; perhaps the most familiar are mushroom-barley and beef- or lamb-barley combinations. Mushroom-barley soup can be made with beef or chicken stock, or with vegetable stock or water, and dried mushrooms,

BARLEY, pearl 3½ oz cooked (½ cup)

Calories	354	Fat	2 g
Protein	13 g	Saturated Fat	<1 g
Carbohydrate	74 g	Cholesterol	0 mg
Dietary Fiber	High	Sodium	12 mg

KEY NUTRIENTS		% RDA Men	% RDA Women
Vitamin B_6	0.3 mg	15%	19%
Copper	0.5 mg	N/A	N/A
Folacin	19 mcg	10%	11%
Iron	4 mg	40%	26%
Magnesium	133 mg	38%	48%
Manganese	1.9 mg	N/A	N/A
Niacin	5 mg	26%	33%
Phosphorus	264 mg	33%	33%
Potassium	452 mg	N/A	N/A
Riboflavin	0.3 mg	18%	23%
Thiamin	0.6 mg	40%	55%
Zinc	3 mg	20%	25%

S=40% or more soluble N/A=Not Applicable N=Not Available

which give it a rich flavor. A popular Polish barley soup called *krupnik* also contains dried mushrooms as well as potatoes and dill. A bowl of meatless barley soup can be enhanced by a dollop of yogurt.

Barley soups that call for beef or lamb are likely to be high in fat and calories. So if you use meat, add it in small amounts. Round out the dish with lots of chopped vegetables—such as onions, carrots, parsnips, and cabbage. Scotch broth is a classic example of a lamb-and-barley soup made with a variety of vegetables—turnips, carrots, leeks, and peas.

Prepare a filling main-dish salad, using cooled, cooked barley as the foundation. Toss sliced mushrooms, chopped tomatoes, or slivered bell peppers with a little oil and vinegar. Add diced chicken or beef, if you like.

Chilled cooked barley can also be turned into a dessert pudding by sweetening and spicing it, then adding dried fruits. Top it off with plain or vanilla yogurt.

Buckwheat

It is surprising to learn that buckwheat isn't related to wheat and isn't a true grain, but rather is the fruit of a leafy plant belonging to the same family as sorrel and rhubarb. Its name comes from the Dutch word *bockweit,* which means "beech wheat"—probably a reference to the plant's triangular fruits, which resemble beechnuts, and their wheatlike uses.

Buckwheat has a strong, nutlike flavor, perhaps the most distinctive of any grain. The particularly robust taste of roasted buckwheat (kasha) may not be immediately appealing, but you'll find that it marries well with other hearty-flavored, densely textured foods, such as beef, root vegetables, cabbage, winter squash, roasted peppers, or eggplant. Nutritionally, it contains significant amounts of the amino acid lysine, more than true grains, like wheat or rice.

The Dutch brought buckwheat to the New World, planting it in their settlements along New York's Hudson River. Indigenous to China, where it is still used for making bread, buckwheat was later introduced into eastern Europe; there it is served as a porridge or as a side dish, like rice. (The word *kasha,* or *kasza,* commonly applied to roasted buckwheat groats, comes from the Slavic languages.) In the United States, this grain is considered a minor crop; most buckwheat is grown in Pennsylvania and the Finger Lakes region of New York State. It's widely available in health-food stores and the kosher section of supermarkets.

FORMS OF BUCKWHEAT Americans are probably most familiar with buckwheat as a flour used to make pancakes. But it can be cooked and offered as an alternative to rice. Buckwheat contains little gluten, and may be a good grain choice for individuals allergic to that protein substance.

The forms of buckwheat on the market include:

Buckwheat grits Sold as buckwheat cereal or cream of buckwheat, these finely ground, unroasted groats cook much more quickly than kasha, developing a soft and creamy texture. They are best as a breakfast cereal or as a rice-pudding-style dessert.

Buckwheat groats, whole These are the raw kernels with their inedible black shells removed. Whole groats are either white (unroasted) or brown (roasted). The white groats have a fairly mild flavor and can be substituted in dishes that call for white or brown rice. Roasted buckwheat has a more assertive flavor.

Kasha Roasted, hulled buckwheat kernels that are cracked into coarse, medium, or fine granules are commonly known as kasha. Enjoy their toasty flavor as an accompaniment to meat or as the basis for a grain-and-vegetable main dish.

PREPARATION Kasha, whole buckwheat, and buckwheat grits can be simmered or baked. The chart on page 297 gives the cooking times.

The package directions on kasha instruct you to sauté the grains first with egg and fat, but this step can be eliminated (simply cook the grain as you would rice) or modified.

Sprouting Like other whole grains, buckwheat groats can be sprouted, ready to eat, in five days. (see directions for sprouting on page 159). Buy

BUCKWHEAT GROATS 3½ oz cooked (½ cup)			
Calories	92	Fat	<1 g
Protein	3 g	Saturated Fat	<1 g
Carbohydrate	20 g	Cholesterol	0 mg
Dietary Fiber	Medium (S)	Sodium	4 mg

KEY NUTRIENTS		% RDA Men	% RDA Women
Magnesium	51 mg	15%	18%
Manganese	0.4 mg	N/A	N/A

S= 40% or more soluble N/A=Not Applicable N=Not Available

BUCKWHEAT COOKING TIMES

Per ½ Cup Uncooked	Liquid (cups)	Cooking Times	Yield (cups)
Groats, unroasted, whole	1	15 minutes	1¾
Groats, roasted, whole	1	13 minutes	1½
Kasha	2½	12 minutes	2

fresh seeds with their hulls from a health-food store; packaged kernels won't sprout.

BUCKWHEAT AND EGGS

Many recipes for buckwheat dishes call for a beaten egg to be mixed into the kernels before cooking. The addition of the egg keeps the kernels separate as they cook, so that they have the consistency of rice rather than oatmeal. As cooking grains absorb water, their cell walls rupture and release the starches contained inside, thus causing the grains to stick together. Egg albumin—a protein—acts as a sealant, strengthening the outer cells walls of the kernels and preventing them from rupturing. The egg also supplies the buckwheat with essential amino acids, making a complete protein. It does, however, add fat and cholesterol, but only slightly: A half cup of cooked kasha prepared with egg will have about 1 gram of fat and 43 milligrams of cholesterol. To avoid the added fat and cholesterol but still get the protein benefit, use an egg white instead of a whole egg.

SERVING SUGGESTIONS Buckwheat has much to recommend it beyond its use as a pancake flour. The grain makes a delicious side dish with poultry or meat. Instead of pouring a rich gravy over it, serve it with defatted pan juices from the cooked meat: Pour the juices into a shallow pan and place in the freezer for a few minutes to allow the fat to solidify, then lift it off and discard it.

To get used to its assertive flavor, you may want to combine buckwheat with a milder grain, such as brown rice, at first. Mixing it with vegetables also tempers its earthiness. Stir chopped onion, carrots, celery, and sliced mushrooms into whole groats or kasha before or after cooking.

Cooked kasha is excellent for stuffing meat, poultry, fish, or vegetables such as tomatoes, peppers, or winter squash. To make the fillings, blend the kasha with chopped vegetables, mushrooms, or fresh or dried fruits.

Experiment with cold, cooked groats, or kasha, as the principal ingredient in a main-dish salad. Combine the grain with tuna, chopped vegetables (try mushrooms and artichoke hearts), and a yogurt or a vinaigrette dressing for an unusual lunch dish. Or, use cooled, cooked kasha, as you would bulgur wheat, to make tabbouleh, a Middle Eastern salad that's perfect for hot weather: Combine the kasha with finely chopped tomatoes, scallions, fresh parsley, and mint; add a generous amount of lemon juice and a little olive oil, and refrigerate until the mixture is well chilled and the flavors blended.

Add whole groats or kasha raw to soups and stews to thicken them, or try cooked groats or kasha as a base for a meat or vegetable stew. A favorite dish among eastern European Jews is *kasha varnishkes*—the roasted kernels are combined with bowtie pasta. Cook the kasha in beef, chicken, or vegetable stock; use any small pasta you like. Serve the mixture as a side dish or, with yogurt stirred in, as a meal on its own.

Prepare a kasha pilaf with nuts and dried fruits and flavor it with Indian spices or curry powder. Bake a kasha casserole with vegetables, part-skim ricotta cheese or low-fat cottage cheese, and tomato sauce or canned tomatoes.

For dessert, sweeten cooked kasha, combine it with fresh fruits, and serve it like rice pudding. At breakfast, cook buckwheat grits in milk or a milk/water mixture for a hot cereal.

Millet

The smallest of our familiar grains, millet surpasses whole wheat and brown rice as a source of some B vitamins, copper, and iron. Its protein content varies greatly, depending upon the variety, but, in general, it is similar to that of wheat. Like most grains, however, millet is deficient in the amino acid lysine, so its protein availability is enhanced when it is eaten with beans or other legumes, which are rich in lysine. Millet is usually tolerated by people who are allergic to wheat.

An easily cultivated, fast-growing grain, millet was an important food in Europe in the Middle Ages, but it was supplanted by other grains, such as barley. However, it has long been a staple in North Africa, where it probably originated, and it is widely consumed in India, China, and Asia as well. In India and Ethiopia, finely ground millet is made into flatbreads called *roti* and *injera,* respectively. (Millet has no gluten, and so cannot be used for raised breads.) In the United States, millet is known principally as feed for birds and poultry. However, pearl millet, which is the major type grown for human consumption, can be found in health-food stores and some supermarkets, always hulled and usually in whole-grain form. The tiny, pale yellow or reddish orange beads of millet can be cooked like any other grain. Occasionally, you may also see cracked millet sold as couscous (though the packaged couscous available in North America is most often made from semolina).

PREPARATION Millet is cooked by the same methods as other grains.

Simmering Use 1½ cups liquid to ½ cup of grain. If the grain is kept covered and undisturbed while simmering, it will be fluffy and separate, like rice. However, if it is stirred frequently and a little liquid is added from time to time, the millet will have a creamy consistency, similar to mashed potatoes. If you sauté millet first, as for a rice pilaf, the cooking time will be cut in half. *Cooking time:* about 25 minutes. Makes about 2½ cups.

Steaming This method is most frequently used with cracked millet to make couscous. Soak the grain in water for about an hour, then steam it (traditionally, over a pot of simmering stew). *Cooking time:* 30 minutes.

SERVING SUGGESTIONS Millet is delicate and bland, so it can be combined with almost any flavoring. Prepare it as a hot cereal (cooked in either water or skim milk), and enhance it with fresh or dried fruits, a pinch of spice, and some skim milk or yogurt. Apples blend particularly well with millet.

Cook the grain as a casserole, with onions, bell peppers, cauliflower, and tomato sauce, or substitute it for rice, as a base for a meat or vegetable stew, chili, or beans. Make a millet pilaf with chicken or vegetable stock and chopped dried apricots. Incorporate cooked millet into meat loaf or hamburger mixtures to stretch them. Add raw millet to soup about 45 minutes before it is done, or stir cooked millet into soup just before serving,

MILLET 3½ oz cooked (½ cup)			
Calories	119	Fat	1 g
Protein	4 g	Saturated Fat	<1 g
Carbohydrate	24 g	Cholesterol	0 mg
Dietary Fiber	Medium	Sodium	2 mg

KEY NUTRIENTS		% RDA Men	% RDA Women
Copper	0.2 mg	N/A	N/A
Folacin	19 mcg	10%	11%
Iron	1 mg	10%	7%
Magnesium	44 mg	13%	16%
Manganese	0.3 mg	N/A	N/A
Phosphorus	100 mg	13%	13%
Thiamin	0.1 mg	7%	10%

S=40% or more soluble N/A=Not Applicable N=Not Available

long enough to heat the grain through.

Unlike other grains, millet is too soft to be used cold as a basis for salads; in addition, it tends to solidify as it cools. But it can be mixed while warm with a tart vinaigrette and chopped raw vegetables, such as cucumbers and tomatoes, for a light side dish.

For a simple but delicious dessert, sweeten millet with brown sugar or honey, flavor it with vanilla or almond extract, and stir in fresh or dried fruits, such as berries, raisins, or dates, and yogurt. Or, add a few tablespoonfuls of whole millet to cookie dough for a more interesting, crunchy result.

Oats

Oats have probably been cultivated since the first century A.D. With the exception of a few countries such as Scotland, where the grain has long been a staple food for humans, it has been used primarily for animal fodder. Brought to the New World by English colonists, oats were planted in Massachusetts in the mid-1600s, and were first packaged in the United States for wide distribution in 1852. Over the years, however, the grain has gained very little in popularity with consumers; even today, only about 5 percent of the world's oat crop is used as food for humans. However, interest in the grain is growing in this country because of highly publicized studies showing that oats, and particularly oat bran, can lower cholesterol levels when eaten as part of a low-fat diet. Americans consume about 11 pounds of oats per person per year—mostly as hot oatmeal, but also as an ingredient in cold cereals, muffins, cookies, cakes, and breads.

Oats are an excellent source of complex carbohydrates and contain about 50 percent more protein than bulgur wheat, and twice as much as brown rice. The grain offers impressive levels of iron and manganese, and also supplies good quantities of copper, folacin, vitamin E, and zinc. Oats are higher in fat than other cereal grains, but the fat is 80 percent unsaturated and the total amount is still low.

Furthermore, oats are a good source of dietary fiber, both soluble and insoluble. The soluble fiber is largely in the form of a gum called beta glucan, which is primarily responsible for lowering cholesterol levels. One study in which the subjects ate a bowl of oatmeal and five oat bran muffins a day reported 19 percent reductions in cholesterol levels. Other studies have shown that eating as little as 2 ounces dry (the equivalent of 1⅓ cups cooked) of oats or oat bran a day can lower cholesterol levels. (That serving of oats contains 5 grams of fiber.) Although oat bran (sold as a separate product) contains more dietary fiber than oatmeal or other forms of oats, some bran is present in all types of oat products since the grain is not refined (the bran and germ are not removed).

Oat bran is just as effective at reducing cholesterol levels as two widely prescribed cholesterol-lowering drugs—and costs much less, according to a University of Maryland study. When the researchers compared oat bran and the drugs cholestyramine resin and colestipol for cost and effectiveness, they found that the drugs and the oat bran produced similar results, but the oat bran cost about $1100 a year less.

Adding oat products (or other foods high in soluble fiber) to a low-fat diet should produce some cholesterol-lowering results, particularly if your cholesterol level is elevated: Soluble fiber is credited with having a greater cholesterol-lowering effect on individuals with elevated cholesterol levels than on those whose levels fall within the "safe" range.

FORMS OF OATS Since neither the bran nor the germ is removed from oats, almost all forms of the grain are similarly nutritious. (The only exception is oat bran, which has a different nutrient makeup than whole oats.) The differences among them relate to size and whether they have been precooked or not.

Oat bran This outer layer of oat groats has a finer texture and a lighter color than wheat bran. It is sold in bulk or packaged as a hot cereal.

Oat groats These are whole oat kernels, which can be cooked like rice or other whole grains. Groats take longer to prepare than any other form of oats, but if they are presoaked in cold water for an hour, they will cook in about half the time of unsoaked groats.

Rolled oats Probably the most familiar form, rolled oats have been heated and pressed flat with steel rollers so that they cook more quickly. Whole groats processed this way are sold as *old-fashioned* oats and cook in about 5 minutes, while *quick-cooking* oats are sliced before heating and pressing; they are ready in about 1 minute. *Instant* oats have been precooked, dried, and pressed very thin; they require only the addition of boiling water to form a very smooth, hot cereal. Packets of instant oatmeal, unlike other oat cereals meant to be eaten hot, often contain added salt, sugar, flavorings, and colors.

Steel-cut oats Often imported in tins from Ireland or Scotland, steel-cut oats are groats that have been thinly sliced lengthwise. They require a fairly long cooking time and have a chewy, hearty consistency.

PREPARATION Whole groats should be picked over and rinsed, but rolled oats and oat bran require no preparation before cooking. Most of the time, oats are simmered, but they can also be baked. The chart on page 301 gives the proportions of water to grain and cooking times for each form of oats.

Like other grains, oats can be cooked in the microwave, but this method is not any faster than stovetop cooking since the grain still needs time to absorb the liquid.

Granola Although oats are the principal grain in granola, many of the commercial brands are exceedingly high in fat because of both the type of oil (sometimes highly saturated tropical oil) added to the oats before they are toasted, and the ingredients, such as coconut, nuts, and seeds, that are used in abundance. To make your own low-fat version, toast rolled oats (quick or old-fashioned) on a baking sheet in a 300° oven (stir frequently). For a sweet granola, stir in honey to taste before toasting, but watch the oats very carefully while they are in the oven, as the honey makes them more likely to scorch. After toasting, mix in your choice of wheat germ, bran, chopped dried fruits, or, in moderation, chopped nuts, or sunflower or pumpkin seeds. Let cool and store in a plastic bag in the refrigerator.

Muesli This is another cold cereal made with uncooked oats. Like granola, mass-market muesli is often high in fat and calories, but you can prepare your own fairly easily. Mix uncooked rolled oats with the following grain products to taste: rolled wheat flakes, bite-sized shredded wheat, wheat nuggets, 100 percent bran shreds, oat or wheat bran, or wheat germ. Stir in any of your favorite dried fruits and a small amount of unsalted, coarsely chopped nuts or seeds. Store in an airtight container in the refrigerator.

SERVING SUGGESTIONS While all types of oats can be eaten as a hot breakfast cereal, there are many other ways to incorporate this grain into your diet. If you enjoy hot oatmeal, serve it with skim milk or yogurt instead of butter and cream. To enhance it, mix in some chopped fresh fruits

OAT COOKING TIMES

Per ½ Cup Uncooked	Liquid (cups)	Cooking Times	Yield (cups)
Groats	1	6 minutes (let stand 45 minutes)	1¼
Steel-cut oats	2	20 minutes	1
Old-fashioned rolled oats	1	5 minutes	1
Rolled oats, quick	1	1 minute (let stand 3 to 5 minutes)	1
Oat bran	1	6 minutes	1

or a fruit purée; if you prefer it sweet, add a little brown sugar, maple syrup, or molasses. For a change of pace, simmer oats along with another grain, such as kasha, or use apple juice instead of water to cook the cereal. Chopped dried fruits can be heated with the old-fashioned or quick oats; they will plump and soften, adding sweetness to the cereal as they cook. Flavor with a pinch of cinnamon, nutmeg, or allspice, or a dash of vanilla, almond, or coconut extract.

Serve homemade granola with fresh fruit and yogurt, skim milk or fruit juice; sprinkle it over fruit salad or yogurt. To prepare an extra-thick breakfast shake, combine oat bran with skim milk, yogurt, and fresh fruit in a blender or food processor.

If muesli is mixed with milk and refrigerated overnight, it will have the consistency of cooked cereal. If you prefer to keep it crunchy, stir in milk or yogurt just before serving. Either way, grate some apple (the traditional muesli fruit) or other fresh fruit over the cereal for a finishing touch.

Groats can be prepared pilaf-style, like rice or wheat berries (in flavor, groats resemble these more than they do oatmeal), and served as a side dish; toss in some toasted sunflower or pumpkin seeds for crunchy texture. Combine cooked groats with steamed vegetables and chopped scallions, season with soy sauce, and offer as an accompaniment to chicken or a main dish of grilled vegetables.

Steel-cut oats or groats work well in soups and stews; precook the oats first unless it will take longer than 2 hours to cook the soup. Rolled oats, on their own or ground into a coarse meal, can be relied on to thicken soups and sauces. Consider oats when you are looking for full-bodied stuffings for poultry and vegetables, such as peppers, squash and tomatoes. Plain toasted oats nicely complement salads, soups, and desserts, and provide a wonderful crisp breading for baked chicken or fish. Keep in mind that oats can be useful as extenders in ground meat or poultry recipes.

ADDED OAT BRAN

Oats and oat bran are added to a wide variety of packaged foods—breads, cookies, muffins, cold cereals, and even potato chips. Don't rely on these, however, to help reduce your cholesterol levels. Most don't contain enough oats or oat bran to be of much value; others are high in fat, thereby offsetting any cholesterol-reducing benefit the oats might have. Many of these products are also high in sugar, sodium, or both. Nutritionally, it is best to add plain oats or oat bran to your own bread, muffin, and cookie recipes. If you choose to purchase a packaged product, check food labels carefully. Remember that ingredients are listed in descending order by weight. Oats or oat bran should be high on the list. Products that contain tropical oils—coconut, palm, or palm kernel—or hydrogenated oils should be used sparingly, since they can contribute significant amounts of saturated fat to your diet.

Rolled oats and oat bran make flavorful additions to yeast breads, but must be combined with wheat flour since oats contain no gluten, which is necessary for dough to rise. Use no more than one

OAT BRAN 3½ oz cooked (½ cup)

Calories	40	Fat	1 g
Protein	3 g	Saturated Fat	<1 g
Carbohydrate	11 g	Cholesterol	0 mg
Dietary Fiber	High (S)	Sodium	1 mg

KEY NUTRIENTS		% RDA Men	% RDA Women
Magnesium	40 mg	11%	14%
Manganese	1 mg	N/A	N/A
Phosphorus	119 mg	15%	15%
Thiamin	0.2 mg	14%	18%

S=40% or more soluble N/A=Not Applicable N=Not Available

OATS 3½ oz cooked (½ cup)

Calories	62	Fat	1 g
Protein	3 g	Saturated Fat	<1 g
Carbohydrate	11 g	Cholesterol	0 mg
Dietary Fiber	Low (S)	Sodium	1 mg

KEY NUTRIENTS		% RDA Men	% RDA Women
Iron	1 mg	10%	7%
Manganese	0.6 mg	N/A	N/A
Phosphorus	76 mg	10%	10%

S=40% or more soluble N/A=Not Applicable N=Not Available

part oats to four parts wheat flour. If you like bread with a hearty texture, measure rolled oats directly from the package; for a finer texture, process them in a blender or food processor to make coarse or fine oat flour.

For cookies, muffins, pancakes, quick breads, and other baked goods leavened with baking soda or baking powder, you can use up to one part oats to two parts wheat flour, creating a more satisfying texture while adding nutritional value. Old-fashioned and quick-cooking oats can generally be substituted for oatmeal, although you may need to add a little extra liquid. If you don't want to experiment, process old-fashioned oats briefly in a blender or food processor to give them the finer consistency of quick oats.

Quinoa

An ancient grainlike product that has recently been "rediscovered" in this country, quinoa (pronounced *keen*-wah) is not a true grain (neither is buckwheat or amaranth), but it looks like one and has similar uses. It is related to leafy vegetables such as Swiss chard and spinach, and its foliage can be cooked and eaten like that of its more familiar cousins. Quinoa is unusual among the grains because it has a delicate taste and light flavor—so it can be substituted for almost any other grain.

Nutritionally, quinoa might be considered a supergrain. It offers more iron than other grains and contains high levels of potassium and riboflavin. It is also a good source of magnesium, zinc, copper, manganese, and folacin. Quinoa has excellent reserves of protein, and like the other nontrue grains, is not low in the amino acid lysine.

Though quinoa is a recent introduction to the North American larder, this crop, native to the Andes, sustained the Incas just as amaranth did the Aztecs, who lived farther north. In a parallel sequence of events, the cultivation of quinoa, like that of amaranth, may also have been suppressed by the Spanish conquistadors. However, this valuable food plant survived in remote areas and has been cultivated continuously for over five thousand years. Quinoa thrives in poor soil, arid climates, and mountainous altitudes. Today, most quinoa is imported from South America, although it is being cultivated on the high slopes of the Colorado Rockies.

Quinoa's survival through the millennia may be attributed to the resinous, bitter coating that protects its seeds from birds and insects—and also shields them from the intense radiation of high-altitude sunlight. This coating, called saponin, is soapy and must be removed in a strong alkaline solution to make the grain palatable (in South America the water used in this process is made into a shampoo). Most quinoa sold in this country has already been cleansed of its saponin.

Quinoa grains are about the same size as millet, but flattened, with a pointed, oval shape. The color ranges from pale yellow through red and brown to black. Quinoa cooks quickly to a light, fluffy texture. As it cooks, the external germ, which forms a band around each grain, spirals out, forming a tiny crescent-shaped "tail," similar to a bean sprout. Although the grain itself is soft and creamy, the tail is crunchy, providing a unique texture to complement quinoa's delicate flavor.

Quinoa is more expensive than most grains. However, during cooking, it increases about three to four times in volume, so you get reasonable value for your money. Since this grain is still a relatively new one, at least to the American market, you're most likely to find it in health-food and specialty stores.

PREPARATION Quinoa should be rinsed to remove any powdery residue of saponin. Place the grain in a fine strainer and hold it under cold running water until the water runs clear; drain well. Brown the grain in a dry skillet for 5 minutes before simmering or baking to give it a delicious roasted flavor.

Simmering Use 1 cup liquid to ½ cup of grain; cook until the grains are translucent and the germ has spiraled out from each grain. *Cooking time:* 15 minutes. Makes about 2 cups.

SERVING SUGGESTIONS Quinoa lends itself nicely to any recipe for pilaf or baked grain casserole; remember to adjust the cooking time, as necessary. It can also be used as the basis for a vegetable soup (or add it to your favorite soup). When cooking braised chicken, add quinoa and broth to the pot, for a variation on arroz con pollo.

The hearty flavor of buckwheat combines especially well with quinoa. Serve it plain, or with a sauce, or with puréed cooked vegetables, or with a low-fat gravy made from defatted chicken stock. Try this grain combination in a cold or hot pilaf along with carrots, onions, garlic, and red pepper.

Quinoa's light, unsticky texture makes it an ideal choice for a warm-weather salad. Mix cooled, cooked quinoa with chopped raw or cooked vegetables and fresh herbs, then toss it with a vinaigrette or soy-sauce dressing. If you need a more substantial dish, add tuna, chicken, tofu, or beans.

Mix quinoa into your favorite rice pudding recipe, or cook it in fruit juice or with dried fruits, then offer it for dessert or breakfast.

QUINOA 3½ oz dry (½ cup)

Calories	374	Fat	6 g
Protein	13 g	Saturated Fat	<1 g
Carbohydrate	69 g	Cholesterol	0 mg
Dietary Fiber	N	Sodium	21 mg

KEY NUTRIENTS		% RDA Men	% RDA Women
Vitamin B_6	0.2 mg	10%	13%
Copper	0.8 mg	N/A	N/A
Folacin	49 mcg	25%	27%
Iron	9 mg	90%	60%
Magnesium	210 mg	60%	75%
Manganese	2.3 mg	N/A	N/A
Niacin	3 mg	16%	20%
Phosphorus	410 mg	51%	51%
Potassium	740 mg	N/A	N/A
Riboflavin	0.4 mg	24%	31%
Thiamin	0.2 mg	13%	18%
Zinc	3 mg	20%	25%

S=40% or more soluble N/A=Not Applicable N=Not Available

Rice

To Americans, rice is the most familiar food eaten in grain form. It is commonly served as a side dish in American households, but elsewhere it forms the basis for most meals. In fact, half the world's peoples eat rice as their staple food. In some languages, the word for "eat" means "eat rice." In China, Japan, and Southeast Asia, for instance, the annual per capita consumption of rice is 200 to 400 pounds; in the United States, the per capita consumption is about 17 pounds. Though rice is grown on every continent except Antarctica, China produces more than 90 percent of the world's rice crop. The United States, though it accounts for only 2 percent of the world's rice, is, due to low consumption, a major exporter of this grain.

Rice was first grown in the American colonies in the late seventeenth century; by 1726, the grain was being exported from Charleston, South Carolina. Today, the major rice-growing states are Arkansas, Louisiana, Mississippi, Missouri, Texas, and California (where rice was first introduced to feed the thousands of Chinese immigrants in the California territory at the time of the Gold Rush).

Rice thrives in warm climates with abundant supplies of fresh water. The type of rice grown in the United States and some other parts of the world is called paddy rice. It is cultivated in fields that are surrounded by levees or dikes, which allow the fields to be flooded with water for most of the growing season. The purpose of the flooding is to subdue weed growth. The fields are drained before the rice is harvested (by machine, in industrialized countries, by hand, in less-developed ones). Another type of rice, upland rice, can be grown in wet soil and doesn't require flooding.

In general, rice is a good source of B vitamins, such as thiamin and niacin, and also provides iron, phosphorus, and magnesium. Although rice is lower in protein than other cereal grains, its protein quality is good because it contains relatively high levels of the amino acid lysine.

RICE BRAN

Like oat bran, rice bran is enjoying a reputation as a cholesterol fighter. Researchers at the USDA have found that rice bran lowers blood cholesterol in animals just as much as oat bran. But scientists are interested in more than the fiber content of the rice.

Because of the composition of the rice kernel and the way it is milled, the processed bran ends up containing rice germ, which is rich in oil. Scientists in Japan and India have found that this highly unsaturated oil also has a substantial cholesterol-lowering effect. Although brown rice is exceedingly nutritious, it is not a concentrated source of fiber or oil.

Rice bran has been available in health-food stores for some time without arousing much enthusiasm: In its natural state, it tastes like sawdust and has a short shelf life. But a range of products containing rice bran are now available—including rice cakes and cereals—that not only taste better, but have been heat stabilized to reduce spoilage. Rice bran is also available packaged like wheat germ. An ounce of one brand contains 8 grams of dietary fiber—of which 2 grams are soluble—and 6 grams of fat. It also has 100 calories, 4 grams of protein, and generous amounts of thiamin, niacin, magnesium, and iron. Rice bran can be used just like wheat germ: Sprinkle it on cereal, salad, and yogurt or add it to baked goods. Unlike oat bran, rice bran doesn't turn gummy when cooked.

Unfortunately, this important food source is usually eaten in most parts of the world in its least nourishing form—that is, milled and polished to remove the bran and germ, which contain valuable nutrients. In the United States, white rice—as this refined form is called—is enriched with two B vitamins—thiamin and niacin—and iron. But in many countries where it constitutes the bulk of the diet, enrichment is not a common practice. As a result, beriberi—a potentially fatal thiamin-deficiency disease—and other nutrient-deficiency diseases have been serious problems. Furthermore, in some of these lands, rice is prewashed and cooked in a large amount of water (which is later discarded), thereby increasing the loss of water-soluble B vitamins.

FORMS OF RICE Rice can be classified according to size: long-grain, medium-grain, and short-grain. *Long-grain rice* accounts for about 75 percent of the domestic crop. The slender grains are four to five times longer than they are wide. If properly cooked, they will be fluffy and dry, with separate grains.

Medium-grain rice is about twice as long as it is wide and cooks up moister and more tender than long-grain. It is popular in some Asian and Latin American cultures, and is the type of rice most commonly processed to make cold cereals.

Short-grain rice may be almost oval or round in shape. Of the three types of rice, it has the highest percentage of amylopectin, the starch that makes rice sticky, or clump together, when cooked. Easy to eat with chopsticks, it is ideal for dishes like sushi.

All the above-mentioned types of rice are available in both brown and white forms.

Brown rice This rice has had only its husk removed during milling. With the bran intact, it retains more fiber, folacin, iron, riboflavin, potassium, phosphorus, zinc, and trace minerals, such as copper and manganese, than any other type of rice. Moreover, brown rice is the only form of the grain that contains vitamin E. It also has a richer flavor and a chewier texture than white rice, and takes longer to cook, though quick-cooking and instant forms are now sold.

White rice (milled rice) The most popular form of rice has been completely milled to remove the husk, bran, and most of the germ. There are several types of white rice.

Enriched white rice has thiamin, niacin, and iron added after milling to replace some of the nutrients lost when the bran layer is removed. As a result, it is higher in these nutrients than brown rice.

Parboiled rice, also called converted rice, has been soaked and steamed under pressure before milling, which forces some of the nutrients into the remaining portion of the grain so that they are not totally lost in the processing. Enriched parboiled rice is similar to regular white rice in terms of thiamin, niacin, and iron, but it has more potassium, folacin, riboflavin, and phosphorous, though not as much as brown rice. The term "parboiled" is slightly misleading; the rice is not precooked, but is actually somewhat harder than regular rice. As a consequence, it takes a little longer to cook than regular white rice, but the

COMPARING RICE 3½ ounces dry (½ cup*)

	Calories	**Iron** (mg)	**Zinc** (mg)	**Thiamin** (mg)	**Niacin** (mg)	**Folacin** (mcg)	**Vitamin B_6** (mg)
Brown	370	2	2	0.4	5	20	0.5
Parboiled, enriched	371	4	1	0.6	4	17	0.4
Parboiled, unenriched	371	2	1	0.1	4	17	0.4
White, enriched	365	4	1	0.6	4	8	0.2
White, unenriched	365	1	1	0.07	2	8	0.2
Wild rice	357	2	6	0.1	7	95	0.4

**Makes 1 to 2 cups cooked.*

WILD RICE

Wild rice is not a grain but a grass seed from a different botanical family, *Zizania aquatica.* Native to North America, it was once basic to the diet of the Chippewa and Dakota tribes. Today, almost all wild rice is actually cultivated in paddies in Minnesota. Although increasingly popular, it is expensive. Specialty or gourmet shops usually stock it; you may find it in larger supermarkets, too.

Nutty and rich in flavor, wild rice has about twice the protein of other rices, as well as more significant levels of the B vitamins, providing 48 percent of the RDA for folacin for men (53 percent for women), 35 percent of the niacin RDA for men (45 percent for women), and 20 percent of the vitamin B_6 RDA for men (24 percent for women). While its high price may deter you from making it a regular part of your diet, you will find that a little goes a long way. It blends well with other rices and even on its own, 1 cup dry cooks up to 3 or 4 cups, which is enough for six servings.

Wild rice is prepared in much the same way as regular rice, though it must be rinsed first. Add 1 cup of wild rice to 4 cups of boiling water, return to a boil and simmer for 30 to 45 minutes. (Darker wild rice needs a longer cooking time.) If you like a chewy texture, reduce the cooking time. Cooked wild rice will keep for a week in the refrigerator, and six months in the freezer.

grains will be very fluffy and separate after they have been cooked.

Instant white rice, which actually takes about five minutes to prepare, has been milled and polished, fully cooked and then dehydrated. It is usually enriched and only slightly less nutritious than regular enriched white rice, but it lacks the satisfying texture of regular rice.

Arborio is a starchy white rice, with an almost round grain, grown mainly in the Po Valley of Italy. Traditionally used for cooking the Italian dish risotto, it also works well for paella and rice pudding. Arborio absorbs up to five times its weight in liquid as it cooks, which results in grains of a creamy consistency.

Aromatic rices These are primarily long-grain varieties that have a toasty, nutty fragrance and a flavor reminiscent of popcorn or roasted nuts. Most of these can be found in grocery stores, but a few may be available only at gourmet shops.

Basmati, the most famous aromatic rice, is grown in India and Pakistan. It has a nutlike fragrance while cooking and a delicate, almost buttery flavor. Unlike other types of rice, the grains elongate much more than they plump as they cook. Lower in starch than other long-grain types, basmati turns out flaky and separate. Although it is most commonly used in Indian cooking, basmati can also be substituted for regular rice in any favorite recipe. It is fairly expensive compared to domestic rice.

Jasmine is a traditional long-grain white rice grown in Thailand. It has a soft texture and is similar in flavor to basmati rice. Jasmine rice is also grown in the United States, and is available in both white or brown forms.

Certain types of rice—some sold only under a trade name—have been developed in the United States to approximate the flavor and texture of basmati rice. These include: Brown and white *Texmati,* developed to withstand the hot Texas climate; *Wehani,* which has an unusual rust-colored bran that makes it turn mahogany when cooked; and *Wild pecan,* or *popcorn rice,* which is not a wild rice, but a tan (because not all of the bran has been removed) basmati hybrid, with a pecanlike flavor and firm texture.

Glutinous rice (sweet rice) Popular in Japan and other Asian countries, this type of short-grain rice is not related to other short-grain rices. Unlike regular table rice, this starchy grain is very sticky and resilient, and turns translucent when cooked. Its cohesive quality makes it suitable for rice dumplings and cakes, such as the Japanese *mochi*, which is molded into a shape.

PREPARATION Domestic packaged rice is almost always very clean, but when using imported rice or rice purchased in bulk, it's a good idea to spread it on a clean surface and pick it over, removing any defective grains or debris.

Don't rinse domestic packaged rice before cooking: Not only is the rice clean, but the starchy coating on enriched rice contains nutrients that will be lost if the rice is washed. However, you should rinse imported rices, such as basmati or jasmine, since these may be dirty or dusty. (There is no nutrient loss, as these are not enriched.) Also, rinse any rices sold in bulk in open barrels or bins. In Hispanic markets you may find white rice coated with glucose; this coating is harmless and doesn't need to be rinsed.

Basmati rice is usually soaked before cooking, but this preliminary step may result in a seepage of water-soluble B vitamins into the soaking liquid. If you decide to soak it (for 30 minutes to 2 hours), use the liquid to simmer the rice, too.

Rice is cooked in a variety of ways throughout the world, but simmering is the method most familiar to Americans. As long as the cooking liquid is not discarded, you can use any method. Each turns out a slightly different-textured rice. See the chart below for cooking times for simmering rice.

Rice can be cooked in liquids other than water—for example, broth, fruit juice, or tomato juice—but be aware that acid ingredients will lengthen the cooking time. When using an acidic liquid, such as fruit or tomato juice, dilute it to at least half strength with water.

Brown and aromatic rices do not need to be enhanced, as they have enough flavor on their own; it is worth adding a pinch of salt to white rice, however, to alleviate its natural flatness. If you're trying to avoid salt, squeeze some lemon juice over the rice; if added toward the end of the cooking time, the lemon will also help to keep the rice white. Another way to boost the flavor of white rice is to serve it mixed with an equal amount of brown rice (to cook them together, you

RICE COOKING TIMES

Per ½ Cup Uncooked	Liquid (cups)	Cooking Times	Yield (cups)
Brown, long-grain	1	25 to 30 minutes	1½
Brown, short-grain	1	40 minutes	1½
Brown, instant	½	5 minutes	¾
Brown, quick	¾	10 minutes	1
White, long-grain	1	20 minutes	1¾
White, instant	½	5 minutes (let stand 5 minutes)	1
Converted	1⅓	31 minutes	2
Arborio	¾	15 minutes	1½
Basmati, white	½	15 minutes	2
Jasmine	1	15 to 20 minutes	1¾
Texmati long-grain, brown	1 (plus 2 tbs.)	40 minutes	2
Texmati long-grain, white	¾ (plus 2 tbs.)	15 minutes	1¼
Wehani	1	40 minutes	1¼
Wild	2	50 minutes	2
Wild pecan	1	20 minutes	1½

should start the brown rice first, then stir in the white rice about 20 minutes before the brown rice is done).

Fluff rice with a fork before serving, no matter which cooking method you've chosen. For drier rice, fluff it, then cover the pan again and let it stand for 10 to 15 minutes. Consider cooking more rice than you need for a meal, as it reheats well if you add a few tablespoonfuls of extra liquid. Cooked rice will keep for about a week in the refrigerator.

SERVING SUGGESTIONS Rice dishes run the gamut from basic to elaborate. Plain steamed or simmered rice, of course, is a fine accompaniment to almost any meal, especially if there are meat juices or a sauce to moisten and flavor the grain. Use brown and aromatic rices with savory foods, sauces, and seasonings, rather than in delicate dishes where their pronounced flavors may overpower subtler ingredients.

It's easy to vary the flavor of any rice by cooking it in broth and adding herbs, spices, or other seasonings at the start. Sauté chopped onions or garlic in a little broth, then add the remainder of the broth and bring it to a boil before stirring in the rice.

Add cut-up vegetables to rice during or after cooking, if you like. For a main dish, add cooked beans or chunks of cooked meat or poultry to the cooked rice. Add slivered nuts, bits of dried fruits, and sweet spices—such as cinnamon, cardamom, and ginger—for an Indian-style pilaf. Dress hot cooked rice with a vinaigrette, some salsa, or herbed yogurt. For a "green rice" dish, simply add a generous quantity of chopped fresh herbs—such as parsley, cilantro, or dill—to the freshly cooked grains.

Use hot rice as a base over which to serve your favorite stir-fry, curry, gumbo, goulash, or stew. Or, substitute rice for pasta in a number of dishes: Top a plate of rice with your favorite tomato or other pasta sauce, or prepare lasagna with layers of rice instead of noodles. Mix cooked rice into a poultry, fish or vegetable stuffing.

Pilaf is one of the most familiar rice dishes. Its preparation calls for the rice to be browned before it is simmered. Sauté chopped onions, then add the rice and cook, stirring for 2 to 3 minutes, or until the rice is opaque or slightly browned. Then add boiling broth (the same amount as for simmering), cover, and cook over low heat until the liquid is absorbed and the rice is tender. Pilafs may be seasoned with sweet spices, such as cinnamon, ginger or cardamom, and enhanced with nuts or dried fruits.

RICE MIXES

Among the most popular packaged grains are rice mixes, which typically come with seasonings or sauces for preparing pilafs. The rice may be brown, regular, parboiled, or instant; sometimes it is combined with vermicelli or orzo (types of pasta). Such mixes may have a high sodium content—as much as 1000 milligrams per ¾ cup serving. They may also contain hydrogenated fats or recommend the addition of fat during cooking. If the seasoning is packaged separately, try using only half the contents of the packet to reduce the sodium content. To cut fat, avoid products with hydrogenated oils and eliminate the fat called for in the directions.

There's really no need to buy a ready-made mix: It's almost as easy, probably tastier, and certainly cheaper to add your favorite spice, fresh or dried herbs, and other seasonings to rice during or after cooking. To save time, combine your favorite dry seasonings in small packets and keep them on hand for rice cooking.

Risotto is traditionally made with arborio rice, but other types of medium-grain rice work equally well. To turn out creamy rice, a large quantity of liquid is gradually stirred in, and the rice is cooked, uncovered. First, sauté some chopped onions (and garlic, if desired) in a little oil or broth, then stir in the rice and sauté until it is opaque. Then add a small amount of hot broth (or wine)—about ½ cup liquid to 1 cup of rice—and cook, stirring, until the liquid is absorbed. Continue stirring the rice, and gradually add 3 to

4 more cups of broth or water, 1/2 cup at a time; do not add more until each 1/2 cup is absorbed. Cook and stir until the rice is tender and creamy, 25 to 30 minutes. Other ingredients may be incorporated when the rice is almost done. A generous quantity of grated Parmesan is usually stirred into the rice before serving, but a moderate amount will approximate the flavor of this classic dish, with less fat. Risotto is subject to many variations. Use part wine, part broth as the cooking liquid; add vegetables, such as diced squash, tomatoes, mushrooms, or shredded greens; stir in a few tablespoonfuls of lemon juice just before the rice is done.

Cold leftover rice can be transformed into a tasty, yet low-fat version of fried rice: Stir-fry the rice, along with chopped onions and vegetables, in a little oil (use a nonstick pan, if possible). You can add a beaten egg white (instead of the usual whole egg) for a more authentic texture.

Rice is frequently added to broth-based, tomato or vegetable soups (cook the raw rice in the soup, or add cooked rice just before serving to heat it through). To thicken soup, cook rice in it, then use a slotted spoon to transfer the rice to a food processor or blender and process until puréed. Or, simply purée some cooked rice with a little liquid and add it to a soup instead of cream.

Treat cold, cooked rice as you would potato or pasta salad. Experiment with artichoke hearts, chopped red or yellow bell peppers, tomatoes, green beans, corn, or peas; boost the protein content by combining the rice with lentils, beans, or chick-peas. Or, add tuna, chicken, or ham and cubes of tropical fruit, such as mango, papaya, or pineapple. Here's an opportunity to sample your favorite ethnic flavors without elaborate preparation: Season the rice salad with curry powder for an Indian touch, use soy sauce and sesame oil for an Asian flavor, give it a Mexican accent with hot peppers, cumin, and cilantro, or dress the rice with balsamic vinegar, olive oil, and herbs for an Italian emphasis.

Use freshly cooked or leftover rice of any type as a breakfast cereal; eat it cold or reheat it in the microwave. Stir in dried fruits, yogurt, spices, or sweetening, if desired.

For a more nutritious dessert, prepare rice pudding with skim milk (use a double boiler to prevent scorching). All types of rice are suitable for puddings, even aromatic or brown rice.

RICE, white, enriched 3½ oz cooked (½ cup)

Calories	129	Fat	<1 g
Protein	3 g	Saturated Fat	<1 g
Carbohydrate	28 g	Cholesterol	0 mg
Dietary Fiber	Low	Sodium	2 mg

KEY NUTRIENTS		% RDA Men	Women
Iron	1 mg	10%	7%
Manganese	0.5 mg	N/A	N/A
Niacin	1.5 mg	8%	10%
Thiamin	0.2 mg	13%	18%

S=40% or more soluble N/A=Not Applicable N=Not Available

RICE, brown, long grain 3½ oz cooked (½ cup)

Calories	111	Fat	1 g
Protein	3 g	Saturated Fat	<1 g
Carbohydrate	23 g	Cholesterol	0 mg
Dietary Fiber	High	Sodium	5 mg

KEY NUTRIENTS		% RDA Men	Women
Magnesium	43 mg	12%	15%
Manganese	1 mg	N/A	N/A
Niacin	2 mg	11%	13%
Phosphorus	83 mg	10%	10%

S=40% or more soluble N/A=Not Applicable N=Not Available

Rye

Most Americans have never eaten rye except in commercial bread and crackers. However, most commercial rye bread is made only in part with rye flour; the rest is usually refined wheat. In addition to its hearty taste, whole rye offers more protein, iron, and B vitamins than whole wheat.

Closely related and very similar in appearance to wheat (except for the bluish gray color of the grain itself), rye probably originated in Asia and spread westward as a weed infesting fields of wheat and barley. It was eventually recognized as a food plant and was first cultivated in eastern Europe during the fourth century B.C. Rye thrives where it is too wet and cold for other grains, and so has been widely consumed in Scandinavia, eastern Europe, and Russia for hundreds of years. In the United States, rye was introduced by British and Dutch settlers and became a staple in colonial New England. A two-grain loaf, made from rye and cornmeal, was also popular in the northern colonies. And for years, New Englanders ate rye as a cereal grain, like rice or barley.

Rye contains 20 percent more protein, by weight, than bulgur, and 86 percent more protein than brown rice.

During the twentieth century, rye production has decreased considerably both here and abroad. Although still favored for breadmaking in Scandinavia and parts of eastern Europe, today the grain ranks eighth among cereal crops in world production. In the United States, which ranks eighth in the world as a rye producer, only a quarter of the annual crop is set aside for human food; the rest is used for the production of rye whiskey and other spirits, and for animal feed.

FORMS OF RYE The nutrient content of the whole rye products listed below is far better than that of refined rye-flour products.

Cracked rye This type cooks more quickly than whole groats. It can be added to soups, or cooked and eaten as a pilaf or hot cereal.

Rye flakes These resemble rolled oats and are made by the same process: The berries are heated and then pressed with steel rollers. Like oatmeal, rye flakes can be cooked as a hot breakfast cereal or mixed into bread, quick bread, and muffin recipes.

Whole rye berries Also called whole kernels or groats, rye berries resemble wheat berries. They can be cooked as a main-dish casserole or a side dish, or added to soups. You can shorten the cooking time for whole rye berries considerably by soaking them in cold water overnight in the refrigerator. To conserve nutrients, use the soaking liquid in cooking. Beef, chicken, or vegetable stock, or fruit juice, can be substituted for water.

PREPARATION The chart below gives cooking times, grain to liquid proportions, and yields for rye. (The cooking time for rye berries reflects overnight soaking.)

SERVING SUGGESTIONS To temper its robust flavor, cook rye along with milder-tasting grains.

RYE COOKING TIMES

Per ½ Cup Uncooked	**Liquid** (cups)	**Cooking Times**	**Yield** (cups)
Rye berries	1½	1 hour, 55 minutes	1½
Rye flakes	1½	1 hour, 5 minutes	1¼

Try simmering rye berries with wheat berries or brown rice; combine cracked rye with cracked wheat; and cook rye flakes in combination with oatmeal. To enjoy rye's distinctive flavor on its own, use rye berries in wheat-berry recipes, cracked rye in cracked-wheat recipes, and rye flakes in oatmeal dishes.

RYE DISEASE

Rye is particularly susceptible to a fungus called ergot, which is toxic to humans, causing convulsions, mental derangement, alternating chills and hot flashes, and gangrene. Poisoning from ergot was widespread from the eleventh to the sixteenth centuries in Europe, and some historians believe that it may have been a factor in precipitating the riots among the French peasants that led to the French Revolution. Ergot forms purplish black masses that are easily identified in the grain, and if found, are separated out from the grain before processing. Grain that contains more than 0.3 percent ergot is not used, and so commercial rye products are perfectly safe to consume.

RYE 3½ oz dry (⅔ cup)

Calories	335	Fat	3 g
Protein	15 g	Saturated Fat	<1 g
Carbohydrate	70 g	Cholesterol	0 mg
Dietary Fiber	High	Sodium	6 mg

KEY NUTRIENTS		% RDA Men	% RDA Women
Vitamin B_6	0.3 mg	15%	19%
Copper	0.5 mg	N/A	N/A
Vitamin E	1 mg	10%	13%
Folacin	60 mcg	30%	33%
Iron	3 mg	30%	20%
Magnesium	121 mg	35%	43%
Manganese	3 mg	N/A	N/A
Niacin	4 mg	21%	27%
Phosphorus	374 mg	47%	47%
Riboflavin	0.3 mg	18%	23%
Thiamin	0.3 mg	20%	27%
Zinc	4 mg	27%	33%

S=40% or more soluble N/A=Not Applicable N=Not Available

Make an old-fashioned rye casserole by baking or simmering rye berries in broth with chopped nuts and raisins. Because rye takes so long to cook, add it presoaked or partially or fully cooked to vegetable soups and hearty stews. Cooked rye berries, seasoned with herbs and mixed with chopped vegetables or fruits, can be used to make an unusual but delicious poultry stuffing.

Cook cracked rye in fruit juice with dried fruits, or prepare it like kasha (by browning it in a skillet before simmering in broth) and serve it as a main dish.

Rye flakes can be used as a meat extender in meat loaves and meatballs and as a thickener for soups. Toasted, they lend flavor and texture to granola (see page 300 for instruction on making your own granola).

Triticale

Unlike many of the other grains, triticale (pronounced tri-ti-*kay*-lee) does not have a history that covers several millennia. It was developed only a little more than a century ago, in 1875, when a Scottish botanist crossed wheat with rye in hopes of creating a food grain with the good baking qualities and high yield of wheat and the robust growing habit and protein content of rye. The few seeds he was able to germinate from the hybrid were sterile, but, in 1937, a French researcher succeeded in producing a fertile cross of wheat and rye. Subsequent

TRITICALE 3½ oz dry (½ cup)			
Calories	336	Fat	2 g
Protein	13 g	Saturated Fat	<1 g
Carbohydrate	72 g	Cholesterol	0 mg
Dietary Fiber	High	Sodium	5 mg

KEY NUTRIENTS		%RDA Men	%RDA Women
Copper	0.5 mg	N/A	N/A
Folacin	73 mcg	37%	41%
Iron	3 mg	30%	20%
Magnesium	130 mg	37%	46%
Manganese	3 mg	N/A	N/A
Niacin	1 mg	5%	7%
Phosphorus	358 mg	45%	45%
Potassium	332 mg	N/A	N/A
Riboflavin	0.1 mg	6%	8%
Thiamin	0.4 mg	27%	36%
Zinc	3 mg	20%	25%

S=40% or more soluble N/A=Not Applicable N=Not Available

research beginning in the 1950s led to great improvements in the new grain, called triticale after the Latin genus names for wheat (*Triticum*) and rye (*Secale*).

Although perhaps not the supergrain it was once claimed to be, triticale does combine rye's ability to survive cold temperatures with the disease resistance of wheat to produce a grain with a substantial protein content. Depending on growing conditions, triticale ranges from 14 percent to 20 percent protein, by weight. It also has enough gluten, unlike rye, to be used alone as a bread flour. Triticale is a good source of some of the B vitamins: It has more thiamin and folacin than either wheat or rye, but less niacin and B_6 than either of its parent grains. Its nutlike flavor is richer than that of wheat, but not so assertive as that of rye. Triticale is not grown in great quantities, and therefore is more likely to be found in health-food stores or through mail-order sources.

FORMS OF TRITICALE Triticale comes in the same forms as wheat or rye:

Cracked triticale These have a shorter cooking time than the whole berries. You can make your own cracked triticale by processing whole berries in a blender until they are coarsely chopped.

Triticale berries Like wheat berries, whole triticale berries have not been stripped of their nutritious bran and germ. They are twice the size of wheat berries, and need to be soaked overnight in the refrigerator before cooking.

Triticale flakes Like rolled oats, these are triticale berries that have been steamed and flattened.

PREPARATION Triticale berries are particularly flavorful when they have been browned before cooking. Sauté ½ cup of uncooked triticale in a small amount of oil until brown, then proceed with cooking.

Simmering Add ½ cup triticale berries to 1½ cups of boiling water. Lower heat and simmer until done. *Cooking time:* 1 hour, 45 minutes. Makes about 1¼ cups.

SERVING SUGGESTIONS Triticale can be substituted for wheat berries or bulgur in any recipe (see page 315). Prepare tabbouleh with cracked triticale or serve the grain as a hot breakfast cereal. Whole or cracked berries make a wonderful pilaf, as well as an interesting stuffing (cooked) for fish or poultry. They can also be added (uncooked) to soups and stews to thicken them, or mixed into ground beef or turkey in meatballs, burgers, and meatloaf to "stretch" the meat.

Wheat

As the most important cereal crop in the world, wheat—mainly in the form of bread and noodles—nourishes more people than any other grain. Unlike many other grains, such as oats, corn, sorghum, and millet, wheat is not typically used as animal feed but is processed directly into human food (although wheat bran and germ, the nutrient-dense by-products of flour refining, are given to livestock). The bulk of the wheat grown is milled into flour—usually white flour. But there are forms of wheat, with their bran and germ intact, that can be eaten as a main or side dish. Whole wheat is a highly nutritious food, offering a good supply of protein, B vitamins, and minerals, including iron, magnesium, and manganese.

Wheat is one of the oldest cultivated grains. Probably descended from a wild grass, and first grown in western Asia six thousand years ago, it was milled into flour for bread in ancient Egypt and was the grain of choice during the Roman Empire. Wheat fell behind barley, rye, and potatoes as a staple food in Europe for hundreds of years during the Middle Ages, but it reemerged as the preeminent grain in the nineteenth century. It was brought to the New World by European settlers in the 1700s, and by the mid-nineteenth century was established in what would later be America's wheat belt.

Today, the United States ranks among the top five wheat-growing nations in the world, exporting one-half of its annual wheat crop to other nations.

FORMS OF WHEAT The thousands of known varieties of wheat all fall into one of six classes, determined by the planting season, hardness of the grain, and the color of the kernel. Hard Red Winter, Hard Red Spring, Soft Red Winter, Hard White, Soft White, and Durum wheat are the major classes. Winter wheats are planted in the fall; they lie dormant during the winter, revive to grow again in the spring, and are harvested early in the summer. Spring wheats are planted in the spring and harvested late in the summer.

THE ANTICANCER FIBER

Scientists at New York Hospital–Cornell Medical Center have found that wheat bran can have a beneficial effect on people who have precancerous polyps of the colon. The magic ingredient—insoluble fiber.

The four-year-long study followed fifty-eight men and women at very high risk of colorectal cancer because of an inherited condition characterized by the continuing development of numerous polyps in the colon and rectum. (The polyps first appear at an early age, and over time, they gradually enlarge and become malignant.) Half the subjects had their regular diet supplemented by a wheat-bran cereal high in insoluble fiber (they ate a total of 22.4 grams of fiber per day); the others were given a low-fiber look-alike cereal (they ate an average of 12 grams of fiber per day, about as much as the average American consumes). The study was double-blind; neither the researchers nor the subjects knew who was eating which cereal. The results: Over the course of the study, polyps were more likely to have shrunk both in size and number in the people on the high-fiber wheat cereal.

Oat bran and other foods rich in soluble fiber have received extensive publicity in recent years, but this study serves as a reminder that you shouldn't scrimp on wheat bran, whole wheat, and other sources of insoluble fiber—especially if you have a family history of colorectal cancer.

The hard wheats have a higher protein-to-starch ratio than the soft wheats. Durum, the hardest wheat of all, is processed into semolina and used to make pasta. Hard Red Winter and Hard Red Spring wheats are milled into bread flour and all-purpose flour, as are Hard White wheats. Soft Red Winter and Soft White wheats produce flours that are well suited for making cakes, crackers, cookies, and pastries. (For information on the various types of wheat flour, see page 329.) Any of these wheats (except durum) may be combined in the whole-wheat products listed below.

Bulgur A processed form of cracked wheat (but with a more pronounced flavor), bulgur is produced by a method similar to that used for converted rice: The whole-wheat kernels are steam cooked and dried, then the grain is cracked into three different granulations. Traditionally, the coarsest grain is used for pilaf; the medium, for cereal; and the finest, for tabbouleh. Bulgur requires less cooking time than cracked wheat. It can also be "cooked" by soaking, without heat.

Cracked wheat This product is made from wheat berries that have been ground into coarse, medium, and fine granulations for faster cooking. Cracked wheat has an agreeably wheaty flavor and can replace rice or other grains in most recipes; it cooks in about 15 minutes and retains a slight crunchiness afterward. You can offer it as a breakfast cereal, mix it into baked goods, or substitute it for bulgur in tabbouleh—a Middle Eastern cold grain salad (see under Serving Suggestions below)—and other main dishes.

It's possible to make cracked wheat at home by processing wheat berries in a heavy-duty blender. Process 2 cups of wheat at a time on high speed for about 4 minutes.

Farina Also sold as Cream of Wheat, farina is made from the endosperm of the grain, which is milled to a fine granular consistency and then sifted. Although the bran and most of the germ are removed, this cereal is sometimes enriched with B vitamins and iron. Farina is most often served as a breakfast cereal, but can also be cooked like polenta.

NEW PRODUCTS FROM ANCIENT GRAINS

There are over thirty thousand varieties of wheat, all of which developed from one common ancestor called wild einkorn. The wheats most commonly grown today are different genetically from this original wheat, but two ancient strains are now being marketed, mostly in health-food stores. Called kamut and spelt, these were among the wheats found growing when humans first walked the earth.

Similar nutritionally to modern wheats, kamut and spelt are available mainly in the form of flours and pastas. Even though they are botanically considered forms of wheat, they may be labeled "wheat-free"—presumably to attract the attention of those with wheat allergies. One packaged spelt product says it is an "alternative to wheat" and its product-information flyer states that it is "perfect for wheat-sensitive people." But whether or not spelt or kamut can be tolerated by individuals with wheat allergies or gluten sensitivity has yet to be established by scientific research, and those with such allergies should consult their doctors before experimenting with these grains.

Rolled wheat (wheat flakes) These are whole wheat berries that have been flattened between rollers and are not to be confused with ready-to-eat wheat-flake breakfast cereals. Rolled wheat flakes resemble rolled oats, but are thicker and firmer; you can add them to baked goods or cook them as hot cereal.

WHEAT COOKING TIMES

Per ½ Cup Uncooked	**Liquid** (cups)	**Cooking Times**	**Yield** (cups)
Whole Berries	1½	1 hour, 10 minutes	1¼
Cracked Wheat	1	15 minutes	1
Bulgur	1	15 minutes	1½
Wheat Flakes	2	53 minutes	1

Wheat berries Also called groats, these are whole wheat kernels that have not been milled, polished, or heat treated. Wheat berries are brown and nearly round in appearance; they take over an hour to cook, but the time can be reduced if they are presoaked. Wheat berries have a robust, nutlike flavor that goes well with other hearty foods. They can be used for grain-based main dishes, served as a side dish, or added to soups and yeast-bread doughs.

WHEAT GERM VS. WHEAT BRAN

For years people have been buying wheat germ to sprinkle on breakfast cereals, yogurt, and salads, as well as to add to baked goods and casseroles. Now, with nutritionists emphasizing the importance of fiber, wheat germ has been joined on supermarket shelves by wheat bran. What are the nutritional differences between the two?

***Wheat germ* contains a fair amount of polyunsaturated fat, deriving 25 percent of its calories from fat. Wheat germ is a good source of thiamin, vitamin E, iron, and riboflavin. One ounce (about 3 tablespoons) supplies 9 grams of protein and 3 grams of dietary fiber. Defatted wheat germ is available, but it's lower in vitamin E; unlike regular wheat germ, it doesn't have to be stored in the refrigerator.**

***Wheat bran* is also a nutritional storehouse; it offers niacin, magnesium, and iron. One ounce (about ½ cup) contains 5 grams of protein, 1 gram of fat, and 12 grams of dietary fiber.**

If you eat whole-wheat cereals and baked goods, then you're already getting the germ and the bran. Otherwise, try adding some packaged wheat germ and bran to your diet; you'll be enhancing the nutrient value of the foods, as well as their flavor and texture.

Wheatena This is the trade name for a very finely cracked wheat product sold for use as a hot cereal. It has a pleasantly nutlike flavor and is among the most nutritious of hot cereals.

PREPARATION Packaged whole wheat products do not require rinsing, but those bought in bulk should be picked over and washed to remove dust or debris before cooking.

Wheat berries, cracked wheat, and bulgur are most frequently cooked by simmering, but they can also be baked in casseroles. The cooking times and liquid-to-grain ratios are provided in the chart on page 314.

Sprouting Whole-wheat berries can be sprouted; use them like bean sprouts, or allow them to grow longer and eat this so-called wheat grass. For directions on sprouting wheat, see page 159.

Steeping Bulgur is often cooked by this method. Place the bulgur in a shallow dish and pour enough boiling water or broth over it to cover by ½ inch (about 2 cups liquid to 1 cup of bulgur). Cover the dish and let stand for at least 30 minutes, or until the bulgur has softened and absorbed the liquid. If necessary, drain off any excess liquid before continuing with the preparation of the dish.

SERVING SUGGESTIONS Whole wheat products, with their rich, satisfying flavor and texture, provide an excellent base for meatless meals; they can also be served as accompaniments to meat, fish, or poultry or added to soups and salads. To temper their robust flavor, combine wheat berries or cracked wheat with milder-flavored grains, such as rice or barley.

Cook wheat berries, cracked wheat, or bulgur as you would pilaf: First, sauté the uncooked wheat with garlic and onion in a small amount of oil or broth. Then simmer the grain and add chopped vegetables, herbs, and spices. Bulgur can be substituted for rice in any recipe.

To make tabbouleh, prepare 1 cup of bulgur by the steeping method. When the grain is tender, add about ⅓ cup of freshly squeezed lemon juice, 2 tablespoons of olive oil, a good handful of chopped fresh parsley, dill or mint, a few diced plum tomatoes, about ½ cup chopped scallions, minced garlic, and salt and pepper to taste. You can, if you like, add other chopped cold vegetables, such as cucumber, bell peppers, or celery;

BULGUR WHEAT 3½ oz cooked (½ cup)			
Calories	83	Fat	<1 g
Protein	3 g	Saturated Fat	<1 g
Carbohydrate	19 g	Cholesterol	0 mg
Dietary Fiber	High	Sodium	5 mg

KEY NUTRIENTS		% RDA Men	% RDA Women
Folacin	18 mcg	9%	10%
Iron	1 mg	10%	6%
Magnesium	32 mg	9%	11%
Manganese	0.6 mg	N/A	N/A

S=40% or more soluble N/A=Not Applicable N=Not Available

cubed turkey or water-packed tuna; or beans or chick-peas. Serve the tabbouleh well chilled.

Experiment with different forms of wheat in casseroles, along with such hearty ingredients as winter squash, roasted bell peppers, or eggplant.

Wheat serves as a good meat extender and thickener, while adding dietary fiber and reducing the fat content of the food. Cooked cracked wheat or wheat berries can be combined with ground beef or turkey to make meatballs or meat loaf. Or, they can be mixed with salads for a more substantial dish. These wheat products are also delicious in soups, stews, and chilies and will help thicken these dishes.

Cooked wheat berries, cracked wheat, or bulgur make excellent fillings for hollowed-out vegetables, such as squash, peppers, or cabbage.

Bread

The beauty of bread is its simplicity. Flour and liquid are the main ingredients, along with yeast and sometimes salt, and these basics yield a nourishing and tasty food—one that is high in complex carbohydrates, protein, and B vitamins, and comes in a wide variety of shapes, textures, and flavors. Practically every culture has its own type of bread, and many have more than one. Pumpernickel, pita, bagels, baguettes, crumpets, chapatis, tortillas, matzo, rye, sourdough, and whole wheat—these are but a few of the types of breads popular around the world. Add optional ingredients, such as sweeteners and fats, and the varieties of bread become truly innumerable.

But of all these various types, breads fall into just two categories: unleavened, and leavened or raised. (Quick breads—those leavened with baking powder or baking soda—are discussed in the box on page 321.) Unleavened breads were the first breads; early on, humans discovered that gruel made from grain and water could be cooked on hot stones to form what we now call flat bread. Types of unleavened breads still popular today include matzo, tortillas, and chapatis.

The invention of raised breads by the ancient Egyptians appears to have been a chance occurrence—the result of wheat dough becoming accidentally contaminated with airborne wild yeasts that caused it to expand. When baked, the slightly risen bread was tastier and lighter than usual, and the Egyptians eventually learned to produce raised breads by using a piece of dough from a previous batch to start another. This and other Egyptian techniques of bread-baking were adopted by the Hebrews and also by the Romans, who spread them throughout their empire. But it took thousands of years of breadmaking before the process that made dough rise was fully understood. Louis Pasteur discovered in the 1850s that yeast was a living organism that multiplied and caused fermentation, producing the carbon dioxide that makes dough rise. Until then, the term *yeast* had been used to refer to the froth of any fermenting liquid.

Though the ingredients in bread are simple, their interaction is complex. Each component plays a specific role in the flavor and texture of the finished product.

WHAT MAKES SOURDOUGH SOUR?

Sourdough bread is made from a living culture called a starter. A classic sourdough starter consists of a mix of water and flour that ferments as it traps wild yeasts from the air. These organisms give the bread its characteristic "sour" flavor, and also serve as leavening agents. Sourdough bread made in one area seldom tastes the same as sourdough bread made in another area—even if the same starter was used. This is because different environments contain different yeasts and bacteria.

Once established, a sourdough starter can be kept alive indefinitely. When a portion is removed to make bread, additional flour and water are mixed in to replenish the starter for future use.

The first raised breads made by the Egyptians were a form of sourdough. More recently, gold miners in California used the Egyptian method of "starting" bread with a piece of dough from a previous batch; hence the beginnings of San Francisco sourdough. Today, most sourdoughs are made with a starter for flavor, but with ordinary yeast as the leavening agent. It is possible to leaven bread with a sourdough starter alone, but it may produce a dense, heavy loaf.

Flour is, of course, the main ingredient; in simple breads, it provides all the nutrients. For raised breads, wheat flour is ideal: It is uniquely suited for bread-making, because when it is mixed with liquid, some of its proteins combine to form gluten. Well-developed gluten is essential to the success of raised breads. It works with yeast and starch to form a network of cells elastic enough to expand during the leavening process, yet strong enough to contain the gases produced by the yeast, so that the dough does not collapse and the resulting bread is light. Gluten also traps starch between its layers and, as the bread bakes, the starch gelatinizes. Together the gluten and gelatinized starch give bread its structure and texture. (Flours made from hard wheats contain the most protein, and so can develop the most gluten. See Flour, page 329.)

Other types of grains can produce gluten, but not to the extent that wheat can. Rye, the next-best gluten producer, is a poor second to wheat. Breads made solely from low-gluten flours will be dense and heavy. As a result, most raised breads contain at least some wheat flour. Any grain (or vegetable starch, such as ground dried potatoes, lentils, or soybeans) can be used to make unleavened breads; corn, for example, is the flour most commonly used in tortillas.

Liquid is used in raised breads to help dissolve and distribute the yeast through the flour, and is necessary for the formation of gluten and the gelatinization of starch. Many kinds of liquid can be used; all have a different effect on the dough's development. Water produces a bread with a crisp, thick crust; milk, another popular choice, produces a bread with a tender, brown crust and helps keep bread fresh. Depending on the amount added, milk may also add to the nutritional quality of bread by providing lysine, the amino acid that is lacking in the flour, thereby producing a complete protein. Other liquids—such as the water that potatoes have been cooked in, fruit juice, or beer—have different effects on the texture and flavor of the bread.

Yeast is a single-cell fungus that will multiply rapidly, given the right conditions. Yeast leavens bread because it ferments the simple carbohydrates naturally present in the flour, producing carbon dioxide and alcohol as waste products. Bread rises when the gluten traps the carbon dioxide in the dough. (The alcohol is largely evaporated during baking.) This is the main function of yeast, but it also modifies the elasticity and stickiness of the dough and is responsible for bread's characteristic flavor and aroma. There are many types of yeasts, but those used in breadmaking are strains of *Saccharomyces cerevisiae.*

Salt not only adds flavor to bread, but also affects the actions of the yeast and gluten. It is possible to make bread without any salt at all, but a small amount of salt will help strengthen the gluten, make the dough easier to handle, and prevent the yeast from multiplying too rapidly. Too much salt, however, will make the dough tough and will halt entirely the reproductive action of the yeast.

DOES TOAST HAVE FEWER CALORIES?

Many diet plans call for a slice of dry toast with a meal, as though toast were a special diet food. It may look more austere, but a slice of toast has the same 60 to 70 calories that a slice of bread has. Toasting removes only moisture. So if you're watching calories, eat your bread plain or toasted, as you like. Just don't add butter—or even margarine.

Sugar is an optional ingredient in bread, but it is often added. Its main function is to provide a readily available form of energy for the yeast at the start of the process, thus helping the bread to rise faster (though dough containing a lot of sugar will take longer to rise because the sugar acts as a preservative, slowing the action of the yeast). Sugar also contributes flavor, helps to keep the bread tender by retaining moisture, and aids in browning.

Fat is another optional ingredient that is frequently used in commercial breads. Fat adds flavor, makes the loaf more tender, and helps the bread brown better. It also helps to increase the dough's elasticity so it can expand even more without letting carbon dioxide escape, thereby producing a loaf with greater volume.

FORMS OF BREAD The flavor, texture, and nutritiousness of a loaf of bread depends on its ingredients and the proportions in which they are combined. How bread is baked also affects flavor and texture. Most breads are either pan-baked or hearth-baked. *Pan breads,* baked in loaf-shaped metal pans, have a soft crust. *Hearth breads*—freeform breads baked in brick ovens, on baking stones, on baking sheets, even on hearths—are crustier. Some breads, such as bagels, are boiled before baking; others, such as crumpets, are "baked" on a griddle; and in Asian cultures, some breads are steamed.

Another basic distinction is whether a bread is white or whole wheat. *White pan bread* made with enriched white wheat flour is the most popular type of bread in the United States. Enriched white flour is not equivalent nutritionally to whole wheat flour. Of the twenty-two nutrients decreased during the milling of white flour, only four—niacin, thiamin, riboflavin, and iron—are replaced when the flour is enriched. Enriched white bread is lacking in copper and zinc and has about 75 percent less dietary fiber. Breads made with unenriched flours are low in B vitamins as well.

Whole wheat bread is another matter. On the one hand, it has more vitamins, minerals, and fiber than enriched white bread. On the other hand, it is not the nutritional champion it has been presented to be: Bread made from wheat flour—white or whole wheat—has no vitamin C, vitamin A, or vitamin B_{12}, and is very low in calcium and vitamin E. In order to be labeled "whole wheat," bread must be made from 100-percent whole wheat flour. Breads labeled "wheat," "cracked wheat," or "sprouted wheat" usually contain white flour; for example, "wheat" breads usually contain about 75 percent white flour. Check the ingredient list: Whole wheat flour should be the only type listed.

Other breads are variations on white and whole wheat. The list below describes the types you are most likely to find in the supermarket. Home bakers, because they can choose from literally thousands of recipes and combine ingredients to their preference, have more options open to them.

Bagels These doughnut-shaped rolls—usually made from high-protein flour, yeast, and salt—are boiled before they are baked in the oven. Plain

COMPARING BREADS 3½ ounces

	Serving size	Calorie	Fat (g)	Protein (g)	Iron (mg)	Niacin (mg)	Riboflavin (mg)
Bagels	1½ Bagels	294	3	10	3	4	0.3
Croissants	1 Croissant	412	21	9	4	2	0.2
English muffins	2 Muffins	246	2	9	3	4	0.3
French bread	3 Slices	286	3	9	3	4	0.3
Italian bread	3 Slices	283	<1	10	3	3	0.2
Matzo	3 Crackers	397	1	10	0	0	0
Multi-grain	4 Slices	260	4	8	3	4	0.4
Pita	2 Pitas	275	2	10	2	4	0.2
Pumpernickel	3 Slices	250	3	9	3	3	0.5
Rye	4 Slices	260	4	8	3	3	0.3
Sourdough	3½ Slices	271	1	8	2	3	0.3
Tortillas (corn)	3 Tortillas	217	3	7	2	1	0.1
White	4 Slices	260	4	8	3	4	0.3
Whole wheat	3½ Slices	250	4	11	3	4	0.2

bagels, sometimes called water bagels, may be varied with poppy or sesame seeds, raisins, garlic, or onion. Whole wheat varieties are sometimes available. Softer, golden egg bagels are made with whole eggs. Most bagels are made with little or no shortening, making them dense. Egg bagels, however, contain some added fat and cholesterol.

Croissants The amount of butter and sugar in these French crescent rolls makes them more like pastry than bread. The butter makes them flaky and tender, but also high in fat; an average croissant gets 46 percent of its calories from fat.

English muffins Made from high-protein white flour, these small, chewy muffins are similar to white bread nutritionally. They are traditionally baked on a griddle or skillet rather than in an oven. Honey-wheat varieties are made from mostly white flour and contain honey, but you may be able to find whole wheat varieties.

French or Italian True Italian and French breads are hearth breads made from flour, yeast, water, and salt. Loaves made at local bakeries (and not produced for long-distance shipping) usually contain few preservatives, and little or no fat or sugar. Look for whole wheat varieties.

High fiber There is no legal definition of terms such as "high fiber," but many breads still promote the fiber content on the label. Whole wheat breads do have more fiber than white—about 2 grams per slice, versus 0.5 grams per slice in white breads. If bread has added wheat or oat bran, soy flour, seeds, nuts, or other whole grains such as oats, it's likely to be higher in fiber, but the increase depends on the amount of these ingredients added. Some of these breads have three times the fiber of white bread; others are only marginally higher.

Matzo Though most people think of matzo as a cracker, it is an unleavened bread. Plain matzo is made from flour (some are made from 100-percent whole wheat flour), water, and sometimes salt. Unlike many other packaged crackers, matzo contains no fat. Egg matzo contains whole eggs and is usually made with apple cider or juice instead of water.

Multi-grain A host of "healthful" multi-grain breads have appeared on the market in the past few years. These breads may contain such ingredients as oats, oat bran, corn, barley, alfalfa sprouts, sunflower seeds, soy flour, sesame seeds,

ADDITIVES IN BREAD

In addition to the vitamins and minerals added to enrich white breads, commercial bakers often use other additives to improve the texture, appearance, and keeping quality of their products. Additives are often listed on the label (and their purpose is usually identified as well). Below is a list of common additives in bread and their functions.

Type	Function/Comment
Dough conditioners *(Sodium stearoyl 2-lactylate; calcium stearoyl lactate; barley malt; ethoxylated and succinylated monoglycerides; polysorbate 60)*	Mechanically kneaded dough can become weak and is easily over-mixed. Dough conditioners act on the gluten and starch in the dough to help strengthen it and increase its elasticity. The resulting loaf is fine-textured and light.
Preservatives *(Sodium propionate; calcium propionate)*	These extend the shelf life of bread and retard mold growth. Sodium propionate increases the sodium content of bread. Calcium propionate boosts the calcium content of the bread slightly.
Colorings *(Caramel coloring; molasses)*	Add color. May be added to impart the darker color people associate with whole grains. Artificial colorings are rarely added to breads.
Yeast nutrients *(Ammonium and calcium salts; monocalcium phosphate)*	Nourish yeast so it produces carbon dioxide at a faster rate. Sugar also serves to boost yeast production.
Wheat gluten	Increases the strength of the dough to support heavy ingredients such as fruit or nuts. May be added to high-fiber breads. Usually blended with low-protein flours. Increases protein content of bread.
Emulsifiers *(Propylene glycol monoesters; monoglycerides; diglycerides; lecithin)*	Help to blend the water and oil in the bread. Contribute to soft texture. These add nothing to the nutritional value of the bread, whereas milk or egg—natural emulsifers—do.
Bleaching agents *(Oxides of nitrogen; chlorine gas; nitrosyl dioxide; chlorine dioxide; benzoyl peroxide; acetal peroxide; azodicarbonamide)*	Whiten and mature white flour. The bleaching agents won't be listed on the label, which will just list bleached flour.

and nuts. A few even contain added wheat germ or bran. Some multi-grain breads are indeed higher in fiber, and the added ingredients can boost the bread's nutritional content, but most still contain white flour as their primary ingredient and may have sweeteners and fats added as well. Moreover, many of these breads contain very little of the "healthful" ingredients; check the ingredient list.

Pita The flatness of this round "pocket" bread (as it is sometimes called) may make you think it is unleavened, but pita bread is made with yeast. The rounds of dough puff during baking, then deflate, leaving a hollow in the middle. Often the other ingredients are just flour and water, though some types have sweeteners or oil added. Whole wheat varieties are available.

Pumpernickel Really a form of rye bread, pumpernickel is usually made with refined rye wheat flours; the darker color comes from added caramel or molasses, so pumpernickel has no nutritional advantages over white or rye breads. Small, thinly sliced, square rye loaves are sometimes labeled pumpernickel; these may be made with 100-percent dark, or unbolted, rye flour, which retains some of the bran and germ.

Reduced calorie A slice of white bread (about an ounce) has 65 calories, and a slice of whole wheat about 70, but some breads claim "Only 40 calories per slice" or "25 percent fewer calories" on their labels. Some breads are lower in calories because they contain more fiber, usually in the form of cellulose. Cellulose may be derived from many plant sources, including pharmaceutical-grade wood cellulose or wheat bran. Other breads have fewer calories per slice simply because they are sliced thinner.

Rye Bread made with 100-percent rye flour will be dense and heavy. As a result, many rye breads contain at least some wheat flour (usually enriched white flour); most deli-style rye breads contain only 20 to 40 percent rye flour. A bread can contain as little as 3 percent rye flour and still be called rye bread. Most of the rye flour used is bolted—or sifted—to remove the bran and germ. Look for breads made with dark (unbolted) rye flour, or those made with mixed rye and whole wheat flours.

Sourdough Sourdough breads are leavened with a "starter" (see page 317). As with any type of bread, the nutritional value of sourdough bread depends on the type of flour used and the ingredients added; the sourdough starter makes it no more or less healthful than other breads. Traditional San Francisco-style sourdough is made from white flour.

QUICK BREADS

Quick breads are leavened with baking powder or baking soda instead of yeast. They are called quick breads because no rising time is required. At baking temperatures, the leavening reacts with water and acid in the batter or dough to form carbon dioxide, and the quick bread rises.

Like yeast breads, quick breads are made from flour, liquid, and sometimes salt, but they usually contain eggs, sugar, and fat as well. There are three types of quick bread mixtures that differ in the proportions of ingredients:

Pour batters **are thin, usually made with an even ratio of flour to liquid. Examples include pancakes, waffles, and popovers.**

Drop batters **consist of two parts flour to one part liquid. They are thick and need to be spooned into the baking pan. Muffins, quick bread loaves, and coffee cakes are made from drop batters.**

Soft doughs **are firm enough to handle. They contain three parts flour to one part liquid. Biscuits and scones are the most common types of soft-dough quick breads.**

The ingredients in pour batters and drop batters are usually stirred just until the ingredients are mixed, to avoid the overdevelopment of gluten. Soft doughs are usually kneaded briefly—about ten to twenty strokes—to develop some gluten. Over-mixing or over-kneading produces a quick bread with a heavy, dense texture.

Homemade quick breads can be healthful as well as delicious. For example, you can substitute whole wheat flour, bran, oatmeal, or wheat germ for 25 percent of the white flour in recipes; reduce the amount of sugar called for by 25 percent; sweeten with dried fruits such as apricots, which add beta carotene, or prunes, which add fiber and iron; and use highly unsaturated vegetable oils instead of butter or margarine. For every two eggs, use one egg white and one whole egg. If just one egg is called for, use two egg whites.

Store-bought quick breads can be high in calories and fat, and low in nutrients and fiber. For example, store-bought bran muffins may contain more hydrogenated oils, sugar, and eggs than they do oat or wheat bran; if the muffin feels heavy in your hand (some are 5 ounces or more) and has a sticky surface, it is likely to have as many calories and fat as a cupcake. Be sure to read nutritional labels and ingredient lists, and choose products with the least fat and sugar.

Tortillas These unleavened breads originated in Mexico, but are now available in supermarkets everywhere. They are usually made from corn or wheat flour. Corn tortillas are made from cornmeal and water; flour tortillas contain white wheat flour, vegetable shortening or lard, water, and salt. Corn tortillas contain 3 to 4 grams of fat in 3½ ounces; flour tortillas can contain 4 to 10 grams in the same size serving. The cornmeal used in tortillas is sometimes treated with lime, which makes some of its nutrients more available (see Corn, page 84). Both corn and flour tortillas are usually found in the grocer's refrigerator case or in the freezer. Flour tortillas may also be found on grocery shelves.

SHOPPING TIPS Choose the freshest bread possible. Commercially packaged breads are usually marked with expiration dates; they'll be fresh on that date and for a few days afterward. In bakeries or supermarket bake shops, buy bread made that day. Although commercially packaged breads usually contain preservatives that prevent mold formation, mold can still develop, especially in hot or humid weather, so inspect the bread carefully through the wrapper.

Commercial breadsticks can be high in fat and calories, so be careful about how many you eat. Most are made with oil, and some contain high-fat ingredients such as sesame seeds. Just three breadsticks (1 ounce) of one brand have 130 calories and 4 grams of fat (28 percent of the calories coming from fat). Three sesame breadsticks (1 ounce) have 150 calories and 7 grams of fat (42 percent fat calories). To find fat-free breadsticks, check the ingredient list.

Check the ingredient list for the primary type of flour used and for the addition of fat, sweeteners, and other ingredients. Most commercial breads contain additives that retard staling; dough conditioners and emulsifiers may also be added. A list of common additives in bread is presented in the chart on page 320. The additives used in bread are safe, and some may even be healthful; for example, calcium propionate, added to retard mold formation, slightly boosts the calcium content of bread.

The ingredient list and nutrition labeling can also help you sort out claims made on the front of the package. Ingredients are listed in descending order by weight, so if a bread claims "whole-grain goodness," and the first ingredient is enriched white flour, you know that the bread is not much better nutritionally than plain white bread.

STORAGE To prevent bread from becoming stale and moldy, keep it at room temperature. Refrigerating bread helps keep it mold-free, but bread stales quickly—even if well wrapped—at temperatures between 20° and 50°. When it's warm, mold will form more quickly, but most families will finish a loaf of bread before this occurs. Commercial breads also contain additives that prevent mold. If a small amount of mold forms on bread, the mold and a generous slice of the bread underneath can be cut away, but excessively moldy bread should be discarded.

Be sure to keep the bread tightly wrapped, or enclosed in an old-fashioned bread box to protect it against drying air. You can keep soft breads in plastic bags, but use paper bags for crusty breads. If bread has turned stale, you can freshen it by reheating it quickly in a hot oven. Stale bread is also fine for toast, croutons, or breadcrumbs.

If you suspect you will not be able to finish a loaf of bread before it spoils, freeze it. Seal the loaf in an airtight plastic bag and put it in a freezer set to 0°. Use frozen bread as needed, thawing it at room temperature first. Frozen bread can go straight into the toaster without thawing.

PREPARATION Store-bought bread is convenient and, of course, requires no preparation at all, save for toasting or filling with sandwich ingredients. But there is an alternative: Making your own bread is not as difficult or time-consuming as you might think.

First, the flour, yeast, liquid, salt, and any other ingredients are blended together. Once the mixture is too stiff to be stirred with a spoon, the dough is kneaded by hand or food processor. Kneading helps develop gluten and evenly disperses the yeast. The dough is then put in a covered bowl and left to rise in a warm (about 80°), draft-free spot. During this period, the yeast ferments and multiplies, producing the carbon dioxide that fills the air pockets created during kneading. When the dough has risen sufficiently, it should be "punched down" to release excess carbon dioxide and further stimulate the yeast, then set aside to rise again (this second rising takes about half as long as the first). The dough is then shaped into the pan, left to rise again for 30 minutes to an hour, and then baked. Bread is done when the crust is evenly brown on all sides, the loaf has slightly shrunk away from the sides of the pan, and the loaf sounds hollow when thumped.

SERVING SUGGESTIONS Good bread can make any meal more satisfying. If you're trying to cut calories, you'd do better to trim portion sizes of meat or skip the butter or mayonnaise than to eliminate the bread. There's such an enormous range of breads to try—most of them low in fat—that this can be an excellent way to add variety to your meals.

When you're toasting bread for breakfast, go beyond the usual sliced supermarket bread. Sliced bagels and English muffins fit most toasters and are pleasingly dense and crunchy when toasted. Pumpernickel and rye bread also make good toast—tasty with low-fat cream cheese. Whole toasted pitas can be used like pizza or pastry crust, with sweet or savory toppings: Try sweetened cottage cheese with cinnamon and raisins for a breakfast "Danish," or try a savory spread of herbed cottage cheese. Generous slabs of French or Italian bread can be lightly browned in a toaster-oven and topped with slices of ripe pear and a sprinkling of Parmesan cheese. If you're accustomed to eating your toast with butter, try just a scraping rather than a whole pat; better yet, sample some fat-free spreads such as jam, jelly, honey, applesauce, all-fruit spread, apple butter, or prune butter. Make your own portable breakfast-on-a-bun as a healthier alternative to fast-food biscuit breakfasts (such biscuits are high in fat, and so is the sausage they usually contain). Warm or toast a small roll or bun and fill it with a scrambled egg (just the white, preferably) and a little shredded Cheddar cheese. Better still, grab a whole-grain roll along with a container of yogurt and a piece of fruit for a quick morning meal.

CHOOSING YOUR CRUST

Making bread at home not only gives you control over the ingredients you use, but also allows you to create the texture you desire. To many people, the crust is the best part of the bread, and it is easy to develop the crust to your liking, whether you prefer it crisp or soft.

Crisp: **Brush the tops of the loaves with water or egg white before baking. For a very crisp crust, brush before baking and several times during the first 15 minutes the bread is in the oven. Another trick is to put a pan of water in the oven prior to baking and keep it there during the first 10 minutes of cooking time. If you bake hearth breads on a baking stone, this will also produce a crisp crust.**

Glazed: **Before baking, brush the loaf with an egg wash—mix a whole egg or an egg yolk and a tablespoon of water or milk.**

Soft: **Brush the bread with melted butter as soon as it is done, then cover the loaf with a towel as it cools.**

At lunch time, the sandwich rules. Vary your bread choices here, too, and opt for low-fat spreads and fillings. Instead of butter, margarine, mayonnaise, or regular cream cheese, use jam or fruit spread, low-fat ricotta or cottage cheese, low-fat mayonnaise, or "light" cream cheese. Mustard, ketchup, chutney, and relish are all low-fat condiments; plain yogurt mixed with mustard and herbs can also stand in for mayonnaise. Favorite sandwich fillings such as bologna, salami, hamburger, peanut butter, ham and cheese, or tuna salad with mayonnaise are high in fat; satisfying alternatives include grilled vegetables, smoked turkey, well-seasoned bean spreads, tuna salad dressed with yogurt, or a bacon-less BLT with mustard. If cheese sandwiches are your favorite, make one with less than one ounce of cheese and fill out the sandwich with slices of apple, pear, tomatoes, or cucumber, or lettuce or sprouts. If you can't resist peanut butter, mix a teaspoonful with some large-curd cottage cheese instead of spreading 2 tablespoonsful on your sandwich; you'll keep your favorite flavor but get much less fat.

Pita bread can be filled with chick-pea salad or a salad of raw or cooked vegetables. Crusty rolls are good for an adaptation of the Provençal *pan bagnat,* which literally means "bathed bread": Halve the rolls, hollow them out slightly, then fill them with tuna, lettuce, sliced tomato, bell pepper, and cucumber. Drizzle the filling with a little vinaigrette and sprinkle with fresh basil or parsley. Press down on the filled roll, wrap it well and refrigerate it for several hours before serving.

Serve substantial whole-grain bread or rolls alongside a bowl of soup and a salad for a complete supper. Or include the bread *in* the soup or salad: Country-style vegetable soups can be thickened by adding crumbled bread (fresh or stale). Croutons—either bite-sized ones, or full-sized slices to float atop French onion soup—can be made by toasting bread cubes or slices in a toaster oven, rather than sautéing them in butter or oil. (For extra flavor, rub the bread with a cut garlic clove before toasting.) A Florentine salad called *panzanella* is a combination of tomatoes, red onion, basil, and cubes of sturdy bread that have been soaked in water and then squeezed dry; the salad is dressed with red-wine vinegar and olive oil.

If you end up with stale bread, don't throw it out; there are many uses for it. You can accumulate stale bread slices in the freezer and then, when you need breadcrumbs, process the frozen bread in a food processor or blender (or grate it by hand). Breadcrumbs also freeze well if kept in a tightly closed plastic bag. (If you need breadcrumbs quickly and there is no stale bread on hand, dry out fresh bread in a low oven and then process as above.) Breadcrumbs can be used to coat poultry or fish before baking, as a casserole or gratin topping, or for thickening sauces. Cubes of stale bread are fine to use for poultry, fish, or vegetable stuffings, as croutons in salad, or they can be used with sliced apples or pears for a Brown Betty.

BREAD, white 3½ oz (4 slices)

Calories	267	Fat	4 g
Protein	8 g	Saturated Fat	1 g
Carbohydrate	50 g	Cholesterol	0 mg
Dietary Fiber	Low	Sodium	538 mg

KEY NUTRIENTS		% RDA Men	% RDA Women
Calcium	108 mg	14%	14%
Folacin	34 mcg	17%	19%
Iron	3 mg	30%	20%
Manganese	0.4 mg	N/A	N/A
Niacin	4 mg	21%	27%
Phosphorus	94 mg	12%	12%
Riboflavin	0.3 mg	18%	23%
Thiamin	0.5 mg	33%	45%

S=40% or more soluble N/A=Not Applicable N=Not Available

BREAD, whole wheat 3½ oz (3½ slices)

Calories	246	Fat	4 g
Protein	10 g	Saturated Fat	1 g
Carbohydrate	46 g	Cholesterol	0 mg
Dietary Fiber	High	Sodium	627 mg

KEY NUTRIENTS		% RDA Men	% RDA Women
Vitamin B_6	0.2 mg	10%	13%
Copper	0.3 mg	N/A	N/A
Folacin	50 mcg	25%	28%
Iron	3 mg	30%	20%
Magnesium	86 mg	25%	31%
Manganese	3 mg	N/A	N/A
Niacin	4 mg	21%	27%
Phosphorus	220 mg	28%	28%
Riboflavin	0.2 mg	12%	15%
Thiamin	0.4 mg	27%	36%

S=40% or more soluble N/A=Not Applicable N=Not Available

Stale bread makes good French toast, which can be turned into a lowfat breakfast or dessert dish if you use just the egg white and some skim milk (flavored with cinnamon and vanilla extract) as the soaking liquid, and cook the toast in a non-stick skillet with little or no butter or oil. When quick breads are slightly stale, they can be sliced and toasted for breakfast. Crumbs of sweet quick breads can be sprinkled on fruit yogurt or applesauce for a simple dessert.

Cereals (Ready-to-Eat)

A bowl of cold cereal and milk is the fastest and, undoubtedly, the most popular American breakfast; in many households, it's also an afternoon or bedtime snack. As a cholesterol-conscious public has steered away from the old-fashioned breakfast of bacon, eggs, and flapjacks, cereals have come to the fore as the best alternative—do-it-yourself meals that are good choices nutritionally. Most cereals offer substantial levels of complex carbohydrates, provide fair quantities of protein, and, thanks to enrichment and fortification, supply good amounts of vitamins and minerals. Some are excellent sources of dietary fiber, furnishing up to 14 grams in just an ounce—about half the amount of dietary fiber experts recommend you consume daily. Despite all the nutrients found in cold cereals, however, you still must shop with care. Some cereals are loaded with sugar, others are made with lots of fat, and still others are laden with so much sodium that a 1-ounce serving may have more sodium than an ounce of potato chips.

Unlike other grain products, such as bread, noodles, and even porridge (the prototypical hot cereal), all of which were made thousands of years ago, cold cereals are a recent development. In 1894, Dr. John Harvey Kellogg, the manager of a health sanitarium in Battle Creek, Michigan, created a wheat-flake cereal as an alternative to traditional breakfast foods. A few years later, Kellogg experimented with corn flakes. By the early part of the twentieth century, Kellogg's Corn Flakes, Shredded Wheat, and a baked-wheat-and-barley mixture called Grape Nuts (invented by C.W. Post, who was a patient at the Battle Creek sanitarium) came to dominate the cold cereal market. By 1950, there were twenty-six brands of ready-to-eat cereals available; today, there are more than a hundred brands.

According to one survey, 49 percent of American adults say they usually eat cold cereal for breakfast.

Most ready-to-eat cereals are made from rice, wheat, corn, or oats, but some contain less-familiar grains, such as barley, amaranth, and quinoa. Usually the grains have been processed by one of several methods—exploded into puffs, pressed into flakes, shredded and spun into little biscuits, or extruded into some fanciful shape. The first step entails milling the grains into flour, either whole (with the bran and germ included) or refined. Water is added to make dough, which is shaped and then toasted or baked; flaked cereals are usually toasted, for example, while shredded wheat biscuits (which are formed from ribbons of dough) are baked. At various points in this process, cereal manufacturers may add sugar in one of its many forms (such as corn syrup or molasses), salt, preservatives, and, in enriched or fortified cereals, vitamins and minerals; many cereals are also supplemented with flavorings and such

COMPARING CEREALS 1 ounce dry

	Cups per ounce	Calories	Fat (g)	Total Carbohydrates (g)	Simple Carbohydrates (g)	Dietary Fiber (g)	Sodium (mg)
Amaranth flakes, *such as Health Valley*	½	90	1	20	N	3	5
Bran buds, *such as All-Bran*	⅓	70	1	22	5	10	260
Bran flakes, *such as Post*	⅔	90	0	23	5	5	210
Children's cereal, *such as Froot Loops*	1	110	1	25	13	1	125
Corn flakes, *such as Kellogg's*	1	110	0	24	2	1	290
Crisped rice, *such as Rice Krispies*	1	110	0	23	3	1	290
Nugget cereal, *such as Grape Nuts*	¼	110	0	23	3	3	170
Oat bran, *such as Cracklin' Oat Bran*	½	110	3	21	7	4	140
Psyllium cereal, *such as Fiberwise*	⅔	90	1	23	5	5	140
Puffed wheat	2⅓	103	<1	23	<1	2	1
Raisin bran, *such as Kellogg's*	¾	120	1	31	12	5	210
Shredded Wheat, *such as Nabisco*	⅔	90	0	23	0	3	0
Toasted O's, *such as Cheerios*	1¼	110	2	20	1	2	290
Wheat flakes, *such as Nutri-Grain*	⅔	100	0	24	2	3	170

N=Not Available

ingredients as nuts, raisins, and marshmallows.

Often a cereal's identity is pegged to one or more of these additives, such as sugar "frosting" on corn flakes or raisins in bran flakes. Here is a closer look at three elements that are commonly used in promoting many of today's cereals.

Enrichment and fortification Over 90 percent of the ready-to-eat cereals on the market today are enriched or fortified. *Enriched* means that thiamin, riboflavin, niacin, iron, and sometimes calcium are added to some milled grain products to approximate levels normally present in the grain before processing. A cereal labeled *fortified* can have any nutrient in any amount added to it, as long as those nutrients are listed on the label. Most cereals are fortified so that a single serving (usually an ounce) provides 10 to 25 percent of the U.S. RDA for the nutrient added. Some brands, however, supply 100 percent of the U.S. RDA for these nutrients in a single serving. While these super-fortified cereals don't pose any danger, you're wasting your money by paying their premium price. There's no reason to get 100 percent of any nutrient from a breakfast cereal or from any other single source: Except, perhaps, for iron, the nutrients added to cereal are readily available in other foods normally eaten during the day. (However, the iron in cereals may not be readily absorbed by the body.)

BREAKFAST AND PERFORMANCE

Researchers have never proved that routinely skipping breakfast is harmful to the health of adults. It is possible, however, that negative effects may be felt by those who normally eat in the morning, and then suddenly stop. Although there are no adequate studies on whether physical or mental performance is altered by omitting breakfast, there's considerable anecdotal material supporting the idea that children who do not eat breakfast have a decreased attention span.

The argument for having a good breakfast is based on the belief that the body needs refueling after about 12 hours of overnight fasting. Foods do affect blood-sugar (glucose) levels, but the links between blood sugar and performance, mood, and feelings of hunger and tiredness are not fully understood. In any case, the effect on glucose levels will depend on the specific food and the individual. Eating nutritious foods that satisfy you through the morning does make sense, however, particularly for children and adolescents.

High fiber Many people look to bran cereals for their daily fiber intake—and often they equate dietary fiber with wheat-bran cereals. It's true that wheat-bran cereals are an excellent source of insoluble fiber, the type that assists the passage of food through the digestive system, thereby helping to prevent constipation. Insoluble fiber has also been linked to the prevention of colon cancer and other bowel-related health problems. However, some cereals, particularly those that contain oats, rice, and barley, also supply soluble fiber, which may be effective in lowering blood cholesterol levels.

The fiber content of cereals ranges from less than a gram (in crisped rice) to 14 grams per serving (All-Bran with Extra Fiber). It's best to get fiber throughout the day from a variety of sources. But if you are not eating enough fruits, vegetables, and other grains, then, at least, have a high-fiber cereal for breakfast. As a general rule, high-fiber cereals offer 7 or more grams of fiber per ounce; 3 to 6 grams is considered a moderate amount of fiber.

At least two cereals on the market contain psyllium, a grain high in soluble fiber that is primarily used in over-the-counter bulk laxatives. Some consumer groups and state attorneys general have criticized its inclusion, saying that the grain makes the cereal a "drug" and warning about possible side effects. (The labels do carry a warning about possible allergic reactions to psyllium in sensitive people.) Meanwhile, one manufacturer has petitioned the FDA to classify psyllium as a GRAS (generally recognized as safe) component in cereals. In any case, psyllium is hardly a miracle fiber source. One of these brands contains 5 grams of dietary fiber per ounce, 3 grams of which are soluble; the other furnishes 11 grams, 3 grams of which are soluble.

Sweeteners Most commercial cereals are sweetened to varying degrees. Some manufacturers use plain sugar (sucrose), while others add brown sugar, honey, molasses, malt, corn syrup, or fructose in the form of dried fruits or fruit juice. All sweeteners provide empty calories (except for dried fruits, which can contribute some nutrients and fiber). There are many cold cereals that contain only a few grams of sugar per serving, but some sweetened brands, particularly those that have been designed to appeal to children, have more than 12 grams. Still other cereals are enhanced with artificial sweeteners, which supply fewer calories.

SHOPPING TIPS Since cereals usually keep well, and since most of them are stamped with a "best used before" date, selecting a fresh cereal is relatively straightforward. Deciding which cereal to choose on its nutritional merits is another matter entirely. Not only can the list of ingredients be lengthy, but the practice of using technical names (such as pyridoxine hydrochloride for vitamin B_6) for vitamins and minerals can be very confusing.

And most labels don't differentiate between the two types of fiber, soluble and insoluble. Nevertheless, if you keep your own special concerns in mind—which probably include more fiber and less salt, sugar, and fat—you can find what you want in a cereal. Below are a few guidelines to assist you in interpreting the complex nutritional information on a cereal box.

1. Make sure a grain is the first item on the ingredient list. Then you can be assured that the grain is the main ingredient. If it is identified as "whole," the cereal should be even more nutritious. And the shorter the ingredient list, the better.

2. Watch serving sizes when comparing cereals. Cereal manufacturers use 1 ounce as the standard serving size, but people usually eat more than that. Bear in mind that 1 ounce of puffed wheat or rice is about a cup (and supplies 50 calories), while 1 ounce of a dense cereal like granola may equal just 1/4 of a cup (and supplies 125 calories).

3. Look at the "Carbohydrate Information." This section may give you information on the complex carbohydrates, sugar, and fiber content. In general, the ratio of carbohydrates to protein should be about 8 to 1. If the cereal provides 30 grams of carbohydrates for every 2 grams of protein, you are probably getting too much added sugar.

4. If you are trying to reduce your sodium intake, look for a cereal containing little or no sodium. Most cold cereals contain 200 to 300 milligrams per serving, but there are some no-sodium cereals available. (An ounce of salted potato chips, by contrast, has about 130 milligrams of sodium.)

5. Check the label for fat content. Most cereals are low in fat, but be on the alert for the addition of oils, such as coconut or palm kernel (which are highly saturated), and for high-fat ingredients, such as nuts and seeds. Not only does fat increase the calorie content, but it can also offset the cholesterol-lowering benefit of any soluble fiber in the cereal. Granola cereals are almost always high in fat because they usually contain nuts, coconut, and coconut oil. Look for brands that are fat-free or make your own (see page 300).

6. Don't count on cereals to supply protein. Most cereals, even the high-protein kind, provide only 3 to 5 grams of protein per ounce. Simply adding a cup of milk offers at least twice as much protein as the cereal itself.

WHERE'S THE FRUIT?

Cereal ads and boxes show bowls of cereal overflowing with fruit or close-ups of fruit-filled spoonfuls of cereal. But when the fruit is added by the manufacturer, you may be getting more hype than fruit. According to the Center for Science in the Public Interest, one brand of fruit-containing cereal has just 1.3 ounces of fruit in an entire 14-ounce box. A study by the Connecticut Agricultural Experiment Station and the Connecticut Department of Consumer Protection found that the proportion of dried fruits by weight in cold cereals ranged from as little as 3 percent to 33 percent. Raisin bran cereals, for example, were found to have, on average, a raisin content of 22 percent—that's 3.3 ounces of raisins in a 15-ounce box of cereal, or less than a quarter of an ounce of fruit per 1-ounce serving. To benefit from the added fiber and nutrients in fruit, you'd be better off adding your own—dried or fresh—to your favorite cereal.

STORAGE Unopened, cold cereals can be stored for about a year in a cool, dry place. Once opened, they'll keep about three months. Just be sure to tightly seal the box's inner wrapping to prevent the cereal from turning soggy or stale.

Some cereals have BHA or BHT added to the packaging material. These additives—which must be indicated on the package if they are present—help to extend the shelf life of cereals by preventing the oils present in whole grains from turning rancid. Though both additives are on the FDA's GRAS list, questions about their safety have been raised, and they are being investigated. Their use is diminishing, and generally, they are not necessary if the cereal does not contain added fat.

SERVING SUGGESTIONS Perhaps you have a favorite cereal that you eat on a daily basis. For a change of flavor, liven it up with a second cereal—use two or three different kinds of flakes, or combine different puffed or waffled cereals. Or, mix textures: shredded and waffled cereals, flakes and nuggets, "o's" and puffs. Sprinkle toasted wheat germ over cereal for a nutritional boost and extra crunch.

Instead of regular low-fat or skim milk, flavor plain milk with vanilla, almond, or other flavoring extract, or try low-fat chocolate milk (or make your own with cocoa or syrup). Flavored yogurt, if briskly stirred, can also be poured over cereal (or add some cereal to a bowl of yogurt). Create a breakfast "parfait" by layering yogurt, fruit, and cereal in a tall glass or dessert goblet. Although the idea may initially sound odd, pour some fruit juice over a crisp cereal for a surprisingly tasty treat. Experiment with apple, pineapple, or white grape juice; the sweetness may even tempt kids away from heavily sugared cereals.

Fresh and dried fruits perk up a bowl of cereal while adding more fiber, vitamins, and minerals. Choose from among sliced bananas, peaches, or nectarines, chopped or grated apple or pear, whole or sliced berries, dark or golden raisins, or chopped dates, figs, or apricots. (Conversely, crushed cereal makes a delicious topping for a bowl of fresh or cooked fruits.)

Besides their premier role as a breakfast food, cereals can be used throughout the day as snacks and crunchy additions to a variety of recipes. Toss chunky cereal shapes with pretzel sticks and dried fruits for a low-fat trail mix or after-school nosh. Popular cereal-based party mixes, consisting of margarine, nuts, seasoned salt, and Worcestershire sauce, are filled with unnecessary fat and sodium; you can approximate their flavor with a homemade version, by combining cereal, pretzels, and flavorful (but low-sodium) seasonings, such as chili powder or curry powder. Puffed cereal, heated briefly in the oven and dusted with spices, can be served instead of popcorn, or combined with it.

Blend crushed cereal into muffin or waffle batter or cookie dough. Use crushed cereal in place of graham crackers or chocolate wafers when making cookie crusts for pies. (If you use a nonstick pan, you can substitute fruit juice for the melted butter and reduce fat even further.) Crushed nonsweet cereals are excellent for breading baked chicken or fish, or for topping casseroles. Sturdy cereals provide a healthy alternative to sautéed croutons.

For a finishing touch, sprinkle small nugget-type cereals or crushed flakes over puddings and frozen desserts.

Flour

Flour is a soft dry powder that is usually ground from grain, though it can also be made from vegetables, fruits, legumes, or nuts—even from fish. The primary use of flour is in baked goods, such as bread, cakes, and muffins, where it serves as the primary source of complex carbohydrates and nutrients. But flour plays other roles in cooking—it's used to thicken soups, stews, and gravies; meats are often coated with flour before sautéing or pan frying to help them brown better; and cake and muffin pans are floured before adding batter to prevent sticking.

For thousands of years, flour was milled by grinding kernels of grain between stones. Although you can still find stone-ground flour, today most flour is milled by the roller process, in which seeds are alternately put through a series of high-speed steel rollers and mesh sifters. The rollers crack the grain, allowing the endosperm (the largest part of the seed) to be separated from the bran and germ. The endosperm is then ground to the desired consistency. For whole-grain flours, the bran and germ are returned to the flour at the end of the process.

TYPES OF FLOURS Ideally suited for making bread and other baked goods, wheat flours are the most popular and familiar of all the different types of flours. Wheat is unique among the grains because it has the potential to produce gluten, a protein that gives dough its strength and elasticity and so is an important element in the texture of baked goods.

Most flours consist of a blend of hard and soft wheats, which affects a flour's gluten content: Hard wheats are higher in protein than soft wheats, and therefore produce more gluten. Because the production of flour isn't standardized, flours from two manufacturers may consist of different blends, which will produce varying results in the kitchen. For example, all-purpose flours sold in the southern region of the United States contain a higher proportion of soft wheat, good for making the light, airy biscuits that are popular there. In northern states, by contrast, the preference is for breads rather than biscuits, and the all-purpose flour used in bread-making contains a higher proportion of hard wheats.

Refined wheat flour

More than 90 percent of the wheat flour we eat is white, or refined, flour, which consists of only the ground endosperm of the wheat kernel. White flour is popular because it produces lighter baked goods than whole wheat flour and has an unequaled ability to produce gluten.

When the bran and germ are removed from the wheat kernel, twenty-two vitamins and minerals are decreased, along with dietary fiber. Therefore, thirty-five states require that white flour be enriched with iron and the B vitamins thiamin, riboflavin, and niacin. Some manufacturers add calcium and vitamin D as well. If a flour has been enriched, the label will say so.

There are many types of white flours:

All-purpose flour (also known as family, plain, white, or general-purpose flour) Made from a blend of hard and soft wheats, this type of flour has a "middle of the road" protein and starch content that makes it suitable for either breads or cakes and pastries. All-purpose flour is available presifted—that is, milled to a finer texture. This aerates the flour to make it lighter than standard all-purpose flour. However, all flour, whether labeled presifted or not, has a tendency to settle and become more compact in storage, so the benefit of presifting isn't always apparent.

Bleached flour When freshly milled, flour is slightly yellow. To whiten it, manufacturers either let the flour age naturally or speed up the process by adding chemicals (such as benzoyl peroxide or acetone peroxide) that bleach it. This process gives the flour more gluten-producing potential, but naturally aged flours develop more gluten as well.

Bread flour This is made entirely from hard wheat; a high gluten content helps bread rise quickly. (It's also available in whole wheat form.)

Bromated flour Some manufacturers add a maturing agent such as bromate to flour in order to further develop the gluten and to make the kneading of doughs easier. Other maturing agents include phosphate, ascorbic acid, and malted barley.

Cake flour Finer than all-purpose flour, cake flour is made entirely from soft wheat. Because of its low gluten content, it is especially well suited for soft-textured cakes and cookies.

Durum flour Since it has the highest protein content of any flour, durum flour can produce the most gluten. The dough made from it is frequently used for pasta.

Farina This granular product, milled from the endosperm of any wheat but durum wheat, is primarily used in breakfast cereals and pasta.

Gluten flour Made so that it has about twice the gluten strength of regular bread flour, this flour is used as a strengthening agent with other flours that are low in gluten-producing potential.

***Instant flour* (*instant-blending, quick-mixing, or granulated flour*)** Instant flour pours easily and mixes with liquids more quickly than other flours. It is used to thicken sauces and gravies, but is not appropriate for most baking because of its very fine, powdery texture and high starch content.

***Pastry flour* (*cookie or cracker flour*)** This flour has a gluten content slightly higher than cake flour but lower than all-purpose flour—making it well suited for fine, light-textured pastries.

Self-rising flour Soft wheat is used to make this flour, which contains salt, a leavening agent such as baking soda or baking powder, and an acid-releasing substance. However, the strength of the leavener in some flours deteriorates within two months, so it's important to purchase only as much as you need during that period. Self-rising flour should never be used in yeast-leavened baked goods.

Semolina This yellow granular product is ground from durum wheat. Its high protein content makes it ideally suited for making commercial pasta, and it can also be used to make bread.

Whole wheat flour

Since roller-milling separates the bran and the germ from the endosperm, the three components actually have to be reconstituted to produce whole wheat flour. (The germ and bran are visible in the flour as minute brown flecks.) Whole wheat flour is higher in fiber, vitamin E, some B vitamins and trace minerals, and protein than enriched white flour. You may also find it called graham flour in the supermarket.

Because of the presence of bran, which reduces gluten development, baked goods made from whole wheat flour are naturally heavier and denser than those made with white flour. Many bakers combine whole wheat and white flour in order to gain the attributes of both. Whole wheat pastry flour is also available.

When whole wheat flour is *stone-ground,* the kernels of wheat are crushed between two heavy, rotating stones, so that the bran and germ remain. Because oil in the germ is released during this process, stone-ground flour is more susceptible to rancidity. Nutritionally, there is no difference between stone-ground flour and roller-milled flour.

Non-wheat flours

Non-wheat flours have little or no gluten, so they need to be combined with wheat flours to produce well-leavened baked goods. Some manufacturers sell them premixed; otherwise, you have to mix them yourself. (As a starting point, mix one part non-wheat to four parts wheat flour.) Many of these flours are available in specialty and health-food stores.

Amaranth flour Milled from the seeds of the amaranth plant, this flour boasts a higher percentage of protein than most other grains, and it has more fiber than wheat and rice. It is also higher in lysine, which some food scientists believe makes it a more complete protein than flour made from other grains. Amaranth flour can be used in cookies, crackers, baking mixes, and cereals. However, it can be expensive and hard to find.

Arrowroot flour The roots of the tropical maranta plant are the source of this flour, often used as a thickener. It is almost entirely starch. Because of its easy digestibility, it is also an ingredient in biscuits for infants and young children.

Buckwheat flour A common ingredient in pancake mixes, buckwheat flour is also used to make Japanese *soba* noodles. It is available in light, medium, and dark varieties (the dark flour boasts the strongest flavor), depending on the kind of buckwheat it is milled from.

Cornmeal Ground from either yellow or white corn, cornmeal has a granular consistency. It is often sold de-germed in order to extend its shelf life, but you can find unbolted cornmeal, which

DEALING WITH BUGS IN FLOUR

Grain products in all stages of growth, processing, and packing are prey to beetles, moths, weevils, and their eggs. These insects are perfectly harmless—in fact, the FDA allows wheat flour to contain an average of fifty insect fragments per 50 grams (nearly 2 ounces). But even well beyond that level of contamination, the product isn't hazardous to your health. Its just not as pure as it might be, given modern processing methods. Of course, once infestation levels reach the point that bugs are clearly visible, most people won't want to eat the food, even though it poses no risk.

Infestation often occurs in the fields or in warehouses. Insects and their residues—including eggs—probably inhabit flour by the time it reaches your shelves. If you find evidence of insects in a new purchase, you can always take the flour back to the store for a refund. It might be easier, however, to simply sift or pick out any fragments.

However, bug problems can get out of hand, especially if grain products aren't stored properly. Follow these tips:

- **Store whole-grain flours in your freezer to prevent insect eggs from hatching.**
- **If you find evidence of bugs, remove the infested items from your home as soon as possible. If left in the kitchen garbage, the insects could contaminate other foods.**
- **Empty the cabinet and wash all surfaces with soap and water; pay special attention to cracks and crevices. Vacuum-clean the cabinet, if possible.**
- **Transfer other grains from the same cabinet to glass containers with tight-fitting lids. Watch these potential problem areas carefully.**
- **Continue to check for infestation. The bugs may reappear if you don't clean well enough. If you haven't seen anything for two months, your cabinet is probably insect-free.**

contains both the bran and germ. Cornmeal is widely used in breads, pancakes, and muffins. A coarsely ground cornmeal called *polenta* is used to make the Italian dish of the same name. Cornmeal from blue corn is popular in Southwestern cuisine. More finely ground cornmeal is called corn flour.

Oat flour Milled from either the entire oat kernel or the endosperm only, oat flour is frequently used in ready-to-eat breakfast cereals. You can make your own to use in baking by grinding rolled oats in a blender.

Potato flour (potato starch) Potatoes are first steamed, then dried and ground, to make this flour. It is used as both a sauce thickener and in bread, cakes, and pancakes.

Rye flour In combination with wheat flour, rye flour is most commonly used in breads. Light, medium, and dark varieties (with dark having the strongest flavor) are available. Light rye flour may be labeled "bolted," which means the flour has been sifted to remove the bran and germ. Dark rye flours are often unbolted, and so contain a good deal more fiber. There are no industry-wide standards for measuring bran in rye flours, so the amount varies among manufacturers.

Soy flour Defatted soybeans are ground to make a very high-protein flour, which can be used with wheat flour to greatly increase the protein content of baked goods.

Tapioca flour Milled from the dried starch of the cassava root, this flour forms a thick gel when heated with water and is often used to thicken puddings, fruit pies, and soups.

Triticale flour A hybrid of wheat and rye, triticale is higher in protein than other non-wheat flours but still needs to be combined with a wheat flour to produce a satisfying texture.

STORAGE TIPS Flour doesn't keep forever and is more susceptible to spoilage than you might think. If flour is stored improperly or for too long, it can develop an off flavor or give unpredictable results in baking. Flour can absorb moisture from the air. The fat from the germ in whole grain flours can go rancid with time.

White wheat flour, de-germed cornmeal, potato flour, arrowroot, and tapioca can be stored at room temperature for six to twelve months in a tightly covered container. Whole-grain flour keeps for less than a month at room temperature, so store it in a tightly covered container in the freezer; it will stay fresh for up to a year. You can use the flour directly from the freezer.

Pasta

Probably no food has undergone a greater transformation in the mind of the health-conscious public than pasta. For years Americans dismissed it as a fattening filler, a food that gave you calories and barely any nutrients. But, increasingly, pasta is regarded as an ideal basic food (a view that has been prevalent in other cultures for centuries). It is rich in complex carbohydrates, high in protein, low in fat, and not especially fattening. Easy to prepare, pasta is also one of the most diverse foods made from grains, available in hundreds of shapes and sizes, and used in hundreds of different dishes worldwide. Americans seem to be catching on to pasta's advantages: In the past decade, consumption of spaghetti and similar pastas generally identified with Italian names increased by almost 50 percent. These Western-style pastas are still the most familiar in the United States, but Americans are also discovering Asian pastas—the noodles and stuffed dumplings that have long been important in China, Japan, Korea, Vietnam, and other Asian countries.

All types of pasta have one thing in common: They are prepared from a dough, or paste (*pasta* means "paste" in Italian) that is made by mixing finely ground grain or flour with water. It may be hard to believe that such a simple food could be nutritious. Yet 82 percent of the calories in spaghetti and similar pastas come from complex carbohydrates; the remaining calories are mostly protein—enough so that 5 ounces of cooked spaghetti (about 1 cup) supply almost as much protein as a whole egg. Spaghetti-type pastas (which are made from refined wheat that has been enriched) also offer good levels of B vitamins and iron, contain no sodium, and furnish a fair amount of dietary fiber; pastas made from whole wheat are even better, providing more nutrients and 5 grams of dietary fiber in a 3½-ounce cooked serving (compared to 1.6 grams in the same amount of regular pasta).

A tablespoon of grated Parmesan cheese adds flavor to pasta, but only 25 calories and 2 grams of fat. It's fairly high in sodium, however, with a tablespoon providing nearly 100 milligrams.

As for the notion that pasta is fattening, consider that 3½ ounces of cooked spaghetti topped with a quarter cup of tomato or tomato-and-vegetable sauce has about 160 calories—about the same number as 3½ ounces of roasted, boneless chicken breast (without the skin), and nearly 60 fewer calories than 3½ ounces of select (the leanest cut) sirloin steak, trimmed and broiled. Both of these foods contain more fat than pasta, which is virtually fat-free. Pasta becomes a fattening food only when it is topped with lots of cheese or with high-fat, high-calorie sauces made with lav-

COMPARING PASTAS
3½ ounces cooked (¾ cup)

	Calories	Protein (g)	Iron (mg)	Thiamin (mg)	Niacin (mg)	Riboflavin (mg)	Phosphorus (mg)	Magnesium (mg)
Buckwheat noodles (soba)	99	5	1	0.1	1	0.03	25	9
Corn pasta	126	3	1	0.1	1	0.02	76	36
Egg Noodles	133	5	1	0.03	0.4	0.02	69	19
Fresh pasta	131	5	1	0.2	1	0.2	63	18
Somen	131	4	1	0.02	0.1	0.03	27	2
Spaghetti, enriched	141	5	1	0.2	2	0.1	54	18
Spaghetti, high protein	164	8	1	0.3	2	0.2	50	30
Spaghetti, spinach	130	5	1	0.1	2	0.1	108	62
Spaghetti, whole wheat	124	5	1	0.1	1	0.05	89	30

ish amounts of butter, oil, heavy cream, or meat.

Many of the names given to pasta shapes are Italian, but the Italians hardly have a monopoly on this food. Although the origin of pasta hasn't been established, the evidence indicates that various forms developed independently in many cultures. The Chinese may have eaten noodles as early as 5000 B.C. It is widely believed that Marco Polo brought pasta to Italy from the Far East in 1295, but if he did, it was probably to compare it to the pasta already there, since the Etruscans, who occupied part of what is now Italy, were making pasta as early as 400 B.C. The history of pasta in the United States is much clearer. Thomas Jefferson was the first to bring it to the New World, in the late 1700s, after tasting some during a visit to Naples while he was the American ambassador to France. The first pasta factory in the United States opened in 1848 in Brooklyn, New York, but pasta remained a relatively uncommon food until the late nineteenth century, when Italian immigrants introduced the dried wheat pastas that have since become the most popular type in this country.

FORMS OF PASTA Wheat is the principal ingredient for Western-style pastas, as well as for the most familiar types of Asian noodles sold here. But each group of pastas makes use of other ingredients and particular manufacturing methods to offer a range of options in flavor, texture, size, and nutritional content.

Western-style pastas

The pastas that we associate with Italy—among them spaghetti (from *spago,* or "strand"), rigatoni (from *rigati,* meaning "grooved"), vermicelli ("little worms"), and linguine ("little tongues")—are most commonly made from semolina. This granular product, milled from durum wheat, yields high-quality pasta with a golden color, mellow flavor, and sturdy texture. (Like white flour, semolina has had the bran and germ removed during milling.) Durum wheat is the hardest of all the wheats, meaning that it's highest in protein. Wheat doughs, when kneaded, develop gluten—a tough, elastic protein substance formed from other proteins in the wheat—and the harder a wheat is, the more gluten it will have. Dough made from semolina is high in gluten, which gives it the resiliency and strength to stand up to the mechanical pasta-making process and to hold its shape during cooking.

Most dried pastas are made from 100-percent semolina, but some manufacturers market versions that combine semolina with other wheat flours, such as farina, which is the coarsely ground endosperm of a wheat that is not as hard as durum. (Farina is a prime ingredient in many breakfast cereals.) When cooked, these combined-wheat pastas are whiter and softer than 100-percent semolina pasta.

Pasta makers use molds or dies to fashion the many different shapes that range from plain spaghetti to intricate cartwheels and bowties. Most Western pastas are classified according to whether they are long or short; round, tubular, or flat; smooth or ridged; solid or hollow. While some names for the various shapes are fairly standard, others are not, particularly in Italy, where one shape can come in several different sizes and have several different names.

Despite the various Italian names used to identify most of the shapes popular in the United States, the FDA legally defines all dried pasta as either macaroni or noodles.

Macaroni This designation is applied to an array of pasta shapes and sizes, whether strands (like spaghetti), tubes (like elbow macaroni, penne, and cannelloni), or shells (conchiglie), to mention just a few. Macaroni must be primarily composed of semolina, farina, and/or flour milled from durum wheat; these three components can be used separately or in any combination, along with water. Optional ingredients, such as egg whites, salt, or flavorings, are permitted. Some types of macaroni—spaghetti and vermicelli, for example—must also conform to certain size designations.

Noodles In addition to the guidelines set for macaroni, noodles must also contain no less than 5½ percent egg by weight. As a result, noodles have some fat and cholesterol. (Some manufacturers make noodles from egg whites, which have neither cholesterol nor fat.) The protein content of macaroni and noodles is about the same (when cooked). Although the egg in noodles adds protein, most of these noodles are prepared by combining semolina with softer wheats, such as farina, which have less protein than semolina.

Pasta is also available in less-standard forms that are finding their way onto supermarket shelves:

Corn and other flours Besides wheat, pastas can be made from corn, rice, and even vegetable starch. *Corn* pasta—which has about half the

PACKAGED PASTA SAUCES

Supermarkets carry a wide array of packaged pasta sauces—classic marinara in jars, "fresh" sauces in plastic cartons (refrigerated in the dairy section), crushed tomatoes or sauce in aseptic packages, dried sauces in envelopes, and ready-to-heat sauces in boilable or microwavable pouches. You'll find sauces containing meats, vegetables, and/or cheese, as well as cream sauces and pesto.

If you're looking for a healthful sauce, however, the manufacturers don't make it easy for you. The labels on most sauces don't provide nutritional data, but merely list the ingredients. If the first three items are cream, cheese, and oil, you can bet the product is high in fat (though some products are harder to judge). Some of the sauces derive close to 90 percent of their calories from fat; a single serving may supply as much fat as you should eat all day.

If you're following a low-salt diet, the sodium content of these sauces, obviously, is of concern—check not only for salt, but also for other sodium sources, such as monosodium glutamate, disodium phosphate, and sodium citrate, as well as for high-sodium cheeses. Since their recommended serving sizes are comparatively small, most of the sauces average 500 milligrams of sodium per serving. That amount may be acceptable if you're not sodium sensitive. Otherwise, look for brands labeled "no salt added." Many of the tomato-based sauces also contain some form of sugar—even the "no sugar added" varieties, which are usually sweetened with fructose (fruit sugar). This is not a drawback, but does add a few calories.

Spaghetti
Whole wheat spaghetti
Corn spaghetti
Amaranth spaghetti
Jerusalem artichoke spaghetti
Beet spaghetti
Red bell pepper and basil spaghetti
Fettuccine
Squid ink fettuccine
Linguine
Spinach linguine
Vermicelli
Capellini

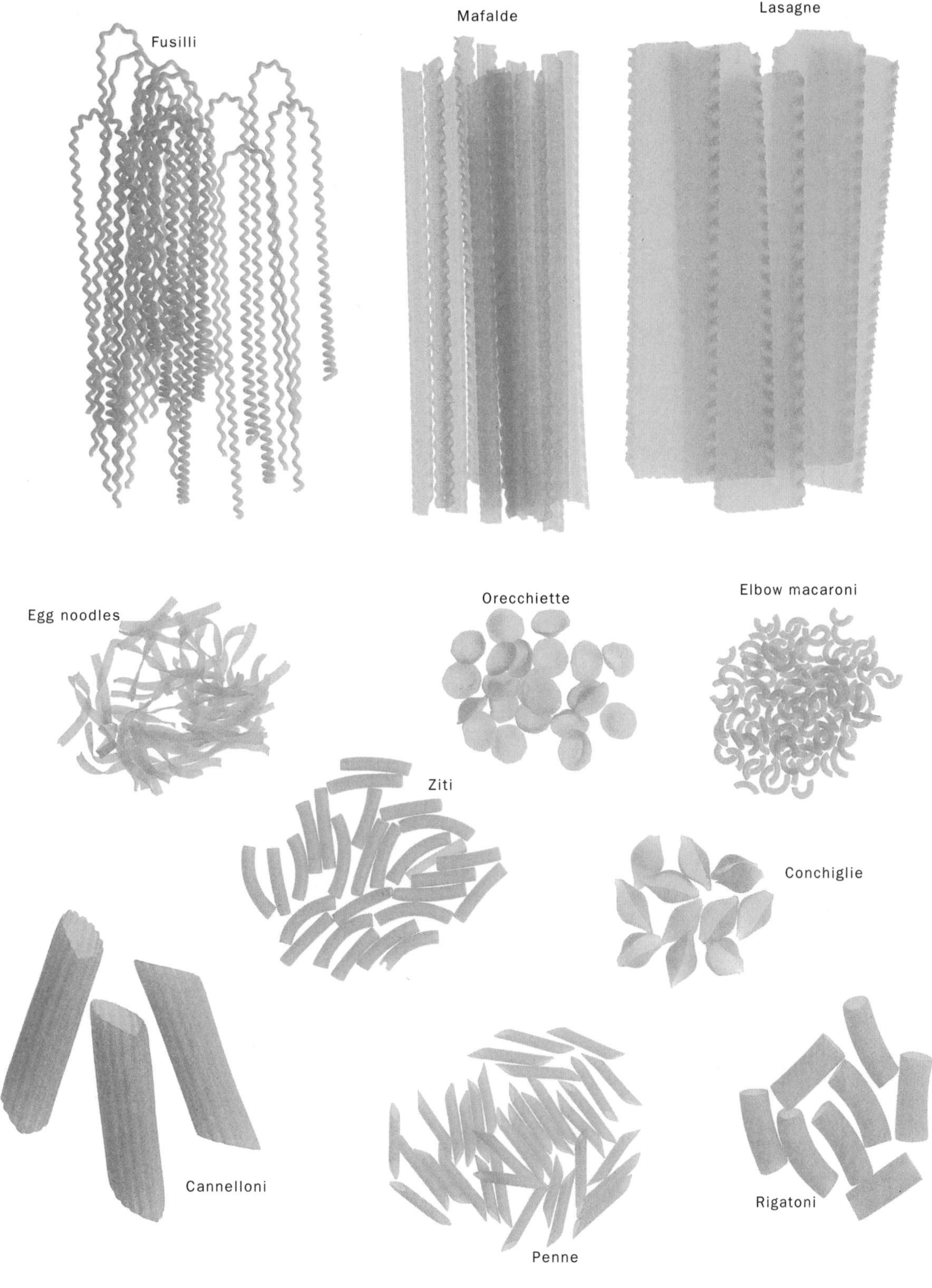
Fusilli
Mafalde
Lasagne
Egg noodles
Orecchiette
Elbow macaroni
Ziti
Conchiglie
Cannelloni
Penne
Rigatoni

COUSCOUS

Popular in northern Africa, couscous is made from semolina that has been precooked and then dried. It is different from both Western and Asian pastas; the tiny grains resemble rice or grits more than they do noodles. Couscous is not enriched, and so contains fewer B vitamins and iron than macaroni or noodles.

Unlike other pastas, which are cooked in large volumes of water, couscous (like rice) is cooked in a small amount of water so that all of it is absorbed. Quick-cooking ("instant") couscous is prepared by steeping it in boiling broth or water for 5 minutes. Regular couscous is first rinsed, then spread in a pan and left to plump for 10 minutes, and stirred and rubbed to break up any lumps. It is then steamed (traditionally, over the pot of stew with which it will be served), uncovered, for about 30 minutes. The grains are rinsed and rubbed again to separate them; another 30 minutes of steaming follows.

Couscous can be served as a "neutral" side dish with meat or poultry or as a bed for an elaborate stew that may contain meat, vegetables, dried fruits, chick-peas, nuts, and fragrant seasonings, including saffron, turmeric, ginger, and cinnamon. In Morocco, couscous is often partnered with a fiery hot condiment called harissa, made from chili peppers, olive oil, lemon juice, herbs and spices.

Couscous can be combined with cooked vegetables for a hot main dish, or used like bulgur (see Wheat, page 313) to make a salad with chopped vegetables and greens. Instant couscous can be quickly transformed into a breakfast cereal; cook in milk, sweeten, and serve with raisins or other dried fruits.

protein of regular pasta, but otherwise is nutritionally comparable—is a good alternative for people allergic to wheat. However, corn pasta deviates from the federal standards for macaroni and noodles, and consequently is labeled "substitute." Pastas made from other flours aren't usually free of wheat—for example, *amaranth* or *quinoa* are combined with whole wheat flour to produce a high-fiber pasta nutritionally similar to whole wheat pasta. When quinoa is used on its own, it yields a pasta slightly higher in protein. Also available is a pasta containing a mixture of wheat flour and flour from the *Jerusalem artichoke*, a tuber. The resulting product has a slightly higher protein content than semolina pasta.

Flavored pastas Some pastas are colored and flavored with vegetable pureés (such as spinach, tomatoes, or beets), that add visual appeal and a hint of flavor. Spinach pasta is higher in dietary fiber than plain semolina pasta. Pasta products can also be seasoned with saffron, garlic, pepper, or other herbs or spices.

Fresh pasta Made from durum or other types of wheat flour, water, and, usually, whole eggs, fresh pasta has a higher moisture content and softer consistency than dried. It is used mainly for dumplings, such as ravioli and tortellini, but also for spaghetti, fettuccine, and other shapes that are sold dried. Fresh pasta colored with vegetable purées is also available. When made with whole eggs, fresh pasta is slightly higher in fat than dried pasta and contains 66 milligrams of cholesterol per 6-ounce cooked serving. In addition, if it is stuffed with cheese or meat, as with ravioli or tortellini, fresh pasta can be high in fat and cholesterol; if it is stuffed with vegetables or seafood, the fat content is likely to be low.

High-protein pasta Enriched with soy flour, wheat germ, yeast, or dairy products, this type of pasta contains 20 to 100 percent more protein than standard pasta. Although it tastes like regular pasta, it may cook up stickier.

Whole wheat pasta Since this type of pasta is made from whole wheat flour or whole wheat durum flour, it is higher in nutrients than semolina pasta. As a result of enrichment, however, semolina pasta is higher in thiamin, riboflavin, niacin, and iron than whole wheat. But whole

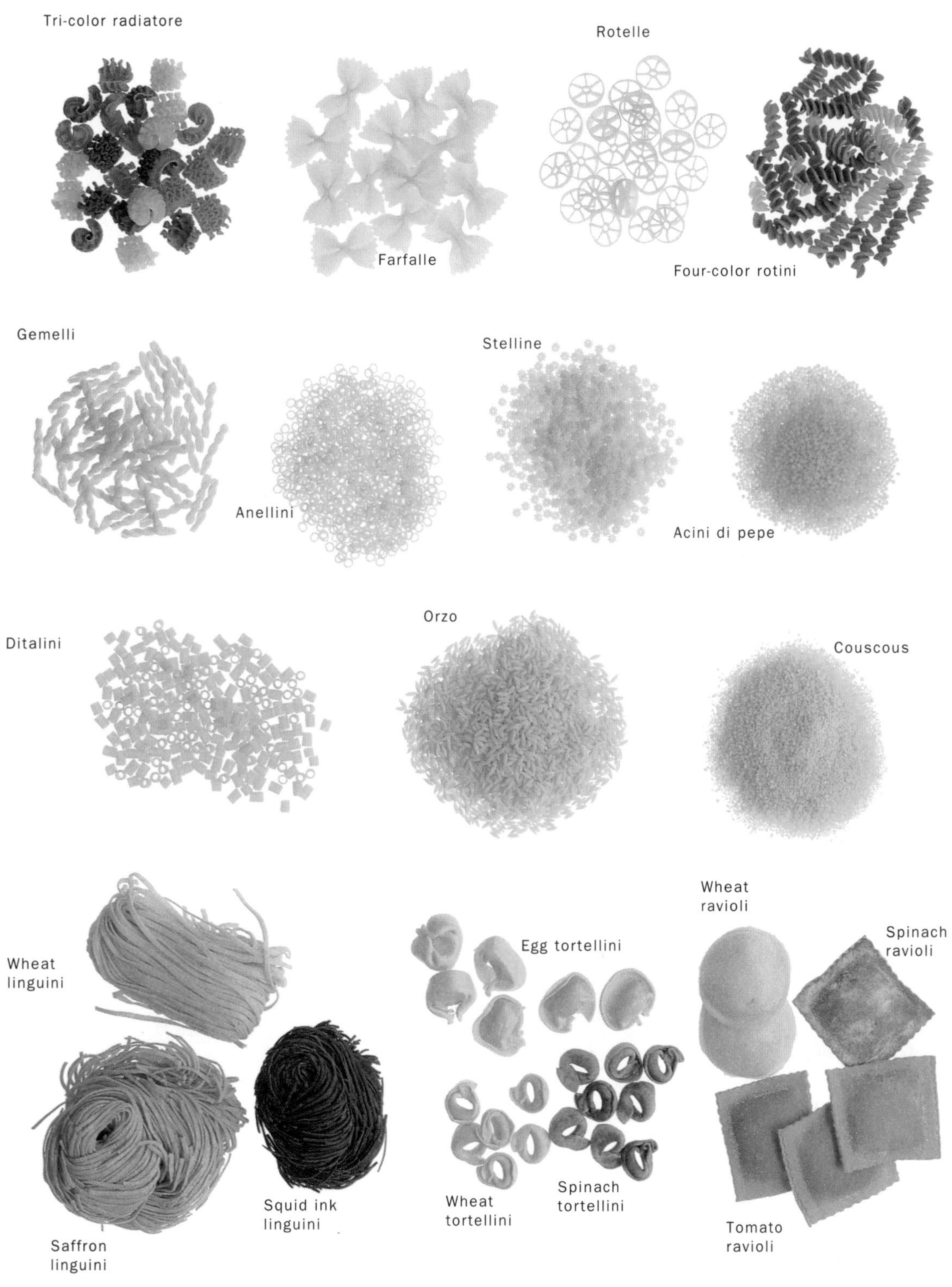
Tri-color radiatore
Rotelle
Farfalle
Four-color rotini
Gemelli
Stelline
Anellini
Acini di pepe
Orzo
Ditalini
Couscous
Wheat ravioli
Spinach ravioli
Egg tortellini
Wheat linguini
Squid ink linguini
Wheat tortellini
Spinach tortellini
Tomato ravioli
Saffron linguini

wheat pasta is a good source of these nutrients, and contains about five times the amount of fiber found in semolina (when comparing the two in their dried state). Moreover, whole wheat pasta is significantly higher in folacin, vitamin B_6, magnesium, phosphorus, potassium, zinc, and trace minerals, such as manganese and copper. Still, whole wheat pasta has a distinctive robust taste that takes getting used to, as well as a chewier texture than semolina pasta when cooked.

Asian noodles

Like Western pasta, the noodles that are an integral part of the national cuisine in Asian countries are used in a multitude of ways: served either as an accompaniment to meat and vegetable dishes, or, on their own, hot or cold, with toppings or dipping sauces; added to soups or salads; made into dumplings and pancakes; and prepared as stuffings. Whereas the majority of Western noodles are made from wheat, the most popular Asian noodles are prepared from a variety of flours. Since many Asian noodles do not include semolina, farina, durum flour, or eggs, they don't conform to government standards for macaroni or noodles and so may be called "alimentary paste" or "imitation noodles." The FDA has begun to allow Asian noodle manufacturers to label their product "Asian noodles." The basic noodle types are listed below, according to their major ingredients. Because of language differences and the many dialects in each language, there are numerous names for each type of noodle, and these are shown in the chart on page 342.

Bean thread noodles Made from mung bean flour, these semitranslucent noodles turn clear when cooked. They can be quickly stir-fried or braised with other ingredients. The noodles are nearly pure starch, containing almost no protein, vitamins, or minerals (other than iron).

Buckwheat noodles These flat, gray noodles, known in Japan as soba, are made from buckwheat and wheat flour, or just buckwheat flour. They are rich in protein. They may be served hot (usually in a broth) or chilled, accompanied by a dipping sauce. In Japan, soba are eaten for lunch or as a snack, and are essential to a traditional dish prepared at New Year's.

Egg noodles Like their American counterparts, Asian egg noodles are made with wheat and are available fresh and dried. These versatile noodles are added to soups, boiled and topped with meat or sesame sauce, or eaten cold with a dressing of oil, soy sauce, or sesame sauce. Fresh, they are also used to make wontons and egg rolls.

Rice noodles Dried rice noodles, which are usually sold coiled in plastic bags, are either thread-thin or spaghettilike. Typically, they are boiled or stir-fried for use in salads or soups. Fresh rice noodles, a standard feature of the Chinese brunch called dim sum, are sold in wide sheets, for making dumplinglike dishes, or cut into ¾-inch-wide ribbons. They are precooked and are ready to eat once boiling water is poured over them. Like bean threads, rice noodles are almost pure starch and low in protein.

Japanese *ramen* (wheat noodles), when packaged as an instant-soup "lunch in a mug," are precooked by steaming and then dried by deep-frying, leaving them with a residue of about 18 percent oil by weight. The fat used is often highly saturated lard or palm oil. Another drawback is the high sodium content of the seasoning packet that comes with *ramen*.

Wheat noodles Non-egg wheat noodles come in a variety of shapes, thicknesses, and colors, and are sold fresh or dried. Their nutritional value is close to that of Western-style wheat pasta, except that the sodium content may be higher. Two types are especially popular: Udon, usually served in broth, are thick and chewy; somen, most often eaten cold, are very thin and fine. Wheat noodles are used in lo mein and chow mein dishes.

SHOPPING TIPS It is difficult to tell when a particular batch of dried pasta was made (though some packages are stamped with "sell by" dates).

Wheat-egg noodles
Wonton wrappers
Fresh rice noodles
Soba
Bean-thread noodles
Whole wheat udon
Somen
Rice sticks
Rice vermicelli
Thin egg noodles
Wheat noodles

NAMES FOR ASIAN NOODLES

	Chinese	Japanese	Korean	Vietnamese
Bean thread noodles	fen si; fun sie	sarifun; harusame	dang myun	bun tau
Buckwheat noodles	qiao mian	soba	naeng myun	
Egg/wheat noodles	dan mian; don mein			
Rice noodles	sha he fen; sa ho fun; gan he fen; gon ho fun			uot; banh pho
Wheat noodles	gan mian; sun mian	somen; udon; ramen	mil gougsou	mi soi

Luckily, dried pasta keeps almost indefinitely, so "freshness" isn't a particular concern. Just be sure that the package is intact and hasn't been exposed to water, and that the pasta inside is not broken.

Fresh pasta—regular or Asian—is perishable, however, and should be displayed in a refrigerated case or in a freezer. Buy it from a shop with a high turnover; if it is packaged, check the "sell-by" date. Keep in mind, too, that a pound of fresh pasta won't serve as many people as a pound of dried (since the fresh absorbs much less water during cooking).

Most supermarkets routinely stock 20 to 30 pasta shapes, which may seem like more than enough. But the Italians have created over 600 pasta shapes, and 150 of them are available in the United States, mostly in speciality and gourmet food shops.

STORAGE Store dried pasta in a cool, dry place and it will keep for many months. As an extra precaution, remove the pasta from its original package and place it in an airtight container.

Store fresh pasta tightly wrapped in plastic wrap; it will keep for a week in the refrigerator or a month in the freezer. Fresh Asian noodles will keep for a day or two under refrigeration, or for three months in the freezer, if tightly wrapped. Fresh rice noodles become stiff when cold, so they are often sold at room temperature and will keep for a day or two; refrigerated, they can last for up to a week.

Leftover cooked pasta will keep for a day or two if refrigerated; dress it lightly with oil to prevent clumping. To serve hot, add to boiling water for 30 seconds and drain or reheat in a microwave oven; place the pasta on a platter or in a casserole dish and cover with vented plastic wrap before you heat it.

PREPARATION Both Western and most Asian pastas should be cooked in boiling water, which softens and properly hydrates them. Since pasta is cooked in more water than it absorbs during cooking, some of the water-soluble B vitamins added during the enrichment of the semolina are lost. Still, one study found that one-half to three-fourths of the B vitamins in pasta are retained during cooking.

Cooking pasta is not difficult but does require attention. The two main rules for perfect pasta are: Use plenty of water and don't overcook. Lots of water helps the pasta cook evenly and prevents clumping and sticking. Pasta is best when it is cooked to the "al dente" stage—tender but firm to the bite. Mushy pasta has been overcooked.

Choose a sufficiently large pot—one that can comfortably hold 4 quarts of water per pound of pasta. Lots of water prevents the pasta from sticking, making it unnecessary to add oil. Many recipes suggest adding salt, but doing so increases the sodium content. And, if you eliminate it, the pasta won't be affected. In fact, you'll probably find that you don't miss the salt. To add flavor, squeeze some fresh lemon juice into the water just before you add the pasta.

When the water reaches a rolling boil, uncover the pot and add the pasta in small batches to keep the water boiling steadily. Boil, uncovered, stirring occasionally with a fork to separate the pieces. The cooking time depends on the type of pasta and its shape or thickness. Package directions are generally accurate if you're cooking the whole package at once but often overestimate the time for smaller amounts. Begin checking the pasta about halfway through the recommended cooking time. Remove a piece from the pot, run it under cool water, and bite it. If it's still hard and white in the middle, continue cooking. If it's almost cooked through, taste another sample in 45 seconds. The pasta is done when it is translucent in the center and no longer hard, but still firm. (Pasta that is to be baked, stir-fried, used in soups or stews, or cooked further in some other way should be undercooked slightly.)

Drain the pasta immediately in a colander. Shake the colander gently to remove as much water as possible. Do not rinse pasta unless you are going to serve it cold, as in a salad, or you need to handle it, as with lasagna or manicotti. Rinsing pasta removes more water-soluble B vitamins, and simply makes the pasta cold.

Place the drained pasta in a warm bowl and toss lightly with a small amount of sauce or oil. Once it's been transferred to plates, add more sauce, if you wish.

Fresh pasta, corn pasta, and pastas made from a combination of wheat and other grains are cooked in the same manner as dried semolina pasta. However, they require less cooking time and will quickly go from tender-firm to soft and gummy. Begin checking fresh pasta after a minute of cooking, corn pastas and wheat/grain combinations after 2 minutes.

Fresh and dried Asian noodles, whether wheat, wheat-and-egg, or buckwheat, are cooked in the same way as other pastas. Special care must be taken to stir the noodles after they have been added to the water to prevent clumping. Thin fresh noodles will cook in about 30 seconds; dried noodles will take anywhere from 2 to 20 minutes, depending on thickness.

Both rice noodles and bean threads in all their forms have been cooked during the manufacturing process, so they need to be only briefly heated before serving. The flavor and texture of dried rice noodles benefit from soaking before use in recipes. Soak the noodles for 15 or 20 minutes in hot water, then quickly rinse them to wash away excess starch, which would otherwise turn clear soups cloudy. (Since they aren't enriched, you don't have to worry about losing water-soluble nutrients.) Boil the noodles for 2 to 10 minutes, depending on thickness. Thin rice noodles can also be stir-fried directly after soaking. Bean threads require 10 to 30 minutes of presoaking. Thin noodles can be added immediately to soups or stir-fries; thicker noodles must be boiled for about 5 minutes. Bean threads are done when they turn perfectly clear.

SERVING SUGGESTIONS Whether you're satisfied with the basics (spaghetti with red sauce and a sprinkling of cheese) or seek more exotic combinations (soba noodles with stir-fried shiitake mushrooms), you'll find pastas to keep you happy for many, many meals.

PASTA YIELDS

The label on most packages lists 2 ounces of dry pasta as the serving size, but this amount is more suitable as an appetizer than as a main dish. If pasta is the centerpiece of your meal, 4 ounces of dry pasta is a more reasonable serving size. Keeping that in mind, the chart below shows cooked yields for different pasta shapes.

	Dry measure	Cooked yield
Spaghetti	2 ounces	1 cup
	1 pound	8 cups
Elbows	½ cup (2 ounces)	1 cup
	1 cup (3½ ounces)	1¾ cups
Orzo	½ cup (3 ounces)	1½ cups
	2½ cups (1 pound)	6½ cups
Egg noodles	1⅓ cups (2 ounces)	1½ cups
Fresh pasta	3 ounces	1 cup

Most Americans associate "tomato sauce" with Italian pastas. Although the first tomato sauces originated in southern Italy, they have come to be identified with the whole country. Tomato sauce lends itself to many variations. A homemade version can be quickly prepared; it doesn't need to simmer on the stove top all day. Cook some chopped onions and garlic in a little broth until softened, then add chopped fresh tomatoes or canned plum tomatoes, tomato paste, and/or tomato purée. If you prefer a more intense flavor, use sun-dried tomatoes. Season with black pepper, oregano, basil, and a pinch of sugar, if necessary; add salt if you're not watching your sodium intake. Enhance the sauce with sliced mushrooms, chopped bell peppers, hot peppers, or black olives. Or, add cooked (fresh or frozen) vegetables to the sauce shortly before serving; try chopped broccoli or spinach, or diced zucchini or carrots. Cook until the flavors are well blended. If you are fond of meat sauce, add a small portion of browned lean ground beef or ground turkey, or serve the sauced pasta with meatballs made of lean ground beef or turkey.

In the summer, a fresh, uncooked tomato sauce is always satisfying. Just toss hot, cooked pasta with chopped ripe tomatoes, fresh basil, and a little olive oil; to vary the basic recipe, experiment with other herbs and vegetables. Serve the dish hot or at room temperature.

Cream and cheese sauces make luscious toppings for pasta, but they should be saved for special occasions since their fat content can be astronomical. Fettuccine Alfredo is one of the most popular cream-sauced pastas, but the amounts of butter and heavy cream in traditional recipes contribute substantial fat and calories. You can make a similar sauce with much less fat and cholesterol by substituting puréed cottage cheese for the cream and butter; then flavor it with a sprinkling of grated Parmesan cheese, black pepper, and some dried basil. If the sauce is too thick, add a little pasta cooking water or chicken broth. For a garlicky sauce, toss some garlic cloves into the pot with the water for boiling the pasta. When the pasta is done, fish out the garlic, squeeze it from its skin, and mash it into the puréed cheese. Toss hot, well-drained fettuccine with the sauce.

Don't confuse the crispy "chow mein noodles" sold in cans with the spaghetti-like wheat noodles used in the restaurant dish called chow mein. The canned noodles are fried in hydrogenated vegetable oil; they contain 237 calories and 14 grams of fat per cup (about an ounce and a half).

Macaroni and cheese is another favorite pasta dish that can benefit from some judicious fat cutting. If you are planning to use a sharp cheese, such as well-aged Cheddar, reduce the amount given in the recipe. Low-fat cottage cheese can replace the white sauce that is often mixed into baked macaroni: Purée the cottage cheese and add a little mustard (its flavor underscores that of the sharp Cheddar). Thin the cheese purée with low-fat yogurt or low-fat sour cream, if necessary, to create a sauce. Stir shredded Cheddar or another favorite cheese into the sauce—try half of the amount called for in a standard recipe. The sharper the cheese, the less you need. A low-fat sauce can also be made with evaporated skim milk, which is as thick as cream. For variety and extra nutritional value, combine cooked cauliflower or broccoli florets or other vegetables with the macaroni before baking.

The fat content of baked pasta dishes, such as lasagna and manicotti, can be trimmed by using part-skim ricotta and part-skim mozzarella. (There are non-fat versions of both these cheeses available in some parts of the country.) Or, consider pot-style or dry-curd cottage cheese, which is low in fat and works well in such dishes. In meat-filled baked pastas, substitute cooked ground skinless turkey for ground beef or pork.

A great favorite with many pasta lovers is pesto, a paste of olive oil, pine nuts, Parmesan cheese, and basil. Its rich flavor can be approximated by

MATCHING SHAPES TO SAUCES

There are no strict rules governing the choice of a sauce to accompany a specific pasta shape. But you'll find through trial and error that certain sauces go best with particular shapes or weights of pasta. Here are some suggested partnerings:

- **In general, serve long, solid pastas, such as spaghetti and linguine, with tomato or seafood sauces or a very light cream sauce.**
- **Hollow or notched pastas, such as shells, elbows, ziti, rigatoni, or fusilli, are designed to trap sauce, so use meat, vegetable, or other chunky sauces.**
- **Thick noodles, such as fettuccine, work well with creamy sauces, as do some short pastas, like rotini (spirals).**
- **Manicotti and jumbo shells can be stuffed with low-fat cheese or vegetables and then baked with tomato or meat sauce.**
- **Small pasta shapes, such as alphabets, stars, acini di pepe, and orzo, are best in broths and soups; orzo can be cooked like rice, or added to rice.**
- **Fresh pastas will absorb more sauce than dried, so choose light sauces, such as a tomato-based primavera.**
- **Short, hearty shapes, such as ziti, penne, fusilli, and radiatore (also called ruffles or nuggets), are ideal for pasta salad. They hold their shape during cooking, provide bite and texture to the dish, and won't be overwhelmed by the dressing.**

combining cottage cheese (and garlic, if you like) with lots of fresh basil; process to a smooth purée in a food processor or blender. For a truer pesto flavor, add a little olive or walnut oil or a few pine nuts or walnuts. You can produce variations on pesto with other herbs, such as parsley or cilantro. Toss a few spoonfuls of pesto with hot pasta just before serving.

Pasta goes well with a variety of vegetables and legumes. Along with a light sauce, toss pasta with strips of roasted eggplant or bell pepper; broiled button or wild mushrooms; quartered artichoke hearts; or steamed zucchini cut into julienne strips. Or, use steamed or sautéed greens, particularly strongly flavored ones, such as arugula, escarole, or broccoli raab, with hot pasta. For a delicious main course that is both nutritious and attractive, prepare pasta primavera. The dish combines pasta with an assortment of lightly cooked fresh vegetables, such as green peas, snow peas or sugar snaps, broccoli, carrots, or asparagus. Although pasta primavera is sometimes made with a rich cream sauce, you can readily substitute a marinara sauce or the lightened versions of pesto or Alfredo sauce described above.

When you eat pasta together with legumes, such as beans or lentils, you get complete protein and a satisfying meal. Add pasta to bean soups—for a simple version of the Italian classic *pasta e fagioli*—or create a sauce of whole and puréed chick-peas, lentils, cannellini, or fava beans.

Pasta gives body and texture to both thick soups and simple broths. Add tiny pasta shapes, such as fine egg noodles, stelline or pastina, or broken pieces of spaghetti or capellini, to clear broths. Stuffed pastas, such as ravioli, tortellini, or agnolotti, can be served in beef or chicken broth for a light meal. Medium-sized pasta shapes, such as elbows, shells, or ditalini, are preferred for heartier vegetable or tomato soups, stews, and chowders. To keep the pasta from overcooking in the soup, partially cook the pasta first in water, then add it to the soup and simmer for just a few minutes before serving.

Pasta salads have an ever-growing following. You can concoct hundreds of tempting, low-fat pasta main dishes by combining cooled pasta with raw or cooked vegetables; lean meat, poultry, or seafood; beans or chick-peas; and a light dressing. Chunky pasta shapes, such as radiatore, rotini, cavatelli, and medium shells, work well in salads. Use freshly blanched, steamed, or grilled vegetables, or any cooked vegetables you happen to have on hand (or can pick up at the salad bar). Add strips of skinless chicken or turkey, canned tuna or salmon, or cooked shrimp. Try some of the dressing ideas described on page 113, or use a low-fat bottled dressing. That picnic classic, macaroni salad—perhaps the original American pasta salad—can be lightened with a low-fat mayonnaise or yogurt dressing. For extra flavor in pasta salads (or for a simple pasta side dish) add garlic, herbs, and a squeeze of lemon juice to the cooking water before adding the pasta.

THE SHAPE OF PASTA

Commercial pasta is produced by mixing enriched semolina and sometimes other hard wheat flours with a small amount of water to form a stiff dough, which is mechanically kneaded to form gluten—a type of protein that gives dough its form and strength. The dough is then forced through dies—metal plates with variously shaped holes drilled into them. Long, solid pastas, such as spaghetti or linguine, are pushed through dies with round or oval holes. Hollow pastas are extruded through dies with pins in the center of the holes. Elbow macaroni is shaped by a die with a notched pin, which forces the dough to pass through more quickly on one side, causing the pasta rods to curve.

The die also affects the pasta's texture and appearance. Teflon-lined dies, popular in the United States, result in a smooth, polished pasta with a high yellow color. Imported pastas usually go through brass dies, which yield a rougher texture and whiter color. (Egg noodles, on the other hand, are rolled by machine into thin sheets that are mechanically sliced to the desired length and thickness.) Once the pasta is shaped, mechanical knives cut it into the appropriate lengths. The pasta is then carefully dried on racks or, with short pastas such as elbow macaroni, on conveyor belts.

Asian noodles are often served like Western-style noodles: hot, with sauce; cold, with a sauce or dressing; or in soup. For a dish that's not strictly authentic but does boast Asian flavors, combine Asian noodles with stir-fried vegetables that have been seasoned with soy sauce, ginger, garlic, and hot peppers. Add noodles to miso broth, or to chicken broth flavored with ginger.

Szechuan cold noodles are probably the best-known Asian pasta preparation. This popular restaurant dish can be made with Chinese egg noodles or Japanese buckwheat noodles (soba); its pungent sauce is based on sesame paste or peanut butter. Unfortunately, it is likely to be high in fat. You can whip up a similar sauce at home by blending peanut butter, soy sauce, sesame oil, and chicken broth; experiment with different proportions and opt for the one with the least possible fat. Toss a small amount of the sauce with a generous portion of cooked noodles and serve well chilled, with a sprinkling of fresh cilantro leaves and chopped scallions.

Cellophane noodles provide interesting texture when mixed into salads with cooked vegetables, well-seasoned beef or chicken strips, fresh herbs, and a lime vinaigrette. These glassy noodles also make wonderful additions to broth.

BUCKWHEAT NOODLES 3½ oz cooked (1 cup)

Calories	99	Fat	<1 g
Protein	5 g	Saturated Fat	<1 g
Carbohydrate	21 g	Cholesterol	0 mg
Dietary Fiber	N	Sodium	60 mg

KEY NUTRIENTS		%RDA Men	%RDA Women
Manganese	0.4 mg	N/A	N/A

S=40% or more soluble N/A=Not Applicable N=Not Available

SPAGHETTI, enriched 3½ oz cooked (¾ cup)

Calories	141	Fat	<1 g
Protein	5 g	Saturated Fat	<1 g
Carbohydrate	28 g	Cholesterol	0 mg
Dietary Fiber	Low	Sodium	1 mg

KEY NUTRIENTS		%RDA Men	%RDA Women
Iron	1 mg	10%	6%
Manganese	0.3 mg	N/A	N/A
Niacin	2 mg	11%	13%
Thiamin	0.2 mg	13%	18%

S=40% or more soluble N/A=Not Applicable N=Not Available

Chapter 6

LEGUMES, NUTS, AND SEEDS

The dried beans and peas collectively called legumes, and the dried fruits that constitute nuts, are all storehouses of concentrated nutrients, especially protein—in fact, they have more protein than any other vegetable food. Although the protein is incomplete (being deficient in one or more amino acids), this problem is easily overcome when they are served with complementary foods, such as grains. Their rich nutritional endowment can be attributed to the fact that legumes and nuts are seeds; that is, they contain within their small pods or shells the means to reproduce themselves, along with enough nutrients to sustain the new plants until they can draw nutrients from the soil.

These two foods, however, have very different roles to play in a healthful diet. Nuts are a nourishing snack food with one significant drawback—they are very high in fat, as are most other seeds. Hence, their contribution to a diet should be a modest one. Legumes, on the other hand, are low in fat, inexpensive, and versatile (they can be used in a variety of interesting dishes). Consequently, they deserve to be a culinary mainstay. For years, many Americans have shied away from legumes, in the belief that they have no value other than as starchy "fillers," or that they cause gas, or that they take too long to prepare. But more and more people have begun to sample these pod-borne vegetables, and they are discovering that any problems associated with legumes are either untrue or exaggerated—and that this food, which was once looked down upon as "poor man's meat," is actually an ideal alternative to meat and other fatty sources of protein.

Legumes

By far the best plant source of protein, legumes are edible seeds enclosed in pods. Although they all belong to a single plant family (called Leguminosae), legumes come in a myriad of forms. The pods may grow on short, erect plants (as soybeans do), on climbing vines (like lima beans), or on trees (for example, carob beans). Sweet clover—the flower generally used in commercial honey production—is a legume, too. Some legumes, such as lima beans and peas, are eaten both fresh and dried; others, such as mung beans, are most commonly consumed as sprouts. Another legume, the peanut, is eaten as a nut (see page 362). Carob beans are made into a cocoa substitute, and both carob and guar beans serve as thickeners in food processing. Fenugreek seeds are often ground and blended into spices (it's one of the dominant flavors in curry powder). Alfalfa and jack beans are valued as animal fodder. Though mesquite, a leguminous shrub that grows in the American Southwest, is best known as a barbecue fuel, its seeds are edible.

Beans are a boon to diabetics. Because these nutritious seeds are digested slowly, they cause a gentle rise in blood sugar. As a result, diabetics who eat a substantial amount of beans require less insulin to control their blood sugar.

This entry will cover only those legumes we eat as mature, dried seeds—namely, beans, dried peas, and lentils. Archaeological evidence shows that these legumes are among the oldest agricultural crops, dating back perhaps ten thousand years. They have been found in Egyptian tombs and are frequently referred to in the Bible. (The "mess of pottage" for which Esau sold his birthright to Jacob was a dish of lentils.) Beyond their worldwide use as food, legumes have an important agricultural value; they produce nitrogen as they grow, and so play an active role (with grains, which deplete the nitrogen in the soil) in crop rotation programs.

In the United States, dried peas and lentils are grown only in a region called the Palouse, centered in eastern Washington and northwestern Idaho. Michigan is the leading state in the production of most other dried beans, except for dried lima beans, which come from California. The United States exports legumes to India, South America, and Europe.

If you enjoy canned baked beans, opt for a vegetarian version—less than 1 percent of the calories will come from fat. Baked beans with franks are the worst fat offenders, deriving 42 percent of their calories from fat. Baked beans with pork would be a better choice, with 13 percent of their calories coming from fat.

In addition to protein, legumes are well stocked with energy-giving complex carbohydrates, B vitamins, zinc, potassium, magnesium, calcium, and iron. But it is the protein content of these pod-borne seeds that stands out: On average, legumes contain about 22 percent protein by dry weight, more than any other plant food. And the protein comes in a package that is relatively low in calories, cholesterol-free, virtually fat-free, and generally high in dietary fiber.

Although the protein in most legumes, like that in all vegetable products, is incomplete, this deficiency can be easily overcome by serving them with rice (or other grains), nuts, or a small amount of an animal product, such as poultry, fish, egg white, or low-fat yogurt. These foods complete the protein in legumes by providing complementary amino acids.

The one bean that doesn't require a complement is the soybean, which contains the most protein of any legume, and is the only vegetable food whose protein is complete. However, soybeans are high in fat. The fat is mostly unsaturated, but it contributes about 47 percent of soybeans' calories.

To see how notable a protein source legumes are, compare 3½ ounces of cooked kidney beans with the equivalent serving of broiled sirloin (Choice grade). The beans offer 9 grams of protein, yet do not contain any fat or cholesterol. The beef supplies about 30 grams of protein, but with the protein come 9 grams of fat (about one third of that is saturated fat) and about 90 milligrams of cholesterol.

Despite the long cooking time required for some legumes, you needn't worry about nutrient loss. Analysis by the USDA has found that beans requiring up to 75 minutes of cooking retained from 70 to 90 percent of most vitamins and minerals. The B vitamins and folacin were most affected by cooking: Beans retain about 65 and 50 percent, respectively, of these water-soluble vitamins.

Beans are also a good source of iron. A cup of most cooked legumes supplies about 25 percent of the RDA of iron for women, 40 percent for men. Of course, the iron in legumes, like that in all non-animal foods, is nonheme iron, which the body does not absorb as well as the heme iron in beef or other animal foods. By consuming foods rich in vitamin C (such as tomatoes or red bell peppers) along with beans you increase the absorbability of the iron.

Legumes are second only to wheat bran as the best plant source of dietary fiber, containing about 9 grams of fiber per cup, cooked. Both types of fiber, soluble and insoluble, are present: The former has been shown to help lower blood cholesterol levels and control blood sugar; the latter increases stool bulk, alleviates some digestive disorders, and may help to prevent colon cancer. Black, navy, and kidney beans are among the highest in fiber.

Ounce for ounce, cooked beans provide almost as much calcium as milk: Skim milk supplies 38 milligrams of calcium per ounce, cooked white beans offer 26 milligrams per ounce, and soybeans provide 29 milligrams per ounce. In addition, freshly cooked beans, peas, and lentils are low in sodium. (Canned beans, however, may be high in sodium.)

With their rich nutritional values, legumes are an outstanding food buy—the cheapest protein source of all, with no waste (unlike meat or poultry). And they keep well, so it's a good idea to always have some on hand. Legumes are easy to cook and tremendously versatile; they add interest to casseroles, soups, salads, and sandwiches.

VARIETIES Legumes come in a few different shapes and a rainbow of colors. The list below will help you to identify the different varieties and use them to their best advantage. Many of these beans are available canned as well as dried. Unlike dried varieties, canned beans require no soaking or cooking, and so are a convenient pantry staple. Their only drawbacks are their sometimes overly soft texture and high sodium content.

Adzuki beans (also called azuki beans) These small red beans, often found in Chinese or Japanese markets, have a soft texture and a slightly sweet flavor. They are available dried, and processed in the form of red bean paste, which

CHICK-PEAS 3½ oz cooked (¾ cup)

Calories	164	Fat	3 g
Protein	9 g	Saturated Fat	<1 g
Carbohydrate	27 g	Cholesterol	0 mg
Dietary Fiber	Medium	Sodium	7 mg

KEY NUTRIENTS		% RDA Men	% RDA Women
Copper	0.4 mg	N/A	N/A
Folacin	172 mcg	86%	96%
Iron	3 mg	30%	20%
Magnesium	48 mg	14%	17%
Manganese	1 mg	N/A	N/A
Phosphorus	168 mg	21%	21%
Potassium	291 mg	N/A	N/A
Thiamin	0.1 mg	8%	11%
Zinc	2 mg	13%	16%

S=40% or more soluble N/A=Not Applicable N=Not Available

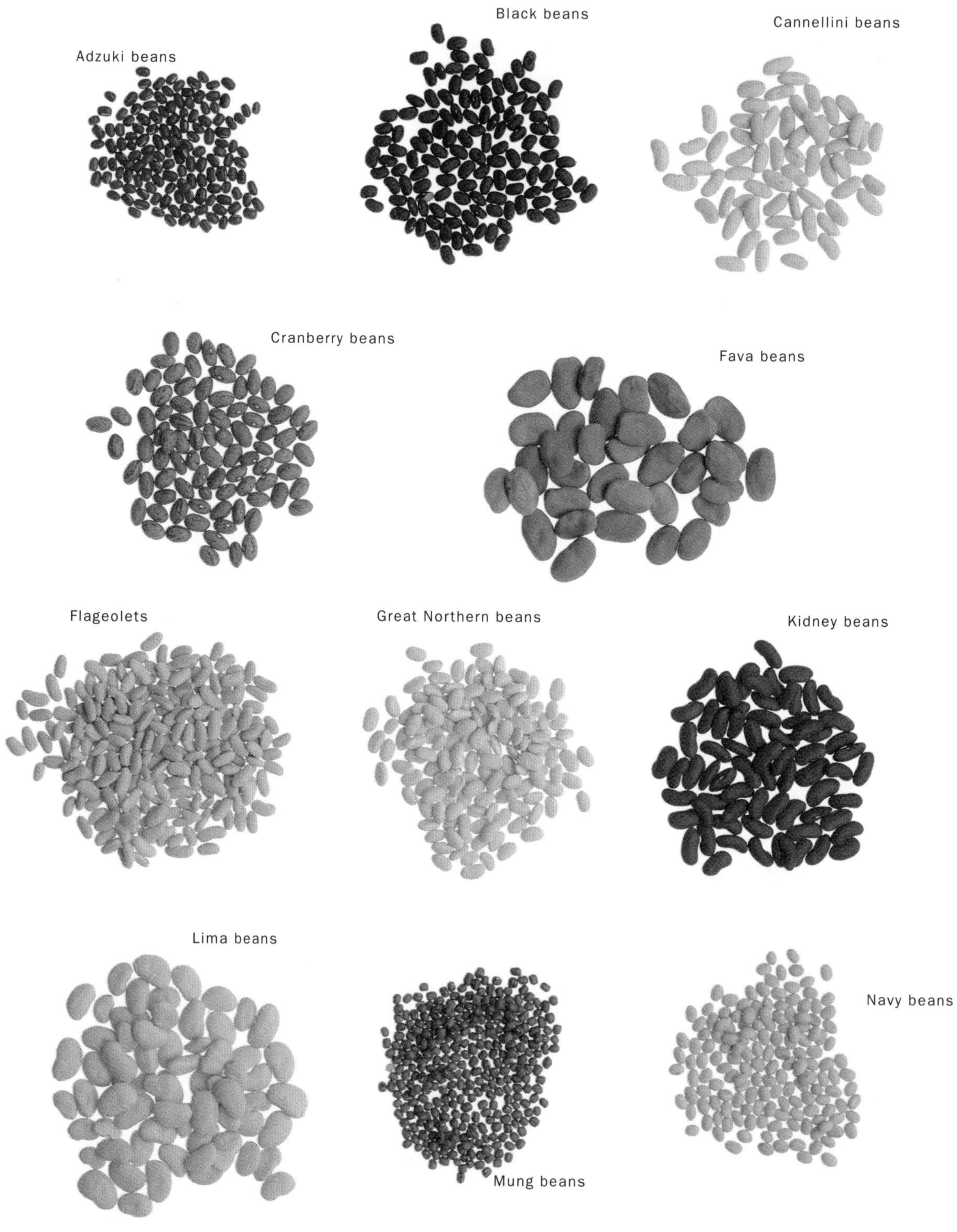
Adzuki beans
Black beans
Cannellini beans
Cranberry beans
Fava beans
Flageolets
Great Northern beans
Kidney beans
Lima beans
Mung beans
Navy beans

COMPARING LEGUMES 3½ ounces (½ cup cooked)

	Calories	**Fat** (g)	**Protein** (g)	**Iron** (mg)	**Calcium** (mg)
Adzuki beans	128	<1	8	2	28
Black beans	132	<1	9	2	27
Black-eyed peas	76	<1	5	1	17
Chick-peas	164	3	9	3	49
Cranberry beans	136	<1	9	2	50
Fava beans	110	<1	8	2	36
Great Northern beans	118	<1	8	2	68
Kidney beans	127	<1	9	3	28
Lentils	116	<1	9	3	19
Lima beans	126	<1	8	2	29
Mung beans	105	<1	7	1	27
Navy beans	142	1	9	3	70
Pinto beans	137	<1	8	3	48
Soybeans	173	9	17	5	102
Split peas	118	<1	8	1	14

consists of mashed red beans, shortening, and sugar. The paste is used in making Asian desserts. Try cooked adzuki beans with rice, barley, or other mild-flavored grains.

***Black beans* (*turtle beans*)** These pea-sized, jet black oval beans have an earthy flavor and a soft, mealy texture. A staple throughout much of Latin America, they are used in such dishes as black beans and rice, refried beans, bean burritos, and, of course, black bean soup. They are also popular in Japanese and Chinese cooking.

***Black-eyed peas* (*cowpeas, black-eyed beans*)** Marked by a single black spot on their skin, these kidney-shaped, creamy white legumes have a pealike flavor and firm, resilient texture (if not overcooked). They are available dried, canned, or frozen; fresh black-eyed peas can be found during the summer months in certain areas. One popular use is in Hoppin' John, a southern New Year's specialty that also includes bacon and rice. Try them in salads, too.

Cannellini These large white kidney beans are sold in canned form. They are often used in Italian dishes, such as minestrone.

***Chick-peas* (*garbanzos, garbanzo beans, ceci*)** Tan-colored and roughly the size and shape of small hazelnuts, chick-peas have a nutlike flavor and a very firm texture. Popular in Indian, Latin, and Middle Eastern cooking, they can be tossed with pasta, added to salads, or mashed to make hummus. Chick-peas can also be roasted for snacks, and are the basis for falafel, a Middle Eastern dish in which the mashed beans are formed into balls and deep-fried.

Hummus is a Middle Eastern dip made from chick-peas, olive oil, and tahini (a paste made from sesame seeds). The mixture is high in fat and calories: A half cup contains 210 calories and 10 grams of mostly unsaturated fat (43 percent fat calories).

Cranberry beans These nutty-flavored oval beans, available fresh or dried, have splashes of pink on their beige skins. Use them in casseroles, chilies, soups, and stews.

***Fava beans* (*broad beans*)** Dried favas look like large lima beans; they have a mealy, granular texture and an assertive flavor. Their thick skins need to be peeled before eating. Popular in Italian cuisine, they combine well with pungent herbs and other strong-flavored ingredients.

Flageolets These kidney-shaped, pale green beans are actually immature kidney beans. In France, they are traditionally eaten with lamb, but they can be served on their own as a side dish, added to soups and stews, or used in cold salads.

Great Northern beans Kidney-shaped, these are the largest of the white beans. Their mild flavor makes them ideal in any baked bean recipe or casserole, as well as in soups and stews.

Kidney beans Named for their shape, these large, meaty beans may be dark red, light red, or white. Kidneys are the favorite choice for chili, and are also good in soups and casseroles.

Lentils These tiny, disk-shaped legumes grow just one or two to a pod and come in many colors. A wide variety of lentils are used in Europe, the Middle East, India, and Africa; in the United States, red, brown, and green lentils are the most common. They cook quickly, need no presoaking, and have a distinctive, somewhat peppery flavor. Use them in soups, cook them with other vegetables, or serve them cold, in salads. Brown and green lentils hold their shape well after cooking and are excellent for salads; red lentils cook more quickly and work best in purées and other dishes where softness is an advantage. Lentils sold as *dhal* have had the outer skins removed, and so are much lower in dietary fiber than other lentils.

Lima beans One of the most widely available beans, limas come in two sizes: large limas, called Fordhooks or butter beans, and baby limas, a smaller, milder-tasting variety. Both are sold frozen as well as dried and canned. Their starchy texture and substantial size make them a satisfying addition to casseroles and soups; combine them with corn and other vegetables for variations on succotash (see Corn, page 87).

Mung beans Most familiar in the form of bean sprouts, mung beans are small greenish-brown, yellow, or black legumes. They cook more quickly than most dried beans and become soft and sweet-tasting. Look for them in health-food stores and Asian markets.

Navy beans (small white beans, pea beans) A smaller version of Great Northern beans, these are denser, less mealy, and more mildly flavored. They can be used in recipes that call for Great Northern or white beans.

Pinto beans These medium-sized long "painted" beans are a reddish tan, mottled with brown flecks. The most popular beans in the United States, they contain more fiber than any other legume. Their earthy flavor makes them a favorite in Mexican dishes; they can be substituted for kidney beans in chili.

Red beans Medium-sized oval beans with a terra-cotta color, these have a rich, savory flavor that makes them the perfect choice for chilies or soups, or for combining with rice.

Soybeans The preeminent legume crop in the world, the soybean is a staple in Asian countries. Soybeans are eaten both fresh and dried, but are found in many other forms as well. Soybean oil is used in cooking and in making margarine and salad dressings; soy protein has become a meat substitute, a milk substitute, and an important ingredient in baby formula. Soy flour helps to enrich pasta and breakfast cereals. Tan-colored

PINTO BEANS 3½ oz cooked (½ cup)

Calories	137	Fat	1 g
Protein	8 g	Saturated Fat	<1 g
Carbohydrate	26 g	Cholesterol	0 mg
Dietary Fiber	High	Sodium	2 mg

KEY NUTRIENTS		%RDA Men	%RDA Women
Vitamin B_6	0.2 mg	10%	13%
Copper	0.3 mg	N/A	N/A
Iron	3 mg	30%	20%
Folacin	172 mcg	86%	96%
Magnesium	55 mg	16%	20%
Manganese	0.6 mg	N/A	N/A
Phosphorus	160 mg	20%	20%
Potassium	468 mg	N/A	N/A
Thiamin	0.2 mg	13%	18%

S=40% or more soluble N/A=Not Applicable N=Not Available

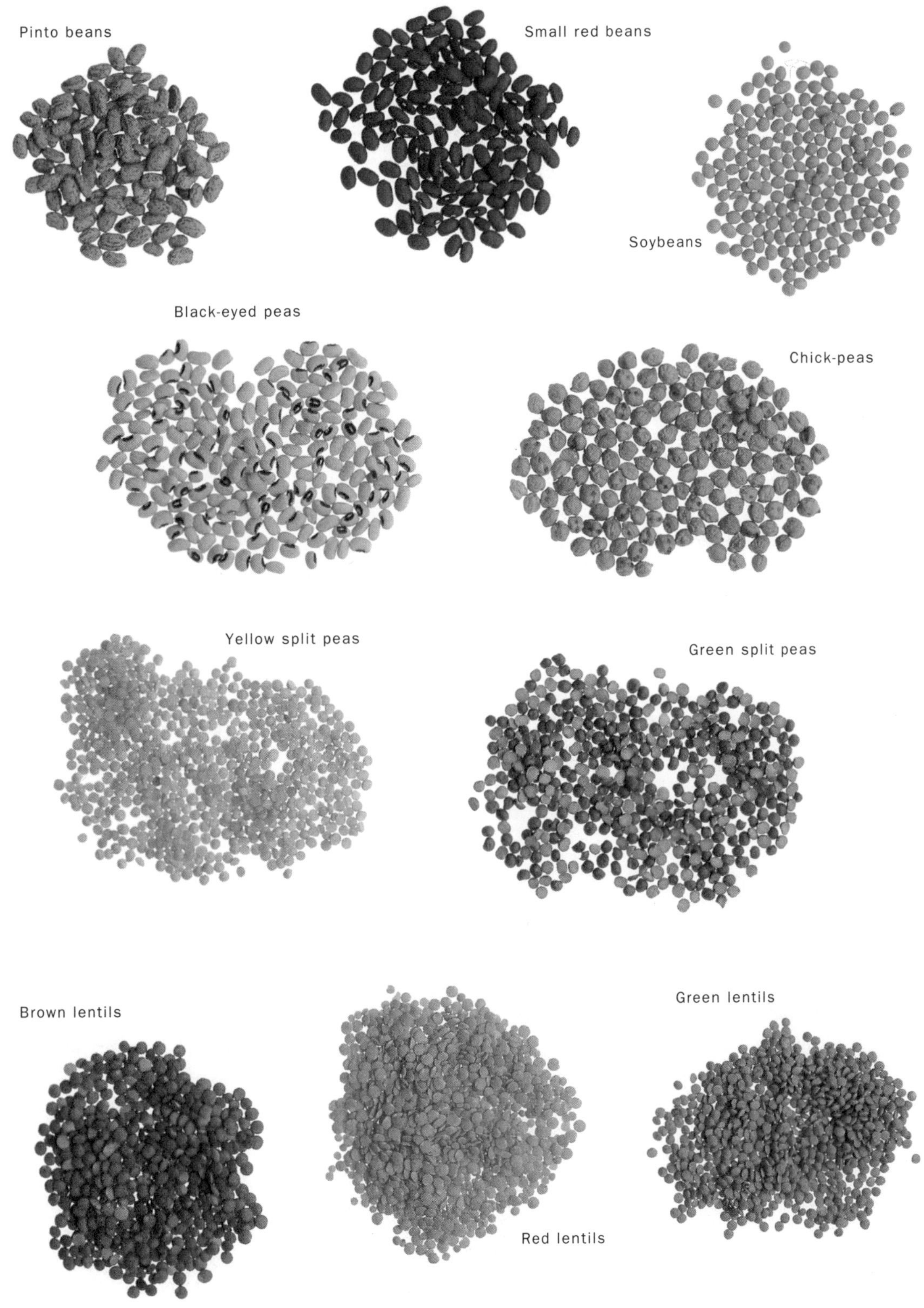
Pinto beans
Small red beans
Soybeans
Black-eyed peas
Chick-peas
Yellow split peas
Green split peas
Brown lentils
Green lentils
Red lentils

dried soybeans, which are available at most health-food stores, are dense, pea-sized beans that should be cooked with robust ingredients, as their flavor is rather bland. Roasted soybeans are also sold as a snack food; like the peanuts they resemble, "soy nuts" are high in fat.

Split peas These favorite soup ingredients are classified as "dry legumes," to differentiate them from fresh green peas. Once these peas are dried and their skins removed, they split apart naturally. Removing the skins also lowers their fiber content. Green split peas are favored in the United States and Great Britain, while yellow split peas, which have a more pronounced nutlike flavor, are preferred in Scandinavian and other northern European countries. Neither type requires presoaking, and both cook quickly. In addition to soups, they make wonderful side-dish purées. Whole dried peas are available in some areas; they work well in casseroles, since they hold their shape better than split peas.

SHOPPING TIPS When buying packaged legumes, look for undamaged boxes or bags of uniformly sized, brightly colored beans, peas, or lentils. If you buy beans in bulk, examine them carefully for insect damage, which sometimes shows up as pinhole-sized marks. Check that the legumes are not cracked or broken.

Dried beans, peas, and lentils are sold at most supermarkets, although for some varieties you may need to visit a health-food store, an ethnic food store, or a gourmet food shop. In specialty stores, colorful mixtures of beans are sold packaged, ready to be made into soup, but you can choose your own combinations of different-colored beans, provided the cooking times are the same (or combine beans after cooking). Canned beans are also widely available; if you don't find the type you're looking for in the canned vegetable aisle of your supermarket, check the sections stocked with Italian or Latin American foods.

STORAGE Store legumes in well-sealed containers at cool room temperature; they should keep for up to a year. If left in a warm, humid environment, dry legumes will take longer to cook. Do not mix a new supply of beans, split peas, or lentils with older legumes; the mixture of old and new stock will cook unevenly.

Store any leftover cooked legumes in tightly closed containers in the refrigerator, where they will keep for three to four days.

THE GAS PROBLEM

For many people, a major obstacle to eating beans is that these foods contain certain indigestible complex sugars that can cause flatulence, often accompanied by indigestion and bloating. These sugars pass undigested into the large intestine, where they are fermented into gas. Some people, though, aren't affected at all, and others only mildly.

There are a few quick ways to reduce the gas-producing properties of beans: During preparation, discard the water after soaking the beans; then boil the beans in a large quantity of fresh water.

It is also advisable to eat beans in small amounts—a ½-cup side-dish serving rather than a big bowl of bean chili—along with low-fat foods (which are easier to digest than fatty foods). In addition, beans should not be served with other gas-producing foods, such as cabbage. Those who suffer distress may find it helpful to consume beans early in the day rather than at dinner, when their system is winding down.

Legumes also contain small amounts of toxic substances known as lectins, which can cause some of the gastrointestinal distress that has come to be associated with these foods. However, lectins are easily destroyed by thorough cooking of the legumes. (The cooking times in the chart on page 355 are more than sufficient.)

LEGUME COOKING TIMES

Dried legumes expand, on average, to two to three times their size after cooking in water. The chart below shows cooked yields per half cup (about 3½ ounces) of dried beans, lentils, and split peas, along with the amount of water to add and cooking times. All these legumes, except lentils and split peas, need to be soaked beforehand. Soybeans require overnight soaking in the refrigerator.

Per ½ Cup Uncooked	**Liquid** (cups)	**Cooking Time**	**Yield** (cups)
Adzuki beans	2	40 minutes	1½
Black beans	2	1 hour 20 minutes	1⅓
Black-eyed peas	2	1 hour	1½
Cannellini beans	1½	1 hour 35 minutes	1½
Chick-peas	2	1 hour 5 minutes	1½
Cranberry beans	2	1 hour 5 minutes	1½
Fava beans	2	30 to 40 minutes	1
Flageolet beans	2	1 hour 10 minutes	1½
Great Northern beans	2	1 hour	1½
Kidney beans	2	55 minutes	1½
Lentils, green (whole)	1½	35 minutes	1½
Lentils, orange (whole)	1½	20 minutes	1⅓
Lima beans	2⅔	45 minutes	1⅓
Mung beans	2	35 to 45 minutes	2
Navy beans	2	1 hour	1½
Pinto beans	2	1 hour	1½
Red beans	1½	45 minutes	1½
Soybeans	2	2 hours 25 minutes	1⅓
Split peas	2	30-35 minutes	1

PREPARATION All dried legumes should be picked over before cooking; spread them on a white kitchen towel so that you can easily see and discard any dirt, debris, or damaged specimens. Then place the legumes in a strainer and rinse them under cold water.

Lentils and split peas are cooked in water—or, to add flavor, in chicken or beef stock—until tender (see the chart above for cooking times). Adjust the cooking time according to the final use you have planned: For salads, remove the lentils or peas from the heat while they are still firm; for soups and purées, cook them until they are very soft.

Dried beans, which have tough skins, are normally soaked before cooking. If you don't have time to presoak beans, expect the cooking time to be lengthened by an hour or more. You can quick-soak beans in an hour, or let them soak for 8 hours or overnight. (The longer soaking eliminates more of their gas-producing sugars.) For either method, place the beans in a large pot (they will double in size soaking) and add enough water to cover them (about 10 cups of water per pound of beans, or two to three times the beans' volume in water). Bring the water to a boil and cook for 2 minutes. For quick soaking, remove the pot from the heat and let stand, covered, for an hour. For long soaking, let the beans stand for at least 6 hours. (For longer soaking, or in warm weather, place the pot of beans in the refrigerator.)

With either method, discard any beans that float to the top after soaking and pour off the soaking water. Then add the required amount of fresh water or broth (see the chart on page 355 for directions); the liquid should cover the beans by about 2 inches. Bring the liquid slowly to a boil, skimming off the scum that rises to the surface. When the liquid boils, reduce the heat, partially cover the pot, and simmer until the beans are tender. Stir occasionally, and add more water, if necessary. Don't keep beans at a rolling boil, or their skins may split. The beans are done when they can be easily pierced with the tip of a knife.

COOKING OUT THE TOXINS

Dried legumes contain a number of potentially toxic substances. Those in soybeans, for example, can interfere with the actions of certain vitamins and the absorption of iron and zinc. Lima beans (and other legumes too, but in negligible amounts) contain cyanogens that are converted to hydrogen cyanide when the plant tissue is damaged, as by chewing. Fava beans can cause favism, a disease that results in the breakdown of red blood cells, in some individuals of Mediterranean or Asian decent. All legumes have within them substances that can make red blood cells clump together.

Fortunately, these various substances are, for the most part, rendered harmless during the normal preparation of beans—soaking and cooking. (Sprouting, too, can have the same effect in some cases.) Moreover, in the case of lima beans, American and European governments have limited the production of this legume to the safest types (that is, the varieties with the lowest cyanogen contents). Favism, however, cannot be prevented by heating or soaking the fava beans, but it is a rare disease; susceptible individuals should simply avoid eating the beans. The best way to protect against any adverse effect is to always cook dried legumes thoroughly and never eat them raw.

Legumes can be cooked in a microwave, but the process takes almost as long as stovetop cooking. Place the legumes in a large microwaveable baking dish with twice their volume of water, cover and bring to a boil on 100 percent power, then reduce to 50 percent power and cook until tender. Crockpots and slow cookers are ideal for cooking legumes; follow the manufacturer's instructions.

If you plan to use canned beans, rinse and drain them thoroughly before cooking to eliminate some of the sodium in the canning liquid. Plan to cook them for as short a time as possible (just to heat them through).

Many types of dried legumes can be sprouted; see page 159.

SERVING SUGGESTIONS Legumes absorb the flavors of the foods they're cooked with, thus making them a versatile ingredient for casseroles, soups, stews, salads, and even sandwiches. They readily take up the flavors of herbs and spices, garlic and onions, soy sauce, vinegar, and salad dressings.

It's easy to combine legumes with the grain-based foods that complement their protein make-up. Try dishes such as tabbouleh with pinto beans, lentil and rice soup, marinated chick-peas in a pita pocket, Cuban-style black beans and rice, tuna and lentil salad on rye bread, bean and barley soup, Boston baked beans with brown bread, or bean burritos on corn tortillas. Any cooked legumes can be formed into patties for vegetarian "burgers" and served on whole wheat buns, while chili and chili-like legume stew can be served on a crisp roll, like a sloppy joe.

Aside from familiar tomato-flavored baked beans, there are many ways to cook beans, lentils, and peas in hearty baked casseroles or on the stovetop. Use cooked (or canned) beans in combination with vegetables such as eggplant, bell peppers, escarole, potatoes, or green beans. Or, try a casserole or skillet dish of beans with pasta or rice (or other grains, such as bulgur or kasha). Experiment with Mexican-style seasonings (hot peppers, garlic, cilantro), Italian ones (garlic and oregano, basil, sage, or rosemary), or use the tra-

TOFU

A versatile cooking ingredient, tofu is a creamy white soy product sold in small blocks. It is made by coagulating the protein of soy beans, in somewhat the same way as cheese is produced. The soybeans are ground with water to produce soy milk, and an ingredient is added to form the soy protein into curds. If the coagulant is calcium sulfate (magnesium sulfate is another common coagulant), the resulting product has a high calcium content.

Tofu is sometimes called "the cheese of Asia," and some types are similar in appearance to a block of farmer cheese; however, unlike cheese, tofu is very bland. In fact, tofu's greatest assets as an ingredient are that it can be cooked in many ways, and can absorb other flavors. Tofu can be stir-fried, broiled, grilled, sautéed, or baked (if marinated first in a spicy sauce, it will have a meaty taste.) It can be puréed to make dips, spreads, salad dressings—even thick shakes and cheesecakes. When mashed, it can be substituted for cottage cheese, ricotta, or even ground beef.

With only about 145 calories per 3½ ounces of firm tofu, this soy product is a good, high-protein substitute for meat, whole-milk products, and mayonnaise. But it is also high in fat, with about 9 grams per 3½ ounces, though the fat is mostly unsaturated.

The basic types of tofu are soft (or silken) and firm. Soft tofu comes in thick, straight-edged blocks; the firm type, which looks more like a tiny pillow, has compressed edges. In Asian markets, tofu is often sold in bulk—the blocks float in tubs of water. Individual water-packed plastic containers are now found in the produce section of many supermarkets.

If you buy tofu from an open tub, shop at a store that has a good turnover, and sniff the tofu to be sure it does not smell sour. Packaged tofu should have a freshness date stamped on its wrapping to guide you. With either type, rinse the tofu when you get it home, place it in a container of fresh cold water, and store it in the refrigerator; change the water daily.

Other soy products similar to tofu are made with soy beans and grains. They include:

***Miso:* A pungent, salty seasoning paste that originated in Japan, miso is made from a combination of soybeans and a grain such as rice or barley. It is fermented with a special mold to produce its distinct, complex flavor. This soy product makes a flavorful soup base or seasoning, but should be used in moderation, as its sodium content can exceed 900 milligrams per tablespoon.**

***Tempeh:* This soy food, a useful meat substitute, originated in Indonesia. To make it, soybeans are cooked, usually with grains, and then aged with a special culture that binds the mixture into a firm substance that can be sliced, or formed into patties. Tempeh contains even more protein than tofu, and is a bit more flavorful.**

You'll find tempeh and prepared foods based on it in health-food stores. A 3½ ounce serving of tempeh has about 200 calories and 8 grams of fat. It also supplies about 12 percent of the RDA for calcium and 23 percent of the RDA of iron for men, 15 percent for women.

ditional New England baked bean ingredients, which include molasses, vinegar, dry mustard, and onions. If you like the taste that salt pork imparts to baked beans, consider substituting some lean ham instead. Since lentils are commonly used in Indian cooking, they're an obvious choice for cooking with the spices of that cuisine: curry powder or its components, including turmeric, cumin, coriander, cayenne, and ginger.

Legume salads—served warm, at room temperature, or chilled—are a delicious way to enjoy legumes in warm weather. A light coating of a vinaigrette dressing works especially well with starchy legumes. For best results, add the vinaigrette while the beans or lentils are still warm, so that they absorb the flavors of the dressing.

LENTILS 3½ oz cooked (½ cup)			
Calories	116	Fat	1 g
Protein	9 g	Saturated Fat	1 g
Carbohydrate	20 g	Cholesterol	0 mg
Dietary Fiber	High	Sodium	2 mg

KEY NUTRIENTS		% RDA Men	% RDA Women
Vitamin B_6	0.2 mg	10%	13%
Copper	0.3 mg	N/A	N/A
Folacin	181 mcg	91%	100%
Iron	3 mg	30%	20%
Magnesium	36 mg	10%	13%
Manganese	0.5 mg	N/A	N/A
Phosphorus	180 mg	22%	22%
Potassium	369 mg	N/A	N/A
Thiamin	0.2 mg	13%	18%

S=40% or more soluble N/A=Not Applicable N=Not Available

Combine beans or lentils with fresh greens, herbs, and raw vegetables, and/or with pasta, cooked vegetables, and meat or poultry. Or, prepare some of these more interesting salad combinations: white beans and tuna with fresh dill; chick-peas with lemon juice, cumin, and ground coriander; lentils and arugula or watercress; kidney beans with fresh snap beans; black-eyed peas with corn kernels, diced carrots, and celery.

Black beans are a marvelous soup ingredient, as are lentils and split peas. For a smoky-flavored pea soup without fatty sausage or ham, try adding some smoked turkey. Cook any kind of legumes in broth, adding herbs and chopped vegetables. Leave the ingredients whole, or purée all or some of the solids for a thick, creamy soup.

SOY MILK

Grinding soybeans with water produces soy milk, which looks like whole milk. It can be used by people who are allergic to cow's milk, or by vegans who eat no animal products. Soy milk is sold in an assortment of flavors. Plain, it is approximately equivalent in calories to skim milk, but has about ten times the fat content (about 5 grams per cup). Unlike cow's milk, this soy product supplies a negligible amount of calcium.

Mashed mild-flavored beans are a good stand-in for cream cheese or sour cream in dips; a thick bean dip can be transformed into numerous appetizing sandwich spreads. Blend hand-mashed or puréed kidney beans or lentils with salsa, chopped tomatoes, and a little Monterey Jack cheese; combine white beans with tuna and lemon juice, chick-peas with garlic and parsley, or kidney beans with puréed roasted garlic. Thick bean, pea, and lentil purées also make tempting side dishes. To mash or purée legumes, cook them until very tender and then mash them with a potato masher, put through a food mill, or process in a food processor.

Nuts and Seeds

We tend to use nuts and seeds only as a snack food, or in salads and desserts. Yet these foods are much more nourishing than most snacks. Indeed, in some parts of the world where meat is forbidden, nuts are still a staple food, just as they were in ancient times. Nomadic peoples first gathered nuts growing in the wild, and around 10,000 B.C. settled populations began to cultivate nut trees. Almonds and pistachios are mentioned in the Old Testament, and the Romans are known to have dined on almonds, hazelnuts, chestnuts, pine nuts, and walnuts. Native Americans taught the European colonists to prepare hickory nuts, chestnuts, pecans, black walnuts, beechnuts, and acorns. Nuts and seeds are also versatile cooking ingredients, and for centuries they have been processed into butterlike pastes, ground into nutritious flours, pressed for fragrant cooking oils, and pulverized with water to produce beverages that resemble milk or coffee.

Most nuts are the seeds or dried fruits of trees; and the majority have hard, woody outer husks that protect the softer kernels inside. The edible seeds we eat, such as those of the pumpkin and sunflower, grow on vegetable or flower plants, and their hulls, which are softer than those of nuts, are sometimes edible. Peanuts are actually a type of legume, but are commonly classified as nuts. All of these foods have substantial reserves of protein: Nuts derive from 8 to 18 percent of their calories from protein, seeds from 11 to 25 percent. Although the protein is incomplete—except for peanuts, nuts and seeds are deficient in the amino acid lysine—it can be complemented by consuming legumes or animal products along with the nuts or seeds. Almonds, Brazil nuts, filberts, and sesame seeds contain good amounts of calcium, and other nuts and seeds have at least a small quantity of this important mineral. Most nuts are also rich in potassium and relatively high in iron. Their oil-rich kernels are one of the best vegetable sources of vitamin E; in addition, they supply the B vitamins thiamin, niacin, and riboflavin (although roasting can destroy much of the thiamin—one reason to eat raw, or unroasted, nuts). The minerals magnesium, zinc, copper, and selenium are also well represented in nuts.

Similarly, seeds—sunflower, pumpkin, squash, and sesame—supply iron, potassium, and phosphorus. (An ounce of sesame seeds furnishes about three times the iron in an ounce of beef liver.) Even more than nuts, seeds contain healthy amounts of dietary fiber, particularly when they are eaten with their shells or hulls.

Along with these nutrients, however, comes fat, usually a great deal of it, which is the principal reason that nuts are less attractive than legumes or grains as a nonmeat protein source. Most nuts derive between 70 and 97 percent of their calories from fat. (One exception is chestnuts, which contain 8 percent fat calories.) Most of the fat in nuts is unsaturated, which can help to lower blood cholesterol levels, but some nuts—especially coconuts, Brazil nuts, macadamias, and cashews—contain more saturated fat than others. The high fat content of nuts and seeds also contributes to their high calorie count; just an ounce of sesame seeds, for example, contains almost as many calories as 3 ounces of broiled, trimmed sirloin steak.

Chestnuts are the only nut with any vitamin C. Three and a half ounces of chestnuts provide 43 percent of the RDA for vitamin C.

It's best to use nuts and seeds sparingly. But even in small amounts they have much to offer in the way of distinctive flavors and textures, as well as protein, vitamins, and minerals. An ounce of roasted peanuts, for example, contains 167 calories and supplies 11 percent of the protein RDA for the average man, 13 percent for the average woman. If you eat an ounce of raw or dry-roasted nuts as an occasional snack, lunch on a lightly spread peanut-butter sandwich, or top your green salad with a spoonful of sunflower seeds, you'll gain some nutritional benefit without consuming excessive quantities of fat and calories.

TYPES OF NUTS Nuts and seeds are indeed varied. They grow all over the world, in assorted sizes and shapes, and are marketed in a variety of forms—with or without shells; whole, chopped, or slivered; raw, dry-roasted, or oil-roasted; salted, sugared, spiced, or plain; packaged or loose. While some types of nuts can be eaten as is from the tree, most are dried to preserve them (and improve their texture and flavor).

Whether you choose nuts in the shell or shelled is mostly a matter of convenience. Nuts keep better in their shells, but, of course, they require cracking before you can eat or cook with them. Most nuts in their shells and some shelled nuts are sold raw, that is, unroasted. Raw nuts have the advantage of no added fat, but their flavor is rather bland compared with that of roasted nuts, and they do not keep as well.

Commercial "roasting" of shelled nuts is actually a form of deep frying, and the fat used is often highly saturated coconut oil. The process adds about 10 calories per ounce of nuts, or a little more than a gram of fat (mostly saturated fat, if coconut oil is used). Roasted nuts are usually heavily salted, too, although you can sometimes find unsalted roasted cashews and peanuts. Nuts can be roasted or toasted at home without fat.

Dry-roasted nuts are not cooked in oil, so they are slightly lower in calories and fat than oil-roasted nuts. Like regular roasted nuts, however, they may be salted or contain other ingredients, such as corn syrup, sugar, starch, MSG, and preservatives.

The descriptions that follow will help you choose the nuts and seeds richest in nutrients and alert you to those that are highest in fat.

Almonds These are the fruit seeds of sweet almond trees, which are closely related to peach trees. You can see the family resemblance if you crack a peach pit to reveal the kernel inside, which looks like an almond. Highly nutritious, almonds contain more calcium than any other nut, along with healthy amounts of iron, riboflavin, and vitamin E. They also have the highest dietary fiber content of any nut or seed, supplying 3 grams of fiber per ounce. Cultivated in central California (where they are the state's largest tree crop), the nuts come in a variety of forms: almonds with shells; whole natural almonds (shelled but not skinned); whole blanched almonds (with the dark brown inner skin removed); sliced natural and blanched almonds; blanched slivered almonds; roasted blanched slivered almonds; chopped natural almonds; diced roasted salted almonds; dry-roasted almonds; almond butter; almond paste; and almond oil.

Brazil nuts The fruit of a tall evergreen tree that grows wild in the Amazon basin, Brazil nuts grow in clusters of one to three dozen within a single large, globular hard shell that resembles a coconut. Each nut has a three-sided shell that is roughly the shape and size of a navel-orange segment. The large, creamy-meated kernels are fairly rich in calcium, phosphorus, and thiamin. They are available raw (with shells and shelled), roasted, and dry-roasted.

Cashews These nuts are the seeds of a tree that is native to Africa and South America. Today, however, most cashews are imported from India. The kidney-shaped nuts grow in a double shell at the top of small pear-shaped fruits. Cashews are always sold shelled, because their shells contain a caustic oil (the cashew is related to poison ivy); in fact, the nuts must be carefully extracted to avoid contamination with this oil. Cashews are a good source of iron and folacin (a B vitamin). They're lower in total fat than most nuts and seeds, but are relatively high in saturated fat. In the United States, these flavorful nuts are more popular for snacking than for cooking, yet they make a par-

ALMONDS, whole 3½ oz dry roasted (¾ cup)

Calories	587	Fat	52 g
Protein	16 g	Saturated Fat	5 g
Carbohydrate	24 g	Cholesterol	0 mg
Dietary Fiber	High	Sodium	11 mg

KEY NUTRIENTS		% RDA Men	% RDA Women
Calcium	282 mg	35%	35%
Copper	1.2 mg	N/A	N/A
Vitamin E	21 mg	210%	263%
Folacin	64 mcg	32%	36%
Iron	4 mg	40%	27%
Magnesium	304 mg	87%	109%
Manganese	2 mg	N/A	N/A
Niacin	3 mg	16%	20%
Phosphorus	548 mg	69%	69%
Potassium	770 mg	N/A	N/A
Riboflavin	0.6 mg	35%	40%
Zinc	5 mg	35%	42%

S=40% or more soluble N/A=Not Applicable N=Not Available

ticularly delicious nut butter. They're sold raw, roasted, or dry roasted.

Chestnuts Once abundant in America, chestnut trees were almost totally wiped out by a widespread tree blight in the early decades of the twentieth century. Some of the American trees were replaced with Chinese trees, but the majority of the chestnuts we eat are imported, mostly from Europe. These glossy-shelled, mahogany-colored nuts develop inside prickly burrs, which break open when the nuts are ripe. When first picked, chestnuts are starchy, but after a few days of curing, some of the starch turns to sugar and the large, soft nuts develop a gentle sweetness.

Nutritionally a breed apart from other nuts, chestnuts are mainly composed of carbohydrates, and are low in fat and calories.

Chestnuts are almost always cooked. Roasted or boiled chestnuts have the consistency of potatoes, and are often served as a vegetable side dish or used in poultry stuffing; they're especially popular at Thanksgiving and Christmas.

Chestnuts are most commonly sold in their shells; these shells are rather soft and can be peeled off easily once the nuts are cooked. In gourmet food shops and some supermarkets, you'll also find jars of peeled chestnuts in syrup (the French *marrons glacés*), cans of sweetened chestnut purée for making desserts, and bags of chestnut flour for baking.

CHESTNUTS 3½ oz roasted (¾ cup)			
Calories	245	Fat	2 g
Protein	3 g	Saturated Fat	<1 g
Carbohydrate	53 g	Cholesterol	0 mg
Dietary Fiber	High	Sodium	2 mg

KEY NUTRIENTS		% RDA Men	% RDA Women
Vitamin B_6	0.5 mg	25%	31%
Vitamin C	26 mg	43%	43%
Copper	0.5 mg	N/A	N/A
Folacin	70 mcg	35%	39%
Iron	1 mg	10%	6%
Manganese	1 mg	N/A	N/A
Magnesium	33 mg	9%	12%
Phosphorus	107 mg	13%	13%
Potassium	592 mg	N/A	N/A
Riboflavin	0.2 mg	12%	15%
Thiamin	0.2 mg	13%	18%

S=40% or more soluble N/A=Not Applicable N=Not Available

Coconuts Here is another fruit seed, like the almond, although we rarely see the fruit in which it grows. More familiar is the egg-shaped, hairy shell of the nut itself. Coconuts grow on the tropical coconut palm, and most of the ones sold in the United States come from Central America and Puerto Rico. Unlike most nuts, the coconut shell does not contain a softer kernel; instead, the shell itself is lined with a layer of rich white "meat," and the hollow at the center of the coconut is filled with a thin, slightly sweet liquid that can be used as a beverage. Another characteristic that distinguishes coconuts from other nuts is that nearly all of its substantial fat content is saturated. Coconut oil, used in many processed foods in this country, is the most highly saturated of all vegetable oils. Moreover, coconut has no redeeming vitamin or mineral assets (though it is high in dietary fiber). Therefore, it is best to eat the nut in very small quantities.

You can buy whole coconuts and crack them yourself, or choose from several types of prepared coconut on the market. The processed forms have been shredded and dried, and may be sweetened, toasted, and/or creamed. Coconut cream, which is the coconut's liquid blended with coconut meat, is a very rich, fatty product used in cooking and concocting drinks. It is sold in cans, or you can make it yourself from fresh coconut.

Filberts and hazelnuts Most people think that these two names are interchangeable, but the filbert is a small European tree, while the hazel, a wild shrub, is its close American relative. Filberts are larger and have a fringed husk. Most of the U.S. supply comes from Turkey. These sweet, acorn-shaped nuts are rich in folacin and are a fair source of calcium, iron, and magnesium. Filberts come with shells and shelled, and are eaten as dessert nuts and used in baking.

Macadamias These "gourmet" nuts were named for Dr. John Macadam, the Australian who reputedly discovered that they were deliciously edible. Indigenous to Australia and now one of the best-known products of Hawaii, macadamias have a sweet, delicate taste and creamy, rich texture. However, they contain more fat and calories than any other nut. On the plus side, macadamias supply significant amounts of iron, magnesium, and thiamin.

Most commonly eaten as a dessert nut, macadamias are nearly always sold shelled, as their shiny round shells are very thick, requiring some 300 pounds of pressure to crack them. They are harvested five to six times a year, but the demand still exceeds the supply, and, as a result, these are usually very expensive.

Peanuts The most familiar nuts to Americans, these are, in fact, not true nuts, but the shell-enclosed seeds of a leguminous bush or vine. The peanut pods develop below the ground, and both the shell and kernel are quite soft before the peanuts are dried.

Peanuts have more protein than any other nuts, and their fat content falls in the moderate range for this class of foods. They are a good source of thiamin, niacin, and folacin, and also provide significant amounts of iron and magnesium. Peanuts are rich in dietary fiber.

Americans eat nearly 12 pounds of peanuts per person, per year.

Three major types of peanuts are grown in the American South and Southwest: Runners, which were introduced in the 1970s and are now the most popular type, are primarily made into peanut butter; Virginia peanuts are sold roasted in the shell; and Spanish peanuts, small round nuts with a reddish-brown skin, are used in candies and in peanut butter, and are also packed as salted nuts.

In the United States, peanuts are mostly eaten dried or roasted, as a snack, in candies, or in the form of peanut butter; in other parts of the world, they are consumed like other legumes, pressed for their oil, or ground into a high-protein, partially defatted flour.

PEANUTS 3½ oz dry roasted (⅔ cup)

Calories	585	Fat	50 g
Protein	24 g	Saturated fat	7 g
Carbohydrate	22 g	Cholesterol	0 mg
Dietary Fiber	High	Sodium	6 mg

KEY NUTRIENTS		% RDA Men	% RDA Women
Vitamin B_6	0.3 mg	15%	19%
Copper	0.7 mg	N/A	N/A
Vitamin E	1 mg	10%	13%
Folacin	145 mcg	73%	81%
Iron	2 mg	20%	13%
Magnesium	176 mg	50%	63%
Manganese	2.1 mg	N/A	N/A
Niacin	14 mg	74%	93%
Phosphorus	358 mg	45%	45%
Potassium	658 mg	N/A	N/A
Thiamin	0.4 mg	27%	36%
Zinc	3 mg	20%	25%

S=40% or more soluble N/A=Not Applicable N=Not Available

Nearly half the peanuts grown in the United States are made into peanut butter. Americans consume 800 million pounds of peanut butter a year, which translates to over 3 pounds per person. Peanut butter is especially popular among children; 92 percent eat peanut butter at least twice a week.

Raw peanuts can be cooked like beans or roasted fat-free at home. Peanuts are also sold oil-roasted, dry-roasted, blanched, and boiled (a product very popular in peanut-growing regions). Peanuts are the only nuts sold partially defatted. They are roasted under pressure in safflower or sunflower oil, a process which—strange as it seems—removes about 60 to 80 percent of the fat. Defatted peanuts are available salted and unsalted. There are a number of peanut products available, too—namely peanut oil and, of course, peanut butter.

Pecans The seeds of a species of hickory native to North America, pecans grow wild from Illinois to the Gulf of Mexico. They are also commercially cultivated across the South and Southwest. The nuts develop in clusters and have smooth oblong or round shells. Cultivated pecans are bred for thin ("paper") shells, which are easier to crack than the hard shells of wild pecans. Pecans are among the highest in fat and lowest in protein of all the nuts. Hickory nuts are wild relatives of cultivated pecans. Pecans are sold with and without shells.

Pine nuts (pignoli, piñon nuts, Indian nuts) These are all names for the seeds of various types of nut pine trees, which grow in several areas of the world. The seeds come from pine cones, and range from orange-pit size (from the Mexican and American trees) to more than 2 inches in length (from the South American nut pines). To harvest them, the pine cones are dried to free the nuts, then the nutshells are cracked to release the kernels. Because of the intricacy of harvesting pine nuts, they are quite expensive.

Slender ivory-colored pignoli are an important cooking ingredient in the Mediterranean region, while the piñons of the American Southwest have been a staple of the Native American larder since ancient times. Pine nuts are also rich in thiamin, iron, and magnesium. In general, European species of pine nuts are richer in protein and lower in fat than the American varieties, but American pine nuts offer more vitamins and minerals. European pine nuts (Italian pignoli are the most widely available in this country) are sold shelled; American pine nuts, or piñons, are sold shelled or with shells.

Pistachios Imported pistachio nuts became a popular snack food in the 1930s. Today, the evergreen trees that bear pistachios are grown in California for the American market. These peanut-sized nuts, which have beige shells and green kernels, supply good amounts of iron, thiamin, and phosphorus. Pistachios are usually eaten as a snack—their shells split naturally as the nuts mature, making them easy to crack by hand—but they are also a flavorful ingredient when used in cooking. They are sold shelled or in the beige shells, which are sometimes bleached or dyed. Pistachios come salted or unsalted, "natural" or roasted.

ARE PISTACHIOS REALLY RED?

In their natural state, the shells are tan. In the 1930s, however, pistachio importers began dying the shells red to make their product distinctive to consumers, and to disguise blemishes that occurred during harvesting. In general, imported pistachios are dyed; those grown in California are usually sold with tan shells, but some are still dyed to meet the demand of customers who either prefer pistachios that way, or wouldn't recognize them in their natural state.

You might think that since the shells are not eaten, dying them makes little difference in terms of food safety. Nevertheless, the kernels inside may be affected since the shells naturally split open when the nuts are ready to be harvested. Moreover, many people eat pistachios by cracking open the shells with their teeth. To be perfectly safe, especially if you eat pistachios frequently, choose tan over red.

Pumpkin seeds The seeds of pumpkins and other winter squashes (such as butternut) are edible. Enclosed in teardrop-shaped shells thin enough to crack open with your teeth, the flat kernels are second only to peanuts in protein content. They are lower in fat than most nuts and are an excellent source of iron.

Pumpkin seeds are sold shelled or unshelled, roasted or raw, for snacks and cooking. You can also scoop out the seeds when you're carving a Halloween jack-o'-lantern (or cooking winter squash); rinse the seeds, dry them, and then toast them in the oven.

Sesame seeds These tiny oval seeds, which grow on a tall annual plant, are basic to many of the world's cuisines, including those of Africa, India, and China. Dark sesame oil is a staple cooking ingredient in Asia; *tahini,* a spread also known as

CAUTION ON PEANUTS

Peanuts can be a source of aflatoxin, a mold that grows on peanuts as well as on corn and other crops. If ingested in large amounts, it is known to contribute to liver cancer. Although it is impossible to produce a peanut crop completely free of aflatoxin, you need not worry that the peanuts and peanut butter you buy are likely to be unsafe. The FDA has set a maximum permissible level for aflatoxin of 20 parts per billion, and the USDA inspects peanut shipments for any sign of the mold; they will ban any crop with detectable contamination. In addition, most American food processors have established rigorous programs to monitor the presence of aflatoxin, and, generally, peanut products fall considerably below the allowable 20 parts per billion.

Thus, commercial peanut butter and commercially packaged roasted and dry-roasted-peanuts are likely to be safe. Another protective factor: Any added salt helps to prevent the mold from forming. However, you should take the following precautions when buying and using peanuts and freshly ground peanut butter:

- **Look carefully at the peanuts you buy in the shell. Discard any that are discolored, shriveled, or show signs of mold.**
- **Peanut butter that is ground in a store may not be as safe as commercial brands. Peanuts that sit around after they have passed inspection may pick up mold if not stored properly. Also, freshly ground peanut butter won't contain any added salt, so it should be refrigerated to slow rancidity.**
- **If peanut butter from any source becomes moldy, don't just skim off the mold. Throw the whole container out.**

the "butter of the Middle East," is made from ground sesame seeds; and *halvah* is a rich Turkish candy made from ground sesame seeds and honey. Sesame seeds were brought to America with the slave trade, and are still used in several popular southern recipes. They are even more familiar in this country as a topping on breads, buns, and rolls.

Most of the sesame seeds sold in the United States are grown in Latin America. You can buy hulled or unhulled sesame seeds; the unhulled, which are darker in color, have the bran intact and are an excellent source of calcium, iron, and phosphorus.

Sunflower seeds These seeds come from the center of the tall daisylike sunflower that is native to North America. The plump, nutlike kernels of the confection sunflower grow in teardrop-shaped, gray-and-white shells (another type, the oil sunflower, has black-shelled seeds). Sunflowers have long been a staple of the vegetarian larder, and in the last decade they have become widely popular both as a snack and as a cooking ingredient. Shelled sunflower seeds are sometimes labeled sunflower kernels or nuts.

Compared to pumpkin seeds, sunflower seeds are higher in calcium, thiamin, vitamin B_6, and folacin, but also contain more calories and fat.

Walnuts, black and Persian (English) Native to Europe and western Asia, Persian walnuts are grown in orchards and sold commercially by the hundreds of thousands of tons. California now leads the world in production of these nuts, which are popularly known as English walnuts. Black walnuts, on the other hand, come from a native North American tree, and they are marketed on a very small scale. Both types of walnuts have a hard, wrinkly shell inside a thick hull. The hulls of Persian walnuts are easily crushed and removed; the shells split readily, allowing quick extraction of unbroken nut halves. They are sold in the shell, and shelled, salted or plain, in halves or in pieces. In contrast, black walnuts have very tough, dark outer hulls, and the shells usually have to be broken under so much pressure (some people find it easiest to crush them under the tires

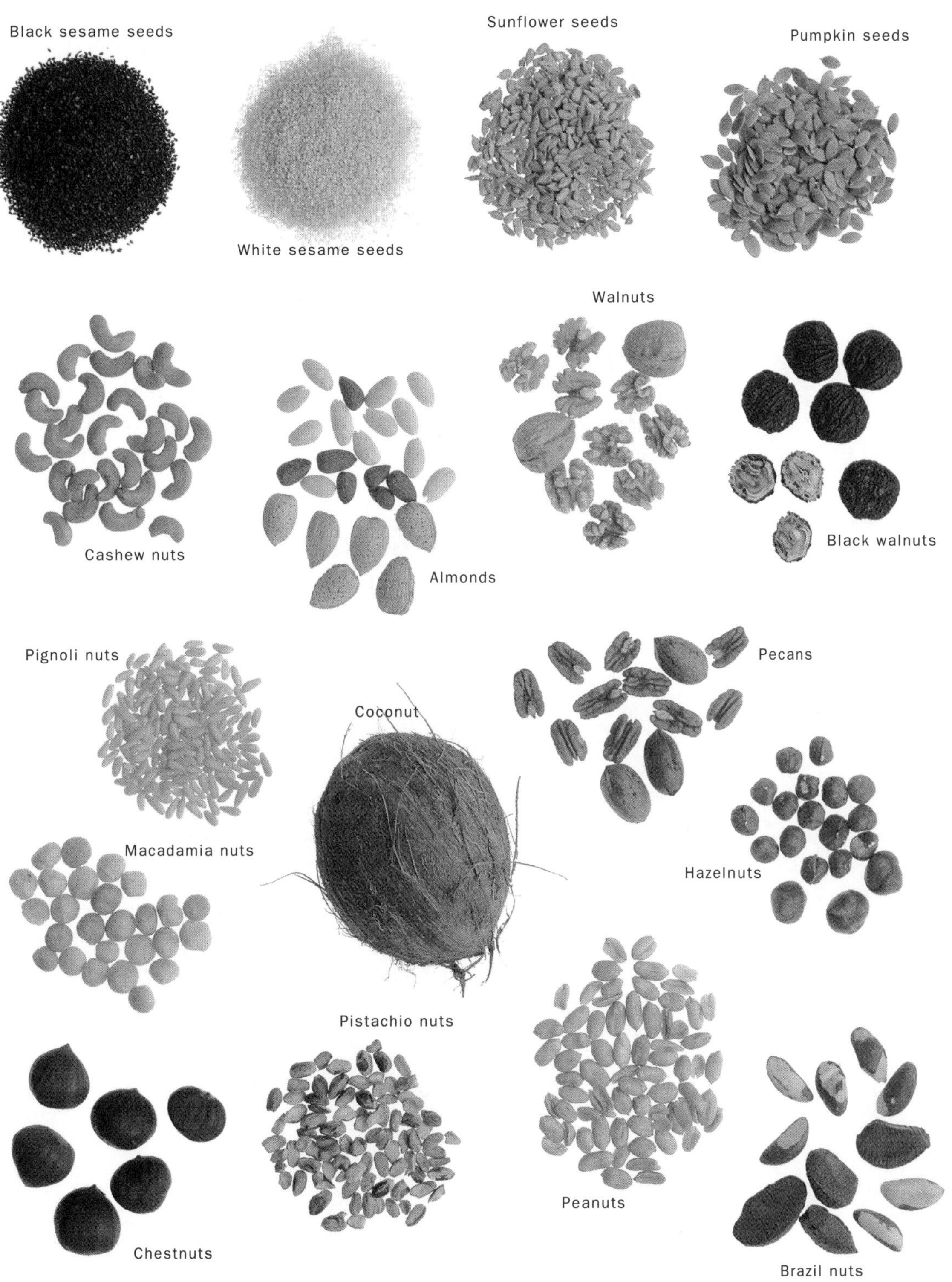
Black sesame seeds
White sesame seeds
Sunflower seeds
Pumpkin seeds
Cashew nuts
Almonds
Walnuts
Black walnuts
Pignoli nuts
Macadamia nuts
Coconut
Pecans
Hazelnuts
Pistachio nuts
Chestnuts
Peanuts
Brazil nuts

of a car) that the nut meats are crushed as well, and have to be picked out in pieces. As a result, black walnuts are usually sold in their shells, though you can sometimes find shelled black walnuts through mail order.

Persian walnuts are higher in fat than black; both types are fair sources of iron and vitamin B_6.

AVAILABILITY Most shelled nuts, sold in vacuum-sealed cans or jars, or cellophane bags, can be found in supermarkets year round. Fresh tree nuts (such as walnuts and filberts) in the shell are more seasonal—supplies are best in the fall and early winter. Chestnuts are most abundant from September through March; coconuts are at their best from October through December.

SHOPPING TIPS When buying packaged nuts, look for a freshness date on a sealed jar, can, or bag. The kernels, if visible, should be plump and uniform in size. If you buy shelled nuts at a candy store, health-food store, or other bulk source, be sure that they're crisp and fresh, not limp or rubbery, musty, or rancid smelling.

When selecting nuts with shells from a basket or bin, choose those with undamaged shells; look out for cracks, scars, or tiny wormholes. Each nut should feel heavy, and the kernel should not rattle when the nutshell is shaken; if it does, the kernel may be withered and dry.

When buying a whole coconut, choose one with a firm shell, free of dark or soft spots. Heft and shake it to see if it is heavy and full of liquid, which are signs of freshness.

STORAGE The high fat content of nuts and seeds makes them prone to rancidity; heat, light, and humidity will speed spoilage. Raw unshelled nuts and seeds, however, keep very well—six months to a year when stored in a cool, dry place.

Shelled nuts and seeds will keep for three to four months at room temperature in a cool, dry place. Keep them in their original package or, once the package is opened, transfer them to plastic bags or freezer containers. For longer storage, keep them in the refrigerator or freezer. In the freezer they'll stay for up to a year. If they are properly wrapped, freezing will not significantly affect the texture or flavor of nuts, and they need not be thawed for cooking purposes. Nuts for eating should be thawed at room temperature and then toasted or freshened in the oven before serving. Don't chop whole nuts until you're ready to use them.

Chestnuts in the shell, stored in a perforated plastic bag, will keep in the refrigerator for about six months.

A whole, unbroken coconut will keep for a month or two at room temperature. Tightly wrap a cracked or opened coconut and use the meat within a week.

PREPARATION Usually all the preparation that's necessary is to crack the nuts that have shells—which can be simple (with peanuts) or challenging (with black walnuts). Use your fingers for soft shells; squeezing two nuts together in your hand works well. For harder shells, use a nutcracker or a small hammer. A nutpick is useful for extracting convoluted kernels, such as those of walnuts.

SUNFLOWER SEEDS 3½ oz dry roasted (¾ cup)

Calories	582	Fat	50 g
Protein	19 g	Saturated Fat	5 g
Carbohydrate	24 g	Cholesterol	0 mg
Dietary Fiber	High	Sodium	3 mg

KEY NUTRIENTS		% RDA Men	% RDA Women
Vitamin B_6	0.8 mg	40%	50%
Copper	1.8 mg	N/A	N/A
Vitamin E	20 mg	200%	250%
Magnesium	129 mg	37%	46%
Manganese	2 mg	N/A	N/A
Niacin	7 mg	37%	47 %
Phosphorus	1155 mg	144%	144%
Potassium	850 mg	N/A	N/A
Riboflavin	0.3 mg	18%	23%
Zinc	5 mg	33%	42%

S=40% or more Soluble N/A=Not Applicable N=Not Available

COMPARING NUTS AND SEEDS 3½ ounces

	Calories	Protein (g)	Fat (g)	PERCENTAGE OF CALORIES FROM Total Fat	Saturated Fat	Polyunsaturated Fat	Monounsaturated Fat
Almonds	589	20	52	80%	8%	17%	52%
Brazil nuts	656	14	66	91%	22%	33%	30%
Cashews, dry-roasted	574	15	46	73%	14%	13%	42%
Chestnuts, European	245	3	2	8%	2%	3%	3%
Coconuts, raw	354	3	33	85%	76%	1%	3%
Filberts/ Hazelnuts	632	13	63	89%	7%	9%	70%
Macadamias	702	8	74	95%	14%	1%	74%
Peanuts, dry roasted	567	26	50	78%	11%	25%	38%
Pecans	667	8	68	91%	7%	23%	57%
Pine nuts/ Pignoli	515	24	51	89%	14%	37%	33%
Pine nuts/ Piñons	568	12	61	97%	14%	41%	36%
Pistachios	577	21	48	75%	9%	11%	51%
Pumpkin seeds, shelled	541	25	46	76%	15%	35%	23%
Sesame seeds	573	18	50	78%	11%	35%	30%
Sunflower seeds, shelled	570	23	50	78%	9%	52%	14%
Walnuts, black	607	24	57	84%	6%	55%	19%
Walnuts, Persian	642	14	62	87%	8%	55%	20%

Brazil nuts are easier to shell when they have been either steamed or frozen.

If shelled nuts seem a little soft (but do not smell rancid), they can be freshened by spreading them on a baking sheet and heating them in a very low oven (150°) for a few minutes.

Chop nuts using a good-sized chef's knife on a large cutting board. For efficient chopping, spread the nuts on the board; hold down the tip of the knife blade with one hand and raise and lower the knife, moving it fanwise across the nuts. A curved chopper used in a wooden bowl works well, too, as does an inexpensive mechanical nut chopper. Pecans and walnuts are soft enough to break by hand, if you need large pieces.

When chopping nuts in a blender, process a small amount at a time and pulse the machine on and off; don't overprocess the nuts, as this will release their oils and turn them to paste. A food processor can handle more nuts, but care must be taken to avoid making nut butter by accident. To make nut butters, see the box on page 369.

Dredge nuts lightly in flour before adding to batter or dough to keep them from settling to the bottom of the mixture.

Most nuts and seeds taste better if they are toasted, roasted, or blanched before you eat or cook with them.

Blanching When applied to nuts, this term refers to removing the papery skin from the kernel. Nuts can be blanched in several different ways. You can drop shelled nuts into a saucepan of boiling water, then remove the pan from the heat and let it stand for a few minutes. Drain the nuts, and when they are cool enough to handle, slip off the skins, or rub them off with a kitchen towel. To dry them, spread the nuts on a paper towel or toast them briefly in a 250° to 300° oven.

You can blanch raw peanuts by placing them in the freezer for a few hours. Oven-toasting peanuts and filberts will enable you to remove their skins. Chestnuts can be blanched in water to make their shells easier to remove.

Boiling European chestnuts can be cooked and served like a vegetable. Blanch and peel the nuts, then cook the kernels in boiling water or broth until tender. *Cooking time:* 35 to 40 minutes.

Roasting chestnuts Chestnuts can be roasted in the oven without fat and then eaten as a snack or used in recipes. To keep them from bursting during roasting and to make them easier to peel, make an "x"-shaped cut in the flat side of each nutshell before roasting. Place the chestnuts in a shallow pan and cover the pan tightly with foil. Shake the pan occasionally during cooking. Peel the chestnuts while they are still warm, taking them from the pan one at a time, and remove their papery inner shell. *Cooking time:* 30 minutes in a 450° oven.

To roast chestnuts over an open fire, cut an "x" in each shell as described above, then wrap the nuts in a sheet of heavy-duty foil that has had a few holes punched in it. Place them about 5 inches from the fire. Or, use a fireplace corn popper or chestnut roasting basket. *Cooking time:* 15 to 20 minutes.

Toasting This method browns and crisps nuts and seeds and brings out their flavor. (Toasting and roasting are slightly different processes; technically speaking, the roasting of shelled nuts requires added fat.) Nuts and seeds can be toasted on the stovetop, or in the oven or microwave; the cooking time will depend on the type of nuts and seeds and whether they are whole, chopped, or slivered.

For stovetop toasting, place shelled nuts or seeds in a single layer in a heavy, ungreased skillet. Toast over medium heat, shaking the pan and stirring them to keep them from scorching, until they are golden brown. Dried shredded coconut can be toasted in the same way. *Cooking times:* for seeds, 3 to 5 minutes; for nuts, 5 to 10 minutes; for coconut, 3 to 4 minutes.

For oven toasting (convenient when you are preheating the oven for baking), place shelled nuts in a shallow baking pan. Stir the nuts occasionally. Cook until they are golden. Peanuts and Brazil nuts can be roasted in their shells. *Cooking time:* 10 to 25 minutes in a 350° oven.

For microwave toasting, spread the nuts in a single layer on a paper plate. *Cooking time:* 1½ minutes at 100 percent power, then stir, let stand for a minute, and cook for another 1½ minutes.

SERVING SUGGESTIONS As a garnish or flavor accent, nuts and seeds particularly enhance

NUTS IN THE SHELL

Buying nuts and seeds in the shell is the best way to keep them fresh, as well as the most economical way to buy them. Still, there is a lot of waste, and it can be difficult to know just how much usable "meat" you're getting. The chart below details the yields from a pound of the various type of nuts and seeds in the shell.

One pound nuts in the shell	Yield/cups shelled nuts
Almonds	1½
Brazil	1½
Chestnuts	2½
Filberts	3½
Peanuts	2
Pecans	2¼
Pistachios	4
Walnuts, black	¾
Walnuts, English	2

NUT AND SEED BUTTERS

Nut and seed butters are simply nuts or seeds ground into a paste. Peanut butter—which was devised by a St. Louis physician in 1890 for elderly and invalid patients—is probably the most famiiiar of these. Other popular types on the market are almond butter, cashew butter, and tahini. The latter is a butter made from ground sesame seeds, and is used in Middle Eastern dishes, such as hummus.

These butters, like the nuts and seeds they're made from, are high in protein, B vitamins, phosphorus, magnesium, and iron. But they also derive 75 percent or more of their hefty calorie count from fat and, in the case of salted products, contain a significant amount of sodium. When choosing nut butters, keep the following in mind:

- Stick to small serving sizes. Two tablespoons of peanut butter—plenty for a sandwich—provides 188 calories, 16 grams of fat. When added to 2 slices of whole wheat bread and two tablespoons of jelly, the calorie count rises to 428, with 38 percent of the calories coming from fat. Reducing the peanut butter to 1 tablespoon and substituting half a medium banana for the jelly will produce a sandwich with 284 calories and 10 grams of fat (or 32 percent of the calories coming from fat).
- The fat in commercial almond and cashew butters and tahini is mostly unsaturated. Most peanut butters, however, include hydrogenated oils—which add saturated fat—to keep the oils naturally present from separating, and to increase its shelf life; if hydrogenated oils are used, they must be listed on the food label. (Commercial peanut butter may also contain extra sugar.) Natural peanut butters, made only from peanuts and sometimes salt, have about 15 percent less fat.
- Nut butters flavored with honey and cinnamon are slightly lower in calories and fat by weight, since the honey and cinnamon take the place of some of the fat. Two tablespoons (about an ounce) of honey cinnamon almond butter has 192 calories and 17 grams of fat, compared to 202 calories and 19 grams of fat in the same serving of regular almond butter.
- You can easily make your own nut butter at home by placing nuts in a blender or food processor, a handful at a time, and processing until they form a paste; add a little salt, if you prefer. For a crunchy butter, chop some nuts as coarse or as fine as you like, then stir them into the butter. Prepare small amounts at a time, since homemade butters don't keep as well as store-bought types.

Commercial nut and seed butters will keep for about a year, unopened, on the shelf. Once opened, they should be refrigerated, especially the "natural" types. Refrigeration will help to prevent the oil from separating and keep the product fresher longer. Commercial nut and seed butters will keep for three to four months in the refrigerator; homemade or store-ground butters will stay for about 10 days.

COMPARING NUT AND SEED BUTTERS (2 tablespoons, about 1 ounce)

	Calories	Protein (g)	Fat (g)	PERCENT CALORIES FROM Total Fat	Saturated Fat	Polyunsaturated fat	Monounsaturated fat
Almond butter	202	5	19	85%	8%	18%	55%
Cashew butter	188	6	16	77%	15%	13%	45%
Peanut butter	188	8	16	77%	14%	24%	36%
Tahini	179	5	16	81%	10%	35%	30%

bland-tasting, smooth-textured foods. A spoonful of chopped nuts or whole seeds will provide a crunchy contrast to foods like low-fat yogurt or cottage cheese, applesauce or apple butter, or hot breakfast cereal. A sprinkling of chopped nuts or whole seeds will add a finishing touch to vegetable, fruit, pasta, or grain salad. Use walnut, hazelnut, or dark sesame oil in the dressing. The traditional Waldorf salad, made with apples, celery, and walnuts, can be varied with other nuts. To keep the nuts crisp, toast them before tossing them with moist salad ingredients.

Try adding walnuts or almonds to a bread-based poultry stuffing, or fold sunflower or pumpkin seeds into a grain stuffing for vegetables, or into a grain casserole. Stir slivered almonds or pistachios into rice pilaf, or toss chopped nuts with pasta.

SUNFLOWER SEEDS AND BAKED GOODS

Sunflower kernels are a good addition to quick breads and muffins, but if you use them in a recipe that calls for baking soda, they'll turn the finished product green. This change in color, which is completely harmless, occurs because the polyphenol compounds in sunflower kernels react under alkaline (basic) pH conditions. (Baking soda is a base.) There is an easy remedy: Just balance the baking soda with an acid ingredient (fruit juice or fruit), molasses, or honey, and the color change will not take place. And if you add sunflower kernels to dark-colored baked goods, such as pumpkin bread or carrot muffins, the greenish tinge won't be noticeable.

Mix finely chopped nuts with breadcrumbs for dredging fish, poultry or meat. Sprinkle baked or sautéed fish or chicken with chopped nuts before serving. Toss cashews or peanuts into Chinese stir-fries. Scatter a few chopped nuts instead of croutons over a bowl of soup.

Nuts can accent a variety of desserts. Add chopped nuts to fillings for baked apples or pears, or to the topping for fruit crisps. When making cakes, cookies, and other desserts, use a smaller quantity of nuts than the recipe calls for, or replace those that are high in fat with lower-fat nuts and seeds. Incorporate chopped nuts or seeds in quick-bread or muffin batters, or sprinkle them over muffin batter just before baking.

Accompany a dessert or snack of fresh or dried fruits with a few nuts in their shells. Create homemade snack mixes by combining pumpkin or sunflower seeds with pretzel sticks, cereal, and dried fruits.

Nut butters are not just for sandwiches. Peanut or sesame butter adds flavor to Szechuan cold noodles (see Pasta, page 346), and thickens and enriches other sauces. If you can afford a modicum of fat in your snacks, try apple slices spread with a little peanut butter, or a pear with almond butter. Or, spread nut butter on a peeled banana, then roll it in crushed cereal; wrap and freeze for an ice cream-like treat. Swirl a teaspoonful of peanut or cashew butter into ice milk or frozen yogurt.

Peanut soup—which originated in Africa and South America and was popularized in the United States by George Washington Carver—is prepared by adding peanut butter to a well-seasoned chicken broth, along with onions, celery, and lemon juice.

Chestnuts are frequently used as a vegetable. Put boiled chestnuts through a food mill and serve like mashed potatoes, or coarsely chop them and add to poultry stuffing. For a holiday meal, toss together cooked, shelled chestnuts and Brussels sprouts.

Serve puréed chestnuts that have been sweetened and flavored with vanilla, for a delicious and unusual dessert. The French usually top them with sweetened whipped cream, but many people find chestnut purée to be sufficiently rich-tasting on its own.

Chapter 7

MEAT AND POULTRY

Americans have always appreciated meat. In colonial days, they hunted game animals for it, and by the early 1800s, as more people left farms to settle in towns, they brought it with them preserved with salt. In the 1870s, the growth of the cattle industry, and new methods of feeding and transporting domestic animals, introduced fresh meat into the average person's daily diet. Meat and poultry became the central focus of meals, and they have remained so, to a striking degree: Americans, who make up only 7 percent of the world's population, eat one third of the world's meat supply.

In the past decade, however, the role of meat and poultry in the American diet has come under greater scrutiny than that of any other food. Nutritionists have recommended that we eat less meat—particularly red meat—because of the total fat, saturated fat, and cholesterol it contains. Vegetarian and semivegetarian diets are in vogue, and many consumers now regard red meats as "bad" foods. Poultry, on the other hand, has come into favor because it is lower in fat. While we are eating more meat and poultry than ever before—176 pounds per person per year—the kinds of meat we choose has changed. Beef consumption has declined steadily since 1976, when Americans reached an all-time high of 89 pounds per person—25 pounds more than we eat today. During the same period, pork consumption has also declined, while that of chicken and turkey has risen. Today, we eat as much poultry as we do beef—64 pounds per person annually.

TWO CONCERNS: FAT AND CHOLESTEROL

Red meat is one of the major sources of fat and cholesterol in the American diet; these substances have long been implicated in various illnesses. Studies have shown that too much dietary fat and cholesterol can increase the risk for heart disease. A high-fat diet also leads to an increased risk of some cancers. For instance, the rate of breast cancer in American women is six times that of Japanese women, and this has been attributed in part to the fact that the Japanese eat much less fat. In addition, a diet high in total fat probably promotes obesity, which itself is a risk factor for heart disease, cancer, and diabetes.

The amount of saturated fat in some meats can pose a threat to health. A diet high in saturated fat can lead to elevated blood cholesterol levels, which, in turn, may result in the coronary arteries becoming clogged, setting the stage for a heart attack. Studies in the United States have found that vegetarians have, on average, blood cholesterol levels 29 percent lower than people who eat meat regularly. Lacto-ovo vegetarians (those who consume only dairy products, eggs, vegetables, and fruit), have, on average, blood cholesterol levels 16 percent lower than people who eat meat regularly.

A high intake of saturated fat may also increase the risk of colon cancer. According to a study of 89,000 female registered nurses published in the *New England Journal of Medicine,* women who ate the most animal fat were almost twice as likely to develop colon cancer as those with the lowest intake. Of all foods the women consumed, beef, pork, and lamb were most strongly linked to colon cancer, particularly if the women had these foods as a main course at least once a day. Women who regularly ate skinless chicken or fish rather than red meats cut their risk by as much as 50 percent.

The amount of cholesterol in meat is also a concern. Fat and saturated fat content vary according to the species of animal, the cut, whether the fat is trimmed or the skin is removed (on poultry), and in some cases, the grade of meat. (The individual entries will tell you which are the leanest types of meat or poultry.) But the cholesterol content of all types of meat, whether it is lean or fatty, is roughly the same—20 to 25 milligrams per ounce. This amount does not fluctuate because cholesterol is found in lean tissue as well as in the fat. However, saturated fat has a far greater effect on blood cholesterol levels than does dietary cholesterol.

THE NUTRIENTS IN MEAT

You don't need to eat meat and poultry to survive; it's possible to get all the nutrients you need from a vegetarian diet, especially if you also include low-fat dairy products and/or fish. But meat and poultry are exceptionally rich in iron, zinc, and vitamins B_6 and B_{12}—nutrients that are difficult to obtain in a meatless diet.

Iron, for example, is essential for the production of hemoglobin in our bodies. But, according to the National Academy of Sciences, about 14 percent of women between the ages of fifteen and forty-four have some degree of iron deficiency. Meat and poultry contain heme iron, the type that is best absorbed by the body; the iron in plant foods, in contrast, is nonheme iron, and is not as well absorbed. For example, about 15 percent of the iron in beef, lamb, chicken, and pork is absorbed by the body, compared to 5 percent in blackstrap molasses and raisins, and 4 percent in navy beans.

About 70 percent of the zinc in the American diet comes from animal products, mostly meat. Chicken and pork contain impressive levels of vitamin B_6. As for vitamin B_{12}, it is not easy to find sources other than animal products, unless you consume fortified soy milk, some nutritional yeasts, or supplements. And, of course, meat and poultry are known for their high protein content, supplying (along with fish) 48 percent of the protein in the American diet. Moreover, the protein in meat, unlike that in vegetables and grains, is complete, meaning that it provides all of the amino acids needed by the body.

BALANCING THE MEAT IN YOUR DIET

Moderation, not abstinence, is the key: It is overconsumption of meat that puts health in jeopardy; small servings will provide significant amounts of nutrients without adding excess fat to your diet. Just 3½ ounces—about the size of a deck of cards—of trimmed, cooked sirloin steak or skinless chicken breast yields more than half of the RDA for protein. The steak also furnishes about a third of the RDA for riboflavin, niacin, vitamin B_6, phosphorus, and iron, about half the RDA for zinc, and one and a half times the RDA for vitamin B_{12}. The chicken offers about 17 percent of the RDA for vitamin B_{12}, about 30 percent of the vitamin B_6, and about 75 percent of the niacin.

Few experts recommend eliminating all meat, or even all red meat, from our diets, because of its nutritional value. In fact, all types can be part of a low-fat diet, if you follow some simple guidelines.

- Eat small portions—about 3½ to 4 ounces.
- Choose lean cuts of beef, pork, or lamb—those that have less than 10 grams of fat in a 3½-ounce serving.

- Substitute chicken or turkey for some of the red meat in your diet; avoid goose and duck, which are much fattier, except on occasion.
- Treat meat as a side dish that complements a meal of vegetables, grains, or legumes.
- Limit fattier cuts of meat, such as prime beef, bacon, and sausage, to special occasions.
- Trim all of the external fat from red meats and remove the skin from poultry.
- Choose low-fat cooking methods—such as roasting, grilling, broiling, and poaching—over frying. Stir-frying and sautéing are acceptable, provided you use little additional fat.

TOUGH OR TENDER

Meat is muscle, made up mostly of water and protein, with some fat. Beef, without external fat, for example, is, on average, 72 percent water, 21 percent protein, and 6 percent fat by weight. Chicken, without skin, is 75 percent water, 21 percent protein, and 3 percent fat. If you looked at a cut of meat or poultry under a microscope, you would see that it is composed of individual, cylindrical muscle fibers. These are held together by thin bands of connective tissue, of which there are two main types: collagen and elastin. Connective tissues are more abundant in those parts of the animal that do a lot of work, because exercise builds connective tissue; this partially accounts for the toughness of cuts from these areas. (Cuts of meat high in connective tissue also tend to be fattier than more tender cuts, because fat is deposited around connective tissue first.) Collagen turns to gelatin when it is heated in liquid—this transformation explains why stewing tenderizes tough cuts of meat. Marinating in an acidic liquid also softens collagen. Elastin is not affected by cooking and can be broken down only by pounding or cutting.

Muscle fibers generally run in only one direction, called the grain. Cutting tough meat across the grain helps to tenderize it in two ways: First, it shortens the muscle fibers, and thus allows you to chew with the grain; second, it breaks up the connective tissues that make meat tough.

THE COLOR OF MEAT

Hemoglobin, the pigment that makes blood red, is not responsible for the red color of beef and lamb and the dark color of chicken or turkey drumsticks. When an animal is slaughtered, most of the hemoglobin is removed as the animal is bled. The color of meat comes instead from myoglobin, another red pigment present in the muscles, which stores oxygen. The parts of an animal containing well-exercised muscles—which require more oxygen—are darker than underused areas. For example, the legs of chickens and turkeys are dark because these animals stand or walk a lot, but their wing and breast meat is white because they hardly fly. On the other hand, goose, duck, and game birds use many of their muscles for flying, and consequently all their meat is dark. As for cattle, a cut of beef from the shoulder, which is involved in walking, is darker than a cut from the loin, which is minimally active. In addition, the type of animal dictates the color of the meat. Beef muscles contain more myoglobin than those of pork or veal.

ARE MEAT AND POULTRY SAFE?

All meat sold in the United States is inspected for wholesomeness by the Food Safety and Inspection Service (FSIS) of the United States Department of Agriculture (USDA), which includes a team of veterinarians. Animals are examined before slaughter for signs of disease, and unhealthy animals are not slaughtered for food.

Every so often, reports appear in the media about excessive hormone, antibiotic, or chemical residues in meat and poultry, and such stories cause great concern among consumers. It's true that hormones—the natural sex steroids estradiol (estrogen), progesterone, and testosterone, as well as two synthetic ones—are used in the raising of livestock, particularly cattle; 70 to 90 percent of the cattle in the United States are given hormones to make them gain weight faster.

These growth stimulants are popular among cattlemen because they save money—savings that are passed on to the consumer. Hormone-treated cattle eat less and reach market sooner, yet gain approximately fifty pounds more lean muscle tissue than an untreated animal. So not only do we save money and resources, but we also get leaner meat. The Food and Drug Administration (FDA) says that hormone-treated beef is safe to eat and, at the prescribed dosages used in feedlots, these hormones have been certified safe. There is virtually no evidence to the contrary. The residues left in meat are so minuscule that each day an average man produces about fifteen thousand times more hormone and the average pregnant women several millions times more than is found in a pound of beef. And many foods naturally contain estrogen: Milk has five times more estrogen, by weight, than hormone-treated beef, and wheat germ, seventeen hundred times more.

Antibiotics are not a part of regular raising practices, but they are prescribed for sick animals. Numerous studies have shown that their minuscule residues are not a risk to human health.

In a recent routine check of levels of 133 animal drugs and pesticides, the FSIS found a violation rate of only about 0.3 percent. All of these transgressions involved illegal amounts of animal drug residues—not pesticides or other chemicals or hormones—and most were only slightly above the legal limits, which are at least a hundred times less than what would be harmful to humans. These violations usually occurred because not enough time had been allowed for the drugs used in treating a sick animal to clear its system before it came to slaughter.

When excessive levels of drugs, chemicals, or hormones are found, they usually occur in the animal's liver, kidneys, or fat—not in the lean tissue. By avoiding organ meats (which are very high in cholesterol), choosing lean cuts, and trimming excess fat, not only do you reduce the amount of fat in your diet, but you significantly reduce the risk of contamination from these substances should they be present.

FOOD POISONING: REDUCING THE RISK

One safety concern that has not been exaggerated is the risk of bacterial contamination in meats and poultry. Every year, at least fifteen hundred to two thousand Americans die, and over six million others get sick, from salmonella and campylobacter poisoning, according to estimates by the Centers for Disease Control. Beef, pork, and chicken, as well as eggs and other meats, can harbor salmonella, while chicken (and raw milk) can house campylobacter organisms. Poultry is more prone to spoilage than other meats, in part because it is sold with its skin, which carries more bacteria than its flesh. Poultry that has been improperly handled is probably the main source of food-borne illness.

The way almost all poultry is raised and processed also contributes to its increased levels of contamination. Chicken production is a highly—but not completely—

automated industry that strives for efficiency: A high-speed production line can slaughter and gut as many as ninety chickens a minute, and generate a great deal of filth. Mechanical eviscerating and other processing methods increase the bacteria count. Recently the industry has come under fire from the press, consumers, and Congress. According to a variety of estimates, at least half of all raw chicken marketed is contaminated with salmonella, campylobacter, or both.

The USDA is responsible for meat and poultry inspection, but in the last decade its performance has reportedly been less than thorough. Although the poultry industry grew, the number of USDA inspectors declined. The USDA seal, according to industry critics, is no longer a guarantee of a clean, wholesome product.

The risks of getting food poisoning from poultry and other foods are eliminated through proper handling and cooking. To prevent food poisoning from meat and poultry, follow the general guidelines below. Other safety tips are included in each entry as they pertain to the particular meat.

- Keep your refrigerator below 40° and the freezer at, or below, 0°.
- Wash your hands thoroughly before and after handling raw meats. Use soap and warm water, and wash for at least 20 seconds, working soap into the hands, including the fingernail area and between the fingers.
- Use a fresh dish towel every time you cook meat.
- Defrost frozen meats only in the refrigerator, in the microwave, or, in some cases, in cold water. Never thaw foods at room temperature. The outside surface thaws before the inside, leaving the outside prone to bacterial contamination and growth.
- After preparing raw meat or poultry, wash the utensils, counter, cutting board—anything that came into contact with the meat—thoroughly in hot, soapy water before preparing other foods.
- Marinate meats and poultry only in the refrigerator. Don't put cooked meat back into an uncooked marinade, and don't serve the marinade as a sauce unless you heat it to a rolling boil for several minutes.
- Don't serve barbecued meat on the plate that previously held the raw meat, and don't use the cooking utensils for serving.

- Never eat meat raw. Steak tartare may be considered a delicacy by some people, but it is dangerous to eat.
- Keep meats at room temperature for no more than an hour before or after cooking, and promptly refrigerate leftovers.
- Cook meats to the recommended internal temperatures. See the individual entries for guidelines.

COOKING MEAT AND POULTRY

Some foods can be enjoyed either raw or cooked, but with meat and poultry, you really don't have a choice. Although carpaccio and steak tartare—both made with raw beef—are still listed on some restaurant menus, health authorities today discourage the consumption of raw meat in any form. As for raw poultry, it has long been recognized as highly unsafe. Cooking renders these foods safe to eat, as well as more palatable and easier to digest.

The question, then, is how to cook these foods for maximum flavor, tenderness, and digestibility while keeping fat to a minimum. If you know where various cuts of meat come from, it will help you choose the right cooking method for each cut: See the individual entries in this chapter for more information.

Cooking meat successfully demands careful timing and temperature control. On the one hand, heat softens connective tissue, making meat tender. But a very high temperature or an excessively long cooking time will harden the protein, rendering the meat tough. High heat also causes moisture loss, resulting in dry meat or poultry. The goal is to cook the food just until the connective tissue is softened, but not so long that the muscle fibers turn tough. Gentle heat is usually best, but for some methods, such as broiling, that isn't an option. The safest and most accurate way to determine doneness is to use a meat thermometer; it will prevent you from serving meat or poultry that is not properly cooked.

The flavors we appreciate in meat and poultry evolve during the cooking process. Heat causes certain compounds in meat to develop the familiar taste and characteristic smell that we associate with it. In addition, high temperatures bring about complex "browning reactions" that make the outer crust of meats, such as roast beef or broiled chops, intensely savory.

Meat and poultry are cooked either by dry- or moist-heat methods. The former, which includes broiling and roasting, allows fat to melt and drain off; the latter, which encompasses braising and stewing, tenderizes leaner cuts of meat. The choice of cooking method also determines how well nutrients will be conserved. Thiamin is the vitamin most at risk; it is destroyed by heat, and also leaches into cooking liquid. (Other B vitamins are similarly affected, but to a lesser degree.) Dry-heat methods will conserve more thiamin than braising or stewing. However, if the liquid from a braised or stewed dish is made into a sauce or gravy, the nutrients will not be lost; the same is true if the broth from poached meat or poultry is used in a sauce or soup. Microwave cooking—which nicely retains the nutrients in vegetables—may not work as well for meat and poultry, as these foods release more liquid when microwaved and lose nutrients in the process.

Beef

The United States was once a nation of confirmed beef eaters, but no longer. In part, concern about fat, saturated fat, and cholesterol, and the role these substances play in cancer, obesity, and heart disease, has steered many people away from beef; since 1976 consumption has dropped 28 percent. According to one survey, one out of every seven men and one out of every eight women in the United States have stopped eating beef entirely.

Today's beef isn't as fatty as that of years past; fat content has dropped about 27 percent since the early 1980s. Noting the preference for low-fat protein, ranchers are crossbreeding traditional breeds with leaner, larger cattle. In addition, cattle are being fed more grass and less corn, and are being sent to market younger so that they will develop less fat. And meatpackers and retailers are trimming more external fat, leaving about 1/10 inch, down from 3/4 inch just five years ago. More than 40 percent of retail cuts of beef have virtually no external fat at all, according to a survey by researchers at the Texas Agricultural Experiment Station at Texas A & M University.

Beef can be a part of a low-fat diet if you follow three simple steps: Choose lean cuts, eat small portions (3½ to 4 ounces, cooked), and trim all visible fat before cooking. Beef is an excellent source of iron, zinc, and vitamin B_{12}—nutrients that can be hard to obtain elsewhere, especially if you are on a vegetarian diet. You don't need to eat slabs of steak or roast to get the nutritional benefits beef has to offer (see the nutritional profile on page 388). Furthermore, trimming the fat has no effect on the vitamin and mineral quality of the meat. Whether the meat is lean or fatty, the levels of these nutrients are approximately the same.

Beef's fat content is widely variable, however, and only the leanest pieces are as low in fat as broiled fish or skinless chicken. There are two factors to consider when choosing a low-fat cut of beef: grade and cut. Grading is a voluntary service established by the USDA and offered to slaughterhouses. Government inspectors evaluate beef carcasses in terms of their marbling, the white streaks or specks of fat within the flesh itself that help give meat its juiciness and distinct flavor. Ironically, the system rewards the production of fatty beef; the cuts with the most marbling are given the highest grade—Prime—followed by Choice and Select. In 1987, to make lean beef more appealing to consumers, the USDA coined the term Select, thus replacing the category Good.

Beef liver is an excellent source of riboflavin, folacin, vitamin B_{12} (a 3½ ounce serving provides over three thousand times the RDA for this vitamin), phosphorus, iron, zinc, niacin, and vitamin B_6. It is also low in fat, furnishing just 5 grams in 3½ ounces, or 27 percent of its calories.

The drawback to liver is its high cholesterol count; 3½ ounces supplies 369 milligrams of cholesterol, more than the recommended maximum daily intake.

On average, a cut of beef graded Select has 5 to 20 percent less fat than Choice beef of the same cut, and 40 percent less fat than Prime. Since grading is not compulsory and costs the meatpacker money, much of the beef in the supermarkets is ungraded—about 44 percent in 1989, according to the American Meat Institute. This ungraded beef is usually of Choice or Select quality and may be sold under the store's brand. Of the beef that is graded, Choice is the most common designation; about 80 percent of the beef graded in 1991 was Choice, 18 percent was Select, and 2 percent was Prime.

Perhaps more important than grade when determining fat content is cut, which refers to the part of the animal from which a piece of meat

VEAL

Delicately flavored and light-textured, veal is a highly versatile meat that comes from very young calves. It is an expensive food and has always been considered a specialty in the United States, where consumption of veal now stands at less than a pound per person each year (down from about 9 pounds per person annually in the 1940s). Italians, by contrast, eat veal as often as Americans eat beef, and a fondness for it extends throughout much of western Europe. The reason for its widespread use overseas is partly tied to economics: There is less grazing land in Europe than in the Americas, hence farmers slaughter male cattle at a young age rather than pay the expense of raising them. Not surprisingly, most of our favorite veal dishes are distinctively European: veal cutlets and scaloppine served with various sauces, stews, and braises, and stuffed veal roasts.

The finest veal comes from animals that are only two to three months old and haven't been weaned. The meat from milk-fed veal is light pink, and the texture is firm but velvety. It is generally available only at restaurants and specialty butchers. The veal sold at supermarkets is usually from older animals—sixteen to twenty weeks old—so that the flesh has become increasingly darker and less tender than that of milk-fed veal.

Veal is somewhat lower in fat than beef—a 3½-ounce serving of trimmed, roasted veal sirloin, for example, contains 6 grams of fat and 168 calories; a similar-sized portion of choice beef sirloin has 9 grams of fat and 211 calories. A lean leg of veal has only 150 calories and 3 grams of fat, or 18 percent of its calories from fat—about the same as skinned chicken breast.

While the cuts of veal are similar to those of beef, there are fewer of them. For the primal cuts, veal is divided up like lamb: *foreshank* and *breast, shoulder, rib, loin,* and *leg* (which includes the *sirloin*). The most popular retail cuts are loin and rib chops, boneless rolled loin roast, boneless shoulder, as well as roasts, cutlets, and scallops made from the leg. The leg cutlets and scallops are the leanest cuts. One good bargain, nutritionally as well as economically, is ground veal; if the meat is taken from the leg or shoulder, it has much less fat than ground beef or lamb.

All cuts of veal are relatively tender. At the same time, veal's lack of marbling means that broiling it tends to yield meat that is dry and tough. Steaks, cutlets, scallops, and chops are best sautéed or braised; the tougher cuts from the lower leg and shoulder benefit most from moist-heat methods—roasting, braising, and stewing.

When you shop for veal, look for light pink, fine-grained meat with little marbling; any fat should be firm and white. (Some veal may carry a USDA grade of Prime or Choice.) Veal should be stored like beef.

Trim off any fat from the meat, including the membrane that surrounds veal scallops; this will prevent the meat from curling as it cooks. Scallops are also usually pounded before cooking to flatten and tenderize them.

comes. Select beef of one cut may have more fat than Choice beef of another cut. For example, 3½ ounces of Select trimmed blade roast (chuck) has 14 grams of fat, as compared to 6 grams of fat in Choice trimmed top round.

CUTS OF BEEF Primal cuts, listed below, are wholesale terms that refer to the sections of the animal. Within the primal cuts are many retail cuts, which are the names given to the steaks and roasts you find in the supermarket. According to the National Livestock and Meat Board, there are some three hundred different retail cuts, and a typical meat counter may display more than fifty cuts at one time. Meat labels always give both the primal and retail cut names. (See illustration page 384.) The list of primal cuts below also identifies common retail cuts.

COMPARING GROUND BEEF **3½ ounces cooked, medium**

	Calories	**Fat** (g)	**Saturated fat** (g)	**Cholesterol** (mg)
Regular ground beef	289	21	8	90
Lean ground beef	272	18	7	87
Extra lean ground beef	256	16	6	84

Brisket The front part of the breast is a boneless cut of beef with lots of fat—218 calories and 10 grams of fat per 3½-ounce serving, trimmed and cooked. Brisket cuts—*flat half brisket, corned brisket, point half brisket,* and *whole brisket*—are best braised or cooked in liquid.

Chuck This cut encompasses meat from the shoulder, arm, and neck of the animal. One of the hardest-working areas of the animal's body, the chuck contains a lot of connective tissue, and, therefore, is not very tender. Chuck cuts include: *chuck eye roast, boneless top blade steak, arm pot roast, boneless shoulder pot roast, cross rib pot roast, blade roast, short ribs, flanken style ribs,* and *stew beef.* (Ground beef is also produced from chuck cuts, among others.) All of these should be cooked in liquid for long periods of time at moderate temperatures; that is the best way to break down the connective tissue and tenderize the meat. The exception is chuck eye roast, which may be roasted. Chuck cuts are relatively fatty, even when trimmed: A 3½-ounce portion of trimmed, braised Select blade roast contains 356 calories and 14 grams of fat.

Flank From this section, which is just behind the belly, comes *flank steak,* also called *London broil* in some parts of the country. It is a flavorful, relatively tender, and lean cut, which is suitable for broiling—though if cooked beyond the medium rare stage, it gets very tough. It can also be braised, panbroiled, or stir-fried. The meat should be cut very thin on a sharp angle across the grain to make it easier to chew.

Foreshank The meat from the front legs of the steer is quite tough, and is used primarily for stew and ground beef. You may also find small steaks labeled *shank cross cuts,* which are well suited for braising or cooking in liquid.

Rib Cuts from the rib are quite tender; however, those from the section nearest the chuck are less tender than the ones from the area nearest the loin. Most rib cuts are packaged as roasts—*rib roast, large end* (near the chuck), *rib roast, small end* (near the loin), *rib eye roast*—but sometimes the roasts are cut into steaks, called *rib steaks* and *rib eye steaks* (also known as *Delmonico steaks*). In general, rib cuts should be roasted, but the steaks can be broiled or grilled. *Back ribs,* another cut from this section, come with the bone intact and should be either roasted or braised.

Round This rear section of the steer is so named because it contains the round bone, or femur. Although the muscles in the round are as hardworking as those in the chuck, meat from the round is more tender because the muscles all run in one direction. The round offers three of the leanest cuts of beef available: *eye of round, top round,* and *round tip.* The Select grade of these cuts has 4 to 5 grams of fat and less than 200 calories per 3 ½-ounce serving, cooked and trimmed. As roasts, these cuts can be roasted or braised; as steaks, they can be broiled or panbroiled. Other cuts from this section include: *boneless rump roast* and *bottom round roast,* which should be roasted or braised, and *round steak,* which should be braised.

Short Loin The tenderest cuts come from the loin, the muscle that does the least work. Two of the leanest cuts of beef—*top loin* and *tenderloin*—are from this section; each cut furnishes about 200 calories and 7 to 9 grams of fat per 3½ ounces, cooked and trimmed. The tenderloin

COMPARING BEEF CUTS

3½ ounces trimmed* and cooked

	Calories	**Fat** (g)	**Saturated fat** (g)	**Cholesterol** (mg)
Arm, choice	219	9	3	101
Arm, prime ††	261	13	5	101
Blade roast, choice	265	15	6	106
Blade roast, prime ††	318	21	8	106
Blade roast, select	238	12	5	106
Bottom round, choice	193	8	3	78
Bottom round, prime ††	249	13	5	96
Bottom round, select	171	5	2	78
Brisket, half point, all grades	212	9	3	95
Brisket, whole, all grades	218	10	4	93
Eye of round, choice	175	6	2	69
Eye of round, prime ††	198	8	3	69
Eye of round, select	155	4	1	69
Flank, choice	237	13	6	71
Porterhouse steak, choice †	218	11	4	80
Rib eye, choice	225	12	5	80
Ribs, whole, choice †	237	14	6	77
Ribs, whole, prime †	280	19	8	81
Ribs, whole, select †	206	10	4	77
Round, select †	172	5	2	78
Round, choice †	191	7	3	78
Shank crosscuts, choice †	201	6	2	78
Short ribs, choice †	295	18	8	93
Sirloin, choice	200	8	3	89
Sirloin, prime ††	237	12	5	89
T-Bone steak, choice †	214	10	4	80
Tenderloin, choice	212	10	4	84
Tenderloin, prime †	232	12	5	84
Tenderloin, select	200	9	3	84
Tip round, choice	180	6	2	81
Tip round, prime †	213	10	4	81
Tip round, select	170	5	2	81
Top loin, choice	209	10	4	76
Top loin, prime †	245	14	5	76
Top loin, select	184	7	3	76
Top round, choice	207	6	2	90
Top round, prime †	215	9	3	84
Top round, select	190	4	1	90

**All cuts are completely trimmed of external fat unless otherwise noted. Cuts marked with † are trimmed to ¼ inch; cuts marked with †† are trimmed to ½ inch. Further trimming of those cuts would lower the calorie, fat, and saturated fat content.*

muscle yields the tenderest meat; from it comes *tenderloin roast* and a number of steaks. *Filets mignons* are small steaks cut from the tenderloin. *T-bone steaks* come from the middle or the loin and include some tenderloin. *Porterhouse steaks* have the most tenderloin. *Shell steaks* or *strip loin steaks* are porterhouse or T-bone steaks without the tenderloin. (These are sometimes called New York or Kansas City steaks.) Roasts from this section can be roasted or broiled; the steaks can be broiled or panbroiled.

AGED BEEF

Before beef reaches consumers, it is always aged for a certain period to improve its flavor and texture. The initial aging occurs after an animal has been slaughtered, which causes its muscles to stiffen (the condition known as rigor mortis). Meat cooked in this state would be very tough; aging allows the muscles to become tender again. The biochemistry behind aging isn't fully understood, but apparently enzymes normally present in the muscles actually digest the protein in the meat, altering both flavor and texture in the process.

Traditional aging—where a carcass of beef is hung for up to three weeks—makes beef even more tender and flavorful. This process is conducted under specific conditions of temperature and humidity, and ultraviolet light is often used to control the growth of microorganisms that could cause spoilage. (The covering of fat on beef carcasses also helps protect them from spoilage.) Because the process is expensive, traditionally aged meat is produced in limited quantities. Most of it is shipped to restaurants, but sometimes local butchers age their own meat. If you find it, expect to pay a premium price.

Short plate The rear of the breast, this section contains tough, fatty meat. Cuts include *skirt steak,* which is the preferred meat for fajitas, *short ribs,* and *spareribs.* Skirt steak can be braised, broiled, or panbroiled; short ribs and spareribs should be braised. Boneless cuts of beef for stew and ground beef also come from this section of the animal.

Sirloin Lying between the round and short loin, this section also contains lean, tender meat. The cuts are primarily steaks—*sirloin flat bone, sirloin round bone, sirloin pinbone,* and *top sirloin steak*—though you may also find *top sirloin butt roast;* some sirloin is ground. Pinbone is closest to the loin and is the most tender, but it has a lot of bone. Flat bone—the center cut—has less waste than the pinbone, but is tougher. Round bone is nearest to the round and is the toughest sirloin cut. Sirloin steaks, which are sold with or without the bone, can be broiled or panbroiled; top sirloin butt roast can be roasted. Sirloin cuts contain 211 calories and 9 grams of fat per $3^1/_2$-ounce serving, trimmed and cooked.

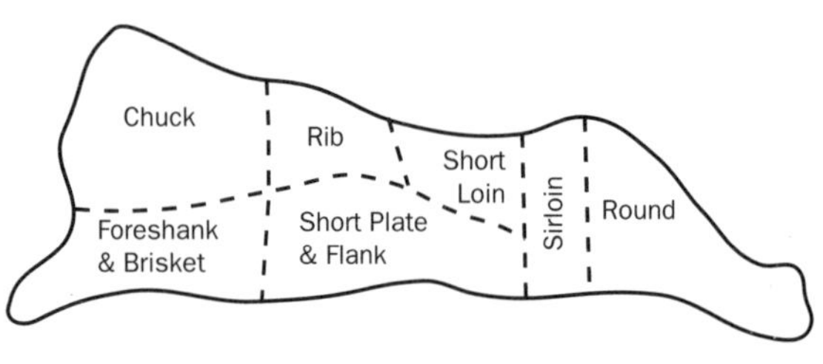

Ground beef Most ground beef comes from the chuck, sirloin, or round. Packages are labeled by cut of beef, by fat content, or both. Evaluating the fat content of packaged hamburger meat can be even more difficult than judging full cuts. While a steak or other cut of beef labeled "lean" must have no more than 10 percent fat by weight, and "extra lean," no more than 5 percent by weight, these standards don't apply to meat that is ground. Ground beef labeled 75 percent lean is 25 percent fat by weight, which is a lot of fat. Since fat has more than twice as many calories as lean meat, a patty made from this meat would derive 77 percent of its calories from fat when raw and 64 percent once cooked (cooking removes water and some fat from the meat). Lean ground beef is, on average, 21 percent fat by weight when raw, and derives 61 percent of its calories from fat when cooked. Extra lean ground beef is, on average, 17 percent fat by weight when raw, and derives 57 percent of its calories from fat when cooked. To get the leanest ground meat, buy a lean cut of sirloin or round and have the butcher trim it of all external fat and grind it for you, or you can do it yourself, using a meat grinder or food processor.

SHOPPING TIPS While cut and grade are good indicators of fat content, you still need to use your eyes when selecting beef. Look for cuts that have little marbling and external fat. If the store has a butcher, you can ask that the external fat be trimmed away.

Fresh beef is easy to spot. Many stores use freshness dates on their labels, so choose the meat with the furthest "sell-by" date. In addition, fresh beef has creamy white fat, not yellow, and feels springy to the touch.

Another means of judging freshness is color. When beef is first exposed to oxygen, it develops a cherry red color, called bloom. The inside of the beef, and any surfaces that are not exposed to oxygen (such as a cut of beef covered by another cut), are dark purple. (If the meat is vacuum packed, all of it will be dark purple, not cherry red, because the packing seals off any oxygen.) As time goes by, exposure to oxygen will cause the meat to turn brown. This color change doesn't mean that the meat is spoiled, only that it isn't as fresh as it could be and should be used immediately.

STORAGE Fresh beef is highly perishable and should be stored in the coldest part of the refrigerator immediately after purchase. Keep the meat in its original wrapping to minimize handling, which reduces the chance of contamination. The smaller the cut of beef, the more surface area is exposed to air, and the faster it will spoil. Large cuts of beef, such as roasts, therefore keep longer than smaller cuts, such as stew chunks. Roasts will keep for four to five days; steaks, three to four days; stew cuts, two or three days; and ground beef, one to two days, but taste best when used immediately.

To keep beef longer, you must freeze it. Although freezing will result in some loss of quality once the meat is thawed, you can minimize the deterioration by taking these steps: Make sure your freezer is set at 0° or lower; setting it even at 10° will cut storage life in half. The faster the meat freezes, the better it will hold its quality when thawed, so cut the beef into small portions before freezing. To create an airtight seal, wrap the beef in vaporproof, plastic-lined freezer paper or aluminum foil. Use a generous sheet of paper, so that you can tuck in all loose ends, and seal each package tightly with freezer tape. Don't forget to label all packages with dates and cuts. Then place each wrapped package in a plastic freezer bag. Roasts and steaks will keep for 6 to 12 months in the freezer; stew cuts, for 3 to 4 months; and ground beef, for 2 to 3 months. To help prevent food poisoning, thaw meats in the refrigerator.

PREPARATION Trim the fat before cooking. External fat and seam fat—the fat between individual muscles in a cut of beef—are the biggest sources of fat in beef. You can't remove the seam fat until the meat is cooked, but external fat can be taken off beforehand. Trimming external fat completely before cooking results in a 19 percent reduction in fat content, according to researchers at Texas A&M University. And pretrimming has no negative effect on flavor, tenderness, or juiciness (except in the case of beef brisket).

A marinade containing acidic ingredients, such as wine or vinegar, can add flavor to beef and help tenderize tough cuts. Make enough marinade to completely cover the meat, and place in a covered non-metal container in the refrigerator. (Or, place the marinade and the meat in a tightly sealed plastic bag, turning it occasionally to cover all sides.) Let the meat marinate for at least 6 hours, but not more than 24 hours; otherwise, the meat will turn mushy. Marinating for 15 minutes to 2 hours can add flavor, but does not tenderize the beef.

If you want to use the marinade as a sauce, cook it at a rolling boil for several minutes before serving. Uncooked marinade becomes contaminated from raw meat sitting in it and is therefore not safe to consume.

Rubs are blends of seasonings that are applied all over the surface of meat just before cooking. Their purpose is to flavor, not tenderize. For a more pronounced flavor, coat the meat several hours before cooking and refrigerate.

A tender cut of meat can turn tough as it cools. As meat heats, the collagen in the connective tissue turns to soft gelatin. When the meat cools, the gelatin thickens, making the meat tougher than when it was hot.

An easy way to tenderize meat is to pound it with a mallet. This technique, which involves breaking up the connective tissue, is useful for moderately thin cuts, such as eye of round, top round, and round tip.

TIMETABLE FOR BROILING BEEF

		MINUTES PER SIDE	
Cut	**Thickness**	**Rare**	**Medium**
Rib eye	1 inch	7	10
	1½ inches	12	15
	2 inches	17	23
Rib	1 inch	7	10
	1½ inches	12	15
	2 inches	17	23
Tenderloin	1 inch	7	10
	1½ inches	9	11
Top loin	1 inch	7	10
	1½ inches	12	15
	2 inches	17	23
Sirloin	1 inch	10	13
	1½ inches	13	15
	2 inches	20	23
Flank	1½ inches	6	7
Top round	1 inch	10	15
	1½ inches	15	17
Hamburgers	3 inches	7	13

Roasting and broiling The amount of time it takes to cook beef depends on a number of factors: cut, size, thickness, temperature, whether the meat is bone-in or boneless, and whether it is lean or fatty. So cooking time charts, like the ones below left and on page 387, can serve only as approximate guidelines. The best way to ensure that beef is properly cooked is to use a meat thermometer. Beef is cooked to the rare stage when it has reached an internal temperature of 140°; medium is reached at 160°; and well done is reached at 170°. The longer the meat cooks, the more fat is released.

Stir-frying The key to stir-frying is to cut the meat into very thin slices so that they cook quickly. Thinly sliced meat also goes further. Semi-freezing the meat firms it and makes it easier to slice into thin strips: Cut flank or round steak into 2-inch-wide strips, wrap the sections in foil or plastic, and place them in the freezer for 10 to 15 minutes, or just until the meat is slightly firm to the touch. Slice the meat in ¼-inch widths across the grain and marinate. Just before cooking, add a small amount of oil to the marinade mixture and stir. The light coating of oil on the beef will help to prevent sticking, a common complaint of less-experienced cooks. *Cooking time:* 3 to 5 minutes.

SERVING SUGGESTIONS Beef can have a place in a low-fat diet if it is served as a side dish or as part of a meal, rather than as the main course. Try complementing vegetables, salads, or grains with small portions of meat. You'll find that hearty foods, such as bulgur, rice pilaf, wild rice, acorn squash, or roasted or baked potatoes, all complement beef. Or, broil a cut of flank steak, eye of round, top round, or round tip and slice it thinly across the grain. Serve small portions atop a salad of mixed greens, red and yellow cherry tomatoes, radishes, and cucumbers. Toss with a low-fat dressing (see page 113).

For a healthy way to enjoy beef, prepare some kebabs. On each skewer, alternate chunks of top

TIMETABLE FOR ROASTING BEEF

Cut	Oven Temperature	Approximate Weight (lbs)	MINUTES PER POUND Rare	Medium	Well done
Rib eye	350°	4 to 6	14 to 16	16 to 18	18 to 20
Rib, rolled	300°	4 to 6	28 to 30	31 to 33	36 to 38
Rib, standing	300°	5 to 8	20 to 22	23 to 25	27 to 30
Sirloin	300°	8 to 12	20 to 22	23 to 25	27 to 30

The following roasts should be cooked until medium rare; the internal temperature should be 145°.

			MINUTES PER POUND
Eye of round	350°	3 to 6	14
Rump, rolled	300°	4 to 6	30 to 33
Rump, standing	300°	5 to 7	23 to 25
Sirloin tip	300°	3 to 5	30 to 33
Tenderloin	450°	4 to 6	8 to 9
Top round	300°	3 to 5	30 to 33

round or sirloin tip with vegetables, such as mushrooms, peppers, cherry tomatoes, onions, shallots, and summer squash. Include whole cloves of garlic if you like; the flavor mellows and turns nutty as they're grilled or broiled. You can marinate the meat beforehand, if you wish. Broil or grill the kebabs 4 to 5 inches from the heat for 3 to 5 minutes per side, until the beef reaches the desired doneness.

Stir-fry beef with vegetables, such as bamboo shoots, napa cabbage, bok choy, water chestnuts, baby corn, snow peas, and scallions. Or, experiment with red and green sweet peppers, carrots, celery, and broccoli.

For lower-fat versions of such favorites as beef stew or pot roast, buy lean cuts, like top or bottom round, rather than chuck. The preparation for either dish involves browning the meat first, to add flavor: Dredge the meat in flour, shake off the excess, and brown the meat in a nonstick skillet or Dutch oven, using a tablespoon of olive oil. To brown the meat without adding fat, broil it (don't dredge it in flour beforehand). The meat is then simmered in a liquid, such as wine, whole or crushed canned tomatoes with juice, beef broth, vegetable juice, or a combination of these. It is generally seasoned with oregano, basil, marjoram, thyme, and bay leaf. A stew or pot roast can be made a day ahead, but it must be refrigerated once it's cooled; the fat will congeal at the top for easy removal.

CORNED BEEF

Corned beef is beef brisket that has been cured in much the same way as ham. A seasoned brine that contains salt, seasonings, and sodium nitrite is injected into the cut of beef; this solution preserves the meat (though it still needs refrigeration). In Anglo-Saxon times, the beef was preserved with grains of salt about the size of corn kernels, hence the term corned.

Since brisket is a fatty cut of beef, it is not surprising that corned beef is high in fat. A 3½ ounce portion has 251 calories and 19 grams of fat, or 68 percent fat calories. The salting solution contributes a lot of sodium—1134 milligrams.

To cut back on fat when making beef stew, use less meat than the recipe calls for and round out the dish with wholesome vegetables, such as mushrooms, parsnips, summer squash, carrots, celery, turnips, potatoes, and sweet potatoes. Potatoes will also thicken the liquid, but you might want to substitute barley. Serve beef stew over rice, couscous, or millet.

When an occasion calls for the elegance of roast beef, be sure to trim all the visible fat from the meat and keep the serving sizes small. Succulent beef tenderloin is an excellent low-fat cut that cooks faster than traditional roasts. Rub it lightly with Dijon mustard, finely chopped parsley, and garlic before roasting. Broiled or grilled vegetables—such as potatoes, peppers, eggplant, or tomatoes—make delicious accompaniments. Lightly brush the vegetables with olive oil flavored with oregano and pepper, and broil until tender and golden.

Cut back on the fat in fajitas by substituting top round steak for the usual, fattier skirt steak. Marinate the meat in a mixture of lime juice, tomato juice, chopped cilantro, garlic, oregano, and finely chopped hot peppers. Grill or broil the steak along with bell peppers and onions. Slice it thinly across the grain and serve it in warm corn tortillas. (Flour tortillas often contain lard.)

Use lean ground beef for meat loaf or meatballs. To make these extra lean, combine ground beef with ground turkey breast. Mix in beaten egg whites, chopped onions, and garlic, Worcestershire sauce, ketchup, and herbs. Before adding ground beef to spaghetti sauce or chili, or using as a filling, brown it in a nonstick skillet and drain off the fat.

Marinades are wonderful for tenderizing lean cuts, such as flank steak or eye of round. Blend wine, vinegar, citrus juice or yogurt with fresh or dried herbs, chopped onions, and crushed garlic. A pinch of sugar will offset the sharpness of the acid ingredients. To make a richer marinade, use red, white, or balsamic vinegar with Dijon mustard, minced shallots, and tarragon. A mixture of lemon juice, lemon zest, finely chopped chives, basil, and dry mustard will provide a lighter-tasting version. For an Asian flavor, combine low-sodium soy sauce with fresh ginger, scallions, cilantro, and rice wine vinegar.

To add flavor to the more tender steaks or roasts—such as T-bone, porterhouse, and filet mignon—prepare a dry rub. Combine dried basil, oregano, and rosemary, then rub the mixture into the meat. Or, create a paste from thyme, dry mustard, pepper, and a small amount of olive oil. Brush the mixture on the meat just before broiling or grilling.

Concoct your own barbecue sauce, but use less sodium and sugar than bottled brands. Mix low-salt ketchup and tomato paste with brown sugar or honey, Worcestershire sauce, garlic, and vinegar.

BEEF, top loin, select 3½ oz trimmed/cooked

Calories	184	Fat	7 g
Protein	29 g	Saturated Fat	3 g
Carbohydrate	0 g	Cholesterol	76 mg
Dietary Fiber	None	Sodium	68 mg

KEY NUTRIENTS		% RDA Men	Women
Vitamin B_6	0.4 mg	20%	25%
Vitamin B_{12}	2 mcg	100%	100%
Iron	3 mg	30%	20%
Magnesium	27 mg	8%	10%
Niacin	5 mg	26%	33%
Phosphorus	218 mg	27%	27%
Potassium	396 mg	N/A	N/A
Riboflavin	0.2 mg	12%	15%
Zinc	5 mg	33%	42%

S=40% or more soluble N/A=Not Applicable N=Not Available

Chicken

Chicken is the most versatile of meats. It can be prepared in many ways—roasted, broiled, grilled, or poached, in soups, stews, and pot pies—and with a variety of seasonings, toppings, and sauces. No wonder, then, that it is a staple in practically every culture's cuisine. In the United States, simple roast chicken is a favorite. In Italy, chicken is sautéed with tomatoes, mushrooms, and wine and served *alla cacciatore*. The Spanish combine chicken with shellfish and rice to produce *paella*. Shredded chicken is used as a filling for tacos and enchiladas in Mexico. In India, chicken marinated in yogurt and baked in a special clay oven is called *tandoori*. The Japanese and Chinese use chicken in stir fries, often flavored with soy sauce and ginger. A favorite of French cooks is *coq au vin*, or chicken in wine.

Consumption of chicken in the United States has risen steadily since the 1940s, when revolutionary changes in breeding and marketing methods made it more abundant and affordable. USDA production figures show that in 1934 (the first year records were kept) thirty-four million broiler chickens were produced. Today, the industry processes that many in a little over one working day. The price paid for chicken (and other poultry) today, when adjusted for inflation, is only one-third of the price paid in the early 1960s. As a result, annual consumption of chicken has doubled since 1968, from 25 pounds per capita to 49 pounds.

But low price isn't the only factor contributing to chicken's increased popularity. More and more people have made a conscious decision to eat less red meat and more poultry in an effort to lower the fat in their diets. When cooked, light-meat chicken without the skin is 33 to 80 percent leaner than trimmed cooked beef, depending on the beef's cut and grade. Chicken breast, the leanest part of the chicken, has less than half the fat of a trimmed Choice grade T-bone steak. Moreover, the fat in chicken is less saturated than the fat found in beef.

Yet chicken is comparable to beef in quantity and quality of protein, with 3½ ounces of roasted chicken breast supplying 49 percent of the RDA for protein for the average man, and 62 percent for the average woman. Both foods supply approximately the same amounts of other vitamins and minerals, except that beef has slightly more iron and zinc.

Still, not all the chicken we eat is low in fat. If you eat chicken with the skin, you'll more than double the amount of fat and saturated fat; chicken skin derives 80 percent of its calories from fat, 23 percent of them from saturated fat. Dark-meat chicken supplies about the same amount of fat as light meat with the skin—about 10 grams of fat in 3½ ounces roasted—and dark meat is slightly higher in cholesterol as well. Dark meat with the skin is the fattiest of all, with 16 grams of fat per 3½ ounces roasted, deriving 56 percent of its calories from fat.

Fast-food chicken can be just as fatty as hamburgers. At McDonald's, for example, six Chicken McNuggets have 270 calories and 15 grams of fat—that's half of the calories coming from fat.

As with beef, chicken is graded for quality by the USDA only if the processors request and pay a fee for it. As a result, many processors have developed their own standards, and you often find ungraded chickens on the market. The chickens you do find on the market with a USDA grade are likely to be Grade A; lesser quality Grade B and C chickens are usually sold to food manufacturers for use in processed and packaged products. The fat content of the chicken is not a primary criterion for a top USDA rating (which is unlike the grading system for beef). Grade A birds are meaty, well shaped, free of feathers, and have a layer of fat. The skin must be unbroken, free of cuts, tears, bruises, or blemishes. A chicken with a bruised wing could have the wing cut off and be rated Grade C, but if the rest of the bird were of better quality, it would be cut up and the parts sold as Grade A.

TYPES OF CHICKEN Chicken is divided into classes based on age and sex. The meat from small, young chickens is usually leaner than that from larger birds.

Broiler/fryers The most popular type of chicken, broiler/fryers are six to eight weeks old and weigh 2½ to 5 pounds. They are meaty, tender, all-purpose birds, and despite their name can be roasted, grilled, poached, steamed, or sautéed as well as broiled and fried. They are not a good choice for stewing, however, as their meat will become dry and stringy.

Capons These are male chickens that have been surgically castrated. This practice results in large birds at a young age, so the meat remains tender. They are usually slaughtered when fifteen to sixteen weeks old, and they weigh 9½ to 10½ pounds. Capons have a large proportion of white meat but a thick layer of fat underneath the skin, which makes the white meat fattier than that of other chickens. They are best roasted.

Roasters These birds are a little older and larger than broiler/fryers. They are generally brought to market when they are three to five months old and weigh 3½ to 6 pounds. Roasters have tender, flavorful meat. They can be roasted, grilled, braised, or stewed.

Chicken liver—which is often chopped and used in sandwiches—is relatively low in calories and fat, but it contains 631 milligrams of cholesterol in 3½ ounces. That's double the maximum amount of cholesterol experts say you should consume in a day.

Rock Cornish hens Developed in the 1800s in the United States by crossing a Cornish game cock with the White Plymouth Rock chicken, Rock Cornish hens weigh ¾ to 2 pounds—the perfect size for serving one person, though a 2-pound bird could serve two people. These plump-breasted birds are very low in fat, and generally come onto the market at five or six weeks of age. You may occasionally find them fresh, but they are often sold frozen. The traditional way to serve Rock Cornish hens is roasted and stuffed, but they can also be broiled, braised, or sautéed.

KOSHER POULTRY

Kosher poultry is no more nutritious than regular poultry. Nor is it less likely to harbor salmonella or other bacteria. Kosher foods comply with a set of religious dietary laws, but they contain the same amount of fat and cholesterol as their non-kosher counterparts.

Kosher poultry is salted after slaughter to draw out the blood. This may kill some salmonella and other bacteria, but the birds are not salted long enough to kill all disease-causing bacteria. In addition, contamination can occur later on; like other poultry, kosher poultry is mechanically eviscerated and processed.

The salt used in koshering may increase the sodium content—500 milligrams of sodium in 8 ounces of kosher meat versus 150 milligrams in non-kosher, according to one study. This may be significant if you're on a low-sodium diet. Some producers claim to wash their birds to remove excess sodium.

Stewing chickens These mature hens are usually twelve months old and weigh 4 to 6 pounds. Their meat is flavorful but tough, making them excellent candidates for stewing, braising, and making stock.

Free-range chickens These are chickens that have been allowed to run freely in the farmyard and scratch for their food, unlike most chickens, which are raised in coops. Some people feel that free-range chickens have a better flavor because the exercise develops their muscles. Exercise also toughens muscles, but free-range chickens are usually slaughtered at a young age, so the meat remains tender. They are no more nutritious than

COMPARING CHICKEN PARTS
3½ ounces cooked

Broiler/Fryers	Calories	Fat (g)	Saturated fat (g)	Cholesterol (mg)
Breast, with skin	197	8	2	84
Breast, without skin	165	4	1	85
Dark meat, with skin	253	16	4	91
Dark meat, without skin	205	10	3	93
Drumstick, with skin	216	11	3	91
Drumstick, without skin	172	6	1	93
Leg, with skin	232	13	4	92
Leg, without skin	191	8	2	94
Light meat, with skin	222	11	3	84
Light meat, without skin	173	6	1	85
Wing, with skin	290	20	5	84
Wing, without skin	203	8	2	85
Roasters				
Dark meat, without skin	178	9	2	75
Light meat, without skin	153	4	1	75
Stewers				
Dark meat, without skin	258	15	4	95
Light meat, without skin	213	8	2	70
Capons				
Meat and skin	229	12	3	86

other chickens, however, and may come at a premium price. In addition, they are processed in the same way as other chickens, and therefore are just as prone to salmonella contamination.

Chicken parts According to the National Broiler Council, over 50 percent of chicken is purchased cut up as parts. You can purchase whole or half breasts with the bone in, or boneless, skinless chicken breast fillets. Drumsticks and wings are also sold separately. Chicken breasts can be roasted (usually referred to as baked), broiled, grilled, or sautéed. Drumsticks and wings can be baked, broiled, or grilled.

SHOPPING TIPS One way to get a really fresh chicken is to check the "sell-by" date on the store's label. Chicken can reach the supermarket as early as the next morning after slaughter. The sell-by date is seven to ten days from slaughter and it's the last day recommended for sale. However, the bird will remain fresh for up to three days afterward if properly refrigerated.

When shopping for a whole chicken, look for a well-shaped bird with a plump, rounded breast, and more breast than leg. You can tell the approximate age of a bird by pressing against the breastbone; if it is pliable the chicken is young and will have tender meat. Chicken parts should be moist and plump. Both whole chicken and chicken parts should have a clean smell.

The color of the skin has no bearing on quality or nutritional value. The poultry industry turns out white and yellow chickens to suit consumer preferences, which vary from region to region. The color of the skin depends on the breed and what the chicken was fed. If the chicken was fed substances containing yellow pigment, such as marigold petals, its skin will be yellow. No matter what the color of the skin, make sure it does not appear transparent or mottled.

Frozen poultry should be rock-hard and show no signs of freezer burn or ice crystals inside the package. Choose packages from below the freezer line in the grocer's case. If there is frozen liquid inside the package, it is likely that the chicken has been defrosted and then refrozen. This does not mean that the chicken is spoiled, but the taste will suffer since the juices that make a bird flavorful have seeped out.

STORAGE Fresh chicken is highly perishable and should be stored immediately in the coldest part of your refrigerator. To minimize handling, keep the chicken in its original store wrapping. Be sure that the fluids from the package do not leak onto other foods in the refrigerator; if the package seems leaky, overwrap it in plastic or aluminum foil, or place it on a plate to prevent the contamination of other foods. Fresh raw chicken will keep in a home refrigerator for two to three days; once cooked, it will keep for three to four days.

If you buy whole birds with the giblets, store the meat and giblets separately since the giblets will spoil before the meat. Open the store wrapping and remove the giblets. Rinse the chicken, pat it dry with paper towels, and rewrap it loosely in heavy-duty plastic, aluminum foil, or butcher paper. The giblets should be discarded or stored in a container and used within one day.

To freeze chicken, remove it from the store wrapping, wash it, and pat it dry with paper towels. Wrap it in freezer paper or aluminum foil, taking care that odd-shaped parts are fully covered and the package is airtight. Do not try to freeze a whole bird in a home freezer; cut it into parts first. Chicken will keep in a 0° freezer for 12 months.

PREPARATION Keep chicken refrigerated until you are ready to cook it. Wash the chicken in cold running water and pat it dry with paper towels. Pluck out any stray feathers remaining with your fingernails or a pair of tweezers.

Never thaw frozen chicken at room temperature; the outside thaws first and becomes susceptible to bacterial growth during the time it takes for the inside to thaw. Leave it in the refrigerator to defrost on a plate to catch the drippings. Allow three to four hours of thawing time per pound of chicken; chicken parts may thaw more quickly. Use a microwave oven for thawing only if you plan to cook the chicken right away; if that is not possible, refrigerate it until cooking time.

Cut away any visible fat on the chicken, but don't remove the skin before cooking. Researchers from the University of Minnesota found that it doesn't matter whether you remove the skin before or after cooking in terms of fat content. No significant amount of fat is transferred from the skin to the meat during cooking. Skinning poultry before cooking only leads to drier—not leaner—meat. Remove the skin before eating the chicken, and be sure to remove any visible fat left on the meat.

Chicken meat around the bones may turn dark during cooking. This is most common in young broiler/fryers, since their bones have not calcified completely, allowing the pigments in hemoglobin from the marrow to seep out. It's safe to eat the darkened meat.

Chicken breasts often have a tough white tendon under the fillet, a small tender piece that is tucked underneath the main part of the breast. If the breast is boneless, you can easily remove this tendon with a sharp paring knife. To tenderize boneless chicken breasts, pound them lightly between two sheets of plastic wrap. This also flattens the breasts to a uniform thickness for even cooking.

Keep raw poultry away from other foods, especially salad greens or any food that will be served raw or cooked only briefly. Be sure to thoroughly wash your hands, the countertop, sink, cutting board, and utensils with hot, soapy water.

Salmonella and other bacteria in poultry can't penetrate a cut on your hand—they have to be eaten to make you sick. The reason you must wash your hands after handling raw poultry is to avoid spreading the possibly contaminated juices to other foods.

Marinate chicken pieces in the refrigerator, not at room temperature. Chicken can spoil if it sits out even for three hours on a warm day. Don't use the marinade as a sauce unless you bring it to a rolling boil for several minutes before serving. Better yet, make extra marinade and store it separately until you are ready to serve it.

(For information on stuffing a whole chicken, and healthy stuffing ideas, see page 420.)

Baking in parchment Boneless, skinless chicken breasts stay moist and tender without the addition of fat when they are baked in cooking parchment or aluminum foil. Place the chicken breast in the center of a square of parchment or foil and top it with thinly sliced vegetables—mushrooms, summer squash, and red peppers—and add seasonings. Tightly wrap and bake in a 425° oven. *Cooking time:* 10 to 15 minutes.

Frying Fried chicken—chicken that has been coated, breaded, and deep fried—is popular in the United States. Unfortunately, it is one of the unhealthiest ways to prepare chicken, since the breading absorbs a lot of the oil used in frying. Light-meat chicken with skin, batter-dipped and fried, contains 277 calories and 15 grams of fat—49 percent fat calories—per 3½ ounces. If you prefer fried chicken, fry it without breading or batter and remove the skin before eating. Skinless light-meat chicken that has been fried without a coating contains 192 calories and 6 grams of fat—28 percent fat calories—in 3½ ounces.

Oven frying This method produces crisp chicken without the trouble of dealing with hot oil, or consuming the extra fat. Dip the chicken in buttermilk, then roll it in a mixture of dry breadcrumbs, parmesan cheese, pepper, paprika, and dried oregano. Cook in a 425° oven, in a broiler pan so the fat drips out. *Cooking time:* 35 to 40 minutes.

Poaching Poaching in water or broth is the best way to prepare chicken that will later be eaten cold. Use a heavy hand with seasonings: Try dried (but not ground) rosemary, sage, thyme, and oregano; or ginger, garlic, and scallions. When poaching chicken breasts, strain the seasonings out of the poaching liquid after the chicken is cooked and reduce it. Mix ⅓ cup low-fat plain yogurt with a tablespoon of flour and mix well. Add the yogurt to the reduced liquid to make a sauce to serve over the cold chicken. When poaching a whole chicken, use the cooking liquid as the base for chicken soup. *Cooking time:* for

TIMETABLE FOR ROASTING CHICKEN

	Oven Temperature	Time
Chicken, whole unstuffed		
1½ to 2 pounds	350°	40 to 50 minutes
2½ to 3 pounds	350°	70 to 80 minutes
5 to 6 pounds	350°	1½ to 1¾ hours
Capon		
9½ pounds	325°	3¾ to 4¾ hours
Rock Cornish hen		
1 to 1½ pounds	375°	1 to 1¼ hours

breasts, about 15 minutes; for whole chicken, 35 to 40 minutes.

Roasting and broiling Of all the cooking methods, roasting a whole bird at a low temperature melts away the most fat. Cooking times vary by the size of the bird and the cooking method (see charts at right and on page 393). Whole chicken is cooked when the white meat registers 180° on a meat thermometer. When the chicken is thoroughly cooked, the juices will run clear, not pink, and the flesh will turn white. Bone-in parts should be cooked to an internal temperature of 170° and boneless parts to 160°.

When grilling chicken, don't add barbecue sauce until 15 minutes before the chicken has finished cooking. Barbecue sauces contain sugar and spices, which can burn or become scorched under high heat, leaving the chicken with a bitter taste.

Steaming Place boneless chicken and sliced vegetables in a shallow heatproof dish. Set the dish on a rack in a large covered skillet or Dutch oven. Add 1 inch of water to the skillet, cover, and cook on the stovetop until the chicken is cooked through. A concentrated, flavorful broth remains in the dish and can be used as a sauce over the chicken. *Cooking time:* 5 to 8 minutes.

Stir-frying Boneless chicken breasts are best for stir-frying because they are easily sliced and cook quickly. Slice the chicken into 1/4-inch pieces, cutting across the grain. *Cooking time:* 3 to 4 minutes.

Homemade chicken broth It's easy to make your own broth to use in cooking or as the basis for soups. It's healthier, too, than buying canned broth, since you can control the amount of salt you add and can remove fat from the stock after cooking. Use stewing chickens, chicken backs, or the leftover carcass from a roast chicken. Place the chicken in a large stockpot with yellow onions with the skins on (to add color), celery ribs, carrots, bay leaves, whole peppercorns, thyme, and salt. Cover the ingredients with water and bring to a boil. Remove any scum that floats to the top, reduce to a simmer, and cover. Once done, strain the liquid to remove the vegetables, bones, and any meat pieces. Let the stock cool completely and refrigerate. Remove any fat that congeals at the top. *Cooking time:* 3 to 4 hours.

TIMETABLE FOR BROILING CHICKEN

	Weight	Time (minutes)
Breast half, with bone	1 to 1¼ pounds	25 to 35
Breast, boned	4 to 5 ounces	12 to 15
Cornish game hen	1 to 2 pounds	30 to 40
Drumsticks	5 ounces	16 to 20
Half chicken	1¼ to 1½ pounds	28 to 32
Thighs	5 ounces	16 to 20

SERVING SUGGESTIONS Roast chicken is one of the simplest dishes to prepare. To add flavor, you can coat the bird with different mixtures and use a variety of seasonings in the cavity; the flavors will penetrate the meat. The mixtures will drip into the roasting pan, and the pan juices can be defatted after cooking and served as a sauce.

Try one of the following: Mix a teaspoon or two of olive oil with dried ground rosemary, sage, or basil and rub the mixture lightly over the entire surface of the bird. For a Chinese flair, combine soy sauce, honey, cooking sherry, and a touch of sesame oil and brush it all over the chicken. Place two or three whole scallions in the cavity, along with a few slices of unpeeled fresh ginger and crushed garlic cloves. For lemon chicken, thinly slice a lemon and drape the slices over the entire surface of the chicken. Halve a lemon and an onion and place them in the cavity. Combine a tablespoon of olive oil with finely chopped garlic, ground pepper, and oregano. Place half of the mixture in the cavity and drizzle the rest over the chicken.

To marinate chicken parts, try a combination of

CHICKEN, breast, no skin 3½ oz cooked			
Calories	165	Fat	4 g
Protein	31 g	Saturated Fat	1 g
Carbohydrate	0 g	Cholesterol	85 mg
Dietary Fiber	None	Sodium	74 mg

KEY NUTRIENTS		% RDA Men	% RDA Women
Vitamin B_6	0.6 mg	30%	38%
Vitamin B_{12}	0.3 mcg	15%	15%
Iron	1 mg	10%	7%
Magnesium	29 mg	8%	10%
Niacin	14 mg	74%	93%
Phosphorus	228 mg	29%	29%

S=40% or more soluble N/A=Not Applicable N=Not Available

CHICKEN, dark meat, no skin 3½ oz cooked			
Calories	205	Fat	10 g
Protein	27 g	Saturated Fat	3 g
Carbohydrate	0 g	Cholesterol	93 mg
Dietary Fiber	None	Sodium	93 mg

KEY NUTRIENTS		% RDA Men	% RDA Women
Vitamin B_6	0.4 mg	20%	25%
Vitamin B_{12}	0.3 mg	15%	15%
Iron	1 mg	10%	7%
Niacin	7 mg	37%	47%
Phosphorus	179 mg	22%	22%
Riboflavin	0.2 mg	12%	15%
Zinc	3 mg	20%	25%

S=40% or more soluble N/A=Not Applicable N=Not Available

red wine, Dijon mustard, crushed garlic, tarragon, pepper, and a dash of olive oil. Or try white wine, lemon zest, chopped fresh dill, cayenne pepper, and a touch of olive oil. For a Southwestern touch, combine lime juice, zest of lime, minced garlic, finely chopped hot peppers, chili powder, ground cumin, pepper, and a small amount of olive oil.

Chicken breasts are good stir-fried with broccoli florets, scallions, fresh ginger, and peanuts. For a healthy chicken chow mein, add cooked Chinese egg noodles, a small amount of chicken broth, soy sauce, red pepper flakes, and cornstarch to thicken (dissolve in cold water first) to the above mixture just before it's finished.

Studies have shown that chicken soup—and other hot drinks—can help alleviate cold symptoms by increasing the flow of nasal secretions. The taste and aroma of chicken soup may be part of the therapy. Nothing will cure a cold, but a bowl of hot soup offers as much relief as anything.

Classic paella—made with chicken, mussels, clams, shrimp, and rice—is time-consuming to prepare. But you can make the following version as an everyday dish. Brown pieces of roasting chicken and set them aside. In the same pan, sauté onions, garlic, and saffron. Then add white rice, chopped tomatoes, chicken broth, green peppers, green beans, roasted red peppers, chopped parsley, bay leaves, and the chicken pieces. Cook covered until the liquid is absorbed, the rice is tender, and the chicken is cooked through. Remove the bay leaves before serving.

Hunter's chicken (chicken cacciatore) is a flavorful stew dish. First roast red and green bell peppers and slice them. Then saute garlic, onions, and celery in a large skillet. Add pieces of stewing or roasting chicken and brown them. Next, add about 1 to 2 cups of white wine and reduce the juices to a glaze. Stir in chopped tomatoes, roasted peppers, and chopped parsley and continue cooking until the chicken is cooked through. Serve with a hearty bread to sop up the delicious sauce.

Duck

In colonial times, wild duck was an important part of the dinnertime menu. But it's fair to say that duck hasn't come close in popularity to chicken or turkey in many years. Americans now eat an average of only about 3/4 pound of duck annually per capita. Perhaps this is because duck is considered sophisticated fare—more difficult to prepare than chicken or turkey and with a more complicated flavor. Ducks also have a large chest cavity (so they contain a smaller proportion of meat to bone), and all of their meat is dark.

Duck is also quite high in fat—a 3½-ounce serving of skinless cooked duck has about 200 calories, 50 percent coming from fat. When duck is served with the skin, the fat percentage rises to 75 (and the calories to 337). Much of this fat resides in a thick layer under the skin, and it is not only a drawback nutritionally, but can cause the duck to appear and taste greasy after cooking. (The released fat can also become a fire hazard during the cooking process.) It is possible, however, to reduce some of this fat content when preparing a duck, allowing you to enjoy it as a rich-tasting occasional treat.

The most widely sold domestic duck is the white Pekin, which was brought to the United States from China in the nineteenth century. Young white Pekin ducks are often sold as Long Island ducklings, though only a third or so of domestic ducks are raised on Long Island, New York. The majority come from duck farms in the Midwest. The ducklings are eight weeks old or younger, and weigh from 3 to 5½ pounds.

SHOPPING TIPS Ducks are available fresh on a limited basis from late spring through late winter, but 90 percent of the duck supply is sold frozen. If you purchase a fresh duck, check that the skin is clean, odor-free, and feather-free—and off-white, not yellow. Frozen ducks should be plump-breasted and wrapped in airtight packages. If you buy the duck in a supermarket, check the "sell-by" date.

STORAGE As with other poultry, keep duck in its original wrapping but overwrap it with aluminum foil to catch any leakage. Store fresh duck in the coldest part of the refrigerator, where it will keep for up to three days. (Wrap and store any giblets separately.)

Because duck is widely available frozen, there is no sense in freezing fresh duck. Store-bought frozen duck should be placed in the freezer in its original wrapping. Date the package and use it within three months. (Some frozen birds carry an expiration date.)

To store cooked duck, remove the meat from the bones, wrap it in foil or in a covered plastic container, and place it in the coldest part of the refrigerator; eat it within three days.

PREPARATION To defrost a frozen duck, place it on a dish in the refrigerator; a 5-pound bird will thaw in 24 to 36 hours. Alternatively, you can submerge the duck in a pot or sink full of cold water. (Warm water thaws the bird too quickly and can cause bacteria to flourish.) Change the water every 30 minutes. Thawing will occur in about 3 hours.

Before cooking a fresh or thawed duck, check for any feathers and remove them, and also remove any visible fat. Then rinse the bird under cold water and pat it dry. For roasting, leave the bird whole; for broiling or grilling, cut the bird into halves or quarters. Cook the duck with the skin on, but remove the skin before eating.

Although you can stuff a whole bird, virtually any stuffing will absorb a great deal of fat as the bird cooks. Prepare and serve stuffing on the side. You can add extra flavor to the duck by putting onion halves, some pieces of celery, and apple or orange quarters into the chest cavity.

DUCK, no skin	3½ oz cooked		
Calories	201	Fat	11 g
Protein	23 g	Saturated Fat	4 g
Carbohydrate	0 g	Cholesterol	89 mg
Dietary Fiber	None	Sodium	65 mg

KEY NUTRIENTS		% RDA Men	% RDA Women
Vitamin B_6	0.3 mg	15%	19%
Vitamin B_{12}	0.4 mcg	20%	20%
Copper	0.2 mg	N/A	N/A
Vitamin E	2 mg	20%	25%
Iron	3 mg	30%	20%
Niacin	5 mg	26%	33%
Phosphorus	203 mg	25%	25%
Riboflavin	0.5 mg	29%	38%
Thiamin	0.3 mg	20%	27%
Zinc	3 mg	20%	25%

S=40% or more soluble N/A=Not Applicable N=Not Available

Use a meat thermometer when cooking a whole duck; the bird is done when the internal temperature reaches 180°.

Broiling Prick the skin of each part all over and remove any visible fat. Lay the parts with the skin side down on a broiling pan and place the pan 4 inches from a preheated broiler. Be careful when broiling duck parts: The released fat can smoke and may catch fire. To avoid this, check the broiling pan every 2 minutes and sprinkle salt directly on any fat that collects in the pan. Broil until golden on one side, turn and continue broiling until the other side is golden and the inside is slightly pink and juicy. If the duck browns too quickly, lower the broiling rack. Keep in mind that a boned duck breast cooks faster than one with the bone in. *Cooking time:* 35 to 45 minutes.

Roasting Thoroughly prick the duck's skin all over, being careful not to pierce the flesh. Place the bird with the breast side up on a rack inside an uncovered roasting pan. To prevent the released fat from smoking, pour a small amount of stock or water—to a level of ½ inch—in the bottom of the roasting pan. (If you use stock, defat it after cooking and use it as a sauce for the duck.) As the bird cooks, continue pricking the skin and basting the bird with the drippings to help release more fat. If areas of the bird seem to brown too fast, shield them with aluminum foil. *Cooking time:* 5 minutes in a 450° oven, then lower temperature to 350° and roast for 20 minutes per pound. Allow the bird to stand 15 minutes before carving.

SERVING SUGGESTIONS To marinate duck before cooking, combine dry red wine, red wine vinegar, olive oil, prepared mustard, chopped shallots, tarragon, and black pepper. For a sweeter flavor, use orange juice, orange zest, white wine vinegar, soy sauce, honey, sherry, and minced fresh ginger and garlic. Marinate for 3 to 4 hours, and afterwards pat the duck dry with paper towels to remove any excess moisture. Reserve the marinade, first skimming off any visible fat that has solidified on the surface. Bring the marinade to a rolling boil for several minutes and serve it as a sauce with the duck.

Good stuffings to serve with duck include a combination of breadcrumbs, chopped apple, chopped cooked prunes or apricots, chopped parsley, tarragon, and pepper. Or try cooked wild rice, sautéed chopped shallots, green pepper, celery, chopped spinach, and sage.

Serve duck with a basmati rice pilaf and braised leeks or onions. For a side dish, cook carrots, cauliflower, zucchini, or white kidney beans in an herbed broth, then purée and serve with grilled tomatoes.

Game

Any bird or animal that is hunted for food can rightly be considered game. These range from everyday creatures, such as squirrel or rabbit, to exotic big-game animals like hartebeests and Cape Buffalo. The meat from game is generally more intensely flavored than meat from domesticated animals. Both types of meat are high in protein and minerals, but game is lower—sometimes significantly lower—in fat and cholesterol than domesticated meats. In most states, wild game can only be hunted in season, and it cannot be sold commercially. But you don't have to be a hunter to sample game. The most popular game animals are raised on carefully managed farms or preserves and the meat is distributed for sale in restaurants, supermarkets, and specialty stores—you can also order game by mail.

Farm-raised game is meatier and more tender than wild game, and also has a bit more fat—but less than beef or pork. This is because the fat in game animals is concentrated on the back or under the spine, rather than being dispersed as marbling throughout the meat. Whereas the percentage of fat calories in beef varies from 20 percent to 60 percent, most big-game meats derive only about 13 to 14 percent of their calories from fat. The low fat content is one reason why venison and other game steaks are chewy. However, using a stock or marinade can help keep them from becoming overly tough and dry.

Farm-raised game is usually available at any time of year in frozen form. Fresh meat, particularly from large game animals, is more seasonal.

TYPES OF GAME There are many different game animals, but they can be divided into two basic categories: feathered and furred.

Feathered game

After duck and goose, the most popular domestic game bird in the United States is pheasant. It is followed in popularity by two of its relatives, quail and partridge.

Partridge This small bird (about 1 pound) resembles a baby pheasant, but has darker meat and a stronger flavor. Young partridge is best roasted; older birds should be braised.

Pheasant The domestic bird weighs 2 to 3 pounds, and a hen is considered more tender and flavorful than a cock. Baby pheasant, usually sold frozen, is considered a delicacy. Available fresh or frozen, it is best roasted.

Quail More mildly flavored than its cousins, the quail is a tiny bird—weighing about 5 ounces—that has almost no fat. The bobwhite, or American quail, is hunted in the wild (and is popular in the South), and there are several other varieties raised on quail farms. Sautéing is usually the preferred cooking method, but you can also roast quail.

Furred Game

These animals range from large (deer, bear, buffalo, wild boar) to small (rabbit, hare, opossum, squirrel). Buffalo, rabbit, and deer are the most common animals raised on game farms.

Buffalo (bison) Except for color, individual cuts of buffalo meat resemble those of beef. But buffalo is one of the leanest meats, with about two-thirds the calories of similar beef cuts. Steaks are good broiled; larger cuts can be roasted; and you can also try buffalo burgers.

Deer (venison) Originally, "venison" meant the meat of any hunted animal, but it now refers to deer and other antlered animals, such as moose and elk. The best meat comes from young males; as with beef and lamb, the loin and ribs provide the tenderest cuts. Roasting or broiling is preferred for tender cuts. If the meat is from an older animal, braising is best.

Rabbit A young rabbit weighs about 3 pounds, has tender meat that tastes somewhat like poul-

COMPARING GAME 3½ ounces

	Calories	**Fat** (g)	**Saturated fat** (g)	**Cholesterol** (mg)
Antelope, roasted	150	3	1	126
Bear, simmered	259	13	N	N
Bison, roasted	143	2	1	82
Buffalo, roasted	188	6	3	58
Caribou, roasted	167	4	2	109
Deer, roasted	158	3	1	112
Elk, roasted	146	2	1	73
Moose, roasted	134	1	1	78
Rabbit, roasted	154	6	2	64
Rabbit, stewed	173	4	1	123
Water buffalo, roasted	131	2	1	61
Wild boar, roasted	160	4	1	N

N=Not Available

try, and is excellent roasted or stewed. The meat of hare, a larger rabbit relative, is tougher and gamier; it should be marinated, then braised or stewed.

SHOPPING TIPS Whether you buy game meat from a specialty shop or at a supermarket, try to check on how old the animal was: Age is the critical factor that determines taste and tenderness as well as the best cooking method. Most often, the game you buy will come frozen. Be sure the package is intact and that it doesn't contain any frozen liquid, which might indicate that the meat has been thawed and refrozen. With fresh game, the meat should be moist and springy to the touch; it should never feel soft.

STORAGE The rules for other meats apply here. Keep frozen game in a 0° freezer. Store fresh game in the coldest part of the refrigerator and use it within one or two days.

PREPARATION AND SERVING SUGGESTIONS Game is traditionally aged by hanging it for anywhere from a few days to a few weeks, which tenderizes the meat and improves its flavor. Meat you buy from a reputable retailer will have been properly aged. Before cooking, trim away visible fat, which can impart a disagreeable flavor to some game meats. The guidelines and suggestions that follow are for popular game animals, but they can be applied to most other game.

Pheasant can be roasted like chicken or duck. Insert a meat thermometer into the breast of the pheasant and place it in 400° preheated oven, then reduce the temperature to 350° and cook for 20 to 25 minutes per pound, or until the thermometer registers 170°. Try serving pheasant with an orange sauce: Remove any fat released into the pan, then add chicken broth thickened with cornstarch to the defatted pan drippings. To this mixture, add a little cider vinegar, honey, orange juice, and orange rind, and bring it to a boil in the oven or on the stovetop; cook, uncovered, for 5 to 8 minutes. Accompany the pheasant and sauce with spiced apples, braised red cabbage, and rice pilaf. As with any poultry, it's a good idea to remove the skin before eating, since that's where much of the fat is.

Small game birds like quail have very little fat, so feel free to add a grain stuffing—try wild rice mixed with fresh cooked chestnuts, chopped celery, pine nuts, and a little sage. Or roast quail Asian style, brushing the birds with a honey-and-soy-sauce glaze. Place the birds, trussed, in a 450° oven, and reduce the temperature to 350°. Roast 35 to 45 minutes if unstuffed, 45 minutes to 1 hour if stuffed. Serve quail with sweet-and-sour beans and bulgur pilaf.

Rabbit can be used as an alternative to chicken, especially in stews. Dredge rabbit pieces in seasoned flour and then brown quickly in a small amount of oil in a nonstick skillet. Add shallots, garlic, diced celery, carrots, chopped parsley, and dry red wine or chicken stock. Cook over low heat, covered, for 1 to 2 hours or until rabbit is tender, stirring mixture several times to ensure even cooking. Defat the cooking liquid before serving. For a variation, after the rabbit is browned, try adding Italian canned tomatoes, tomato paste, chicken broth, carrot chunks, oregano, and pepper. Allow to simmer until the rabbit is nearly done, then add Italian green beans and serve over egg noodles.

Venison can generally be cooked like beef, although venison tends to be leaner and a little tougher. Many recipes call for draping fat over a roast or larding, but this isn't necessary. Choose venison loin, which is a more tender cut and cooks quickly. Rub a 2-pound loin with garlic cloves, salt, and pepper. Lightly brown in a nonstick pan with a small amount of oil, and then transfer the loin to a roasting pan and roast in a 450° oven for 20 to 30 minutes. The meat should be slightly pink at the center.

VENISON 3½ oz cooked

Calories	158	Fat	3 g
Protein	30 g	Saturated Fat	1 g
Carbohydrate	0 g	Cholesterol	112 mg
Dietary Fiber	None	Sodium	54 mg

KEY NUTRIENTS		% RDA Men	% RDA Women
Copper	1 mg	N/A	N/A
Iron	5 mg	50%	33%
Niacin	7 mg	37%	47%
Phosphorus	226 mg	28%	28%
Potassium	336 mg	N/A	N/A
Riboflavin	0.6 mg	35%	46%
Thiamin	0.2 mg	13%	18%
Zinc	3 mg	20%	25%

S=40% or more soluble N/A=Not Applicable N=Not Available

For sauce, skim any excess fat from the pan and add chopped scallions, garlic, and sliced mushrooms to the pan. Roast the vegetables for an additional 10 to 15 minutes. Add red wine or beef broth and deglaze the pan, cooking the sauce 10 to 15 minutes or until the flavor has mellowed. Thinly slice the venison and serve the sauce along with a combination of wild and brown rice, dilled carrots, and green beans.

Venison steaks can also be marinated in a combination of red wine, olive oil, juniper berries, bay leaves, salt, and pepper for a few hours before broiling. Pat dry and set the steaks on a broiler rack and broil 4 to 5 minutes per side, or until slightly pink at the center. The marinade can be reduced and served with the steaks, along with braised Brussels sprouts and a gratin of leeks and mashed potatoes.

Goose

Before turkey was introduced to Europe in the sixteenth century, the citizens feasted on goose. Though not popular in the United States, this rich-tasting bird with its moist, dark meat is still the favorite for festive occasions in Scandinavia and central European countries. Whether wild or domestic, goose is as fatty as duck—roasted without its skin, a 3½-ounce slice of roasted skinless goose contains 13 grams of fat; in fact fat makes up nearly 50 percent of its calories. So, from the health standpoint, goose is definitely a fowl to be savored only on occasion.

Domestic geese usually weigh between 6 and 14 pounds; those under 9 pounds are younger birds—less than six months old—and are often more tender than older birds.

SHOPPING TIPS Like ducks, geese are generally sold frozen, though you can sometimes find fresh birds between Thanksgiving and Christmas. Because frozen birds are shipped to market from July through December, they can be hard to find in the spring and the early part of summer. Geese usually have to be ordered from a butcher—they are not readily available in supermarkets. Check to see that the goose you are buying is free of feathers and that it has a clean smell. Frozen birds should be solidly frozen and there should be no tears in the wrapping.

STORAGE A fresh goose will keep two to three days, but use it as soon as you can. A frozen bird will keep in a 0° freezer for six months.

PREPARATION As with all poultry, rinse the goose and pat it dry with paper towels before cooking. Whatever method you choose—roasting is the preferred method—carefully prick the skin all over without piercing the flesh so that the fat is released during cooking. Exercise care when cooking: A goose releases even more fat than a duck does, and as the fat accumulates, it can begin to smoke and may even catch fire. (For that reason, broiling goose isn't recommended.) Goose is done when it has reached an internal temperature of 180°.

Poaching Poach the goose in water flavored with carrots, onions, celery, bay leaves, and peppercorns. When the goose is done, pour off the stock and brown the bird in the oven, which will cook out even more fat. Strain the stock and skim off any surface fat with a spoon. You can then make a light gravy by reducing the defatted stock and combining it with cornstarch. *Cooking times:* for poaching a young bird, 1 hour; for older birds (10 pounds or more), 2 hours. To brown the goose, bake for 5 to 10 minutes (or until browned) in a 450° oven.

Roasting Thoroughly prick the goose's skin all over, being careful not to pierce the flesh. Place the whole goose with the breast side up on a rack inside an uncovered roasting pan. Pour a small

GOOSE, no skin 3½ oz cooked

Calories	238	Fat	13 g
Protein	29 g	Saturated Fat	5 g
Carbohydrate	0 g	Cholesterol	96 mg
Dietary Fiber	None	Sodium	76 mg

KEY NUTRIENTS		% RDA Men	% RDA Women
Vitamin B_6	0.5 mg	25%	31%
Vitamin B_{12}	0.5 mcg	25%	25%
Copper	0.3 mg	N/A	N/A
Vitamin E	3 mg	30%	38%
Iron	3 mg	30%	20%
Phosphorus	309 mg	39%	39%
Potassium	388 mg	N/A	N/A
Niacin	4 mg	21%	27%
Riboflavin	0.4 mg	24%	31%
Zinc	3 mg	20%	25%

S=40% or more soluble N/A=Not Applicable N=Not Available

amount of stock or water—to a level of ½ inch—in the bottom of the pan to help prevent the released fat from smoking. (If you use stock, defat it after cooking and use as a sauce for the goose.) As a further precaution, use a bulb baster to remove the fat as it collects in the roasting pan. While the bird cooks, continue pricking the skin and basting the bird with the drippings to help release more fat. If areas of the bird seem to brown too fast, shield them with aluminum foil. *Cooking time:* 15 minutes in a 450° oven, then lower the oven temperature to 350° and roast for 20 minutes per pound. Allow the bird to stand 15 minutes before carving.

SERVING SUGGESTIONS Potatoes are the traditional stuffing for goose—but it's a good idea to cook the stuffing separately so that it won't absorb released fat. Boil the potatoes first, then dice them and sauté the chunks in a skillet with chopped scallions, parsley, oregano, and pepper. Cook the mixture in a separate dish alongside the goose as it roasts.

Good side dishes for goose are applesauce and braised onions, or a colorful cabbage slaw made from red and green cabbage, carrots, and a sweet-and-sour dressing. A salad made with chicory, roasted peppers, and artichoke hearts also complements goose nicely.

Lamb

While Americans display a fairly hearty appetite for beef, they have never shown much enthusiasm for lamb. Annually, we consume, on average, a pound of lamb per person, a fraction of our beef consumption. Yet sheep are the most numerous livestock in the world, and lamb or mutton (the flesh of mature sheep) is the principal meat in parts of Europe, North Africa, the Middle East, and India. Dishes featuring lamb range from roasted whole leg of lamb seasoned with assertive herbs—a specialty in Italy and southern France—to Greek *moussaka* (a ground-lamb dish), to savory kebabs, curries, and stews prepared in countries as disparate as Iraq, India, and Ireland. In these countries, as well as in New Zealand (where average per capita consumption of lamb and goat averages more than 60 pounds a year), people have taken full advantage of lamb's robust taste. Moreover, it lends itself magnificently to all kinds of seasoning and a variety of cooking methods.

As with beef, modern breeding methods have improved lamb's taste and texture. In ages past, the meat from sheep was relatively tough and stringy, because the animals were bred for wool as well as for meat, and because they were often on the move from pasture to pasture, which made them exceptionally lean. In the eighteenth century, English breeders produced animals that were chunky and compact, yielding plenty of meat. Most of the lamb sold in American markets comes from descendants of these English breeds. Today, however, animals are raised either for wool or for meat; as a result, lamb has become consistently more flavorful and tender.

The meat is also leaner, thanks to breeding and to the extensive trimming of the external fat—on average only ¼ inch or less is left on retail lamb. Like beef, lamb is graded for quality. The same category names are used—Prime and Choice—but these terms do not indicate the same differences in fat content as they do in beef. The majority of lamb to reach the market is Choice, which, nutritionally, is comparable to Choice beef: Many corresponding cuts contain the same amount of internal fat, and offer similarly significant levels of protein, iron, zinc, and vitamin B_{12}.

In the United States, meat that is labeled "lamb" comes from sheep that are less than a year old. Most of our lamb, in fact, is from animals that go to market at five to seven months of age. The term "spring lamb" is sometimes applied to meat that is marketed during spring and summer months. In decades past, these were the primary months fresh lamb was available, but modern breeding techniques have ensured that lamb is plentiful throughout the year. Consequently, the expression no longer has any practical meaning.

You may sometimes encounter meat labeled "yearling mutton," which comes from an animal between one and two years old; it is more strongly flavored than lamb. Meat from animals older than two years is classified as "mutton," which is seldom sold in the United States.

About 11 percent of lamb sold in the United States is imported, mostly from New Zealand. It arrives fresh and vacuum-packed. Imported lamb comes from younger animals that are generally grass fed (rather than grain fed); it has a stronger taste than domestic meat.

CUTS OF LAMB The cut of lamb is the best indicator of fat content, as well as to the tenderness of the meat. Lamb has fewer retail cuts than beef. In general, leaner cuts, such as the foreshank and parts of the leg, are less tender than cuts from areas where the muscles are little used, such as the loin and rib. However, because lambs are smaller, younger animals than beef cattle, even lean cuts are more tender than corresponding cuts of beef.

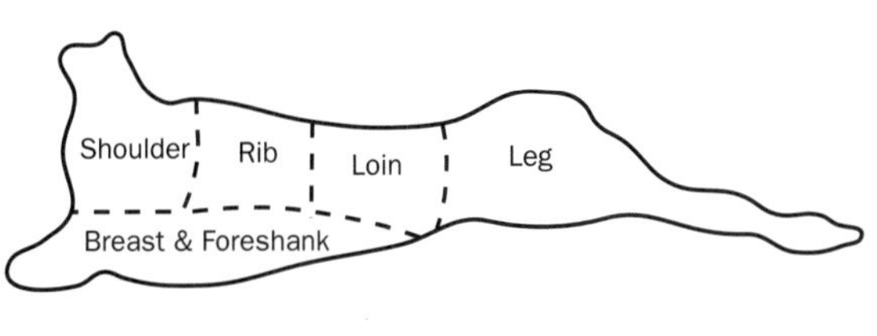

Primal cuts—the divisions of lamb made by wholesalers—are given below, since they are used consistently throughout the country and are indicative of fat content. The most common names for retail cuts, which are used to identify the smaller cuts of meat sold in supermarkets and butcher shops, are also included, along with the preferred cooking methods. (Information on fat and calorie content pertains to cuts that have been trimmed of external fat.)

Breast and foreshank Whole breast can be purchased unboned, or boned and rolled; it is usually roasted or braised, often with a stuffing. However, the meat is fatty and not as tender as the other cuts. This section includes *spareribs* and *riblets* (single-ribbed strips), both relatively inexpensive cuts that contain more bone than meat; they can be grilled or braised. The *foreshank,* which is connected to the breast, is a lean, stringy cut—only 29 percent of its calories come from fat. It is usually tenderized by cooking in liquid for long periods. Shank meat is also ground and cubed for stewing.

Leg The most popular cut of lamb, the leg can be roasted whole, or boned and either rolled (for roasting) or flattened (for broiling). It can also be subdivided into two basic parts: the sirloin (or butt), which is well marbled, and the shank, or lower half, which is much leaner. Cuts from the sirloin include *sirloin roast* and *sirloin chops. Leg steaks* from the center leg are suitable for broiling or grilling. The *hind shank* is among the leanest cuts of lamb, with only 180 calories (33 percent of which come from fat) per 3½ ounces. Sometimes called *shank half roast,* it can be roasted or braised. The shank meat can also be cut up for stews or pounded for cube steak.

Loin This section, considered the choicest part of the lamb, yields an excellent roast. When both sides of the loin are used, the result is a *saddle of lamb.* More frequently, the section is divided into *loin chops,* which have about 216 calories per 3½ ounces, 40 percent of them fat calories. Chops can be braised, broiled, or baked.

COMPARING LAMB CUTS **3½ ounces trimmed and cooked**

	Calories	**Fat** (g)	**Saturated fat** (g)	**Cholesterol** (mg)
Arm	192	9	4	86
Blade	209	12	4	87
Foreshank	187	6	2	104
Leg	191	8	3	89
Loin	202	10	4	87
Rib	232	13	5	88
Shank	180	7	2	87
Shoulder	204	11	4	87
Ground lamb	283	20	8	97

Rib A *whole rib,* also known as a rack, can be purchased for roasting, but it is heavily marbled meat with a thick outer layer of fat. In fact, over 50 percent of its calories come from fat, even after trimming. *Rib chops* can be trimmed of more of their fat to yield tender, juicy meat.

Shoulder The hardest-working muscle has a good deal of fat, in addition to many bones. Sold whole with the bone intact, it is tastiest braised or stewed. Or, it can be sold boned as *rolled boneless shoulder roast* (which can also be braised). *Shoulder lamb chops* (which may be subdivided into blade chops and arm chops) are less expensive than rib or loin chops, and are somewhat leaner: The calories in arm chops are only about 40 percent fat. Shoulder chops can be cooked like other chops, or they can be cut up and used for stews or kebabs. Meat from the *neck,* which is taken from the front of the shoulder, is also good for stewing, or it can be boned and ground.

Ground lamb Usually made from shank and neck meat, as well as other trimmings, ground lamb may contain a good deal of fat. You can reduce the fat content by buying a shoulder cut and asking the butcher to trim and grind it (or do so yourself). Use ground lamb as you would ground beef.

SHOPPING TIPS Prepackaged lamb sold in supermarkets is ordinarily dated for freshness, so be sure to check the label. Other signs of freshness are firm, pinkish red meat (lamb darkens with age); bones that are reddish at the joint (and also moist); and fat that is creamy white. When buying from a butcher, ask that the external fat be trimmed.

STORAGE Store lamb in the coldest part of the refrigerator immediately after purchase; keep it in its original wrapping (either plastic wrap or butcher's paper), but check that the wrap is securely sealed. As a general rule, the larger a cut is, the longer it keeps. Hence, whole roasts will keep up to five days; chops and steaks, for two to four days; and lamb that has been ground or cubed for stewing, for one or two days.

For longer storage, fresh lamb should be frozen. Make sure your freezer is set at 0° or lower. To create an airtight seal, wrap the lamb in vaporproof, plastic-lined freezer paper or aluminum foil. Overwrap the package, tucking in all loose ends, and then seal it tightly with freezer tape. Be sure to label all packages with dates and cuts. Place each wrapped package in a plastic freezer bag.

Large cuts of lamb can be frozen for six to nine months, and small chops, cubes, and ground lamb can be kept for three to four months.

To help prevent food poisoning, thaw the lamb in the refrigerator or defrost it in a microwave oven set on low power.

PREPARATION While most retail cuts are sold trimmed of most external fat, some cuts, such as the leg or shoulder, may be sold with some of the fat intact. Trim it carefully before cooking: too much fat is not only unhealthy, but can also give cooked lamb a strong flavor. Do the same for cubes of lamb used for stewing or kebabs.

Some lamb cuts may also retain pieces of the fell, a papery membrane that covers surface fat. Butchers often leave the fell intact on large cuts, since it helps the meat retain its shape and natural juices. Any fell on small cuts should be removed, as it can distort the shape of the meat during cooking.

Since most cuts of lamb are naturally tender, they don't need to be tenderized further before cooking with dry-heat methods, such as roasting, grilling, or broiling. One advantage of dry-heat methods is that they allow the fat to drip off during cooking. The firmest cuts, though, like the shank and shoulder, will benefit from moist-heat cooking methods, such as poaching or braising. The long, slow simmering helps to tenderize the meat and allows its juices and flavors to blend with those of the other ingredients.

With dry-heat methods, the meat should be cooked until it is slightly pink; cooked longer, it will lose a good deal of its flavor. Cooking times will vary, according to cut and size, but, in general, the meat should be cooked slowly over low, moderate heat, until the internal temperature is 135° to 140°. Braised or stewed lamb should be cooked to the desired degree of tenderness.

When roasts and other large pieces of lamb are finished cooking, let them sit for 15 or 20 minutes before carving.

SERVING SUGGESTIONS Lamb often has a strong flavor, which can be mellowed by cooking it with fresh herbs and spices along with garlic, leeks, onions, and shallots or scallions.

Breast of lamb is a lean cut that tastes delicious when stuffed. To prepare a Middle Eastern type of stuffing, lightly sauté finely chopped garlic. Stir in cooked rice or couscous, chopped parsley, raisins, ground cinnamon, and a sprinkling of chopped almonds. Or, sauté mushrooms, leeks, garlic, chopped carrots, parsley, and oregano; combine the mixture with breadcrumbs. Spread either stuffing on the lamb, then roll and tie the breast. Brown the rolls in a large, heavy skillet before braising or roasting them in the oven.

The breast can also be marinated before it is stuffed: Blend red wine vinegar, chopped ginger, garlic, and prepared mustard and use to marinate the meat in the refrigerator for 3 or 4 hours. Blanch fresh spinach or herbs, pat dry, and lay the leaves on top of the lamb. Roll the lamb tightly so the leaves are in the center, and tie with kitchen string. Roast in a 425° oven for 15 or 20 minutes; reduce the temperature to 325° and continue roasting until done.

Many people consider leg of lamb to be the classic spring roast. Traditional recipes need only be slightly adapted to produce more healthful results. For example, many recipes call for roasting potatoes and other vegetables along with the lamb, but the fat that drips from the meat is then absorbed by the vegetables: It's better to cook

LAMB, leg 3½ oz cooked

Calories	191	Fat	8 g
Protein	28 g	Saturated Fat	3 g
Carbohydrate	0 g	Cholesterol	89 mg
Dietary Fiber	None	Sodium	68 mg

KEY NUTRIENTS		% RDA Men	% RDA Women
Vitamin B_6	0.2 mg	10%	13%
Vitamin B_{12}	3 mcg	150%	150%
Folacin	23 mcg	12%	13%
Iron	2 mg	20%	13%
Niacin	6 mg	32%	40%
Phosphorus	206 mg	26%	26%
Potassium	338 mg	N/A	N/A
Riboflavin	0.3 mg	18%	23%
Thiamin	0.1 mg	7%	10%
Zinc	5 mg	33%	42%

S=40% or more soluble N/A=Not Applicable N=Not Available

them separately. Give the lamb flavor, without fat, by adding garlic: Make ½-inch slits all over the lamb and insert a sliver of peeled garlic into each one. Place the roast in a pan and rub the entire leg with rosemary, basil, chopped parsley, and pepper. Season onions, carrots, parsnips, and potatoes with rosemary and roast in a separate pan.

Loin, rib, or shoulder chops are easy cuts to cook. Season them by rubbing with paprika and cayenne pepper; with ground coriander, cumin, and basil; or with finely chopped ginger, cilantro, and allspice, before grilling or broiling. Serve with a sauce made from chopped fresh mint, white wine vinegar, and honey. Or, broil the chops plain and sprinkle with grated lemon zest, finely chopped scallions, parsley, and lemon juice just before serving.

Shank is the best cut for soups and stews. Make an Indian lamb curry by combining broiled pieces of shank with sautéed onions, garlic, and fresh ginger. Season to taste with curry powder, ground cumin, and ground coriander. Cover with chicken or beef broth and water, and simmer for about an hour. Then add chunks of vegetables, such as potatoes, carrots, and peas, and cook until tender. Serve with basmati rice and raita, a refreshing mixture of cucumbers and plain yogurt. Or, prepare a French-style stew by adding chunks of broiled lamb to sautéed whole shallots or chopped leeks and garlic. Stir in a few tablespoons of flour and cook, stirring constantly, until the flour is no longer visible. Add chunks of unpeeled new potatoes and turnips, red wine, bay leaf, and rosemary. Simmer until the meat is tender, then stir in whole mushrooms and cook briefly. A hearty winter soup can be concocted by combining a small amount of broiled lamb with defatted beef broth and canned or cooked white navy beans, barley, carrots, celery, pearl onions, canned whole tomatoes, tomato paste, thyme, and bay leaves. Simmer for 30 or 40 minutes, or until the barley is tender. Remove the bay leaf before serving.

Use ground lamb as you would ground beef or turkey. Be sure to brown the meat first to remove some of the fat when preparing a sauce or a stuffing. To reduce the fat in ground lamb, "stretch" the raw meat with cooked rice, chopped scallions, parsley, allspice, and ground cinnamon, then shape into meatballs and cook.

Pork

Because so many pork products—especially bacon, sausage, spareribs, and hot dogs—are high in fat, pork has a dubious reputation among health-conscious consumers. Consumption of pork has declined 11 percent since 1980; today we eat 46 pounds of pork per person per year, which is 28 percent less than our beef consumption. Yet recent research has shown that, in many cases, "fat as a pig" is no longer an accurate statement. Improved ways of breeding, feeding, and raising pigs mean that fresh pork, on average, is 31 percent lower in fat, 29 percent lower in saturated fat, 14 percent lower in calories, and 10 percent lower in cholesterol than it was in 1983.

Pork's improved fat profile doesn't mean that it's as lean as skinless turkey or chicken breast or lean fish. Only the leanest cuts approach the low fat content of these meats; other lower-fat cuts are comparable to the leanest cuts of beef. Still, pork is an excellent source of B vitamins—it's the leading food source of thiamin, a B vitamin necessary for the conversion of carbohydrates into energy and important for normal functioning of the cardiovascular and nervous systems. Pork also supplies good amounts of iron, zinc, and high-quality protein. Moreover, the fat in pork is slightly less saturated than that in beef.

As with beef, the guidelines for including pork in your diet are to choose lean cuts, eat small portions (3½ to 4 ounces cooked), and trim all visible fat before cooking. You can't rely on a grading system for pork, unlike beef, to give you a clue to the fat content of the cut. Because fresh pork is consistent in quality, there is no grading system used, though as with beef, pork is inspected by the USDA for wholesomeness.

CUTS OF PORK Like beef, pork is divided into primal, or wholesale, cuts that refer to the part of the animal they come from. Pork is further subdivided into retail cuts, which are the ones found in the supermarket. For fresh pork, the cut determines the fat content and cooking method.

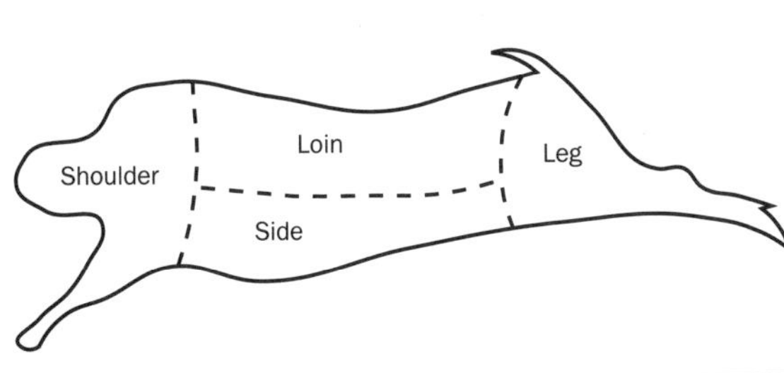

Only one-third of the pork produced each year is sold fresh. The rest is cured, smoked, or processed. Curing was once a method of preserving meat so that it would be available throughout the winter. Today, pork is cured for flavor; though the method lengthens cured pork's storage life, most cured pork must be kept refrigerated. The primary curing ingredients are salt, sugar, and sodium nitrite (the latter substance has been linked to the development of stomach cancer). Other chemicals that may be added are sodium ascorbate or erythorbate, which speed up the cure time; sodium phosphate, which helps retain some moisture in the cured product; water; and flavorings.

Since salt and other sodium-containing substances are necessary for curing the meat, cured pork products can be exceptionally high in sodium—just 3½ ounces of cured ham, for example, can contain more than one-third of the maximum recommended daily intake of sodium. Some lower-sodium products are available, however.

Since the nutritional makeup and preparation methods of fresh and cured pork differ, they are discussed separately below.

The iridescent film that appears on some cooked hams is harmless. Ham has a high fat and water content and these substances ooze out and react with the nitrites used in curing, causing a reflection like oil on a puddle.

Fresh pork

Leg Fresh hams come from this section of the hog. The whole leg can be sold as a ham that weighs 10 to 14 pounds. More often, it is divided into *butt half* and *shank half* (the butt half is much meatier). These cuts are sold with or without the bone. You may also find *top leg (inside roast).* Sometimes slices are cut from the leg and sold as *leg cutlets.* Fresh ham supplies 45 percent of its calories in the form of fat. It can be roasted, though it is sometimes dry; for that reason, braising can be a better method. Top leg can be roasted or braised, and leg cutlets can be broiled, braised, or sautéed.

Loin This part of the pig supplies the largest number of fresh cuts and also the leanest, with meat that is tender and flavorful. The loin is divided into three parts: *blade loin,* nearest the shoulder; *center loin,* and *sirloin,* nearest the leg. You may also find *top loin* chops. The cuts from either end are not as tender as the center loin, and thus the center loin is most expensive. You'll find both roasts and chops with or without the bone. Thick chops—an inch or more in thickness—can be broiled, sautéed, or braised. Roasts can be roasted or braised.

Tenderloin is sometimes sold on its own as a

roast, though more often it is included as part of loin or sirloin chops. It is about a foot long and 2 inches in diameter at its thickest point. It's well worth searching for; not only is the meat exceptionally tender, but the tenderloin is the leanest cut of fresh pork, with just 26 percent of its calories coming from fat. Roast or braise the whole tenderloin; it cooks rapidly. Or slice it into medallions and sauté the slices.

The loin is also the source of the impressive *crown roast,* which is two *center rib roasts* fastened together in a circle to form a hollow that can be stuffed and then roasted. Crown roasts are usually ordered from a butcher, since the backbone must be removed or cracked and the rib ends must be trimmed. *Country-style ribs* are not true spareribs, but are cut from the shoulder end of the loin. Meatier and leaner than spareribs, they can be braised, broiled, or roasted.

Shoulder From this section come two large pork roasts, *Boston* (or *shoulder*) *butt* and *picnic shoulder,* which is really the foreleg of the pig. A Boston butt roast is flavorful, but contains a lot of sinew; it is best braised to dissolve this connective tissue. Picnic shoulder can be roasted or braised. You can also cut these roasts into chunks, marinate them, and grill or broil them for kebabs.

Side The only fresh cut from this section is *spareribs.* These are quite fatty (and should be eaten infrequently). They are best roasted, broiled, or braised; you can reduce the fat in spareribs if you parboil them before cooking.

Cured pork

Bacon Pork belly, which comes from the side of the hog, is called bacon once it has been cured and smoked. A solution of brine and water is injected into the pork belly; a smoked flavor may

COMPARING PORK CUTS **3½ ounces trimmed and cooked**

	Calories	**Fat** (g)	**Saturated Fat** (g)	**Cholesterol** (mg)
Bacon*	576	49	17	85
Blade loin	247	15	5	93
Boston butt, fresh	273	16	6	116
Canadian bacon*	185	8	3	58
Center loin	199	9	3	79
Center rib, boneless	214	10	4	83
Country-style ribs	234	14	5	86
Ground pork	297	21	8	94
Ham, canned, extra lean*	136	5	2	30
Ham, cured, extra lean	145	6	2	53
Ham, cured, lean*	157	6	2	55
Ham, fresh, butt half	206	8	3	96
Ham, fresh, shank half	215	11	4	92
Loin, whole	187	8	3	77
Picnic shoulder, fresh	228	13	4	95
Sirloin	216	10	4	86
Spareribs	397	30	11	121
Tenderloin	164	5	2	79
Top loin	194	7	3	78

**Contains over 1000 milligrams of sodium*

also be injected, or the bacon may be smoked after it is cured. *Pancetta* is an Italian-style bacon; the whole pork belly is rolled into a sausage shape and then sliced into bacon strips. Bacon is very high in fat, saturated fat, and sodium.

Because of shrinkage, a pound of raw bacon—about 20 slices—cooks up to about four ounces. Three slices of bacon cooked—less than an ounce—has 109 calories and 9 grams of fat. That's 74 percent fat calories.

Canadian bacon A leaner alternative to regular bacon, Canadian bacon is smoked and cured pork loin. (In Canada and Great Britain, it is called back bacon.) It's used in much the same way as bacon, though it resembles ham in appearance and taste. Three and a half ounces of this meat will supply 185 calories, 41 percent of them coming from fat.

Ham True ham is pork leg that has been cured and sometimes smoked. There are many types of ham on the market. Most hams are brine (or wet) cured, whereby the pork leg is injected with a solution of water, salt, sodium nitrite, and sugar. Some hams are dry cured; the meat is rubbed with salt, sugar, sodium nitrate, sodium nitrite, and seasonings. These may also be called country hams. The dry curing process draws out moisture and intensifies the color and flavor of the meat.

Most hams are sold "fully cooked," that is, they have been cooked to a high enough internal temperature to make them safe to eat. Hams that require cooking will be marked as such on the label.

The types of ham on the market include *bone-in hams,* which contain the shank bone and are available whole or in sections; *semi-boneless hams,* which have had the shank bone removed, leaving the round leg bone; *boneless hams,* which have been rolled or molded and packed in a casing; and *canned hams,* brine-cured ham pieces that have been molded, vacuum sealed, and fully cooked. *Picnic ham* is not a true ham but comes from the shoulder, not the leg.

Ham is further divided by the percentage of protein it contains by weight. Because the curing solution can add greatly to the weight of the ham, the USDA has categorized ham in the following way: Products labeled "ham" have no added water and are at least 20.5 percent protein. "Ham with natural juices" is at least 18.5 percent protein. "Ham—added water" is at least 17 percent protein. "Ham and water product" can contain any amount of water, but must state the percentage of added ingredients on the label.

You'll also find some hams labeled lean or extra lean. Lean hams must contain no more than 10 percent fat by weight; extra lean hams, no more than 5 percent.

SPECIALTY HAMS

There are many ways of curing and smoking hams, each producing different flavors. Here are some of the different types of cured ham:

Black Forest ham: **This is a German ham that is smoked over pine wood. It is often dipped in beef blood to produce its black surface.**

Smithfield ham: **The USDA specifies that these country hams must originate in Smithfield, Virginia. Until 1966, they had to come from pigs fed nothing but peanuts, but that regulation was dropped because of the cost of raising peanut-fed hogs.**

Prosciutto: **This golden-pink Italian-style ham is dry-cured and air-dried, but not smoked. It is always eaten uncooked and is usually thinly sliced and served with figs or melon, or added to cooked dishes at the last minute. True prosciutto, called Parma ham, is made in Parma, Italy. Prosciutto is also made in the United States and some is imported from Switzerland and Canada.**

Westphalian ham: **This German ham is smoked with juniper berry and beechwood. It has very dark flesh.**

SHOPPING TIPS Look for cuts of fresh pork that are well trimmed of fat; retailers are now trimming the external fat on pork to about ⅛ inch. The meat should be pinkish-gray to pink in color; the leg and shoulder cuts tend to be darker than

SAUSAGE

Technically, sausage can be made from any kind of chopped or ground meat—even from poultry or fish—but most of the familiar varieties are pork-based. The meat is highly seasoned and sometimes smoked; it's the seasoning that gives each variety of sausage its individual flavor. For example, Mexican *chorizo* is seasoned with vinegar, garlic, cumin, and hot peppers; Italian *link* is seasoned with garlic, wine, fennel, and for the hot variety, red pepper; Polish *kielbasa* is usually smoked and contains garlic, pepper, paprika, and herbs.

Sausage is very high in fat, calories, and sodium (see chart below). Dry and semi-dry sausages may have been cured with sodium nitrate and sodium nitrite, which may be linked to stomach cancer, if eaten in excessive amounts. When you eat sausage, do so in moderation. Use it as a flavoring for foods, rather than as a main course.

Every scrap of federally inspected meat from the animal carcass can be used in making sausage, and sometimes animal fat is added. *Blood sausage* is made from blood, pork fat, and seasonings. *Liverwurst* is made from pork liver. *Mortadella,* which can be made from pork or beef, is larded with fat.

Sausage may be stuffed into a casing or sold in bulk like ground beef. There are four types of sausage: *fresh,* which is made from raw meat and sometimes contains grains or breadcrumbs, must be thoroughly cooked before eating; *semi-dry,* a smoked and partially dried sausage; *dry,* which is fully dried and may be smoked or not; and *cooked,* which is ready to eat, but may be served hot. It is important that you know which type of sausage you are buying so you can prepare it correctly.

Fresh sausage will keep for only a day or two in the refrigerator. Semi-dry sausages will keep for two to three weeks, dry sausages for four to six weeks. Cooked sausages will keep for a week.

COMPARING SAUSAGES 3½ ounces

	Calories	**Fat** (g)	**Sodium** (mg)
Blood sausage	278	35	680
Bockwurst, pork, raw	307	28	1105
Bologna, pork	247	20	1184
Bologna, turkey	199	15	878
Bratwurst, pork, cooked	301	26	557
Chorizo, beef and pork	455	38	1235
Hot dogs (2), beef and pork	320	29	1120
Hot dogs (2), chicken	257	19	1370
Italian sausage, pork, cooked	323	26	922
Kielbasa, beef and pork	310	27	1076
Liverwurst, pork	326	29	860
Mortadella, beef and pork	311	25	1246
Pepperoni, beef and pork	497	44	2040
Pork sausage, fresh, cooked	369	31	1294
Salami, beef and pork	250	20	1065

the loin cuts. Pork tenderloin is deep red, however. The fat should be creamy white. The bones, if present, should be red and spongy at the ends; the whiter the bone ends, the older the animal was when it was slaughtered and the less tender the meat will be.

When choosing cured pork products, be sure to read the label. It will tell you what type of product you're getting and also give you important information about how to cook and store it.

STORAGE Since the fat in pork is less saturated that that of beef, it turns rancid faster. Fresh pork will keep for two to three days in the refrigerator depending on the size of the cut (smaller cuts spoil more quickly). Keep pork in its original store wrapping in the coldest part of the refrigerator. Cooked pork will keep in the refrigerator for four to five days.

Cured pork products keep much longer than fresh pork. Vacuum-packed bacon is often marked with a "sell-by" date; the unopened bacon will keep until a week after this date. Once opened, it will keep for about a week if tightly wrapped. Slab bacon—often available from a deli counter—will keep for several weeks if tightly wrapped and refrigerated. Canadian bacon will keep for three to four days if sliced, up to a week if in large pieces.

Cured hams keep for about a week in the refrigerator. If the ham is vacuum-packed or sealed in plastic, leave it in its wrapping. If not, rewrap it tightly in aluminum foil. Canned hams should be refrigerated; they will keep for up to six months if unopened. Once opened, tightly wrap the leftovers and use within a week. Some canned hams do not need refrigeration, but be sure to check the label. If in doubt, refrigerate. Dry-cured hams should be refrigerated; they'll keep for six months.

PREPARATION Trim all external fat from fresh pork before cooking. Be sure to wash everything that comes in contact with the raw meat in hot soapy water to guard against contamination.

Because of many warnings over the years about pork and trichinosis, most cooks think it's necessary to cook pork to the well-done stage to eliminate this risk. Today, however, trichinosis has been virtually eliminated; most hogs are not fed food scraps (which can carry the parasite), and those that are, by federal law, are fed scraps that have been cooked to destroy parasites. Moreover, most hogs are raised on sanitary lots. These changes have led to a decreased infection rate among hogs; according to the Food Safety and Inspection Service, as little as 0.1 percent of the pork supply nowadays may be infected with *Trichinella spiralis,* the parasite that causes trichinosis. Researchers have also discovered that this parasite is destroyed at 137°, and so the recommended internal temperature of cooked pork has been lowered from 170° to 160° (which allows for

TIMETABLE FOR ROASTING PORK
(Roast in a 325° to 350° oven.)

Cut	Weight (lbs)	Minutes per pound
Boston butt*	3 to 4	40 to 45
Loin, boneless	3 to 5	20 to 30
Loin, with bone	2 to 4	20 to 25
Crown roast*	6 to 10	20 to 25
Leg (fresh ham)*	3 to 4	38 to 45
Tenderloin**	½ to 1½	20 to 30

**Roast to an internal temperature of 170° F.*
***Roast in a 425° to 450° oven.*

TIMETABLE FOR BROILING PORK

Cut	Thickness	Minutes per side
Loin chops		
with bone	¾ inch	4 to 6
boneless	¾ inch	3 to 5
with bone	1½ inches	10 to 11
boneless	1½ inches	8 to 9
Tenderloin		16 to 21 (total)
Ribs		45 to 60 (total)

a margin of safety). At that stage of doneness, the meat is still juicy and slight traces of pink may remain. When cooking a roast, you can remove it from the oven at 155° and let it stand for 15 minutes before carving; during that time, the temperature will rise to 160°.

Roasting and broiling As with other meats, cooking times for pork depend on the size and thickness of the cut, the cooking method, and whether the meat is boneless or boned. Use the charts on page 411 as general guidelines, but always use a meat thermometer to make sure the pork is fully cooked.

Unlike fresh pork, cured ham will retain its rosy color even when fully cooked. This is because the nitrites used in curing the pork react chemically with the myoglobin in the meat to form nitrosomyoglobin, which stays pinkish red even at high temperatures.

PORK, top loin 3½ oz cooked			
Calories	194	Fat	7 g
Protein	30 g	Saturated Fat	3 g
Carbohydrate	0 g	Cholesterol	78 mg
Dietary Fiber	None	Sodium	45 mg

KEY NUTRIENTS		% RDA Men	% RDA Women
Vitamin B_6	0.4 mg	20%	25%
Vitamin B_{12}	0.6 mcg	30%	30%
Iron	1 mg	10%	7%
Niacin	5 mg	26%	33%
Phosphorus	221 mg	28%	28%
Potassium	354 mg	N/A	N/A
Riboflavin	0.3 mg	18%	23%
Thiamin	0.6 mg	40%	55%
Zinc	2 mg	13%	17%

S=40% or more soluble N/A=Not Applicable N=Not Available

HAM, cured, extra lean 3½ oz			
Calories	145	Fat	6 g
Protein	21 g	Saturated Fat	2 g
Carbohydrate	2 g	Cholesterol	53 mg
Dietary Fiber	None	Sodium	1203 mg

KEY NUTRIENTS		% RDA Men	% RDA Women
Vitamin B_6	0.4 mg	20%	25%
Vitamin B_{12}	0.7 mcg	35%	35%
Vitamin C	21 mg	35%	35%
Iron	2 mg	15%	10%
Niacin	4 mg	21%	27%
Phosphorus	196 mg	25%	25%
Riboflavin	0.2 mg	12%	15%
Thiamin	0.8 mg	53%	72%
Zinc	3 mg	20%	25%

S=40% or more soluble N/A=Not Applicable N=Not Available

Cured hams that are not marked "fully cooked" must be treated like fresh pork; cook them to an internal temperature of 160°. Even hams that are marked fully cooked may benefit from cooking to 140° to improve flavor. The surface of country-style hams may be coated with a mold that is a normal part of the curing process. These hams must be scrubbed with a stiff-bristled brush to remove the mold and excess salt on the surface. The ham must then be soaked for several hours and then simmered before baking. Most country-style hams come with detailed directions for preparation.

When broiling pork loin or chops, place the meat on a rack 4 inches from the heat; ribs should be placed 5 inches from the heat.

SERVING SUGGESTIONS Add flavor to a pork loin roast by making ½-inch slits all over the meat and inserting slivers of peeled garlic. Rub the entire roast with dried sage mixed with a small amount of olive oil and pepper. Or make an apricot-ginger glaze for a pork loin roast: Mix together apricot preserves, Dijon mustard, tomato paste, minced ginger and garlic, and enough apple juice to make the mixture the consistency of honey. Brush over the meat before roasting.

Use pork loin or tenderloin to make medallions for an elegant entrée that cooks quickly. Slice the raw meat into ¾- to 1-inch rounds. Lightly dredge them in flour and brown them in a nonstick skillet in a little olive oil. Add sage, pepper, white wine, and a little broth (or caraway seeds, orange zest, brown sugar, and orange juice) to the pan and simmer for 3 to 5 minutes, or until the pork is cooked through.

Pork loin cutlets, like turkey cutlets, can be used in scaloppine dishes. See page 419.

For a Cajun twist, season loin pork chops with thyme, paprika, cayenne pepper, and garlic powder before broiling.

Pork chops can also be stuffed, provided they are at least 3/4-inch thick. Slit them in the center and stuff them with a mixture of sauteed chopped apples, shallots, bell peppers, celery seeds, and a small amount of pine nuts, if desired. Secure the opening with a toothpick and brown the chops in a skillet with a small amount of oil. Add a little apple juice, more celery seeds, and pepper, then cover and braise 15 to 20 minutes.

The flavor of fresh pork blends well with sweet accompaniments. Applesauce is traditionally served, but try cranberry sauce, too. Other good side dishes include prunes poached in wine, baked acorn squash drizzled with honey, or red cabbage cooked with chopped apples, onions, and a little cider vinegar.

For Chinese-style sweet-and-sour pork, slice pork loin into 1/4-inch strips and stir-fry with fresh or canned pineapple chunks, red bell peppers, scallions, fresh ginger, garlic, and soy sauce. Serve over brown rice.

If your diet can tolerate the high sodium content of cured ham, you can use lean or extra-lean ham in pasta and rice salads. Combine cooked pasta or rice with diced carrots, peas, corn kernels, broccoli florets, and cubes of ham. Make a light vinaigrette from white wine vinegar, chived dry mustard, and a little olive oil, and toss lightly to combine ingredients.

Turkey

Turkeys originated in the Americas millions of years ago, and the Pilgrims, landing in Massachusetts in 1620, found them a valuable game bird. Four wild turkeys were served as part of the first Thanksgiving feast in 1621, starting a tradition that has endured to this day. Benjamin Franklin regarded the turkey so highly that he proposed naming it the official bird of the United States instead of the bald eagle, declaring that ". . . the Turkey is a much more respectable Bird, and withal a true native of America."

In the past, turkey was regarded as a once-a-year treat at Thanksgiving or Christmas—90 percent of all turkeys were sold during November and December—and many cooks felt that whole birds entailed too much work to serve at other times of the year. But today more people are making turkey a part of their regular diet. Turkey breast is the leanest of all meats, supplying just 135 calories and less than a gram of fat per 3 1/2-ounce serving, skinned. In addition, turkeys are now produced in greater numbers and are available in many forms, in contrast to a few years ago when turkeys were mostly available whole. Consumers can select the parts they prefer, such as whole or half breasts, cutlets and tenderloins; these cook much faster than a whole bird. Convenience and nutritional awareness have contributed to a 133 percent increase in turkey consumption over the last two decades.

As with chicken, almost all of the fat in turkey is found in the skin. However, turkey meat is so low in fat that eating 3 1/2 ounces of roasted breast meat with skin would furnish only 153 calories, 18 percent of them coming from fat. The dark

COMPARING TURKEY PARTS
3½ ounces cooked

Fryer/Roasters	Calories	Fat (g)	Saturated Fat (g)	Cholesterol (mg)
Breast, without skin	135	1	<1	83
Breast, with skin	153	3	1	90
Dark meat, with skin	182	7	2	117
Dark meat, without skin	162	4	1	112
Leg, with skin	170	5	2	70
Leg, without skin	159	4	1	119
Light meat, with skin	164	5	1	95
Light meat, without skin	140	1	<1	86
Wing, without skin	163	3	1	102
Wing, with skin	207	10	3	115
Young hens				
Dark meat, with skin	232	13	4	84
Dark meat, without skin	192	8	3	80
Light meat, with skin	207	9	3	74
Light meat, without skin	161	4	1	68
Young toms				
Dark meat, with skin	216	11	3	91
Dark meat, without skin	185	7	2	88
Light meat, with skin	191	8	2	75

meat is higher in fat than the light meat, but it is still relatively lean if eaten without the skin, deriving 22 to 38 percent of its calories from fat. (Dark meat with the skin, however, adds significantly to your fat intake; 3½ ounces has between 7 and 13 grams of fat, supplying 35 to 50 percent of its calories.)

Turkey is high in the nutrients for which meat is known. It is not only an excellent source of protein, but also of niacin, vitamin B_6, vitamin B_{12}, and phosphorus. It also has good amounts of iron, zinc, riboflavin, and magnesium.

TYPES OF TURKEY The wild turkeys of yesteryear have largely been replaced—at least for food—by domestic turkeys, which are farm-raised birds bred for their broad breasts and juicy, flavorful flesh. Domestic turkeys weigh 6 to 24 pounds and have large breasts in relation to their legs and wings—they are so out of proportion, in fact, that domestic turkeys cannot fly more than a few feet at a time.

Most of the turkeys found on the market are young and will have tender meat. The most common types of turkey are:

Prestuffed turkeys that are sold frozen are perfectly safe, provided they aren't thawed before cooking—bacteria can multiply in the stuffing as the turkey thaws. Never buy a *fresh* prestuffed turkey.

Fryer/roasters The youngest and most tender turkeys available, fryer/roasters are under sixteen weeks old at slaughter. Their small size—5 to 9

TURKEY COLD CUTS

Many of the traditional cold cuts—ham, salami, and pastrami, for example—are now being made with turkey. Unfortunately, they are not as lean as turkey itself. A number of them are made from dark meat, and some brands contain high-cholesterol organ meats, such as the heart and gizzard. As a result, these cold cuts are often high in fat and almost always loaded with sodium. One brand of turkey bologna (advertised as "80 percent fat free" by weight) derives 77 percent of its calories from fat, and has 1100 milligrams of sodium in a 3-ounce serving.

Look for cold cuts—such as turkey breast, turkey pastrami and turkey ham—that have a gram or less of fat per ounce (at least 95 percent fat free by weight). Turkey bologna and salami tend to be nearly as rich in fat as their beef counterparts. Turkey "breast" cold cuts are low in fat, but they are not solely composed of turkey; the meat has been processed and filled with additives, such as modified food starch. The fat content of turkey roll depends on whether it is made primarily from dark or light meat; it contains gelatin, sugar, and other fillers and flavorings. Sliced fresh turkey from the deli counter is a healthier option.

When buying turkey cold cuts, be sure to check the ingredient list carefully for sodium and sugar. Sodium comes in many forms besides salt. Look out for any additive that has sodium as part of its name, including monosodium glutamate (MSG), which is commonly found in turkey products. In addition, barbecued and smoked products are not only high in sodium, but may contain nitrites (a potential carcinogen). Look for low- or no sodium cold cuts. Be advised that the sugar in cold cuts may appear on the label as dextrose, corn syrup, or honey.

pounds—makes them good choices for small families. They can be roasted, broiled, or grilled.

Hens These female turkeys, five to seven months old, weigh between 8 to 18 pounds. Some cooks believe that hens have a larger proportion of white to dark meat. Hens can be roasted, broiled, or grilled.

Toms There are those cooks who believe that the only relevant difference between a tom and a hen is size—tom turkeys weigh up to 24 pounds. Others insist that toms have tastier meat. Like hens, toms can be roasted, broiled, or grilled.

Mature hens or toms These are older turkeys and are not often found on the market. They are best stewed or poached.

Turkey parts Turkey is available in sections. All-white-meat *breasts* come in whole or half form, with the bone in or boneless. *Breast steaks* are crosswise cuts ½ to 1 inch thick; breast steaks that are ¼ to ⅜ inch thick are called *cutlets. Tenderloins* are the whole muscles on the inside of the turkey breast. Tenderloins are also sliced lengthwise into ½-inch-thick steaks, called *tenderloin steaks. Thighs* and *drumsticks* are all-dark-meat sections sold separately or together as *hindquarters. Wings* are white-meat sections sold with the bone in.

Ground turkey Provided that it's made from mostly light meat, ground turkey can be a leaner substitute for ground beef. Packaged ground turkey often contains dark meat, however, and may derive 54 percent of its calories from fat. But some processors do sell turkey ground from breast meat only (check ingredients labels). You can be sure of very lean ground meat if you buy fresh turkey parts—breast cutlets or tenderloins, for example—and have the butcher grind them for you, or grind them yourself. Ground turkey can be substituted for ground beef, but it needs more seasoning; tomato juice, egg white, and herbs will add moisture and flavor.

SHOPPING TIPS Like chicken, turkey is graded by the USDA if the processors request and pay for

TIMETABLE FOR THAWING TURKEY

	TIME	
Weight (lbs)	**Refrigerator**	**Cold Water**
8 to 12	1 to 2 days	4 to 6 hrs
12 to 16	2 to 3 days	6 to 8 hrs
16 to 20	3 to 4 days	8 to 10 hrs
20 to 24	4 to 5 days	10 to 12 hrs
Turkey halves, quarters or half breasts	1 to 2 days	4 to 6 hrs

it. The graded turkey sold in supermarkets is Grade A, which means that it is well shaped, free of feathers, and has a layer of fat. Check that the skin is unbroken, free of cuts, tears, bruises, or blemishes. When buying turkey parts, choose those which are moist and pink. The skin, if any, should be creamy white, not bluish.

The sell-by date on fresh turkey is seven days after the bird has been processed. The turkey is fresh until then, and for a day or two afterward. Don't buy fresh turkey—whole or parts—unless you plan to cook it within that time period.

Be wary when buying self-basting birds. Some basting solutions are made simply from broth and seasonings, but others contain highly saturated coconut oil, partially hydrogenated soy or corn oil, or butter. Be sure to read the ingredient list carefully.

Frozen turkeys should be rock hard and stored well below the freezer line in the refrigerated case. Make sure the package is tightly sealed and the turkey is free of freezer burn and ice crystals. Avoid packages that have a lot of frozen liquid in them; the fluid indicates that the turkey was defrosted and refrozen. If frozen turkey is properly handled at the store and at home, there should be no difference in quality between fresh and frozen birds.

When buying a whole bird, make sure to select one that will fit into your oven. The number of people you plan to feed will determine the size of bird you buy. Allow 3/4 of a pound per person, a pound if you want leftovers. If the bird is over 12 pounds, you should allow 1/2 to 3/8 pound per person, since larger birds have a greater proportion of meat to bone.

STORAGE As soon as you get fresh turkey home from the store, place it in the coldest part of the refrigerator. To reduce the chance of contaminating other foods with salmonella, store turkey in its original tight wrapping, except if you have purchased a whole bird with the giblets. Remove the giblets from the turkey and store them in a separate container; they should be used or frozen within 24 hours. Rewrap the turkey in butcher paper or heavy-duty aluminum foil. Above all, see that the package does not leak juices onto other foods; overwrap the turkey or place it on a platter in the refrigerator.

If you can't use the turkey within one or two days of purchase, freeze it. However, home freezers are not cold enough to quick-freeze a whole bird so as to eliminate the risk of salmonella. It is therefore essential that the turkey be cut into parts first. Rinse the turkey parts in cold water and dry them with paper towels, then wrap them in heavy-duty aluminum foil or freezer paper, and seal the package tightly. Turkey parts will keep for six months in a freezer set at 0°. If you've bought a whole frozen bird, it will keep for up to a year, but just remember that you do not know how long it stayed in the store's freezer.

Once cooked, turkey will keep for three to four days in the refrigerator. Carve all of the meat from a turkey carcass and wrap and store it within two hours of removing the bird from the oven. Always store turkey, gravy, and stuffing separately. (Gravy and stuffing should be used within two days; bring leftover gravy to a rolling boil before serving.) You can also freeze leftover turkey, stuffing, and gravy for up to a month. Wrap the turkey securely in freezer paper or heavy-duty aluminum foil.

PREPARATION Keep turkey refrigerated until you plan to use it. Rinse it under cold running water, and pluck out any stray pinfeathers with your fingernails or a pair of tweezers. (If you're preparing a whole bird that has previously been frozen, remove the giblets and the neck before rinsing.) Be sure to wash the counter top, sink, utensils, and your hands with hot, soapy water after handling raw turkey.

Never thaw a frozen turkey at room temperature. The turkey will thaw from the outside in, leaving the surface prone to bacterial growth before the inside has fully thawed. The safest way to thaw a frozen turkey is in the refrigerator. The length of time it takes will depend on the size of the bird. (See chart on page 416.) Place the turkey in a shallow baking pan or on a tray to catch the moisture as the bird defrosts.

Defrosting a turkey in cold water takes a shorter time, but requires some vigilance. Check the wrapping to make sure there are no tears, then place the wrapped bird in the sink or a large container and cover the turkey with cold water. (If the package is torn, place the turkey in a tightly sealed plastic bag.) Change the water every 30 minutes to keep it cold. This method significantly reduces thawing time.

You can thaw turkey in your microwave, if it will fit. Plan to cook the turkey immediately after thawing.

Whether you're preparing a whole bird or turkey parts, leave the skin on during cooking. The skin will help keep the meat moist and juicy, and won't increase the fat content of the turkey as long as it is removed before eating.

LOW-FAT GRAVY

Most of the pan drippings used to make gravy consist of fat and brown solids. To make a low-fat gravy from pan drippings, remove the bird from the cooking pan, then drain all juices into a fat skimmer, preferably one with a spout set close to the bottom. Let the drippings sit until the fat rises, then pour out the clear broth. You can also pour the drippings into a jar and use a bulb baster to remove the fat—or refrigerate it to congeal the fat. Otherwise, simply skim the fat from the juices in the roasting pan—there will be some fat left, but considerably less. Proceed with the gravy recipe. Juices can be thickened with flour if you add a small amount at a time. Have some defatted turkey or chicken broth on hand to make up a sufficient volume, if necessary.

Starchy stuffings—such as those made with bread or rice—are especially prone to bacterial contamination; the bacteria in the raw poultry can get into the stuffing and multiply. Consider cooking the stuffing separately from the turkey; it will save you time and work. In addition, an unstuffed turkey cooks faster than a stuffed one. Before roasting, simply flavor the cavity with some chopped onion, celery, apple and herbs. Add a clove or two of garlic if you like.

If you decide to stuff the bird, do so just before you're ready to cook it. Stuff the bird loosely (tightly packed stuffing cooks more slowly, and stuffing expands as it cooks). Fold the neck skin over the back and secure with skewers or toothpicks. Tie the legs together with clean string, or use metal "hock-locks," if they're provided. Once the turkey is cooked, check the internal temperature of the stuffing with a meat thermometer; it is done at 165°. Never let a stuffed turkey sit at

TIMETABLE FOR BROILING AND GRILLING TURKEY PARTS

	Weight/Thickness	Time (minutes)
Breast steaks	¾ lb	15 to 20
Drumsticks	½ to 1 lb	50 to 75
Tenderloins	½ lb	15 to 20
Thighs	½ to 1 lb	50 to 75
Wings	½ to 1 lb	50 to 75
Burgers	¾ inch thick	5 to 6 per side
Whole breasts*		
unstuffed		15 to 18 per lb
stuffed		18 to 24 per lb

**Cook in a covered kettle grill*

TIMETABLE FOR ROASTING TURKEY
Roast in a 325° oven

Weight (lbs)	**TIME** (hours)	
	Unstuffed	**Stuffed**
4 to 6 (breast)	1½ to 2¼	2 to 2¾
6 to 8	2¼ to 3¼	3 to 3½
8 to 12	3¼ to 4	3½ to 4½
12 to 16	4 to 4½	4½ to 5½
16 to 20	4½ to 5	5½ to 6½
20 to 24	5 to 5½	6½ to 7
Drumsticks, quarters, thighs	2 to 3½	N/A

N/A=Not applicable

room temperature. Remove the cooked stuffing from the turkey immediately and serve it separately; keep the remaining stuffing in a warm oven (200°), or refrigerate it in a tightly closed container.

Broiling or grilling Turkey parts can be broiled or grilled on a barbecue, like chicken parts, as well as broiled in the oven. Whole turkeys or turkey breasts can be cooked in a covered kettle grill. Be sure the rack is 6 to 8 inches from the heat source. Turn turkey parts occasionally as they cook; they will take an hour or more, depending on size and thickness. For whole birds and breasts, use a meat thermometer.

Roasting Place the whole turkey, breast side up (or turkey breast, round side up), in a shallow roasting pan. Insert a meat thermometer into the thickest part of the thigh muscle or directly into the breast, if cooking just a breast; be careful not to touch the bone. Roast the turkey, uncovered, in a 325° oven for the appropriate length of time (see chart above), until the thermometer reaches 180°, or 170° when cooking the breast alone. If areas of the turkey brown too quickly, shield those parts with aluminum foil.

If you don't have a meat thermometer, some turkeys and turkey breasts are sold with a pop-up thermometer that lets you know when the turkey is done. Another test: A turkey is done when the leg moves up and down easily and the hip joint gives readily. Or, pierce the thickest part of the inner thigh with a fork; the turkey is done if the juices run clear, not pink. Let the turkey stand 15 minutes before carving.

HEALTHY HOLIDAY MEALS

Keeping holiday occasions nutritious is often a matter of ensuring that the accompaniments to the main course, which is often turkey, are not high-fat foods. When you factor in the appetizers, side dishes, and desserts, along with the rest of the day's meals, a person's typical Thanksgiving or Christmas day intake could reach nearly 5000 calories, almost half of them derived from fat. Lower the calorie count by making simple substitutions in your holiday fare.

- **Offer raw vegetables with salsa as an appetizer instead of chips and dip, or crackers with cheese.**
- **Instead of candied sweet potatoes, substitute plain sweet potatoes or butternut or acorn squash, sweetened with a drizzling of maple syrup.**
- **Serve steamed green beans or broccoli with a sprinkling of Parmesan cheese instead of butter.**
- **In place of creamed onions, prepare a combination of whole pearl onions and steamed Brussels sprouts.**
- **Forgo canned cranberry sauce, which contains a lot of sugar, and make your own version, following the directions on page 212.**
- **For dessert, try the healthy pumpkin pie on page 170 or baked apples.**

Other roasting methods combine roasting and steaming techniques to produce a moist and flavorful bird. Set the turkey on a roasting rack in a roasting pan and add about 3½ cups of water to the bottom of the pan; if the water evaporates, add more. The juices and drippings will run into the water in the pan, which can later be defatted and serve as the basis for a gravy.

Cooks differ over the advantages of basting. Many take the position that basting is not necessary since it cannot penetrate the turkey, and that

SAFE TURKEY TIPS

Short-cut methods for cooking turkey seem to circulate during the holiday season. Unfortunately, many of these time-savers are unsafe practices, which may result in food poisoning. To be sure of serving a safe bird, follow these precautions:

- **Never partially cook a bird with the intention of finishing the job later at home or at a relative's house. The turkey may not reach a high enough internal temperature during either cooking period to kill any bacteria that are present.**
- **Don't try to save time by prestuffing a turkey, even if you plan to refrigerate it before cooking. Bacteria can grow quickly in starchy stuffing. Stuff the bird right before you're ready to cook it. To cut down on preparation time, mix the dry stuffing ingredients as early as the night before and refrigerate the mixture, separately, in a tightly covered container until you are ready to cook the turkey.**
- **It's not safe to roast a turkey overnight in an oven set at a low temperature. It takes too long for the turkey to reach a temperature high enough to kill the salmonella bacteria that may be present in the raw meat. Turkey—and other meats and poultry—should never be cooked at temperatures lower than 325°.**
- **Don't travel with a hot turkey, unless your destination is very close by. Hot foods must be kept at a constant temperature of 140° or above to be safe.**
- **If traveling with a raw turkey, remember that it cannot remain unrefrigerated for more than 2 hours. If your trip will take longer, pack the turkey in a cooler loaded with plenty of ice or cold packs. It's even safer to start with a frozen bird rather than a fresh one; the cooler will approximate refrigerator conditions, and the bird will begin to thaw en route.**

opening the oven door to baste will reduce the oven temperature and therefore increase cooking time. Other cooks feel that basting prevents the light meat from drying out. You'll have to experiment and see which option you prefer. If you do decide to baste, use defatted chicken or turkey stock instead of pan drippings, which are a concentrated source of fat. But if you prefer the pan drippings, skim the fat from them before you baste. To maintain an even oven temperature, baste no more often than every 30 minutes.

SERVING SUGGESTIONS For everyday cooking, try turkey parts. A turkey breast can be served for dinner one night, and any leftovers can be incorporated into other meals throughout the week. Complement the turkey with mashed potatoes (with defatted gravy, if desired), minted peas, and sautéed onions.

Leftovers are easily used. Spread apple butter on rye bread, then prepare a sandwich with leftover turkey and tomatoes. Or, cube the turkey and use in your favorite chicken salad recipe with a low-fat yogurt dressing.

Turkey cutlets are an inexpensive substitute for veal in scaloppine dishes. For turkey Marsala, gently pound the cutlets between two sheets of plastic wrap to flatten and tenderize them. Lightly dredge the cutlets in flour, shake off the excess, then brown them in a small amount of oil and remove them from the pan. In the same pan, briefly sauté some mushrooms, and then deglaze the pan with Marsala wine. Return the cutlets to the pan until they are heated through.

Pounded turkey cutlets make wonderful stuffed vegetable rolls. Season the cutlets with thyme, Dijon mustard, and pepper. Place blanched and drained cabbage leaves, carrots cut into julienne strips, and slices of green or red peppers in the center of each cutlet. Tightly roll each cutlet and secure with a toothpick. Brown the rolled cutlets in a small amount of olive oil and remove from

TURKEY, breast, no skin 3½ oz cooked			
Calories	135	Fat	1 g
Protein	30 g	Saturated Fat	<1 g
Carbohydrate	0 g	Cholesterol	83 mg
Dietary Fiber	None	Sodium	52 mg

KEY NUTRIENTS		% RDA Men	Women
Vitamin B_6	0.6 mg	30%	38%
Vitamin B_{12}	0.4 mcg	20%	20%
Iron	2 mg	20%	13%
Magnesium	29 mg	8%	10%
Niacin	7 mg	37%	47%
Phosphorus	224 mg	28%	28%
Zinc	2 mg	13%	17%

S=40% or more soluble N/A=Not Applicable N=Not Available

TURKEY, dark meat, no skin 3½ oz cooked			
Calories	162	Fat	4 g
Protein	29 g	Saturated Fat	1 g
Carbohydrate	0 g	Cholesterol	112 mg
Dietary Fiber	None	Sodium	79 mg

KEY NUTRIENTS		% RDA Men	Women
Vitamin B_6	0.4 mg	20%	25%
Vitamin B_{12}	0.4 mcg	20%	20%
Copper	0.2 mg	N/A	N/A
Iron	2 mg	20%	13%
Niacin	3 mg	16%	20%
Phosphorus	196 mg	25%	25%
Riboflavin	0.2 mg	12%	15%
Zinc	4 mg	27%	33%

S=40% or more soluble N/A=Not Applicable N=Not Available

the pan. Add lemon juice, fresh chopped basil, pepper, and a pat of butter to the pan. Heat and stir for a moment, and pour over the turkey rolls. You can serve the rolled cutlets with fresh lemon wedges.

Use ground turkey as you would ground beef. For burgers, mix the turkey with mustard, Worcestershire sauce, thyme, egg white, and breadcrumbs before cooking. To make meatballs, combine ground turkey with cooked rice, egg white, parsley, and oregano. Brown in a nonstick pan and add to spaghetti sauce. Or, prepare turkey chili: Brown the ground meat in a deep, heavy skillet and add whole canned tomatoes, tomato paste, cooked kidney beans, minced garlic, chili powder, and cayenne pepper. Simmer until the mixture is cooked through and the flavors have developed (about 15 to 20 minutes). You can use ground turkey in a half-and-half mixture with lean ground beef if you like.

Stuffing can be made in a low-fat version, too. One way to cut back dramatically on fat is to omit the butter called for in most recipes and use vegetable stock or wine to hold the stuffing together. Use cooked rice (white, brown, aromatic, wild, or a combination of these), croutons, or cornbread as a base. Lightly sauté chopped celery, carrots, and onions in stock, then mix the vegetables with chopped parsley, sage, oregano, or thyme. Combine the vegetables with the rice or bread and stir in a little chicken stock or white wine to moisten the mixture. Add raisins, chopped apple, or dried apricots, if desired.

For a chestnut stuffing—chestnuts, unlike other nuts, are exceptionally low in fat—combine cooked rice, sautéed onions, garlic, mushrooms, cooked shelled fresh chestnuts, and thyme. Moisten the mixture with chicken or turkey stock. If you prefer meat in your stuffing, replace the traditional fatty sausage with ground light-meat turkey seasoned with thyme, pepper, and sage or with cubes of lean smoked ham. (Be sure to cook the meats thoroughly before adding them to the stuffing.)

Chapter 8

FISH AND SHELLFISH

Though Americans have traditionally favored meat far above fish and shellfish, in the past decade these water-borne foods—which have long been appreciated by creative cooks—have become increasingly popular among the public at large. Since the early 1980s, annual consumption has risen by almost 25 percent, to nearly 16 pounds per capita. In part, this is due to the fact that fish and shellfish are no longer limited to a few familiar choices such as swordfish, fillet of sole, and shrimp. Today, many supermarkets display a suprising array of fish and shellfish from local waters and, increasingly, from other regions and even other countries. But certainly another reason behind the growing enthusiasm for these foods is their nutritional value. Like meat and poultry, fish and shellfish offer an excellent source of protein, yet unlike these animal foods, they are relatively low in calories, fat, and cholesterol. They contain some cholesterol, as do all animal products, but most fish or shellfish is no higher in cholesterol than skinless chicken breast or lean beef. Shrimp is the exception, with 195 milligrams per 3½ ounce serving, as compared with 72 milligrams in a similar serving of lobster and 70 to 85 milligrams in light meat chicken (without the skin). The good part is that all fish and shellfish are low in saturated fat. Whitefish such as flounder, cod, and haddock, as well as shellfish, are very low in total fat. They're also a good source of vitamin B_{12}, iodine, phosphorus, selenium, and zinc.

In addition, some of the fat in fish, unlike the fat in meat and poultry, appears to promote health. Fish fat, which takes the form of oils, contains certain types of polyunsaturated fatty acids—known as omega-3s—that have anti-clotting properties and thus may be protective against heart attack and perhaps high blood pressure. Like other unsaturated fats, fish oils can help lower blood cholesterol levels when they replace saturated fats in the diet. They may also help control inflammatory responses in the body that cause such conditions as arthritis and psoriasis (a chronic skin condition characterized by redness and scaling). Omega-3s are distributed throughout the fish's flesh, so you should still trim and discard any visible fat as well as the liver, and avoid eating the skin, since contaminants, if present, are most likely to settle in these three areas.

Eating even a serving or two of fish per week (any kind of fish) is associated with a lower risk of heart disease. Research suggests that the higher the fat content of fish, the greater the cardiovascular benefits. Fish with a moderate to high fat content include striped and freshwater bass, butterfish, carp, catfish, halibut, herring, mackerel, mullet, ocean perch, orange roughy, pompano, rainbow trout, sablefish, salmon, sardines, shad, smelt, swordfish, and tilefish. Most canned fish also retains most of its omega-3's.

Fish oil supplements are another story. You should avoid cod liver oil and other fish oil supplements, which may contain toxic levels of vitamins A and D, as well as environmental contaminants that often concentrate in the fish's liver. Large doses of fish oil may also thin the blood excessively and may increase your risk for certain kinds of stroke. And there is no evidence that taking fish oil supplements provides the same protection against heart attacks as eating fish.

HOW SAFE IS SEAFOOD?

Not so long ago, food poisoning from eating raw fish or shellfish was considered the only possible hazard associated with enjoying these foods. But in recent years, frequent headlines about pollutants in both fresh and salt water, coupled with reports about contamination due to improper shipping and handling within the seafood industry, have led increasing numbers of people to wonder if many varieties of fish, whether cooked or raw, are hazardous. It is true that fish and shellfish are among the most perishable of commodities—even when properly refrigerated, they don't last as long as chicken or beef. Even fish from the purest water has to be handled carefully. Complicating matters is the fact that lakes, rivers, and oceans here and all over the world are polluted with sewage, industrial waste, and heavy metals such as mercury and lead, as well as other contaminants. There are U.S. government agencies that inspect fish (fresh and canned) and make rules about where food fish may be harvested. But fish and shellfish are not subject to mandatory federal inspection; enforcement is largely the responsibility of each state, and the quality and effectiveness of state programs vary greatly. Funds to finance these programs are always short, and consumer groups have long complained that more vigilance and more funding are needed.

Any fish or shellfish may carry some bacteria and viruses—and animals from sewage-polluted waters may carry large doses of them. Many varieties of fish commonly carry the larvae of tapeworms and roundworms. Cooking will kill all such parasites and microorganisms. (Of course, if bacteria reach a certain level, the fish will be unfit for consumption no matter how much you cook it.) But heat won't eliminate mercury, lead, or such industrial pollutants as polychlorinated biphenyls (PCBs). These compounds were once widely used in electrical insulation, pesticides, plastics, inks and dyes, and other industrial products, and they seeped into the food chain in various ways. Banned by the U.S. government in 1979, PCBs persist in the environment. When they accumulate in the body they can cause birth defects, and are classified as probable carcinogens. PCBs are not the only possible contaminant: Chlordane, dioxin, DDT (which is also banned but still present), and the heavy metals are also of concern.

Nevertheless, in a detailed report published in 1991 by the National Academy of Sciences, a committee of experts on seafood safety concluded that *fish and shellfish—if cooked—are safe and wholesome and that Americans should be eating them.* The report did point out that these animals are more subject to chemical contamination than food animals raised on land, because they feed not just on plants but on other animals, and they filter gallons of water through their bodies daily. Chemicals that may be present have "an opportunity to become more concentrated through bioaccumulation." Another problem is that the potential ill effects from consumption of these chemicals are not obvious and dramatic (like food poisoning from eating bad clams, for example). Indeed, the effects are very hard to detect. Maybe the consumption of small amounts of PCBs or mercury might slightly raise the risk of cancer or of birth defects. But, as the Academy's report admitted, "the current state of knowledge on these subjects must be regarded as quite tentative." Clearly, consumers as well as scientists would like a lot more information about fish—where they were caught or harvested, how they've been handled, what pollutants they may contain, and what the longterm effects of such pollutants may be on human health.

Many fish and shellfish, including catfish, salmon, trout, carp, oysters, and mussels, are now raised by aquaculture, or fish farming. The quality of the fish depends on conditions at the fish farm. Contrary to what many people imagine, farm-raised fish don't necessarily live in nice clean tanks. The water the fish are raised in may be polluted with agricultural runoff, pesticides, or river water. The fish farmers may also add drugs (including antibiotics and sulfa drugs) to prevent or treat disease, or put hormones into the water. As with other fish, proper handling in processing and transporting is important, too. The FDA inspects fish farms, but some critics believe the inspection system is inadequate.

SAFETY GUIDELINES

Following two basic rules can help minimize the risk from contamination. Eat fish and shellfish in reasonable amounts—that is, in modest portions no more than three times a week—and choose different varieties, so you aren't likely to always be eating fish from the same area. In addition, follow the suggestions in this chapter for purchasing, storing, handling, and cooking fresh fish and shellfish. Before you eat freshwater fish caught locally, check with the local health department to make sure the waters are safe.

It's best to simply avoid eating raw fish or shellfish, including sushi—the risk of illness is too high. Even the freshest fish may harbor various kinds of bacteria and other potentially harmful organisms. Certain shellfish—clams, oysters, mussels—live by filtering 15 to 20 gallons of water a day. If the water they inhabit is polluted, they'll retain bacteria and viruses along with the microscopic foodstuffs they absorb. Raw shellfish can thus be a source of hepatitis, gastroenteritis, and other diseases. Raw fish, as used in sushi, sashimi, ceviche, and other dishes, may be a source of parasites, such as tapeworms and roundworms, as well as bacteria and viruses. (Marinating raw fish in lemon or lime juice is not the equivalent of cooking—it won't kill all bacteria and parasites.) It's true that a well-trained sushi chef may know how to purchase and handle fish so as to minimize the risk of illness and parasitic infection. But while sushi chefs are licensed in Japan, there's no way to check their credentials in this country. Preparing and eating raw fish at home is definitely not recommended, since this practice has proved the most common source of parasitic infection from fish in this country. If you make gefilte fish or other dishes that use raw, ground fish, remember not to sample it until it's cooked.

If you can't bear to give up raw fish, the FDA recommends that the fish first be frozen to destroy parasites. The temperature must be −4°, and the fish must stay frozen at least three days. Recently, the FDA took samples from fifteen sushi suppliers in Seattle. Out of ninety-two pieces, seven (one in thirteen) contained up to three parasitic larvae. But all had been killed by proper freezing. Freezing does not kill bacteria, however.

There's very little information on how any pollutants in fish might affect fetuses or very young children, but it makes sense for pregnant and nursing women (and women who think they may be pregnant), as well as small children, to eat fish only once or twice a week, and to avoid species such as salmon, swordfish, and other large game fish that may contain PCBs or heavy metals. And, of course, pregnant and nursing women, the very old and very young, and anyone coping with a serious illness should take no chances with raw fish and shellfish.

The surest way of getting untainted seafood is to buy it from a reputable source, whether it's a fish seller or a supermarket with a well-stocked fish department. Not only is the seafood likely to be properly handled and displayed, but the people who work there can answer questions you might have about storing and preparing your purchase once you get it home. The information in this chapter does the same; with it, you can choose and prepare most popular fish or shellfish on the market with the expectation that it will be safe, nutritious, and good to eat.

Fish

Fish and shellfish share the same waters, but they are distinct creatures. A fish is a vertebrate—it has a backbone, which shellfish lack. Fish also move by means of fins, breathe through gills, and, typically, have scales—three other traits that separate them from shellfish. Furthermore, the texture and flavor of fish is often more delicate than that of shellfish.

Another distinction is in the astonishing range of fresh fish that is available. More than two hundred species of fish are caught in American waters alone, and hundreds more are available worldwide. The varieties that appear in markets have shifted over the years. Some traditionally popular species, such as striped bass and pompano, are relatively scarce (and therefore expensive) due to overfishing and pollution, while species that were once overlooked, such as shark, skate, and Pacific cod, are being commercially harvested to meet the increasing demand of consumers. Because of more sophisticated fishing methods and improved refrigeration and shipping, fishermen are able to bring fish to market that were previously either uncatchable or too perishable. We rely increasingly on imports from Canada, Latin America, and even New Zealand. Furthermore, aquaculture—the science of breeding and raising fish on fish "farms"—is making a rapidly growing contribution to the market supply of both fresh and saltwater species.

Most fish markets, therefore, now offer many kinds of fresh fish. It's true that a handful of species—including tuna, pollack, cod, salmon, and flounder—account for at least three-quarters of all the fish we eat. But other varieties are growing in popularity, and many are available nationwide or over a fairly large area of the country. For the adventurous consumer, this is a boon; having such a broad choice is inspiring if you enjoy cooking fish, and it also helps lower any risk of contamination from a particular species.

Keep in mind that as far as preparation goes, you have considerable latitude when it comes to choice. Many fish have similar characteristics, so that it's fairly easy to find a suitable substitute when a particular species isn't available. Nearly all thin fillets from white-fleshed fish, for example, are mild tasting and flaky, whether the fish is flounder, cod, or turbot.

It's simplest to think of fish, both from a health standpoint and a cooking standpoint, as lean or fatty. Lower-fat (or lean) fish have less than 5 grams of fat in a 3½-ounce cooked serving; fatty fish have more than 5 grams. Only a few fish are truly high in fat, with more than 10 grams of fat per 3½ ounces. These fish—which include Pacific herring, Atlantic mackerel, pompano, salmon, sardines, and shad—are very rich in omega-3s. (Though lower in fat, trout, whitefish, sablefish, and tuna, fresh and canned, are also good sources of omega-3s.)

Most fish can be categorized as either roundfish or flatfish, according to their bone and body structure. (Tuna, which has a unique cross-shaped skeleton, fits neither category; nor do shark or skate, which have cartilage rather than bone.) The distinctions between flatfish and roundfish are especially important if you are cleaning and boning fish yourself, but even if you buy prepared fillets, an understanding of the structural differences will help you understand what you're getting.

The flounder is the clearest example of a flatfish: This platter-like fish has both eyes on one side of its head, and it swims with the broad side of its flat, oval body parallel to the ocean floor. The backbone divides the fish in half lengthwise, and two sets of ribs fan straight up and down from the backbone in a single plane, making the fish more or less one dimensional. Two even rows of fin bones project inward from the dorsal and ventral fins along the top and bottom edges of the body; these can easily be removed by trimming the perimeter of the fish. Each side of a flatfish yields two thin fillets; only the very largest flatfish, such as halibut, are thick enough to cross-cut into steaks.

Roundfish, such as striped bass, red snapper, and salmon, have thicker, more bullet-shaped bodies, and their spines lie deeper within this rounded form. One set of ribs projects straight up from the spine, while a double row of bones fans vertically from the bottom of the backbone. The bones supporting the fins project inward at various angles. A roundfish is more complicated to fillet than a flatfish, but it yields thicker fillets and, if the fish is reasonably large, meaty steaks.

Market forms of fish

Unlike beef, with its myriad cuts and grades and elaborate nomenclature, the forms in which you'll find fish in the market are simple and few.

A *whole* fish (sometimes called a "round" fish) comes to you just as it was caught. If you choose a whole fish, you'll likely have the fish seller prepare it for you, drawing or dressing it or cutting it into steaks or fillets. If the fish is filleted, about half the total weight of a whole fish will be discarded as fins, scales, skin, head, and bones.

A *whole drawn* fish has been eviscerated through a small opening so that it is not split. The gills and usually the scales are removed, but the head and tail are left intact.

A *whole dressed* fish has been first split and then eviscerated; it is also scaled, and the fins, head and tail are cut off. The backbone (which runs through the center of the fish) can be removed if you want to stuff the fish. When small fish such as rainbow trout, which are commonly pan cooked, are sold this way, they are referred to as pan dressed. Pan-dressed fish may have their tails left on and their backbones removed.

Fillets are the meaty sides of the fish, cut away from the backbone. Most of the other bones are also taken out when fish is filleted, but fine bones called "pins" may remain; these can be removed before or after you cook the fish. Sometimes the skin is removed, but often with fatty fish such as salmon, snapper, or bluefish, the skin is left on to help hold the fish together while it cooks. If both sides of the fillet are left connected at the top, it is called a *butterfly* fillet; if joined at the bottom, it's a *kited* fillet. Fillets are the most popular form of fish in the United States. They can be cooked in many different ways—sautéed, steamed, broiled, poached—and are easy to eat because they are basically boneless.

Steaks are thick cross-cut slices from dressed large roundfish such as salmon, or from thick flatfish like halibut. Steaks are usually surrounded by a band of skin and have a section of the backbone in the center. Dense fish steaks can be grilled or broiled, braised, or cut up for use in chowder; steaks of fish with more delicate flesh are good for poaching and baking.

Fish fingers are strips cut from fillets or steaks.

VARIETIES The following listing covers species of fresh fish that are available nationwide or in many areas of the country. Names of fish often vary with the region: Various types of North American flounder, for instance, are locally called "sole"—French sole, Pacific sole, sand sole, lemon sole, even Dover and English sole—even though no North American fish is truly a sole. Some flounders are given market names like sanddab, fluke, plaice, or turbot. This listing includes the most familiar market nomenclature and also takes note of regional differences and widely-used names, even if they are technically not the correct ones.

Bass A number of different freshwater and saltwater species are called "bass" or "sea bass." The *striped bass,* also called striper or rockfish, is a large fish with firm, well-flavored flesh. Once abundant on both coasts, striped bass has become much rarer because of overfishing and contamination with PCBs, and commercial fishing is now banned in most Eastern states and in California.

COMPARING FISH **3½ ounces cooked**

	Calories	**Fat** (g)	**Saturated Fat** (g)	**Cholesterol** (mg)
Bass, freshwater	153	5	1	91
Bluefish	166	6	1	79
Carp	162	7	1	84
Catfish	155	6	1	58
Cod, Atlantic	105	1	<1	55
Flounder	117	2	<1	68
Haddock	112	1	<1	74
Halibut	140	3	<1	41
Herring	203	12	3	77
Lingcod	114	1	<1	70
Mackerel, Atlantic	262	18	4	75
Monkfish	102	2	<1	34
Mullet	150	5	1	63
Orange roughy	169	9	<1	27
Perch	117	1	<1	115
Pike	113	1	<1	50
Pollack	113	1	<1	92
Pompano	211	12	5	64
Red snapper	128	2	<1	47
Rockfish	121	2	<1	44
Salmon, sockeye (red)	216	11	2	87
Sea bass	124	3	1	53
Shad	263	18	6	101
Shark	174	6	1	68
Smelt	124	3	<1	90
Swordfish	155	5	1	50
Tilefish	147	5	1	64
Trout, rainbow	151	4	1	73
Tuna, bluefin	184	6	2	49
Tuna, yellowfin	145	1	<1	60

Fish farms, where bass are harvested year-round, are becoming the principal source of this fish.

White bass is a small freshwater fish of the Great Lakes region, the South, and the Southwest; it is caught by sport fisherman and is also sold commercially, usually whole.

Both types of bass can be baked, poached, broiled, grilled, sauteed, or steamed whole. (Also see Sea bass.)

Bluefish This plentiful Atlantic fish is a great fighter, making it popular with sport fishermen. However, it ranges over a wide area during its life-span and is exposed to many contaminants, including PCBs. In samples dating from 1985, some large bluefish were found to contain PCB residues that exceeded the "level of tolerance" considered safe by the FDA, and even small bluefish may not be safe to consume constantly, according to the 1991 National Academy of Sciences report on seafood safety. Although its exceptionally rich flavor has given bluefish a "high-fat" reputation, it actually has only 6 grams of fat per 3½-ounce cooked serving. The bluefish you'll find in the market average 3 to 6 pounds; they are sold whole, dressed, and as fillets. The rather dark flesh is tasty baked or grilled (the flesh lightens when cooked).

Butterfish Called butterfish in the Eastern United States, and Pacific or California pompano in the West, this small silvery fish is usually sold whole, drawn, or dressed. Suitable for broiling, baking, or pan frying, it has a delicate flavor and soft, rather dark flesh that firms and lightens when cooked.

Carp This freshwater fish is a favorite with two diverse ethnic groups: Chinese cooks like to poach or steam it whole, while Eastern European Jews use it in making gefilte fish and also serve it poached, with a sweet-and-sour sauce. The flesh of carp is somewhat coarse, and parts of the fish can be tough. It is also a difficult fish to skin and bone, so you may prefer to buy fillets, although it is commonly sold dressed or split lengthwise. Try this fish baked, broiled, steamed, or poached.

Catfish Best known in the South, this tasty freshwater fish has become increasingly popular in recent years and is now one of America's favorite fish. Though once caught in rivers and streams, it is now farmed in ponds and sold fresh and frozen all over the country. The fish has a smooth but tough skin that can be difficult to remove, so it's preferable to buy fillets or nuggets. Although traditionally they are fried, catfish is also delicious baked, grilled, poached, sauteed, or in stews.

Cod Among the five most popular fish eaten in the United States, Atlantic cod is one of the mainstays of New England fisheries. A similar fish called Pacific cod is caught on the West Coast. (Haddock and pollack, described below, are also members of the cod family.) Cod is sold whole—at a weight of up to 10 pounds—dressed, and in fillets and steaks. The flesh is firm, white, and mild in flavor, and this very lean fish can be cooked by almost any method; try it broiled, baked with tomato sauce, or in chowder. Small cod (under 3 pounds) are sometimes marketed as scrod; they are sweeter and more tender than full-grown cod.

Flounder This widely available flatfish, which can be found on nearly every American coastline, has a mild flavor and light texture that have made it a longstanding favorite. The flounder family includes the true sole (caught only in European waters), European turbot, and fluke. Winter flounder from New England is sometimes called "lemon sole," and other flounders are offered as "gray sole," "petrale sole" (a Pacific flounder), or "rex sole." If you see Dover sole on a restaurant menu, it may be imported from England (and will be priced accordingly) or it may be a type of Pacific flounder that is sometimes called by this name in the United States.

Flounder is sold whole, dressed or filleted, fresh and frozen. This very low-fat fish can be broiled, sautéed, stuffed and baked; the whole fish can also be steamed.

SHOULD YOU BE WARY OF SCAVENGER FISH?

No. It's not really true that scavenger fish or bottom feeders—catfish and flounder as well as shrimp, crab and lobster—feed mainly off waste. They eat whatever swims or floats by them. And even when dead organic matter is consumed by these bottom-feeding fish, they digest it and use it to form proteins, fats, and carbohydrates. They are not necessarily more likely to be contaminated than other fish.

Haddock A smaller version of the cod, this lean North Atlantic fish can be substituted for cod in most recipes, although its flesh may be slightly softer.

Halibut A flatfish, like flounder, halibut is found in both the North Atlantic and northern Pacific waters. This very large fish is usually marketed in fillets or steaks, more commonly frozen (or thawed) than fresh. Poach, bake, broil, or sauté halibut steaks as you would salmon; you can

CANNED FISH

Not only are canned versions of fish a convenient way to add fish to your diet, but if you choose carefully, they provide the same health benefits as fresh fish, being low in calories, fat, and sodium, and high in protein, B vitamins, and omega-3 fatty acids.

Choose canned fish packed in water, not oil. The vegetable oil that is commonly used doubles the calories in the fish and adds up to ten times more fat. Only 15 percent of the calories in water-packed tuna come from fat, compared to over 60 percent in the oil-packed version. Draining the oil removes about a third of the calories and half the fat, but can also remove the valuable omega-3 fatty acids. One study found that while draining water-packed tuna removed only about 3 percent of the omega-3s, draining oil-packed tuna removed 15 to 25 percent.

Added salt is another nutritional concern with canned fish. Processors usually add four to ten times the amount of sodium naturally found in fresh fish. Fortunately, "low-salt" and "no salt added" varieties are available. "Low salt" tuna usually has about 50 percent less sodium, and tuna marked "no salt added" contains 90 percent less. Rinsing regular tuna or other canned fish can also remove most of the sodium.

Canned tuna is probably the most familiar type of canned fish, but it's not the only type available. Salmon and sardines also come canned, and they offer some nutritional advantages over tuna. If eaten with the bones, these fish can supply significant amounts of calcium—175 to 467 milligrams per 3½-ounce serving. Salmon is high in vitamin B_{12} and sardines are rich in iron. However, both fish are higher in fat than canned tuna, even when packed in water. Water-packed tuna contains 1 to 2 grams of fat per 3½ ounces. Water-packed red salmon has about 9 grams; pink salmon about 6 grams (the redder the salmon, the fattier and moister it is).

Canned water-packed sardines are even higher in fat—19 grams per 3½ ounces. Sardines are also higher in cholesterol than either tuna or salmon, containing 99 to 117 milligrams per 3½ ounces compared with 47 to 70 milligrams in tuna and 41 milligrams in salmon.

also substitute firm, white-fleshed halibut fillets in flounder or sole recipes.

Herring See the box on pickled and smoked fish, page 435.

Lingcod A popular Pacific coast fish, lingcod is not a true cod, but has tender, delicate white flesh like its namesake. Whole lingcod, which weigh 3 to 10 pounds and up, are usually sold dressed, and markets also carry fillets and steaks. Try this fish baked, poached, or grilled.

Mackerel This oily fish is related to tuna, and like that fish, it has outer layers of red meat and lighter interior meat. The proportion of red and light meat varies with the species, as does the percentage of fat. All types of mackerel, though, are higher-fat fish and rich in omega-3s. Most of the commercial catch is canned, but fresh mackerel is also available from the waters off California as well as the eastern coasts of the United States and South America. Spanish mackerel and jack mackerel have relatively light, mild-flavored meat, while Atlantic, Pacific, and king mackerel, or kingfish, have more red flesh and a pronounced flavor. Fresh mackerel is very perishable, so shop for it with particular care. This fish is marketed dressed or in fillets, and can be poached, baked, or broiled. A citrus or vinegar marinade helps temper its richness.

Mahi-mahi This is the Hawaiian name for a fish that is also called "dolphin" or "dolphin fish" because of its resemblance to that mammal (it is *not* actually related to the true dolphin, which is a type of porpoise). Caught primarily in Pacific waters, it is most often sold in fillets or steaks, fresh or frozen, with the skin attached to hold the fish together during cooking. Mahi-mahi has dense, sweet, moist flesh something like swordfish, and it can be cooked in the same ways: baked, broiled, or poached. Despite its rich flavor, mahi-mahi is a lean fish.

THE SCOOP ON CAVIAR

Most people eat caviar, if at all, in small amounts and rarely. As an occasional treat, caviar is not bad; it has fewer calories and more nutrients than an equivalent amount of potato chips, if you're ever offered the choice.

Whether it's the expensive "real" kind, made from sturgeon roe, or the much cheaper roes of salmon, lumpfish, and whitefish, caviar is high in protein: 4 grams per tablespoon. A tablespoon also contains 100 percent of the RDA for vitamin B_{12}, 10 percent for iron, and 4 percent for calcium, along with some potassium, phosphorus, and vitamin A. As for calories, there are 40 per tablespoon, or fewer than 80 per ounce. There are no nutritional differences between one type of caviar and another, but there are differences in taste, texture, color, and price.

A tablespoon of any fish roe contains 94 milligrams of cholesterol, almost a third of the recommended maximum daily allowance. However, caviar has a moderate fat content—about 2 grams per tablespoon—and, like other fish, it supplies some omega-3s.

Fresh sturgeon caviar labeled malossol (Russian for "lightly salted") contains approximately 4 percent salt as a preservative, which works out to about 240 to 300 milligrams of sodium per tablespoon. The sodium content of economy-class caviars (which may be made from "injured" eggs) can go as high as 700 milligrams per tablespoon.

Monkfish You won't find whole monkfish for sale at your market; this fish is so ugly that the head is cut off, and its thick, tapering tail section is sold whole or in fillets. Also called goosefish or anglerfish (*lotte* in French), monkfish has appeared on many American restaurant menus in recent years (it has long been popular in France). Its texture and flavor are often compared to lobster, and you can substitute this lean fish for lobster meat or scallops in many recipes. (Monkfish is sometimes referred to as "poor man's lobster.") It can be poached, sautéed, stir-fried, cut into medallions, or used in chowders and soups.

Mullet Most of our saltwater mullet comes from Florida, with silver and striped mullet the most common species. This fish has distinctive areas of dark and light meat: The dark meat is strong-flavored and oily, while the light flesh is mild and sweet. Buy mullet dressed for baking, broiling, grilling, or sautéing; it is also sometimes sold in fillets.

Orange roughy This small saltwater fish is mostly imported from New Zealand and sold in the form of frozen fillets. It has become quite popular, probably because its firm, slightly sweet white flesh possesses an adaptable "neutral" flavor like that of flounder. Orange roughy can be cooked by almost any method, and substituted for other mild-flavored, white fleshed fish such as cod, haddock, and halibut.

Perch Although some species of saltwater fish are commonly called perch (see Rockfish), the true perch is a freshwater fish; yellow perch and walleye from the Great Lakes are the most familiar American types. Most perch are caught by sport fishermen. Weighing 3 pounds or less, this fish has firm, flaky white flesh and is sold whole, dressed, and as fillets. Small perch is most commonly sautéed, but can also be baked, broiled, or poached.

Pike This slender freshwater fish, also called pickerel, comes from the Great Lakes and other northern U.S. and Canadian lakes. Its intricate bone structure can make filleting this fish difficult. The flesh is flaky and somewhat dry, so it's best to bake pike with a moist stuffing or a sauce, or poach it; small whole fish are often sauteed. Pike is one of the leanest of all fish, with less than 1 gram of fat per serving.

Pollack (Alaska and Atlantic) Tons of mild white Alaska pollack from the Pacific go into fish sticks and surimi (see page 444), making it one of the top ten fish in the American diet. Atlantic pollack, a different species, is richer and more flavorful. Though sometimes called Boston bluefish, it is not related to true bluefish. It has a dark layer of flesh just under the skin on one side, which can be removed for a milder flavor. Cook this lean fish as you would cod—bake, broil, poach, sauté, or use it in chowders and soups.

Pompano Sometimes called Florida pompano, this silvery fish is caught in the Atlantic off the southern U.S. coast, but overfishing has limited the supply so that pompano these days is fairly expensive. You can buy whole fresh or frozen pompano. Its rather oily, firm white meat has a delicate flavor and is best cooked by broiling, grilling, or baking in parchment.

Rockfish (ocean perch) Fish of this large family go by many names. The Atlantic species is called Atlantic ocean perch, rosefish, or redfish; some of the many Pacific varieties may be called rockfish, rock cod, Pacific ocean perch, or even Pacific red snapper (although they are quite different from cod, freshwater perch, and true red snapper). All types of rockfish/ocean perch have mild, firm white flesh, and have become very popular throughout the United States. Market size is 2 to 5 pounds and the fish are sold mostly in the form of thick fillets, which can be cooked by just about any method.

Sablefish Though it is commonly called "black cod," this northern Pacific fish is not a cod, nor is it a butterfish, another name often applied to sablefish fillets. A high fat content gives it a soft texture and a rich taste that is surprisingly mild. Fillets, fresh or frozen, are the most common market form, but sablefish is also sold whole (weighing about 3 to 15 pounds) or cut into steaks. The fish is excellent broiled, though baking, poaching, and steaming are also suitable methods. It is also available smoked.

Salmon One of the most delicious fish, salmon—especially the fattier species—is also rich in omega-3s. In fresh and canned form, it is one of the most popular fish with Americans (as is smoked salmon). This is the most familiar anadromous fish—that is, it lives in the ocean except during the spawning season, when it swims into coastal rivers and streams. Most salmon sold fresh in the United States, and all of our canned salmon, comes from Pacific waters. Any Atlantic salmon comes mostly from Canada or Norway.

Several types of salmon are sold commercially. *Chinook,* or king salmon, the largest and fattiest fish, has firm, usually deep red flesh. Chinook is sold fresh, frozen, and smoked. *Sockeye* (also called red or blueback), the finest canned salmon (but also sold fresh), has deep-red meat and the next-highest fat content. *Coho,* or silver salmon, is a small fish with medium-red, less fatty flesh; it is sold fresh. *Chum,* or dog salmon, is a lower-fat fish with firm, sometimes coarse, pale flesh. Pink, or humpback, salmon, the smallest and leanest of all, has soft, bland, pink flesh; most pink salmon is canned.

Depending on the size of the fish, fresh salmon is sold whole, in fillets, and in steaks; it can be broiled, grilled, sauteed, poached or baked, and is so moist and flavorful it needs little adornment.

Sea bass (groupers) Various species, including the large, diverse family of fish known as groupers, are marketed under this name (sometimes spelled "seabass"). Most have firm, lean, white flesh. One of the most popular species is *black sea bass,* a small fish (usually under 5 pounds) found in the Atlantic; it is marketed mostly in the Northeast, and is popular as a steamed or fried dish in Chinese restaurants. Usually sold fresh and whole, and sometimes filleted, it can also be baked, broiled, or poached.

Red and black groupers are taken from southern Atlantic waters and the Gulf of Mexico. Weighing from 3 to 20 pounds, they are sold fresh as steaks or fillets, which are best broiled, poached, or sautéed, or stuffed and baked. Grouper is also good in soups and stews. The same cooking methods are also suitable for *white sea bass,* a West Coast fish from a different family that typically weighs 10 to 15 pounds and is sold whole, pan-dressed, or in thick fillets or steaks.

Shad This fish is famous for its tasty roe as well as its rich flesh: Shad is one of the fattiest of all fish. An anadromous fish like the salmon, shad is at its best in spring, when it enters inland waters on both the Atlantic and Pacific Northwest coasts to spawn. Females bear large sacs of roe weighing up to 3/4 pound each, which are considered a great delicacy (some people prefer the roe to the fish itself). Female shad average about 8 pounds, males about 4 pounds. This fish has rich, sweet flesh but is unfortunately very bony—it has 360 bones, to be exact. It's best to buy fillets if you are not familiar with this fish, as it is difficult to bone. Sometimes the roe is sold with the fish, and sometimes it is marketed separately. Because of its high fat content, shad remains moist and delicious when baked or broiled.

Saltwater fish are generally no higher in sodium than freshwater fish. Fish have an internal regulatory system that prevents them from depositing sodium from the water in their flesh.

Shark (mako, dogfish) If you aren't a fish lover, you may nevertheless find this notorious predator appealing as food. Shark has a lean, meaty, "unfishy" texture, a mild flavor, and is free of bones, due to its cartilaginous skeleton. *Mako shark,* which can weigh up to 1000 pounds, is similar to swordfish in texture and flavor. *Dogfish* is a small shark (averaging about 2 feet long) with firm, rich flesh. Other types of shark, such as *thresher, blue,* and *blacktip,* also appear on the market. Shark is usually sold in thick steaks, and sometimes in fillets. The meaty flesh holds up well in grilling and can also be baked or poached. (Fresh shark may have a slightly ammoniac odor, which can be lessened by soaking the fish in salted water, milk, or water and lemon juice for a few hours, then rinsing it before cooking. If shark has a *strong* odor of ammonia, it has not been properly treated after it was caught; pass it up.)

Skate (ray) This flat, kite-shaped ocean creature is a relative of the shark. Like the shark, it has tough skin instead of scales, and a cartilaginous skeleton rather than bones. Usually just the triangular "wings" (not the body itself) are eaten; it's easiest to buy skate skinned and filleted. Skate flesh has striations of muscle that make it resemble crabmeat in texture; its flavor is similar to that of scallops or other shellfish. Try skate baked, broiled, or poached.

Like shark, skate may have a slight odor of ammonia when you buy it. If it does, follow the suggestions given for preparing shark, above. Unlike most seafood, skate improves with a little aging: Storing it in the refrigerator for a day or two will tenderize it.

Smelt This small, delicately flavored fish is related to salmon. Some species live in fresh water, while others are found in the Pacific and the Atlantic. *Rainbow smelt* and *eulachon* are the major commercial species. Because smelt are small and are usually eaten whole, they are most commonly sold dressed or drawn. The soft bones are edible, but the fish is also easy to bone once it's cooked. Smelt are very often deep-fried or sautéed, but they can also be broiled, grilled or baked.

Snapper There are a number of snapper species in U.S. waters, and *red snapper,* caught off the southeastern coast, is by far the best known. Because this fish is in great demand, other species (such as mutton snapper and silk snapper) may be falsely advertised as red snapper in markets and restaurants. You can recognize the real thing by its bright red skin (usually left on the fillets to identify it) and its light-colored flesh. Because red snapper tends to be expensive, you're more likely to find it in a restaurant than in your fish market. If you can buy a dressed 4- to 6-pound fish, show it to best advantage by baking, grilling, poaching, or steaming it whole; bake or broil fillets.

Sole See Flounder.

Swordfish Highly prized by sport fishermen,

swordfish can be found on both U.S. coasts. This large saltwater fish has meaty, rich-tasting flesh. The problem with swordfish is that, in a number of tests, many fish have been found to contain large concentrations of mercury. Other big fish, such as tuna and shark, are also susceptible to mercury contamination, but swordfish have been found to contain the highest levels. Since this problem was discovered, the FDA has monitored both domestic and imported swordfish very closely. Swordfish is usually sold in boneless loins (a lengthwise quarter-section of the whole fish), steaks, or chunks, fresh or frozen. Its exceptionally firm flesh makes it a good choice for kebabs; or, broil, poach, or bake swordfish steaks.

Tilefish Caught in deep Atlantic waters, tilefish average about 10 pounds. This fish was not very popular until a few years ago, but now is increasingly available and worth seeking out for its firm, pinkish-white flesh that has some of the sweetness of lobster or scallops. You'll find whole tilefish and fillets in the market. It can be substituted for other white-fleshed fish such as cod, where its sweet flavor will be a bonus. Use tilefish in chowders, or bake, broil, poach, or steam it.

Trout (freshwater) Related to salmon, trout are freshwater fish that, in markets, range from 1½ to 10 pounds whole. *Rainbow trout,* the most frequently available, is sold fresh or frozen throughout the country all year. It is an immensely popular game fish, but only farm-raised rainbows are sold commercially. *Steelhead trout* is an ocean-going rainbow trout that breeds (and tastes) like salmon; it is now also farmed. Trout generally have mild, sweet flesh, though texture, flavor, and fat content vary. Generally, the larger the fish, the higher the fat content. *Lake trout* is a large recreational fish caught in deep lakes in the Northeast, Midwest, and Canada; commercial lake trout come mainly from the Great Lakes and are available dressed or in fillets or steaks. (Some species of Great Lakes fish, including trout, have been found to contain disproportionately high concentrations of contaminants.)

Smaller trout are sold whole or dressed. They are often sautéed, but can also be broiled, grilled, or baked; try whole larger fish (or trout steaks or fillets) poached or baked. Substitute large trout for salmon in recipes.

Tuna Americans eat more tuna than any other fish. Although about 95 percent of it is consumed in canned form, the fresh fish is also extremely popular. Tuna is a large saltwater fish (depending on the species, it may weight up to 1500 pounds). Some of the more common types caught primarily in the Pacific are *albacore* and *yellowfin; bluefin* abounds off of both U.S. coasts. Tuna has "meaty" flesh, deep red and dense; it is soft and looks almost like beef when raw, but firms up and turns lighter in color when cooked. (Like good beef, fresh tuna should be reddish, not brown, when you buy it.)

Only the Japanese eat more tuna than Americans. There's a big difference in how we eat the fish, however: While American eat most of their tuna in canned form, the Japanese prefer their tuna raw.

Fresh tuna is most commonly sold in steaks or slices. It's tasty marinated and then grilled, poached, baked, broiled, or sautéed.

Weakfish This fish's name comes from its fragile mouth, which tends to break when the fish is hooked. A closely related species that is abundant from the Carolinas to Florida is *spotted sea trout.* The sweet, pale flesh is also rather tender, and should be handled carefully in cooking. Weakfish average 1 to 3 pounds and are abundant on the Atlantic and Gulf coasts. Both fish are sold whole, dressed, and in fillets, and can be substituted for striped bass, or for less flavorful fish such as cod and pollack. Bake whole large weakfish, and grill, broil, or steam smaller fish and fillets.

Whitefish The term "whitefish" is sometimes loosely used to describe various white-fleshed fish, but true whitefish is a species related to trout and abundant in the Great Lakes. It has particu-

PICKLED AND SMOKED FISH

Since fish is one of the most perishable of all foods, it's not surprising that techniques for preserving it were developed before the advent of refrigeration. Pickling and smoking are two time-honored methods. Not only do they help preserve the fish, they also alter and enhance its texture and flavor: Pickled herring and smoked salmon are delicacies quite different from either fish in its fresh state.

Oily fish such as salmon, sturgeon, sablefish, and butterfish are favorites for smoking; trout and whitefish are American smoked favorites. Finnan haddie is a famous Scottish smoked haddock specialty. Herring is sometimes smoked but more commonly pickled. You can choose from Dutch *maatjes* herring (lightly sugar-cured), German Bismarck herring (pickled in vinegar with onions), English kippers and bloaters (salted, cold-smoked herring), and German-Jewish-style *schmaltz* (fat) herring in sour cream sauce.

In addition to cold- and hot-smoked salmon, Scandinavians prepare *gravlax,* salmon cured with salt, sugar, and herbs. Lox is salmon cured in brine, while the salmon that is sold as "Nova Scotia" or "Nova" is cold-smoked. British kippered salmon is brined and then hot- or cold-smoked.

Various types of smoked and pickled fish are sold by the pound at the deli counters of many grocery stores, in fish markets, and in gourmet shops; less-expensive packaged versions are found in the dairy case of many supermarkets. When sold in bulk, these products will not have nutritional labels, so be aware that they can be very high in sodium (777 milligrams of sodium in 3½ ounces of smoked chinook salmon, 335 milligrams in the same size serving of pickled herring). Since they are made from fatty fish, they are relatively high in fat (about 4 grams for the salmon, 7 grams for the herring). Delectable smoked sablefish is especially high in fat, with nearly 20 grams of fat in a 3½-ounce, 254-calorie serving.

Although pickling and smoking do preserve fish to some extent, they do not eliminate the need for proper storage. Unless canned or vacuum-packed, these products should be stored in the refrigerator, where they will keep for about a week. Smoked salmon can be frozen if carefully wrapped, but its texture may change slightly. Also, unless the fish is hot-smoked for a long period of time, or actually cooked, the process of curing, salting, or pickling will not necessarily kill dangerous organisms that may be present in the fish. Freezing at −4° for at least three days will destroy parasites, but this is not appropriate for all types of preserved fish.

larly sweet, moist, delicate flesh and is a favorite for smoking (see box above). Whitefish for market average around 4 pounds and are sold dressed and in fillets. This fish can be baked, broiled, or poached (leave the skin on fillets to hold them together while cooking).

SHOPPING TIPS Since government inspection is not mandated for seafood, it's up to the consumer to find a reliable source for fresh, wholesome fish. You have to trust your senses when shopping for this highly perishable food: Overall quality can be judged by sight, smell, and touch. Start by locating a good fish dealer, either a fish market or a supermarket fish department with a good reputation, a clean appearance, and a knowledgeable staff. Ask questions about unfamiliar fish (and expect informed answers), and let the dealer know if seafood you've bought is ever unsatisfactory: You're entitled to return it if it is less than perfectly fresh.

To preserve freshness, plan your shopping so you can get seafood home and into the refrigerator as quickly as possible. Make the fish store (or the fish counter) the last stop of your shopping trip. In warm weather, or when you may be delayed on the trip home, have the fish packed in ice or bring a picnic cooler to keep it chilled.

Your nose will tell you immediately whether the fish in the shop are fresh; on walking in the door, you should smell only a saltwater scent, not a "fishy," sour, or ammonia-like odor. When buying prepackaged fish, take a closer sniff: Off-odors will penetrate the plastic. (The date on the label will help you choose the freshest fish in the display, but don't place total faith in it. Ask the fish dealer when it was packaged.)

Fish decays much faster than beef or chicken, so it must be kept very cold to forestall bacterial growth. All fish should be displayed on top of clean ice, with metal trays or sheets of paper or plastic to shield the delicate flesh of fish steaks or fillets from direct contact with the ice. (Whole or dressed fish, protected by their scales, can safely be placed directly on ice, and should be covered with some ice as well.) Fish should not be stacked too deeply or displayed under hot lights.

Even if you're normally a bargain hunter when shopping for food, keep this in mind when buying fish: A reduced price may reflect the dealer's attempt to sell older fish before it spoils and becomes unsalable. Examine any sale-priced seafood with particular care.

Whole fresh fish should have tight, shiny scales, and should not feel slippery or slimy. The eyes should be bright and clear, not clouded or sunken in their sockets. Gills should be clean and tinged with pink or red, never brownish or sticky. The surface of a steak or fillet should look freshly cut, and the fish should not be sitting in a pool of liquid. (Prepackaged fish should not contain excess liquid, either.) The flesh should look moist, slightly translucent, and dense, not flaky. Pass up steaks or fillets that are dried out at the edges.

Whether whole or cut, fresh fish is firm and resilient: If you poke it with your finger, the flesh should spring back, not remain indented.

Frozen fish can be of very high quality, but only if it has been handled properly. Sometimes fish are flash-frozen on the boat just after they are caught; later the fish are thawed and sold as fresh. The quality may be comparable or even superior to fresh fish, and such fish needs no special treatment (except that it should not be refrozen when you get it home). When buying pre-packaged frozen fish, be sure that the fish is still solidly frozen when you buy it. Watch out for excessive quantities of ice crystals or water stains on the package, or for cloudy liquid in the package if the wrapping is clear. Avoid fish with freezer burn, which will appear as whitened, cottony-looking patches.

The amount of fish you buy is determined by the form in which it is purchased. When buying a whole fish, allow about twice as much weight per serving as you would for steaks or fillets.

STORAGE It's best to use fish within a day of buying it, although it can be kept an extra day if it is of very high quality and was very fresh when purchased. Whole or drawn fish will keep longer than steaks or fillets; lean fish keeps better than oily fish.

Rinse and rewrap fish when you get it home: Place it on paper towels in a clean plastic bag or tightly covered container, and store in the coldest part of the refrigerator. Or, place the fish in a heavy plastic bag and set it in a pan of ice.

If you want to freeze fish yourself, you'll need a freezer that stays at 0°, preferably a chest-style unit rather than the freezer compartment of a refrigerator. Fish for freezing should be perfectly fresh and of high quality. Thawed fish is sometimes sold as fresh, so be sure to ask the dealer if you suspect this, because fish that has been frozen should not be refrozen. The faster the fish freezes, the better, so freeze whole fish only if they weigh no more than 2 pounds; cut larger fish into fillets or steaks. Rinse and dry the fish and wrap it tightly in heavy-duty freezer paper or polyvinyl chloride (PVC) plastic wrap. Overwrap the package with foil or a freezer bag, then label and date it and freeze it quickly. (Packaged fish should be rinsed and rewrapped.) Freeze fish that you've purchased frozen (and that has not been thawed) in its original wrapping. In general, you can cook frozen fish without thawing it (unless the recipe requires that the fish be soft or flexible, as for rolling or stuffing).

Frozen lean fish will keep for up to six months, fatty fish for about three months.

PREPARATION Fish can be just as easy to prepare as chicken breasts. If you buy dressed fish, fillets, or steaks, there is virtually no additional preparation necessary. Just rinse the fish quickly (or dip it briefly in cold water), then pat it dry before cooking. Always check for bones remaining in a fillet (this is likely with roundfish) by running your finger across the fillet; if you feel the tips of any bones, pull them out with tweezers.

If you want to thaw frozen fish, place it in the refrigerator overnight; do not thaw it at room temperature, where it may be subject to bacterial contamination.

As with raw meat or poultry, you must thoroughly wash all surfaces and utensils (and your hands) used to prepare raw fish; be particularly careful not to bring cooked food into contact with raw fish, or with utensils that were used to prepare it.

Don't marinate fish at room temperature; place the fish and marinade in the refrigerator.

With the risk of bacterial and parasite contamination, it's safer by far to properly cook all seafood. This doesn't mean it should be overcooked, however; fish is delicate, and if overcooked it will be dry and tough. Fish needs to be cooked just long enough to destroy any harmful organisms, and to alter its texture slightly. The cooking of fish should be carefully timed to ensure that it is cooked enough for safety but not beyond the point of moistness and tenderness.

The "10-minute rule" is a standard guide to cooking times devised by the Canadian Fisheries and Marine Service. Simply measure the fish at its thickest point and cook it for 10 minutes per inch of thickness. There are a few modifications: If the fish is stuffed, measure it after stuffing; double the time if the fish is frozen; and add 5 minutes if the fish is cooked in a sauce. Turn the fish (except thin fillets) halfway through the cooking time. (The Canadian rule does not apply to microwave cooking, which is much faster than conventional methods.)

FISH STICKS

These tidy little slabs of fish (often pollack) are coated with crumbs or batter, fried, and frozen; reheated in the microwave or oven, they make a quick, seemingly healthy meal kids dote on. However, there's more to fish sticks (and battered or crumbed fillets, their "grown-up" versions) than fish: Although these foods are an excellent source of protein and omega-3s, quite a bit of fat is used in the coating. A representative brand has 13 grams of fat and 250 calories in just five fish sticks—that's 45 percent of calories from fat. There's also a lot of added sodium (more than 900 milligrams per serving in some brands). Serving fish sticks with ketchup, cocktail sauce, or commercial tartar sauce compounds the sodium problem.

There are some healthier fish sticks on the market, with only about 4 grams of fat per serving and roughly half the sodium. If you seek these out, be sure to look beyond "Light," "Lite," "Healthy!," "New!," and other front-of-the-package claims to read the ingredient and nutritional labels.

Even when applying this rule, it helps to be familiar with the appearance of properly cooked fish as an additional doneness test. The fish should be just opaque: not translucent, but not chalky. The flesh will be firm and moist. When probed with a knife tip, the fish should *barely* flake—if it flakes too easily and falls apart, the fish is already overcooked. For large whole fish, you can use a meat thermometer and cook to 145°. Test for doneness well before the prescribed cooking time has elapsed: Fish will continue to cook by retained heat even after it is removed from the pan or the oven, so it may be best to stop cooking it when it is just a shade underdone.

Use the Canadian rule (and the visual checks described above) for calculating cooking times for fish, using any of the following methods. Remember that frozen fish need not be thawed before cooking as long as you allow for the extra cooking time.

Baking Baking works best with oily fish—dressed and stuffed, or in steaks or large chunks. Leaner fish will need added moisture: Cover the fish with vegetables or sauce, bake it atop a bed of chopped vegetables, or baste it during cooking. Line the baking pan with foil for easier removal of the baked fish, which may stick to the pan, or use a nonstick pan. Bake fish in a preheated 400° to 450° oven.

Baking in parchment or foil packets also keeps fish moist, especially if vegetables or a little liquid (such as broth or wine) are included in the packets. Place the fish on a large square of cooking parchment or foil, fold the wrapping over the contents, crimp the edges together to seal it, and bake until the fish tests done. (If your recipe calls for any acidic foods, such as tomatoes, lemon juice, or wine, don't use foil; the combination of foil and acid can cause the fish to discolor.)

Broiling/grilling Dense, flavorful fish in steaks, fillets at least 3/4 inch thick, or cubes (for kebabs) stands up best to these cooking methods. Whole fish can also be successfully grilled. Fatty fish needs little or no added fat; leaner or more delicate fish can be marinated and basted to provide additional moisture. Whether grilling or broiling, position the rack so the fish is 4 to 6 inches from the heat source.

To eliminate the danger of the fish falling apart when you turn it, grill whole fish in a special hinged basket. Also useful for grilling fish are special grill racks made of a metal sheet perforated with small holes (rather than those made of widely-spaced wires). Give any grill or broiler rack a liberal coating of nonstick cooking spray before grilling fish, and preheat it before placing the fish on it. You can also grill fish on top of a perforated sheet of foil in a covered barbecue.

COD, Atlantic 3½ oz cooked

Calories	105	Fat	1 g
Protein	23 g	Saturated Fat	<1 g
Carbohydrate	0 g	Cholesterol	55 mg
Dietary Fiber	None	Sodium	78 mg

KEY NUTRIENTS		% RDA Men	% RDA Women
Vitamin B_6	0.3 mg	15%	19%
Vitamin B_{12}	1 mcg	50%	50%
Magnesium	42 mg	12%	15%
Niacin	3 mg	16%	20%
Phosphorus	138 mg	17%	17%

S=40% or more soluble N/A=Not Applicable N=Not Available

HALIBUT 3½ oz cooked

Calories	140	Fat	3 g
Protein	27 g	Saturated Fat	1 g
Carbohydrate	0 g	Cholesterol	41 mg
Dietary Fiber	None	Sodium	69 mg

KEY NUTRIENTS		% RDA Men	% RDA Women
Vitamin B_6	0.4 mg	20%	25%
Vitamin B_{12}	1 mcg	50%	50%
Vitamin E	0.9 mg	9%	11%
Iron	1 mg	10%	7%
Magnesium	107 mg	81%	100%
Niacin	7 mg	37%	47%
Phosphorus	285 mg	36%	36%
Potassium	576 mg	N/A	N/A

S=40% or more soluble N/A=Not Applicable N=Not Available

Microwaving The microwave is the answer for people who think cooking seafood is complicated or tricky. You can microwave plain fillets or steaks instead of pan-poaching them, or cook more elaborate sauced or combination fish dishes with ease. Arrange fish in a microwavable dish with thicker portions to the outside for even cooking. For plain fish and most recipes, you'll need to cover the fish with plastic wrap and vent the wrap by turning back one corner or piercing it a few times. Rotate the dish halfway through the cooking time.

Check the fish for doneness before the recommended cooking time has elapsed (especially with an unfamiliar recipe): You can always cook it more, but there's nothing to be done if the fish is overcooked. Remove the fish from the oven when the edges are opaque but the center is still slightly translucent; let it stand for the indicated time after microwaving so it can continue cooking from retained heat. Test again after the standing time elapses, and return the fish to the microwave if it is not fully cooked throughout.

You can also microwave fish in parchment packets (but not foil), as described under *Baking*. And if you need to thaw frozen fish, microwaving is an excellent way to do it. *Cooking times:* for boneless fish, 3 to 6 minutes per pound at 100 percent power (let stand for 3 to 5 minutes after microwaving); for 4-ounce fillets in parchment, 5 to 7 minutes at 100 percent; for thawing frozen fish, 6 to 8 minutes at 30 percent (medium) power. (These times are a rough guide: Consult your microwave oven manual for more specific instructions.)

Poaching This gentle cooking method can be used for almost any kind of firm-fleshed fish, although fish on the lean side work somewhat better, as fatty fish tend to fall apart when cooked in liquid. Fish steaks, fillets, or whole fish can be poached. Immerse the fish in a pan of fish stock, a mixture of water and lemon juice or wine, or water and skim milk. (Although you can improvise a poaching pan by using a roasting pan and a roasting rack, for a large fish the most efficient equipment is a fish poacher—a long, narrow pan fitted with a removable rack.) Bring the liquid to a gentle simmer, partially cover the pan, and poach until the fish is opaque. Or, place the fish in already-simmering liquid and continue as described.

Sautéing Lean fillets or whole, small pan-dressed fish are good sautéed. A light coating of crumbs or flour (dip the fish in milk first to help the coating adhere) or a cornstarch dredge will give the fish a crisp crust and help hold it together during cooking. Use a nonstick pan liberally sprayed with cooking spray or brushed with oil; heat the pan, then add the fish. Cook, turning once (turn carefully to avoid breaking the fish) until the fish is lightly browned on the outside and it tests done on the inside. Remove the fish from the pan promptly.

SALMON, sockeye 3½ oz cooked

Calories	216	Fat	11 g
Protein	27 g	Saturated Fat	2 g
Carbohydrate	0 g	Cholesterol	87 mg
Dietary Fiber	None	Sodium	66 mg

KEY NUTRIENTS		% RDA Men	% RDA Women
Vitamin B_6	0.2 mg	10%	13%
Vitamin B_{12}	6 mcg	300%	300%
Iron	1 mg	10%	7%
Magnesium	31 mg	9%	11%
Niacin	7 mg	37%	47%
Phosphorus	276 mg	35%	35%
Potassium	375 mg	N/A	N/A
Riboflavin	0.2 mg	12%	15%
Thiamin	0.2 mg	13%	18%

S=40% or more soluble N/A=Not Applicable N=Not Available

Steaming Any fish that can be poached, whether whole, steak, or fillet, is also a candidate for steaming—and since the fish is not immersed in cooking liquid, it retains more of its natural flavor. You can also cook flavorful vegetables along with the fish and serve with a well-seasoned sauce. For equipment, you can use a collapsible vegetable steamer lightly coated with nonstick cooking spray or oil. Or the fish can sit on a heat-proof plate atop a steaming rack in a pot or skillet, which should be sufficiently large so that its sides don't touch the edge of the plate. Another option is a wooden Chinese steamer that can be placed in a wok or large skillet. Whichever piece of equipment you choose, use 1 to 2 inches of water as the cooking liquid, to which you can add fresh herbs such as fennel or dill. Bring the water to a boil, place the fish in the steaming basket (or on the steaming rack), cover the pot tightly, and steam the fish until it tests done.

Stir-frying Chunks of lean, dense fish such as halibut or shark can be stir-fried as you would chicken or beef. Lightly coat the fish in cornstarch before frying. Watch the cooking time carefully, or the seafood will overcook and toughen. It's a good idea to stir-fry the fish first, then cook any vegetables or other ingredients. Return the seafood to the pan and toss it quickly to reheat it just before serving.

SERVING SUGGESTIONS If you want to add more fish to your diet, you surely won't want to cook it the same way every time—and you certainly don't have to. Whether you have plenty of time to cook or just a little, whether you're dining alone or feeding a large family, whether your favorite cuisine is Mexican, Italian, Chinese, or Indian, there are dozens of ways to prepare fish for any occasion. Many types of fish—such as flounder, haddock, or striped bass—have a delicate texture and a mild, neutral flavor that provide a ready backdrop to your favorite seasonings and accompaniments. Then there are fish like pompano, bluefish, shark, and skate, whose characteristic flavor or texture becomes the main feature of the dish no matter how they're prepared.

Anchovies are small fish of the herring family. Rarely eaten fresh, they are usually sold in cans or jars and are used as a seasoning. Anchovies go into tuna-and-vegetable *salade Niçoise* and Caesar salad, and are also a popular pizza topping. The tiny fillets are heavily salted and packed in oil; whole anchovies are also sold in bulk, packed in salt. Puréed anchovies go into tubes of anchovy paste, a convenient flavoring and cracker spread.

A good starting point for flavoring fish is lemon juice and zest, which complement almost any kind of fish. Sprinkle fish with lemon juice before and after cooking, drape it with lemon slices before baking, add lemon wedges or juice to poaching liquid, and serve cooked fish with lemon wedges. Try lime or orange juice or zest for a nice change; a flavored vinegar is another possible substitute for the tartness of citrus. Dill, tarragon, basil, parsley, and thyme are some favorite herbs for flavoring fish. Choose a single herb or combine two for flavor variations. Use paprika to add color to baked white fish fillets or pale-colored chowders.

TROUT, rainbow 3½ oz cooked

Calories	151	Fat	4 g
Protein	26 g	Saturated Fat	<1 g
Carbohydrate	0 g	Cholesterol	73 mg
Dietary Fiber	None	Sodium	34 mg

KEY NUTRIENTS		% RDA Men	% RDA Women
Vitamin B_6	0.5 mg	25%	31%
Vitamin B_{12}	4 mcg	200%	200%
Calcium	86 mg	11%	11%
Iron	2 mg	20%	13%
Magnesium	39 mg	11%	14%
Niacin	7 mg	37%	47%
Phosphorus	321 mg	40%	40%
Potassium	634 mg	N/A	N/A
Riboflavin	0.2 mg	12%	15%

S=40% or more soluble N/A=Not Applicable N=Not Available

Use the flavor and texture of the fish as a starting point for determining your cooking method, seasonings, and accompaniments. Lean, mild-flavored fish like flounder or tilefish, when steamed, partner nicely with delicate vegetables like asparagus, summer squash, and snow peas. Bake or grill oilier, more flavorful fish such as catfish and tuna with a robust tomato or curry sauce and assertively flavored vegetables such as eggplant, fennel, and bell peppers. But there's plenty of leeway to experiment with less "logical" combinations: Try jazzing up mild-flavored fillets with a hot Creole sauce, or grilling more assertive fish steaks with a simple lemon and herb sauce.

You can make your own fish sticks, for a reliably tasty dinner that's guaranteed low in fat and sodium: Dip fish fillets or strips in a milk-and-egg-white mixture, then in dry breadcrumbs that you've seasoned with dried herbs. Place the fish on a baking sheet lined with foil and sprayed with nonstick cooking spray; bake in a 400° oven for about 10 minutes. For a low-sodium accompani-

TUNA, canned, water-packed 3½ oz			
Calories	131	Fat	<1 g
Protein	30 g	Saturated Fat	<1 g
Carbohydrate	0 g	Cholesterol	18 mg
Dietary Fiber	None	Sodium	356 mg

KEY NUTRIENTS		% RDA Men	% RDA Women
Vitamin B_6	0.4 mg	20%	25%
Vitamin B_{12}	2 mcg	100%	100%
Iron	3 mg	30%	20%
Magnesium	29 mg	8%	10%
Niacin	12 mg	63%	80%
Phosphorus	186 mg	23%	23%
Potassium	314 mg	N/A	N/A

S=40% or more soluble N/A=Not Applicable N=Not Available

ment, serve the fillets with fresh salsa or an herbed yogurt sauce.

Fish is eaten in every part of the world, and every ethnic and national cuisine has its favorite fish recipes. Among them are many good choices for health-conscious American cooks. Try poached, steamed, or baked fish with Chinese seasonings such as fresh ginger, scallions, and low-sodium soy sauce; or marinate and baste broiled fish with a Japanese teriyaki sauce made of low-sodium soy sauce, sherry, honey, and grated fresh ginger. Serve broiled fish with a zesty homemade Mexican salsa, or substitute fish for chicken or beef in fajitas. For an Italian fish dinner, add fish to homemade or store-bought marinara sauce and serve it over pasta, or poach thick fish steaks in a tomato sauce seasoned with onions, basil, and capers.

There are fish soups, stews, and chowders from every part of the world: Cook up a French bouillabaisse (fish stew), made with an assortment of fish and shellfish, a handful of herbs, and a pinch of saffron; a Finnish-style salmon and potato soup seasoned with allspice and dill; or a simple New England fish chowder with cod or halibut, enriched with milk and crumbled crackers.

Whatever your choice of recipe, there is usually a way to make it lower in fat. Many classic fish recipes call for creamy sauces, but in most cases low-fat yogurt (or other low-fat dairy products) can be used to create healthier versions of high-fat mayonnaise, hollandaise, or tartar sauce. Flavor the yogurt with mustard, vinegar, herbs, capers, chopped pickles, tomato paste, or horseradish. Or add chopped vegetables—scallions, cucumbers, tomatoes, or bell peppers, for instance. When making milk-based chowders, use lowfat or skim milk (with a little cornstarch) instead of whole milk or cream. In recipes calling for cheese sauce or a cheese topping, use a flavorful cheese, finely shredded, so you can use less (try half the amount called for).

When preparing tuna or salmon salad, use a yogurt dressing or a mixture of yogurt and "light" mayonnaise. Highlight the salad with lemon juice, fresh herbs, chopped scallions or chives, pickles, capers, or prepared mustard. Diced celery is popular in fish salads, but other vegetables—tomato, cucumber, red cabbage, bell pepper, or corn kernels, for instance—are good for a change. An unusual addition to tuna salad that few people will be able to identify (even as they enjoy its flavor) is grated apple. You can also purée water-packed canned fish as the basis for a dip; add low-fat yogurt and fresh herbs and serve with breadsticks or vegetable dippers. Or, try your favorite canned-fish salad recipe with leftover poached, broiled, or baked fish.

Combine fresh fish with vegetables, pasta, or grains for a well-rounded meal. Serve poached, baked, or broiled fish on a bed of cooked spinach "creamed" with low-fat yogurt; or present herb-broiled fillets on a salad of Boston or Bibb lettuce and drizzle with a citrus vinaigrette. Bake a whole fish with a bread or grain stuffing: Use a favorite poultry stuffing as a starting point, or improvise a stuffing of couscous, brown rice, wild rice, or kasha. Add chunks of cooked fish (or canned fish) to pasta or grain salad. Turn your favorite potato salad or slaw into a hearty main dish by adding chunks or strips of fresh-cooked fish. Alternate cubes of meaty fish and vegetables on skewers for a light barbecue meal.

Shellfish

Many people who aren't fish eaters will happily consume lobster or shrimp or scallops—foods that are as distinct from one another as they are from fish with fins. Though you're likely to encounter far more types of fish than shellfish in a fish store or on a restaurant menu, shellfish nevertheless exist in hundreds of varieties and offer flavors that range from sweet to briny. Edible shellfish are usually divided into two categories, mollusks and crustaceans. Mollusks include two-shelled bivalves—clams, oysters, mussels, and scallops—as well as univalves such as abalone, which have a shell covering a soft underpart. The tentacled creatures called cephalopods—squid and octopus are the most common types used for food—are a third class of mollusk. Lobster, shrimp, crabs, and crayfish are all crustaceans, whose segmented bodies are covered with armor-like sections of thick or thin shell.

Any of these shellfish is low in calories and is an excellent source of protein, iron, and the trace minerals zinc and copper. Most types also contribute a significant amount of B vitamins and iodine to the diet and are not particularly high in sodium. Nor are they high in cholesterol—though one of the popular misconceptions about shellfish is that it's a cholesterol-rich food. This misunderstanding arose from traditional methods of food analysis that identified as true cholesterol certain fats in shellfish that are merely similar to cholesterol, thereby yielding a cholesterol value for shellfish that was significantly higher than that for most meats. Newer analytical methods indicate that the cholesterol content of most shellfish is only about 50 to 70 milligrams per 3½-ounce serving—lower than that of skinless chicken or turkey breast, cooked. But even shellfish with the highest cholesterol levels are only slightly higher in cholesterol than lean beef, veal, or pork. (The exceptions are shrimp and crayfish, which have nearly twice as much cholesterol as a same-size serving of lean beef.) Shellfish are also low in total fat and saturated fat—factors that have a greater impact on blood cholesterol—and, like fish, they contain omega-3 fatty acids that appear to offer protection against heart disease. However, because of the very low fat content of shellfish, their fat composition is of little importance.

Three and a half ounces of oysters (about fourteen steamed oysters) supply 182 milligrams of zinc—more than *ten times* the RDA.

Many people are aware that eating raw shellfish from contaminated waters can make them sick. However, they may assume that if they heed periodic health prohibitions regarding the eating of raw clams and oysters, they can enjoy them worry-free the rest of the time. Unfortunately, this is no longer the case. Medical authorities warn that the eating of raw shellfish, even when it is certified clean, carries considerable risks. A federal report on seafood safety issued by the National Academy of Sciences in 1991 stated, "The major risk of acute disease [from fish and shellfish] is associated with the consumption of raw shellfish, particularly bivalve mollusks."

The problem lies in the inadequacy of current tests for shellfish contamination and in the policing of the shellfish industry. Because clams and oysters live by filtering 15 to 20 gallons of water per day, those that live in polluted water can become concentrated storehouses of coliform bacteria—pathological microorganisms that can find their way into fresh and salt water from untreated sewage. Because of this, harvesting has been limited to those areas that are certified clean. Unfortunately, the regulation of the shellfish industry is still irregular at best. A handful of agents are charged with overseeing some ten million acres of approved shellfish beds along the Atlantic, Pacific, and Gulf coasts.

Therefore, anyone eating raw shellfish from any area runs a risk of gastrointestinal infection and the diarrhea, nausea, abdominal cramps, and vomiting that go along with it. Shellfish-borne viruses such as hepatitis A pose additional risks for persons not in good health, such as individuals with cancer, diabetes, or any disease that impairs immunity (such as AIDS).

It's true, of course, that many people eat raw shellfish without getting sick. If you decide to take a chance on raw oysters or clams, buy them only from reputable markets and ask the dealer to show you the tag certifying that the shellfish were harvested from state-approved waters. In restaurants you can inquire about the origin of shellfish—though the waiter is hardly likely to know whether they're from polluted beds. And you can go back to the old rule about eating oysters only in months that contain the letter "r": In late spring and summer (May through August), the bacterial count is likely to be higher because the water is warmer. People who gather their own shellfish should obviously exercise great caution; first and foremost, they need to check with local authorities about the safety of any area they intend to harvest.

Inadequately cooked shellfish, too, can be a source of infection. Steamed clams, for example, are typically cooked just to the instant of opening, about a minute or two, so the clam never gets hot enough inside to kill bacteria or inactivate any virus that may be present. If it is health certainty you want, learn to like your shellfish on the well-done side.

VARIETIES The list that follows comprises a representative sampling of the more popular shellfish species in North America. The shellfish are identified by their most common names, although you will find that many varieties have local designations as well.

Clams These bivalves are, for the most part, caught in local waters. Easterners eat Atlantic clams, and Westerners enjoy Pacific varieties, but similar types of clams are harvested—dug from the sand at low tide or scooped from beds in deeper waters—on each coast. They are available all year.

Clams may be hard-shelled or soft-shelled. The edible portion may consist of the muscles that operate the shell; the siphon, or neck (through which the bivalve takes in water); and the foot, which it extends from the shell to propel itself through sand. In general, clams are sweet and a bit chewy; flavor and relative tenderness depend on the size and species.

The hard-shelled clam called a quahog is the largest eastern type, ranging from about 1½ to 6 inches across. The clams called cherrystones and littlenecks are not different species, but just smaller-sized quahogs: Cherrystones measure less than 3 inches across, littlenecks about 2 to 2½ inches. Full-sized quahogs are sometimes called chowder clams, as they can be tough and are best cut up and cooked. (Depending on size, cooked quahogs are used in chowder or baked with a crumb stuffing.)

The *surf clam,* also called a sea or skimmer clam, is the most common eastern species. Large and comparatively tough, it is commonly cut up and used in recipes; most surf clams are canned.

A third type of eastern clam is the soft-shelled *steamer,* which has a long siphon that projects from its thin, brittle shell. As the name suggests, this type of clam—about 2 inches long—is usually steamed, but it can also be shucked and then sautéed or deep-fried.

The Pacific *geoduck* is a large soft-shell clam weighing 2 to 4 pounds, with sweet, tasty flesh. It can be shucked and sautéed, and it also makes a tasty chowder. Wide *razor clams* are named for their resemblance to an old-fashioned straight razor and the sharpness of their shells; usually steamed, they are commercially marketed on the West Coast, but not in the East. There are small Pacific clams called *butter clams* and *littlenecks,*

IMITATION SHELLFISH

Based on a centuries-old process invented by the Japanese, imitation shellfish, called surimi, has become a booming industry in the United States, where it is providing an inexpensive substitute for shellfish. Most American surimi is made from Pacific pollack, a deep-sea whitefish. The filleted fish is ground and refined to remove its natural color, flavor, and odor, and then re-colored, flavored (naturally and artificially), and shaped to resemble crab legs, shrimp, scallops, lobster tails, and the like.

Surimi has less cholesterol than shellfish, and is rich in high-quality protein. It has very little fat (and thus has almost no omega-3s). The fish is cooked, so it's less perishable than fresh fish. The salt (and sometimes monosodium glutamate, or MSG) added to surimi can give it ten times the sodium content of real shellfish, while the content of other vitamins and minerals is lowered in processing. Three and a half ounces of surimi supply about 100 calories, less than a gram of fat, 20 to 30 milligrams of cholesterol, and 143 to 841 milligrams of sodium.

In grocery stores, surimi is labeled "imitation seafood" and sold under various brand names, for example, "Sea Legs." The ingredients must always be listed—for instance, "crab-flavored minced pollack." In some restaurants, however, it may be passed off as real, more expensive, shellfish. But if you know what you are getting, and you aren't on a sodium-restricted diet, surimi is a good way to add low-fat, low-cholesterol fish protein to your diet.

Surimi is sold frozen or "fresh" (thawed), breaded or unbreaded. Since surimi has a gelatin-like texture, it's not good when eaten alone. Use it in salads or sandwiches. Thawed, unbreaded surimi can be used without further cooking in salads and sandwiches. Or, cook surimi as you would shellfish, being careful not to overcook it: Like real shellfish, it will toughen if cooked too long or at too high a temperature.

and large *Pismo clams* (found on the California coast), which are scarce and delicious. *Mud clams* and *white sand clams* are two other varieties found on the West Coast.

Clams are sold fresh, in the shell or shucked and packed in their own juices (liquor). You can also buy shucked clams frozen or canned.

Crabs Found in the Atlantic and the Pacific, these crustaceans can be divided into two categories: swimming crabs, such as the blue crab, and walking crabs, such as the rock crab. Beyond that, there are dozens of different crabs, but a handful dominate the market.

Crabs are sold live, and their meat—delicately sweet, firm yet flaky—is available fresh cooked, frozen, and canned. Fresh crabmeat is sold as lump, backfin, or flake. Lump crabmeat, which consists of large, choice chunks of body meat, is the finest and most expensive. Backfin is smaller pieces of body meat. Flake is white meat from the body and other parts and is in flakes and shreds. Some fresh-cooked crab is pasteurized after cooking, which helps it keep longer. Canned crab is often imported from Asia and may come from a variety of species.

In the East, the hard-shell *Atlantic blue crab* (sold as *soft-shell crab* in the seasons when it is molting) is the premier variety: Live hard-shells are marketed when they are about 5 to 7 inches across and are most abundant in summer. Soft-shells are available from May to September. Boiling and steaming are the easiest way to cook hard-shells; soft-shell crabs are usually sautéed or broiled.

Another East-coast species, the Florida *stone crab,* is unusual in that only its meaty, thick-shelled claws are eaten: When the crab is caught, just one leg is removed and the crab is thrown back—it has the ability to regenerate the missing leg. Stone crabs are caught from October through March.

The Pacific coast from California to Alaska is

the source for the *Dungeness crab,* one of the larger species. Most weigh between 1½ and 3 pounds, but the largest can weigh as much as 4 pounds. Winter and early spring are the prime seasons for live crab.

QUESTIONABLE DELICACIES

Open up a lobster or crab and you will find what many shellfish lovers consider a special treat: The green tomalley, or liver, in a lobster or the so-called mustard, or crab butter (hepatopancreas), in a crab. Since these organs perform the usual functions of the liver in any animal—filtering toxins from the system—they may contain high concentrations of PCBs and other contaminants if the crustacean was harvested from contaminated waters. Therefore, it's safest to discard this particular delicacy.

In some female lobsters you will find another delicacy—coral, or roe, which is perfectly safe to eat. If you're a fan of lobster coral, try to choose a female lobster—its wider abdomen is a clue to its gender.

Alaska king crab, the largest of all crabs, is mostly sold as cooked and frozen meat from the legs and claws. *Snow crabs* are harvested in both the North Atlantic and the North Pacific; like king crabs, their meat is mostly sold cooked and frozen, so it is available all year round.

Smaller crabs include the *rock crab* and the *Jonah crab,* found on both coasts.

Crayfish (crawfish) The growing popularity of Cajun food has enhanced the reputation of the crayfish, which has long been a mainstay of this spicy Louisiana cuisine. Looking like small lobsters, crayfish are found in freshwater lakes, streams, and rivers in Louisiana and some other parts of the country, particularly the Pacific Northwest. They are also farmed in several Southern states. Their peak season in the South is November through June, and they are at their best in early spring.

Crayfish are harvested when about 5 inches long and are most commonly cooked live and served whole, to be dismantled by the diner like a lobster or crab. Their flesh tastes somewhat like lobster, though it is not as dense and rich. Unlike most other shellfish, crayfish (like shrimp) have a relatively high cholesterol content, with about 178 milligrams of cholesterol in a 3½-ounce serving of cooked crayfish.

Crayfish are sold live or fresh frozen; their tail meat is also sold cooked.

Lobster (American) and spiny lobster The king of crustaceans, lobsters contain sweet, firm, succulent meat within their claws, tail, and body cavity. The finest American lobsters (*Homarus americanus*) come from Maine; most of these slow-growing crustaceans are marketed at a weight of 1 to 3 pounds (the smallest are called "chicken" lobsters, the largest, "jumbo" lobsters). However, lobsters weighing 10 pounds or more can be found at some fish markets and restaurants; surprisingly, their meat is no less tender than that of smaller specimens. Lobster is available all year, but the bulk of the catch—some of which comes from Canada and Massachusetts, as well as from Maine—is harvested in the summer and fall.

Southeastern waters and the Pacific yield *spiny,* or *rock, lobsters,* which have coarser meat, all of which is in the tail (these lobsters lack the large claws of Northern lobsters). Frozen cooked rock lobster tails, usually from Australia, New Zealand, or South Africa, are widely available in American supermarkets.

Lobsters must be cooked alive or killed just before they are cooked. They are sold live, fresh cooked, and frozen.

Mussels These slender blue-black bivalves are found on both the Atlantic and Pacific coasts; in their natural state, they attach themselves to surf-washed rocks and spend half their lives submerged and half exposed to the air. Long a favorite food in Europe, these mollusks are growing quickly in popularity with Americans. The diminutive mussel meats, which may be cream-colored to dark orange, are delicately sweet and are usually steamed and served in their attractive shells, baked with a crumb topping, or used in salads or cooked dishes.

Because mussels are severely affected by pollutants, they are now being commercially farmed in "safe" waters. When conditions are optimal, these cultivated mussels are usually superior in quality to wild mussels. Although available year round, mussels are best and most plentiful from October through May; in late spring, their spawning season, they tend to be of inferior quality.

Mussels are sold live, fresh (shucked), and cooked as well as smoked. You can also buy canned mussels.

Octopus Possibly the strangest-looking sea creature we use as food, the purplish-black octopus is a cephalopod—a mollusk whose pliable body consists of tentacles sprouting directly from its head. (*Cephalopod* is a Greek-derived word meaning "headed foot.") Octopus is caught primarily on the Pacific coast and it is also imported; it is usually sold frozen (or thawed) and already dressed (cleaned). The cholesterol level of octopus is quite low—48 milligrams in 3½ ounces, raw, as compared to 233 milligrams in its relative the squid. (Each has only 1 gram of fat, however.) Unlike almost any other type of seafood, octopus calls for long cooking to tenderize its firm, mild-flavored flesh.

Oysters With flavors that range from bland to salty, these plump, mineral-rich bivalves are the prize of epicures, who tend to enjoy them raw or barely cooked. They can also be steamed, baked, or grilled, however. Unfortunately, coastal development and pollution have reduced the number of natural oyster beds, but thanks to commercial oyster farming, these choice bivalves are still in good supply. They are at their best in late fall and winter.

Eastern oysters, named for their place of origin (Bluepoints, Lynnhavens, and Chincoteagues, for example), account for most of the American oyster supply. Western waters produce *Pacific oysters* (which were originally eastern transplants) and *Olympia oysters,* a tiny native western species harvested commercially in Washington state. Most Pacific oysters are graded and marketed by size rather than by name.

Oysters are sold live in the shell and shucked, and in jars and cans.

Scallops Many people who are fond of neither fish nor shellfish like tender-firm scallops, which have a mild, sweet flavor. The nuggets of pinkish-white meat (actually the single muscle that opens and closes this bivalve's handsome fan-shaped shell) are sold shucked and trimmed, so it's an easy form of seafood to prepare and cook. Although scallops are most plentiful during fall and winter, fresh and frozen sea scallops are sold all year.

Bay scallops, which are harvested in shallow Northeastern and Gulf coastal waters, are small—about the size of a quarter in diameter—with a very delicate flavor. *Sea scallops,* found in deeper waters, are larger (about 1½ inches across), much more common, and therefore less expensive than bay scallops. They can be halved or quartered to use in recipes that call for bay scallops, although their flavor is more pronounced. A third type, *calico scallops,* are small sea scallops from Florida that are sometimes sold as bay scallops. They are the least expensive scallops; because the shells are steamed to open them, these scallops reach the consumer in a partially cooked state.

There are many traditional ways of serving scallops raw, including ceviche (or seviche), in which they are marinated in lime juice. However, while the marinade changes their color and texture, it doesn't eliminate the risk of parasites. At the very least, scallops used in ceviche should first be frozen for several days at −4°. Otherwise, serve scallops sautéed, simmered, grilled, or baked.

Shrimp (prawns) Shrimp ranks second to tuna as Americans' favorite seafood. Like chicken, its dense white meat has a fresh, mild flavor that combines well with many ingredients. You can buy shrimp already shelled and cleaned (deveined) or even precooked to use as a quick,

COMPARING SHELLFISH 3½ ounces cooked

	Calories	**Fat** (g)	**Saturated Fat** (g)	**Cholesterol** (mg)
Clams	148	2	<1	67
Crab, blue	102	2	<1	100
Crab, king	97	2	<1	53
Crawfish	114	1	<1	178
Lobster, northern	98	1	<1	72
Mussels	172	5	1	56
Oysters, eastern	137	5	1	109
Scallops	112	1	<1	53
Shrimp	99	1	<1	195

convenient recipe ingredient—though these prepared shrimp are considerably more expensive than raw, unpeeled shrimp.

Almost all shrimp caught are frozen at sea for optimum freshness, and they suffer virtually no loss of quality in freezing. The shrimp are thawed for sale, or sold frozen (thawed shrimp should be labeled "previously frozen").

Some three hundred species of shrimp are sold worldwide, but saltwater shrimp are generally designated as warm- or cold-water species. *Warm-water shrimp* are caught in tropical waters. Much of the U. S. catch is harvested in the South Atlantic and the Gulf of Mexico, and coastal waters off Latin America and Asia supply warm-water shrimp for import. Warm-water species are classified by shell color—white, pink, and brown shrimp—though the differences in their appearance and flavor are hard to detect. Rock shrimp, another warm-water variety, has a hard-to-peel shell but unusually sweet meat. *Cold-water shrimp,* caught in the North Atlantic and northern Pacific, possess firmer meat and a sweeter flavor; they are usually sold cooked and peeled.

Shrimp come in a wide range of sizes; the larger the shrimp, the higher the price. (In some areas of the country, very large shrimp may be called prawns, a term used in many other countries to refer to shrimp of any size. But in the United States, shrimp is the standard name for all types and sizes.)

Shrimp are low in fat and calories, but higher in cholesterol than most seafood, with about 195 milligrams of cholesterol per 3½-ounce serving.

Fresh-frozen shrimp are sold in bulk; whole, shelled, and shelled and deveined, and either raw or cooked. You can also buy canned or packaged frozen cooked shrimp. Size classifications range from Tiny (150 to 180 shrimp per pound) through Colossal (10 shrimp or less per pound). Larger shrimp may cost more per pound, but this doesn't necessarily mean they taste any better than their smaller counterparts.

Squid More streamlined than its relative the octopus, this cephalopod is netted on both coasts and is sometimes marketed as "calamari," its Italian name. The squid's hollow body (or mantle), usually ivory-colored with purplish patches, is perfect for stuffing once it has been cleaned out and the head removed. In addition, the mantle (also called the tube) may be lightly scored and cut crosswise into rings or bite-size pieces for sautéing, poaching, steaming, or for adding to sauces, soups, or stews. The tentacles can be chopped into pieces and eaten as well. Squid is tender, with a mild flavor. It contains a sac of brownish-black ink (used as protective camouflage in its ocean habitat); some recipes call for the ink to be used in cooking the squid.

Squid is sold both whole and dressed, either fresh or frozen, and is available all year. It is one of the few types of seafood high in cholesterol—

a $3\frac{1}{2}$-ounce uncooked portion has about 233 milligrams of cholesterol.

SHOPPING TIPS In many states, the harvest of oysters, clams, and mussels is monitored by the National Shellfish Sanitation Program. Packaged shellfish bear a sticker from the state agency; items sold in bulk have a tag that the fish dealer should show you on request (although there's no way of proving that the tag came with the shellfish you're buying). As with finfish, your nose and eyes can tell you a lot about the merchandise. Shellfish should smell briny-fresh, and look bright and clean. Shells should be hard (except for soft-shell crabs and clams) and moist.

Shellfish that are sold live offer specific signals of freshness: Hard-shelled bivalves should be tightly closed (so that you can't pull them apart), or should close tightly when the shell is tapped; don't buy clams, oysters, or mussels with open or cracked shells. The protruding necks of soft-shell clams should retract when you touch them. Lobsters, crabs, and crayfish should be active, moving their legs when touched; a lively lobster will tuck its tail under its body when lifted. Choose crustaceans that feel heavy for their size.

Freshly shucked bivalves, cooked lobster, shrimp, and crab, and any other shellfish not sold live should smell perfectly fresh, with no trace of ammonia or a "fishy" smell. Look for glossy, plump scallops with a definite sweet smell. Shucked oysters or clams should be submerged in their own clear liquor. If sold still frozen, shrimp should be solidly encased in ice.

Cooked shrimp should be purchased the same day they were cooked (the same is true of cooked crab or lobster). If cooked in the shell, shrimp should be pinkish-orange, with opaque rather than translucent flesh. Cooked crab and lobster should have bright orange-red shells. Crabmeat should be snowy white (meat from some parts of the crab may be tinged with brown or red). Be especially wary when buying cooked lobster tails, as dealers sometimes cook lobsters that have died, rather than killing them for cooking. If the lobster was alive when it went into the pot, the tail will be tightly curled. Fresh-cooked seafood should not be displayed alongside raw fish or shellfish, as bacteria can migrate from the raw to the cooked.

Shop for octopus and squid as you would for fish. Be sure they smell fresh, not fishy, and look moist and shiny. If buying them whole, the eyes should be bright, not cloudy.

CLAMS 3½ oz cooked

Calories	148	Fat	2 g
Protein	26 g	Saturated Fat	<1 g
Carbohydrate	5 g	Cholesterol	67 mg
Dietary Fiber	None	Sodium	112 mg

KEY NUTRIENTS		%RDA Men	%RDA Women
Vitamin B_{12}	99 mcg	495%	495%
Vitamin C	22 mg	37%	37%
Calcium	92 mg	12%	12%
Copper	0.7 mg	N/A	N/A
Folacin	29 mcg	15%	16%
Iron	28 mg	280%	186%
Manganese	1 mg	N/A	N/A
Niacin	3 mg	16%	20%
Phosphorus	338 mg	42%	42%
Potassium	628 mg	N/A	N/A
Riboflavin	0.4 mg	24%	31%
Thiamin	0.2 mg	13%	18%
Zinc	3 mg	20%	25%

S=40% or more soluble N/A=Not Applicable N=Not Available

STORAGE Possibly the most perishable of all foodstuffs, any type of shellfish is highly susceptible to bacterial contamination and growth once it dies or gets too warm. Therefore, when you buy shellfish, it is imperative to keep it alive—or cold—until you are ready to cook and serve it.

Live bivalves can be stored in the refrigerator, covered with wet kitchen towels or paper towels. Don't put them in an airtight container or submerge them in fresh water, or they will die. The key is to keep them truly cold: if possible, at 32° to 35°. Within that range, oysters, clams, and mussels should keep (in a live state) for about four to seven days. Be sure to remove any that die (look for open shells) during that period so they do not contaminate the remaining bivalves. Shucked oysters, clams, and mussels should be kept in tightly covered containers, immersed in their liquor; they, too, should keep for up to a week.

It's best to cook and eat live lobsters, crabs, and crayfish the same day they are purchased. Fresh-cooked lobster or crabmeat will keep for two to three days in the refrigerator. Pasteurized packaged crabmeat will keep for about six months, unopened.

Uncooked shrimp and scallops should be stored like fish and used the same day you buy them.

You can freeze shucked raw bivalves in their liquor in airtight containers; scallops are better if cooked before freezing. Do not freeze raw shrimp (sold thawed, as "fresh"), as they have already been frozen: Cook them first. Or, buy frozen shrimp and be sure they are still solidly frozen when they reach your home freezer. Cooked, shelled, and deveined shrimp can be frozen in airtight packaging and kept for no more than two months. Freeze all cooked shellfish in airtight containers or tightly sealed heavy-duty freezer bags. Most types of frozen raw or cooked shellfish will keep for two months if the freezer is set at 0° or colder. Be sure to thaw frozen shellfish in the refrigerator, not at room temperature.

PREPARATION Some types of shellfish are as easy to prepare as fish: Scallops, dressed octopus, shrimp purchased shelled and deveined, and shucked bivalves are ready to be cooked. However, bivalves, crustaceans in their shells, and whole squid need specialized preparation that can be somewhat involved. A fish seller may be able to help you by explaining some of these procedures before you attempt them for the first time.

Unless you have experience shucking live mussels, clams, or oysters, it's safer and faster to have this service performed by the fish seller. If that isn't possible, or you want to store the bivalves unshucked, then do it yourself. First discard any animals with broken or gaping shells—they have died and are not fit to eat. To prepare the remainder, scrub the shells (with a stiff brush, if necessary) and rinse under cold running water. Scrape any tough encrustations from the shells with a sturdy knife. Pull the stringy "beards"—the fibrous dark tufts protruding from the shells—off mussels before rinsing them, if you like (some people prefer to leave them on).

All bivalves should be rinsed—and preferably swirled about—in several changes of cold water to loosen the grit they accumulate. Some people like to take this a step further and purge the grit by soaking bivalves in salt water—usually a gallon of water to which 2 teaspoons of salt have been added. You can also try using a cup of cornmeal instead of, or in addition to, the salt. Let the bivalves sit in this solution in the refrigerator for 2 to 3 hours.

Mussels are steamed to open them for serving; clams may be shucked before or after cooking, depending on the dish; and oysters are opened while alive. Shelling clams and oysters is easier if you have the right tools: An oyster knife has a very short, strong blade and a guard to protect your fingers; a clam knife is about the size of a paring knife, but has a stronger blade and a rounded tip. It's not uncommon for the knife to

LOBSTER 3½ oz cooked

Calories	98	Fat	<1 g
Protein	21 g	Saturated Fat	<1 g
Carbohydrate	1 g	Cholesterol	72 mg
Dietary Fiber	None	Sodium	380 mg

KEY NUTRIENTS		% RDA Men	% RDA Women
Vitamin B_{12}	3 mcg	150%	150%
Copper	1.9 mg	N/A	N/A
Vitamin E	1 mg	10%	13%
Magnesium	35 mg	10%	13%
Phosphorus	185 mg	23%	23%
Potassium	352 mg	N/A	N/A
Zinc	3 mg	20%	25%

S=40% or more soluble N/A=Not Applicable N=Not Available

slip while you're applying pressure to open a shell, so wear a pair of work gloves to protect your hands on these occasions.

Clams Hard-shell clams are easier to open if you place them in the freezer for 10 minutes before opening them. Hold a clam in your gloved palm, rounded side up, with the shell's hinge toward your wrist. Working over a bowl to catch the juices, push the knife blade between the shell halves from the front (use the fingers of the hand holding the clam as a vise to press the knife into the shell toward the heel of your hand). Twist the knife when it is well inside to separate the half-shells. Cut the muscles on each side of the hinge, then cut the interior muscles to free the clam. Soft-shell clams are easier to open (you can use a regular paring knife); you'll also need to pull off the dark membrane that covers the edible "neck" of the clam.

Oysters To shuck an oyster, place it on top of a folded cloth (or hold it in a gloved hand) with the deeper shell downward. Hold it firmly as you insert the oyster knife between the two halves of the shell and twist the knife to pry the halves apart. Work the blade around to the hinge. Working over a bowl to catch the juices, cut the muscle that holds the shell together, then remove the top half. Slip the knife under the oyster to free it. Strain the oyster liquor before using it, to remove any broken bits of shell.

Shrimp It's not difficult to shell and devein shrimp once you know how. You can shell the shrimp before cooking, or cook them with the shells on, which some people feel adds flavor to the dish. To prepare uncooked shrimp, use a small sharp knife to make a shallow cut down the back (outer curved side) of each shrimp, then pull off the shell and legs. (Remove the tail portion of the shell, or leave it on for decoration.) Use the knife tip or a metal skewer to pick out the black intestinal vein at the back; working under cold running water will help free the vein. Remove shells from cooked shrimp by peeling off the shell with your fingers. Devein as described above.

SHRIMP 3½ oz cooked

Calories	99	Fat	1 g
Protein	21 g	Saturated Fat	<1 g
Carbohydrate	0 g	Cholesterol	195 mg
Dietary Fiber	None	Sodium	224 mg

KEY NUTRIENTS		% RDA Men	% RDA Women
Vitamin B_{12}	1 mcg	50%	50%
Copper	0.2 mg	N/A	N/A
Iron	3 mg	30%	20%
Magnesium	34 mg	10%	12%
Niacin	3 mg	16%	20%
Phosphorus	137 mg	17%	17%
Zinc	2 mg	13%	17%

S=40% or more soluble N/A=Not Applicable N=Not Available

Always thaw frozen shrimp (in the refrigerator) before cooking it.

Crabs and lobsters If you plan to boil live lobsters or hard-shell crabs, you can simply drop them headfirst into boiling water. If you plan to cook them by another method, such as broiling, they need to be killed first. If you want the fish seller to perform this task for you, be sure to make your purchase shortly before you plan to cook the shellfish; or you can do it at home using a heavy chef's knife.

To kill a crab, place it upside down on a cutting board, lay the knife lengthwise on the belly of the crab and strike it firmly with a mallet to cut the crab in half. Break off the shells, first the bottom belly flap and then the top shell; remove and discard the spongelike gills. Then twist off and crack the legs and claws to extract the meat. Remove the body meat as well, pick over all the meat for shell bits, and it is ready to cook. Soft-shell crabs can be killed by cutting off the head with a sharp knife or large shears, but this is commonly done by the fish seller.

To kill a lobster for broiling or grilling, place it belly-down and insert a knife tip at the junction of the body and tail shells. Cut the body in half lengthwise, remove the stomach and black intestinal vein, and crack the claws. Rinse the lobster well.

Squid and octopus Both these cephalopods are commonly sold dressed and ready to cook. Wash them thoroughly before cooking. Squid cooks very quickly. Octopus, however, is tough and needs to be precooked before using it in a prepared dish. Place the cleaned octopus into boiling, salted water and simmer until the skin can be peeled off. This may take anywhere from 15 to 60 minutes, depending on the octopus's size and age. Some cooks feel that octopus must be pounded with a mallet to tenderize it before cooking; others find that cooking alone is sufficient.

ADDING FLAVOR TO CRABS

Crabs are often cooked in what is called "crab boil," which is simply water seasoned with a traditional combination of spices. The spice mixture can be purchased in any area where live crabs are sold (or by mail order). Or, you can make your own by adding to the salted cooking water a few whole mustard seeds, dill seeds, coriander seeds, allspice berries, a whole clove, a bay leaf, a blade of mace, and a pinch of Cayenne or crushed red pepper. The spices can be added directly to the water, or, for easy removal, placed in a square of cheesecloth and tied with a piece of string. Add a squeeze of lemon juice to the water as well.

If you do not salt the water too heavily, use the cooking water as a base for a seafood soup after cooking the crabs and removing the spices. The same mixture can be used to add flavor to lobster or shrimp.

When it comes to cooking shellfish, the trick is to heat them sufficiently to destroy harmful organisms, but not so long as to make the flesh too tough. This requires careful monitoring, as shellfish can be toughened by just seconds of overcooking. Cooking times vary depending on size and species, but most types of shellfish undergo a characteristic change when cooked, and these alterations can help you judge doneness: Shrimp flesh turns opaque and its color changes from grayish-green to pink or orange; the shells of oysters, clams, and mussels will open (those that don't should be discarded); shelled oysters plump and their edges curl; scallops turn opaque and their flesh is just firm, not soft; the shell of a live lobster or crab will turn from green or blue to scarlet, and its flesh will turn from translucent to opaque.

In some cases these changes may take place before the flesh reaches an internal temperature compatible with safe eating. Bivalves should be cooked to an internal temperature of 145°, which usually requires at least 6 minutes. Live lobsters should be cooked to 165°, which you can test with an instant-reading thermometer that can be inserted through a vent at the end of the tail. (You can also test lobster for doneness by tugging on one of the small legs—it should pull off easily.) With crabs, the apron (a triangular flap of shell on the crab's belly) will loosen when the flesh is cooked.

Like fish, shellfish lend themselves to a variety of cooking methods:

Baking Many types of shellfish respond well to this method if the baking is carefully timed. In some cases, as with clams or mussels, it helps to protect the food from the full intensity of the dry heat with a sauce or coating, a topping of vegetables, or by combining the shellfish with other ingredients in a casserole.

Squid is often baked with a stuffing; soft-shell crabs may be given a crumb coating, mussels a crumb topping. Live oysters can be baked until they open, or you can open them first and then bake them on the half shell with a sauce or stuffing (oysters Rockefeller are made with a breadcrumb-and-spinach stuffing). Precooked oysters or clams may be baked with crumb stuffing or a sauce to keep them moist. Halved lobsters will stay moist during baking if you top the flesh with a crumb "stuffing."

Scallops or peeled shrimp turn out moist if baked in parchment or foil packets; top the seafood with lemon and herbs for flavor. To bake in packets, place the shellfish on a large square of cooking parchment or foil, fold the wrapping over the contents, crimp the edges together to seal it and bake until just done—about 5 minutes, or according to the recipe.

Boiling Live lobsters, crabs, and crayfish are often cooked by dropping them into boiling water, which cooks them quickly. Shelled or unshelled shrimp to be served cold or used in a recipe are usually boiled first. Cook shellfish at a rolling boil. For extra flavor, use fish stock instead of plain water, or add a few lemon wedges to the water.

Squid and octopus are also boiled. Squid should be timed carefully as it can easily overcook; octopus, on the other hand, may require an hour or more of simmering to tenderize it.

Broiling/grilling Shellfish cooks very quickly under a hot broiler or over hot coals. Place halved lobster flesh-side up under the broiler; shrimp and scallops can be grilled on skewers or broiled in the oven. A marinade or baste will keep the shellfish moist as it cooks. Bivalves in their shells can be cooked on a grill until the shells open. Shucked oysters, clams, or scallops can be oven-broiled if given a crumb coating to protect them from the intense heat—a good alternative to frying them. King crab legs can also be broiled if basted to keep them moist.

Microwaving Shellfish responds very well to microwave cooking: The food stays moist and there's certainly no faster way to cook it. The various types of shellfish have different requirements for microwaving.

Arrange bivalves in a microwavable dish, hinges toward the outside of the dish. Cover loosely with plastic wrap and microwave until the shells open and the seafood tests done. Place shrimp (shelled or unshelled) on a plate with their thicker portions to the outside; cover with plastic wrap. Lobster tails can be microwaved the same way. Scallops are cooked as you would fish (see page 438). Squid and octopus can be microwaved with a stuffing, instead of baking.

Poaching This cooking method works well for many types of shellfish: shrimp in or out of the shell, scallops, shucked oysters and clams, cut-up squid, and octopus. Poach shellfish in fish stock, or a mixture of water and lemon juice or wine (flavor the poaching liquid with herbs, if you like). Bring the liquid to a gentle simmer, add the shellfish, partially cover the pan, and poach until the shellfish is done.

Sautéing This method for cooking many types of shellfish—shrimp, scallops, shucked clams and oysters, soft-shell crabs, crayfish, and cut-up octopus and squid—traditionally requires quite a bit of butter or oil, both for flavor and to keep the delicate shellfish from sticking to the pan and breaking apart. For a healthier low-fat sauté, be sure to use a nonstick pan; spray it with cooking spray or brush it lightly with oil. A light dredging in flour or breadcrumbs will also help keep the shellfish from breaking up. As a further precaution, shake the pan gently and turn the food carefully. Remove the shellfish from the pan promptly when it is done, or it will continue to cook (and will be likely to overcook) from the heat retained by the pan.

Steaming Bivalves in their shells are often served simply steamed, or are steamed to open them before continuing to cook them by another method. Lobsters and hard- or soft-shell crabs can also be steamed; for crabs, a flavorful broth is used, seasoned with cloves, ginger, and whatever other spices you care to use.

Rather than steaming them in a rack *over* boiling water, bivalves and crustaceans are often steamed *in* a small amount of liquid: Place them in a pot with about 1 to 2 inches of boiling liquid (water, wine, or seasoned broth), cover, and steam over high heat until the bivalves open (but for a minimum of 6 minutes for safety's sake). Discard any shells that do not open. Steaming also provides a gentle, fat-free method for cooking shrimp and scallops (though you can use a collapsible steamer or steaming rack for these types of shellfish).

Stir-frying This Asian technique cooks shellfish in very little time and can be done with a minimum of oil. Stir-fried shellfish with an assortment of vegetables makes a quick, nutritious main dish. Shelled shrimp, crab, lobster, and crayfish, scallops, shucked bivalves, and even squid can be stir-fried. Cut the shellfish into small pieces so it cooks evenly; coat it lightly with cornstarch or marinate it briefly in a cornstarch–soy sauce broth before cooking. Be sure to remove the shellfish from the pan as soon as it's done: Stir-fry vegetables separately, then return the shellfish to the pan to reheat briefly just before serving.

SCALLOPS 3½ oz cooked			
Calories	112	Fat	1 g
Protein	23 g	Saturated Fat	0 g
Carbohydrate	3 g	Cholesterol	53 mg
Dietary Fiber	None	Sodium	265 mg

KEY NUTRIENTS		% RDA Men	% RDA Women
Calcium	115 mg	14%	14%
Iron	3 mg	30%	20%
Phosphorus	338 mg	42%	42%
Potassium	476 mg	N/A	N/A

S=40% or more soluble N/A=Not Applicable N=Not Available

SERVING SUGGESTIONS Happily, many of the traditional ways of serving shellfish are healthfully low in fat. The old-fashioned clambake is a great example: An assortment of seafood—crabs, lobsters, clams, and mussels—along with potatoes, corn on the cob, and onions, is baked in a pit on the beach under a blanket of seaweed. The foods flavor each other with their natural juices. If you don't live near a beach, you can make a rough approximation of a clambake by layering the ingredients in a tall stockpot (shellfish at the bottom) and steaming them. Fresh spinach can stand in for the seaweed in the cooking pot.

OUT OF THE FRYING PAN

What do shellfish have in common with potatoes? They are low-fat, highly nutritious foods—unless you choose to eat them fried, as many people do. A 3½-ounce serving of boiled or steamed shrimp, for instance, has less than 100 calories and derives less than 10 percent of those calories from fat; an equivalent portion of breaded, deep-fried shrimp, on the other hand, packs about 240 calories—more than 45 percent of them coming from fat. In the case of clams, the calories go from 148 (12 percent from fat) to 202 (50 percent from fat).

Shellfish is so versatile it can be combined with quite a variety of other ingredients, both for flavor and to round out the meal nutritionally. Mild-flavored scallops are compatible with delicately flavored vegetables such as asparagus and mushrooms, but can also be prepared with a robust garlic and tomato sauce. Similarly, shrimp can be served with a light lemon and herb sauce, curried Indian-style, or cooked in the Creole manner with hot peppers and a multitude of spices.

Except for time-honored favorites like deep-fried shrimp, calamari, and the like, most high-fat shellfish dishes can be updated with lighter ingredients. Instead of tartar sauce, hollandaise, or cream-based sauces, try low-fat or nonfat yogurt as a sauce base: See pages 481-482 for some suggestions. Tomato-based cocktail sauces and fresh tomato salsas are good nonfat choices, too. Make crab Louis or shrimp salad with a yogurt dressing rather than mayonnaise. You can even prepare "creamed" seafood dishes such as lobster Newburg if you use a slimmed-down white sauce made with little butter and low-fat milk instead of the cream-and-egg-based original. The Provençal version of coquilles St. Jacques (scallops) is a classic recipe that can be made without much added fat: Flour-dredged scallops are sautéed, then wine and herbs are added to the pan to make a sauce. The scallops and sauce are then transferred to individual baking dishes, topped with breadcrumbs and grated cheese, and baked until browned. If you sauté in a nonstick pan and keep the cheese to a minimum, you'll turn out a meal that's healthful as well as delicious.

It's hard to beat melted butter as a dipping sauce for lobster, crab, or clams, but you can try a low-oil lemon vinaigrette (see page 113), a lemony herbed yogurt dip, a Chinese-style accompaniment of rice, vinegar, and shredded fresh ginger—or simply ample squeezes of fresh lemon juice. Serve steamed mussels and clams with their own flavorful juices as a sauce.

Shellfish can be added to other favorite dishes for a healthy portion of high-quality protein—and great appetite appeal. Incorporate shellfish in green or cooked-vegetable salads; add it to hot or cold pasta dishes. Try a cold rice salad with shrimp, mussels, or scallops and diced steamed vegetables; or add cooked shellfish to hot rice dishes such as risotto and pilaf. Serve squid or scallops, stir-fried with mushrooms and bell peppers, over brown rice. For a Mediterranean-style seafood pizza, top a pizza crust with herbed tomato sauce, then with scallops and shrimp—no cheese needed. Don't forget the Thanksgiving classic, oyster stuffing, made by adding cooked, quartered oysters to a bread stuffing.

Make kebabs with shrimp, scallops, even mussels, clams, or oysters, and vegetables; broil them in the oven or grill them on the barbecue.

If you prefer creamy seafood chowders and soups, substitute low-fat or skim milk for the usual cream and butter. Or take your cue from such classic seafood soups as bouillabaisse and cioppino and cook the ingredients in a flavorful broth rather than using cream for richness. Or make a Manhattan-style chowder with a tomato base. In any case, do take advantage of whatever shellfish is best in the market: rely on its fine flavor instead of adding high-fat ingredients.

Chapter 9

DAIRY AND EGGS

Milk and eggs are basic, nutrient-rich foods. Milk is the sole nourishment for infant mammals; eggs contain the nutritional material to sustain unborn birds and reptiles. Human beings have been consuming eggs and the milk of other animals for thousands of years, and both foods are still among the most nutritious available to us. Milk and milk products—including cheese and yogurt—are the most important dietary sources of calcium, providing about three quarters of this mineral in the American diet. And both milk and eggs provide a roster of other vitamins and minerals, along with ample supplies of protein. Because the protein is complete, dairy foods complement the protein in legumes and grains, by supplying the amino acids present in low amounts in some non-animal protein sources.

From a culinary standpoint, these foods are widely enjoyed and remarkably versatile. Eggs and dairy products can be eaten alone, but they are also used to enhance innumerable other foods: They can lighten cakes or thicken sauces and soups, and they serve as accompaniments, flavorings, or sauces in hundreds of different dishes, from breakfast cereals to vegetables. In many others—from the omelet to the sundae—they are the central ingredient. But despite the universal appreciation for milk and eggs, they have several drawbacks when it comes to health concerns. With dairy products, the most serious shortcoming is that the fat in milk is mainly saturated. In addition, some dairy products are also quite high in sodium. The downside to eggs is their cholesterol content: One egg contains about two thirds of the total suggested daily maximum intake. Whole eggs are high in fat, too, containing about 5 grams per large egg.

AVOIDING THE FAT

Should you give these foods up entirely in order to limit your fat and cholesterol intake? Not really. Eggs do no harm if eaten occasionally. They may be high in cholesterol, but the fat they contain is primarily unsaturated. The whites are fat free and an excellent source of protein. And during the past decade manufacturers have created an astonishing variety of low-fat or nonfat dairy products that preserve the taste, texture, and nutritional value of whole milk products. As a result, consumers have a wider choice than they have ever had before when it comes to buying milk, sour cream, yogurt, ice cream, and cheese, not to mention various "imitation" versions of these products.

In low-fat or nonfat forms, these products have an important role to play in the American diet, given their rich supply of calcium—a mineral that as many as two thirds of American women, and one half of American men, should be consuming in greater quantities. Calcium intake is the primary factor in building strong bones. It's vital to start consuming adequate amounts of calcium in childhood—especially between the ages of eleven and twenty-four—and continue to do so through adulthood. Calcium plays a role in preventing osteoporosis—a loss of bone mass and subsequent weakening of bones that occurs in postmenopausal women and occasionally in older men. The link between calcium and osteoporosis is not clear-cut, but getting enough calcium is one way a woman can help reduce her risk of getting the disease. One of the reasons that milk and dairy products are reliable sources of well-utilized calcium is that they contain lactose (or milk sugar) and vitamin D, which enhance calcium's absorption. It's also easy to remember that 3 to 5 cups of milk or servings of other calcium-rich dairy products will supply the 800 milligrams of calcium you need each day.

DAIRY AND EGG SAFETY

Most milk comes from large dairy cooperatives, where milk from many farms is pooled and then processed to a uniform standard. The milk is pumped directly from the cows' udders—via milking machines—to steel tanks, and from there to refrigerated trucks. These modern practices contribute to our safe, reliable milk supply—a far cry from the days when raw milk, sold from open pails or cans, was a common vehicle for the spread of disease.

Today, less than 1 percent of the 280 million glasses of milk consumed by Americans daily is raw—that is, unpasteurized. Yet this small percentage of raw milk has gotten increased attention in recent years as the source of serious and sometimes fatal occurrences of food poisoning. Raw milk and products made from it become excellent vehicles for infection from a variety of bacteria, and in the nineteenth century raw milk caused widespread outbreaks of disease. That's why pasteurization—a mild heating process that kills dangerous microorganisms—is considered one of the greatest advances in food sanitation. Today, raw milk and products made from it are still legally sold in some states, but that doesn't mean that they are safe to consume. In 1987, sixty-two Californians died from listerial bacteria in cheese made from unpasteurized milk, and sixteen thousand Midwesterners were struck by salmonella poisoning—the most common type of foodborne illness—after drinking improperly pasteurized milk.

Some proponents of raw milk contend that it is more nutritious, because the heat of pasteurization destroys some nutrients. In fact, the nutrient loss is minimal, and there is no evidence that raw milk enhances resistance to disease, another claim that has been made for it. Very few dairies still produce what is called certified milk, which is processed under extremely rigid sanitary standards in an attempt to preserve its cleanliness without pasteurization. However, even certification is no guarantee that milk is not contaminated. Many states have banned the sale of any raw milk, certified or not, and the Centers for Disease Control calls raw milk "unsafe"; the FDA considers it "a public health problem." These statements would seem to be enough to convince any consumer that the dubious benefits of raw milk in no way outweigh its risks.

Raw eggs should be given the same wide berth as raw milk. Eggs have also been implicated as the major cause of severe outbreaks of salmonella. The majority of cases involving this kind of salmonella have occurred in northeastern states, and over three quarters of the outbreaks are thought to have been caused by Grade A, whole fresh eggs. Researchers suggest that the salmonella bacteria in these recent outbreaks can come from inside the hens, and hence are inside the eggs, rather than by the usual route of cracked or dirty eggshells. Tips on how to make sure your eggs are safe are on page 486.

Milk

Milk, the foundation for all other dairy products, is in itself an exceptional food. Rich in high-quality protein, milk is also a pre-eminent source of calcium. In addition, it supplies vitamins A and D, riboflavin, other B vitamins, phosphorus, and magnesium. For years, whole milk was considered the healthy standard, a requisite for robust children and a beverage adults were encouraged to continue drinking after childhood ("you never outgrow your need for milk" ran the advertising jingle). Between 1970 and 1990, however, whole milk consumption steadily declined, dropping more than 50 percent, as weight- and health-conscious Americans, learning the harmful effects of dietary fat and cholesterol, begun to question the value of the all-American drink.

MILK AND KIDS

Most pediatricians recommend that children should drink a quart of milk a day (which can be consumed in the form of yogurt or other dairy products as well) to get the nutrients that milk provides. Whole milk is the best—and only—choice for children under the age of two; low-fat milk products aren't good for babies and toddlers because their rapidly growing bodies need the fat milk provides. After age two, however, switch your children to low-fat milk and dairy products to help foster in them a lifetime habit of low-fat eating.

Yet as whole milk consumption was dropping, low-fat and skim milk were increasing in popularity: Today, Americans drink more milk in these two forms than whole milk. Fortunately, when its fat content is reduced, milk's other nutrients remain intact. The most important one, perhaps, is calcium, and milk is the leading source of this mineral in the American diet. Calcium is nearly as important for adults as it is for children, since the body is continually replacing bone over a lifetime. Although calcium occurs in many other foods, including green leafy vegetables, it is in its most usable form in milk. Just two cups of skim milk a day provides 75 percent of the adult RDA for calcium—for under 200 calories. A fair amount of phosphorus, which works in balance with calcium to build bone, is another of milk's nutritional assets.

Like meat, milk provides high-quality protein, and it is very well balanced in its amino acid makeup. Yet unlike the protein in many meats, the protein in low-fat and skim milk does not come packaged with fat. Milk is particularly high in the amino acid lysine, which is limited in many plant foods, especially grains, making milk an ideal complement to cereals, bread, and other grain products. Two cups of skim milk a day provides 27 percent of the RDA for protein for the average man, 33 percent for the average woman.

Low-fat and skim milk are required by the FDA to be fortified with vitamin A, a fat-soluble vitamin that is largely lost when milkfat is removed. And all milk is fortified with vitamin D, which is present naturally in milk in small amounts. A deficiency of vitamin D can interfere with the body's absorption of calcium, leading to rickets, a disease characterized by bone malformation that affected many American children in the early twentieth century. Adding vitamin D to milk has been credited with the virtual elimination of rickets in this country.

The words "pasteurized" and "homogenized" are so commonly seen on milk cartons that most people probably think these two processes are required by federal law. In fact, pasteurization—heating milk to destroy disease-causing bacteria, as well as yeasts and molds—is required for Grade A milk sold in interstate commerce, but within each state or locality, compliance is voluntary. Most parts of the country do comply with the pasteurization guidelines set by the U.S. Public Health Service and the FDA, so that 99 percent of all milk sent to market is pasteurized.

As explained on pages 456-457, unpasteurized, or raw, milk is considered an unsafe food product. Pasteurization not only ensures the safety of the milk supply, but also increases its shelf life. At the same time, it doesn't significantly affect the nutritional values of milk.

Homogenization, which distributes the milkfat evenly through the milk, is another process we take for granted. It was developed around 1900, but until the 1950s it was common for milk to arrive at stores and households unhomogenized, with a layer of cream at the top of each bottle. You could skim off the cream and use it separately, or shake the bottle to remix the cream with the milk.

Today, almost all fluid milk is homogenized by forcing it through a small opening under high pressure. This breaks down the fat into particles so tiny they remain emulsified in the milk rather than floating to the top.

For some people, the lactose in milk is a problem, not a benefit. Lactose consists of two chemically combined sugars, glucose and galactose. Many people cannot digest more than a small amount of milk because of a deficiency of lactase, an intestinal enzyme that breaks lactose into its two constituent sugars to render it absorbable. Humans produce peak amounts of lactase in infancy, when milk is necessary for survival; thereafter, the supply begins to diminish. Many adults are unable to drink milk or eat dairy products without symptoms such as gas, bloating, diarrhea, and cramps. Lactose intolerance affects 5 to 10 percent of Americans of northern European origin; it is more common among Blacks, Asians, Jews, some Mediterranean and Hispanic peoples, and Native Americans.

Still, millions of people like milk and other dairy products, and want to continue enjoying them throughout their lives. Most lactose-intolerant people can eat at least some dairy products as part of a meal but not alone; most can even drink a full glass of milk with meals. Cultured dairy products, such as yogurt and buttermilk are easier for lactose-intolerant people to digest. There's very little lactose in cheese (it is removed in the process of cheesemaking), so that is rarely a problem. Lactose is present, however, in fluid, evaporated, condensed, and powdered milk.

Lactase-treated milk is sold in many supermarkets, and lactase is also available in a liquid form that can be added to dairy products. To use one of these products you must add it at least 24 hours before eating the dairy products, to give it time to act on the lactose. Lactase is also available as tablets to be taken with dairy products, but these are quite inefficient.

TYPES OF MILK Buying milk is no longer a question of telling the milkman to leave one bottle or two. Not only is the milkman almost a thing of the past, your local supermarket may carry ten or more different types of fresh milk, as well as canned and dried forms. There are kinds of milk and cream with different fat contents, with various components added or removed, and others that are flavored to appeal to a variety of tastes. Although most milk is sold fresh for immediate consumption, some forms of dairy products are processed and packaged so they can be kept on the shelf for emergency use.

Milk solids (consisting of milk's protein, carbohydrates, minerals, vitamins, and, sometimes, fat—everything but the water) may be added to standardize the milk-solid content of milk from different sources. These solids add protein to any type of milk, and lend opacity, body, and flavor to low-fat and skim milk. Milk is graded according to its quality and intended use. All the fluid milk we buy in the stores is Grade A; Grade B and C milks are processed into cheese and other dairy products.

Whole milk By Federal law, whole milk must contain at least 3.25 percent milkfat and 8.25 percent milk solids by weight—which means it derives about 50 percent of its calories from fat. Because of this relatively high fat content, whole

COMPARING MILK 3½ ounces (½ cup)

	Calories	Fat (g)	Saturated Fat (g)	Cholesterol (mg)	Calcium (mg)
Buttermilk	40	1	<1	4	116
Evaporated skim	78	<1	<1	4	290
Evaporated whole	134	8	5	29	261
Low-fat, 1%	42	1	1	4	123
Low-fat, 2%	50	2	1	8	122
Skim	35	<1	<1	2	123
Whole, 3.3%	61	3	2	14	119
Whole, 3.7%	64	4	2	14	119

milk is best used only for infants and young children up to age two, not older children or adults.

CHOCOLATE MILK: A HEALTHFUL ALTERNATIVE? **Many children—and adults, too—have trouble drinking as much milk as they should: Milk flavored with chocolate syrup or cocoa may be more appealing, but people worry about the nutritional value of chocolate milk. There's no cause for concern. If made with 1-percent or skim milk, chocolate milk is relatively low in fat: A cup of 1-percent chocolate milk contains 3 grams of fat, which contribute 17 percent of its calories. (The chocolate syrup, though loaded with sugar, is low in fat—less than 1 gram per 2-tablespoon serving.) And the amounts of calcium and other nutrients remain about the same. Because of the sugar, though, chocolate milk has about twice the calories of plain milk.**

It is commonly believed that the chocolate in chocolate milk "binds" calcium and makes it difficult for the body to absorb the mineral. Chocolate does contain oxalic acid (a chemical that occurs in many plants), which tends to combine chemically with calcium to form calcium oxalate—a compound thought to make the calcium unusable. But milk contains a lot of calcium, while the amount of chocolate typically added to milk contains only a little oxalic acid; hence there's plenty of "free" calcium left over. Only about 6 of the 250 milligrams of calcium in a cup of low-fat chocolate milk are "tied up" as calcium oxalate. One study found that cocoa does not inhibit calcium absorption to any significant degree.

Low-fat milk (1-percent or 2-percent) This designation covers milk that contains from 0.5 to 2 percent milkfat. However, those low percentages (and the "low-fat" designation itself) are deceptive. "Two-percent milk" refers to the milkfat percentage by *weight,* and much of milk's weight is water. Once you subtract the water from 2-percent milk, for example, you're left with a product that contains 20 percent fat by weight; such milk actually derives 35 percent of its *calories* from fat. "One-percent"milk gets 23 percent of its calories from fat. Drinking 2-percent milk is a good way to wean yourself from whole milk at first, but is too high in fat as a permanent choice, unless your diet is otherwise very low in fat. Skim milk is the preferred choice, but since many people find low-fat milk more appealing, 1-percent milk is a good compromise.

Skim milk or nonfat milk This type of milk has as much fat as possible removed: It may not contain more than 0.5 percent milkfat by weight, and usually contains less than half a gram of fat per cup, deriving just 5 percent of its calories from fat. Skim milk has about half the calories of whole milk. It is the best choice for most adults, and is the only type of milk that should be consumed by people on strict low-fat diets.

Specialty milks

In addition to catering to the need for milk with varying fat contents, dairies supply specialty milk in response to particular health concerns and taste

ICE CREAM AND FROZEN TREATS

Real ice cream is made from milk and/or cream. By law, products labeled ice cream must contain at least 10 percent milkfat by weight, and this makes them rich indeed; real ice cream gets about 48 percent of its calories from fat, much of it saturated. In recent years, other frozen desserts have joined ice cream in the supermarket freezer. You'll find high-fat premium ice creams, nonfat, nondairy frozen desserts, and everything in between. Fortunately, many of these ice cream clones provide the same flavor and texture as real ice cream, and some do it with much less fat.

So-called super-premium ice creams have up to 20 percent milkfat by weight and derive 60 percent or more of their calories from fat. "Light" versions of super-premium ice creams generally approach the fat content of standard ice creams.

Frozen dairy desserts—which cannot legally be called ice cream because they do not meet the Federal government's specifications—have largely replaced the old-fashioned watery ice milks. They may also be called gourmet ice milk. Most are made of skim milk. Some list water as the first ingredient.

In an attempt to match the texture of ice cream, the new frozen desserts use an array of ingredients such as Simplesse (a fat substitute made from proteins of egg whites and milk), polydextrose and maltodextrin (food-starch derivatives), and a variety of natural gums (such as guar and cellulose). These products range in fat content from 0 to 4 grams per ½ cup. Some may be sweetened with artificial sweeteners, which further reduce their calorie count.

Frozen yogurt may or may not be low in fat, depending on whether it is made from whole milk and cream or skim milk. In general, though, frozen yogurts contain 3 to 4 grams of fat per ½ cup. There are nonfat frozen yogurts, too.

Some frozen desserts are made from tofu and are dairy-free: They thus contain no lactose or cholesterol. Still, some of the tofu products are high in fat, though the fat is largely unsaturated.

Another category of frozen desserts is fruit-based. Sherbets usually contain some dairy products as well as fruit, while sorbets, fruit ices and fruit-juice bars usually do not contain dairy products. Most are cholesterol- and fat-free.

If your diet is otherwise healthy and ice cream is a sometime treat—not a daily ritual—you can probably enjoy an occasional small serving of even the richer frozen desserts. However, if you want to keep your daily diet very low in fat (or have been advised to do so by your doctor), you're better off sticking with fruit-based sorbets or ices, or one of the nonfat dairy (or dairy-free) products. When choosing a frozen dessert, read nutritional information and ingredient lists carefully, and keep these points in mind:

- When buying and serving frozen desserts, watch those "extras": Even the most virtuous low-fat product becomes a heavyweight if mixed-in ingredients such as crumbled cookies (or a thick chocolate coating) are added. The same is true if you dress up your fat-free frozen yogurt with nuts, hot fudge and whipped cream. Try fresh berries or a sprinkling of crunchy breakfast cereal instead.
- Watch out for the shrinking serving size. Ice cream manufacturers usually use 4 ounces (about ½ cup) as a standard serving size. In an effort to make their products appear ever lighter, some give calorie and fat information for a smaller than average serving—3 or 3½ ounces. If you aren't aware of the difference, you may end up making unfair comparisons.
- "Light" and "lite" can be used to signify anything the manufacturer chooses—for instance, lighter color or texture. Fat and calorie content may be unaffected.
- Choose a frozen dessert that has less than 4 grams of fat per 4-ounce serving (standard ice cream has about 8 grams of fat per serving, premium brands about 17 grams). A product marked "fat-free" generally has less than half a gram of fat per serving.

preferences. For instance, the widespread recognition of lactose intolerance among the American population has brought lactose-reduced milk to the dairy case; the growing awareness of osteoporosis prompted the development of calcium-fortified milk. Buttermilk, though not as popular a drink as it once was, is now a low-fat product that has many cooking uses.

Acidophilus milk This type of milk (usually low-fat or skim) has the same nutritional value as the milk from which it is made. It differs from regular milk in that the bacterium *Lactobacillus acidophilus* has been added to it. (Unlike acidophilus yogurt, however, acidophilus milk isn't fermented.) Some people believe that acidophilus milk is good for digestive upsets, or can help combat lactose intolerance. However, a study undertaken by the Mayo Clinic failed to find that acidophilus milk is useful in the treatment of irritable bowel syndrome; neither did this type of milk forestall the digestive problems caused by an inability to digest lactose.

Another benefit attributed to acidophilus milk is that it can help restore beneficial bacteria to the intestines after taking antibiotics (it's believed that *L. acidophilus* is normally present in the intestines); this could be true, but even the National Dairy Council, which would like to see the public consume more milk products of every kind, says there is no evidence that acidophilus milk will provide any permanent digestive benefits. Still, acidophilus milk can't hurt you, and if you like the taste there is no reason not to drink it.

Buttermilk Originally a by-product of butter-making, buttermilk is now made by culturing milk—usually skim or low-fat—with a lactic-acid culture. Some buttermilk, because of culturing, may have a lower lactose content and so may be better tolerated by lactose-intolerant people. Sometimes a small amount of butter is added for a smoother flavor and texture, but generally buttermilk gets just 20 percent of its calories from fat. A small amount of salt may also be added. However, buttermilk is not usually fortified with vitamins A and D.

Calcium-enriched milk You can pack even more calcium into a glass of milk with this low-fat milk, which is fortified with 500 milligrams of added calcium per cup.

IS GOAT'S MILK BETTER?

Goat's milk contains most of the same nutrients as cow's milk. The calcium content of goat's milk is slightly, but not significantly, higher than that of cow's milk. Still, goat's milk is deficient in vitamin B_{12} and folacin, which are essential for the formation of normal red blood cells. Moreover, goat's milk is higher in fat, and is rarely sold in low-fat or skim versions.

Goat's milk contains a higher percentage of small fat globules, which in theory are more easily broken down by digestive enzymes—so some people think it is more digestible than cow's milk. But homogenization reduces the size of the fat globules in cow's milk, too. No human studies have ever shown that either homogenized cow's milk or goat's milk is more quickly digested than other kinds of milk. Goat's milk contains lactose in the same amounts as cow's milk, so it is not the answer for people with lactose intolerance.

If you like the tangy taste of goat's milk, just make sure it has been pasteurized. In some states it is legal to sell raw goat's milk at farm stands, in spite of the high risk of bacterial contamination.

Lactose-reduced milk The enzyme lactase is added to this product to help lactose-intolerant people digest it more easily. Its flavor is slightly sweet, but it has virtually the same nutrient values as regular 1-percent milk.

Low-sodium whole milk Although salt is not added to milk, dairy products are naturally fairly high in sodium. Low-sodium milk has been treated to replace about 95 percent of its natural sodium with potassium. Its sodium content is about 6 milligrams per cup, compared with 120 per cup in regular whole milk. The treatment almost doubles the milk's potassium content (from 370 to 617 milligrams per cup).

Milk in other forms

Canned, dried, or "boxed" milk, which can stay ready on your pantry shelf for months, is obviously useful for those times when you suddenly run out of milk and it's inconvenient to go to the store. But some of these products have special qualities that make them unique cooking ingredients as well, so they needn't be used only as temporary replacements for fresh milk. For example, evaporated skim milk can be whipped for a rich, fat-free topping that has about one-tenth the calories of whipped heavy cream.

Dry milk powder To make familiar nonfat dry milk (whole dry milk is mostly used in food manufacturing), the water is partially evaporated from fluid milk, then the milk is sprayed in a drying chamber to further dehydrate it. You reconstitute the resulting powder by adding water, usually in a proportion of about 1 cup of water to 3 tablespoons powdered milk. Instant nonfat dry milk, which consists of large, flakelike particles, dissolves quickly and smoothly.

Nonfat dry milk can also be used in recipes—or stirred into liquid milk—to add protein and calcium with minimal calories and no fat. A tablespoon of nonfat dry milk contains 94 milligrams of calcium, 27 calories, and no fat, and has added vitamin A and D.

Evaporated milk This kitchen-cabinet standby is made by removing more than half of the water in milk and then canning and heat-sterilizing it. Since the cans can be stored at room temperature, this milk product is convenient to keep on hand for cooking and for emergencies. It is fortified with vitamin D and may also have added vitamin A. To use evaporated milk in place of fresh milk, reconstitute it with an equal amount of cold water (or use it undiluted in recipes that so specify).

Evaporated milk comes in whole and skim forms. Nutritionally, skim is preferred—it contains less than a gram of fat per cup compared to 18 grams of fat in a cup of whole—and it is a versatile ingredient for low-fat cooking. Undiluted, it is as thick as heavy cream, and can be substituted for cream in soups and sauces; if it is very well chilled, you can even whip it.

Sweetened condensed milk This was one of the first canned foods to appear on the market. Created in 1856, condensed milk was a soldiers' staple during the Civil War. Like evaporated milk, it is made by removing about half the water content of liquid whole milk. However, a large amount of sugar is added to sweetened condensed milk, and so it is commonly used to make ice cream, puddings, and candies. Undiluted, it contains 982 calories per cup.

THE DRUG QUESTION

Does milk contain drug residues? Antibiotic drugs given to cows can and do pass into milk, and millions of samples are tested each year to detect residues. Some surveys have turned up signs of drugs that are illegal in dairy cows—though often the levels are so low as to be barely detectable. The FDA has taken corrective steps. But some investigators believe that FDA rules are not tough enough and insist that milk should be free of all antibiotic residues. A fair goal—yet even FDA critics conclude that you're better off drinking milk than not drinking it, and that the U.S. milk supply is safe.

Ultra-high temperature (UHT) or ultrapasteurized milk These dairy products are processed at temperatures higher than those used in regular pasteurization, thereby lengthening shelf life. In fact, UHT milk, packed in brick-style cartons (like juice boxes) that are presterilized and aseptically sealed, can be stored at room temperature for about six months. Once opened, however, it must be refrigerated.

Cream

The fatty layer that rises to the top of unhomogenized milk, cream was once the *sine qua non* of gourmet cooking. Today's health-conscious cooks have found ways to make rich-tasting sauces, soups, and desserts without cream, but a small quantity of any type of cream, judiciously used (not poured over oat-bran cereal at break-

COMPARING CREAM
3½ ounces (½ cup)

	Calories	Fat (g)	Saturated Fat (g)	Cholesterol (mg)
Half and half	130	12	7	37
Heavy cream	345	37	23	65
Light cream	292	31	19	69
Sour cream	214	21	13	116

fast), does add a unique flavor and texture to recipes. As usual, when using a high-fat ingredient, you'll want to balance it by composing the meal mainly of low-fat foods.

Sweet creams In ascending order by fat content, these are: Half-and-half (or cereal cream)—a mixture of milk and cream—with a milkfat content of not less than 10.5 percent but not more than 18 percent by weight; light cream (or coffee cream or table cream), with not less than 18 percent but not more than 30 percent milkfat; light whipping cream, with not less than 30 percent but not more than 36 percent milkfat; and heavy cream, with 36 percent milkfat or more.

Sour creams Dairy sour cream, sour half-and-half, lowfat, light, and fat-free sour cream are all made by culturing cream and/or milk with lactic acid bacteria. Sour cream must contain at least 18 percent milkfat by weight. Sometimes rennet and/or nonfat milk solids are added to give sour cream more body.

Sour half-and-half, as well as low-fat and light sour cream, are made like sour cream, using half-and-half. Fat-free sour cream (labeled as a sour-cream alternative because it does not meet the federal standard of identity for sour cream) is made from cultured skim milk. Cholesterol-free sour cream alternative is made with skim milk and vegetable oil.

SHOPPING TIPS The milk products in your local supermarket or convenience store will nearly always be marked with a sell-by date. Generally, the date is determined by the producer, although in some areas it may be regulated by a local authority. A common standard for setting an expiration date is eight to twelve days from the time the milk is pasteurized.

Since the lower part of a refrigerated display case is colder than the top, select a carton from the bottom of the display if possible. Try not to buy more milk than you need; a larger size is no bargain if it goes bad before you finish it. If you're not sure you'll be able to use a full half gallon, you're better off buying two quarts and leaving the second carton unopened until needed. Opening milk and exposing it to warm air activates bacteria, causing the milk to spoil more quickly, even if it is re-refrigerated.

Liquid or powdered nondairy coffee lighteners are made with vegetable fats, so they may be cholesterol-free but they are not fat-free. If palm or coconut oil is used, you'll get saturated fat with none of real milk's vitamins and minerals. And the most popular brands of coffee creamer have more calories per serving than light cream.

Milk can also spoil if it hasn't been kept under constant refrigeration. Just to be sure that the milk or cream you buy is perfectly fresh, sniff the top of the container for any sign of sourness; even cultured products like buttermilk should smell fresh, not bitter or sharp.

It's hard to find milk in glass bottles these days, but translucent plastic jugs are very common. Some studies suggest that milk in translucent plastic containers is more susceptible to significant losses of riboflavin and vitamin A from the effect of the fluorescent lights in supermarkets. Low-fat and skim milks are particularly sensitive to light. Cardboard containers, however, seem to protect against the light.

STORAGE All fresh dairy products should be promptly refrigerated, otherwise they will turn sour within a matter of hours. Dairy products last longer and taste better when kept cold—at 45° or below. If the temperature of milk is allowed to reach 50°, the shelf life is halved. (A 20-minute trip by car on a hot day can raise the temperature of milk by as much as 10°.)

Milk containers should be sealed, closed, or covered, as milk readily picks up flavors and aromas from other foods. It's best to leave fresh milk in its original container, where it should keep for three to five days after purchase.

If you prefer to serve milk or cream in a pitcher or creamer rather than from the carton, pour just the amount you need into the serving container, and don't return any leftover milk or cream to the carton. Cover and store it separately, since it will spoil sooner (and so should be used as soon as possible).

Canned evaporated or condensed milk can be stored at room temperature for six months. Once opened, it should be transferred to a clean, opaque container, covered tightly and refrigerated; the milk should keep for three to five days.

Aseptically packaged UHT milk has a shelf-life of about six months at room temperature. For best flavor, refrigerate it in the sealed package to thoroughly chill it before serving.

Unopened packages of nonfat dry milk should be stored in a cool, dry place. Reseal opened packages, as moisture will make powdered milk lumpy and eventually cause it to spoil. Discard nonfat dry milk if it smells scorched or rancid.

Milk and milk products do not promote mucus buildup in the throat, as many people believe, and therefore don't need to be eliminated from your diet if you have a cold or flu. Whole milk, however, may leave your tongue feeling coated. Switching to skim milk should solve that problem.

PREPARATION Fluid milk is ready to use as it comes from the carton; nonfat dry milk needs to be mixed with water. For richer-tasting milk (and more concentrated nutrients) use ½ cup less water than the package instructions specify for each one-quart envelope of dry milk. For best flavor and texture, mix the milk in a blender, and prepare it far enough in advance to allow for thorough chilling before you serve it.

LOW-FAT WHIPPED CREAM

A tablespoonful of whipped cream is not such a dietary disaster—if you can really limit yourself to one spoonful. If you can't, try whipped evaporated skim milk. Chill it very thoroughly; for best results, pour the undiluted milk in a shallow pan and place it in the freezer until ice crystals form at the edges. Use a chilled bowl and beaters to whip the milk, and serve it within an hour. To stabilize the whipped milk so it does not deflate, add a little unflavored gelatin, using 1½ tablespoons of gelatin per cup of evaporated milk: Warm ⅓ cup of the milk slightly and dissolve the gelatin in it. Chill the mixture, then add it to the remaining ⅔ cup of chilled milk and whip; add a little confectioner's sugar and vanilla, if desired.

You can also make whipped cream from nonfat dry milk that has been reconstituted with ice water. Whip it just as you would cream.

You can also use nonfat dry milk to pack protein and calcium into the meals you cook. For instance, add a few spoonfuls of nonfat dry milk powder to soups, sauces, and gravies. The powder scorches easily, so cook it over low heat; a double boiler eliminates most of the risk of burning. Mix the dry milk into the ground turkey or lean ground beef that you use for burgers, meatloaf, or meatballs; add the powder to a shake made from skim milk or yogurt; or combine it with hot cereal before cooking.

When cooking with any kind of milk, be careful not to boil it, as this will cause a tough scum to form on the surface. Even when milk does not boil, it may scorch. For best results, heat milk over low heat and whisk or stir it frequently.

Cooking milk and other dairy products with acid ingredients, salty foods, and certain vegetables may cause the milk to curdle. To help prevent this, use gentle heat and avoid overcooking. To dilute acidity or saltiness, add a little fresh milk to

MILK, 1% 3½ oz (⅓ cup)			
Calories	42	Fat	1 g
Protein	3 g	Saturated Fat	<1 g
Carbohydrate	5 g	Cholesterol	4 mg
Dietary Fiber	None	Sodium	51 mg

KEY NUTRIENTS		% RDA Men	Women
Vitamin B_{12}	0.4 mcg	20 %	20 %
Calcium	123 mg	15%	15%
Phosphorus	96 mg	12 %	12 %
Riboflavin	0.2 mg	12%	15%

S=40% or more soluble N/A=Not Applicable N=Not Available

MILK, skim 3½ oz (½ cup)			
Calories	35	Fat	<1 g
Protein	3 g	Saturated Fat	<1 g
Carbohydrate	5 g	Cholesterol	2 mg
Dietary Fiber	None	Sodium	52 mg

KEY NUTRIENTS		% RDA Men	Women
Vitamin B_{12}	0.4 mcg	20%	20%
Calcium	123 mg	15%	15%
Phosphorus	101 mg	13%	13%

S=40% or more soluble N/A=Not Applicable N=Not Available

the dish from time to time as it cooks. Evaporated milk, because it has already been heated in processing, also makes curdling less likely.

On the other hand, sometimes you want milk to curdle: If a recipe calls for buttermilk or sour milk and there is none on hand, you can sour sweet milk with vinegar or lemon juice. For a cup of soured milk, place a tablespoonful of the acid ingredient in a measuring cup, then fill to the 1-cup mark with milk. Stir, then let stand for 5 minutes.

SERVING SUGGESTIONS If you're trying to drink more milk (or have your children do so) and aren't so fond of it, you can try lots of different flavorings. If you find skim milk unappealing, try it in milk drinks—the added ingredients will help disguise its thinness. You can combine milk with frozen orange-juice concentrate or other juice concentrates; blend it with fresh or canned fruit juice or nectar; or purée fresh fruit with it. Flavor these drinks with vanilla, almond, or other extracts, spices or instant coffee powder and sweeten with a little honey or sugar if necessary. For a tangy refresher, blend buttermilk with tomato juice and spicy seasonings. Stir the ingredients together, or, better yet, mix them in a blender, and serve the flavored milk well chilled. To enrich and thicken any skim-milk drink, blend in a tablespoon or two of nonfat dry milk.

In cold weather, try hot drinks: Hot milk sweetened with honey, molasses, or maple syrup and flavored with vanilla, cinnamon, or nutmeg is a soothing and nutritious winter warmer. Hot cocoa, made with cocoa powder, sugar, and skim milk, is a low-fat beverage that can stand in for dessert, too.

Buttermilk's tartness makes it usable in many recipes that call for yogurt. Top baked potatoes with buttermilk and chives instead of sour cream. Enrich hot soups with a last-minute addition of buttermilk, or use buttermilk as the base for cold vegetable soups. Make low-fat salad dressings and marinades with buttermilk; substitute it in baking for regular milk, cream, or yogurt.

Evaporated skim milk can be used as a substitute for heavy cream in many recipes, and provides the same rich texture.

Cheese

Rich and delicious, varied and versatile, cheese is made in nearly every country where milk is produced and available. It has almost endless uses—as an appetizer, a salad ingredient, a main course, a soup ingredient, a satisfying sandwich filling, and a basis for creamy sauces. Like all dairy products, cheese is usually high in protein and calcium. But about 8 pounds of milk are used to make 1 pound of most types of cheese, with the result that just an ounce (an average slice) of cheese contains as much fat—most of it saturated—as a cup of whole milk. In fact, most cheeses derive 60 to 90 percent of their calories from fat. Therefore, vegetarians who replace meat with cheese are doing themselves no favor: Substitute Cheddar cheese for trimmed broiled sirloin steak and, ounce for ounce, you end up with almost twice as many calories and six times the saturated fat, as well as more cholesterol and far more sodium.

Despite its nutritional drawbacks, cheese is a popular food. Per capita consumption in the United States is 28 pounds a year, more than twice what is was in the late 1960s. One survey found that cheese is the food that people cutting back on fat find most difficult to trim from their diets. You needn't give up cheese, though. High-fat cheeses can be eaten in small portions without risk to your health. And because cheese is so rich-tasting, a little can go a long way toward enhancing accompanying foods, whether it's on top of a cracker or sprinkled over a serving of pasta. Some types of cheese, such as part-skim mozzarella or ricotta, and low-fat cottage cheese, are low or moderate in fat.

Another option is to choose reduced-fat cheeses (see box, page 469). Since fat is so essential to the taste and texture of cheese, it has been difficult to produce satisfying cheeses that are truly low in fat—many cheeses that are labeled "low-fat" are lower than standard cheeses by only 2 to 4 grams of fat per ounce, which still leaves 5 to 7 grams per ounce. However, new, better-tasting low-fat products are always being introduced, and often these are just as high in calcium and protein as their fat-laden cousins.

CHEESE AND YOUR TEETH

It will never take the place of the toothbrush, but cheese may save you some cavities. Studies conducted in Britain and Canada have shown that eating Cheddar and other aged cheeses after eating sweets seems to somehow counteract the decay-causing action of the sugary food. The reason is not clear: The cheese may simply stimulate saliva production, helping to rinse the sugar away; some substance in the cheese may fight cavity-causing bacteria, or it may favorably change the acid-alkaline balance in your mouth. Still, considering the fat and calorie content of cheese, you're better off reaching for your toothbrush than for a piece of cheese after a meal or snack.

VARIETIES Cheesemaking lends itself to experimentation, and the different kinds of cheese now available number more than a thousand, with new types being created every year. Although the most familiar cheeses are made from cow's milk, milk from goats and sheep—even from buffaloes, camels, mares, or yaks—is also made into cheese.

To turn milk into natural cheese, it is first cul-

COTTAGE CHEESE, 1% 3½ oz (½ cup)

Calories	72	Fat	1 g
Protein	12 g	Saturated fat	<1 g
Carbohydrate	3 g	Cholesterol	4 mg
Dietary Fiber	None	Sodium	406 mg

KEY NUTRIENTS		%RDA Men	%RDA Women
Vitamin B_{12}	0.6 mcg	30%	30%
Phosphorus	134 mg	17%	17%
Riboflavin	0.2 mg	12%	15%

S=40% or more soluble N/A=Not Applicable N=Not Available

COMPARING CHEESES 3½ ounces

	Calories	Fat (g)	Saturated Fat (g)	Cholesterol (mg)	Calcium (mg)	Sodium (mg)
Blue cheese	353	29	19	75	528	1395
Brick	371	30	19	94	674	560
Brie	334	28	17	100	184	629
Camembert	300	24	15	72	388	842
Cheddar	403	33	21	105	721	621
Colby	394	32	20	95	685	604
Cottage cheese, 2%	90	2	1	8	69	406
Cottage cheese, 1%	72	1	<1	4	61	406
Cottage cheese, creamed	103	5	3	15	60	405
Cottage cheese, dry curd	85	<1	<1	7	32	13
Cream cheese	349	35	22	110	80	296
Edam	357	28	18	89	731	965
Feta	264	21	15	89	493	1116
Fontina	389	31	19	116	550	800
Gouda	356	27	18	114	700	819
Gruyère	413	32	19	110	1011	336
Limburger	327	27	17	90	497	800
Monterey Jack	373	30	19	89	746	536
Mozzarella, low moisture, part skim	280	17	11	54	731	528
Mozzarella, low moisture, whole milk	318	25	16	89	575	415
Muenster	368	30	19	96	717	628
Neufchâtel	260	23	15	76	75	349
Parmesan	392	26	16	68	1184	1602
Port Salut	352	28	17	123	650	534
Provolone	352	27	17	69	756	876
Ricotta, part skim	138	8	5	31	272	125
Ricotta, whole milk	174	13	8	51	207	84
Romano	387	27	17	104	1064	1200
Roquefort	369	31	19	90	662	1809
Swiss	376	28	18	92	961	260
Tilsit	340	26	17	102	700	65

tured (like buttermilk or yogurt) with bacteria, then curdled—broken into curds (solids) and whey (liquid)—by the use of a culturing agent such as the enzyme rennin. The whey is drained off from the curds, which, depending on the type of cheese being made, may be pressed to remove more moisture. This fresh cheese may then be aged, or ripened, to further dry it and develop its flavor; often, other ingredients are added to impart the unique characteristics associated with a particular type of cheese. Various natural cheeses are also injected or sprayed with mold or bacteria, washed with beer or brandy, smoked over fragrant wood, or coated with herbs, spices,

LOW-FAT CHEESE

Low-fat cottage cheese may be the all-time best-known diet food. However, there is virtually no aged cheese (with the possible exception of sapsago) that can be classified as low in fat: Most cheeses get about 70 percent of their calories from fat. Cream cheese, although a fresh type, gets 90 percent of its calories from fat. And even whole-milk ricotta gets 60 percent of its calories from fat; creamed cottage cheese has 45 percent fat calories.

The answer to a health-conscious cheese lover's prayers would seem to be the new "reduced-fat," "lower-fat," "low-cholesterol," and "cholesterol-free" cheeses. Made by substituting skim milk, low-fat milk, or even water for whole milk or cream (and/or using vegetable oil instead of butterfat) they come in lots of flavors and styles intended to replicate everything from Cheddar to blue cheese.

The problem is that true cheese lovers will be disappointed in their taste and texture; most low-fat cheeses are processed cheeses, which tend to be bland and rubbery. And though they are lower in fat than some natural cheeses, many of these products don't really rate the designation "low-fat." For example, part-skim mozzarella has about 5 grams of fat per ounce, deriving more than 50 percent of its calories from fat.

A cheese that has one or two grams less fat than the cheese it copies can be legally labeled "lower fat"—even if it still supplies 12 grams of fat per ounce. Low-cholesterol or cholesterol-free cheese may have all its butterfat replaced by vegetable oil—so you get the same amount of fat as in the original cheese. Therefore, check the label of any cheese marked "part-skim," "low-fat," or "reduced fat." In general, cheeses with 3 grams of fat or less per ounce are truly low-fat, but they are rare.

The low-fat and low-cholesterol claims of these cheeses may distract you from another problem—many of them are particularly high in sodium. Extra salt is required to make up for flavor lost with the fat, and sodium phosphate is often used as an emulsifier.

Other imitation cheeses are made from soy milk or tofu. Soy cheese, while cholesterol-free (unless dairy products are added), is still high in fat and may be high in sodium.

or ash. Cheese may be encased in a layer of wax to hold in moisture and prevent the cheese from drying out.

Some natural cheese varieties can be grouped according to their firmness or density; others are classified according to special techniques used in the process of making the cheese. The varieties included here represent those you might find in a specialty cheese shop or a gourmet shop; large supermarkets also carry many of these cheeses.

Cheese can also be divided into two broad categories: natural and processed. The latter, which are made from the former, are described last.

Soft, unripened ("fresh") cheese

If you're looking for "real" cheese that's low in fat and sodium, this is a good place to start. Just a few steps from fresh milk, foods such as cottage cheese and farmer cheese do not have the concentration of fat and sodium that hard cheeses do. They can be made from skim milk and are easy to find in low-fat and even nonfat versions. Neutral in flavor, fresh cheeses can be seasoned to your taste and combined with ingredients from fresh fruit to tomato sauce to add protein to quick snacks or complicated recipes.

Cottage cheese The traditional "dieter's delight," and certainly a healthful food in its low-fat form, cottage cheese exhibits the first stage of all cheesemaking: the separation of milk or cream into curds and whey. To make cottage cheese, the curds are drained and sometimes pressed to form a soft, white, spoonable cheese. You'll find creamed cottage cheese, which is 4 to 5 percent fat by weight (it has small curds and added cream), 2-percent cottage cheese, 1-percent cottage cheese, and dry curd cottage cheese, which has 0.5 percent fat by weight. As with milk, however, the percentage of fat by weight does not give an accurate picture of the percentage of calories from fat. Cottage cheese may contain less than a gram to 5 grams of fat per ½ cup (3½ ounces), contributing from 4 to 39 percent of its calories.

Cottage cheese is usually slightly salted, but is also available in unsalted and even lactose-free versions.

Cream cheese and American Neufchâtel These are the familiar creamy white cheeses that we spread on toast and bagels. Compared to butter, these spreads are preferable in terms of fat content. However, they still pack quite a bit of fat: The fat in cream cheese contributes 90 percent of its calories, the fat in Neufchâtel 80 percent. Light or low-fat cream cheese, on the other hand, has about 75 percent fat calories. For a nonfat cream cheese substitute, try yogurt cheese (see page 480), made from nonfat yogurt.

Farmer cheese (also called hoop, pot, or bakers' cheese) If cottage cheese is placed in a form and the liquid pressed out, it produces a firm, rather grainy white loaf, very low in fat with a mildly tart flavor. Farmer cheese can be sliced or crumbled, and is a good baking ingredient. Sometimes farmer cheese is combined with chopped chives or with fruit to make a savory or sweet cheese.

THE LOW-CALCIUM CHEESES

Many people think cheese and calcium are synonymous. But the truth is that two types of cheese—cottage cheese and cream cheese—are meager sources of calcium when compared to milk, yogurt, or other cheeses. You'd have to eat about 6 cups of low-fat cottage cheese or 10 ounces of cream cheese to meet the calcium RDA. Eating that amount of cottage cheese—if you could stand it—would do your health no harm since it supplies just 12 grams of fat. The cream cheese, on the other hand, would supply 100 grams of fat. There are certainly better ways to meet your calcium needs. For example, if you had an ounce of part-skim mozzarella cheese (210 milligrams of calcium), a cup of skim milk (246 milligrams), and a cup of plain nonfat yogurt (452 milligrams) you'd exceed the calcium RDA—and get just 5 grams of fat.

Mascarpone This Italian curd cheese is like the thickest whipped cream and is usually served as a dessert topping. It is made from cream, and therefore is very high in fat. Yogurt cheese is a healthy substitute.

Mozzarella The familiar pizza cheese is fresh in that it is not aged, but it undergoes a process that differentiates it from other fresh cheeses. The warmed curds are kneaded, and the resulting cheese can be separated into layers or strips. Freshly made mozzarella, sold in Italian grocery stores and now available in many supermarkets, is a soft, bland, delicate cheese. Factory-made mozzarella, which is drier and has more cheese flavor, can be sliced or shredded and used as a topping for pizzas, pastas, and sandwiches. Fresh mozzarella is good with fresh or sundried tomatoes and basil leaves, but it usually comes only in whole milk forms, and therefore is high in fat.

Mozzarella comes in several versions: Whole-milk, part-skim, low-moisture (both whole-milk and skim), "light," and fat-free. Part-skim moz-

MOZZARELLA, part skim 3½ oz

Calories	280	Fat	17 g
Protein	27 g	Saturated Fat	11 g
Carbohydrate	3 g	Cholesterol	54 mg
Dietary Fiber	None	Sodium	528 mg

KEY NUTRIENTS		% RDA Men	% RDA Women
Vitamin A	628 IU	13%	16%
Vitamin B_{12}	0.9 mcg	45%	45%
Calcium	731 mg	91%	91%
Phosphorus	524 mg	66%	66%
Riboflavin	0.3 mg	18%	23%
Zinc	3 mg	20%	25%

S=40% or more soluble N/A=Not Applicable N=Not Available

zarella may sound like a low-fat product, but it gets about 55 percent of its calories from fat (compared with 71 percent for whole-milk mozzarella). Still, part-skim mozzarella is lower in fat than cheese such as Cheddar and Swiss. The lowest-fat forms of mozzarella do not melt as smoothly as whole-milk or even part-skim mozzarella, but they can have 20 to 50 percent fewer calories than the full-fat version. Low-moisture mozzarella is slightly higher in calories and fat (and in protein and calcium) than regular mozzarella, simply because it contains less water.

Ricotta Whey remaining from making other types of cheese was originally the sole ingredient in ricotta, but American ricotta is now made from a combination of whey and whole or skim milk. Ricotta is like a fine-textured cottage cheese and can be eaten by itself, although it is more commonly used in Italian pasta dishes and desserts. It comes in whole-milk, part-skim, and fat-free forms. The part-skim version has about 40 percent less fat than the whole-milk cheese.

String cheese Although snack-size sticks of mozzarella are now sold under this name, true string cheese originated in Syria, and often comes in a braided rope. The flavor is similar to mozzarella, but saltier. Soaking string cheese in water before serving it will remove some of the salt.

Semisoft cheeses

This is the largest category of cheese, comprising many of the best-known cheeses from all over the world. Semisoft cheeses slice well, making them favorites for sandwiches, and they also melt smoothly for cooking. Aged for just a few weeks, they remain relatively moist and delicate in taste—though if left to age further, they will become denser and stronger in flavor.

Unlike hard cheeses, which develop a tough rind, semisoft cheeses often have a wax or plastic coating applied to them. Brick, Limburger, and Liederkranz are actually "washed" cheeses—they are aged in rooms where they pick up natural molds to form a soft rind, then rinsed with salt water (or beer or brandy) to further sharpen their flavors, which are considerably more assertive than those of other cheeses in this category. Softer than other semisoft cheeses, they are almost more spreadable than sliceable.

Bel Paese Bel Paese ("beautiful country") is a smooth, creamy cheese with a mild flavor. It is made in Italy and in the United States. It melts well and is also good to serve with fruit as a dessert cheese.

Brick A truly American cheese, brick is made in rectangular loaves and has numerous holes. When young, brick cheese is sweet and mild; after aging, it tastes somewhat like a mild Limburger or Cheddar. Brick slices well and its shape makes it ideal for sandwiches.

Edam A noted Dutch cheese, Edam is made of part-skim milk and comes in 2- and 4-pound balls and 5-pound blocks covered in red wax (or red cellophane). Unaged Edam is very mild and buttery-tasting; the aged version is rarely sold in the United States.

Fontina Although it originated in Italy, fontina is today made in Switzerland, Denmark, Sweden, and Argentina as well. This ivory-colored cheese is mild and buttery in flavor, excellent for melting in fondues and sauces. Imported Italian fontina has a light brown rind, but American versions—quite different in flavor and texture—often have a red rind.

Gouda One of the best-known Dutch cheeses, Gouda is coated with red or yellow wax. This whole-milk cheese has a rich, mild flavor that sharpens with age. Although Dutch Gouda is made in large wheels and usually sold cut, American versions come in "baby" wheels weighing less than a pound.

Jarlsberg Made in Norway, Jarlsberg is similar to true Swiss cheese (called Emmenthaler) but softer and milder in flavor. Conversely, it is more flavorful and firmer than American Swiss. Jarlsberg is made in 20-pound wheels and sold in wedges.

Liederkranz Despite its German name, Liederkranz was invented in New York State and today is manufactured in Ohio. The small blocks of cheese with a rust-colored rind have a pungent aroma but a mellow flavor. With time, however, the flavor becomes quite strong, so pay attention to the date on the package.

Limburger Unwrap a block of Limburger and you're greeted with the pungent aroma for which it is famed. Limburger has a velvety coating of strong-smelling mold, and the foil wrapping holds in the striking bouquet. The flavor is quite robust as well.

Muenster or Munster (American) Virtually unrelated to the German monastery-made cheese of the same name, American muenster is a rather bland, ivory-colored cheese with pin-sized holes. It combines well with more flavorful ingredients.

Port Salut Originally made in a Trappist monastery in France, Port Salut is a strongly flavored, pale yellow cheese with an orange skin. Danish esrom is a similar cheese.

Provolone Once made from water-buffalo milk, provolone is today made from cow's milk. The flavor is mild and the cheese ivory-colored and elastic when young; it can be used like mozzarella at this stage. After aging, provolone deepens in color and flavor and develops a drier texture. Smoked provolone, which has a tangy smoke flavor, is made by natural smoking or by adding a smoke-flavored liquid. Though it is commonly made in sausage-shaped loaves or spheres and sold in slabs or slices, provolone is sometimes formed into whimsical small shapes; these are usually smoked.

Tilsit This Dutch cheese (also made in Finland, Norway and the United States) has an assertive taste and aroma. It is made in loaves that are sold wrapped in foil. Danish havarti is similar to tilsit.

Soft-ripened

Brie, Camembert, and similar cheeses are sprayed on the surface with different strains of penicillin and then aged, during which time they develop soft, edible rinds. Despite their luxuriously creamy texture and delicious flavor, these cheeses are actually somewhat lower in calories than firm cheese such as Cheddar. (Camembert and Brie have about 90 calories and 7 grams of fat per ounce, while Cheddar has about 110 calories and 9 grams of fat.) The soft-ripened cheeses get 60 to 75 percent of their calories from fat; those known as double- and triple-crèmes have extra cream added and are higher in fat. Explorateur, Boursault, and Boursin are in this category.

If you buy a whole cheese, let it ripen, if necessary, at room temperature for a few days. Once cut, such a cheese is unlikely to ripen properly. A properly ripe cheese will look plump and feel soft if you squeeze it gently. Once cut, it should appear to be melting slowly, but not runny and liquid. An underripe cheese will have a chalky, hard center layer.

Brie The best known of these cheeses, Brie is made in northern France and comes with a downy white coat in wheels that range in size from about 5 to 10 inches in diameter. It is often sold cut into wedges. Brie has a rich, buttery flavor with an underlying tang. You can also buy American-made versions of Brie, which tend to be blander in taste.

CHEDDAR 3½ oz

Calories	403	Fat	33 g
Protein	25 g	Saturated Fat	21 g
Carbohydrate	1 g	Cholesterol	105 mg
Dietary Fiber	None	Sodium	621 mg

KEY NUTRIENTS		% RDA Men	% RDA Women
Vitamin A	1059 IU	21%	26%
Vitamin B_{12}	0.8 mcg	40%	40%
Calcium	721 mg	90%	90%
Folacin	18 mcg	9%	10%
Magnesium	28 mg	8%	10%
Phosphorus	512 mg	64%	64%
Riboflavin	0.4 mg	24%	31%
Zinc	3 mg	20%	25%

S=40% or more soluble N/A=Not Applicable N=Not Available

Camembert Like Brie, this soft cow's-milk cheese also has a velvety white rind; it may be slightly reddened in spots when the cheese is fully ripe. The interior is soft and creamy yellow. Camembert is made in Normandy in flat disks about 5 inches in diameter, and is often sold foil-wrapped and enclosed in a thin wooden box. American cheesemakers produce their own versions of Camembert.

Firm (hard) cheeses

To many people, "cheese" means Cheddar, the predominant cheese in this category. Robust but not pungent in flavor, firm cheeses are popular for cooking—think of macaroni and cheese, fondue, and French onion soup—and also for serving with crisp apples and pears. Because they dehydrate as they age, these cheeses are more concentrated sources of calcium than softer products.

Cheddar Originally an English cheese, Cheddar has become immensely popular in the United States and Canada. In fact, it is America's favorite cheese, accounting for about a third of the total cheese consumption. It ranges from white to deep orange in color; yellow and orange cheddars are colored with annatto, a natural coloring that does not affect the taste of the cheese. Cheddar is a very versatile cheese, good for sandwiches and snacks, as well as for cooking and grating.

Young Cheddar is mild and easily sliceable; the flavor sharpens and the texture becomes more crumbly with age. Cheddar is made in flat wheels weighing from 12 to 78 pounds, in "midget" and "peewee" wheels of 5 or 11 pounds, and in "longhorn" loaves that weigh about 12 pounds. The wheels are wrapped in cheesecloth and wax, so Cheddar does not develop a rind (some Cheddar is aged in plastic packages instead). In stores, Cheddar comes packaged in whole wheels, in wedges, chunks, sticks, and shredded.

Other British Cheddar-type cheeses are tart Caerphilly (which originated in Wales), creamy Scottish Dunlop, crumbly Cheshire, sharp Gloucester, mild Leicester, and Derby, which comes in a popular sage-flavored version.

Colby This cheese was developed in Wisconsin at the end of the nineteenth century. It looks like Cheddar but is blander, moister, and softer.

Gruyère This cheese originated in Switzerland, but it is also made in France. Its winy, nutlike bouquet makes Gruyère a favorite cooking cheese, commonly used in quiche; it is also excellent for eating along with fresh fruit. Gruyère is ivory-yellow with a wrinkled rind; the cheese has tiny eyes (or none) and, if well aged, it may show small cracks.

Monterey Jack A mildly flavored white California cheese, Monterey Jack was developed from the local cheeses made by Spanish missionary fathers in the eighteenth century. It is made in 6- to 12-pound wheels and usually sold in sticks, bricks, or wedges. Somewhat softer than colby when young, it is sometimes made with bits of jalapeño peppers and sold as "Pepper Jack."

Swiss The true "Swiss cheese" is Emmenthaler (or Emmentaler), a glossy, moist, golden yellow cheese with large "eyes" and a smooth brown rind stamped with the word "Switzerland." (The familiar holes, or eyes, of Swiss cheese are caused by gas pockets that develop as the cheese ripens.) It has a sweet, nutlike tang and is a favorite for sandwiches and for cooking. This "Switzerland Swiss" is made in 200-pound wheels and usually aged for ten months to a year. It is sold in wedges, or sliced. Appenzeller is another Swiss cheese that resembles Emmenthaler.

Versions of "Swiss" cheese are made throughout the world—in the United States, Finland, the Netherlands, Austria, and Denmark. Most are blander than Switzer-land Swiss, and also less expensive.

Very hard (grating) cheeses

As cheese ages, it loses moisture, becoming denser in texture and more concentrated in flavor (and calcium content). A boon to the fat-conscious cook, these cheeses, grated finely and used sparingly, can go a long way as a seasoning.

Most grating cheeses come in large, heavy wheels and are sold by the piece (an irregular chunk if the cheese is too hard for smooth slicing). To really enjoy the flavor of grated cheese, buy a chunk and grate it yourself: The flavor is markedly better than that of pre-grated cheese in a jar or a cardboard shaker box, which despite its preservative content can never have the robust flavor of just-grated cheese. These cheeses can be frozen if wrapped well, and will grate easily without thawing, so you can always keep them on hand. Sliced into slivers or shavings, they can be used in salads, or eaten with fruit.

Some cheeses contain a naturally occurring chemical called tyramine which can cause vascular headaches—such as migraines—in people prone to them because it causes blood vessels to dilate. Ripe cheese, such as Camembert, Cheddar, and blue cheese, is high in tyramine. Cottage cheese and processed cheeses have very little or none.

Asiago An Italian cheese now also made in the United States, asiago is most commonly sold aged, for grating. Aged asiago is granular, like Parmesan, but somewhat more pungent in flavor.

***Dry Jack* (*Dry Monterey Jack*)** An aged skim- or part-skim-milk version of the American cheese of the same name, Dry Jack is similar in flavor and uses to Parmesan.

Parmesan Aged true Parmesan, produced in a restricted area around Parma, Italy, is marked "Parmigiano-Reggiano"; versions made in other parts of Italy are simply called *granas* (grainy or granular cheeses). Parmesan-type cheeses are made in the United States as well. A fine, aged Parmesan is straw-colored and has a uniquely flaky, crystalline texture. Its flavor is nutty-sweet and complex. American Parmesan is softer, paler in color, and tends to be saltier.

Romano Sometimes made from sheep's milk (and called pecorino romano), this is another Italian cheese that is also made in America. It is cream-colored with a thin brown rind. Romano is saltier than Parmesan, but can be used in many of the same ways.

Sapsago A Swiss product, Sapsago is a rock-hard grating cheese made from skim milk; it has less than 3 grams of fat per ounce. Flavored with a special type of clover (which also colors it green), it is used as a seasoning. Sapsago comes in a 3-ounce, foil-wrapped, short cone shape.

Blue-veined cheeses

Mold is usually considered an unwelcome intruder in our food, but blue cheese is a notable exception: Roquefort, Gorgonzola and Stilton—the great blues of France, Italy, and England—are referred to as "the Kings of Cheeses." There are good blue cheeses made in Denmark, Germany, and the United States, but these three are the most popular worldwide.

The discovery of the delicious flavor of mold-ripened cheese, like the discovery of wild yeast as a dough leavener, was undoubtedly accidental; however, cheesemakers have learned how to carefully preserve the particular molds that give the best flavor. Blue cheeses are inoculated with these molds (which are related to penicillin) by different methods, and then allowed to ripen in a controlled atmosphere until they are streaked with bluish-green veins and develop some of the finest flavors in the cheese world. The flavors are relatively mild in young blues, then intensify as the cheeses age.

People who are allergic to penicillin should probably not eat blue cheeses and some other soft cheeses, since they may experience a reaction to the penicillium molds used to produce the cheese.

Although blue cheeses get about 74 percent of their calories from fat, they are so strongly savory you need use only a small amount. They go particularly well with low-fat foods such as fruits or salads. The sodium content of these cheeses ranges from about 400 to 500 milligrams per ounce, however.

Gorgonzola The most famous Italian blue cheese, Gorgonzola has veins that are more green than blue. The body of the cheese is white, with a thin, edible rind. Made in 13-pound wheels, Gorgonzola is sold in full and partial wheels and wedges.

Stilton England's contribution to the blue cheese tray is milder than its famous French and Italian cousins. Stilton has a smooth, hard, brown rind and a creamy yellow interior with an even pattern of blue veins. It is made in 18-pound cylinders that are sold in sections, and in 5-pound forms to sell whole.

Goat's- and sheep's-milk cheeses

Now quite popular in the United States, imported and domestic goat's-milk cheeses display a pleasant tartness when young; this can develop into a mild gaminess or a striking pungency as the cheese ages.

You might like to try one of the milder cheeses, then progress to the stronger (longer-aged) varieties if the flavor appeals to you. Goat's milk is higher in fat than whole cow's milk, but it is slightly lower in cholesterol. Sheep's milk is also higher in fat than whole cow's milk; the best-known cheeses made from it are Roquefort and feta.

Chèvre This is simply the generic French name for goat's-milk cheeses. They range from fresh, soft, cream-cheese types with just a faint tartness to rock-hard, aged cheeses with an undeniable pungency. Some are treated with mold to form a soft rind, while others are formed into log shapes and coated with herbs or ashes. The mild *Montrachet* and the larger and slightly stronger *Bûcheron* are two of the most familiar French chèvres. Older, stronger French examples include *Valençay* (pyramid-shaped and sometimes coated with ash) and *Crottin de Chavignol,* one of the sharpest goat cheeses. Many American goat cheeses have come on the market in the last twenty years or so, often echoing their French forebears in shape and flavor. You may be able to find them in low-fat versions.

Feta Greece is the home of this chalky-white, porous, brined, sheep's- or goat's-milk cheese. You may have eaten cubes of salty feta in a Greek salad. To reduce the sodium content when using it at home, drain it and rinse it in fresh cold water.

Roquefort One of the world's greatest cheeses, Roquefort is a blue-veined cheese made in southern France. It is aged in limestone caves, as it has been since the fifteenth century. The cheese, which is made in 6-pound forms, is firm and white with blue-green veins and has a very high sodium content.

AMERICAN CHEESE, processed 3½ oz			
Calories	375	Fat	31 g
Protein	22 g	Saturated Fat	20 g
Carbohydrate	2 g	Cholesterol	94 mg
Dietary Fiber	None	Sodium	1430 mg

KEY NUTRIENTS		%RDA Men	%RDA Women
Vitamin B_{12}	0.7 mcg	35%	35%
Vitamin A	1210 IU	24%	30%
Calcium	616 mg	77%	77%
Phosphorus	745 mg	93%	93%
Riboflavin	0.4 mg	24%	31%
Zinc	3 mg	20%	25%

S=40% or more soluble N/A=Not Applicable N=Not Available

Processed cheeses

More than half the cheese produced in the United States goes into making processed cheese, which is most commonly sold in the form of slices or spreads. Many consumers appreciate its uniformity of color, flavor, and texture (typified by its dependable melting quality). Processed cheese is marginally lower in protein, vitamin A, calcium, and iron than many natural cheeses, and is higher in sodium.These products are made by melting one or more types of ground natural cheese with an emulsifier to form a smooth mass; pasteurization, an integral part of the process, improves the keeping quality of these foods. Pasteurized process cheese food may have added dairy ingredients other than cheese, such as cream or nonfat milk solids, and may be flavored with sweeteners, fruits, vegetables, or meat. Rather than being shaped into forms and sliced, processed cheeses are poured onto a chilled surface in their liquid state and cut into "slices" when the cheese re-congeals.

Pasteurized process cheese spread has additional ingredients that make it soft and spreadable. It is sold in pots, tubes, and even aerosol cans. (When natural cheeses are blended without heating and flavored to make a spread, the product is called cold-pack or club cheese.)

American cheese is a term that can be applied to Cheddar, colby, and other natural cheeses, but to most people it means the perfectly square slices that have been a lunchbox staple for decades. This American cheese is a pasteurized process cheese made from Cheddar or a combination of Cheddar and colby cheeses.

SHOPPING TIPS Use four of your five senses when choosing cheese: In addition to tasting the cheese if possible, sniff it, feel it, and above all, take a close look at it. Soft-ripened cheese such as Brie or Camembert should feel plump and full, and look fresh and white, not sunken, dry, or browned; there should be no sharp, ammonia-like smell. A knowledgeable salesperson will help you choose a soft-ripened cheese you can serve immediately, or one that will ripen in a few days. Semisoft and firm cheeses should look moist but not oily on the surface, and should feel resilient. Cheeses with holes should show a slight gleam (but not an oily slick) in their eyes.

When buying precut, packaged cheese, or fresh cheeses like cottage cheese, the freshness date and physical appearance of the cheese and the package are your best cues. Be sure the package is sealed.

STORAGE Cheese must be well wrapped to protect it from picking up other aromas in the refrigerator, and also to prevent its flavor from migrating to other foods. Foil is the best wrapping; plastic wrap traps moisture that may cause cheese to mold more quickly. Placing the wrapped cheese in a covered container provides an extra measure of protection for strong-smelling cheese. Wax-coated cheeses need no further wrapping until they are cut. They will lose moisture, however, becoming more dense and flavorful with time. Check cheese for mold from time to time.

IS MOLDY CHEESE SPOILED?

Even if kept wrapped and refrigerated, cheese may develop fuzzy spots of multicolored mold on its surface. Does this mean you have to throw the cheese away? If it's a dry cheese—a firm or very hard variety such as Cheddar or a Parmesan—and the mold is limited to a small spot, it is probably safe to cut off the moldy portion to a depth of about ½ inch and use the remaining cheese. However, with softer, moister cheeses, such as mozarella, ricotta, or cottage cheese, thread-like branches of mold may have penetrated deep beneath the surface. Although many food molds are harmless, some are toxic or carcinogenic. In the case of softer cheese, it's better to throw it away.

Generally, the softer the cheese, the more perishable it is. Ripe Brie will keep for just a few days, while Cheddar will keep for a month or more, and Parmesan can be stored for several months. Whole cheeses keep longer than cut ones: A whole Edam or Gouda can be stored in the refrigerator for a year or more.

After serving cheese, rewrap any left-over portions, and refrigerate or freeze them. If they have not survived in a presentable form, use them for cooking.

Most cheeses can be frozen. Although they may lose some moisture and become rather brittle and difficult to slice, they will be fine for melting or cooking. Thaw the cheese in the refrigerator for about 24 hours before using.

A slightly underripe Brie or other soft-ripened cheese can be wrapped in foil or plastic and left at cool room temperature for a day or two to bring it to perfect eating condition. Once ripe, keep it wrapped and refrigerated. It should keep for three to four weeks.

Keep cottage cheese and ricotta tightly covered in the original container; they should be good for about one week after the marked date. Storing the carton upside down—make sure it's tightly closed—will help seal out air and keep the contents fresh longer. Farmer cheese and cream cheese should keep for about two weeks.

Pasteurized process cheese spreads will keep indefinitely in their unopened jars at room temperature; once opened, they will keep for three to four weeks.

PREPARATION All cheeses—except the soft, unripened fresh cheeses—taste best at room temperature. As with wine, the subtleties of their flavor are "numbed" by cold. The textures of soft-ripened cheeses, especially, are at their best when at room rather than refrigerator temperature. When serving cheese, remove it from the refrigerator at least an hour before serving time (but keep it wrapped so the cut surfaces don't dry out). It's best to take out only the amount you think you'll need, so you don't end up repeatedly warming and chilling the cheese.

Cheese grates better when cold; if you're cooking with cheese, you might even put the cheese in the freezer for 15 minutes to ½ hour before grating or shredding it.

High heat will toughen cheese: Warm or melt it gently, preferably in combination with other ingredients. Use shredded or grated cheese for melting into sauces or soups, and stir it in after you turn off the heat; the residual heat of the food will melt the cheese. Well-aged cheese usually melts more smoothly than young cheese.

To make serving and cooking cheese easier, you might try a few inexpensive gadgets. A cheese plane, which looks like a pie server with a slit cut in it, shaves thin slices from Cheddar, Swiss, and the like. You can also buy a wire cheese cutter that adjusts for slices of different thicknesses. A rotary (drum) grater is very effective for finely grating hard cheeses; some have interchangeable drums for varying the coarseness of the shreds. Many types of cheese can be grated in a food processor fitted with the steel blade.

SERVING SUGGESTIONS Like meat, cheeses are best used as a condiment or seasoning rather than as the main part of a meal. Top a vegetable, grain, or bean casserole with shredded Cheddar, or sprinkle a bowl of pasta with grated Romano; serve an appetizer of marinated artichoke hearts or mushrooms topped with shaved Parmesan: Melt a bit of crumbled blue cheese in a bowl of tomato soup; fill pita bread with chopped vegetables and slivers of Swiss; or top Italian bread with slabs of ripe tomato and a thin slice of mozzarella. Instead of a thick grilled-cheese sandwich, top an open-face turkey sandwich with a little shredded Swiss and broil until melted. When you make English-muffin or pita "pizzas", add some vegetables and go light on the cheese.

Don't let cottage cheese be the bane of your weight-loss diet. Vary it with the addition of herbs, chopped vegetables, fresh fruit, spices, or a little grated sharp cheese. Use flavored cottage cheese as a spread for toast or sandwiches: A toasted mini-pita filled with sweetened, spiced cottage cheese and raisins is a healthy substitute for a morning danish or doughnut. Purée cottage cheese to use instead of sour cream on baked potatoes. Mix a little crumbled blue cheese or goat cheese with cottage cheese or low-fat cream cheese for a lower-fat sandwich or appetizer spread.

Flavorful goat cheeses can be crumbled and tossed with pasta or cooked vegetables, or melted on top of an open-face sandwich. Young chèvre is a nice change from cream cheese as a breakfast bread spread. Slices of Montrachet and similar goat cheeses can be quickly broiled and served atop a salad of bitter or tart greens.

When serving cheese and fruit as a dessert,

watch the proportions: Accompany a generous platter of fruit with a modest amount of cheese. Experiment with different combinations; some classic pairings are pears with blue cheese or Swiss cheese; grapes with Brie or Camembert; and apples with Cheddar.

Yogurt

Not so long ago most Americans considered yogurt a product for health-food faddists. At that time, relatively few people were aware that yogurt had been a staple in certain parts of Asia, the Middle East, and Eastern Europe for centuries. Yogurt has been commercially produced in the United States since 1940, but didn't become popular until about thirty years later.

Since the 1970s, however, more and more people have discovered the delightfully tart, subtle flavor of this cultured dairy product. Its reputed health benefits have been widely publicized as well: One national advertising campaign featured vigorous hundred-year-old denizens of the Georgian steppes who attributed their longevity to nothing less than yogurt. With consumers seeking more healthful foods, the American yogurt market expanded sixfold between 1970 and 1990.

Many medicinal claims have been made for yogurt throughout the ages: It has been—and is—touted as a cure for everything from insomnia to yeast infections, as a cancer preventive and a life-extender. Few if any of the claims have been proven by medical research, but it is unarguable that low-fat or nonfat yogurt is a nutritious and healthful food—an excellent source of calcium and protein, and a good source of riboflavin, phosphorus and vitamin B_{12}. It can be eaten as is, or dressed up with added ingredients. Plain yogurt also helps fat-conscious cooks by standing in for mayonnaise, heavy cream, whipped cream, or sour cream, as the occasion requires. Such versatility, along with its pleasantly tangy flavor and creamy texture, makes yogurt an easy food to add to your daily meals. Nonfat and low-fat yogurt are obviously the best choices, but even whole-milk yogurt contains slightly less fat than liquid whole milk.

Yogurt is made by curdling milk with purified cultures of two special bacteria—*Lactobacillus bulgaricus* and *Streptococcus thermophilus*—that cause the milk sugar (lactose) to turn into lactic acid. The pasteurized (and usually homogenized) milk is inoculated with the cultures, then warmed in an incubator for several hours; during this time the yogurt thickens and develops its distinctive flavor. Nonfat milk solids are often added to thicken the yogurt; this also adds protein.

In some types of yogurt, the bacteria survive the processing; in other cases, the milk is pasteurized again after the cultures are added, and the bacteria are destroyed. This is more often the case in Swiss-style brands. Many frozen yogurt products are pasteurized after culturing, too. Check the ingredient listing for "active yogurt cultures" or "living yogurt cultures." Yogurt that has been pasteurized subsequent to culturing will be labeled "heat-treated after culturing."

Because yogurt is cultured, it is more digestible than milk for some people with lactose intolerance: The live cultures create lactase, the enzyme in which lactose-intolerant people are deficient. However, the amount of lactose remaining varies from 25 to 80 percent. Active cultures also aid in

COMPARING YOGURTS 3½ ounces (½ cup)

	Calories	**Fat** (g)	**Saturated Fat** (g)	**Cholesterol** (mg)	**Calcium** (mg)
Low-fat, plain	63	2	1	6	183
Low-fat, fruit	99	1	1	5	138
Nonfat, plain	56	<1	<1	2	199
Whole	61	3	2	13	121

the digestion of casein, a milk protein. And there is some medical evidence that live yogurt cultures may help to restore the "friendly" bacteria in the intestines, after the bacterial balance of the digestive system has been upset by the use of antibiotics.

KEFIR

A close cousin of yogurt, kefir also has its roots in Eastern Europe. It was originally a beverage made from mare's milk, fermented with a cultured "starter"—akin to a sourdough starter—until it developed a low alcohol content. A modern version sold in the United States is made in much the same way as yogurt but using different cultures. It tends to be somewhat less tart than plain yogurt. Kefir can be made from whole or lowfat milk, and is sold plain and fruit flavored.

VARIETIES Plain, or unflavored, yogurt is the original and most versatile of yogurts. It contains 110 to 140 calories per cup. However, most of the yogurts sold in the United States are fruit flavored, and fall into two categories: Sundae-style yogurts, in which the fruit is at the bottom of the container and must be stirred in; and blended, custard-like, Swiss- or French-style yogurts, in which the fruit is distributed throughout the yogurt. Yet another type of yogurt is flavored with vanilla, coffee, or fruit juice (but no fruit solids). Flavored and fruited yogurts range from about 100 calories per cup (for artificially sweetened nonfat vanilla) to 307 (for some whole-milk sundae-style yogurts).

Yogurt is produced in nonfat, low-fat, and whole-milk versions. Lowfat yogurt typically contains from 2 to 5 grams of fat per 8-ounce serving; whole-milk yogurt may contain 6 to 8 grams of fat per 8 ounces. Some brands of whole milk yogurt (called farm-style) come with a layer of yogurt cream on top. To reduce the fat content, lift this off and discard it rather than stirring it in.

In order to thicken or stabilize yogurt and increase its shelf life, some brands of yogurt have added gelatin, starches, pectin, or gums. These additives are not harmful, but they sometimes give the yogurt a slightly "unnatural" stiffness or thickness.

Some yogurts contain artificial flavors or colors, as well as natural and artificial sweeteners such as sugar, honey, molasses, corn syrup, fructose, saccharine, or aspartame. A cup of regular sweetened vanilla, lemon or coffee yogurt contains the equivalent of 3½ teaspoons of sugar; fruit flavors may have as much as 7 teaspoons per cup. Some extra-rich yogurts have egg yolks added.

Hard and soft-serve frozen yogurt can be a healthy treat, but there is quite a range of products and not all of them are good choices. Nonfat frozen yogurt is the best choice; although it has plenty of sugar added, it still has half the calories of some premium ice creams and, of course, no fat. Low-fat versions are the next best. Other types of frozen yogurt may be enriched with whole milk or cream, raising their calorie and fat content significantly but still leaving it far below that of most ice cream (see page 461). Sauces, toppings, or mix-ins like nuts, cookies, and candies, can also increase the calorie and fat content of a serving of frozen yogurt.

Fruit-flavored yogurt drinks, like yogurt, vary

YOGURT CHEESE

Yogurt thickens when the whey is drained from it. The resulting mildly tart yogurt "cheese," or curd, can be substituted for cream cheese, sour cream, or crème fraîche in recipes, used to make low-fat dips and spreads, or sweetened and served as a dessert. You can buy an inexpensive yogurt cheese "funnel" or make your own out of common kitchen items. Use any type of plain yogurt that does not contain gelatin, as gelatin keeps the whey from draining off. Fruited yogurts will not work well, but flavored yogurts that do not have solids in them (such as vanilla, coffee, or lemon) can be made into tasty dessert cheeses by this method.

To make yogurt cheese, line a strainer or colander with dampened cheesecloth, a clean white cloth napkin or towel, or paper towels; place the strainer over a bowl. (You can also use a simple funnel-shaped drip coffee filter—the type that sits atop the cup or pot—lined with a paper filter.) Stir the yogurt, then spoon it into the strainer. Cover the strainer with plastic wrap and place the strainer and bowl in the refrigerator.

The thickness of the resulting product will depend on the type of yogurt you use and how long it drains. As a rule of thumb, an hour or two will yield a sour-cream-like yogurt; six to eight hours, or overnight draining, will produce a yogurt "cream cheese."

For appetizer dips and/or sandwich spreads, flavor the yogurt cheese with herbs, spices, or chopped vegetables. For instance, add minced garlic and fresh or dried herbs such as basil, thyme, dill, oregano, or tarragon. Or flavor the cheese with chili or curry powder, chopped scallions or chives, puréed roasted bell peppers, capers, anchovies, or mustard. Add shredded carrots, chopped cooked spinach or puréed artichoke hearts.

For dessert, sweeten the yogurt cheese with honey, brown sugar, or frozen fruit-juice concentrate, and flavor it with vanilla or almond extract, nutmeg, cardamom or ginger; fold in grated citrus zest or chopped dried fruit, if desired; serve with fresh fruit (it's especially good with bananas or berries) or plain cookies. You can make a chocolate cheese spread for fruit slices (or a simple frosting for cake or cookies) by adding cocoa powder to sweetened yogurt cheese.

Lightly thickened yogurt cheese can be used instead of mayonnaise in tuna or chicken salad. When cooking with yogurt cheese (using it to make sauces or creamy soups, for example), take the same precautions you would with regular yogurt (see page 481).

widely in both sugar and fat content. But almost any of these products is a good alternative to a milkshake that is made with whole milk and ice cream.

SHOPPING TIPS All commercial yogurts are freshness dated. Be sure to check the date, and select the latest-dated carton you find on the shelf. Nutrition labeling will alert you to the carbohydrate content, which can be a tip-off to how much sugar is in the yogurt. If you prefer fruited yogurt, select one made with fresh fruit rather than preserves.

If you like yogurt as a light snack, or are buying it for children, look for 4- or 6-ounce cups rather than the more common 8-ounce ones.

More than 85 percent of the yogurt sold in the United States is fruit-flavored, with strawberry the most popular flavor.

STORAGE Keep yogurt in its original container in the refrigerator. An unopened container of yogurt with live cultures should keep for about ten days past the freshness date; pasteurized yogurt will keep even longer. However, check to see that the yogurt looks and smells fresh when you open it.

PREPARATION Most people eat yogurt straight from the carton. But yogurt is also a wonderful ingredient for healthful cooking, as long as some adjustments are made, especially when substituting it for cream or mayonnaise. Drain off any excess liquid and stir the yogurt before spooning it out of the carton. Expect some difference in texture because of yogurt's low fat content, and a slightly tart flavor because of its mild acidity. You may need to add a pinch of sugar or salt to some recipes. The acidity can be counteracted in baking, if necessary, by adding ½ teaspoon baking soda for each cup of yogurt (don't do this, however, if you are on a low-sodium diet); if the recipe calls for sour cream or buttermilk, no such modification is necessary.

Stovetop cooking with yogurt can present problems: The yogurt will "break" or curdle if heated to too high a temperature. To prevent this, have the yogurt at room temperature, and stir it well before adding it to hot food. As an extra precaution, stir a tablespoon of cornstarch into each cup of yogurt before adding it. It's also a good idea to add the yogurt over very low heat, or, better yet, after removing the pan from the heat.

Yogurt can be used to marinate meat, and will tenderize it to some extent because of its acid content.

SERVING SUGGESTIONS If you sweeten plain yogurt yourself, with sugar, honey or frozen juice concentrate, you can control the amount of sweetener rather than settling for the excessive amount in some pre-flavored yogurt. You may not need to add any sugar if you stir in fresh fruit, such as whole berries, sliced bananas, chopped peaches or nectarines, or grated apples or pears. Or, use yogurt as a dip for fruit slices. Applesauce or apple butter are good mix-in possibilities, as are raisins or chopped dates, figs or prunes; top with a sprinkling of wheat germ or your favorite breakfast cereal. Or, instead of adding ingredients to the yogurt, spoon it over breakfast cereal or a bowl of fresh sliced fruit.

Flavor plain yogurt with vanilla, almond or coconut extract, or spice it with ground cinnamon, cardamom or ginger—even cocoa powder (which will require some sweetener) or chocolate syrup. Make a low-fat shake by blending yogurt with fresh or frozen fruit.

Its current popularity has made yogurt a sort of food-label buzzword. Today, even candy and frozen desserts are made "healthier" with yogurt, and here some caution is required. When plain yogurt is flavored with sugar, honey, preserves, granola, nuts, or chocolate, it takes on their calories (and fat). When a mixture of oil and sugar has a little yogurt powder added to make a coating for peanuts or raisins, the result can hardly be called a healthy snack. And when a frozen yogurt bar is coated with chocolate, its calorie content more than doubles.

On the savory side, you can season plain yogurt with your favorite dip ingredients—scallions or chives, chili or curry powder, herbs or mustard, salsa or chili sauce; serve raw vegetables or oven-toasted tortilla triangles for dippers. Chopped or grated vegetables—carrots or bell peppers, for instance—can also go into plain yogurt. Stir some plain yogurt into hot tomato or vegetable soup, or add a dollop to chilled gazpacho. Cucumbers and yogurt are a refreshing warm-weather combination (see page 90).

You can give your home cooking a substantial

YOGURT, plain, low-fat 3½ oz			
Calories	63	Fat	2 g
Protein	5 g	Saturated Fat	1 g
Carbohydrate	7 g	Cholesterol	6 mg
Dietary Fiber	None	Sodium	70 mg

KEY NUTRIENTS		% RDA Men	% RDA Women
Vitamin B_{12}	0.6 mcg	30%	30%
Calcium	183 mg	23%	23%
Phosphorus	144 mg	18%	18%
Riboflavin	0.2 mg	12%	15%

S=40% or more soluble N/A=Not Applicable N=Not Available

YOGURT, fruit, low-fat 3½ oz			
Calories	99	Fat	1 g
Protein	4 g	Saturated Fat	1 g
Carbohydrate	19 g	Cholesterol	5 mg
Dietary Fiber	None	Sodium	53 mg

KEY NUTRIENTS		% RDA Men	Women
Vitamin B_{12}	0.4 mcg	20%	20%
Calcium	138 mg	17%	17%
Phosphorus	109 mg	14%	14%
Riboflavin	0.2 mg	12%	15%

S=40% or more soluble N/A=Not Applicable N=Not Available

health boost by substituting plain yogurt for sour cream, mayonnaise, heavy cream, or whipped cream. Yogurt makes thick, creamy salad dressings, adds a lively tang to tuna salad, and is a fine topping for baked potatoes. It can also "stretch" rich foods like guacamole. If you don't find yogurt palatable for these uses, try mixing it with mayonnaise or sour cream instead of using it straight. Yogurt can be substituted for milk, buttermilk, or sour cream in many baking recipes.

Yogurt makes a tangy marinade for chicken, fish, or meat; the Indian dish tandoori chicken is probably the best-known example of yogurt-marinated food.

For a basic marinade, just add a little lemon juice to plain yogurt. For an Indian flavor, add curry powder or its components, including cumin, coriander, and cayenne pepper.

You can create homemade frozen yogurt desserts yourself instead of buying over-sweetened commercial products. Just stir the yogurt (add fruit or other flavorings, if desired) and freeze it for a few hours. Thaw slightly and stir again before serving. You can also make frozen yogurt in an ice-cream maker.

Eggs

The egg is an inexpensive source of high-quality protein (about 6 grams in a large egg) and an important source of vitamins B_{12} and E, riboflavin, folacin, iron, and phosphorus. These attributes should make it one of nature's near-perfect foods, but the egg has one drawback: Its yolk contains about two-thirds of the total suggested daily maximum intake of cholesterol.

When Americans began to be cholesterol-conscious, the egg was one of the first foods they stopped eating: Following a gradual decline since World War II in per capita consumption of fresh eggs came a markedly steeper drop of some 22 percent between 1980 and 1990. (Interestingly, consumption of food products containing eggs rose significantly in that same decade, probably due to the increased use of eggs in manufactured foods and fast foods. This suggests that, although Americans are conscious of the cholesterol content of fresh eggs, they are not as well-informed about the egg—and cholesterol—content of processed foods.)

In the years since cholesterol became a widespread concern, research has shown that saturated fat has a greater effect on blood cholesterol levels than dietary cholesterol does—and eggs are not a major source of saturated fat. A whole large egg contains about 5 grams of total fat, of which less than 2 grams are saturated. By comparison, a 3½-ounce broiled extra-lean hamburger patty and an ounce of Cheddar cheese each contain 6 grams of saturated fat.

Another point in favor of the egg: Differences

in the way cholesterol content is measured have resulted in eggs with a lower cholesterol content. A study performed by the Egg Nutrition Board (whose values were accepted by the USDA) found that a large egg contains about 210 milligrams of cholesterol—nearly 25 percent less than the formerly accepted figure of 275 milligrams. In response to these findings, the American Heart Association has raised its weekly acceptable egg intake for healthy people from three whole eggs (or egg yolks) to four. Those with elevated cholesterol still need to limit themselves to one whole egg or egg yolk each week.

Laying hens produced an average of 250 eggs per year in the United States in 1980, compared with 151 eggs per year in 1945.

Egg whites, though, can be used freely: It is the yolk that contains all of the fat and cholesterol (as well as the major concentration of calories, B vitamins, and minerals). The white is almost pure protein—protein that is considered nearly perfect because of its exemplary balance of amino acids. Even if you are very concerned about your consumption of cholesterol, you can still take partial advantage of the egg's culinary usefulness and nutritional value by cooking with egg whites alone.

In recent years, a new health concern has been raised about eggs—salmonellosis (salmonella-caused food poisoning). Formerly found only when a cracked shell had allowed the bacteria (which are present in the chicken's intestines) to contaminate the contents of the egg, salmonella bacteria have now been found in clean, uncracked eggs. Therefore, washing the eggs before cracking them and observing other careful handling techniques may not be enough to protect you from infection. To safeguard your health, the eggs must be cooked at high enough temperatures to destroy the bacteria. Undercooked egg dishes, such as soft-cooked or sunny-side-up fried eggs, or recipes made with raw eggs, such as Caesar salad dressing or eggnog, carry the risk of salmonellosis. (For ways to prevent salmonellosis, see the box on page 486.)

USDA egg grades—AA, A, and B—indicate freshness as well as other aspects of quality. Federal grading is not mandatory, but most eggs sold in the United States are inspected by the USDA, marked with that agency's seal, and assigned a grade. Some packers comply with state standards comparable to the federal grading rules; some states also have their own grading seals. Eggs that do not bear the USDA grade seal must be Grade B or better. Most eggs that are assigned Grade B end up in egg products rather than being sold fresh.

Grading is based on the condition of the inside and outside of the egg, including the cleanliness, soundness, shape, and texture of the shell, the thickness and clarity of the albumen (white), the size and shape of the yolk, the presence of blood spots, and the size of the air cell or pocket (eggs dry as they age, so the fresher the egg, the smaller the air pocket). The interior of the egg is evaluated by one of two methods. Candling, or rotating the eggs over a high-intensity light, shows the size of the air cell and the condition of the yolk (this process was originally performed with candles, hence its name).

The breakout method is just what it sounds like—breaking a random sample of eggs and evaluating them visually and with special measuring devices. USDA-graded eggs are also required to be washed with a disinfectant and then sprayed with oil to replace the natural protective coating that is washed away.

TYPES OF EGGS Most supermarkets carry just one or two types of eggs: white and/or brown hen's eggs. Most white eggs come from the Single Comb White Leghorn breed of hen. Brown eggs, which are preferred over white eggs by consumers in New England and some other parts of the country, are produced by Rhode Island Red, New Hampshire, and Plymouth Rock hens. The color

EGG SUBSTITUTES

As an alternative to experimenting with egg whites in order to lower the cholesterol content of your favorite recipes, you might like to try some of the commercial egg substitutes on the market. They come in frozen, refrigerated, or powdered form, and most have egg whites as their basic ingredient. Some have vegetable oil, flavoring, and color added to give the effect of yolk; these can be used in recipes or cooked like scrambled eggs. Other products contain no eggs at all, and are intended to produce the leavening effect of beaten eggs when used in baked goods. You can also buy meringue powder (look for it at stores that sell cake-decorating supplies); this product takes the worry out of using uncooked egg whites in decorative icings and similar recipes.

The calorie content of supermarket egg substitutes ranges from about 15 to 60 calories per serving (compared with about 80 calories for a whole egg). Most have no (or negligible) cholesterol, but some contain as much as 4 grams of fat per serving. As always, careful reading of labels is your best guide.

of the shell—and, for that matter, the color of the yolk—has no bearing on the egg's quality or nutritional value. Duck, goose, or quail eggs are available at some gourmet shops or, locally, direct from the farm.

SHOPPING TIPS Almost all the eggs you'll find in the supermarket will be graded AA or A, and the two are very nearly comparable. Eggs are also sorted by size (actually by weight) when they are graded, and packed as Peewee, Small, Medium, Large, Extra Large, or Jumbo. There is a difference in weight of 3 ounces per dozen between each size and the next. Medium eggs are appropriate for many cooking uses, but baking recipes, which tend to be more specific in their requirements, often call for Large eggs.

Grading tells you a lot about the eggs you buy. Still, the way the eggs are handled after they leave the packing plant can determine their condition when you take them home. Refrigeration is vitally important to freshness: Eggs age as much in one day at room temperature as they do in one week of refrigerated storage. Therefore, buy eggs only at stores that keep them in chilled cases. Look for a date or freshness code on the carton. All USDA-inspected eggs are required to carry a three-digit number that indicates what day of the year they were packed (i.e., January first is 001; December thirty-first is 365). Look for the highest-numbered carton you can find. If kept refrigerated, the eggs should be good for four to five weeks from the packing date. In some states and localities, egg cartons must be marked with expiration dates after which they should not be sold.

When eggs are sold at a farm or at a nearby outlet, they may be displayed in "flats," or cardboard trays. It's best to be sure of their source when buying eggs locally; they may not be graded or dated, so the seller's reputation is your only assurance of quality. And the eggs should always be kept under refrigeration if that farm-fresh quality is to be preserved.

Check eggs carefully before purchasing, looking for cracks, breaks, or excessive dirt. Gently jiggle each egg to make sure the egg is not cracked at the bottom and stuck to the carton. And be sure that the carton is packed at the top of your grocery bag, or the eggs may not survive the trip home. Get them home and into the refrigerator quickly.

STORAGE Check again to make sure that no eggs have been broken in transit; remove any cracked eggs and discard them. It's not necessary or desirable to wash or wipe eggs before storing them, since this will remove their protective coating.

Store eggs in their original carton in the coldest part of the refrigerator. (The molded rack in the refrigerator door is not a good place to store eggs; they're exposed to warm air every time the refrigerator is opened.) The carton also protects the eggs from aromas of strong-flavored foods in the refrigerator; eggs can absorb odors right through their porous shells. Large-end-up—the way the eggs come in the carton—is the best way to keep them: The yolk remains centered in the white, away from the air pocket at the large end of the egg.

Although fresh eggs will keep for four to five weeks, their quality declines with time; the whites become thinner and the yolks flatter. For best flavor and appearance, use eggs that are less than one week old for frying or poaching; reserve older eggs for hard-cooking, scrambling, and baking.

Hard-cooked eggs can be refrigerated for up to one week. Since the cooking washes the protective coating from the shells, it's best to store them in a carton or covered container. Mark unshelled hard-cooked eggs with a penciled "x" to distinguish them from fresh eggs. (If you forget which is which, place the eggs on their sides and spin them. A hard-cooked egg, with its yolk immobilized in the center, will spin smoothly and easily, while a raw egg will wobble.) You can also peel hard-cooked eggs and place them in a bowl with cold water to cover them.

When using egg substitutes instead of fresh eggs, you need not worry about salmonella, because such products are pasteurized. Commercial products made with eggs—such as mayonnaise, eggnog, or chocolate mousse—are safe, too, because they are made with pasteurized eggs.

Eggs can be frozen, but not in their shells. Whites and yolks can be frozen together if they are beaten just until blended, then placed in small containers and tightly sealed. To freeze whites alone, separate them, then place them in containers and seal. Yolks need to be combined with salt, sugar, or corn syrup in order to be usable when thawed: For every four yolks, beat in 1/8 teaspoon of salt or 1½ teaspoons of sugar or corn syrup; seal in containers and label as to whether you've added salt or sweetener. Thaw frozen eggs overnight in the refrigerator, and cook them thoroughly or use them in recipes as soon as they are thawed.

PREPARATION In cooking, the two parts of the egg perform different functions. The yolk acts as a fat and, to some degree, as a protein, enriching, thickening, and emulsifying mixtures; it also adds color and flavor. Egg whites take in air when beaten, trapping air bubbles. The protein coagulates when heated, creating the structure that causes a cake to rise while baking. Egg white serves as a binder and thickener as well.

Cooking times will be more predictable and whites will beat to a fuller volume if eggs are brought to room temperature. To do this quickly, place them in a bowl of warm water for a few minutes.

It's possible to trim cholesterol and fat from egg recipes by cooking with fewer yolks than whites. Substitute two whites for one whole egg for up to half the eggs in scrambled eggs or omelets. In other recipes, try substituting two egg whites plus 1 teaspoon of vegetable oil for each whole egg; this significantly reduces the cholesterol and saturated fat content of the dish, but drops the total fat content by only about 1 gram per egg. Sometimes you can simply substitute two egg whites for each whole egg, but only experimenting with your favorite recipes will tell which of them can be adapted this way: Eggs do perform very specific functions, especially in baking and sauce-making, and sometimes there's just no workable substitute or modification.

Beaten whites are the basis for meringue and angel food cake, which are both healthy dessert choices because they are low in fat. Here are some tips on separating eggs and on beating egg whites for successful baking.

PREVENTING FOOD POISONING

The most effective way to prevent salmonellosis is to throughly cook eggs. In order to kill the bacteria, eggs must reach an internal temperature of 160°, or be cooked at 140° for at least 3 minutes, effectively pasteurizing them. This translates to a 7-minute boiled egg, a 5-minute poached egg, or a 3-minute-per-side fried egg. Both the yolk and white should be firm. Omelets, scrambled eggs, and French toast should be cooked until dry (at least one minute of cooking at 250°—"medium" stovetop heat—is recommended for scrambled eggs). Bake soft meringue toppings for at least 20 minutes at 325°. Cook soft custards thoroughly (most recipes call for minimal cooking, or for simply adding hot milk to raw eggs and stirring), and refrigerate them immediately.

You can take other steps to keep salmonellosis from striking:

- **Buy the freshest eggs you can find, refrigerate them, and use them promptly, as the bacteria multiply with time.**
- **Wash utensils and containers used for raw eggs with soap and hot water (wash your hands, too).**
- **Refrigerate all cooked egg dishes within two hours.**
- **Be careful not to allow cooked food (or food that will be eaten raw, such as fruits or vegetables) to come in contact with raw eggs.**
- **Make eggnog and ice cream with cooked custard bases rather than raw eggs (or find some eggless ice cream recipes).**
- **Be sure that custard pie fillings and pasta fillings made with eggs and cheese are thoroughly baked.**
- **When adding eggs to batter, crack them one at a time into a cup. If any shell falls in, discard the egg and use a clean cup for the remainder.**
- **Don't taste raw cookie dough or cake batter once eggs have been added.**

Separating eggs It's easiest for the inexperienced cook to use an egg separator. More practiced cooks break eggs by rapping them sharply downward on the edge of a bowl at the egg's "beltline." As the two pieces of shell are gently pulled apart and then held upright, the yolk will be left in one of the halves. After emptying the half-shellful of white into a small bowl, the yolk is carefully tipped from one shell half into the other, which causes any remaining white to flow into the bowl. The yolk can be discarded or saved for another use.

Beating egg whites Beat the eggs just before you need them, not in advance. The other ingredients, the baking pans, and the oven should be ready. Use a large, deep bowl, and be sure it's free of grease. Begin beating with a whisk, an egg beater, or an electric mixer at slow speed; once the eggs are foamy, gradually increase the speed and beat until the whites are firm but not dry. When you lift the mixer out of the eggs, it should pull the whites into glossy peaks that neither fold over nor break; when you tilt the bowl, the whites should not slide. (If the recipe directs you to beat the eggs to soft, not stiff, peaks, the tips of the peaks should curl over as you lift the beater from the bowl.) Where a recipe calls for adding sugar to the egg whites, add it very gradually, just about a tablespoonful at a time, or it may decrease the volume of the beaten whites.

LEFTOVER YOLKS

If you're learning to do without egg yolks, you may be wondering what to do with this nutritious but cholesterol-laden food—other than throw it away. One of the best options is to separate the eggs, then hard-cook the yolks (as if poaching them) and feed them to your cat or dog. You can even crumble hard-cooked yolks and put them out on a bird feeder, where they will be thoroughly appreciated.

Either lemon juice or cream of tartar—both acidic ingredients—may be added when beating egg whites.

They help to stabilize the beaten whites so they do not deflate so readily. Either ingredient will slow the aeration of the egg whites, so do not add lemon juice or cream of tartar until the whites have been beaten to the foamy stage.

The standard methods of cooking eggs are familiar to most people; here are some tips on the basic techniques.

Frying The steam-basting method lets you fry an egg with a minimal amount of fat and for a safe length of time, but it still leaves it moist and tender: Spray a nonstick skillet with cooking spray (or brush it lightly with oil or butter), heat it over medium-high heat, and crack in the egg. Reduce the heat to low and cook for one minute, then add 1 teaspoon of water, cover the skillet tightly and cook for at least 6 minutes longer.

Omelets Making a perfect omelet is something of an art and requires a little practice. Omelets can be made with whole eggs, or by replacing some of them with whites alone (see guidelines above). For a simple firm omelet, beat the eggs with a fork until blended, adding 1 tablespoon of milk or other liquid for each egg. Spray a nonstick skillet thoroughly with nonstick cooking spray or brush it with a little oil or butter; heat the skillet over medium heat. Pour in the eggs and reduce the heat to low. As the eggs begin to set at the edges, lift the edges with a thin spatula and tilt the pan to let the uncooked eggs run to the bottom. When the eggs are firm, place a filling, if you are using one, on top of one side of the omelet and fold the other side over it. Or, simply fold the cooked omelet and slide it out of the pan.

Poaching Traditionally, poached eggs are served with runny yolks, but for safety reasons you must cook them until firm. Bring an inch or two of water to a simmer in a saucepan or small skillet. Break an egg into a cup, then, holding the cup just above the surface of the water, gently slide the egg into the pan. Cook until the white and yolk are firm (at least 5 minutes). Lift the egg out using a slotted spoon, and drain it on paper towels.

Some cooks prefer to stir up a "whirlpool" in the simmering water (using the handle of a wooden spoon) before adding the egg; this helps the white to form into a fairly smooth round shape rather than trailing in shreds. Also, adding a little vinegar to the water will cause the white to coagulate more quickly, making for a tidier poached egg.

Poached eggs can be cooked in advance and kept in a bowl of cold water. Reheat them by dropping them into boiling water for a few seconds. Eggs poached and served in broth, soup, or tomato sauce make an unusual main dish.

Scrambling Scrambled eggs can be made successfully with whites only, or with one whole egg plus one or two whites (see guidelines above). Break the eggs into a bowl and beat them with a fork until blended (add a few spoonfuls of milk and any seasonings, as desired). Spray a nonstick skillet with cooking spray or brush it with a little oil or butter and heat the skillet over medium heat. Pour in the eggs. As the eggs begin to set, gently draw a spatula across the pan to break up the eggs into curds. Continue to cook until no liquid egg is visible.

MICROWAVE CAUTION

You can cook eggs in the microwave, but be careful: If the membrane that surrounds the yolk is left intact, the yolk may explode when you cut into it after cooking. For safety's sake, break the egg into a cup and pierce the yolk with a needle before cooking. Or scramble the white and yolk together.

Soft- and hard-cooking Eggs should never really be "soft-boiled" or "hard-boiled," because rapidly boiling water can be turbulent enough to crack the eggs as they cook. It's best to start eggs in cold water that's brought slowly to a simmer. Place the eggs in a pan, add just enough water to cover them, and bring to a boil over medium-high heat. As soon as the water comes to a boil, turn off the heat and let the eggs stand in the water for at least 7 minutes for soft cooked and 15

EGG 3½ oz (2 large eggs)			
Calories	149	Fat	10 g
Protein	12 g	Saturated Fat	3 g
Carbohydrate	1 g	Cholesterol	425 mg
Dietary Fiber	None	Sodium	126 mg

KEY NUTRIENTS		% RDA Men	% RDA Women
Vitamin A	635 IU	13%	16%
Vitamin B_{12}	1 mcg	50%	50%
Folacin	47 mcg	24%	26%
Phosphorus	178 mg	22%	22%
Iron	1 mg	10%	6%
Riboflavin	0.5 mg	29%	38%

S=40% or more soluble N/A=Not Applicable N=Not Available

EGG WHITE 3½ oz (whites of 3 large eggs)			
Calories	50	Fat	0 g
Protein	11 g	Saturated Fat	0 g
Carbohydrate	1 g	Cholesterol	0 mg
Dietary Fiber	None	Sodium	164 mg

KEY NUTRIENTS		% RDA Men	% RDA Women
Vitamin B_{12}	0.2 mcg	10%	10%
Riboflavin	0.5 mg	29%	38%

S=40% or more soluble N/A=Not Applicable N=Not Available

to 17 minutes for hard-cooked. (The eggs will reach an internal temperature of 165°, which destroys salmonella bacteria.) For easy peeling, drop hard-cooked eggs into cold water as soon as they are done, and then peel them immediately. Peel under cold running water. This also helps prevent the grayish layer that sometimes forms around a hard-cooked egg yolk.

SERVING SUGGESTIONS For most health-conscious people, the two-egg breakfast is a thing of the past. However, one or two eggs can serve as a substantial and healthful lunch or dinner main dish, if prepared by a low-fat method and served with well-chosen accompaniments. Combine fried (steam-basted), boiled, or scrambled eggs, or omelets with sauces or fillings that do not add extra fat. Serve eggs with boiled or baked potatoes, grains, or whole-grain breadstuffs, and forgo the rich sauces. Tomato-vegetable sauces are a good choice, and are traditional in dishes such as *huevos rancheros* and Spanish omelets; salsa is good with almost any kind of eggs.

Vegetables make the healthiest omelet fillings. If you are an omelet fan, skip the cheese, ham, or bacon fillings at home or when eating out, and opt for a spinach or onion omelet or an *omelet aux fines herbes* (seasoned with chopped fresh parsley, chives, or other herbs).

Italian frittatas, or open-face omelets, are easy to make and often include fresh vegetables such as spinach, broccoli, asparagus, or mushrooms: Stir beaten eggs into diced or sliced vegetables and cook in a skillet until set. A light sprinkling of cheese, browned under the broiler, gives the frittata a savory topping.

You can even make deviled eggs a low-cholesterol appetizer by filling the hard-cooked whites with a well-seasoned filling that's not made from the yolks. Try yogurt-dressed potato salad or an herbed cottage cheese or tofu mixture. You can also make an egg-white-only egg salad (or use just half as many yolks as whites). Chopped egg whites make a healthful garnish for spinach or other salads.

Many egg-based dishes, such as quiche, are traditionally made with cream, whole milk, high-fat cheese, and butter. Experiment with substituting skim milk, cottage cheese, reduced-fat cheeses, margarine, or olive or vegetable oil for a more heart-healthy recipe. Add fresh vegetables or cooked legumes if possible.

Seek out egg-white only-recipes for soufflés, cakes, and cookies. Meringue cookies and angel food cake, based on egg whites, are nearly fat-free (unless they include chocolate, coconut, or nuts).

APPENDIXES

Appendix A

Cooking Glossary

COOKING HAS A great effect on the flavor and texture of the foods we eat, and also on their nutritional value. With improved knowledge of the physical and chemical changes that cooking causes in food, and greater understanding of the value and conservation of vitamins, minerals, and other valuable food constituents, cooking methods have undergone a minor revolution in recent decades.

Tastes have changed, too. During the first half of this century, overcooking was the rule: In an effort to make them more digestible, many foods were boiled or stewed for hours. Under such treatment, vegetables and fruits turned mushy, while meat and poultry were rendered stringy and savorless—their flavors obliterated and their nutritional value decimated.

Today, the quality of "freshness" is appreciated even in cooked foods. Both dry heat methods such as roasting and baking, and moist heat techniques such as blanching, steaming, and braising, are used by health-conscious cooks to produce crisp-tender vegetables, bright-colored fruits, and moist, flavorful meats and poultry. These techniques help conserve nutrients as well as taste and texture: The cook need only give some attention to details such as cooking time and temperature, how much liquid to add, whether or not to cover the pan, and the importance of serving certain cooked foods promptly. Even healthy frying (sautéing and stir-frying) is feasible if broth or a small amount of vegetable oil is used instead of large quantities of butter or animal fat.

The glossary that follows presents the most common cooking techniques for the foods described in this book. A general understanding of how these processes work will help you choose techniques for cooking a wide range of foods with healthful, delicious results.

BAKING This dry-heat method cooks food by surrounding it with heated air in an oven or covered barbecue grill. Vegetables, grains, legumes, meat, poultry, and fish (as well as casseroles and cakes) can be cooked by this method. Firm fruits, such as apples, pears, peaches and plums, can be baked with spices and sweetener for a healthy dessert. The food may be covered to keep it moist (wrapping chicken or fish in cabbage or lettuce leaves is a good way to keep it moist during baking), or left uncovered to let the air circulate around the food and evaporate the moisture.

Potatoes are the most familiar baked vegetable. Other sturdy root vegetables (such as beets and rutabagas), as well as winter squash, can also be baked. Onions and garlic can be baked to render them sweet and mild. Place the vegetables on a baking sheet or in a shallow baking dish, or wrap them in foil. Sprinkle halved or cut vegetables with a few tablespoons of liquid and cover them to keep them from drying out. Bake in a moderate oven (about 350°) until the vegetables are tender when pierced with a knife.

Grains are baked in a casserole or baking dish in much the same way you would simmer them on the stovetop: Stir in a measured amount of liquid and any seasonings or additional ingredients, then cover and bake in a 350° to 400° oven until the liquid is absorbed and the grain is tender. Baking should take the same amount of time as simmering, or slightly longer.

Dried beans and peas (legumes) are usually precooked and then slow-baked with other ingredients, such as onions, molasses, and tomato sauce, to flavor them.

Chicken parts, thick chops, whole fish, and fish steaks can be baked; both "fully-cooked" and "cook before eating" hams are also "baked" (actually roasted). In order to keep them from drying out, marinate chicken, meat, or fish beforehand, cook in a sauce or coating (a crumb crust, for instance), or cook some vegetables in the same pan. Covering the food with foil or a lid will help keep it moist. Use a shallow baking dish and turn the food occasionally for even cooking.

To bake fruits, core or pit the unpeeled fruit. Stuff the fruits, if desired, with chopped dried fruit or nuts, and place them in a baking dish with a small amount of liquid—pan juices, fruit juice, or wine. Cover with foil and bake in a 325° oven until tender, basting occasionally with the liquid.

BAKING IN PARCHMENT Also called cooking en papillote, this method seals moisture into lean chicken breasts or fish fillets. You can use special cooking parchment, but it's possible to obtain a similar result with aluminum foil. Cut large squares of foil (parchment is usually cut in a large heart shape for this purpose); place a boneless chicken breast or fish fillet on each square. For a one-dish meal, place the chicken or fish on a bed of cooked rice, and top with thinly sliced vegetables, then season with your favorite herbs and spices. Fold the wrapping over the contents, crimp the edges together to seal it, and bake in a 400° to 425° oven.

BLANCHING Also called parboiling, blanching means cooking food quickly in a large quantity of rapidly boiling water. Immersing food in lots of water can leach out nutrients, but the brief cooking time minimizes this nutrient loss. Blanching is used to cook tender vegetables and to precook sturdier ones before finishing them with another technique such as braising or baking.

To blanch vegetables, bring a large pot of water to a boil. Drop in the vegetables a few at a time, then cover and return the water to a boil. Cook just until the vegetables are bright-colored and barely crisp-tender. (You may want to use a timer, as blanching often takes a minute or less.) Drain the cooked vegetables in a colander and cool them under cold running water (or place the colander in a bowl of ice water). This stops the cooking and sets the bright color.

A very brief blanching also loosens the skins of tomatoes, peaches, and plums, making them easier to peel.

BOILING Though blanching, microwaving, or steaming are preferred for cooking vegetables because these methods help preserve nutrients, some vegetables cook more efficiently when they are boiled. The nutrient loss will be minimal if a few guidelines are followed. Use just enough water to prevent scorching: Try ½ cup for a pound of vegetables. Bring the water to a full rolling boil, then add the prepared vegetables, cover the pan, and increase the heat, if necessary, to return the water quickly to a boil. Then adjust the heat to maintain a slow boil. (When boiling strong-flavored vegetables such as cabbage or Brussels sprouts, lift the lid for a few seconds to allow the smelly sulfur compounds in these vegetables to disperse.) Check during cooking to be sure the water does not boil away. If you want to retain any nutrients released into the cooking water, use it in the finished dish, or reserve the water for use in soups or sauces.

When cooking potatoes, beets, and similar vegetables in their skins, you can use plenty of water, as the skin protects against nutrient loss. Since these vegetables take longer to cook than, say, broccoli or asparagus, it's important to use enough water to keep the pot from boiling dry in the course of cooking.

BRAISING This moist-heat method cooks meat, poultry, or vegetables slowly in their own juices plus a little added liquid. Slow cooking in liquid softens the connective tissue of meat without hardening the protein, so this is one of the best methods for tenderizing and flavoring lean cuts of meat that would be tough, stringy, and insipid if broiled or roasted. Pot roast is a familiar example of braised meat. (By contrast, tender cuts of meat will be rendered tough by this cooking method.)

Whether you're cooking meat, poultry, or vegetables, you can use wine, broth, juice, or beer for braising instead of water. The liquid will cook down to a thick, savory sauce to serve with the food, thus preserving nutrients that might otherwise be lost. Vegetables are often braised along with meat and poultry; they add flavor as well as contributing moisture.

Sometimes foods are precooked before braising: Strongly-flavored vegetables such as rutabagas and Brussels sprouts are better if they are blanched first. Fatty meats, such as short ribs, can also be blanched before braising to remove some of the fat. Meat and poultry may also be seared or browned before braising to intensify their flavors and produce better color.

To braise meat or poultry, first brown the meat, if desired, in a lightly oiled nonstick pan—a deep skillet or Dutch oven works well. (Dredging the food in flour first helps brown it and thickens the cooking liquid.) Pour off any excess fat, then add a small amount of boiling liquid—to a depth of not more than ½ inch. Adjust the heat so the liquid simmers, then cover the pan tightly and cook until the meat is very tender, adding more boiling liquid if necessary. You can braise on the stovetop or in a low (300° to 325°) oven. Remove the meat when it is done and continue to cook down the liquid until it forms a thick sauce. If possible, braise the meat the day before you plan to serve it; when refrigerated, the fat will congeal on the surface of the liquids and can then be easily removed.

To braise vegetables, place them in a heavy skillet with enough liquid to cover the bottom; cover, and simmer over low heat until tender, basting occasionally.

BROILING AND GRILLING Properly done, broiling and grilling yield meat, poultry, and fish that is crisp on the outside and juicy on the inside. These methods are also good alternatives to frying for vegetables such as eggplant, tomatoes, and summer squash. Oven broilers heat the food from the top, while barbecue grills heat it from the bottom. (Also, see Panbroiling, page 493.)

These cooking methods work well for tender cuts of meat such as steaks or chops that are from 1 to 2 inches thick, kebabs, thick ground-meat patties, bone-in poultry parts, and thick fish steaks or whole fish; very lean meats and thin chicken or fish fillets can quickly toughen or overcook under the high heat. Marinating and basting help keep broiled foods moist and flavorful. Be careful with sugary barbecue sauces, however, as they can quickly scorch and burn.

For healthier broiled foods, use a pan with a rack that allows fat to drip off (this will also prevent flare-ups caused by burning fat). Keeping the fat out of the fire is even more important when grilling, because when animal fat drips onto a barbecue fire, it can produce substances that may be carcinogenic. So when barbecuing, trim all visible fat. As a further precaution, push the hot coals to the sides of the barbecue and place a foil pan of water under the meat; any fat will then drip into the pan rather than onto the coals. Never broil or grill meat until it is blackened; if this occurs inadvertently, scrape or cut off the charred area.

Grill or broil meat about 4 inches from the heat source; chicken and turkey should be 6 to 8 inches from the heat. Start poultry pieces with the bone side toward the heat—bone-side up for broiling, bone-side down for grilling. Have the broiler hot—trying to broil or grill at a low temperature results in dried-out, gray meat rather than juicy, well-browned food. Turn it halfway through the cooking time, using tongs to avoid piercing it and releasing juices. Be careful not to overcook and dry out meat when broiling.

Sturdy vegetables can be broiled, too. Place halved or thickly sliced vegetables (or whole baby vegetables) on a broiler rack. Brush them lightly with oil (or baste them during broiling with broth or juice) and broil about 4 inches from the heat. When the vegetables begin to brown, turn them and broil the other side.

When grilling vegetables on the barbecue, it's best to use a wire grilling basket rather than placing the food directly on the grill, where it is likely to stick and break apart.

FRYING Cooking food in a deep or shallow pan of hot fat is obviously not a healthful method; however, sautéing and stir-frying can be modified so that little or no fat is added to the food.

MICROWAVING This newest way of cooking is, for some foods (such as vegetables), also the healthiest. It's undeniably fast, and little or no liquid is used. When microwaving vegetables, cover or wrap them to hold in moisture and help them cook more evenly; the exception is hard-shelled or tough-skinned vegetables, such as winter squash and potatoes; do not cover these, but do be sure to pierce them several times before cooking, or they may explode. When cooking whole vegetables, such as potatoes, arrange them in a circle for even cooking. Don't add salt to vegetables before cooking them in a microwave, as it will toughen them.

Meats and poultry can't be browned in a microwave, as they can with other cooking methods. Fish, on the other hand, lends itself very nicely to microwaving: It doesn't require browning, and it retains nearly all of its moisture when microwaved, as though it had been perfectly poached.

Microwave cooking times will vary with the quantity of food and the type of oven you use: The owner's manual is your best guide to the correct times. Test for doneness after the shortest cooking time, if a range of times is given. To ensure that food cooks evenly in a microwave, it should be stirred several times, or the platter or dish it is on should be turned midway through the cooking time.

PANBROILING (PANGRILLING) Steaks, chops, patties, and small whole fish can be cooked by this stovetop version of oven broiling. Unless the meat is very lean, no added fat is needed. Use nonstick cooking spray or a little oil if necessary. (Fish will probably require some oil in the pan.) Heat a heavy (preferably nonstick) skillet sizzling hot; as the food will be cooked by contact with the hot metal, you need a skillet that can take and retain fairly high heat. Place the meat or fish in the pan and cook, uncovered, until one side is browned, then turn and cook the other side. Cook thick cuts of meat slowly over medium heat, thinner cuts over medium-high heat; pour off fat as it accumulates. Special stovetop grilling pans with raised grids allow the fat to drain off for healthier cooking.

POACHING This method calls for cooking food in barely simmering water on the stovetop. Eggs are the food most commonly poached, but poaching is also a gentle cooking technique for meat, poultry, and fish, producing a mild-flavored food that goes well with assertive sauces or accompaniments. Chicken breast is often poached for chicken salad; poached beef is good with a robust horseradish or mustard sauce. Fruit can also be poached, singly or in combination, as a dessert or main-dish accompaniment. For best flavor, poach food in well-seasoned broth, a combination of broth and wine, or fruit or vegetable juice, as appropriate.

When poaching meat, poultry, or fish, place the food in cold liquid and bring it to a bare simmer—never a rapid boil. Partially cover the pan, or use a lid cut from parchment paper, which allows excess steam to escape while holding in the heat. When the food is cooked, you may strain the poaching liquid and cook it down (thicken if necessary) to serve as a sauce. Or, use savory poaching liquid as a soup base.

Fruit is usually added to boiling sugar syrup, which helps hold its shape as well as sweetening it, but you can also poach fruit in water, wine, or fruit juice; add whole or ground spices to the poaching liquid for added flavor. Cook fruit in a small amount of barely simmering liquid, partially covered. Turn the fruit occasionally, and baste it with the cooking liquid if it is not completely immersed.

PRESSURE COOKING Long before the microwave arrived on the scene, the pressure cooker was the secret to quick cooking. It's also a healthy method, since this type of pot in effect steams the food, and does so in minutes. You do need to time the cooking carefully; as with microwaving, pressure cooking can overcook vegetables in seconds. Follow the instructions that come with your pressure cooker for the correct cooking times and techniques.

Some foods require special procedures, especially if you're using an older pressure cooker. Grains must be rinsed before cooking to remove excess starch, which can block the steam valve during cooking. Foam clogging the valve can also be a problem with dried beans. With both beans and grains, adding a few teaspoons of oil will help prevent excessive foaming. Don't fill the pot more than one-third full, to allow plenty of space for the grains or beans to expand.

ROASTING A standard cooking method for large cuts of meat and whole chickens, turkeys, and other poultry, roasting is not a demanding technique, but it does require careful temperature regulation and timing. A constant moderate temperature (300° to 350°) causes less shrinkage and conserves more nutrients than a hot oven, while producing equally flavorful results. (It was once thought that initial high heat "sealed in" juices, but this is now known not to be true.)

Traditionally, meat for roasting had a liberal layer of fat on it. Leaner cuts and lean poultry were "larded" or "barded," that is, strips of fatty pork or bacon were inserted through or wrapped around the food to keep it moist. Neither is a healthy option, but leaner roasts do benefit from marinating and/or basting (with broth, not fatty pan drippings). Rubbing the meat with a teaspoon of vegetable oil will also help without adding much fat. Poultry cooked in its skin—which can be removed before the bird is eaten—has a natural protective coating, but basting with broth, fruit juice, or cider will help keep a roasting bird moist. (It is best to baste chicken or turkey only at half-hour intervals to avoid lowering the oven temperature and increasing the cooking time.)

Cooking both meat roasts and poultry on a rack allows fat to drip off. Cooking vegetables or fruit with a roast also supplies moisture; however, if the potatoes, onions, carrots, or apples you place in the pan are sitting in drippings, they will not be a healthful addition to your meal. Place them on the rack or on top of the meat, or consider them simply as seasonings to be discarded.

To roast beef, lamb, or pork, prepare the meat and place it on a rack in an open roasting pan. Place the roast in a preheated, moderate oven and cook until a meat thermometer inserted in the thickest portion of the roast registers the correct temperature. Remember that the size, shape, and cut of the roast, its temperature when placed in the oven, and the accuracy of your oven thermostat can affect cooking time. A good meat thermometer—and your own experience—are your best guides.

When cooking a chicken or turkey, place it breast-side up on a rack in a roasting pan. Roast, uncovered, in a 325° oven until the thermometer shows that the bird is done. If parts of the bird brown too quickly, protect them with a loose tent of foil. Do not, however, closely cover a roasting bird (or other meat) with foil, or it will steam rather than roast.

Allow a roast to stand for 15 to 20 minutes before carving; this lets the meat finish cooking and also allows the juices to be reabsorbed evenly throughout the meat so they are not lost during carving.

Vegetables can be roasted, too. Sturdy ones such as white and sweet potatoes, winter squash, eggplant, turnips, carrots, beets, onions, and garlic develop a rich, sweet flavor when baked at a high temperature—in a 450° to 500° oven. Leave the vegetables whole, or halve or quarter large ones; roast them with the skin on. Brush the vegetables with a little oil, or baste them lightly with broth or juice so they do not dry out. Potatoes in their jackets and corn on the cob in its husk are sometimes roasted right in the coals of a barbecue fire; other vegetables can be roasted this way, too, if convenient, and their charred skins peeled when they are done.

SAUTÉING Sauté comes from the French word *sauter,* which means "jump," which is what the food should do in the pan when you cook by this method. Sautéing is sometimes referred to as panfrying, but whatever term you use, the key is to use a very hot skillet so that the food cooks quickly. You can sauté vegetables, and thin cuts of meat such as pork medallions, veal scallops, and boneless chicken breasts, as well as fish fillets, and whole small fish. The food may be breaded or dusted with flour; chicken may be sautéed without the skin. Also, grains such as rice or kasha are sometimes sautéed before simmering to intensify their flavor.

Sautés traditionally call for butter and/or oil; if you use a nonstick pan, you can manage with very little fat. Alternatively, use a nonstick cooking spray or sauté in a small amount of broth or even water. (Such liquids do not get as hot as fat, so the cooking process changes slightly in character.) The pan should be big enough to hold the food without crowding, or it will steam rather than sauté.

For quick cooking, cut the food into small, uniform pieces (dice, strips, or slices). Heat a skillet or sauté pan (with a tablespoon of fat or a few tablespoonfuls of broth) until hot but not smoking. Add the food and immediately begin to shake the pan, tossing the food and stirring it or loosening it with a spatula if it begins to stick. (When sautéing meat or poultry, turn it with tongs rather than a fork, so you do not pierce it and release juices.) If using broth or water, add more as the liquid evaporates.

SIMMERING Most Americans cook rice by this basic method, and it works equally well for other whole and cracked grains. By using a measured quantity of liquid (so none is poured off after cooking), you conserve most of the nutrients in the grain. You can simmer grains in water, broth, milk, or juice for added flavor (acidic juices will slow the cooking, so they should be added after the grain is partially cooked).

To simmer, bring a measured amount of liquid to a boil in a pot with a tight-fitting cover. Stir in the grain and re-cover the pot. When the liquid returns to a boil, reduce the heat so that it simmers and cook, covered, until the grain is tender and the liquid is absorbed. It's best not to uncover the pot during cooking, but you may want to check it once—quickly—toward the end of the cooking time to make sure that the liquid has not been absorbed prematurely, allowing the grain to scorch.

To simmer grains that have been precooked by toasting or sautéing, bring the measured amount of liquid to a boil in a separate pot, then stir the liquid into the skillet of grain. Cover tightly, reduce heat, and simmer.

Finely cracked cereals used for porridge, such as cream of wheat or cream of rice, are stirred into rapidly boiling water and then stirred constantly for about a minute to keep them from lumping. They are then simmered, covered or uncovered, until thick. Stir occasionally to keep the cereal from sticking, and be sure to add more boiling water if necessary.

STEAMING This is an ideal cooking method; because the food is not immersed in water, most nutrients are retained. Almost any food that can be boiled or simmered can also be steamed: It works well for vegetables and can also be used for boneless chicken breasts, fish, and some grains. Use a metal steaming basket or a bamboo steamer, or improvise a steamer, if necessary, with a metal strainer or colander. Place the food in the steamer over boiling water, using a pot with a tight cover. A large steamer that leaves space for the steam to circulate around and through the food does the most efficient job. If the water threatens to boil away before the food is done, add more boiling water from a kettle.

STEEPING Bulgur and other cracked grains, such as barley grits, can be cooked this way, and will be slightly chewier than if they were simmered. Place the grain in a saucepan or heatproof bowl and pour boiling liquid over it, using ½ cup water for each cup of grain. Cover and let stand for 15 to 30 minutes, or until most of the liquid has been absorbed; drain in a strainer if necessary, then fluff with a fork before serving.

STEWING Similar to braising, stewing is used to cook meat or poultry with vegetables in a large amount of liquid, producing a hearty one-pot meal. You can also stew meat by itself and serve it with vegetables that you've cooked separately. Stews are usually made with relatively small cubes of meat or cut-up poultry. Browning the meat before stewing makes a more flavorful dish; dredging the meat in flour first enhances the browning and helps thicken the stew. Pour off any accumulated fat after browning, then add enough boiling liquid (water, broth, or wine) to cover the meat. Cook, covered, until the meat or poultry is tender. Time the addition of vegetables so that they will be done at the same time as the meat. You'll want to add dense, firm vegetables such as carrots or turnips earlier than more delicate ones like mushrooms or peas.

When you cook stewed meat or poultry ahead of time, you can refrigerate it to make removal of fat from the broth easier. In addition, stews often improve in flavor after standing for a day.

STIR-FRYING Rapid stir-frying has attained great popularity in recent years: A stir-fry of mixed vegetables or meat and vegetables is a colorful, satisfying meal or side dish. Use a wok or a heavy non-stick skillet and you can stir-fry with a minimum of oil (about a tablespoon). Or, you can stir-fry with broth, adding more as the liquid evaporates.

Cut the food into thin, uniform pieces. If you are using more than one vegetable, start with the densest, then add more delicate vegetables toward the end; some require just seconds in the wok. Or, stir-fry each vegetable individually, remove it to a dish when cooked, and stir-fry the next. (When cooking meat and vegetables, cook the vegetables first, then remove them from the pan and set aside.)

Heat the oil or broth in the pan until very hot but not smoking; toss in the food and stir constantly with two spatulas, tossing until the vegetables are crisp-tender.

Fats and Oils

In a healthful diet, fats and oils should be used sparingly. Even in small amounts, they can contribute a significant amount of fat and calories. Just a tablespoon of vegetable oil contains 120 calories and 14 grams of fat; the same amount of butter or stick margarine has 100 calories and 11 grams of fat. Moreover, not all fats and oils are the same; some, like butter and coconut oil, are highly saturated; others, like canola oil, olive oil, and safflower oil, are highly unsaturated. Below you'll find information on butter, margaine, and the various types of vegetable oils.

Vegetable oils

A tablespoon of oil here and there may not seem like a big deal, but vegetable oils account in large part for a major shift in American eating habits in recent years. These oils are simply fat in liquid form. While we have cut back on animal fats, in 1989 we consumed about 68 percent more vegetable oil than we did in 1969—in our cooking oils, margarines, baked goods, fried foods, mayonnaise, and salad dressings. Our total fat consumption has, as a result, risen slightly.

Nutritionists agree that we should increase the ratio of polyunsaturated to saturated fats in our diet to help lower blood cholesterol levels and thus reduce the risk of heart disease. Moreover, some research suggests that monounsaturated fats—abundant in olive oil and canola oil—are almost as good in lowering cholesterol.

However, no vegetable oil is 100 percent unsaturated. Corn, soybean, safflower, and other kinds of oil all contain some saturated fatty acids. In fact, coconut and palm kernel oil actually contain a higher percentage of saturated fatty acids than animal fats do.

Despite these substantial variations, many shoppers do not know which type of vegetable oil is in the cooking or salad oil they buy. According to a survey by the National Sunflower Association, price and brand loyalty were found to be key considerations, rather than the type of oil. Shoppers also reported that they were attracted to their brand because of its "low cholesterol" content. They were apparently unaware that no vegetable product contains cholesterol, which is found only in animal products.

Consumers are even less aware of the type of "invisible" oil in processed foods such as crackers, cakes, frozen dinners, snack foods—even nondairy creamers. Soybean oil is the most commonly used oil in processed foods, and is also used in bottled salad dressings and mayonnaise. Coconut and palm kernel oils, the only vegetable oils high in saturated fat, are also frequently used.

To minimize your consumption of oils, take the following steps:

- Read labels on store-bought foods and cut back on those containing coconut or palm kernel oil, which have a long shelf life but are highly saturated. Also cut down on foods with hydrogenated oils, since hydrogenation only makes the fat more saturated.
- Heat cooking oil before adding food. The food will sit in the oil for a shorter time and absorb less of it.
- Stir-fry vegetables and meat (cut up in small pieces). Using this method, you can cook food faster and with very little oil.

- Use a spray-on vegetable oil, such as Pam, which can coat a pan satisfactorily with a mere ¼ teaspoon of oil.
- Make your own salad dressing, using two parts safflower or sunflower oil to one part vinegar or lemon juice. Add fresh or dried herbs, garlic, or mustard.

Butter and Margarine

A bewildering array of margarine products and substitute butters—semisoft spreads, squeezable liquids, even powders—has expanded what used to be a small corner of the dairy section in the supermarket. Three out of four Americans today use margarine regularly, often because they think it is better for them than butter. Are they making the right choice?

If you're trying to follow a "heart-healthy" diet, you should limit your use of butter, since most of its calories come from saturated fat, and it contains a fair amount of cholesterol. Of course, if your diet is sensibly low in fat and cholesterol, a daily pat of butter won't hurt you. But if you or members of your family eat a lot of butter, switching to a butter substitute or blend can make a big difference.

Here are some of your options:

Margarines As in butter, 100 percent of margarine's calories come from fat, but the fat is largely polyunsaturated; good for spreading and cooking. None of the major brands have any cholesterol, since almost all are made from vegetable oils (though the Food and Drug Administration does allow lard—which is animal fat—to be used).

Vegetable-oil spreads These contain less than the 80 percent fat by weight required in a margarine, but may nonetheless be no better than regular margarine.

Diet or reduced-calorie margarines One way to cut fat is to use a "diet" margarine. Though all of its calories still come from fat (about 45 percent

VEGETABLE OILS: A FAT BREAKDOWN

The chart below lists the breakdown of fatty acids in various oils. The higher the ratio of unsaturated to saturated fatty acids, the more healthful the oil. This doesn't mean that you should merely add unsaturated oils to your diet. The trick is to cut down on all *fats. But when you do eat fat, try to make it as unsaturated as possible.*

	FATTY ACID CONTENT			
Oils, least to most saturated	**Poly-unsaturated** (%)	**Mono-unsaturated** (%)	**Saturated** (%)	**Unsaturated/ Saturated Fat Ratio**
Canola	32%	62%	6%	15.7:1
Safflower	75%	12%	9%	9.6:1
Sunflower	66%	20%	10%	8.6:1
Corn	59%	24%	13%	6.4:1
Soybean	59%	23%	14%	5.9:1
Olive	9%	72%	14%	5.8:1
Peanut	32%	46%	17%	4.6:1
Sesame seed	40%	40%	18%	4.4:1
Cottonseed	52%	18%	26%	2.7:1
Palm kernel	2%	10%	80%	0.2:1
Coconut	2%	6%	87%	0.1:1

Note: These percentages do not add up to 100% because other fat-like substances make up the total composition.

fat by weight), it is diluted with water, so it has half the fat and calories of regular margarine per tablespoon.

Butter-margarine blends These are anywhere from 15 percent to 40 percent butter. Thus they contain some of butter's cholesterol and saturated fat, as well as its taste.

Sprinkle-on powders Made from carbohydrates, these powders are virtually fat- and cholesterol-free. They melt well on hot, moist foods like baked potatoes. But they won't do for spreading on toast, in recipes, or for sautéing.

How much saturated fat a margarine or spread contains depends both on which vegetable oil it contains and how it was made. When shopping for a margarine or spread, let the ingredients label be your guide:

- Most margarine products tell how much saturated and polyunsaturated fats they contain. Look for one with at least twice as much polyunsaturated as saturated fat. If a brand doesn't give you a breakdown of fats, be suspicious.
- Although all the oils commonly used in margarines are high in polyunsaturated fat and low in saturated fat, they vary substantially. Those lowest in saturated fat are safflower, sunflower, and corn oil, in that order.
- If a hydrogenated or partially hydrogenated oil is listed first, the product is likely to be more saturated. To make oil solid and prolong its shelf life, manufacturers add hydrogen molecules—a process called hydrogenation. It transforms good unsaturated vegetable oil into a more saturated kind of fat.
- The softer or more fluid a margarine is, the less saturated it is likely to be. For this reason, liquid or tub margarines are almost always better than stick margarines. One sign of a high polyunsaturate content is a liquid oil as the first ingredient listed, rather than a partially hydrogenated oil.
- Margarine with water listed as the first ingredient has one-third to one-half less fat than the average margarine.
- Watch the sodium content, which tends to be relatively high. Salted margarine is just as undesirable as salted butter. Unsalted varieties are available.

Appendix C

Herbs and Spices

AN EXCELLENT WAY to enhance the flavors of food when you're cutting back on fat is to use herbs and spices creatively. The following guide will help you choose appropriate seasonings for different foods.

Fresh herbs are becoming more widely available all the time: Look for them in the produce department or at greengrocers'. Buy fresh herbs as needed: Wrap them in damp paper towels, place in plastic bags, and refrigerate. If using fresh herbs in a cooked dish, add them toward the end of the cooking time so that their delicate flavors are not lost. Dried herbs (as well as spices) can stand up to longer cooking. Store dried herbs and spices in airtight containers in a cool, dark place to conserve their flavors and aromas.

ALLSPICE Whole or ground, this Jamaican berry can be used with sweet and savory foods. Add a few berries when making chicken, beef, or fish stock, pot roast or beef stew; add ground allspice to mulled cider, fruit compote and other fruit desserts, and pumpkin pie.

ANISE Its licorice-like flavor makes this seed a favorite for spice cakes, cookies, and other desserts. Whole or ground anise seed also goes well with fruit (try it in applesauce) and a little of this spice adds an intriguing note to braised beef or cooked cabbage.

BASIL Essential to Italian cooking, this herb blends well with tomatoes and garlic. Its mild sweetness complements any type of meat or poultry, shellfish, and many vegetables. Fresh basil is quite widely available, and the leaves can be used as a flavorful salad ingredient: Try them layered with fresh tomatoes.

BAY LEAF Usually sold dried, brittle bay leaves are most commonly used whole, but you can also buy powdered bay leaves. If using the whole leaves, be sure to add them at the start of cooking to give them time to release their flavor; remove them from the dish before serving. For a subtle savory flavor, add bay leaf to meat, poultry, and fish stocks, meat and poultry stews and braises, vegetable soups and stews, and tomato and other sauces.

CARAWAY The flavor of these seeds is most associated with rye bread, but they are also used in main dishes and salads in German and other Northern European cuisines. Try caraway seeds in potato salad and cole slaw, cucumber salad, meatloaf, or sprinkled over cooked noodles.

CARDAMOM Two dissimilar cuisines—Scandinavian and Indian—both make liberal use of this warmly sweet spice. It's tasty with fruit—ground cardamom goes into Scandinavian-style fruit soups, baked apples, fruit compotes, and gingerbread—and this spice also seasons Swedish meatballs. Use cardamom in homemade curry powder, and in sweet rice pilafs. Try cardamom with sweet vegetables such as winter squash, pumpkin, and sweet potatoes.

CAYENNE This pungent seasoning is made by grinding dried hot red peppers (chiles), and indeed is often called hot red pepper. It is an ingredient of chili powder and is used in Mexican, Indian, Chinese, and Cajun recipes; marinades and barbecue sauces for meat and poultry; and in any dish you want to give a peppery kick. If you're not used to hot food, use just a pinch to begin with, then taste and add more if necessary.

CELERY SEED A mild celery flavor is contributed by the seeds of this familiar salad vegetable; they enhance split-pea soup, fish chowders, tomato sauces and soups, hot or cold potato dishes, and stuffings.

CILANTRO (CORIANDER LEAVES) Also called Chinese parsley, fresh cilantro or coriander looks something like flat-leaf parsley but can be distinguished instantly by its pungent fragrance—which seems to inspire either love or hate. Fresh cilantro is a key ingredient in Mexican, Indian, and Chinese cooking, and is found more and more frequently in supermarkets and greengrocers'. Cilantro retains very little of its flavor when dried, so it's best to use fresh if possible. Add chopped cilantro just before serving to salsa, stir-fries, legume or rice salads, or hot cooked rice; sprinkle it over grilled chicken or fish, or a dish of ripe tomatoes.

CINNAMON In addition to its familiar uses in desserts and fruit dishes, cinnamon is a traditional ingredient in Moroccan and Greek chicken and beef dishes and fruited rice pilafs. Use this spice with winter squash, sweet potatoes, carrots, and parsnips. Serve whole cinnamon sticks as stirrers in hot cider or fruit juice.

CLOVES Whole dried cloves or ground cloves are combined with other sweet spices in apple desserts, gingerbread, and pumpkin pie. Their pungency also enhances pea and bean soups, baked beans, chili, barbecue and tomato sauces, pork and ham, and sweet potatoes.

CORIANDER SEED Whole or ground coriander seeds are quite distinct in flavor from coriander leaves, also called cilantro. Pungently spicy yet sweet and slightly fruity, they are a component of curries and Middle Eastern and Mediterranean dishes, as well as spice cakes and cookies. A touch of coriander perks up savory soups, roast pork, and salad dressings.

CUMIN Whole or ground cumin seeds go into chili powder and many Mexican and Tex-Mex dishes. Cumin is used in the Middle East, and also in India as a component of curry powder; it's usually heated before using to bring out its flavor. Cumin complements beef and lamb, cooked carrots and cabbage, chickpeas, lentils, and other legumes.

DILL SEED Often used in pickling, dill seed is also good in salad dressings, sauces, and marinades, with fish, and in cucumber, carrot, cabbage and potato salads as well as hot cooked cabbage, carrots, and potatoes.

DILLWEED The feathery green leaves of the dill plant have a milder flavor than the seeds, but complement the same foods. Try adding a little dillweed to tuna or salmon salad, or to cottage cheese or yogurt for a savory dip or sauce.

FENNEL SEED Like the vegetable it comes from, fennel seed has a mild licorice flavor (much milder than anise). Try fennel seeds with fish and shellfish, in Italian dishes and sauces, potato salad, and in rye bread and rolls.

GINGER (FRESH) This finger-like root is not, strictly speaking, either an herb or a spice, but it is used as a seasoning. The fresh root has beige flesh covered with a thin tan skin; you peel the skin before grating or slicing the root. Wrap fresh ginger well and store it in the freezer, where it will keep for months; there's no need to thaw it before using it. Try ginger's sweet-pungent flavor in

Japanese dishes, in marinades for chicken or fish, stir-fries, and fruit-salad dressings.

GINGER (GROUND) In its dried, ground form, ginger is most commonly used in gingerbread, spice cake, pumpkin pie and the like. But a pinch of ground ginger will also enhance braised poultry or meat, soups and stews, stuffings, cooked carrots, winter squash, sweet potatoes, and baked or stewed fruit. Try a sprinkling of ginger on a half grapefruit or in rice pudding.

MACE The dried, ground outer coating of the nutmeg berry, mace has a similar flavor to nutmeg but is slightly stronger; taking this into account, mace can be used in the same ways as nutmeg. Mace is the classic spice for poundcake.

MARJORAM (SWEET MARJORAM) This herb is closely akin to oregano and has a related but more delicate flavor. It's especially good in tomato sauce and other tomato-based dishes, with cooked lentils and beans, summer squash, potatoes, fish, lamb, and veal.

MINT Fresh mint leaves add zest to sweet dishes such as fruit salads and fruit soups, melon, berries, and cold fruit beverages (a few mint leaves make an appetizing garnish for such foods). This refreshing herb is also delicious with cooked carrots or peas, in fresh pea soup or chilled yogurt soup, with lamb, and in cold grain salads, such as tabbouleh.

MUSTARD The whole or ground seeds of the mustard plant, or prepared mustard (ground mustard mixed with liquid), contribute a savory, spicy flavor. Mustard is often used in sauces for meat and fish, in marinades, salad dressings, chutneys, pickles, and relishes; it also goes well with cheese. Mustard sparks fish and seafood salads, and also adds rich flavor to cooked spinach and cabbage-family vegetables such as Brussels sprouts and cauliflower.

NUTMEG In earlier times, nutmeg was freshly ground from the dried berry with a small grater; today, most people buy it already ground. Either way, this pungent, sweet spice is a favorite in fruit desserts and baked goods. A pinch of nutmeg also enhances braised or stewed meats and poultry, white sauce (a classic Béchamel sauce is made with nutmeg), cooked spinach, broccoli, cauliflower, and carrots.

OREGANO Like basil, this is considered a quintessential Italian herb, but oregano is also used in Greek and Mexican cooking. Add it to tomato sauces, salad dressings, tomato-based soups such as minestrone, or marinades. Or you can season baked fish, grilled poultry, mushrooms, green beans, and summer squash with this aromatic herb.

PAPRIKA Like cayenne, paprika is made by drying and grinding peppers, but paprika is made from less pungent peppers and has a warmly sweet, rather than a hot, flavor. You'll find it used in many Spanish and Hungarian dishes. Rub poultry with paprika before roasting to add color as well as flavor; sprinkle fish with it before broiling or baking for the same double enhancement. Use paprika in chowders, salad dressings, and whenever a touch of color is needed on a savory dish, for instance with potatoes, cauliflower or puréed soups.

PARSLEY The most widely available of all fresh herbs, parsley comes in flat-leaf and curly-leaf forms, and is one of the most versatile of herbs. Though often used as a garnish (and not eaten), it adds a refreshing "bite" (and vitamin C) whenever it is added to cooked foods. Toss in some freshly chopped parsley just before serving soups and stews, vegetables, sauced pastas, grains, and eggs. Sprinkle parsley over poached, baked, or grilled meat, chicken, or fish. Fresh parsley's flavor and color also brightens salads and dressings. Since fresh parsley is so readily available, you should try to avoid dried parsley, which is virtually flavorless.

PEPPER There are many varieties of this common spice, not just black and white. Black pepper comes from immature berries with their natural coating intact; white pepper berries are fully ripe and have had this outer layer removed. You can find peppers such as Lampong and Tellicherry (both black), Muntok and Sarawak (both white peppers) in gourmet shops; they vary in pungency and flavor. White pepper is preferred for pale-colored foods so it will not show up as dark specks. It's best to buy whole peppercorns and grind them yourself as needed (a simple peppermill is an inexpensive kitchen requisite): Once ground, pepper rapidly loses its flavor. There is hardly a savory dish that cannot be seasoned to advantage with pepper. For an unusual dessert, sprinkle a little finely-ground black pepper over vanilla ice milk or frozen yogurt.

ROSEMARY A branch of fresh rosemary looks like a small sprig of evergreen, and is just as fragrant. If you like its assertive flavor, try using it to season chicken, lamb, pork, flavorful fish such as salmon and tuna, tomato sauces and soups, potatoes, mushrooms, and peas. When you are using fresh rosemary, it is necessary to chop and crush it thoroughly, as its needle-like leaves are quite hard. Even dried rosemary needs to be crushed or crumbled.

SAFFRON The most expensive of spices, saffron comes from a particular species of crocus. The spice is sold as "threads"—the whole stigma of the flower—or powdered, in small glass vials. Just a pinch is needed to add brilliant yellow color and an exotic, slightly bitter flavor to seafood, poultry, Spanish-, Italian-, or Indian-style rice dishes (such as paella, risotto, or pilaf), sauces, and soups. Saffron should be dissolved in a small amount of warm water (just a teaspoonful or so) before adding it to the dish.

SAGE Most familiar as a seasoning for poultry stuffing, sage—sold as whole leaves or crumbled—has a bold flavor and aroma. Try it with any type of poultry, pork, veal, or ham; in cheese sauces; in legume or vegetable soups and seafood chowders; and with cooked mushrooms, lima beans, peas, tomatoes, or eggplant.

SUMMER SAVORY This slightly peppery herb goes particularly well with vegetables, and is especially good with fresh or cooked green beans as well as dried beans. Also use savory with peas, cabbage, Brussels sprouts, potatoes, legumes and in salad dressings. This herb also enhances poultry, fish, lamb, and pork, and is even sometimes used to season cooked fruit.

TARRAGON Essential to French cooking, tarragon has a faint undertone of anise or licorice. It can be overpowering and may overshadow other herbs, so use it with discretion. Tarragon is an excellent choice with poached, baked, or broiled fish or poultry, with shellfish such as crabmeat or shrimp, and with eggs. Try tarragon in vinaigrettes and other salad dressings, and with cooked potatoes, peas, asparagus, carrots, mushrooms, or tomatoes.

THYME This versatile herb, though quite strong in flavor, is compatible with many foods and is essential in Creole recipes. Add a little thyme to tomato sauce, vegetable soup, clam and other seafood chowders, beef stew or pot roast, poultry stuffing, and cooked vegetables such as summer squash and green beans.

Index

Specific types or varieties of foods and nutrients are listed under their own names (for example, "Blackberries," "Salmon," or "Iron") rather than under broader headings ("Berries," "Fish," or "Minerals"). References to shopping and storage tips, food preparation, and serving suggestions are not included in this index since they are a regular feature of every entry.

C

Q

R

S

T

THE UNIVERSITY OF CALIFORNIA
LET THERE BE LIGHT
1868